Lecture Notes in Artificial Intelligence   11649

Subseries of Lecture Notes in Computer Science

Series Editors

Randy Goebel
  University of Alberta, Edmonton, Canada
Yuzuru Tanaka
  Hokkaido University, Sapporo, Japan
Wolfgang Wahlster
  DFKI and Saarland University, Saarbrücken, Germany

Founding Editor

Jörg Siekmann
  DFKI and Saarland University, Saarbrücken, Germany

More information about this series at http://www.springer.com/series/1244

Kaspar Althoefer · Jelizaveta Konstantinova ·
Ketao Zhang (Eds.)

Towards Autonomous Robotic Systems

20th Annual Conference, TAROS 2019
London, UK, July 3–5, 2019
Proceedings, Part I

 Springer

Editors
Kaspar Althoefer
Queen Mary University of London
London, UK

Jelizaveta Konstantinova
Queen Mary University of London
London, UK

Ketao Zhang 🆔
Queen Mary University of London
London, UK

ISSN 0302-9743   ISSN 1611-3349   (electronic)
Lecture Notes in Artificial Intelligence
ISBN 978-3-030-23806-3   ISBN 978-3-030-23807-0   (eBook)
https://doi.org/10.1007/978-3-030-23807-0

LNCS Sublibrary: SL7 – Artificial Intelligence

This Springer imprint is published by the registered company Springer Nature Switzerland AG
The registered company address is: Gewerbestrasse 11, 6330 Cham, Switzerland

Preface

This volume contains the papers presented at TAROS 2019, the 20th Towards Autonomous Robotic Systems (TAROS) Conference, held at Queen Mary University of London, UK, during July 3–5, 2019 (https://www.qmul.ac.uk/robotics/events/taros2019/).

TAROS is the longest running UK-hosted international conference on robotics and autonomous systems (RAS), which is aimed at the presentation and discussion of the latest results and methods in autonomous robotics research and applications. The conference offers a friendly environment for robotics researchers and industry to take stock and plan future projects. It welcomes senior researchers and research students alike, and specifically provides opportunities for research students and young research scientists to present their work to the scientific community.

TAROS 2019 was held at the Queen Mary University of London, the most inclusive university of its kind. The conference programme included an academic conference, industry exhibitions, robot demonstrations and a conference dinner. The program highlights included:

- Keynote lectures by world-leading experts in robotics, including lectures by Professor Veronique Perdereau from Sorbonne University, France, Dr. Francesco Nori from Google DeepMind, UK, and Professor Bruno Siciliano from the University of Naples Federico II, Italy
- An IET-sponsored evening lecture by Professor Aude Billard from the Swiss Institute of Technology Lausanne (EPFL), Switzerland
- Invited talks by Rich Walker from Shadow Robot Company, UK, and Dr Stoyan Smoukov from Queen Mary University of London, UK
- Oral presentations, covering topics of robotic grippers and manipulation, human–robot interaction, robotic learning, robot navigation, planning and safety, robotic sensing, soft robotics, mobile and industrial robots
- Poster presentations, covering topics of swarm and multi-robot system, aerial and space robotics, eversion robots, bio-inspired robots, reconfigurable robots, robot design and testing, human–robot interaction
- Presentations of the finalists of the Queen Mary UK Best PhD in Robotics Award
- Industrial and academic exhibition stands

The TAROS 2019 Organizing Committee would like to thank all the authors, reviewers, and the conference sponsors, including the IET, UK-RAS Network, The Alan Turing Institute, Institute of Applied Data Science, Queen Mary University of London, University of Nottingham (The Rolls-Royce UTC in Manufacturing and On-wing Technology), NCNR, Automata, Ocado Technology, Springer and Frontiers in Robotics and AI.

May 2019

Kaspar Althoefer
Jelizaveta Konstantinova
Ketao Zhang

Organization

General Chair

Kaspar Althoefer   Queen Mary University of London, UK

Program Chairs

Jelizaveta Konstantinova   Queen Mary University of London, UK
Ketao Zhang   Queen Mary University of London, UK

Web Chair

Joshua Brown   Queen Mary University of London, UK

TAROS Steering Committee

Chris Melhuish   Bristol Robotics Laboratory, UK
Mark Witkowski   Imperial College London, UK

Program Committee

Akram Alomainy   Queen Mary University of London, UK
Kaspar Althoefer   Queen Mary University of London, UK
Ahmad Ataka   King's College London, UK
Christos Bergeles   King's College London, UK
Michael Cashmore   King's College London, UK
Kerstin Dautenhahn   University of Waterloo, Canada
Yiannis Demiris   Imperial College London, UK
Sanja Dogramadzi   University of the West of England, UK
Venky Dubey   Bournemouth University, UK
Ildar Farkhatdinov   Queen Mary University of London, UK
Manuel Giuliani   University of the West of England, UK
Hareesh Godaba   Queen Mary University of London, UK
Roderich Gross   University of Sheffield, UK
Dongbing Gu   University of Essex, UK
Marc Hanheide   University of Lincoln, UK
Lorenzo Jamone   Queen Mary University of London, UK
Jelizaveta Konstantinova   Queen Mary University of London, UK
Senka Krivic   King's College London, UK
Barry Lennox   University of Manchester, UK
Honghai Liu   University of Portsmouth, UK
Shan Luo   University of Liverpool, UK

Contents – Part I

Robotic Systems and Applications

Robotic Grippers and Manipulation

Reasoning on Grasp-Action Affordances

Paola Ardón[✉][iD], Èric Pairet[iD], Ron Petrick[iD],
Subramanian Ramamoorthy[iD], and Katrin Lohan[iD]

Edinburgh Centre for Robotics, Edinburgh, UK
paola.ardon@ed.ac.uk

Abstract. Artificial intelligence is essential to succeed in challenging activities that involve dynamic environments, such as object manipulation tasks in indoor scenes. Most of the state-of-the-art literature explores robotic grasping methods by focusing exclusively on attributes of the target object. When it comes to human perceptual learning approaches, these physical qualities are not only inferred from the object, but also from the characteristics of the surroundings. This work proposes a method that includes environmental context to reason on an object affordance to then deduce its grasping regions. This affordance is reasoned using a ranked association of visual semantic attributes harvested in a knowledge base graph representation. The framework is assessed using standard learning evaluation metrics and the zero-shot affordance prediction scenario. The resulting grasping areas are compared with unseen labelled data to asses their accuracy matching percentage. The outcome of this evaluation suggest the autonomy capabilities of the proposed method for object interaction applications in indoor environments.

1 Introduction

One of the most significant challenges in artificial intelligence is to achieve a system that simulates human-like behaviour. Let us consider a robot in a simple task such as finding, collecting and delivering an object in home environments. Given the complexity of home settings, it is hard to provide a robot with every possible representation of the objects contained in a house. It is even harder to feed the robot with all the possible uses of those objects. Instead of learning all possible scenarios, suppose that a reasoning technique allows the system to deduce an object affordance. As a result, offering the opportunity to achieve autonomous capabilities. The term affordance refers to everything that defines the interaction with an object, from the way to grasp it to its inherited ability to perform different tasks [10]. Thus, affordance defines all possible actions depending on the target objects' physical capabilities. For instance, a glass cup looks as if it can be handed over, contain liquids, or pour liquids from it. The characteristics that define the glass cup as a container or graspable object constitute its affordance. According to different theories of human perception, the psychology of perceptual learning compounds the different qualities in the environment

© Springer Nature Switzerland AG 2019
K. Althoefer et al. (Eds.): TAROS 2019, LNAI 11649, pp. 3–15, 2019.
https://doi.org/10.1007/978-3-030-23807-0_1

rather than acquiring associated responses to every object [3,9]. Thus, humans are efficient at deducing affordance for objects with different appearances and similar abilities, e.g. glasses: wine, tumbler, martini, and discern among those with similar features but different purposes, e.g. bowling pin vs water bottle. Nonetheless, in robotics, the most common approach to learn affordances is from labels [4,14,16]. This technique limits the number of learned objects, grasping areas and affordance groups. Moreover, the robot is unable to interact with novel objects. Further, by learning the limited set of responses, it is not possible to deduce the key features that define the objects affordance.

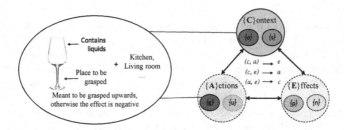

Fig. 1. Affordance map model to create a correlation between the objects properties and their environment to improve on grasp-action affordance.

Using the same analogy as the theories of human perception this paper hypothesises that using the semantic features of the object and its surroundings not only improves the affordance grasping action towards the object but it also allows a reasoning process that, in the long term, offers autonomy capabilities, a solution not yet seen in the current literature. This work summarises an architecture that addresses the previously described challenges. The focus is on affordance reasoning for calculating grasping areas, using a combination of the object and its environment features. Figure 1 shows the foundations of this proposal, which is an extended version of the affordance map presented in [16]. The proposed methodology works with the concept that an affordance relates attributes of an object and the environment to an interactive activity by an agent who has some ability, which relates back to the object causing some affordance. In other words, the attributes of the object and the environment reside in the context of the affordance, the abilities of the agent and the object in the affordance actions and the outcome of this interactive activity in the effects. This work focuses on the integration of the semantic features of the previously mentioned environment in order to obtain a good grasp affordance action, from now on referred to as grasp-action, of the object. The presented framework can reason on the object grasping areas that are strongly related to the affordance group. The reasoning process is based on a Knowledge Base (KB) graph representation. This KB is built using semantic attributes of the object and the environment. For every object explored by the framework, the KB uses weights to relate a subset of attributes. This association then leads to an affordance category which is highly correlated with a grasp-action area. The designed framework is assessed not only using standard learning evaluation metrics, but it is also tested on the zero-shot affordance prediction scenario. Moreover, the resulting grasping areas are compared with unseen labelled data to asses their accuracy matching percentage. The results demonstrate the suitability of the method for grasp-action affordance applications, offering a generalised object interaction alternative with autonomy capabilities.

2 Related Work

Many methods extract viable grasping points on objects, independently on their affordance [1,14]. Others focus explicitly on the task of grasp-action affordance from visual features and model parameters that are learned through reinforcement learning using biologically inspired methods [4,23]. [23], interestingly embraces psychology theories for human development such as the ones presented in [9] to learn from exploratory behaviours the invariants to obtain the best grasps. Contrary, [2,15] focus on the ability-action affordance of the objects. In their work, they use statistical relational learning to learn the ability affordance of different objects, which shows to cope with uncertainty. Other works go beyond the visual representation of the object and combine visual as well as textual descriptors to build a KB [22,25]. This KB is composed of actions learned through reinforcement learning techniques with the purpose of interacting with the object. [8,12] work on the actions and objects relations in a single interface representation to capture the needs of planning and robot control. Another extension is [5], they use these action complexes to extract the best grasping points of the objects. In literature, it is extensive the use of learning techniques such as deep Convolutional Neural Networks (CNN) to build an affordance model based on the visual objects features, resulting in a plausible generalised method given the robustness of their data [6,17]. Unlike these works, this paper presents a methodology that combines attributes of the object and the environment to provide a denser context for object affordance interaction. Thus, allowing it to generalise the grasp-action affordance on similar objects.

3 Proposed Solution

In this paper, a grasp-action area of the object is the result of the relation between the object and its surrounding environment. Figure 1 shows a summary of the proposed affordance model. Let us consider a glass cup in an affordance map relationship. Additional to its inherited affordance action qualities, i.e. contain liquids and being graspable, there are other elements that define its opportunity of interaction. For example the way in which it is being manipulated as well as the features that describe the glass cup itself and its surrounding environment. All these elements together define the affordance of the glass cup. This does not mean they are dependant of each other but rather codefining and coherent together. Bearing this example in mind, in Fig. 1, the context $C = \{c_1, c_2, ..., c_n\}$

is the set of semantic attributes of the glass cup and its environment (such as kitchen and living room), ({o}bject $\cup$ {s}urrounding) $\subseteq$ {**C**}ontext. The set of available actions, $\mathbf{A} = \{a_1, a_2, ..., a_n\}$, is understood as a twofold: (i) the way in which the glass cup can be approached, its suitable grasp-action areas, and (ii) the usages that the glass cup can achieve, its ability-action such as containing liquids, ({g}rasps $\cup$ {u}sage) $\subseteq$ {**A**}ctions. The set of effects of performing those actions, $\mathbf{E} = \{e_1, e_2, ..., e_n\}$, is kept as a simple discretisation between positive or negative effects, such as holding the glass cup correctly in order not to spill the liquid, ({p}ositive $\cup$ {n}egative) $\subseteq$ {**E**}ffects. The key attributes of the affordance reasoning to get those grasp-action areas are enclosed in the form of a KB. These methods are commonly used in artificial intelligence because of their advantages for harvesting data and accessing a more extensive array of queries regarding the essential features of a process, rather than just the result. KBs achieve this task by connecting a collection of attributes through a general set of rules. In this work, the attributes are the features that describe the object and the environment and are connected through a hierarchical set of decisions that result in the object affordance. This section first summarises the object modelling stage, to then reason on the object affordance that is highly correlated with the resulting grasp-action areas as schematised in Fig. 2.

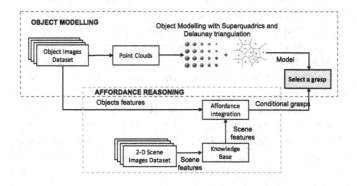

Fig. 2. Proposed framework for grasping affordance reasoning.

A KB is visualised as a graph representation, as illustrated in Fig. 3 where the entities (nodes) are connected by general rules (edges). In this setup, the entities are the target object, the attributes of the object and its surrounding, and the resulting affordance groups. The general rules are the attribute to attribute relation that results from a classification process. The relation between attributes are weighted accordingly, where the higher the weight, the higher the correlation between the two entities. In order to describe objects by their attributes the best practice is to divide their features into base, semantic and discriminative [7]. In this work, the base features, such as edges and colours, are extracted using CNN. The semantic features are visual characteristics of the object as defined in

Table 1. From now on, these features will be referred to as visual semantic features. They are the result of a deep CNN and are divided as (i) shape attributes, these are the set of visual attributes that describe the objects geometrical appearance; (ii) texture attributes, are categories based on visual characteristics of the objects materials; and (iii) environment attributes, which are the scenarios in which the objects are more likely to be found in. This attribute is added with the purpose of facilitating the object affordance reasoning. The implemented KB considers different scenarios in which the object can be located; thus the object is not restricted to a particular environment. For example, a glass containing liquids is more likely to be found in a kitchen and a living room. Finally, the discriminative features are those that offer a comprehensive understanding of the semantic features. They are the result of a predictive decision tree model that uses deep CNN as nodes. The KB is composed of four different Deep Neural Networks that, through the pre-trained CNN, resnet50 [11], extract features from the perceived images. These four different deep learned CNN correspond to the four different visual semantic attributes, as described in Table 1, which result in the deduced set of entities in a graph that defines a grasp-action affordance.

Table 1. Used attributes and entities of the KB graph.

Attribute	Entities per attribute
Shape	Box, cylinder, irregular, long, round
Texture	Aluminium, cardboard, coarse, fabric, glass, plastic, rubber, smooth
Categorical	Container, food, personal, miscellaneous, utensils
Environment	Bathroom, bedroom, play-room, closet, kitchen, living room, office

3.1   Knowledge Base Predictive Model

In this paper, the KB constitutes a data library that builds a predictive model connected through a hierarchical set of decisions, such as the edges on Fig. 3, from now on referred as weights. These decisions are the result of a classification task of the object semantic features, represented as the nodes in Fig. 3. From each of the attributes, $\forall a \in \boldsymbol{A} : \boldsymbol{A} \in [1, ..., K]$, where K is the total number of visual semantic features as described in Table 1, a set of weights represented as a vector $\boldsymbol{\Psi}_{a_k} = [\psi_1, \psi_2, ..., \psi_n]$ is extracted, where n is the total number of entities in that attribute. These $\boldsymbol{\Psi}_{a_k}$ are hierarchically connected with the next attribute a_{k+1}. Then $\boldsymbol{\Psi}_{a_k}$ offers a way to rank on the next best entity candidate. The higher the ψ_n, the higher the probability that the connected two entities among attributes result in a better affordance reasoning. These weights are proportional to the posterior probability distribution obtained from the classification task. Such that the posterior probability distribution is defined as the Bayes rule:

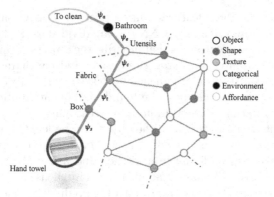

Fig. 3. Example of a cleaning object and the extracted attributes used to build the KB graph. The higher weights **Ψ** (red) create the reasoning to an affordance group. (Color figure online)

$$\widehat{P}(a|x) = \frac{P(x|a)P(a)}{P(x)}, \tag{1}$$

where x is an image belonging an attribute a, $P(a)$ is the posterior distribution and $P(x)$ is a normalisation constant that consists of the sum over a of the multivariate normal density. Figure 3 depicts an example of an object which grasping affordance can be to clean or to hand over. In this example, the weights deduce the best path (shown in red) to the *to clean* grasping affordance. The collected information from each of the deep CNN is then used to learn a decision tree as a predictive model: $(\boldsymbol{y}, Z) = (y_1, y_2, y_3, ..., y_n, Z)$, where Z is the affordance group that the system is trying to reason, and the vector $\boldsymbol{y}$ is the set of features $\{y_1, y_2, y_3, ..., y_n\}$ used for the reasoning task. Thus, the model learns the ranking that reasons on the affordance grasping task $R(x) = \boldsymbol{\Psi}_A^\mathsf{T} \boldsymbol{y}(x)$ where $\boldsymbol{\Psi}_A$ is the transpose of the model parameters from all the attributes and $\boldsymbol{y}(x)$ is the set of visual features of a given image x.

3.2 Calculating the Grasping Points

Once the affordance is deduced, the system selects from the set of grasping points obtained in the object reconstruction stage and limits the grasps depending on the affordance reasoning obtained from the KB. In order to impose such constraints, the space of the previously obtained grasping points is discretised in the third dimension, z, so that the following decision on the grasping area can be made: (i) The grasping region should lie on those points located in the central subspaces of the discretised space for objects that are meant to contain edibles. (ii) For the rest of objects, it is considered as the grasping region those subspaces where the density of grasping points is higher than a threshold, given that the affordance action-effect is not critical.

4   Evaluation

This work's goal is to achieve a system able to reason on the object grasp-action affordance, thus offering autonomy capabilities. As a result, it is of interest to evaluate the KB on (i) its attribute accuracy classification, and (ii) its reasoning efficiency with similar objects.

4.1   System Setup

The setting up of the system consists on collecting the required data for the training and the assessment of the method. This collection is built using two different datasets that are manually organised into entities of the attributes described in Table 1. After passing through the predictive model in the KB, every object in the library is expected to fall into: *to eat, to contain, to hand over, to brush, to squeeze, to clean* or *to wear*. The first set of images is from the Washington-RGB dataset, which contains 300 objects providing the point clouds and the two-dimensional (2-D) images for each one of the instances [13]. The second dataset is the MIT indoor scene recognition that contains 15,620 different 2-D images of 67 different indoor scenes from which this work uses seven of those classes [20]. By unifying these two datasets, the objects are correlated to the environment in which they are more likely to be located. Both datasets are split into 70% for training and the remaining 30% for testing. These subsets are used to train and test a battery of classifiers that help to define good object affordances features. In order to represent the obtained grasping area of the objects, an ellipse with the iCub humanoid robot end-effector dimensions is simulated. The orientation of such ellipse is out of the scope of this work and the focus remains on the position of the grasping area.

4.2   Reasoning on the Affordance

A summary of the accuracies per deep CNN in the KB is presented in Table 2. As a reminder to the reader, the aim of the proposed methodology is not to improve the performance of the individual classifiers. Nonetheless, the illustrated accuracies match the state-of-the-art results shown in [11,13]. To evaluate the overall performance of the KB, the accuracies before and after adding the environment features were collected. Figure 4 shows the data for both cases. A lower accuracy is obtained in the case where the environment features are not included, as illustrated in Fig. 4(a) and (b). Furthermore, Fig. 4(a) not including the environment shows a slightly higher spread among different affordance classes. This misclassification is the case for affordances which objects have a general semantic categorical attribute such as "miscellaneous" or "container". Thus, a percentage of objects are misclassified among the *to contain, to brush, to eat,* and *to squeeze* categories. Regarding grasping, this miscue represents a significant adverse effect, especially for objects which real affordance is *to contain,* and its misclassification results in the system lifting up the object from any point, risking dropping its content. This risk is reduced by 4.24% when adding the environment features, as portrayed in Fig. 4(b), especially in categories such as *to contain, to hand over* and *to eat*. The posterior probability distribution of the affordances categories is also evaluated. Figure 5 shows that while there is a decrement in the distribution for some categories such as *to hand*, there is an increment for others such as *to clean*. This change in the distribution is accredited to the variation in environments where these objects are found.

Table 2. Each of the attributes classification accuracies.

Classifier	Accuracy
Shape	95.71%
Texture	98.83%
Categorical	99.91%
Environment	76.50%

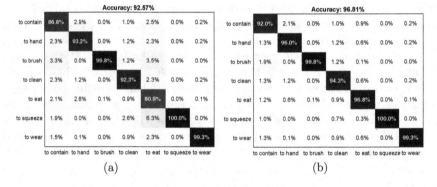

Fig. 4. Affordance category classification performance: (a) before adding environment features, showing an average diagonal accuracy of 92.57%; (b) after including the environment, showing a diagonal average accuracy of 96.81%.

4.3 Zero-Shot Affordance

Considering the changing nature of indoor scenes, it is useful to measure the method's affordance prediction on new objects. In this work, the object affordance is limited to its grasping action and is seen as the combination of the action-effect pair that results from the observations of the object and its environment. Zero-shot affordance, in this case, refers to the affordance prediction of a familiar but previously unseen object. For this part of the experiments, a set of semantically similar objects has been chosen from a third dataset, Cornell [24]. This dataset is used to learn how to grasp objects in other works such as [14,24]. These works exploit the fact that the Cornell dataset contains the three-dimensional (3-D) point cloud of the objects and their corresponding labelled

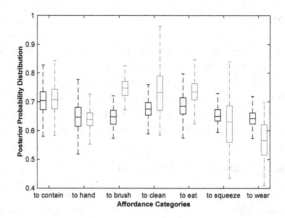

Fig. 5. Distributional posterior probabilities per class of the KB before (shown in black) and after (shown in magenta) the environment features. (Color figure online)

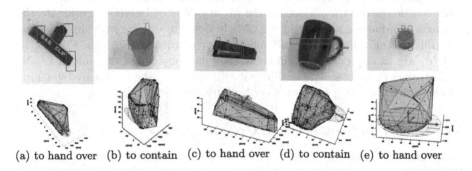

(a) to hand over   (b) to contain   (c) to hand over   (d) to contain   (e) to hand over

Fig. 6. Zero-shot affordance prediction on semantically similar objects. The original images contain the labels (rectangles) for the preferred grasping regions from [14,24]. (Color figure online)

grasping regions in the form of rectangles. From the Cornell dataset, 22 semantically similar objects to the ones used for the training of the KB are chosen, obtaining an average accuracy of 81.3% on the object affordance reasoning. In order to deduce the affordance of an unknown object, the same hierarchical procedure previously explained is followed. The set of weights Ψ_A has ranked a connection of attributes that results in an affordance, depending on the perceived semantics. Furthermore, this hierarchical connection has been learned in a predictive model to result in the grasping areas of the object. Figure 6 shows a sample of the familiar objects tested using the KB with their affordance group and deduced grasping area (shown with the red ellipse). Out of this subset, the most critical case is shown by the ones which affordance is to contain edibles, the cup and the mug in Fig. 6(b) and (d), for which the grasping areas are correctly calculated.

5   Discussion

The proposed methodology is not only able to (i) reason on the object affordance of known and semantically similar objects, but also (ii) to extract a suitable grasp-action region of the target depending on the interpreted affordance. Given these features, this section discusses the performance of the KB on discerning the affordance of semantically similar objects, followed by a comparison of the obtained grasp-action regions with other methods' ground truth data.

5.1   Similar Shape, Different Affordance

One of the most significant arguments for building this framework is to help a robot generalise on object affordances. That is to say, just as humans succeed at generalising an action towards objects of the same category with significantly different shapes, e.g. glasses: wine, tumbler, martini, and differentiate how to manipulate objects with similar shapes but for different purposes, e.g. candle vs water bottle. Given the objects in the library, it is of interest to evaluate the different affordance and grasping regions obtained for objects with similar shape but different affordance thus different preferred grasping regions. Figure 6(b) and (e) are examples of two different everyday objects (a cup and a candle respectively) with considerably different affordance, where the located grasping regions differ according to the deduced affordance of the object.

5.2   Quality on the Calculated Grasping Area

Different works have been done in the field of affordance detection and grasping. However, they commonly learn a labelled set of data in order to be able to identify the grasping regions. Contrary to these techniques, the method presented in this paper deduces the grasping region without any *a-priori* information about the grasping points. Given that the presented method does not train on grasp labels, in order to evaluate its output, it is compared to the ground truth labels of the Cornell dataset. There are works that use deep learning techniques to learn the grasping points of the objects mapped in the Cornell dataset images [14,21,24]. It is worth mentioning that these works do not account for affordance learning but for object classification. They simulate the end-effector with a rectangle, allowing it to account for its orientation, and use point and rectangle metrics to measure the mean square error (MSE) between their ground truth and the obtained grasps. Their proposed point metric computes the centre point of the predicted rectangle and considers the grasp as a success if it is within some distance from at least one of the ground truth rectangles. Contrary to this work, their labelled grasping areas are based on their end-effector control, and kinematic constraints and not on object affordance. Thus, a direct quantitative comparison is not viable. However, it is possible to use a modified version of their proposed point metric. The results of this work can be qualitatively evaluated by visually inspecting the resulting area. Moreover, quantified by the percentage of grasping regions that coincide between both sets of data, i.e., the labelled rectangles of the Cornell dataset and the ellipses of this proposal. In order to obtain such percentage, the Euclidean distance from the centre point of the labelled rectangles, observation a, to the centre point of the superellipsoid, observation b, is measured and expected to be below a set threshold. From the Cornell dataset, a subset of 65 random images was taken, including images from different perspectives of the same object. These images were categorised into an affordance group, illustrating their provided grasping label as a red rectangle on the 2-D image, as seen in Fig. 6. By measuring the Euclidean distance, 88% of the calculated grasps using the KB proposed in this work fall inside the labelled grasping regions. The other 12% falls either close to a valid region, or entirely in a new area given that it has followed the constraints of the grasps depending on the object affordance, as it is the case of the cup in Fig. 6(b).

6   Conclusions and Future Work

Contrary to the available methods, the framework presented in this paper is able to (i) reason on the affordance grasp-action of known and familiar objects without previously acknowledging the grasping areas, thus (ii) offering a reasoning process for object interaction with autonomy capabilities. The results of the evaluation performed on the framework support the hypothesis presented at the beginning of this work: that the grasp-action affordance does not depend solely on the object semantic features but on their combination with the features that describe the environment. The results show that without any *a-priori* awareness on the grasping regions, the designed KB can reason on the object's affordance grasping points. The presented framework has room for improvement. The performance of the KB can be increased by adding more attributes to the base, as well as modifying the predictive model to classify more than one affordance at the time (for example, an object's affordance can be *to hand over* as well as *to clean*). Furthermore, the dynamics and system control schemes of the robot and the environment are considered out of the scope of the presented work. Nonetheless, [18,19] offers a learning-based framework that comprises relative and absolute robotic skills for dual-arm manipulation suitable for dynamic environments, that together with a dense context representation of the scenario semantics offers a complete solution for an interactive object platform.

Acknowledgements. Thanks to the support of the EPSRC IAA 455791 along with ORCA Hub EPSRC (EP/R026173/1, 2017–2021) and consortium partners.

References

1. Ardón, P., Dragone, M., Erden, M.S.: Reaching and grasping of objects by humanoid robots through visual servoing. In: Prattichizzo, D., Shinoda, H., Tan, H.Z., Ruffaldi, E., Frisoli, A. (eds.) EuroHaptics 2018. LNCS, vol. 10894, pp. 353–365. Springer, Cham (2018). https://doi.org/10.1007/978-3-319-93399-3_31
2. Ardón, P., Pairet, È., Ramamoorthy, S., Lohan, K.S.: Towards robust grasps: using the environment semantics for robotic object affordances. In: Proceedings of the AAAI Fall Symposium on Reasoning and Learning in Real-World Systems for Long-Term Autonomy, pp. 5–12. AAAI Press (2018)
3. de Beeck, H.P.O., Torfs, K., Wagemans, J.: Perceived shape similarity among unfamiliar objects and the organization of the human object vision pathway. J. Neurosci. **28**(40), 10111–10123 (2008)
4. Bonaiuto, J., Arbib, M.A.: Learning to grasp and extract affordances: the Integrated Learning of Grasps and Affordances (ILGA) model. Biol. Cybern. **109**(6), 639–669 (2015)
5. Detry, R., et al.: Learning object-specific grasp affordance densities. In: IEEE 8th International Conference on Development and Learning, ICDL 2009, pp. 1–7. IEEE (2009)
6. Do, T.T., Nguyen, A., Reid, I.: AffordanceNet: an end-to-end deep learning approach for object affordance detection. In: International Conference on Robotics and Automation (ICRA) (2018)
7. Farhadi, A., Endres, I., Hoiem, D., Forsyth, D.: Describing objects by their attributes. In: 2009 IEEE Conference on Computer Vision and Pattern Recognition, CVPR 2009, pp. 1778–1785. IEEE (2009)
8. Geib, C., et al.: Object action complexes as an interface for planning and robot control. In: IEEE RAS International Conference on Humanoid Robots (2006)
9. Gibson, J.J.: The Ecological Approach to Visual Perception, Classic edn. Psychology Press, London (2014)
10. Gibson, J.: The theory of affordances. In: Shaw, R., Bransford, J. (eds.) Perceiving, Acting, and Knowing: Toward and Ecological Psychology, pp. 62–82. Erlbaum, Hillsdale, NJ (1977)
11. He, K., Zhang, X., Ren, S., Sun, J.: Deep residual learning for image recognition. In: Proceedings of the IEEE Conference on Computer Vision and Pattern Recognition, pp. 770–778 (2016)
12. Krüger, N., et al.: Object-action complexes: grounded abstractions of sensory-motor processes. Robot. Auton. Syst. **59**(10), 740–757 (2011)
13. Lai, K., Bo, L., Ren, X., Fox, D.: Detection-based object labeling in 3D scenes. In: 2012 IEEE International Conference on Robotics and Automation (ICRA), pp. 1330–1337. IEEE (2012)
14. Lenz, I., Lee, H., Saxena, A.: Deep learning for detecting robotic grasps. Int. J. Robot. Res. **34**(4–5), 705–724 (2015)
15. Moldovan, B., Moreno, P., van Otterlo, M., Santos-Victor, J., De Raedt, L.: Learning relational affordance models for robots in multi-object manipulation tasks. In: 2012 IEEE International Conference on Robotics and Automation (ICRA), pp. 4373–4378. IEEE (2012)
16. Montesano, L., Lopes, M., Bernardino, A., Santos-Victor, J.: Learning object affordances: from sensory-motor coordination to imitation. IEEE Trans. Robot. **24**, 15–26 (2008)

17. Nguyen, A., Kanoulas, D., Caldwell, D.G., Tsagarakis, N.G.: Object-based affordances detection with convolutional neural networks and dense conditional random fields. In: IEEE/RSJ International Conference on Intelligent Robots and Systems (IROS) (2017)

18. Pairet, È., Ardón, P., Broz, F., Mistry, M., Petillot, Y.: Learning and generalisation of primitives skills towards robust dual-arm manipulation. In: Proceedings of the AAAI Fall Symposium on Reasoning and Learning in Real-World Systems for Long-Term Autonomy, pp. 62–69. AAAI Press (2018)

19. Pairet, È., Ardón, P., Mistry, M., Petillot, Y.: Learning and composing primitive skills for dual-arm manipulation. In: Konstantinova, J., et al. (eds.) TAROS 2019. LNAI, vol. 11649, pp. 65–77 (2019)

20. Quattoni, A., Torralba, A.: Recognizing indoor scenes. In: IEEE Conference on Computer Vision and Pattern Recognition, CVPR 2009, pp. 413–420. IEEE (2009)

21. Saxena, A., Driemeyer, J., Ng, A.Y.: Robotic grasping of novel objects using vision. Int. J. Robot. Res. **27**, 157–173 (2008)

22. Sridharan, M.: Integrating knowledge representation, reasoning, and learning for human-robot interaction. In: AAAI Fall Symposium. Artificial Intelligence for Human-Robot Interaction, pp. 69–76. AAAI Press (2017)

23. Stoytchev, A.: Toward learning the binding affordances of objects: a behavior-grounded approach. In: Proceedings of AAAI Symposium on Developmental Robotics, pp. 17–22 (2005)

24. Sung, J., Lenz, I., Saxena, A.: Deep multimodal embedding: manipulating novel objects with point-clouds, language and trajectories. In: 2017 IEEE International Conference on Robotics and Automation (ICRA), pp. 2794–2801. IEEE (2017)

25. Zhu, Y., Fathi, A., Fei-Fei, L.: Reasoning about object affordances in a knowledge base representation. In: Fleet, D., Pajdla, T., Schiele, B., Tuytelaars, T. (eds.) ECCV 2014. LNCS, vol. 8690, pp. 408–424. Springer, Cham (2014). https://doi.org/10.1007/978-3-319-10605-2_27

Design Analysis of a Fabric Based Lightweight Robotic Gripper

Ahmed Hassan$^{(\boxtimes)}$, Hareesh Godaba, and Kaspar Althoefer

Queen Mary University of London, London, UK
ahmed.hassan@qmul.ac.uk

Abstract. The development of grasping mechanisms for various grasping applications have enabled robots to perform a wide variety of tasks in both industrial as well as domestic applications. Soft robotic grippers have been very useful in grasping applications with an added advantage of simpler control mechanisms as compared to rigid grippers. In this paper, a two fingered gripper inspired by the fingers of a human hand is introduced. The gripper is made from fabrics and, hence, compliant, lightweight, completely foldable and boasts a high payload capability. The mechanical design of the gripper is optimized through experiments, a maximum bending angle of 180° is achieved. We demonstrate grasping of a variety of objects using the new gripper.

Keywords: Soft robotic gripper · Pneumatic actuation ·
Fabric based inflatable finger

1 Introduction

Soft robotic grippers have seen tremendous development in recent years. Simple control mechanisms, easy operation, low development and operation costs have made soft robotic grippers one of the prime areas for research and development. As a result of this, numerous soft robotic gripping methods and techniques are being developed.

The techniques of soft robotic grippers can be divided into three broad categories: gripping by actuation, by varying stiffness and by controlled adhesion [1]. In the current paper, we will discuss the development of a soft robotic gripper with fabric-based stiffness controlled fingers. Each of these methodologies has its own merits and demerits. The proposed gripper falls under the category of controlled actuation; using controlled actuation, we can also control the stiffness of the gripper to achieve different gripping forces to handle hard and soft objects.

A common objective concerning the development of robotic gripper is to make them, ideally, as robust and practical as a human hand. To achieve this, numerous gripping devices have been developed, from highly complex and rigid structures like Shadow Dexterous Hand [2] to highly flexible, compliant and under-actuated robotic hands, such as those by Deimel et al. [3]. The main advantages of soft robotic grippers over conventional rigid robotic grippers are that they require far simpler control algorithms, are lightweight and conform well to target objects due to their compliant behavior (Fig. 1).

K. Althoefer et al. (Eds.): TAROS 2019, LNAI 11649, pp. 16–27, 2019.
https://doi.org/10.1007/978-3-030-23807-0_2

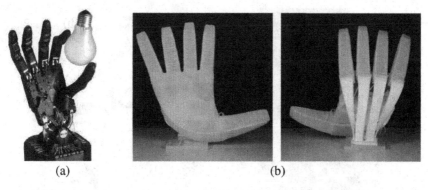

(a)   (b)

Fig. 1. (a) Shadow Robot Dexterous arm comprising of rigid components. The operation of this hand requires a complex control methodology and suffers from a bulky structure due to many pneumatic structures needed to drive hand's fingers [2]. (b) RBO 2 hand, in contrast, is made up of soft pneumatically actuated fingers. This soft structure enables the hand to achieve maximum compliance. Despite the many degrees of freedom in the fingers only a small number of actuators are required [3].

Keeping in mind the advantages of the grippers made of soft and stiffness controllable structures, numerous grasping mechanisms have been developed to cater a wide variety of applications. Manti et al. [4] and Crooks et al. [5] developed grippers which fall under the category of control through actuation. Fluidic elastomer actuators [6–8] are one of the most popular forms in the category of soft grippers. This type of gripper involves a polymer based flexible structure with enclosed internal chambers. When the chambers are pressurized, either by air (pneumatic) or by liquids (hydraulic), the structures bend forming an effective grip. The main advantage of fluidic elastomer actuators is high gripping force and high compatibility. A similar work on fabric based robotic grippers actuated by means of air pressure [9] was proposed as an alternative to polymer based fluidic elastomer actuators for added benefits like low actuation requirement.

Another very popular technique for soft robotic gripping is granular jamming [10, 11]. In this technique, a membrane filled with granules (coffee, aromatic beads, adzuki beans) [12] is used. When the vacuum is created in the membrane, the granules tightly pack together and the friction between the particles cause the structure to become rigid; an object in contact with the gripper's membrane will be wedged between the particles (Fig. 2).

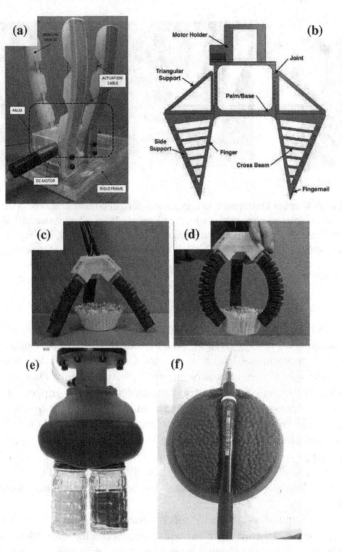

Fig. 2. Robotic grippers using external motors for actuation; (a) Bio inspired soft robotic gripper [4]; (b) Fin-ray inspired high compliance gripper [5]; (c) Fluidic elastomer actuator based gripper in open state; (d) closed state picking up test object [7]; (e) Universal gripper based on granular jamming technique [10]; (f) A gripper showing aromatic beads as jamming medium [12].

Another interesting approach in designing soft grippers is the use of stimuli-responsive materials or smart materials. As the name suggests, the resulting structures exhibit grasping operations when exposed to some specific external stimuli. The external stimuli include chemical change (pH change [13], salt change [14]), humidity change [15], electrical [16], optical [17], thermal [18] and magnetic stimuli [19]. The applications of stimuli responsive soft grippers include micro grippers for assembly of micro-objects, drug delivery systems and surgery.

In this paper, we propose a soft gripper made of airtight fabric actuated using pneumatic pressure. The proposed gripper can be actuated using pneumatic pressure to achieve deformation. Additionally, by controlling the pressure, we can also control the stiffness of the gripper and achieve different grasping forces to handle hard and soft objects.

2 Design of the Proposed Fabric-Based Gripper

The fabric based gripper presented in this paper has fingers made up of an air tight fabric structure. The fabric allows the overall structure to be extremely lightweight. In the unactuated state, the fingers are fully foldable. Upon inflation, the stiffness of the fabric structure increases and enables it to apply forces for grasping.

The human fingers grasp by bending at the joints. In order to replicate bending in the fabric-based finger, a technique to generate asymmetric elongations on either sides of the finger, is employed. This asymmetric elongation is achieved by incorporating a pleated structure on one side of the finger (Fig. 3). When pressure is applied through the inlet, the pleats unfold while the non-pleated side does not change in length. This asymmetric deformation causes the finger to bend (Fig. 4).

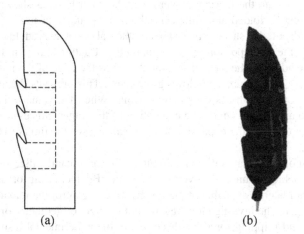

(a)   (b)

Fig. 3. (a) Schematic representation of the fabricated finger in deflated state (b) Actual finger in deflated state

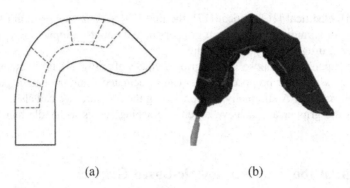

Fig. 4. (a) Schematic representation of the fabricated figure in pressurized state; (b) Actual fabric-based finger in pressurized state.

We fabricate the fingers using a fabric with the tradename *ripstop* [20] sold by UK fabrics online. This material is inherently leak-proof and as such ideal for our purpose since airtightness can be achieved without any extra coating. The ripstop fabric also has a high yield strength capable of sustaining high pressures.

The finger inspired gripper is fabricated as follows. First, a rectangular sheet of fabric is taken (Fig. 5(a)) and a rectangular hole is cut into it, as shown in Fig. 5(b). A separate piece of fabric larger than the cut-out hole is prepared and pleats are introduced to attain a size close to the size of the cut hole. The pleated section with its folds is then sewn onto the fabric to cover the rectangular hole, as shown in Fig. 5(c). The sheet obtained is folded along the central axis perpendicular to the pleats and the overlapping ends of the sheets are sewn together along a curved line. The excess material outside the sewn portion is cut to obtain the structure shown in Fig. 5(d). The seams along the edges of the pleated section as well as the edge of the finger are sealed applying partially cured latex and allowing it to cure. This prevents the air inside from escaping out through the holes caused by sewing. When the actuator is inflated, the pleats unfold to allow for asymmetric elongation of the finger. Since the sewn edge of the finger is inextensible, the expansion in the pleats causes the finger to bend towards the sewn edge.

The amount of extra material sewn into the fabric significantly affects the amount of bending angle achieved under a given air pressure. By increasing or decreasing the amount of extra material available in the finger, we can control the maximum bending angle of the finger. The investigations regarding the effect of geometry of pleats on the bending angle and gripping force are discussed in the experimental results section.

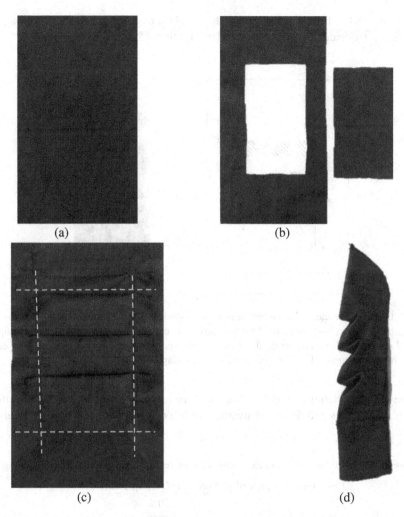

Fig. 5. The step-wise construction process for the finger; (a) fabric cut to size of the finger; (b) section cut-out where extra material will be sewn; (c) stitching of extra material, note the pleats in the fabric to aid in expansion (broken yellow lines highlighting the stitching path); (d) finger completed and edges trimmed. (Color figure online)

To investigate the bending capabilities of the finger, numerous designs with variations in geometry are fabricated and experiments are conducted to understand the working principle in more detail. The design parameters considered in this study are the number of pleats and the degree of overlap in the pleated section. A representative schematic depicting the design parameters is shown in Fig. 6(a). The shaded regions represent the overlapped portions in a pleated structure. The example shown has four independent shaded regions indicating four pleats. For the design shown in Fig. 6, the total number of sections are 4 with each section having a length of 2.5 cm. The degree of overlap is 50%. In our experimental study, fabric-based fingers with 3, 4, 5 and 6 sections are fabricated. A degree of overlap of either 25% or 50% is chosen.

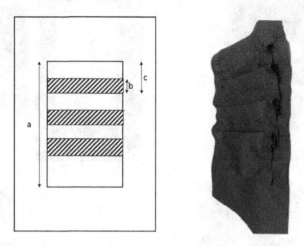

Fig. 6. Design parameters of the finger; a is the total cutout section (same for all the designs i.e. 10 cm), b is the percentage overlap of extra material and c is the Section length (depending upon the total number of sections). For the design shown above, the total number of sections are 4 each section having a length of 2.5 cm, the percentage overlap is 50%.

The design variations which are fabricated for experiments to investigate the effect of number of pleats and degree of overlap are listed in Tables 1 and 2 respectively.

Table 1. Details of design parameters with varying sections and same overlap percentage

Design no.	Number of sections (n)	Overlap percentage
1.1	3	50%
1.2	4	50%
1.3	5	50%
1.4	6	50%

Table 2. Details of design parameters with varying percentage overlap

Design no.	Number of sections (n)	Overlap percentage
2.1	4	25%
2.2	4	50%
2.3	5	25%
2.4	5	50%

3   Experimental Results

The finger designs were actuated by means of air pressure. The experiments were performed using two different levels of air pressure to study the maximum achievable bending angle and applied forces. When the finger is unactuated, the edge with the pleats is nearly straight (as shown in the left image in Fig. 7). When the is actuated using pneumatic pressure, the pleated edge forms a curved shape. The bending angle is given by the angle between the tangents drawn at the base and at the apex in the actuated state (as shown in the middle and right images in Fig. 7).

Fig. 7. Measurement of bending angle for the sample (4 sections, 3 pleats with 25% overlap), the finger in its unactuated state (left), actuated at 20 psi (middle) and actuated at 40 psi (right).

The experimental results for different fabrication designs are shown in Tables 3 and 4 and the corresponding experimental images are shown in Figs. 8 and 9. It is noted that by decreasing the number of sections from 4 greatly limits the bending angle of the finger. Also, the amount of extra material in the finger in the form of overlapped fabric in each section increases the bending capacity of the finger when it is pressurized.

Table 3. Experimental analysis for designs with varying number of sections

Design number	Bending angle		
	Air pressure: 0 psi/0 kPa	Air pressure: 20 psi/137.895 kPa	Air pressure: 40 psi/275.79 kPa
1.1	0°	104°	107°
1.2	0°	157°	162°
1.3	0°	163°	157°
1.4	0°	177°	180°

Table 4. Experimental analysis for designs with varying percentages of overlapping material

Design number	Bending angle		
	Air pressure: 0 psi/0 kPa	Air pressure: 20 psi/137.895 kPa	Air pressure: 40 psi/275.79 kPa
2.1	0°	93°	97°
2.2	0°	157°	162°
2.3	0°	78°	75°
2.4	0°	163°	157°

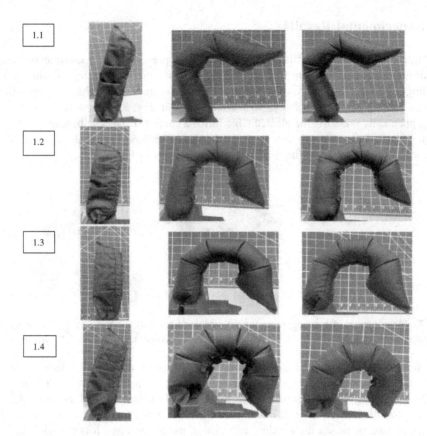

Fig. 8. Experimental demonstrations of finger designs with variable number of sections and same overlap percentage.

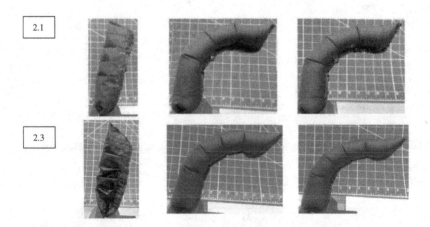

Fig. 9. Experimental images showing the deformation of different finger designs with variable number of sections and overlap percentages at different actuation pressures.

4 Discussion

From the experimental results on our designs with the varying number of sections and the amount of extra material added in the form of percentage overlap, it was found that the amount of extra material added determines the bending angle of the finger. Increasing the number of segments from 3 to 4 increases the bending angle by almost 50% but increasing the number of segments further has a negligible effect on the bending angle as we can see from Fig. 9. Further, the degree of overlap in the pleats has a drastic effect on the bending angle of the finger. When the degree of overlap is increased from 25% to 50% in a fabric finger with 5 segments, the bending angle doubles (Fig. 10).

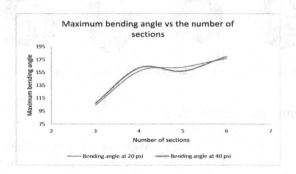

Fig. 10. Bending angle of different finger designs with varying number of segments

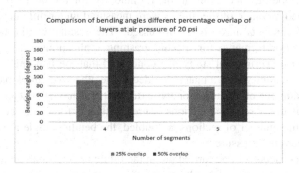

Fig. 11. Bending angle of different finger designs with varying percentage overlap of extra material at air pressure of 20 psi

We finally utilize the fabric-based design to develop a two fingered gripper. A holder with two holes is 3-D printed using Acrylonitrile Butadiene Styrene (ABS). the ends of the two fingers are inserted into the two holed and fastened using cable ties. The two inlets to the two fingers are commonly actuated by one pneumatic source. When pressure is applied, both the fingers bend creating an enclosing structure as shown in Fig. 11. We use the two fingered gripper to grasp a variety of soft and hard objects. The gripper can not only grasp and lift a heavy object such as a plier but also grasp a delicate cup made of Polyethylene terephthalate (PET). This demonstrates the ability of the gripper to control the stiffness and modulate the grasping forces applied to the object (Fig. 12).

Fig. 12. Gripper with two fingered structure demonstrating the gripping operation

5 Conclusions and Future Work

In this paper, we proposed a fabric based finger for grasping applications. the finger boasts of full foldability and low weight (5.06 grams per finger). We conducted a design study of fabric based fingers to understand the effect of geometrical design on the performance of the actuator. Several design variations were fabricated to investigate their bending properties and evaluate their suitability for the development of a soft gripper. The bending angle of the fingers were measured under different pressures and the experimental results have been discussed. The results would be helpful for achieving desired performance for specific grasping applications.

Based on our experimental study, we concluded that the bending of the finger is governed by the amount of extra material added to the otherwise inflexible fabric. Also, increasing the amount of sections for the extra material has almost no effect on the bending angle if the number of sections is greater than 3 for the given length of our finger. Even if the number of sections is doubled, the bending angle remains the same for a given pneumatic pressure.

Further experiments will be carried out in the future to determine more performance metrics such as the forces that can be achieved for different applied pressures and for different finger designs. These studies would be very useful in the development of a gripper suitable for a wide variety of applications involving grasping and manipulation.

References

1. Shintake, J., Cacucciolo, V., Floreano, D., Shea, H.: Soft robotic grippers. Adv. Mater. **30**, 1707035 (2018)
2. Shadow Robot: Dexterous Hand – Shadow Robot Company

3. Deimel, R., Brock, O.: A novel type of compliant and underactuated robotic hand for dexterous grasping. Int. J. Rob. Res. **35**, 161–185 (2016)
4. Manti, M., Hassan, T., Passetti, G., D'Elia, N., Laschi, C., Cianchetti, M.: A bioinspired soft robotic gripper for adaptable and effective grasping. Soft Robot. **2**, 107–116 (2015)
5. Crooks, W., Vukasin, G., O'Sullivan, M., Messner, W., Rogers, C.: Fin ray® effect inspired soft robotic gripper: from the robosoft grand challenge toward optimization. Front. Robot. AI. **3**, 1–9 (2016)
6. Rakotomalala, L., Mapelli, A.: A 3D printed soft gripper integrated with curvature sensor for studying soft grasping. Soins Pediatr. Pueric. **39**, 25–27 (2018)
7. Wang, Z., Chathuranga, D.S., Hirai, S.: 3D printed soft gripper for automatic lunch box packing. In: 2016 International Conference on Robotics and Biomimetics, ROBIO 2016, pp. 503–508 (2016)
8. Marchese, A.D., Katzschmann, R.K., Rus, D.: A recipe for soft fluidic elastomer robots. Soft Robot. **2**, 7–25 (2015)
9. Low, J.H., et al: A bidirectional soft pneumatic fabric-based actuator for grasping applications, pp. 1180–1186 (2017)
10. Amend Jr., J.R., Brown, E., Rodenberg, N., Jaeger, H.M., Lipson, H.: A positive pressure universal gripper based on the jamming of granular material. J. Phys. Condens. Matter. **9**, 341–350 (1997)
11. Brown, E., et al.: Universal robotic gripper based on the jamming of granular material, pp. 1–10
12. Nishida, T., Shigehisa, D., Kawashima, N., Tadakuma, K.: Development of universal jamming gripper with a force feedback mechanism. In: 2014 Joint 7th International Conference on Soft Computing and Intelligent Systems, SCIS 2014, 15th International Symposium on Advanced Intelligent Systems, ISIS 2014, pp. 242–246 (2014)
13. Zhao, L., Huang, J., Zhang, Y., Wang, T., Sun, W., Tong, Z.: Programmable and bidirectional bending of soft actuators based on janus structure with sticky tough PAA-clay hydrogel. ACS Appl. Mater. Interfaces **9**, 11866–11873 (2017)
14. Xiao, S., et al.: Salt-responsive bilayer hydrogels with pseudo-double-network structure actuated by polyelectrolyte and antipolyelectrolyte effects. ACS Appl. Mater. Interfaces **9**, 20843–20851 (2017)
15. Taccola, S., Greco, F., Sinibaldi, E., Mondini, A., Mazzolai, B., Mattoli, V.: Toward a new generation of electrically controllable hygromorphic soft actuators. Adv. Mater. **27**, 1668–1675 (2015)
16. Yang, C., et al.: Reduced graphene oxide-containing smart hydrogels with excellent electro-response and mechanical properties for soft actuators. ACS Appl. Mater. Interfaces. **9**, 15758–15767 (2017)
17. Hubbard, A.M., Mailen, R.W., Zikry, M.A., Dickey, M.D., Genzer, J.: Controllable curvature from planar polymer sheets in response to light. Soft Matter **13**, 2299–2308 (2017)
18. Ongaro, F., et al.: Autonomous planning and control of soft untethered grippers in unstructured environments. J. Micro-Bio Robot. **12**, 45–52 (2017)
19. Ghosh, A., et al.: Stimuli-responsive soft untethered grippers for drug delivery and robotic surgery. Front. Mech. Eng. **3**, 1–9 (2017)
20. PU Coated FR Ripstop: (n.d.). https://ukfabricsonline.com/pu-coated-fr-ripstop. Accessed 25 Apr 2019

A Method to Estimate the Oblique Arch Folding Axis for Thumb Assistive Devices

Visakha K. Nanayakkara[1](✉), Nantachai Sornkaran[2], Hasitha Wegiriya[2],
Nikolaos Vitzilaios[3], Demetrios Venetsanos[4], Nicolas Rojas[5],
M. Necip Sahinkaya[6], and Thrishantha Nanayakkara[5]

[1] Mechanical Engineering Department, CEMAST Campus,
Fareham PO13 9FU, UK
visakha.nanayakkara@fareham.ac.uk
[2] Department of Informatics, King's College London, London, UK
{nantachai.sornkarn,hasitha.wegiriya}@kcl.ac.uk
[3] Department of Mechanical Engineering,
University of South Carolina, Columbia, SC, USA
VITZILAIOS@sc.edu
[4] School of Mechanical, Aerospace and Automotive Engineering,
Coventry University, Coventry, UK
ac6109@coventry.ac.uk
[5] Dyson School of Design Engineering, Imperial College London, London, UK
{n.rojas,t.nanayakkara}@imperial.ac.uk
[6] Department of Mechanical and Automotive Engineering,
Kingston University London, Kingston, UK
M.Sahinkaya@kingston.ac.uk

Abstract. People who use the thumb in repetitive manipulation tasks are likely to develop thumb related impairments from excessive loading at the base joints of the thumb. Biologically informed wearable robotic assistive mechanisms can provide viable solutions to prevent occurring such injuries. This paper tests the hypothesis that an external assistive force at the metacarpophalangeal joint will be most effective when applied perpendicular to the palm folding axis in terms of maximizing the contribution at the thumb-tip as well as minimizing the projections on the vulnerable base joints of the thumb. Experiments conducted using human subjects validated the predictions made by a simplified kinematic model of the thumb that includes a foldable palm, showing that: (1) the palm folding angle varies from 71.5° to 75.3° (from the radial axis in the coronal plane) for the four thumb-finger pairs and (2) the most effective assistive force direction (from the ulnar axis in the coronal plane) at the MCP joint is in the range $0° < \psi < 30°$ for the four thumb-finger pairs. These findings provide design guidelines for hand assistive mechanisms to maximize the efficacy of thumb external assistance.

Keywords: Thumb kinematics · Foldable palm ·
Metacarpophalangeal joint · Thumb assistance

© Springer Nature Switzerland AG 2019
K. Althoefer et al. (Eds.): TAROS 2019, LNAI 11649, pp. 28–40, 2019.
https://doi.org/10.1007/978-3-030-23807-0_3

1   Introduction

Repetitive forceful occupational tasks like handling heavy tools and pipetting are likely to cause long term musculoskeletal impairments and localized muscle tension in the thumb [7,19]. While the thumb is found to be playing a leading role in any grasp [5,9], it has been observed that the basal trapeziometacarpal (TM) joint of the thumb is loaded more than the other joints [11]. The TM joint's unique saddle shape with the wrist bone along with its distinctive muscle and ligament capsule enables substantial movements of the thumb to reach the tips of the other fingers (thumb opposition) and to stabilize any grasp [14].

The human thumb has three joints, namely TM or carpometacarpal, metacarpophalangeal (MCP), and interphalangeal (IP); five intrinsic muscles located in the palm, and four extrinsic muscles connected to the bones via tendons (Fig. 1). The main role of the palmar intrinsic muscles is to move the thumb in different opposition ranges towards the other fingers while flexing, abducting, or medially rotating the thumb proximal joints [14]. In addition, the extrinsic FPL muscle is also dedicated to flex the thumb; the other extrinsic muscles support thumb extension [4]. In this context, it is important to abstract thumb's integrated musculoskeletal arrangement with the palm in a kinematic model of the thumb [18], [13] to design any external assistance to reduce further loading when repetitive tasks are done. Since the MCP joint is more accessible and directly connected to the TM joint, it seems more suitable to provide external support towards the palm.

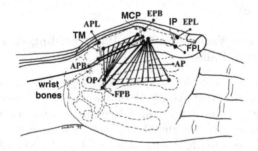

Fig. 1. Thumb muscle arrangement reprinted with kind permission from Colditz [4] and modified to indicate the thumb joints and wrist bones. Three joints: trapeziometacarpal (TM), metacarpophalangeal (MCP), and interphalangeal (IP). Four extrinsic muscles: Extensor Pollicis Brevis (EPB), Abductor Pollicis Longus (APL), Extensor Pollicis Longus (EPL), Flexor Pollicis Longus (FPL). Five intrinsic muscles: Opponens Pollicis (OP), Abductor Pollicis Brevis (APB), Flexor Pollicis Brevis (FPB), Adductor Pollicis (AP), First interossei (FI) (not shown).

Some notable work done to develop thumb assistive devices so far include, a pediatric robotic thumb exoskeleton [1], an articulated parallelogram mechanism to support thumb joint Flexion-Extension (F-E) along with thumb rotation at the base [2], co-actuated RoboGlove to assist all five fingers [8], a tendon-driven, polymer-based wearable robotic hand (Exo-glove Poly) to support thumb F-E [10], and a synergy-based single actuator tendon-driven wearable glove [20]. However, the thumb assistive force direction is not clearly specified and the assistance towards the foldable palm is not investigated in detail in the assistive devices developed so far.

In this paper, we test the hypothesis that an external assistive force exerted at the MCP joint of the thumb is most effective if it is parallel to the oblique arch [16]. Hereafter, we refer to the oblique arch folding axis as the virtual palm folding axis. The effectiveness of external assistance is measured in terms of the force gain at the thumb-tip. Since thumb's integrated musculoskeletal arrangement (Fig. 1) with a foldable palm is not in general incorporated in thumb kinematic models (e.g. [3,18]), a previously proposed thumb kinematic model with a virtual foldable palm joint is adopted in this work to simulate the hypothesis [12]. Simplified model based predictions are tested using experiments on human subjects to understand how a supportive tendon force at the MCP joint contributes to the thumb-tip pinch grip using an assistive tendon driven glove. We observe that the effective assistive force direction range from the experimental results is within the analytically predicted range from the adopted kinematic model.

The rest of this paper is organized as follows: Sect. 2 elaborate the kinematic modeling and experimental methods used to test the hypothesis. The numerical simulation and experimental results are presented in Sect. 3. Finally a discussion and concluding remarks are given in Sects. 4 and 5 respectively.

2   Methodology

2.1   Experiment 1: Variation of the Palm Folding Angle Across Thumb-Finger Pairs

This experiment is conducted to estimate the palm folding angle (γ in Fig. 2(b)) based on the assumption that the MCP joint would exert a force perpendicular to the palm folding axis during a palm folding movement. Therefore, we asked human participants to move the thumb to touch each other finger with a rubber band attached between the MCP joint location of a GECKO-TAC leather glove and an ATI Mini40 (SI-40-2) 6-axis Force/Torque (F/T) transducer mounted on a fixed frame (Fig. 2). Three male and one female subjects participated in this experiment.

The initial force sensor measurement is taken when the hand is open as in Fig. 2(a) with the band in tension. This anatomical position is taken to be as the coronal plane. Then the subjects are asked to move the thumb-tip to reach each finger-tip as shown in Fig. 2(b). Palm folding angle is computed using F/T transducer measurements for these two thumb postures (Fig. 2) for the four thumb-finger pairs.

The coordinate frames are assigned as follows: Force sensor z_s-x_s space coincides with the reference x_o-y_o space (coronal plane *ie.* the plane of the paper). y_s and z_o are normal to the paper. In the data analysis, the force sensor y axis

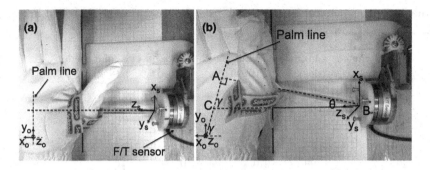

Fig. 2. Experiment 1 to evaluate palm folding angle γ. The reference x_o-y_o axes are in the palmar coronal plane. Force sensor z_s-x_s plane conforms to the reference x_o-y_o plane (plane of the paper). y_s and z_o are normal to the paper. (a) Initial hand position with rubber band in tension. The palm line is taken along y_o direction at the beginning. (b) Thumb and index finger-tip grasp posture with the moved rubber band. Virtual triangle ABC is defined on the x_o-y_o plane, taking the rubber band projection on AB. θ is the angle of the rubber band from the z_s axis.

(y_s) is rotated around z_s to account for the force sensor misalignment. A virtual triangle ABC is defined on the plane x_o-y_o taking the projection of the moved rubber band along AB. Hence the initial and resulting force sensor values are used to find the rubber band movement angle θ (Fig. 2(b)) for each thumb-finger combination. The palm folding arch, approximated as the line AC that goes through the reference is defined such that AB and AC are perpendicular to each other for each thumb-finger pair combination. Therefore, the palm folding angle γ (in the coronal plane) can be computed when θ is known.

2.2   Kinematic Model of the Thumb and Foldable Palm

A simplified 7-DOFs kinematic model proposed in [12] is used to ascertain how thumb-tip force gain depends on the interaction between the palm folding angle and the direction of the assistive force given at the MCP joint (Fig. 3). The coordinate frames for each joint, link connections, and design parameters of the kinematic chain are defined according to the Denavit-Hartenberg (D-H) notation (Table 1) [6].

Each consecutive thumb joint position in Fig. 3 is evaluated using link parameters and transforming frame N corresponding to the Nth joint to the wrist reference frame 0 using the transformation [6],

$$ {}^{0}_{N}T = \prod_{i=0}^{N-1} {}^{i}_{i+1}T \tag{1} $$

where $N = 8$.

The thumb-tip position vector is obtained from the first three elements of the last column of ${}^{0}_{N}T$ in Eq. 1. The Jacobian matrix for the thumb-tip is computed using the symbolic MATLAB function.

Table 1. D-H parameters for the thumb-palm kinematic model illustrated in Fig. 3 [12].

Joint no.	Link twist (deg)	Link length (mm)	Link offset (mm)	Joint angle (deg)
1	90	0	0	θ_1
2	−90	0	l_1	θ_2
3	−90	0	0	θ_3
4	0	l_2	0	θ_4
5	90	0	0	θ_5
6	0	l_3	0	θ_6
7	0	l_4	0	θ_7

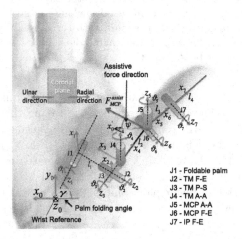

Fig. 3. 7-DOFs kinematic model of the thumb with foldable palm adopted to analyse the effective thumb assistive force direction [12]. $\theta_1 - \theta_7$ are J1-J7 joint rotational movements respectively. Thumb link lengths $l_2 - l_4$ represent thumb bone lengths whereas l_1 is the virtual orthogonal length from TM to J1 axis. Palm folding angle γ is the J1 axis inclination from the radial direction at the wrist reference (in the coronal plane). Assistive force F_{MCP}^{assist} is applied at the MCP joint at variable inclinations of ψ with respect to an axis x_o' parallel to the wrist reference x_o in ulnar direction on the $x_o - y_o$ space.

Thumb joint angle ranges are defined based on extensive precision grasp experiments done in the previous study [12].

Joint torques τ_{pre} are calculated assuming there is an initial unit force F_{tip}^{pre} at the thumb-tip to hold an object,

$$\tau^{pre} = J_{tip}^T F_{tip}^{pre} \tag{2}$$

Similarly, joint torques τ_{assist} due to the assistive unit force F_{MCP}^{assist} exerted at the MCP at variable directions of ψ from the ulnar axis in the coronal plane (Fig. 3) are computed as,

$$\tau_{assist} = J_{MCP}^T F_{MCP}^{assist} \tag{3}$$

where τ^{pre} and τ_{assist} are 7×1 and 4×1 torque vectors respectively, J_{tip} and J_{MCP} are 3×7 and 3×4 Jacobian matrices, F_{tip}^{pre} is the 3×1 unit force vector at the thumb-tip and F_{MCP}^{assist} is the 3×1 external assistive force vector in $x - y$ space. The new thumb-tip force F_{tip}^{post} is given by,

$$F_{tip}^{post} = (J_{tip}^T)^+ (\tau_{pre} + \tilde{\tau}_{assist}) \tag{4}$$

where $(J_{tip}^T)^+$ is the pseudoinverse of J_{tip}^T (assuming full-rank) and $\tilde{\tau}_{assist} = [\tau_{assist}^T \ \mathbf{0}_{1 \times 3}]^T$.

Assistive force gain at the thumb-tip is then evaluated by taking the ratio of the Euclidean norms of F_{tip}^{post} and F_{tip}^{pre}, that is, $|F_{tip}^{post}|/|F_{tip}^{pre}|$.

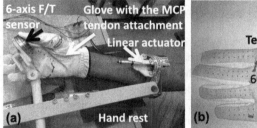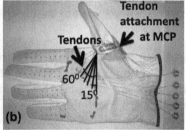

Fig. 4. Experiment 2: (a) Experimental setup to record force sensor and linear actuator data. Customized experimental setup supports the hand to keep in a flat position to obtain a consistent tendon assistance across each thumb-finger pair. (b) Wearable leather glove with attached assistive tendons to the thumb MCP joint $(0° - 60°)$. Each tendon is $15°$ apart.

2.3 Experiment 2: Interaction Between the Palm Folding Angle and the Thumb Assistive Force Direction

This experiment is carried out to find how thumb-tip force gain varies for different combinations of palm folding angles and thumb assistive force directions.

Five tendons are attached to a Velcro ring fastened around the MCP joint location of a GECKO-TAC leather glove as shown in Fig. 4(a). The tendons are attached from $0°$–$60°$ in $15°$ increments. These tendons are braided fishing lines of diameter $0.15\,\mathrm{mm}$.

A linear actuator (L12-50-210-06-I from Firgelli Technologies Inc.) fixed to the experimental setup as shown in Fig. 4(a) controls individual tendon movement of $5\,\mathrm{mm}$. Each tendon goes through a threaded pulley before it is connected to the actuator. The subjects are asked to hold an ATI Mini40 (SI-40-2) 6-axis F/T transducer which is mounted on a movable frame (Fig. 4(a)). While they are maintaining a constant pinch grip force (by looking at the force profile on

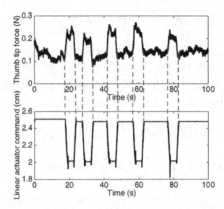

Fig. 5. A representative raw data trial. (*top*) Normal thumb-tip force including resultant pulses. (*bottom*) Corresponding linear assistive pull with five pulses plotted against time. The spikes in the linear actuator control command at the edges come from the internal control action to correct position errors in the transient phase.

the computer in front of them), an assistive force pulse (a linear tendon pull of 5 mm with duration of 5 s) is given at the MCP joint from the linear actuator. Five such pulses are given for each tendon within each thumb-finger pair trial range of 100 s with a sampling frequency of 1000 Hz. A representative raw data set is shown in Fig. 5. The linear actuator and force sensor readings are recorded for ten subjects (five male and five female), four thumb-finger pairs with five tendons for each pair using LabVIEW software, National Instruments Corp., through the data acquisition card.

All the selected subjects for both experiments 1 and 2 are right-handed and have no known thumb injuries or past thumb arthritis with their ages ranging from 25–45. Experimental procedure is approved by the Biomedical Sciences, Medicine, Dentistry and Natural and Mathematical Sciences Research Ethics Panel (BDM REP).

Recorded linear actuator assistive pulse command is smoothed out by applying a 3rd order polynomial Savitzky-Golay filter with frame size 7. Time indexes of the already smoothed assistive force pulses are used to find the resultant force pulses at the thumb-tip sensor measurements (Fig. 5). Then the resultant thumb-tip force vector for each pulse is computed using its 3D base vector (before the pulse) and the corresponding 3D pull vector (after the pulse). The thumb-tip force vector during the assistive pull is projected onto the thumb-tip base vector (F_b) and is added to it, to find the effective thumb-tip pull vector (F_p). The assistive force gain (F_p/F_b) is computed for each pulse taking the norms of F_p and F_b. Then the effective force gain is computed using the average force gains for the five pulses (Fig. 5).

Each input assistive force pulse at the MCP is a linear actuator pull of 5 mm for 5 s (Fig. 5) whereas, in the simulation, it is taken as a unit force vector (Fig. 3). Since thumb-tip force gain is calculated using the forces at the thumb-

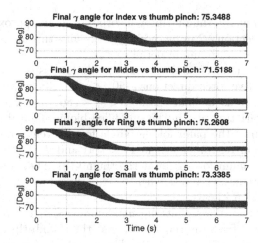

Fig. 6. Palm folding angle γ variation with each thumb-finger tip grasp posture combination across four subjects. Final average γ angle values for each thumb-finger interaction posture (Fig. 2) are marked along with the plots. Note the initial γ is 90° due to the palm axis assignment (Fig. 2(a)).

tip before and after exerting the assistive force at the MCP joint, the input force at the MCP is not taken into account in force gain computation.

Kolmogorov-Smirnov test is performed to check whether the force gain data for all the subject-finger-tendon pairs are normally distributed. Depending on the outcome, non-parametric Wilcoxon rank sum right-tailed, left-tailed, and two-sided (paired) hypothesis tests (equivalent to Mann-Whitney U test) are performed to test the significance of the assistive force direction across thumb-finger pairs, based on a significance level of $p < 0.05$.

3   Results

3.1   Variation of the Palm Folding Angle (Experiment 1)

Figure 6 shows the results of experiment 1 (see methods Sect. 2.1 for more details) suggesting that we can identify a steady state palm folding axis that varies its angle from 71.5°–75.3° across the other four fingers. It should be noted that this approximated axis dynamically varies when the palm folds with the moving MCP joint. Here, we argue that external assistive forces given at the MCP joint will have better efficacy if they are as perpendicular as possible to this palm folding axis.

3.2   Kinematic Model Simulations

A simplified kinematic model proposed in [12] is adopted to further understand how to maximize the efficacy of an external force given at the MCP joint to assist the grip force at the thumb tip by incorporating an approximation for the palm folding axis. Section 2.2 in methodology explains this model that accounts for palm folding and the thumb in detail.

The model based numerical simulation results for assistive force gains with respect to the assistive force directions $-50° < \psi < 50°$ at the MCP joint for different palm joint axis inclinations $50° < \gamma < 80°$ are shown in Fig. 7. In these figures, the variation of γ in the simplified biomechanical model represent a possible variation of the palm folding angle for different thumb-finger pairs. Numerical simulation results shown in Figs. 7(a) and 7(b) show that γ varies around 70° for maximum force gain at the thumb-tip. Therefore our simplified kinematic model prediction agrees with the experimental approximation of the steady state γ angle in Fig. 6.

Figure 7(b) further shows that the maximum assistive force gain ratio of 1:1.6 can be obtained for an initial 1 N force at the thumb-tip when ψ is in the range $10° < \psi < 20°$ for $70° < \gamma < 75°$. These numerical simulation results in Fig. 7 suggests that assistive force direction ψ corresponding to the maximum assistive force gain (as indicated by the colour code) increases with increasing γ, confirming our original argument that the efficacy of an external assistive force at MCP joint can be optimized by having it as perpendicular to the palm folding axis as possible.

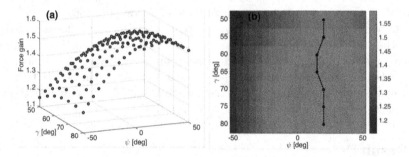

Fig. 7. (a) Assistive force gains at the thumb-tip for the assistive unit forces at the MCP joint calculated using thumb kinematics in Fig. 3 plotted against assistive force directions $(-50° < \psi < 50°)$ and palm folding angle $(50° < \gamma < 80°)$. (b) Maximum thumb-tip assistive force gains from Fig. 7(a) (connected in black dashed lines) with ψ and γ variations. (Color figure online)

3.3 Thumb Assistive Force Direction Across the Thumb-Finger Pairs (Experiment 2)

Experiments are conducted on human subjects to test how far the model based prediction holds when the actual palm folding does not follow a strict linear axis and when the TM joint in practice does not strictly follow a simple three orthogonal axes model. Please see the details of experiment-2 in Sect. 2.3 in methods.

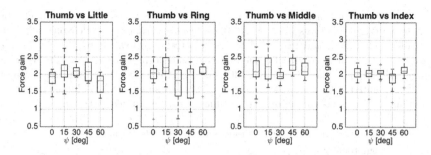

Fig. 8. Boxplots of thumb-tip assistive force gain for the linear actuator assistive force at the MCP joint in pinch grasp with each finger. Each box displays force gain values for an assistive tendon force direction in the range $0° < \psi < 60°$ (Fig. 4) for the ten subjects. $\psi = 60°$ is the tendon closest to the index finger.

Figure 8 shows boxplots of experimental assistive force gains for the assistive tendon directions ψ at the MCP joint for each thumb-finger pair across the ten subjects and five tendon directions. Since the force gain data for all finger-tendon pairs is not normally distributed ($p > 0.05$ Kolmogorov-Smirnov test), non-parametric Wilcoxon rank sum hypothesis test is performed to compare the median force gains.

Table 2 summarizes the outcome across the ten subjects. It shows that the median assistive force gains at $\psi = 15°$, $30°$ and $45°$ are statistically significantly higher than that of $\psi = 60°$ for the thumb-little pair. Moreover, a paired rank sum test confirms that the medians of $\psi = 15°$, $30°$ and $45°$ are not significantly different indicating it is effective to apply forces in any angle between $15°$ and $45°$ for the thumb-little pair. $\psi = 15°$ is the most effective for the thumb-ring pair. For the thumb-middle pair, median force gain at $\psi = 45°$ is significantly higher than that of $\psi = 30°$. A paired rank sum test confirms that the medians of $\psi = 45°$, $\psi = 60°$ pair and $\psi = 45°$, $\psi = 15°$ pair are not significantly different from each other. Hence the tendon directions greater or lower than $30°$ are the most effective for the thumb-middle pair. Significantly lower median force gain at $\psi = 45°$ for the thumb-index pair than $\psi = 30°$ and $\psi = 60°$ and no significant difference among $\psi = 15°$, $30°$ and $60°$, indicates that thumb-index pair can be effectively supported by tendons at $\psi = 15°$ and $\psi = 30°$ directions. Since $\psi = 0°$ is not significantly different from any of the directions and all the thumb-finger pairs are favoured by tendon angle directions $< 30°$, it can be noted that $0° < \psi < 30°$ is the most effective for all the thumb-finger pairs.

Table 2. Comparison of the median force gains in Fig. 8 across the ten subjects for the assistive force directions $0° < \psi < 60°$ using non-parametric Wilcoxon rank sum right-tailed, left-tailed, and two-sided hypothesis tests (equivalent to Mann-Whitney U test). F_g^i - Median force gain for the assistive tendon direction, $\psi = i$ (Fig. 4) from the ulnar direction where $i = 0°, 15°, 30°, 45°, 60°$. Statistically significant p-values (< 0.05) are noted with a * mark. Since $\psi = 0°$ is not significantly different from any of the tendon directions corresponding p-values are not included in the table.

Thumb-finger pair	Wilcoxon rank sum test	Result	p-value
Thumb-little:			
	$F_g^{60°} < F_g^{15°}$	True	0.0378* (<0.05)
	$F_g^{60°} < F_g^{30°}$	True	0.0129* (<0.05)
	$F_g^{60°} < F_g^{45°}$	True	0.027* (<0.05)
	$F_g^{15°} \neq F_g^{30°}$	False	0.9698 (>0.05)
	$F_g^{15°} \neq F_g^{45°}$	False	0.9698 (>0.05)
	$F_g^{30°} \neq F_g^{45°}$	False	0.9698 (>0.05)
Thumb-ring:			
	$F_g^{30°} < F_g^{15°}$	True	0.0226* (<0.05)
	$F_g^{45°} < F_g^{15°}$	True	0.032* (<0.05)
Thumb-middle:			
	$F_g^{45°} > F_g^{30°}$	True	0.0014*(<0.05)
	$F_g^{45°} \neq F_g^{60°}$	False	0.3075 (>0.05)
	$F_g^{45°} \neq F_g^{15°}$	False	0.7913 (>0.05)
Thumb-index:			
	$F_g^{45°} < F_g^{30°}$	True	0.0445*(<0.05)
	$F_g^{60°} > F_g^{45°}$	True	0.0226*(<0.05)
	$F_g^{30°} \neq F_g^{60°}$	False	0.4274 (>0.05)
	$F_g^{15°} \neq F_g^{60°}$	False	0.3847 (>0.05)
	$F_g^{15°} \neq F_g^{30°}$	False	0.6232 (>0.05)

4   Discussion

Our statistical analysis on experimental data confirms the model predictions by identifying the most effective assistive force direction in the range $0° < \psi < 30°$ (Table 2). Multiway Analysis of Variance (ANOVA) of experimental data from ten human subjects too confirm that there is a significant interaction effect between finger pairs (representing γ) and $30° < \psi < 60°$ ($p = 0.023$, $F = 2.76$) while there is no significant interaction effect when $0° < \psi < 30°$ ($p = 0.135$, $F = 1.72$). The variability of force gain across subjects (Fig. 8) can come from thumb anatomical variations [17].

In this work, we consider the initial ψ to build a relationship among ψ, γ, and the thumb-tip force gain. However, ψ changes with the thumb movement. Therefore, from a designer's point of view, knowing the best starting tendon angle would be practically more useful than the final angle that can vary depending on grasp affordances. In our experiment, palm folding angle γ is evaluated assuming that the palmar arches involve palm folding in straight axes [16]. According to the experiment results, average γ angles variation between 71.5° to 75.3° could be due to the size of the palmar muscles of each individual. The γ variations depending on the time (see Fig. 6) may be due to the subjectwise thumb moving strategies to reach each finger tip.

These findings are useful not only for the tendon actuated assistive devices but also for all the actuation mechanisms because the effective direction of actuation is significant to give assistance to the thumb. In the future, it will be interesting to investigate different types of methods to exert assistive forces in control directions such as exoskeletons, both hard [1] and soft [15].

5   Conclusion

Experimental results show that average palm folding angle varies from 71.5° to 75.3° across the four thumb-finger pairs for four subjects. Our numerical results based on the kinematic model of the thumb and the palm predict that the thumb-tip assistive force gain can be maximized by exerting assistive force vectors to the MCP joint in the range 10°–30° from the ulnar axis, for palm folding angle in the range 70°–80° from the radial axis in the coronal plane. This practically means that assistive forces at the MCP joint exerted perpendicular to the palm folding axis maximises the force gain at the thumbtip.

Statistical significance tests on experimental thumbtip force gain data show that the effective assistive force direction at the MCP is $0° < \psi < 30°$ across thumb-finger pairs for ten human subjects. This shows that the moment arm produced by the MCP assistive force around the palm folding axis plays a vital role in thumb tip force gain. This finding also indicates the significance of including foldable palm as an integral part of the kinematic model of the thumb to abstract thumb biomechanics to design assistive devices for the hand.

References

1. Aubin, P.M., Sallum, H., Walsh, C., Stirling, L., Correia, A.: A pediatric robotic thumb exoskeleton for at-home rehabilitation: the Isolated Orthosis for Thumb Actuation (IOTA). In: IEEE International Conference on Rehabilitation Robotics (ICORR), pp. 1–6 (2013)
2. Cempini, M., Cortese, M., Vitiello, N.: A powered finger-thumb wearable hand exoskeleton with self-aligning joint axes. IEEE/ASME Trans. Mechatron. 20(2), 705–716 (2015)
3. Chang, L.Y., Matsuoka, Y.: A Kinematic thumb model for the act hand. In: IEEE International Conference on Robotics and Automation (ICRA), pp. 1000–1005 (2006)
4. Colditz, J.C.: The biomechanics of a thumb carpometacarpal immobilization splint: design and fitting. J. Hand Ther. 13(3), 228–235 (2000)
5. Cotugno, G., Althoefer, K., Nanayakkara, T.: The role of the thumb: study of finger motion in grasping and reachability space in human and robotic hands. IEEE Trans. Syst. Man Cybern. 47(7), 1061–1070 (2016)

6. Craig, J.J.: Introduction to Robotics: Mechanics and Control, vol. 3. Pearson Prentice Hall, Upper Saddle River (2005)

7. De Monsabert, B.G., Rossi, J., Berton, E., Vigouroux, L.: Quantification of hand and forearm muscle forces during a maximal power grip task. Med. Sci. Sports Exerc. **44**(10), 1906–1916 (2012)

8. Diftler, M., et al.: RoboGlove - a robonaut derived multipurpose assistive device (2014)

9. Feix, T., Romero, J., Schmiedmayer, H.B., Dollar, A.M., Kragic, D.: The grasp taxonomy of human grasp types. IEEE Trans. Hum.-Mach. Syst. **46**(1), 66–77 (2016)

10. Kang, B.B., Lee, H., In, H., Jeong, U., Chung, J., Cho, K.J.: Development of a polymer-based tendon-driven wearable robotic hand. In: IEEE International Conference on Robotics and Automation (ICRA), pp. 3750–3755 (2016)

11. Ladd, A.L., et al.: The thumb carpometacarpal joint: anatomy, hormones, and biomechanics. Instr. Course Lect. **62**, 165–179 (2013)

12. Nanayakkara, V., et al.: Kinematic analysis of the human thumb with foldable palm. In: Alboul, L., Damian, D., Aitken, J.M.M. (eds.) TAROS 2016. LNCS (LNAI), vol. 9716, pp. 226–238. Springer, Cham (2016). https://doi.org/10.1007/978-3-319-40379-3_23

13. Nanayakkara, V.K., Cotugno, G., Vitzilaios, N., Venetsanos, D., Nanayakkara, T., Sahinkaya, M.N.: The role of morphology of the thumb in anthropomorphic grasping: a review. Front. Mech. Eng. **3**(5) (2017). https://doi.org/10.3389/fmech.2017.00005

14. Neumann, D.A., Bielefeld, T.: The carpometacarpal joint of the thumb: stability, deformity, and therapeutic intervention. J. Orthop. Sports Phys. Ther. **33**(7), 386–399 (2003)

15. Polygerinos, P., Wang, Z., Galloway, K.C., Wood, R.J., Walsh, C.J.: Soft robotic glove for combined assistance and at-home rehabilitation. Robot. Auton. Syst. **73**, 135–143 (2015)

16. Sangole, A.P., Levin, M.F.: Arches of the hand in reach to grasp. J. Biomech. **41**(4), 829–837 (2008)

17. Santos, V.J., Valero-Cuevas, F.J.: Reported anatomical variability naturally leads to multimodal distributions of Denavit-Hartenberg parameters for the human thumb. IEEE Trans. Biomed. Eng. **53**(2), 155–163 (2006)

18. Valero-Cuevas, F.J., Johanson, M.E., Towles, J.D.: Towards a realistic biomechanical model of the thumb: the choice of Kinematic description may be more critical than the solution method or the variability/uncertainty of musculoskeletal parameters. J. Biomech. **36**(7), 1019–1030 (2003)

19. Wu, J.Z., et al.: Inverse dynamic analysis of the biomechanics of the thumb while pipetting: a case study. Med. Eng. Phys. **34**(6), 693–701 (2012)

20. Xiloyannis, M., Cappello, L., Khanh, D.B., Yen, S.C., Masia, L.: Modelling and design of a synergy-based actuator for a tendon-driven soft robotic glove. In: 6th IEEE International Conference on Biomedical Robotics and Biomechatronics (BioRob), pp. 1213–1219 (2016)

Energy-Tank Based Force Control
for 3D Contour Following

Salua Hamaza[1,3](✉) ⓘ, Ioannis Georgilas[2] ⓘ, and Thomas Richardson[1,3] ⓘ

[1] Bristol Robotics Laboratory, Bristol BS16 1QY, UK
{s.hamaza,thomas.richardson}@bristol.ac.uk
[2] Department of Mechanical Engineering, University of Bath, Bath, UK
i.georgilas@bath.ac.uk
[3] Department of Aerospace Engineering, University of Bristol, Bristol, UK
http://www.brl.ac.uk/

Abstract. Manipulation has been a major topic in robotics since its earlier developments. In the last few years, a new research area has focused in the introduction of manipulation capabilities on mobile robots. Several challenges are faced when mobile robots interact with unknown environments, for which inherent compliance is a key feature to achieve the intended outcome in a safe and robust way. This paper proposes a unified method of force control with energy-tank based methods to tackle 3D contour following. This method is tailored for manipulators that are designed for aerial applications, and addresses the interaction with unknown surfaces by also tackling the safety aspect, i.e. the response generated during contact loss.

Keywords: Manipulation · Mechatronics · Compliance · Control

1 Introduction

Nowadays unmanned aerial vehicles (UAVs) are deployed for a variety of tasks that range from passive observation, e.g. inspection, environmental surveying, infrastructure monitoring, to contact-based applications such as transportation of objects [1,15,17], non-destructive testing [12] and simple maintenance tasks [16,19]. The term *aerial manipulation* has been coined to describe this class of robots that are able to carry out manipulation tasks airborne by means of mechanical devices, i.e. manipulators, mounted on top of the flying platform.

The state-of-the-art in robotic manipulation from the past four decades has demonstrated that compliance is a key aspect [13,20]. Standard manipulation using robotic arms has been augmented with compliance either via software with an active control, or through hardware with the introduction of mechanical elements that resemble a spring-damper system. Likewise, compliance is also a key feature in aerial manipulation thanks to the several advantages that it brings to the aerial system as a whole. Some of these advantages are energy absorbance

© Springer Nature Switzerland AG 2019
K. Althoefer et al. (Eds.): TAROS 2019, LNAI 11649, pp. 41–51, 2019.
https://doi.org/10.1007/978-3-030-23807-0_4

in case of collision [2], force estimation and obstacle detection [24], and improved in-flight stability thanks to the dampening of perturbations [9,10].

In this paper we propose a passivity-based force controller tailored for aerial manipulation, using energy-tank based methods. Such approach is implemented for 3D contour following, and is particularly suited for aerial systems interacting with unknown structures. In fact, the combination of the force-tracking with inherent compliance of the energy-tank based method allows to safely interact with un-modeled environments. The envisioned aerial application for such contour following is to aid indoor navigation of UAVs, for example in a search and rescue scenario. Often UAVs are deployed to enter wrecked buildings after an earthquake or other natural calamities, having only to rely on visual sensing for indoor navigation due to the signal occlusion on GPS tracking. A more robust way to safely navigate and map such unknown environments would be to include tactile feedback to the aerial platform. Contour following is a useful property that aerial manipulators can exploit for example to detect crevices and doorways in which the UAV can fly into.

The proposed control approach is presented and then validated through experiments validating contouring capabilities on different 3D profiles. Experiments also address the case scenario of contact loss with the environment. Overall this approach achieves a good accuracy and shows great potential for its use on-board mobile robots.

1.1   Related Work

Interaction control strategies can be sub-categorised into *direct* and *indirect force control*. The direct approach achieves the force regulation of the end-effector by adopting an integral action on the force error. Such error is often generated by an outer force loop, hence an additional force feedback loop. On the other hand, indirect force control is based on impedance and compliance control where the output force is the result of an inner motion loop; without the explicit closure of a force feedback loop [22]. In the works presented in [3,4] a constrained-based approach that allows to selectively control force, impedance and position has been proposed. Moreover, hybrid position/force control gained popularity in the last two decades as it allows to work in force and motion sub-spaces that are complimentary to each other depending on the task specification. Despite the versatility of hybrid control, the major drawbacks associated with it are the need for an accurate modeling of the contact properties *a-priori* to reach a good performance, and the lack of robustness during contact-loss [18]. In [14] a variable-impedance control applied to an aerial platform is proposed, capable of adjusting the impedance of the multi-rotor and regulate the time-varying interaction forces. However this approach focuses on a time-varying force output for safe and robust compensation of disturbances in the environment rather than force-tracking and contouring. In this paper we propose a force control architecture that includes the concept of energy tanks [5,6] for aerial interaction applications in contour following. This approach is aimed for interaction airborne with 3D surfaces and accounts for the lack of prior knowledge of the environment, therefore avoiding pre-modeled variations in the force-tracking.

2   Modeling

2.1   Rigid Joint Dynamics

The equations of motion of a manipulation system with n rigid joints can be derived using the Newton-Euler approach:

$$\mathbf{M}(\mathbf{q})\ddot{\mathbf{q}} + \mathbf{C}(\mathbf{q},\dot{\mathbf{q}})\dot{\mathbf{q}} + \mathbf{G}(\mathbf{q}) = \tau_m + \tau_{ext} \qquad (1)$$

where $\mathbf{M}(\mathbf{q}) \in \mathbb{R}^{n \times n}$ is the generalised mass matrix, matrix $\mathbf{C}(\mathbf{q},\dot{\mathbf{q}}) \in \mathbb{R}^n$ represents the Coriolis and centrifugal terms, and $\mathbf{g}(\mathbf{q})$ comprises of all gravitational terms acting on the manipulator. On the right side of the equation, τ_m comprises the motor torque and the control input of the system, and τ_{ext} consists of all externally applied torques. Vectors $\mathbf{q}, \dot{\mathbf{q}}, \ddot{\mathbf{q}} \in \mathbb{R}^n$ represent the generalised coordinates of the manipulator and its time derivatives.

2.2   Flexible Joint Dynamics

For a robot with n flexible joints, i.e. an actuator that contains an elastic element such as series elastic actuator (SEA), the above equation is not sufficient to describe the dynamics of the inherent flexible transmission. Following the work proposed in [23], the equation of motion adapted for a flexible joint type of manipulator is:

$$\mathbf{M}(\mathbf{q})\ddot{\mathbf{q}} + \mathbf{C}(\mathbf{q},\dot{\mathbf{q}})\dot{\mathbf{q}} + \mathbf{G}(\mathbf{q}) = \tau_{flex} + \tau_{ext} \qquad (2)$$

$$\mathbf{J}\ddot{\theta} - \tau_{flex} = \tau_m \qquad (3)$$

$$\tau_{flex} = \mathbf{K}(\theta - \mathbf{q}) \qquad (4)$$

where τ_{flex} represents the elastic joint torque, $\mathbf{J} \in \mathbb{R}^{n \times n}$ and $\mathbf{K} \in \mathbb{R}^{n \times n}$ are both diagonal positive definite matrices expressing the motor inertia and the joint stiffness respectively and θ represents the motor position.

3   Control

3.1   Force Control Design

The proposed controller is designed for a generic n-DoF manipulator actuated by DC motors. These type of motors present a linear relationship between the input current and output torque, in accordance with the motor's specifications. To achieve direct force-tracking on the end-effector, a current controller is implemented with a Proportional-Integral control law as follows:

$$\tau_m = J^T(\mathbf{q})\left[K_T\left[k_p\Big(c(t) - c_d(t)\Big) + k_i \int_0^t \Big(c(t) - c_d(t)\Big)dt\right]\right] \qquad (5)$$

where τ_m is the output torque generated by the manipulator and linked to the output force; J^T is the transpose of the Jacobian matrix which only depends on the manipulator's configuration, i.e. the vector of generalised coordinates $\mathbf{q} \in \mathbb{R}^n$. The parameter K_T is the motor's torque-current constant, provided by the motor's manufacturer. k_p and k_i are the proportional and integral gains respectively, and c and c_d are the actual and desired current values.

3.2 Energy Tank Design

Energy tank-based methods have frequently been used in tele-operated manipulation methods [7,8,21] and they have recently been applied to impedance controller with variable stiffness [6]. The role of the energy tank is to act as a storage element and minimise the energy dissipated by the controlled system. Such dissipated energy represents a *passivity threshold*, and the tank being its reservoir. Therefore, the presence of the tank allows to adjust the impedance of the system.

The variable $x_t(t) \in \mathbb{R}$ is the state associated with the tank. The tank energy is:

$$T(x_t) = \frac{1}{2}x_t^2 \tag{6}$$

where $x_t(0) > 0$, and the dynamics are given by:

$$\begin{cases} \dot{x}_t = \dfrac{\beta}{x_t}\left(\dot{\tilde{x}}^T D_d \dot{\tilde{x}} \right) + u_T \\ \tilde{x}(t) = x(t) - x_d(t) \\ u_T = -w(t)^T \dot{\tilde{x}}_t \end{cases} \tag{7}$$

where $\tilde{x}$ represents the state error, and β is defined as:

$$\beta = \begin{cases} 1 & \text{if } T \leq T_{upper} \\ 0 & \text{otherwise} \end{cases} \tag{8}$$

The term $w(t)$ is the tank control input, β is a design parameters that enables the storage of dissipated energy as long as the total tank energy is less than an upper bound T_{upper}. Otherwise, the tank is disabled as β is zero, to avoid excessive storage. The product $(\dot{\tilde{x}}^T D_d \dot{\tilde{x}})$ represents the power dissipated. The extended motor dynamics of the system are described by:

$$\tau'_m = J^T(\mathbf{q})\, \alpha \Big[K_p(F_{ext} - F_{des}) + K_d(\dot{F}_{ext} - \dot{F}_{des}) + \ldots$$
$$\ldots K_i \int_0^t (F_{ext} - F_{des}) \Big] \tag{9}$$

where α is defined as:

$$\alpha = \begin{cases} 1 & \text{if } T \geq T_{lower} \\ 0 & \text{otherwise} \end{cases} \tag{10}$$

where $T_{lower} > 0$ represents the lower bound below which the energy cannot be extracted by the tank, leading to $\alpha = 0$ and preventing singularities to occur.

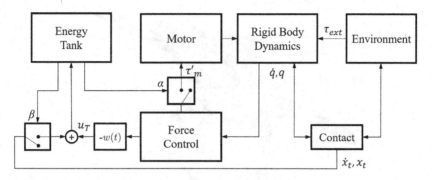

Fig. 1. Block diagram of the control architecture.

3.3 Case Scenario: Contact Loss

Contact loss can be a recurring scenario during manipulation with an unmodeled environment, even more likely to occur if the interaction is performed on-board of a UAV. Aerial vehicles tend to be unstable in the proximity of obstacles, leading to disturbances that often generate altitude loss and drifting. Therefore, it is essential that a manipulator intended for aerial applications is able to cope with contact loss, preventing it from executing unsafe motions. Typically, manipulators that solely operate with force-tracking would try to apply the desired force F_{des} regardless contact with the environment is established. The tank-based design brings an improvement to pure force-tracking as the output force is regulated until the tank energy is drained and the lower bound T_{lower} is reached. However, depending on the remaining energy in the tank, undesired substantial and rapid motion can still occur.

To address contact loss, we propose a port-based control architecture where the controller is switched on and off depending on the contact information sensed at the end-effector. This port-based model works by reading the end-effector states, i.e. position, velocity and current/force, and computing the overall kinetic and potential energy of the manipulator at any given time. During contact loss the output energy quickly reaches higher values as it is dependent on the square of the velocity $\dot{x}_t$. Once the saturation point is met, a signal is sent to the energy-tank control block that forces its drainage by setting $\beta = 0$ (see Eq. (8)). As a result the controller output is set as zero. In Fig. 1 a control block diagram of the passivity-based force control via Energy-Tanks model is illustrated.

4 Manipulator Design

In the aerial manipulation state-of-the-art, a recurrent approach is to employ multi-DoF serial manipulators on top of UAVs, providing n additional DoFs to the overall aerial structure. Despite the dexterity that a higher-DoF manipulator offers in terms of tasks that can be accomplished, there are several drawbacks that come with it. The main problem with the presence of multiple actuators on

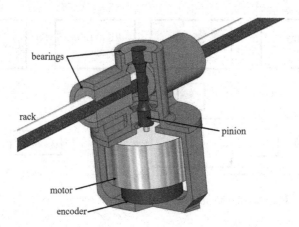

Fig. 2. Drawing of the manipulator's transmission mechanism. The pinion (in green) drives the motion of the toothed rack in a backdrivable way. The encoder measures the relative position of the motor shaft, therefore informing the system on the end-effector's relative position. (Color figure online)

a UAV is the increased payload that causes a shorter battery life and decreased manoeuvrability [11]. Another problem associated with high-DoF manipulators is the higher kinematics and control complexity, which often requires higher processing power and can drastically slow down computation time. In general, most aerial tasks may require limited manipulation capabilities as the exertion of a force on a surface for non-destructive-testing or inspection purposes. Such simple operations can be achieved with a simple 1-DoF manipulator oriented towards the contact surface. Despite its simplicity and limited dexterity, this approach provides a minimal, weight-efficient solution for force-driven tasks.

The proposed design consists of a single-DoF manipulator actuated by a prismatic joint. Amongst the improvements brought up from its previous version seen in [9] there is a more powerful on-board computer, i.e. Raspberry Pi 3 (1.4 GHz 64-bit quad-core ARM Cortex-A53 processor) with Wi-Fi connectivity and logging capabilities. On-board sensing is also integrated in the manipulator, in particular a rangefinder Teraranger One® based on Time-Of-Flight principle and an Maxon® MILE digital encoder on the slider joint that measures the end-effector relative position. Both sensors have a high sampling rate up to 1 kHz and allow for real-time feedback. A Maxon® DC motor actuates the prismatic joint via a pinion-rack transmission and it has its own dedicated motor board, namely a Maxon EPOS 2 24/3 Digital Controller. This controller board is particularly well-suited for real-time control as it provides a sampling rate of 10 kHz on the *current* output. The pinion-rack transmission is made out of lightweight, sturdy aluminium components. The mechanism housing is made out of 3D printed material and holds 4 bearings, 2 radial and 2 linear bearings respectively, within a cross-shaped profile. The bearings allow to distress the motor shaft from any radial tension that might generate during the interaction.

The overall weight on the manipulator, including the hardware, sensing and electronics is 450 g. A Computer-Aided-Drawing of the mechanical design is presented in Fig. 2 illustrating a detail of the transmission mechanism.

To minimise friction on the end-effector and guarantee a smooth contouring even on indentations that might be present on the target surface, a metal ball caster of 15 mm diameter is mounted at the tip. The ball caster is also ideal as it reduces the contact surface to a single point, therefore zeroing the moments of the external wrench τ_{ext} leading to pure force exchange F_{ext}.

5   Experiments

5.1   Experimental Setup

The setup used to validate the proposed control architecture includes the 1-DoF manipulator presented earlier mounted on a stationary base; a 6-axis force/torque sensor to measure the output force and the target surface that we aim to contour follow. The sensor chosen is the Robotiq FT 300, sampling at the rate of 100 Hz. The sensor data act as ground truth measurements rather than a feedback for the controller loop, in fact the estimated force on the end-effector is directly derived from the current information through the use of the torque constant K_T (see Sect. 3.1). Figure 3 illustrates a snapshot of the setup during the experiments with a close up on the 1-DoF manipulator in contact with the sensor.

Fig. 3. Experimental setup: 1-DoF manipulator equipped with a friction-less end-effector, exerting force over a 6-axis Force/Torque sensor.

5.2   Results

Several experiments are conducted to validate the proposed passivity-based force control with energy-tank. For each experiment, a different 3D profile with curvatures of different radius spanning from 1 cm to 10 cm was contoured to validate the robustness of the control approach. The experiments aim to validate the ability to:

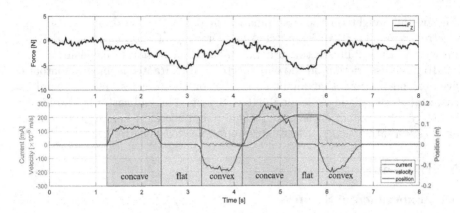

Fig. 4. 3D contour following experiment highlighting the force curve (top) and the end-effector's position, velocity and current states (bottom). (Color figure online)

- 3D contour follow an unknown surface;
- establish a force pushing forwards whilst in contact;
- respond to an external input from the environment (τ_{ext}) in a compliant/ passive way;
- cease any force/motion as contact loss with the target is sensed;
- show the robustness of the controller by contouring differently shaped profiles.

In Fig. 4 the results of a single sample experiment are illustrated, with a focus on the force output generated on the surface (top figure) and the end-effector's position, velocity and current states (bottom figure). To understand the behaviour of the end-effector we can start by looking at the position profile (red line) for which the y-axis lays on the right side of the bottom plot. The manipulator starts at position 0 and moves forwards of about 0.1 m until it reaches a plateau, then goes backwards at about $t = 3.3$ s. The velocity profile (blue line) for which the y-axis lays on the left side, is either positive, when motion forward is generated, or negative when the rack moves backwards. The zero in velocity always follows the position plateau: when the end-effector position is constant, its time derivative is zero. It can be noticed that during the position plateau, the force sensed on the Force/Torque sensor reaches 5 N (green line in the top figure). The presence of the plateau suggests that the target surface is flat (highlighted in the yellow areas), hence no motion is generated in either directions. Positive velocity suggests that the target profile is concave (green areas), viceversa negative velocity results from a convex profile (red areas).

The current profile is displayed as a light blue line in the same graph, with its y-axis on the left side of the figure along with the velocity profile. The current drives the rack at 200 mA and actively moves the end-effector towards the target. As the encoder senses an external force pushing the rack backwards, the *current* output is set as zero and the end-effector responds in a passive way. This occurs every time the manipulator is in contact with a convex profile, causing the end-effector to move backwards. As the targeted contour profile starts to flatten

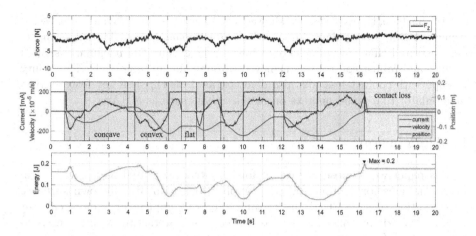

Fig. 5. Experiment demonstrating 3D contour following for longer periods. From top to bottom: force curve; position, velocity and current curves; and the tank energy curve. (Color figure online)

or becomes concave, the current input is set to positive again and the end-effector maintains contact with the surface. The transition between concavity and convexity acts as a trigger on the manipulator as the external wrench is no longer zero: $\tau_{ext} > 0$. In the figure, the phases of the task are highlighted within green, yellow and orange boxes as the manipulator contours a concave, flat or convex profile.

In Fig. 5 another sample experiment is illustrated. As seen above, the position, velocity and current curves are highlighted inside yellow, green and red boxes describing the flat, concave and convex profile respectively of the contoured structure. Additionally, this figure presents a purple area towards the end of the experiment that highlights the "contact loss" section. It is to be noted that the position curve starts at an initial value of 0 and this is just to characterise the start of the experiment, associated with a zero encoder value rather than a specific physical position of the manipulator.

The force curve in the top figure shows on average -2 N of force being exerted by the manipulator, with peaks up to -5 N. Towards the end of the experiment, at $t = 16.2$ s the manipulator experiences contact loss with the environment, as the target surface is purposely removed. As a consequence, the force output on the sensor goes to 0 N, while the manipulator's velocity spikes towards higher values, triggering the *no contact* condition. The energy value inside the virtual tank reaches its upper threshold, as illustrated in the bottom figure (cyan curve). Hence, the tank is instantaneously drained and both current and velocity values quickly move to zero. The effectiveness of the contact less condition can be seen in the position curve (red line) by looking at the displacement of the end-effector since the moment of the contact loss detection: the rack only displaces by 11 mm since the condition is met.

To conclude, the experiments showed a good accuracy in 3D contour following using a 1-DoF manipulator mounted on a stationary base. The experiments demonstrated that continuous contact was kept despite the irregularly shaped profiles and robust control was achieved throughout multiple trials. The ability to cope with contact loss was also demonstrated, as this is a key feature for a manipulator that could operate on mobile robots such as a UAVs.

6 Conclusion

In this paper we propose the use of force control integrated with energy-tank based methods for contour following applications with 3D unknown surfaces. The addition of the virtual energy-tank allows to implement a more efficient passivity-based controller and is most suited when interacting with un-modeled environments. Such controller is validated on a single-DoF manipulator in several experiments and demonstrates the accuracy of the compliant interaction as well as its robustness with fast changing profiles. The specific *contact loss* scenario is also validated during the interaction showing fast response and minimal energy consumption. Overall this approach demonstrates great potential for its use on flying platforms for aerial manipulation applications.

Acknowledgments. This work is supported by the EPSRC Centre for Doctoral Training in Future Autonomous and Robotic Systems (FARSCOPE).

References

1. Augugliaro, F., et al.: The flight assembled architecture installation: cooperative construction with flying machines. IEEE Control Syst. **34**(4), 46–64 (2014)
2. Bartelds, T., Capra, A., Hamaza, S., Stramigioli, S., Fumagalli, M.: Compliant aerial manipulators: toward a new generation of aerial robotic workers. IEEE Robot. Autom. Lett. **1**, 477–483 (2016)
3. Borghesan, G., De Schutter, J.: Constraint-based specification of hybrid position-impedance-force tasks. In: 2014 IEEE International Conference on Robotics and Automation (ICRA), pp. 2290–2296. IEEE (2014)
4. De Schutter, J., et al.: Constraint-based task specification and estimation for sensor-based robot systems in the presence of geometric uncertainty. Int. J. Robot. Res. **26**(5), 433–455 (2007)
5. Ferraguti, F., et al.: An energy tank-based interactive control architecture for autonomous and teleoperated robotic surgery. IEEE Trans. Robot. **31**(5), 1073–1088 (2015)
6. Ferraguti, F., Secchi, C., Fantuzzi, C.: A tank-based approach to impedance control with variable stiffness. In: 2013 IEEE International Conference on Robotics and Automation (ICRA), pp. 4948–4953. IEEE (2013)
7. Franchi, A., Secchi, C., Son, H.I., Bulthoff, H.H., Giordano, P.R.: Bilateral teleoperation of groups of mobile robots with time-varying topology. IEEE Trans. Robot. **28**(5), 1019–1033 (2012)

8. Franken, M., Stramigioli, S., Misra, S., Secchi, C., Macchelli, A.: Bilateral telemanipulation with time delays: a two-layer approach combining passivity and transparency. IEEE Trans. Robot. **27**(4), 741–756 (2011)
9. Hamaza, S., Georgilas, I., Richardson, T.: An adaptive-compliance manipulator for contact-based aerial applications. In: 2018 IEEE/ASME International Conference on Advanced Intelligent Mechatronics (AIM), pp. 730–735. IEEE (2018)
10. Hamaza, S., Georgilas, I., Richardson, T.: Towards an adaptive-compliance aerial manipulator for contact-based interaction. In: 2018 IEEE/RSJ International Conference on Intelligent Robots and Systems (IROS). IEEE (2018, in press)
11. Huber, F., et al.: First analysis and experiments in aerial manipulation using fully actuated redundant robot arm. In: 2013 IEEE/RSJ International Conference on Intelligent Robots and Systems (IROS), pp. 3452–3457. IEEE (2013)
12. Keemink, A.Q., Fumagalli, M., Stramigioli, S., Carloni, R.: Mechanical design of a manipulation system for unmanned aerial vehicles. In: 2012 IEEE International Conference on Robotics and Automation (ICRA), pp. 3147–3152. IEEE (2012)
13. Mason, M.T.: Compliance and force control for computer controlled manipulators. IEEE Trans. Syst. Man Cybern. **11**(6), 418–432 (1981)
14. Mersha, A.Y., Stramigioli, S., Carloni, R.: Variable impedance control for aerial interaction. In: 2014 IEEE/RSJ International Conference on Intelligent Robots and Systems, IROS 2014, pp. 3435–3440. IEEE (2014)
15. Michael, N., Fink, J., Kumar, V.: Cooperative manipulation and transportation with aerial robots. Auton. Robots **30**(1), 73–86 (2011)
16. Orsag, M., Korpela, C., Bogdan, S., Oh, P.: Valve turning using a dual-arm aerial manipulator. In: 2014 International Conference on Unmanned Aircraft Systems (ICUAS), pp. 836–841. IEEE (2014)
17. Pounds, P.E., Bersak, D.R., Dollar, A.M.: The Yale aerial manipulator: grasping in flight. In: 2011 IEEE International Conference on Robotics and Automation (ICRA), pp. 2974–2975. IEEE (2011)
18. Raibert, M.H., Craig, J.J.: Hybrid position/force control of manipulators. J. Dyn. Syst. Meas. Control **103**(2), 126–133 (1981)
19. Ruggiero, F., Lippiello, V., Ollero, A.: Aerial manipulation: a literature review. IEEE Robot. Autom. Lett. **3**(3), 1957–1964 (2018)
20. Salisbury, J.K.: Active stiffness control of a manipulator in Cartesian coordinates. In: 1980 19th IEEE Conference on Decision and Control including the Symposium on Adaptive Processes, vol. 19, pp. 95–100. IEEE (1980)
21. Secchi, C., Franchi, A., Bülthoff, H.H., Giordano, P.R.: Bilateral teleoperation of a group of UAVs with communication delays and switching topology. In: 2012 IEEE International Conference on Robotics and Automation (ICRA), pp. 4307–4314. IEEE (2012)
22. Siciliano, B., Villani, L.: Robot Force Control, vol. 540. Springer, Heidelberg (2012)
23. Spong, M.W.: Modeling and control of elastic joint robots. J. Dyn. Syst. Meas. Control **109**(4), 310–318 (1987)
24. Suarez, A., Heredia, G., Ollero, A.: Lightweight compliant arm with compliant finger for aerial manipulation and inspection. In: 2016 IEEE/RSJ International Conference on Intelligent Robots and Systems (IROS), pp. 4449–4454. IEEE (2016)

Kinematic Control and Obstacle Avoidance for Soft Inflatable Manipulator

Ahmad Ataka[1,2]([✉]), Agostino Stilli[3], Jelizaveta Konstantinova[2],
Helge A. Wurdemann[4], and Kaspar Althoefer[2]

[1] The Centre for Robotics Research (CoRe), Department of Informatics,
King's College London, London WC2R 2LS, UK
ahmad_ataka_awwalur.rizqi@kcl.ac.uk
[2] The Centre for Advanced Robotics @ Queen Mary (ARQ),
Faculty of Science and Engineering, Queen Mary University of London,
Mile End Road, London E1 4NS, UK
[3] The Department of Computer Science,
University College London, London WC1E 7JE, UK
[4] The Department of Mechanical Engineering, University College London,
London WC1E 7JE, UK

Abstract. In this paper, we present a kinematic control and obstacle avoidance for the soft inflatable manipulator which combines pressure and tendons as an actuating mechanism. The position control and obstacle avoidance took inspiration from the phenomena of a magnetic field in nature. The redundancy in the manipulator combined with a planar mobile base is exploited to help the actuators stay under their maximum capability. The navigation algorithm is shown to outperform the potential-field-based navigation in its ability to smoothly and reactively avoid obstacles and reach the goal in simulation scenarios.

Keywords: Kinematic control · Obstacle avoidance ·
Soft manipulator · Bio-inspired robot

1 Introduction

Soft robotics has been at the forefront of the robotics revolution in the last decade. Robots with soft and flexible materials, often taking inspiration from properties of biological organisms in nature, have been developed to handle tasks previously untouched by the rigid robots counterparts. These include minimally invasive surgery [7], whole-body grasping, and manoeuvring in tight space surrounded by cluttered environment [16]. The emergence of smart materials

This work was supported in part by King's College London, the EPSRC in the framework of the NCNR (National Centre for Nuclear Robotics) project (EP/R02572X/1), q-bot led project WormBot (2308/104059), and the Indonesia Endowment Fund for Education, Ministry of Finance Republic of Indonesia.

K. Althoefer et al. (Eds.): TAROS 2019, LNAI 11649, pp. 52–64, 2019.
https://doi.org/10.1007/978-3-030-23807-0_5

and low-cost fabrication techniques have also led to various designs and actuating mechanisms, which include pneumatically-actuated systems [8], tendon-
driven systems [15], or a combined antagonistically tendon-pressure actuation
system [12]. Despite all of these promising developments, new challenges arise in
the field of robot modelling [17], control [14], and navigation [4], mainly due to
the non-linear behaviour of the flexible structure employed.

One of the emerging technologies in the field of soft robotics is the use of
an inflatable structure which enables the robot to grow over a wide range of
length [11]. This type of robot is useful not only due to the compliance of the
material employed but also due to its ability to grow from a tiny size to a very
long structure. Current applications include an antenna reconfiguration [5] and
systems that can be inserted through a narrow opening used in a laparoscopic
surgery [12]. The inflatability of the structure makes this type of robot a prime
candidate for further applications where cluttered environments are present, such
as the nuclear industry or a below-ground environment. However, research on
control and navigation of this type of robot is still in its infancy.

For soft robots in general, the majority of the navigation methods employed in
the literature rely on either an optimization technique [10,13] or sampling-based
planners [19,21]. While practically useful even in complex environments, these
types of methods rely on the availability of a complete or at least near-complete
knowledge of the environment. Recent effort which implemented a neural dynamics approach [6] poses a similar complication, while another method which used
a supervised learning-by-demonstration [20] relies on human interventions for
training. On the other hand, the use of reactive obstacle avoidance, such as presented in [3,9], is very susceptible to a local minima problem, a scenario where
the robot gets stuck in a configuration before reaching the target. Besides, none
of these works deals with the inflatability of the robotic structure which is the
main characteristics of the soft inflatable manipulator in this paper.

In this paper, we present a kinematic control and obstacle avoidance for
the soft inflatable manipulator based on the design presented in [18]. A beam-
theory-based kinematic model based on the previous work in [18] is used. The
position control and obstacle avoidance are based on our previous work in [4]
where we applied reactive magnetic-field-inspired navigation to multi-segments
soft continuum manipulator. Our contribution is twofold:

1. we apply the magnetic-field-inspired navigation as a way to avoid unknown
   obstacle reactively for the soft inflatable arm, and
2. we exploit the redundancy on the beam-theory kinematic model to help the
   robot avoiding the actuators' constraints when navigating the environment.

2 Kinematic Modelling

2.1 Design of the Inflatable Manipulator

The design of the soft inflatable robotic manipulator is based on the previous
works described in [18]. The manipulator consists of a hyperelastic latex bladder

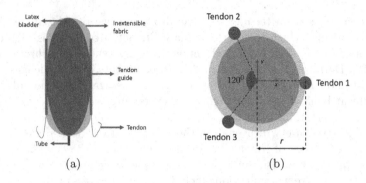

Fig. 1. The mechanical design of the soft inflatable manipulator.

Fig. 2. The manoeuvrability of the soft, inflatable manipulator.

whose endpoint is attached to an inextensible fabric. A hollow tube is connected to the bladder as a means for air to be pumped in. The outer fabric is equipped with three channels where each channel is radially separated by 120° from the other two channels. Three nylon tendons are guided along these channels and fixed at the distal end of the manipulator. The mechanical design of the manipulator is illustrated in Fig. 1. Air can be pumped in through the hollow tube into the bladder to change the state of the manipulator from a deflated state to an inflated state. Since the outer fabric is unstretchable, the radial expansion of the elastic bladder will be constrained up to the cross-sectional area of the outer fabric. This constraint forces the bladder to expand only in the direction of the robot's longitudinal axis, i.e. causing the robot structure to elongate. Once fully inflated, further variations of the air pressure inside the bladder will result in variations of the manipulator's structural stiffness.

Besides the air pressure inside the bladder, length variations of the three tendons will also affect the manipulator's shape. These enable the manipulator to perform not only elongation but also bending in a 3-dimensional environment as shown in Fig. 2. Any difference in the tendons' length will lead to a 3-dimensional bending. The overall combination of the tendons' length and the air pressure will move the manipulator's tip to a particular position. A stepper motor is connected to each tendon via a linear actuator used to control the tension of the tendons. A linear pressure regulator is used for regulating the pressure from an air compressor to manipulate the air pressure inside the latex bladder.

2.2   Beam Kinematic Model

As can be observed in Fig. 2, the segment of the manipulator can be modeled as a circular arc with a constant curvature. Hence, the shape of the segment can be parameterized by a set of configuration space variables $\mathbf{k} = \begin{bmatrix} \kappa \ \phi \ l \end{bmatrix}^T$ which represent a curvature κ, a rotational deflection angle ϕ, and a segment length l. The actuator space variables $\mathbf{q}_A = \begin{bmatrix} f_1 \ f_2 \ f_3 \ p \end{bmatrix}^T$ consist of an air pressure p and force f_i of tendon-i. The workspace variable $\mathbf{x} \in \mathbb{R}^3$ stands for the tip position. The kinematic model maps the actuator space variables $\mathbf{q}_A$ to the configuration space variables $\mathbf{k} = h(\mathbf{q}_A)$ and finally to the workspace variables $\mathbf{x} = g(\mathbf{k})$.

The kinematic model of the inflatable arm is based on the Euler-Bernoulli beam theory as has been described in [18]. As shown in Fig. 1b, the tension f_i of each tendon produces a bending moment $\mathbf{M}$ given by

$$\mathbf{M} = \sum_{i=1}^{3} \mathbf{r}_i \times \mathbf{F}_i. \tag{1}$$

$\mathbf{r}_i$ stands for the vector position of tendon-i with respect to the manipulator's central axis. From Fig. 1b, it can be expressed as $\mathbf{r}_i = \begin{bmatrix} r\cos\left(\frac{2\pi}{3}i\right) \ r\sin\left(\frac{2\pi}{3}i\right) \ 0 \end{bmatrix}^T$, where r stands for the cross-sectional radius. $\mathbf{F}_i$ stands for the tension vector of tendon-i and is defined as $\mathbf{F}_i = \begin{bmatrix} 0 \ 0 \ f_i \end{bmatrix}^T$. The magnitude of the bending moment is proportional to the curvature κ of the manipulator segment as follows

$$\kappa = \frac{|\mathbf{M}|}{EI}, \tag{2}$$

where E stands for the Young modulus of the material while I stands for the cross-sectional moment of inertia which is defined as $I = \frac{\pi}{2}r^4$ for a circular cross section with radius r. The bending moment $\mathbf{M}$ also produces a rotational deflection angle ϕ. We can derive the value of ϕ as follows

$$\phi = \mathrm{arctan2}\left(-M_x, M_y\right). \tag{3}$$

The tension on the tendons and the pressure of the elastic bladder will contribute to the increase of length l. The total force acting on the manipulator is given by

$$F_{tot} = (p - p_0)A - \sum_{i=1}^{3} f_i, \tag{4}$$

where $A = \pi r^2$ stands for the cross-sectional area of the manipulator and p_0 stands for the initial pressure. The increase in the manipulator's length is

$$\Delta l = l - l_0 = \frac{F_{tot}}{EA}l_0, \tag{5}$$

where l_0 stands for the initial length.

Equation (1)–(5) map the actuator space variables $\mathbf{q}_A$ to the configuration variables $\mathbf{k}$. To get the workspace variables $\mathbf{x}$, we use the geometrical property of a circular arc. The homogeneous transformation matrix describing the tip pose of the manipulator with respect to the base, $\mathbf{T}(\mathbf{k}) \in SE(3)$, is described in [17]. The tip position $\mathbf{x} \in \mathbb{R}^3$ can be expressed as

$$\mathbf{x} = \begin{bmatrix} \frac{1}{\kappa} \cos\phi(1 - \cos\kappa l) & \frac{1}{\kappa} \sin\phi(1 - \cos\kappa l) & \frac{1}{\kappa} \sin\kappa l \end{bmatrix}^T. \tag{6}$$

In this paper, we assume that the soft inflatable manipulator is put on top of a mobile platform which is able to move translationally in a planar environment. In this case, the pose of the tip with respect to a static world frame $\mathbb{W}$ is described as $^W\mathbf{T}(\mathbf{q}) = \mathbf{T}_B(\mathbf{q}_B)\mathbf{T}(\mathbf{q}_A)$, where $\mathbf{T}_B \in SE(3)$ stands for a homogeneous transformation matrix of the frame attached to the base with 2 translational degrees of freedom and $\mathbf{q}_B \in \mathbb{R}^2$ stands for the position of the base. Hence, the overall actuator space variables are described by $\mathbf{q} = \begin{bmatrix} \mathbf{q}_B & \mathbf{q}_A \end{bmatrix}^T$. From the kinematic model, we can also derive the Jacobian matrix defined as $\mathbf{J}(\mathbf{q}) \in \mathbb{R}^{3\times6} = \frac{\partial\mathbf{x}}{\partial\mathbf{q}}$ using a numerical computation as described in [4].

3   Tip Navigation and Obstacle Avoidance

3.1   Go-to-Goal Navigation

The geometric control approach, as presented in [4], is used to navigate the tip of the arm towards the desired position. This approach is chosen since it can maintain the manipulator's tip to move at an almost constant speed during the movement. By setting the speed to be small, we can ensure that the motion of the manipulator is slow enough such that its dynamics can be neglected.

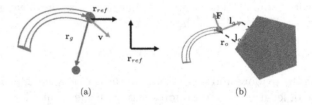

(a)   (b)

Fig. 3. (a) The tip of the manipulator moves with velocity $\mathbf{v}$ and located at $\mathbf{r}_g$ from the goal. $\mathbf{r}_{ref}$ is a static reference vector. (b) The tip of the manipulator generates an artificial current $\mathbf{l}_o$ on the obstacle surface.

Suppose that the manipulator's tip moves with velocity $\mathbf{v}$ as illustrated in Fig. 3a. We can express the direction of velocity vector $\mathbf{v}$ as a rotation matrix with respect to a static unit reference vector $\mathbf{r}_{ref}$ as $\mathbf{R}_v = \mathbf{I} + \hat{\omega}_v + \hat{\omega}_v^2 \frac{1}{1+\cos\phi}$.

Here, $\omega_v = \hat{\mathbf{r}}_{ref}\frac{\mathbf{v}}{|\mathbf{v}|}$, $\cos\phi = \mathbf{r}_{ref}^T\frac{\mathbf{v}}{|\mathbf{v}|}$, while $\hat{\mathbf{l}}$ is defined as a skew-symmetric matrix of a vector $\mathbf{l}$ as follows

$$\hat{\mathbf{l}} = \begin{bmatrix} 0 & -l_z & l_y \\ l_z & 0 & -l_x \\ -l_y & l_x & 0 \end{bmatrix}. \tag{7}$$

$\mathbf{I} \in \mathbb{R}^{3\times3}$ is an 3×3 identity matrix. We can use the same procedure for vector $\mathbf{r}_g = \mathbf{x_g} - \mathbf{x}$ to get the direction of the goal $\mathbf{R}_g$ with respect to frame $\mathbf{r}_{ref}$.

The aim is to rotate the direction of the manipulator's tip from arbitrary orientation $\mathbf{R}_v$ to the goal orientation $\mathbf{R}_g$. The control law is described as follows

$$\hat{\omega}_g = -K_\omega \log(\mathbf{R}_e), \tag{8}$$

where $\mathbf{R}_e$ stands for an error matrix and is defined as $\mathbf{R}_e = \mathbf{R}_g^T\mathbf{R}_v$. Here, $K_\omega \geq 0$ is a constant while the operator $\log(\mathbf{R})$ for any $\mathbf{R} \in SO(3)$ is defined as $\log(\mathbf{R}) = \frac{\beta}{2\sin\beta}(\mathbf{R}-\mathbf{R}^T)$ where $\beta = \arccos(\frac{tr(\mathbf{R})-1}{2})$. The angular speed $\omega_g \in \mathbb{R}^3$ expressed in the goal frame $\mathbf{R}_g$ can be retrieved from $\hat{\omega}_g$ in (8) by exploiting the skew-symmetric matrix definition in (7). To get the angular speed ω_{ref} in the static frame $\mathbf{r}_{ref}$, a matrix transformation is used as follows $\omega_{ref} = \mathbf{R}_g\omega_g$. Lastly, the force needed to generate this required angular speed is given by

$$\mathbf{F}_{gc} = \hat{\omega}_{ref}\mathbf{v}. \tag{9}$$

To generate the initial movement, an additional controller is used as follows

$$\mathbf{F}_v = -K_v(v - v_d)\mathbf{d}, \tag{10}$$

in which $K_v > 0$ represents a positive constant, v_d denotes the desired speed of the manipulator's tip, while $\mathbf{d}$ is defined as $\mathbf{d} = \begin{cases} \frac{\mathbf{r}_g}{|\mathbf{r}_g|} & \text{if } |\mathbf{v}| = 0 \\ \frac{\mathbf{v}}{v} & \text{if } |\mathbf{v}| > 0 \end{cases}$. Similarly, in order to force the manipulator's tip to asymptotically stop at the goal position, a proportional-derivative controller $\mathbf{F}_{pd}$ is employed when the robot is located at a distance smaller than a limit distance r_{gl} to the goal. Finally, the overall control signal to govern the tip's movement to the goal is described as follows

$$\mathbf{F}_{tg} = \begin{cases} \mathbf{F}_{gc} + \mathbf{F}_v & \text{if } |\mathbf{r}_g| \geq r_{gl} \\ \mathbf{F}_{pd} & \text{if } |\mathbf{r}_g| < r_{gl} \end{cases}. \tag{11}$$

3.2   Magnetic-Field-Inspired Obstacle Avoidance

To achieve obstacle avoidance, the magnetic-field-inspired obstacle avoidance based on the previous works described in [1,2,4], is employed. The obstacle avoidance algorithm is inspired by a phenomenon observed when a charged particle moves close to a current-carrying wire. A moving robot (in this case the tip of a soft inflatable manipulator) will induce an artificial current on the closest obstacle surface. The artificial current, in parallel to the real electric current in a wire, produces a magnetic field which affects the movement of the robot in such a way that the robot will avoid collision with the obstacle.

The tip induces an electric current $\mathbf{l}_o$ on the closest obstacle described by

$$\mathbf{l}_o = \mathbf{l}_a - \frac{(\mathbf{l}_a^T \mathbf{r}_o)\mathbf{r}_o}{|\mathbf{r}_o|^2}. \tag{12}$$

Here, $\mathbf{l}_a$ and $\mathbf{r}_o$ denote a unit vector of the tip's movement direction and the closest obstacle position with respect to the robot's tip, respectively. From the geometrical perspective, Eq. (12) defines the artificial current $\mathbf{l}_o$ as a projection of the tip's velocity direction $\mathbf{l}_a$ on to the obstacle surface as illustrated in Fig. 3b. To avoid collisions, the manipulator's tip needs to follow the direction of artificial current $\mathbf{l}_o$. To ensure this behaviour, the vector field $\mathbf{F}_o$ is defined as

$$\mathbf{F}_o = c \quad \mathbf{l}_a \times (\mathbf{l}_o \times \mathbf{l}_a) \quad f(r_o, v), \tag{13}$$

where $c > 0$ denotes a constant, $f(r_o, v) \geq 0$ denotes a positive scalar function, and v denotes the speed of the manipulator's tip. To ensure collision avoidance with the obstacle surface, we set the scalar function $f(r_o, v)$ to be proportional to the speed of the manipulator's tip v and inversely proportional to the distance towards the obstacle surface r_o once the distance between the tip and the closest obstacle is smaller than a limit distance r_l as follows $f(r_o, v) = \begin{cases} \frac{v}{r_o} & \text{if } r_o < r_l \\ 0 & \text{if } r_o \geq r_l \end{cases}$.

3.3   Implementation Strategy

It is not possible to directly apply the proposed vector field to the model of the manipulator described in Sect. 2.2 since it describes only the kinematics, not dynamics of the system. To apply the proposed vector field to the kinematic model without losing its properties, the force $\mathbf{F}_t$ is numerically integrated to generate a task-space velocity $\dot{\mathbf{x}}$ as follows $\dot{\mathbf{x}}(t + \Delta t) = \dot{\mathbf{x}}(t) + \mathbf{F}_t(t)\Delta t$, where Δt stands for a time-integration constant.

For the case of a mobile base, we have a redundant system where $\mathbf{J}(\mathbf{q}) \in \mathbb{R}^{3 \times 6}$. This redundancy can be exploited to ensure that the manipulator's tip can reach the desired target and, at the same time, the manipulator's actuators stay inside their actuating capability. The actuator space velocity $\dot{\mathbf{q}}$ is given by [4]

$$\dot{\mathbf{q}} = \mathbf{J}^+ \dot{\mathbf{x}} + \lambda(\mathbf{I} - \mathbf{J}^+ \mathbf{J})\mathbf{z}, \tag{14}$$

where λ stands for a positive constant, $^+$ stands for a pseudo-inverse operation described by $\mathbf{J}^+ = \mathbf{J}^T(\mathbf{J}\mathbf{J}^T)^{-1}$, and $\mathbf{I} \in \mathbb{R}^{6 \times 6}$ is an identity matrix. The vector $\mathbf{z} \in \mathbb{R}^6$ stands for an arbitrary vector which will be chosen to ensure an actuator constraint avoidance. Each actuator has a target value to be achieved.

For the base, the target position is given by

$$\mathbf{x}_{BT} = l_0 \frac{\zeta(\mathbf{r}_{bg})}{|\zeta(\mathbf{r}_{bg})|} + \zeta(\mathbf{x_g}), \tag{15}$$

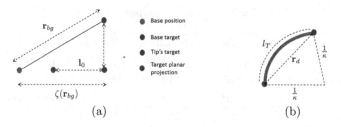

(a)   (b)

Fig. 4. (a) The base (blue dot) will be forced to move to a target position (green dot) located at a distance l_0 from the projection (orange dot) of the goal position (red dot). (b) The length of the manipulator will be forced to reach a target length l_T, i.e. the curve length from the target base position (green dot) to the goal position (red dot). (Color figure online)

where l_0 stands for an initial relaxed length of the manipulator, $\mathbf{r}_{bg} = \mathbf{x}_b - \mathbf{x_g}$ stands for a relative position between the base position $\mathbf{x}_b$ and the goal position $\mathbf{x_g}$, while $\zeta(\mathbf{x})$ is an operation which returns a planar version of a vector $\mathbf{x}$. This base target position will help the pressure avoiding its actuating constraint since it will bring the mobile base closer to the goal position. More specifically, Eq. (15) tries to keep the base located at a planar distance which is equal to the normal length l_0 from the goal position as illustrated in Fig. 4a.

For the tendons, the target value is its mid-value f_T between its minimum f_{min} and maximum tensions f_{max}. For the pressure, the target value is

$$p_T = p_0 + \frac{\sum_{i=1}^{3} f_i}{A} + \frac{l_T - l_0}{l_0} E. \tag{16}$$

Slotting (16) into (4)–(5), we can see that this target pressure will force the manipulator's length l to be l_T. Here, we choose this target length l_T as follows

$$l_T = \begin{cases} \frac{2}{\kappa} \arcsin\left(\frac{\kappa|\mathbf{r}_d|}{2}\right) & \text{if } \kappa \neq 0 \\ |\mathbf{r}_d| & \text{if } \kappa = 0 \end{cases}, \tag{17}$$

where $\mathbf{r}_d = \mathbf{r_g} - \mathbf{x}_{BT}$. This target length l_T is the length of a circular arc which spans from the target base position $\mathbf{x}_{BT}$ to the goal position $\mathbf{r_g}$. Hence, this will make the manipulator easier to achieve the target base position $\mathbf{x}_{BT}$ while at the same time allowing the tip to reach the goal as illustrated in Fig. 4b.

Finally, to achieve these targets, the rate of vector $\mathbf{z}$ is defined as

$$\dot{\mathbf{z}} = (-K_{Pz}(\mathbf{q} - \mathbf{q}_T) - K_{Dz}\dot{\mathbf{q}}), \tag{18}$$

where K_{Pz} and K_{Dz} stand for positive constants while the target vector $\mathbf{q}_T$ is defined as $\mathbf{q}_T = \begin{bmatrix} \mathbf{x}_{BT} & f_T \mathbf{I}_3 & p_T \end{bmatrix}^T$. Here, $\mathbf{I}_3 \in \mathbb{R}^3$ stands for an identity vector. Finally, vector $\mathbf{z}$ is given by $\mathbf{z}(t + \Delta t) = \dot{\mathbf{q}}(t) + \dot{\mathbf{z}}\Delta t$.

Table 1. A list of parameters.

Parameter	Value	Parameter	Value	Parameter	Value
r	0.015 m	E	60000 Pa	p_0	100000 Pa
l_0	0.09 m	K_ω	10	K_v	50
c	1.5	Δt	0.02 m	v_d	0.025 m/s
K_{Pz}	6	K_{Dz}	1	λ	1
r_{gl}	0.05 m	f_{min}	0 N	f_{max}	5 N

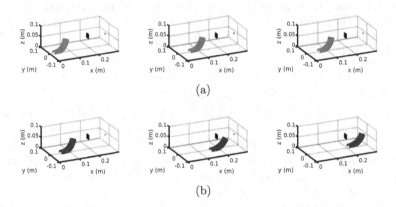

Fig. 5. The soft inflatable arm with a mobile base navigates an environment consisting of a planar obstacles with (a) an electric-field-potential algorithm and (b) a magnetic-field-inspired algorithm. The order of movement is from left to right. (Color figure online)

4   Results and Analysis

In this section, the performance of the proposed algorithm is evaluated in the simulation scenario. The parameters used for the manipulator's modelling and the navigation algorithm are presented in Table 1. In this paper, we consider only static obstacles in the environment whose shape and position are unknown to the manipulator before the movement execution. We assume that the manipulator is equipped with a sensor which is able to detect the surrounding obstacles as far as a distance $r_l = 0.04$ m. In some of the scenarios, we compare the performance of the algorithm with the electric-field-based navigation as described in [3].

The first environment consists of a single planar obstacle (drawn in black) where the manipulator's tip needs to reach the desired position (shown as a red dot) across the obstacle as shown in Fig. 5. We compare the performance of the electric-field-potential algorithm (Fig. 5a) with the proposed magnetic-field-inspired algorithm (Fig. 5b) when applied to the model of the soft inflatable manipulator. We can see how the electric-field-potential algorithm fails to guide the tip of the manipulator to reach the target in Fig. 5a. This is due to the repulsive nature of the potential field involved which cancels the attraction towards

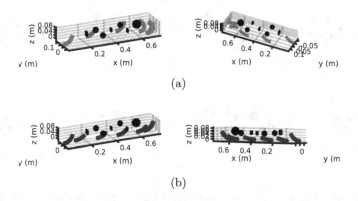

Fig. 6. The soft inflatable arm with a mobile base navigates an environment consisting of multiple obstacles viewed from two different perspectives in the left and the right. (a) The performance of an electric-field-potential algorithm and (b) a magnetic-field-inspired algorithm are shown. The step-by-step configuration starts from left to right in the left pictures and vice versa in the right pictures.

the goal. The magnetic-field-inspired algorithm, on the other hand, does not encounter the same problem since the vector field employed is not repulsive.

The second scenario is where the environment is more complicated as it consists of many planar and spherical obstacles as shown in Fig. 6. Once again, we compare the performance of the electric-field-potential algorithm (Fig. 6a) and the magnetic-field-inspired algorithm (Fig. 6b) when applied to the kinematic model of the soft inflatable manipulator. In this scenario, we can see that when using the electric-field-potential, the robot does not get stuck as is the case in the previous environment. However, we can observe how the motion is less smooth compared to the motion when using the magnetic-field-inspired algorithm in Fig. 6b. This occurs especially in the final stage of the motion where we can observe that the obstacle causes more bending of the robot body in Fig. 6a compared to the robot in Fig. 6b whose shape does not get affected as much. This less smooth motion is caused by the repulsiveness of the vector field employed in Fig. 6a.

In the last scenario, the environment consists of more obstacles and the manipulator is expected to move in succession to several target points. This scenario mimics the situation when the manipulator needs to bring a sensor such as a camera to inspect several locations in an unknown cluttered environment. In Fig. 7, we only show the manipulator's movement when using the proposed magnetic-field-inspired navigation. To better visualise the manipulator's movement, we show the step-by-step motions in each figure from two different perspectives shown in Fig. 7a and b. In each figure, we can observe how magnetic-field-inspired navigation is able to smoothly navigate the manipulator towards each of the target locations without colliding with multiple obstacles.

In all the scenarios presented from Figs. 5, 6 and 7, we can observe that the overall length of the manipulator does not vary too much during the course of

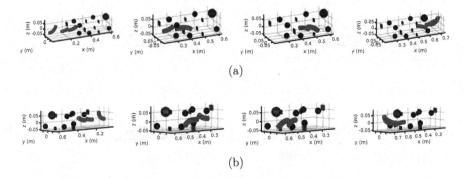

(a)

(b)

Fig. 7. The soft inflatable arm moves to several target points in succession in a cluttered environment viewed from two different perspectives in (a) and (b) using the magnetic-field-inspired navigation.

the movement. This is a direct effect of the redundancy mechanism described in Sect. 3.3 which exploits the redundancy of the manipulator to avoid the actuating constraints when navigating towards the goal.

5 Conclusions and Future Works

In this paper, we have implemented magnetic-field-inspired navigation to guide the soft inflatable manipulator towards a target position while reactively avoiding collision with the environment. The beam-theory-based model is used to model the behaviour of the manipulator which uses a combined antagonistically tendon and pressure actuation. The redundancy in the manipulator combined with a planar mobile base is exploited to help the actuators stay under their maximum capability without affecting the manipulator's movement while navigating the environment. The navigation algorithm is shown to outperform the potential-field-based navigation in its ability to smoothly and reactively avoid obstacles and reach the goal in simulation scenarios. Applying the algorithm to the real soft inflatable manipulator in a real-life environment while considering the dynamics of the system will be the focus of the future works.

References

1. Ataka, A., Lam, H.K., Althoefer, K.: Reactive magnetic-field-inspired navigation for non-holonomic mobile robots in unknown environments. In: Proceedings of the IEEE International Conference on Robotics and Automation, pp. 6983–6988, May 2018. https://doi.org/10.1109/ICRA.2018.8463203
2. Ataka, A., Lam, H.K., Althoefer, K.: Reactive magnetic-field-inspired navigation method for robots in unknown convex 3-D environments. IEEE Robot. Autom. Lett. **3**(4), 3583–3590 (2018). https://doi.org/10.1109/LRA.2018.2853801

3. Ataka, A., Qi, P., Liu, H., Althoefer, K.: Real-time planner for multi-segment continuum manipulator in dynamic environments. In: Proceedings of the IEEE International Conference on Robotics and Automation, pp. 4080–4085, May 2016
4. Ataka, A., Shiva, A., Lam, H.K., Althoefer, K.: Magnetic-field-inspired navigation for soft continuum manipulator. In: 2018 IEEE/RSJ International Conference on Intelligent Robots and Systems (IROS), pp. 168–173, October 2018. https://doi.org/10.1109/IROS.2018.8593592
5. Blumenschein, L.H., Gan, L.T., Fan, J.A., Okamura, A.M., Hawkes, E.W.: A tip-extending soft robot enables reconfigurable and deployable antennas. IEEE Robot. Autom. Lett. 3(2), 949–956 (2018). https://doi.org/10.1109/LRA.2018.2793303
6. Chen, Y., et al.: Safety-enhanced motion planning for flexible surgical manipulator using neural dynamics. IEEE Trans. Control Syst. Technol. 25(5), 1711–1723 (2017). https://doi.org/10.1109/TCST.2016.2628806
7. Cianchetti, M., et al.: Soft robotics technologies to address shortcomings in today's minimally invasive surgery: the STIFF-FLOP approach. Soft Robot. 1(2), 122–131 (2014)
8. Fras, J., Czarnowski, J., Macias, M., Glowka, J., Cianchetti, M., Menciassi, A.: New STIFF-FLOP module construction idea for improved actuation and sensing. In: Proceedings of the IEEE International Conference on Robotics and Automation, pp. 2901–2906, May 2015. https://doi.org/10.1109/ICRA.2015.7139595
9. Godage, I., Branson, D., Guglielmino, E., Caldwell, D.: Path planning for multisection continuum arms. In: Proceedings of the International Conference on Mechatronics and Automation (ICMA), pp. 1208–1213, August 2012. https://doi.org/10.1109/ICMA.2012.6283423
10. Granna, J., Godage, I.S., Wirz, R., Weaver, K.D., Webster, R.J., Burgner-Kahrs, J.: A 3-D volume coverage path planning algorithm with application to intracerebral hemorrhage evacuation. IEEE Robot. Autom. Lett. 1(2), 876–883 (2016). https://doi.org/10.1109/LRA.2016.2528297
11. Hawkes, E.W., Blumenschein, L.H., Greer, J.D., Okamura, A.M.: A soft robot that navigates its environment through growth. Sci. Robot. 2(8) (2017). https://doi.org/10.1126/scirobotics.aan3028, http://robotics.sciencemag.org/content/2/8/eaan3028
12. Maghooa, F., Stilli, A., Noh, Y., Althoefer, K., Wurdemann, H.: Tendon and pressure actuation for a bio-inspired manipulator based on an antagonistic principle. In: Proceedings of the IEEE International Conference on Robotics and Automation, pp. 2556–2561, May 2015. https://doi.org/10.1109/ICRA.2015.7139542
13. Neumann, M., Burgner-Kahrs, J.: Considerations for follow-the-leader motion of extensible tendon-driven continuum robots. In: Proceedings of the IEEE International Conference on Robotics and Automation, pp. 917–923, May 2016. https://doi.org/10.1109/ICRA.2016.7487223
14. Qi, P., Liu, C., Ataka, A., Lam, H.K., Althoefer, K.: Kinematic control of continuum manipulators using a fuzzy-model-based approach. IEEE Trans. Ind. Electron. 63(8), 5022–5035 (2016). https://doi.org/10.1109/TIE.2016.2554078
15. Qi, P., Qiu, C., Liu, H., Dai, J., Seneviratne, L., Althoefer, K.: A novel continuum-style robot with multilayer compliant modules. In: Proceedings of the IEEE/RSJ International Conference on Intelligent Robots and Systems, pp. 3175–3180, September 2014. https://doi.org/10.1109/IROS.2014.6943002
16. Rus, D., Tolley, M.T.: Design, fabrication and control of soft robots. Nature 521, 467–475 (2015). https://doi.org/10.1038/nature14543. http://www.nature.com/nature/journal/v521/n7553/abs/nature14543.html

17. Sadati, S.M.H., Naghibi, S.E., Shiva, A., Walker, I.D., Althoefer, K., Nanayakkara, T.: Mechanics of continuum manipulators, a comparative study of five methods with experiments. In: Gao, Y., Fallah, S., Jin, Y., Lekakou, C. (eds.) TAROS 2017. LNCS (LNAI), vol. 10454, pp. 686–702. Springer, Cham (2017). https://doi.org/10.1007/978-3-319-64107-2_56
18. Stilli, A., Kolokotronis, E., Fraś, J., Ataka, A., Althoefer, K., Wurdemann, H.A.: Static kinematics for an antagonistically actuated robot based on a beam-mechanics-based model. In: 2018 IEEE/RSJ International Conference on Intelligent Robots and Systems (IROS), pp. 6959–6964, October 2018. https://doi.org/10.1109/IROS.2018.8593674
19. Torres, L., et al.: A motion planning approach to automatic obstacle avoidance during concentric tube robot teleoperation. In: Proceedings of the IEEE International Conference on Robotics and Automation, pp. 2361–2367, May 2015. https://doi.org/10.1109/ICRA.2015.7139513
20. Wang, H., Chen, J., Lau, H.Y.K., Ren, H.: Motion planning based on learning from demonstration for multiple-segment flexible soft robots actuated by electroactive polymers. IEEE Robot. Autom. Lett. **1**(1), 391–398 (2016). https://doi.org/10.1109/LRA.2016.2521384
21. Wu, K., Wu, L., Ren, H.: Motion planning of continuum tubular robots based on centerlines extracted from statistical atlas. In: Proceedings of the IEEE/RSJ International Conference on Intelligent Robots and Systems, pp. 5512–5517, September 2015. https://doi.org/10.1109/IROS.2015.7354158

Learning and Composing Primitive Skills
for Dual-Arm Manipulation

Èric Pairet[1,2(✉)] , Paola Ardón[1,2] , Michael Mistry[1] , and Yvan Petillot[2]

[1] Institute of Perception, Action and Behaviour, University of Edinburgh,
Edinburgh, UK
{eric.pairet,paola.ardon}@ed.ac.uk, mmistry@inf.ed.ac.uk
[2] Engineering and Physical Sciences, Heriot-Watt University, Edinburgh, UK
y.r.petillot@hw.ac.uk

Abstract. In an attempt to confer robots with complex manipulation capabilities, dual-arm anthropomorphic systems have become an important research topic in the robotics community. Most approaches in the literature rely upon a great understanding of the dynamics underlying the system's behaviour and yet offer limited autonomous generalisation capabilities. To address these limitations, this work proposes a modelisation for dual-arm manipulators based on dynamic movement primitives laying in two orthogonal spaces. The modularity and learning capabilities of this model are leveraged to formulate a novel end-to-end learning-based framework which (i) learns a library of primitive skills from human demonstrations, and (ii) composes such knowledge simultaneously and sequentially to confront novel scenarios. The feasibility of the proposal is evaluated by teaching the iCub humanoid the basic skills to succeed on simulated dual-arm pick-and-place tasks. The results suggest the learning and generalisation capabilities of the proposed framework extend to autonomously conduct undemonstrated dual-arm manipulation tasks.

Keywords: Learning from demonstration · Humanoid robots ·
Model learning for control · Dual arm manipulation ·
Autonomous agents

1 Introduction

Complex manipulation tasks can be achieved by endowing anthropomorphic robots with dual-arm manipulation capabilities. Bi-manual arrangements extend the systems competences to efficiently perform tasks involving large objects or assembling multi-component elements without external assistance. These systems not only deal with the challenges of single-arm manipulators, such as trajectory planning and environmental interaction, but also require an accurate synchronisation between arms to avoid breaking or exposing the handled object to stress.

Traditional approaches have addressed the aforementioned challenges by means of control and planning-based methods [18]. These methods depend upon

© Springer Nature Switzerland AG 2019
K. Althoefer et al. (Eds.): TAROS 2019, LNAI 11649, pp. 65–77, 2019.
https://doi.org/10.1007/978-3-030-23807-0_6

Fig. 1. iCub humanoid learning to contour an obstacle through kinaesthetic guiding (left), and composing multiple skills to conduct a dual-arm pick-and-place task (right).

an excellent understanding of the exact model underlying the system's and task's dynamics, which are commonly approximated to make the calculations computationally tractable [13]. On top of that, some of these methods lack scalability and generalisation capabilities, involving hand-defining all possible scenarios and actions [3,5]. All these issues have motivated the use of more natural techniques for robot programming, such as (LbD), in which a human movement is recorded to be later reproduced by a robot.

Despite the encouraging possibilities offered by adopting human knowledge for robot control, teaching complex systems, such as dual-arm manipulators, to respond and adapt to a broad case of scenarios remains an open challenge. Particularly, it is expected from a dual-arm system to generalise the provided demonstrations to confront novel scenarios in (a) the task space to deal with the changing requirements about trajectory planning and environmental interaction, and (b) the relative space to ensure the essential synchronisation between arms [12]. However, current learning-based architectures in the literature pursuing autonomy and robustness against the dynamic and unpredictable real-world environments are limited to single-arm arrangements [4,15,17]. Contrarily, learning-based frameworks for dual-arm robots do not generalise to undemonstrated states, thus being limited to highly controlled scenarios [7,19,21].

This paper presents a novel learning-based framework which endows a dual-arm system with a real-time and generalisable method for manipulation in undemonstrated environments (see Fig. 1). The framework models a dual-arm manipulator with a set of dynamic movement primitives laying in two orthogonal spaces to tackle the task's requirements separately from the synchronisation constraints. The modularity of the DMPs is leveraged to (i) create a library of primitive skills from human demonstrations, and (ii) exploit primitive skills simultaneously and sequentially to create complex behaviours. The potential of the proposal is demonstrated in simulation after recording skills with the iCub humanoid through kinaesthetic guiding. The results suggest the proposal's suitability to endow a dual-arm robot with the necessary learning and generalisation capabilities to autonomously address novel manipulation tasks.

2 Dual-Arm System Modelisation

This paper pursues an end-to-end learning-based framework which endows a dual-arm system with enhanced generalisation capabilities, meets the synchronisation constraints, and is easily programmable by non-robotics-experts. This work addresses all these requirements by means of learnable and composable primitive skills represented as dynamic movement primitives (DMPs) [9]. This section firstly overviews DMPs and its use in the literature. It then introduces the proposed typology of actions in a dual-arm system, which allows leveraging the strengths of a DMP-based modelisation in the dual-arm context.

2.1 Dynamic Movement Primitives

DMPs are a versatile tool for modelling and learning complex motions. They describe the dynamics of a primitive skill as a spring-damper system under the effect of a virtual external force called coupling term. This coupling term allows for learning and reproducing any dynamical behaviour, i.e. primitive skill. Importantly, (a) coupling terms can be learnt from human demonstrations, (b) they can be efficiently learned and generated, (c) a unique demonstration is already generalisable, (d) convergence to the goal is guaranteed, and (e) their representation is translation and time-invariant. Because of all these properties, DMPs are adapted to constitute the fundamental building blocks of this work. Next follows an introduction about DMPs and their usage to encode positional and orientational dynamics, and an overview of some coupling terms in the literature.

Positional Dynamics. Let the positional state of a one-degree of freedom (DoF) system be defined by its position, linear velocity and acceleration. Then, the system's state transition is defined with non-linear differential equations as:

$$\tau \dot{z} = \alpha_x(\beta_x(g_x - x) - z) + f_x(\cdot), \tag{1}$$

$$\tau \dot{x} = z, \tag{2}$$

where τ is a scaling factor for time, x is the system's position, z and $\dot{z}$ respectively are the scaled velocity and acceleration, α_x and β_x are constants defining the positional system's dynamics, g_x is the model's attractor, and $f_x(\cdot)$ is the coupling term. The coupling term applying at multiple DoFs at once is defined as $\mathbf{f}_x(\cdot)$. The system will converge to g_x with critically damped dynamics and null velocity when $\tau > 0$, $\alpha_x > 0$, $\beta_x > 0$ and $\beta_x = \alpha_x/4$ [9].

Orientational Dynamics. A possible representation of orientations is the unit quaternion $\mathbf{q} \in \mathbb{R}^4 = \mathbb{S}^3$ [20]. They encode orientations of a system as a whole, thus ensuring the stability of the orientational dynamics integration. Let the current orientational state of a system be defined by its orientation, angular velocity and acceleration. Then, the orientational state transition is described by the following non-linear differential equations:

$$\tau\dot{\boldsymbol{\eta}} = \alpha_q(\beta_q\, 2\log(\mathbf{g}_q * \bar{\mathbf{q}}) - \boldsymbol{\eta}) + \mathbf{f}_q(\cdot), \tag{3}$$

$$\tau\dot{\mathbf{q}} = \frac{1}{2}\boldsymbol{\eta} * \mathbf{q}, \tag{4}$$

where $\mathbf{q}$ is the system's orientation, $\boldsymbol{\eta}$ and $\dot{\boldsymbol{\eta}}$ respectively are the scaled angular velocity and acceleration, α_q and β_q are constants defining the system's dynamics, $\mathbf{g}_q \in \mathbb{S}^3$ is the model's attractor, and $\mathbf{f}_q(\cdot) \in \mathbb{R}^4$ is the coupling term. The operators $\log(\cdot)$, $*$, and $\bar{\mathbf{q}}$ denote the logarithm, multiplication and conjugate operations for quaternions, respectively.

Coupling Terms. Coupling terms describe the system's behaviour, thus being useful to learn and retrieve any primitive skill. They are commonly used to encode the positional [9] and orientational [20] dynamics of a motion. Coupling terms are modelled in each dimension as a weighted linear combination of non-linear radial basis functions (RBFs) distributed along the trajectory. Thus, learning a certain movement relies on finding the weights of the RBFs which closely reproduce a demonstrated skill.

More complex behaviours may be achieved by exploiting an additional coupling term simultaneously with the motion-encoding one. This approach has been used to avoid joint limits and constraining the robot's workspace via repulsive forces pushing the system away from these limits [6]. Coupling terms have also been leveraged for obstacle avoidance with an analytic biologically-inspired approach describing how humans steer around obstacles [8,17]. Another use is for environmental and self-interaction purposes by means of a controller tracking a desired force profile [7]. To the best of the authors' knowledge, the practice of using coupling terms simultaneously has been limited to two primitive skills acting on the same frame or space [15]. Contrarily, this work further exploits the DMP modularity to describe a dual-arm system in two orthogonal spaces with the purpose of facing complex scenarios by composing multiple coupling terms.

2.2 Dual-Arm Primitive Skills Taxonomy

Skills for single-arm manipulation have been well analysed in the robotics community. While some of this knowledge can be extrapolated for a dual-arm manipulator as a whole, their complexity resides in the arms interaction. In the context of manipulation via a dual-arm system, a possible classification of any primitive skill falls into two groups: (a) absolute skills, which imply a change of configuration of the manipulated object in the Cartesian or absolute space $\mathcal{S}_a$, e.g. move or turn an object in a particular manner, and (b) relative skills, which exert an action on the manipulated object in the object or relative space $\mathcal{S}_r$, e.g. opening a bottle's screw cap, or hold a parcel employing force contact.

Each type of primitive skill uniquely produces movement in its space since they lay in orthogonal spaces such that $\mathcal{S}_a \perp \mathcal{S}_r$. It is natural to expect from a dual-arm system to simultaneously carry out, at least, one absolute and one relative skill to accomplish a task. Let us analyse the task of moving a bottle to a particular position while opening its screw cap. Both end-effectors synchronously move to reach the desired configuration (absolute skill). At the same time, the left end-effector is constrained to hold the bottle upright (relative skill), while the right end-effector unscrews the cap (relative skill).

2.3   Dual-Arm DMP-Based Modelisation

Given the variety of primitive skills that a dual-arm system can execute, this work seeks to model the robotic platform in a generalisable yet modular fashion, which accounts for both absolute and relative skills. To this aim, let us consider the closed kinematic chain depicted in Fig. 2 operating in a three-dimensional (3D) workspace $\mathcal{W} = \mathbb{R}^3 \times \mathrm{SO}(3)$. Each arm i, where $i = \{L, R\}$, interacts with the same object $\mathcal{O}$. In this context, the absolute skill explains the movement of the object $\mathcal{O}$ in the workspace $\mathcal{W} = \mathcal{S}_a$, while the relative skill describes the actions of each end-effector i in $\mathcal{S}_r$, i.e. with respect to the object's reference frame $\{\mathcal{O}\}$. Note that $\{\mathcal{O}\}$ is the centre of the closed-chain dual-arm system.

The state of the closed-chain dual-arm system in the workspace can be described by the position/orientation, linear/angular velocities and accelerations of $\{\mathcal{O}\}$ in $\mathcal{S}_a$. As introduced previously, the system's state transition is subjected to its modelled dynamics. Figure 2 illustrates the proposed modelisation of the system's dynamics in $\mathcal{S}_a$ as a set of DMPs acting between the objects's frame $\{\mathcal{O}\}$ and its goal configuration $\mathbf{g}_o$, which accounts for a desired goal position $\mathbf{g}_{o_x} \in \mathbb{R}^3$ and orientation $\mathbf{g}_{o_q} \in \mathbb{R}^4$. Therefore, three positional DMPs as in (1)–(2) and one orientational DMP as in (3)–(4) are required to encode the system's dynamics in the absolute space $\mathcal{S}_a = \mathbb{R}^3 \times \mathrm{SO}(3)$.

In the relative space $\mathcal{S}_r$, the dynamics of each end-effector are modelled as DMPs referenced to the objects's frame $\{\mathcal{O}\}$. Since $\mathcal{S}_r = \mathbb{R}^3 \times \mathrm{SO}(3)$, each end-

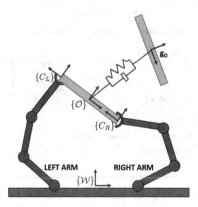

Fig. 2. DMP-based modelisation of a closed-chain dual-arm system in the absolute and relative spaces. This model is extended to deal with rotational dynamics.

effector dynamic's in the relative frame is described by three positional DMPs as in (1)–(2) and one orientational DMP as in (3)–(4).

Any action referenced to the object's frame can be projected to the end-effectors using the grasping geometry **G** of the manipulated object. This allows computing the required end-effector control commands to achieve a particular absolute task. A detailed explanation of this transformation can be found in [12].

3   Learning-Based Dual-Arm Manipulation

To endow a dual-arm manipulator with autonomy and robustness in novel scenarios while being easily programmable and customisable by non-robotics-experts, this work has decomposed and modelled the system's dynamics and synchronisation constraints as primitive skills lying in the system's absolute and relative space. Leveraging the formulated modelisation, this work proposes the framework schematised in Fig. 3 which creates and manages a library of primitive skills. The framework has two components: (i) a learning module that learns a set of primitive skills from human demonstrations, and (ii) a manager module that combines simultaneously and sequentially these primitives to address a wide range of complex tasks in unfamiliar environments.

3.1   Library Generation

A primitive skill is represented by its coupling term and frame of reference, i.e. either absolute or relative. Learning coupling terms only requires a human demonstrator teaching the characteristic skill. As previously introduced, different coupling terms might be better formulated with different mathematical representations, e.g. a weighted combination of non-linear RBFs to encode the dynamics of a task, an analytical obstacle avoidance expression, or among others, a force profile to control the environmental interaction.

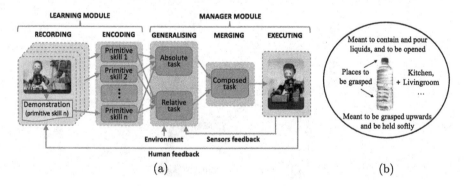

Fig. 3. Scheme of the proposed framework. (a) Learning: a library of primitive skills is learnt from human demonstrations. Manager: the primitives are combined simultaneously and sequentially to confront novel environments. (b) The required primitive skills are selected according to the affordance elements of the dual-arm task.

The modularity offered by the proposed DMP-based formulation and its use in two different spaces tackles the hindrance and ambiguity arising when demonstrating all features of a dual-arm task in an all-at-once fashion. This means that instead of learning a task as a whole, the framework harvests a collection of primitive skills. Creating a repertoire of skills referred to as a library, allows the demonstrator to teach in a one-at-a-time fashion, i.e. to focus on one feature of the demonstration at a time [4]. Moreover, this modular library can be employed for movement recognition purposes, where a demonstrated skill can be compared against the existing ones in the library. If the observed behaviour does not match any existing primitive, it is identified as a new skill and can be added to the framework's library [10].

3.2 Attaching Semantics

The framework needs additional information to successfully conduct a dual-arm manipulation task. Let us consider the robotic task of opening a bottle's screw cap, where the system needs to select a proper sequence of primitive skills in order to succeed (see Fig. 3(b)). This is first a grasping, where each end-effector holds a different component of the bottle, then a synchronous turning referenced in the system's relative space and finally, a placing and releasing primitives. Therefore, in order to ease this action selection, it is essential to attach a semantic description to each primitive skill.

Semantic labels bridge the gap between the low-level continuous representation of primitives and the high-level description of actions and their influence on objects. An approach to tackle the object affordances challenge consists in combining features from the object and their surroundings to infer on a suitable grasp-action based on their purpose of use [1,2]. The combination of such elements builds the relationship between context, actions and effects that provide a cognitive reasoning of an object affordance.

3.3 Library Management

Each coupling term stored in the framework's library represents a particular absolute or relative primitive skill. Reproducing a skill consists in using its coupling term as $\mathbf{f}_x(\cdot)$ or $\mathbf{f}_q(\cdot)$ in (1)–(4). This computation retrieves the skill's required accelerations, which can be integrated over time to obtain the skill's velocities $\dot{\mathbf{y}}_o$ for an absolute primitive or $\dot{\mathbf{y}}_{C_i}$ for the end-effector i relative primitive.

The individual retrieval of primitives already accounts for the inner DMP generalisation capabilities, such as different start and goal configurations, as well as obstacle locations. However, these primitive skills need to be combined to generate more complex movements, such as a pick-and-place task of a bottle accounting for the presence of unexpected obstacles (absolute space), while opening the bottle's screw cap considering the exerted force (relative space).

The presented framework addresses this prerequisite by simultaneously combining different absolute and relative skills as:

$$\begin{bmatrix} \dot{\mathbf{y}}_L \\ \dot{\mathbf{y}}_R \end{bmatrix} = \mathbf{G}^T \sum_{j=1}^{J} w_j \, \dot{\mathbf{y}}_{o_j} + \sum_{k=1}^{K} w_k \begin{bmatrix} \dot{\mathbf{y}}_{C_{L,k}} \\ \dot{\mathbf{y}}_{C_{R,k}} \end{bmatrix}, \tag{5}$$

where $\dot{\mathbf{y}}_i \in \mathbb{R}^6$ describes the linear and angular velocity commands of the $i = \{L, R\}$ end-effector satisfying the set of activated primitive skills, $\mathbf{G} \in \mathbb{R}^{6 \times 12}$ is the global grasp map of the two end-effectors grasp matrices as described in [13], and $\dot{\mathbf{y}}_{o_j} \in \mathbb{R}^6$ and $\dot{\mathbf{y}}_{C_{i,k}} \in \mathbb{R}^6$ are the velocities of the $j \in [1, J]$ absolute and $k \in [1, K]$ relative primitive skill stored in the library. Absolute and relative skill selection is conducted with the weights w_j and w_k, respectively.

The resulting framework does not only combines skills simultaneously, but also sequentially. This allows the execution of a complex task composed of a sequence of primitives. To do so, a primitive skill is executed by initialising it with the full state (pose, velocities and accelerations) of its predecessor primitive skill. Such an initialisation avoids abrupt jumps in the system's state.

4   Results and Evaluation

The proposed framework has been evaluated on the iCub humanoid robot. Particularly, the real platform has been used to load the framework's library with a set of primitive skills learnt from human demonstrations. These skills have been employed in simulation to conduct dual-arm pick-and-place tasks of a parcel in novel scenarios, demonstrating the proposal's potential for humanoid robots.

4.1   Experimental Platform

iCub is an open source humanoid robot with 53 DoFs [11] (see Fig. 4(b)). The most relevant ones in this work are the three-DoFs on the torso, the two seven-DoFs arms equipped with a torque sensor on the shoulder, and the two nine-DoFs anthropomorphic hands with tactile sensors in the fingertips and palm.

iCub operates under YARP. The deployment of the proposed framework on the iCub platform is schematised in Fig. 4. Mainly, four big functional modules can be distinguished: (i) the proposed framework described in this paper (blue blocks), (ii) the real/simulated platform with its visual perception, joint sensors and actuators (magenta blocks), (iii) the end-effectors control via the built-in YARP Cartesian controller [16] and an ad-hoc external torso controller (green blocks), and (iv) the HRI interface to parameterise the desired start and goal configurations for the task, and retrieve the robot's status (red blocks).

4.2   Learning Primitive Skills from Demonstration

For the system to succeed on the dual-arm pick-and-place of a parcel task in novel environments, the framework's library needs to be loaded with the absolute

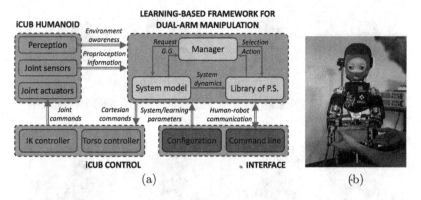

Fig. 4. (a) Layout of the framework deployment on the iCub robot. Note: grasping geometry (GG), primitive skill (PS). (b) iCub humanoid being taught grasp maintenance through kineasthetic guiding. (Color figure online)

primitive skills of (i) pick-and-place dynamics on a horizontal surface, (ii) rotational motion around the z-axis, and (iii) obstacle avoidance. Moreover, since the parcel has to be grasped by lateral contact of both end-effectors, the library also requires a relative skill to ensure grasp maintenance, i.e. prevention of contact separation. All these primitive skills have been demonstrated via kineasthetic guiding on the real iCub humanoid robot. To this aim, all joints have been set in gravity compensation, allowing the demonstrator to physically manoeuvre the robot through each primitive. Figure 4(b) depicts the kineasthetic teaching of obstacle avoidance and grasp maintenance primitives.

During the demonstrations, proprioception information is retrieved via YARP ports to learn the coupling terms $\mathbf{f}_x(\cdot)$ and $\mathbf{f}_q(\cdot)$ in (1)–(4) characterising the different skills. For the pick-and-place and rotational dynamics, the coupling terms are encoded as a weighted linear combination of non-linear RBFs distributed along the trajectory as in [9]. The obstacle avoidance is learnt by finding the best-fitting parameters of the biologically-inspired formulation as in [17]. Finally, the grasp maintenance skill is learnt by setting the parcel's grasping geometry as a pose tracking reference as in [7].

4.3 Experiments on Simulated iCub Humanoid

The evaluation of the framework on the pick-and-place setup has been conducted on a simulated iCub robotic platform. Particularly, the four primitive skills previously learnt and loaded in the framework's library are simultaneously and sequentially combined to conduct three consecutive dual-arm pick-and-place task in novel environments (see Fig. 5).

Given an initial random configuration laying on the table and within iCub's workspace (see Fig. 5(a)), the first action consists of grasping the parcel. This is achieved by retrieving the parcel's configuration, then use the learnt parcel's geometry to compute the grasping points, and finally approach them laterally

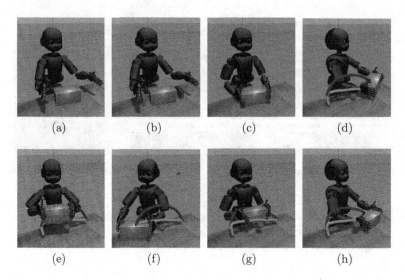

Fig. 5. iCub humanoid succeeding in novel dual-arm pick-and-place tasks by simultaneously and sequentially combining primitive skills. Demonstrated pick-and-place (green trajectory). Framework's response (blue trajectory). Obstacle (red sphere). (a) Parcel initial state. (b)–(c) Grasping parcel laterally. (d)–(f) and (f)–(h) Pick-and-place execution with different start, goal and obstacle configurations. (Color figure online)

via the middle-setpoints displayed as red and blue prisms for the right and left end-effector, respectively (see Fig. 5(a)–(c)). From this stage on, the grasp maintenance skill ensures that both end-effectors are in flat contact with the box to avoid undesired slippage.

The following three consecutive movements require picking-and-placing the parcel between different configurations laying on the central, right and left side of iCub's workspace. The former pick-and-place does not require avoiding any obstacle, thus the built-in DMPs generalisation capabilities are sufficient to address this task (see Fig. 5(c)–(d)). However, the two latter pick-and-place tasks involve adapting the learnt dynamics to address novel scenarios. When the obstacle (red sphere) is collinear with the start and goal positions, i.e. below the demonstrated task (green trajectory), the iCub humanoid circumnavigates the obstacle from the top (see Fig. 5(d)–(f)). Instead, for an obstacle located forward the demonstration, the framework guides the system through a collision-free trajectory near iCub's chest (see Fig. 5(g)–(h)).

The experimental evaluation conducted with the simulated iCub humanoid robot has demonstrated various of the aforementioned framework's features. Having a repertoire of primitive skills available in the framework's library allows exploiting them simultaneously and sequentially to confront complex tasks in novel scenarios. The reported case is one of the 16 successful experiments out of a total of 20 trials. In all cases, the robot had to accomplish the three consecutive dual-arm pick-and-place tasks with different start and goal locations, while avoiding novel obstacles and ensuring grasp maintenance. Failure in any of these tasks made the trial unsuccessful. Interestingly, in the four failed trials one of iCub's forearms collided with the obstacle. This is because the biologically-inspired obstacle avoidance formulation only considers the carried object and should be extended to the object-arm space. The flexibility of the proposed framework could be leveraged to integrate in its library a potential field-inspired approach for obstacle avoidance which also checks for link collisions [14].

5   Final Remarks and Future Work

This work has presented a novel end-to-end learning-based framework which endows a dual-arm manipulator with real-time and generalisable manipulation capabilities. The framework is built upon the proposed extension of the DMP-based modelisation for dual-arm systems, which considers two different frames to reference the movement generation, force interaction and constraints requirements. Based on this arrangement, the proposed framework is twofold: (i) learns from human demonstrations to create a library of primitive skills, and (ii) combines such knowledge simultaneously and sequentially to confront novel scenarios.

The suitability of the proposed approach has been demonstrated in a dual-arm pick-and-place setting, where the iCub humanoid first learnt a repertoire of primitive skills from human demonstrations and then composed such knowledge to successfully generalise to novel scenarios. The framework is not restricted to the presented experimental evaluation nor platform. Any system capable of learning from demonstrations can benefit from this work. Moreover, the framework's modularity allows loading to its library any primitive skill that might be required for dual-arm manipulation purposes.

Future work will significantly extend the library of primitive skills such that more challenging dual-arm manipulation behaviours can be addressed within the framework. In this regard, imminent efforts will focus on learning force-dependant primitive skills or other actions requiring complex synchronisation between end-effectors, such as the opening of a bottle's screw cap or succeeding in the peg-in-a-hole tasks.

Acknowledgments. This work has been partially supported by ORCA Hub EPSRC (EP/R026173/1) and consortium partners.

References

1. Ardón, P., Pairet, È., Petrick, R., Ramamoorthy, S., Lohan, K.S.: Reasoning on grasp-action affordances. In: Konstantinova, J., et al. (eds.) TAROS 2019, LNAI, vol. 11529, pp. 3–15. Springer, Heidelberg (2019)
2. Ardón, P., Pairet, È., Ramamoorthy, S., Lohan, K.S.: Towards robust grasps: using the environment semantics for robotic object affordances. In: Proceedings of the AAAI Fall Symposium on Reasoning and Learning in Real-World Systems for Long-Term Autonomy, pp. 5–12. AAAI Press (2018)

3. Argall, B.D., Chernova, S., Veloso, M., Browning, B.: A survey of robot learning from demonstration. Robot. Auton. Syst. **57**(5), 469–483 (2009)
4. Bajcsy, A., Losey, D.P., O'Malley, M.K., Dragan, A.D.: Learning from physical human corrections, one feature at a time. In: Proceedings of the 2018 ACM/IEEE International Conference on Human-Robot Interaction, pp. 141–149. ACM (2018)
5. Billard, A., Calinon, S., Dillmann, R., Schaal, S.: Robot programming by demonstration. In: Siciliano, B., Khatib, O. (eds.) Springer Handbook of Robotics, pp. 1371–1394. Springer, Heidelberg (2008). https://doi.org/10.1007/978-3-540-30301-5_60
6. Gams, A., Ijspeert, A.J., Schaal, S., Lenarčič, J.: On-line learning and modulation of periodic movements with nonlinear dynamical systems. Auton. Robots **27**(1), 3–23 (2009)
7. Gams, A., Nemec, B., Ijspeert, A.J., Ude, A.: Coupling movement primitives: Interaction with the environment and bimanual tasks. IEEE Trans. Robot. **30**(4), 816–830 (2014)
8. Hoffmann, H., Pastor, P., Park, D.H., Schaal, S.: Biologically-inspired dynamical systems for movement generation: automatic real-time goal adaptation and obstacle avoidance. In: 2009 IEEE International Conference on Robotics and Automation, ICRA 2009, pp. 2587–2592. IEEE (2009)
9. Ijspeert, A.J., Nakanishi, J., Hoffmann, H., Pastor, P., Schaal, S.: Dynamical movement primitives: learning attractor models for motor behaviors. Neural Comput. **25**(2), 328–373 (2013)
10. Ijspeert, A.J., Nakanishi, J., Schaal, S.: Movement imitation with nonlinear dynamical systems in humanoid robots. In: 2002 Proceedings of the IEEE International Conference on Robotics and Automation, ICRA 2002, vol. 2, pp. 1398–1403. IEEE (2002)
11. Metta, G., Sandini, G., Vernon, D., Natale, L., Nori, F.: The iCub humanoid robot: an open platform for research in embodied cognition. In: Proceedings of the 8th Workshop on Performance Metrics for Intelligent Systems, pp. 50–56. ACM (2008)
12. Pairet, È., Ardón, P., Broz, F., Mistry, M., Petillot, Y.: Learning and generalisation of primitives skills towards robust dual-arm manipulation. In: Proceedings of the AAAI Fall Symposium on Reasoning and Learning in Real-World Systems for Long-Term Autonomy, pp. 62–69. AAAI Press (2018)
13. Pairet, È., Hernández, J.D., Lahijanian, M., Carreras, M.: Uncertainty-based online mapping and motion planning for marine robotics guidance. In: 2018 IEEE/RSJ International Conference on Intelligent Robots and Systems (IROS), pp. 2367–2374. IEEE (2018)
14. Park, D.H., Hoffmann, H., Pastor, P., Schaal, S.: Movement reproduction and obstacle avoidance with dynamic movement primitives and potential fields. In: 2008 8th IEEE-RAS International Conference on Humanoid Robots, Humanoids 2008, pp. 91–98. IEEE (2008)
15. Pastor, P., Hoffmann, H., Asfour, T., Schaal, S.: Learning and generalization of motor skills by learning from demonstration. In: 2009 IEEE International Conference on Robotics and Automation, ICRA 2009, pp. 763–768. IEEE (2009)
16. Pattacini, U., Nori, F., Natale, L., Metta, G., Sandini, G.: An experimental evaluation of a novel minimum-jerk cartesian controller for humanoid robots. In: 2010 IEEE/RSJ International Conference on Intelligent Robots and Systems (IROS), pp. 1668–1674. IEEE (2010)
17. Rai, A., Meier, F., Ijspeert, A., Schaal, S.: Learning coupling terms for obstacle avoidance. In: 2014 14th IEEE-RAS International Conference on Humanoid Robots (Humanoids), pp. 512–518. IEEE (2014)

18. Smith, C., et al.: Dual arm manipulation: a survey. Robot. Auton. Syst. **60**(10), 1340–1353 (2012)
19. Topp, E.A.: Knowledge for synchronized dual-arm robot programming. In: 2017 AAAI Fall Symposium Series. AAAI Press (2017)
20. Ude, A., Nemec, B., Petrić, T., Morimoto, J.: Orientation in cartesian space dynamic movement primitives. In: 2014 IEEE International Conference on Robotics and Automation (ICRA), pp. 2997–3004. IEEE (2014)
21. Zöllner, R., Asfour, T., Dillmann, R.: Programming by demonstration: dual-arm manipulation tasks for humanoid robots. In: IROS, pp. 479–484 (2004)

DE VITO: A Dual-Arm, High Degree-of-Freedom, Lightweight, Inexpensive, Passive Upper-Limb Exoskeleton for Robot Teleoperation

Fabian Falck[✉], Kawin Larppichet, and Petar Kormushev

Robot Intelligence Lab, Dyson School of Design Engineering,
Imperial College London, London, UK
{fabian.falck17,kawin.larppichet17,p.kormushev}@imperial.ac.uk
https://www.imperial.ac.uk/robot-intelligence/

Abstract. While robotics has made significant advances in perception, planning and control in recent decades, the vast majority of tasks easily completed by a human, especially acting in dynamic, unstructured environments, are far from being autonomously performed by a robot. Teleoperation, remotely controlling a slave robot by a human operator, can be a realistic, complementary transition solution that uses the motion intelligence of a human in complex tasks while exploiting the robot's autonomous reliability and precision in less challenging situations.

We introduce DE VITO, a seven degree-of-freedom, dual-arm upper-limb exoskeleton that passively measures the pose of a human arm. DE VITO is a lightweight, simplistic and energy-efficient design with a total material cost of at least an order of magnitude less than previous work. Given the estimated human pose, we implement both joint and Cartesian space kinematic control algorithms and present qualitative experimental results on various complex manipulation tasks teleoperating Robot DE NIRO, a research platform for mobile manipulation, that demonstrate the functionality of DE VITO. We provide the CAD models, open-source code and supplementary videos of DE VITO at http://www.imperial.ac.uk/robot-intelligence/robots/de_vito/.

Keywords: Upper-limb exoskeleton · Teleoperation · Remote control · Semi-autonomous control · Human-in-the-loop control · Manipulation

1 Introduction

Robots have proven to reliably outperform humans on low-variability, repetitive tasks which guarantee constraints suiting an autonomous operation. However, in spite of rapid advances in robotics in recent decades, robots cannot autonomously handle the vast majority of typical human tasks acting in unstructured, dynamic environments where plans and motions cannot be easily derived by a machine [7]. For instance, in the DARPA Robotics Challenge, robots have to complete a

---

F. Falck and K. Larppichet—Equal contribution.

© Springer Nature Switzerland AG 2019
K. Althoefer et al. (Eds.): TAROS 2019, LNAI 11649, pp. 78–89, 2019.
https://doi.org/10.1007/978-3-030-23807-0_7

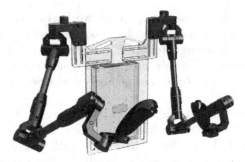

Fig. 1. CAD model of the DE VITO, an upper-limb exoskeleton consisting of two arms and the electronics body.

course in almost full autonomy and solve tasks, such as driving and egressing a vehicle, opening a door and a valve, drilling or climbing stairs [2]. In spite of the highly predefined, static environment, the competition illustrated the limitations of robots in such settings which are easily solvable by a human. To give a second example, in the context of social assistance robotics, especially manipulation tasks can have a challenging nature due to their high task complexity and variability introduced by interacting humans [6]. Both examples show that while robots are in principle equipped with super-human sensor (e.g. 3D LIDAR, 360-degree vision) and actuator (e.g. AC servo motor, hydraulic motor) hardware, their capabilities lack the cognitive capabilities of making sense of these inputs and produce flexible actions. This is why robots operating in non-predefined, complex environments had little to no impact on our everyday lives up until now. Therefore, we argue that *teleoperation*, controlling a robot remotely (i.e. at a physical distance) by a human operator, can be an approach to utilize the motion intelligence and creativity of a human for such tasks while exploiting the robot's autonomous reliability and repetitive precision in all other situations. Such a human-in-the-loop, semi-autonomous operation can be an important and realistic complementary approach to integrate robots effectively and act as a transition solution in the years ahead [11].

While various human-robot interfaces exist to control a robot, this work proposes an upper-limb exoskeleton we call *DE VITO (Design Engineering's Virtual Interface for TeleOperation)*. Figure 1 shows the rendered CAD model of DE VITO. The exoskeleton passively measures the state of a human arm (master) with its seven degrees of freedom. This in turn controls a slave robot through a kinematic mapping procedure. In designing DE VITO, we aim at and achieve the following five design goals for our system: (1) A *few-component, high degree-of-freedom (DOF), dual-arm* design, without sacrificing in measurement precision on manipulation tasks and in comparison to previous designs that have a small number of DOFs (2) *Passive* measurement with minimal impact on the human operator (3) A *lightweight and wearable* and therefore portable suite directly mounted on the operator (4) *Low-energy*, highly optimized electronic components (5) An *inexpensive* design with an estimated total material cost of at least an order of magnitude less than previous work which is crucial to make the exoskeleton design more widely accessible. Potential applications of DE VITO are, for example, as a teaching interface in imitation learning, as an interface in dual-arm coordination experiments, as a virtual reality control interface, or as a teleoperation interface in hazardous or highly complex environments (e.g. social assistance robotics).

The main contributions of this work are as follows: (1) A discussion of state-of-the-art upper-limb exoskeleton literature, examining their design characteristics (2) the mechanical and electronic design of DE VITO and a comparison of three kinematic control procedures (3) qualitative experiments that demonstrate DE VITO's functionality on Robot DE NIRO [6], a mobile manipulation research platform, in several complex manipulation tasks.

The remainder of this work is organized as follows: In Sect. 2, we discuss the related work. In Sect. 3, we derive and explain technical details of the design of DE VITO. In Sect. 4, we discuss our experiments with DE VITO on Robot DE NIRO and conclude our work in Sect. 5.

2   Related Work

In this section, we discuss prior work on controlling a robot arm system through a human-operated, teleoperation method or device during manipulation. In a review by Field et al., the authors classify motion capturing methods into four categories: (1) optical, through computer vision systems that capture the human pose either with passive or active markers or markerless (2) inertial, by measuring acceleration and rotational velocities with triaxial accelerometers and gyroscopes (3) magnetic, by measuring electromagnetic fields caused from mounted transmitters and (4) mechanical, by directly measuring the joint angles through potentiometers. In this work and while discussing related approaches during this section, we focus on a *mechanical* exoskeleton design to capture the motion of a human arm for the following reasons: First, while an optical system can provide highly accurate pose estimates, the fastest real-time, analog convolution operations have a frame rate of 166 Hz (upper-bound estimate, since frame rate would drop in multilayer architecture) [5]. This would introduce a significant latency into the control loop. Furthermore, a user would have to actively avoid visual occlusion relative to one or multiple cameras. Second, while inertia sensors can capture a large range of motion, they lack the accuracy and also the sampling frequency required for a reactive teleoperation system. Third, a mechanical design is inexpensive, lightweight and can easily provide sampling rates of about 1 kHz. In addition, a mechanical exoskeleton could feed a physical interaction with the environment back to the user, a crucial feature for controlling the robot on manipulation tasks in the real world [9].

Various reviews have discussed the current state-of-the-art of mechanical exoskeletons [8]. A first key design challenge is the shoulder joint of the exoskeleton. With regards to the kinematics of the exoskeleton, it is problematic that the human arm's centre of rotation is changing during the motion as this causes a small misalignment of the rotation axis. One way to overcome this issue is by preventing and compensating the misalignment through an internally exerted force onto the human arm [10]. The majority of designs, however, estimate the arm pose with a passive approach, as this allows a more natural, user-friendly interaction. To prevent the rotational centre from moving in passive designs, the shoulder joint (compare Sect. 3.1), consisting of a ball and socket joint, is often imitated by three connected revolute joints. However, this technically simple solution comes at the cost a potential gimbal lock, if two rotational axes are colinear or lay within the same plane. If gimbal lock applies, the exoskeleton's degree of freedom is reduced by one. Considering this additional singularity point, previous work proposed to, for example, place the shoulder joint at enough distance from the operator such that the singularity cannot be reached within the workspace of the robot [15], or introduced additional, redundant degrees of freedom to the exoskeleton [14]. For our design, we propose a passive measurement with the shoulder joint. being very close to the operator, making the design compact and wearable, while placing the singularity point in a favorable (because not important during operation) pose of the exoskeleton.

Moreover, we want to highlight three particularly promising mechanisms to measure internal rotation and briefly discuss the differences to our design, all illustrated in Fig. 2. Perry et al. propose a semi-circular bearing design which isolates each joint (no interacting joint measurements in one-dimensional rotations) allowing a precise, isolated measurement [16]. However, this design is both heavy ($\approx$10 kg in total) and expensive. In comparison, the Toyota T-HR3 Master Maneuvering System is linked by four bars and therefore requires at least four revolute joints and numerous moving parts to operate, making its design overly complicated [1]. Kim et al. propose a design with non-90-degree linkage of rotation axes, which is based on only three revolute joints (like ours). However, in any arm motion, multiple joints are involved in the measurement process, overcomplicating the procedure [12]. In comparison, our design aims at a simplistic (few moving parts), lightweight and inexpensive (one single joint with an encoder used in [1,12,16] has a cost higher than the total material cost of our work) design without sacrificing in measurement precision.

3   Design and Implementation

3.1   Human Arm Motion

The purpose of DE VITO is to estimate the pose of a human arm by measuring its joint angles. In order to understand possible motions of a master operator, we first review the simple arm model (ignoring minor misalignment due to human joint translation) in human kinesiology. The human arm consists of seven degrees of freedom, illustrated in Fig. 3: Three rotations at the glenohumeral (shoulder) joint (1–3), one rotation at the elbow joint (4), one rotation at the radioulnar joint on the forearm (5) and two rotations at the wrist joint (6–7). The Range of Motion (RoM) is defined as the maximum span of a human arm in positive and negative direction with regards to a given reference frame. It was empirically

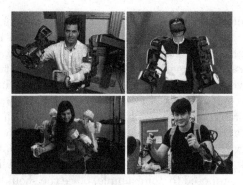

Fig. 2. Comparison of internal rotation measurement approaches. Semi-circular bearing design (top left) [16], four-bar linkage design (top right) [1], three non-90-degree linkage design (bottom left) [12], our offset linkage design (bottom right).

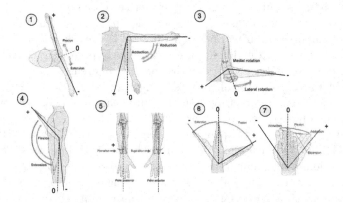

Fig. 3. Degrees of freedom of a human arm. 1–3: glenohumeral joint, 4: elbow joint, 5: radioulnar joint, 6–7: wrist joint. The thin black lines indicate the positive and negative range and the null reference. Figures adapted from [4].

studied by Boone et al. on a set of human male subjects [3] and is listed together with the covered range of motion of our exoskeleton design in Table 1.

3.2 Mechanical Design

We explain the mechanical design of DE VITO by first discussing the upper part (shoulder joint), then the lower part (wrist joint and end-effector control).

As discussed in Sect. 2, the placement of the shoulder joint in an upper-limb exoskeleton is difficult, due to the moving rotational centre in a human arm, and important, as gimbal lock can reduce the degrees of freedom of the exoskeleton. While the singularity point cannot be avoided, the exoskeleton can be designed in such a way that gimbal lock occurs either outside of the workspace of the robot (compare [15]) or at least in an operationally less important pose.

Figure 4 compares the CAD models of three design variants (A to C) for the right arm differing in the placement of the shoulder joint, also known as

Table 1. Comparison of the range of motion (RoM) between a human arm [3] and our proposed exoskeleton design. The first value of RoM represents maximum positive, the second maximum negative span in degrees with regards to the given reference frame in Fig. 3.

Anatomic part	Joint description and type	Motion description	Human arm RoM [deg.]	Exoskeleton RoM [deg.]	Coverage percentage [%]
Shoulder	Glenohumeral joint (ball and socket joint)	Flexion/extension	(158, 53)	(110, 55)	78
		Adduction/abduction	(0, 170)	(0, 110)	64
		Medial/lateral rotation	(70, 90)	(110, 110)	100
Elbow	Elbow joint (hinge joint)	Flexion/extension	(146, 0)	(110, 110)	75
Forearm	Radioulnar joint (pivot joint)	Pronation/supination	(71, 84)	(110, 110)	100
Wrist	Wrist joint (saddle joint)	Flexion/extension	(73, 71)	(110, 55)	88
		Adduction/abduction	(33, 19)	(25, 180)	100

singularity placement. All CAD models were designed using Fusion 360. In all three renderings, the camera pose is the same with gravity pointing downwards. The green arrows indicate rotational degrees of freedom. The three variants are shown in the pose of their kinematic singularity, occurring when the rotational axis along the upper-arm linkage (joint 3) is colinear with the first rotational axis at the shoulder joint (joint 1). The red arrows indicate the rotational direction of this kinematic singularity. In variant A, gimbal lock occurs when both arm linkages point forwards and are colinear with the sagittal axis and removes the rotational degree of freedom within the transverse plane, which is highly unfavourable as it lies in the most used workspace area of a robot. In variant B, gimbal lock occurs when both arm linkages point outwards being colinear with the frontal axis, prohibiting a rotational movement in the transverse plane. While this pose is infrequent during normal operation, it can be relevant to specific manipulation tasks, such as picking up an object and placing it in a box on the side of the robot. In variant C, gimbal lock occurs in the "relaxed pose" when both arm linkages point downwards, being colinear with the longitudinal axis and prohibiting rotational movement in the frontal plane. This singularity pose is by far the most favorable for two reasons: First, operation is unlikely in this pose. Second, it is outside of the workspace of most upper-body manipulation robots, such as the Baxter arms of DE NIRO which we use in the experimental section. Therefore, we chose variant C for our final design.

The lower part of the exoskeleton is illustrated in Fig. 6. It was designed in such a way that the forearm rotational axis (pronation/supination; blue dashed line) is perpendicular with the pitch and yaw axis of the controller (purple dashed lines) which allows a comfortable and ergonomic motion to rotate the end-effector. On top of the first joint, we mount a Nunchukcontroller typically used as a controller for a Nintendo Wii game console. The Nunchuk's two buttons are mapped to open and close a gripper and, in the case of an emergency, to immediately disable teleoperation (Baxter arms remain on last published coordinates) in accordance with the industrial robot ISO 10218. The small joystick, which is controllable by the thumb, is used for fine manipulation movements in the transverse plane.

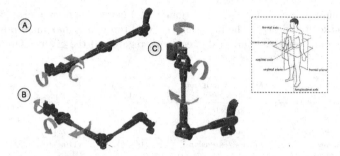

Fig. 4. CAD models of three design variants (right arm only) for the shoulder joint. The green arrows indicate rotational degrees of freedom, the red arrows indicate the rotational direction of kinematic singularity, if the rotational axis along the upper arm linkage is colinear with the last rotational axis at the shoulder joint. Variant C is chosen as our final design. Source of right-hand image: [13]. (Color figure online)

The complete mechanical design (CAD model and kinematic diagram) is illustrated in Fig. 5. As before, the green arrows indicate the seven rotational degrees of freedom of the design. Its corresponding Denavit-Hartenberg (DH) parameters are listed in Table 2. The total weight of the design is 3.2 kg (including the central electronics board), with each arm contributing 0.85 kg. This fulfills our initial goal of a lightweight, portable design that can be easily carried for prolonged amounts of time in operation mode. With regards to manufacturing DE VITO, all seven joints were 3D printed from ABS+, particularly suited for robust designs and good at avoiding warping. For manufacturing the links, we use carbon fiber fishing rod with a diameter of approximately 18 mm.

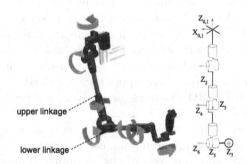

Fig. 5. CAD model of one arm of DE VITO (without central body) and its corresponding kinematic diagram. The green arrows represent the seven degrees of freedom of the arm. The brown arrows represent the seven Z and the X vectors in DH notation. Note that all other X and Y vectors follow from the right-hand rule and the initial coordinate frame. (Color figure online)

Table 2. DH table of DE VITO. a_i represents the length of the common normal of joint axes i and $(i-1)$, α_i represents the angle between two adjacent joint axes, and d_i represents the offset along Z_{i-1} to the common normal.

Index i	a_i	α_i	d_i	θ_i
1	0	0	0	θ_1
2	0	$\frac{\pi}{2}$	0	θ_2
3	0	$\frac{\pi}{2}$	0.37	θ_3
4	0	$-\frac{\pi}{2}$	0	θ_4
5	0	$\frac{\pi}{2}$	0.33	θ_5
6	0	$-\frac{\pi}{2}$	-0.07	θ_6
7	0	$\frac{\pi}{2}$	-0.07	θ_7

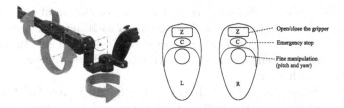

Fig. 6. CAD model of the lower part of DE VITO (left) and Nunchuk interface to control an end-effector (right). The green arrows indicate the rotational degrees of freedom. (Color figure online)

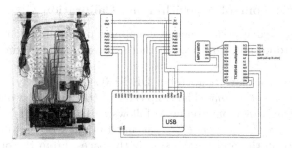

Fig. 7. Circuit board body (left), and corresponding wiring diagram (right) of DE VITO. The circuit board's main components are one Arduino mega, one I2C multiplexer, one MPU6050 breakout, and two terminal blocks.

The electronic components of the exoskeleton mainly comprises one Arduino mega, one MPU6050 breakout, one I2C multiplexer, two terminal blocks, and potentiometers described below. All components except for the potentiometers are mounted on a central circuit body covered in a plastic frame and worn on the back of the operator. A program running on the Arduino mega reads all sensor measurements and forwards them to a ROS node to compute the forward and inverse kinematics, as explained in Sect. 3.3. In order to use this very inexpensive and energy-efficient micro controller, we conducted a low-level hardware and code optimization by (1) parallelizing potentiometer measurements with an interrupt handle (2) increasing the clock speed of the Arduino mega to the maximum, yet stable value (3) adjusting the encryption and minimizing the number of bytes during serial communication from 63 to 23 bytes per reading sample. Doing so, we achieve an effective sampling rate of the serial communication of 720 Hz, a ten-times increase compared to before the optimization, which is sufficient for reactive, precise feedback for the manipulation tasks in Sect. 4.

The MPU6050 is functioning as an IMU sensor. It allows to measure the yaw of the operator (rotation around the longitudinal axis) and therefore enables, if required, the slave-robot to turn on the spot. The I2C multiplexer is required to communicate with multiple same-address devices and furthermore allows extending DE VITO with additional sensors in future work. The circuit board body together with its corresponding wiring diagram is illustrated in Fig. 7.

In order to measure the joint angles, we use seven rotary potentiometers per arm, omitting expensive encoders in the related work, with an electrical angle of rotation of 260°, being sufficient to cover the range of motion of all exoskeleton joints. Due to the limitation of the Arduino mega to 10 bits per analog signal, the resolution of the potentiometers is limited to $\frac{260 \text{ deg.}}{2^{10}} \approx 0.25°$. In our experiments, we found this sensitivity to be more than sufficient for smooth, precise teleoperation by a human.

The approximate total material cost of the design is 200 GBP, including 3D printing materials ($\approx$70 GBP), carbon tubes and mechanical parts ($\approx$60 GBP) and electronic parts ($\approx$70 GBP), making our design at least an order of magnitude less expensive than prior exoskeleton designs discussed in Sect. 2.

3.3   Kinematic Control Algorithm and Calibration

In the following, we define the kinematic mapping procedures from the exoskeleton pose to the robot pose which we further explore in the experimental section. In the following, θ_i^{master} and θ_i^{slave} refer to the i-th joint angle of the master (exoskeleton) and the slave (e.g. Robot DE NIRO), respectively.

(1) *Joint space one-to-one*: The simplest way to align the two spaces spaces is by mapping each angle one-to-one as follows: $\theta_i^{slave} = \theta_i^{master} + \theta_i^{offset}$, where θ_i^{offset} is an offset angle of joint i that accounts for the difference in the null reference in both spaces. From the operator's perspective, this control procedure is most intuitive, as, for example, a rotation of the i-th exoskeleton joint by an angle β directly results in a rotation of the i-th robot arm joint by β. However, it comes at the disadvantage that the range of motion of the master operator (human) limits the range of motion of the slave (robot), although the latter is typically larger.

(2) *Joint space scaled*: To overcome this shortcoming, we use joint-specific factors c_i that linearly scale the mapping as follows: $\theta_i^{slave} = c_i * \theta_i^{master} + \theta_i^{offset}$. By upscaling the master angles, the operator can access a larger range of motion of the slave robot. However, controlling the slave robot this way is less intuitive and is therefore subject to experiments.

(3) *Cartesian space*: In addition to the joint space control procedures, we provide a more high-level, Cartesian control approach controlling the end-effector pose of the slave robot $P_{\text{end-effector}}^{\text{slave}}$, given the pose of the exoskeleton's end-effector $P_{\text{end-effector}}^{\text{master}}$. The control procedure consists of three steps: First, we calculate the slave's end-effector pose (6 DOFs) as follows: $P_{\text{end-effector}}^{\text{slave}} = P_{\text{end-effector}}^{\text{master}} + d_{\text{offset}}$, where d_{offset} is an offset pose to guarantee operation in the slave robot's workspace. This remains one DOF undefined (nullspace), which is why we impose a constraint on the elbow joint, fixing it in a specific rotation. Figure 8 illustrates two different elbow joint constraints which can be switched between by the user depending on the exact manipulation task at hand. Third, we use Robot DE NIRO's inverse kinematics solver to compute the joint angles and actuate accordingly.

4   Experiments

In the following, we describe our qualitative experiments and results that demonstrate DE VITO's general functionality. The experiments apply the exoskeleton

Fig. 8. Comparison of two imposed elbow constraints (1 and 2) under Cartesian space control. Note that while the human pose is approximately identical (left), the robot pose differs depending on the elbow constraint (right).

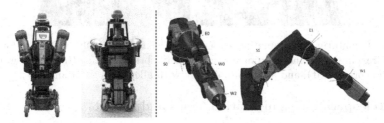

Fig. 9. Left: Robot DE NIRO [6], a research platform for mobile manipulation, used as the experimental slave robot of this work, right: Baxter arms for manipulation and their seven degrees-of-freedom at shoulder (S), elbow (E) and wrist (W). Source of figures on right-hand side: [17].

to teleoperate in complex manipulation tasks which would require – if at all explored by current literature – a computationally costly training procedure to perform them autonomously.

4.1 Experimental Platform

As the experimental platform and slave-robot for our experiments, we use Robot DE NIRO [6], a research platform for mobile manipulation, and integrated the communication of both systems via the Robot Operating System (ROS). DE NIRO is a humanoid robot with Baxter dual-arms mounted on top of a QUICKIE electric wheelchair base. The Baxter arms have seven degrees of freedom each and are mainly made of twist and bend joints. The control loop cycle frequency of the Baxter arms, including receiving an asynchronous message and execution, is 1 kHz, therefore not limiting the exoskeleton control effectively sampled at a frequency of 720 Hz [17]. For our experiments, we will not make use of DE NIRO's navigation capabilities and will only operate the robot in stationary mode. Furthermore, DE NIRO is equipped with a large amount of sensors, including a Microsoft Kinect RGB-D camera, a 360-degree camera rig, ultrasonic and infrared proximity sensors and 2D and 3D LIDARs. DE NIRO together with two functional views of its Baxter arms is illustrated in Fig. 9. In addition, we optionally use an HTC Vive as an immersive interface for the user that displays the Kinect sensor data and allows controlling DE NIRO in virtual reality.

Fig. 10. Qualitative manipulation experiments with Robot DE NIRO as the slave robot: Grasping a cup and handing it over (top left), brick stacking (top right), grasping a bottle (bottom left), and a peg-in-hole task with allen keys (bottom right).

4.2   Teleoperated Manipulation Tasks and Results

We tested the functionality of the exoskeleton qualitatively on four manipulation tasks, illustrated in Fig. 10: Grasping and handing over cups and bottles, stacking bricks and a peg-in-hole task. We drew three key insights from these experiments: First, all manipulation tasks could be completed by untrained human subjects teleoperating Robot DE NIRO, demonstrating the general functionality of DE VITO. Second, we found that the scaled control procedure described in Sect. 3.3 can be easily learned by a human and empirically fine-tuned the scaling factors c_1 to c_7 as $\{1.0, 1.2, 1.5, 1.0, 1.3, 1.5, 1.5\}$, considering the trade-off between a larger effective range of motion of the robot (what the exoskeleton actually maps to) with the effective precision of the exoskeleton (too large scaling factors cause a overly reactive procedure). Third, we found the Cartesian space control to be most intuitive and easy to use for subjects, as their visual feedback can be focussed on the end-effector pose.

5   Conclusion

In this work, we introduced DE VITO, a dual-arm, passive, wearable, and simplistic upper-limb exoskeleton to teleoperate robots in complex manipulation tasks and demonstrated its general functionality in qualitative experiments. DE VITO's design has several limitations: There is no haptic feedback on the exerted force, e.g. in the form of touch, to the user, making tasks such as grasping soft or elastic objects difficult. In addition, although the precision of the manipulation actions through DE VITO is remarkable given its inexpensive, low-energy and light-weight design, further research and experiments are required to evaluate the degree to which general manipulation tasks are solvable with the exoskeleton. We will in addition integrate DE VITO with Robot DE NIRO to experiment with a semi-autonomous, combined use case for manipulation.

References

1. Ackerman, E.: Toyota gets back into humanoid robots with new T-HR3 (2018). https://spectrum.ieee.org/automaton/robotics/humanoids/toyota-gets-back-into-humanoid-robots-with-new-thr3
2. Ackerman, E., Guizzo, E.: DARPA robotics challenge finals: rules and course (2018). https://spectrum.ieee.org/automaton/robotics/humanoids/drc-finals-course
3. Boone, D.C., Azen, S.P.: Normal range of motion of joints in male subjects. J. Bone Joint Surg. **61**(5), 756–759 (1979)
4. clinicalgate.com: Upper limb - general description (2015). https://clinicalgate.com/upper-limb-2/
5. Debrunner, T., Saeedi, S., Kelly, P.H.: AUKE: automatic kernel code generation for an analogue simd focal-plane sensor-processor array. ACM Trans. Archit. Code Optim. (TACO) **15**(4), 59 (2019)
6. Falck, F., Doshi, S., Smuts, N., Lingi, J., Rants, K., Kormushev, P.: Human-centered manipulation and navigation with Robot DE NIRO. In: 2018 IEEE/RSJ International Conference on Intelligent Robots and Systems (IROS) Workshop Towards Robots that Exhibit Manipulation Intelligence (2018)
7. Fang, B., Guo, D., Sun, F., Liu, H., Wu, Y.: A robotic hand-arm teleoperation system using human arm/hand with a novel data glove. In: 2015 IEEE International Conference on Robotics and Biomimetics (ROBIO), pp. 2483–2488. IEEE (2015)
8. Gopura, R., Kiguchi, K., Bandara, D.: A brief review on upper extremity robotic exoskeleton systems. In: 2011 6th IEEE International Conference on Industrial and Information Systems (ICIIS), pp. 346–351. IEEE (2011)
9. Hirche, S., Buss, M.: Human-oriented control for haptic teleoperation. Proc. IEEE **100**(3), 623–647 (2012)
10. Jarrasse, N., Morel, G.: Connecting a human limb to an exoskeleton. IEEE Trans. Robot. **28**(3), 697–709 (2012)
11. Kemp, C.C., Edsinger, A., Torres-Jara, E.: Challenges for robot manipulation in human environments [grand challenges of robotics]. IEEE Robot. Autom. Mag. **14**(1), 20–29 (2007)
12. Kim, B., Deshpande, A.D.: Controls for the shoulder mechanism of an upper-body exoskeleton for promoting scapulohumeral rhythm. In: 2015 IEEE International Conference on Rehabilitation Robotics (ICORR), pp. 538–542. IEEE (2015)
13. Krishnan, R.H., Devanandh, V., Brahma, A.K., Pugazhenthi, S.: Estimation of mass moment of inertia of human body, when bending forward, for the design of a self-transfer robotic facility. J. Eng. Sci. Technol. **11**(2), 166–176 (2016)
14. Lu, J., Haninger, K., Chen, W., Gowda, S., Tomizuka, M., Carmena, J.M.: Design of a passive upper limb exoskeleton for macaque monkeys. J. Dyn. Syst. Measur. Control **138**(11), 111011 (2016)
15. Nef, T., Mihelj, M., Kiefer, G., Perndl, C., Muller, R., Riener, R.: ARMin-exoskeleton for arm therapy in stroke patients. In: 2007 IEEE 10th International Conference on Rehabilitation Robotics, ICORR 2007, pp. 68–74. IEEE (2007)
16. Perry, J.C., Rosen, J., Burns, S.: Upper-limb powered exoskeleton design. IEEE/ASME Trans. Mechatron. **12**(4), 408–417 (2007)
17. Research Robotics: Baxter research robot SDK wiki - arm control overview and hardware specifications (2015). http://sdk.rethinkrobotics.com/wiki/Arm_Control_Overview, http://sdk.rethinkrobotics.com/wiki/Hardware_Specifications

A Novel Probabilistic Projection Model for Multi-camera Object Tracking

Jiaxin Lin[1,2(✉)], Chun Xiao[1], Disi Chen[2], Dalin Zhou[2], Zhaojie Ju[2], and Honghai Liu[2]

[1] School of Automation, Wuhan University of Technology,
Wuhan 430070, China
tiao_ju@163.com

[2] Intelligent Systems and Biomedical Robotics Group, School of Computing,
University of Portsmouth, Portsmouth, UK

Abstract. Correlation Filter (CF)-based algorithms have achieved remarkable performance in the field of object tracking during past decades. They have great advantages in dense sampling and reduced computational cost due to the usage of circulant matrix. However, present monocular object tracking algorithms can hardly solve fast motion which usually causes tracking failure. In this paper, a novel probabilistic projection model for multi-camera object tracking using two Kinects is proposed. Once the object is found lost using multimodal target detection, the point projection using a probabilistic projection model is processed to get a better tracking position of the targeted object. The projection model works well in the related experiments. Furthermore, when compared with other popular methods, the proposed tracking method grounded on the projection model is demonstrated to be more effective to accommodate the fast motion and achieve better tracking performance to promote robotic autonomy.

Keywords: Object tracking · Correlation filter · Multi-camera ·
Multimodal target detection · Projection

1 Introduction

Object tracking plays an important role in the field of computer vision. It can be used in video surveillance, human-robot interaction, augmented reality, etc. While a great many tracking algorithms have been proposed and improved constantly, challenges caused by background clutter, fast motion, occlusion and other factors still exist.

In recent years, a lot of research works focus on two kinds of trackers: correlation filter-based tracker and deep learning-based tracker. Correlation filters use circulant matrix to conduct dense sampling and improve computational efficiency by exploring matrix theory and kernel trick in the frequency domain [9, 10]. Correlation filter-based methods are steadily improved from aspects of color information [4], back-ground information [11], unwanted boundary effects [5] and scale variation [3, 6]. Deep

Supported by grant of the EU Seventh Framework Programme (Grant No. 611391), National Natural Science Foundation of China (Grant no. 51575412, 51575338 and 5157540).

K. Althoefer et al. (Eds.): TAROS 2019, LNAI 11649, pp. 90–100, 2019.
https://doi.org/10.1007/978-3-030-23807-0_8

learning-based trackers, such as Modeling and Propagating CNNs in a Tree Structure for Visual Tracking (TCNN) [12] and Multi-Domain Convolutional Neural Networks (MDNET) [17], succeed in getting high-level semantic information while the heavy computational load constrains their development.

Even though many nontrivial works have been done, there are still certain flaws. Almost all present trackers are based on monocular camera systems and recognized as single camera tracking (SCT). This indicates that we can get the information about the object from only one perspective. Once the object moves faster than the tracker can accommodate, total tracking loss may occur. In order to alleviate or further solve the problem, this paper proposes a novel probabilistic projection model for multi-camera object tracking based on two Kinects. The fast discriminative scale space tracking (fDSST) algorithm is conducted separately in two simultaneous videos. After each train-detection cycle, we use multimodal target detection to estimate whether the object is lost or not. If loss happens, the probabilistic point projection derived from the information of the other Kinect is adopted to choose a better tracking position.

The structure of this paper is as followed. Section 2 demonstrates the related work including a brief description of CF-based trackers, inter-camera tracking (ICT) and probabilistic models used in robotic area. Section 3 gives the formulation about fDSST algorithm. Section 4 gives probabilistic projection model for two Kinects. Section 5 proposes the framework of multi-camera tracking. Experiments are described in Sect. 6 followed by a conclusion in Sect. 7.

2 Related Work

Object tracking algorithms using correlation filter can be traced back to the article [1] published in 2010 by Bolme et al. The basic idea is that the similarity of two functions can be revealed by their cross-correlation. The filter is called Minimum Output Sum of Squared Error (MOSSE) filter and its tracking speed reaches 669 frames per second (fps). It is well known that better tracking performance requires more samples. But computation of extensive samples will reduce efficiency. This problem is solved in the literature [10], where Henriques et al. speed up the computing by using the matrix property of circulant matrix in the frequency domain. In case of dense sampling, it still retains a speed of more than 300 fps. Then Dual Correlation Filter (DCF) which expands the one-dimensional grayscale feature into multi-channel features and further advances the tracking results is proposed in [9]. Danelljan introduces color features [4] into correlation filter on this basis. The color information is divided into 11 directions, so that the image information input of this algorithm is richer than the previous grayscale features and histogram of oriented gradients (HOG) features. The Spatially Regularized Discriminative Correlation Filters (SRDCF) algorithm is an extension of DCF. The DCF suffers the boundary problem caused by cyclic samples. Accordingly, the regularization term (originally is a constant multiplied by the filter) is improved in [5] and replaced by a position-dependent function multiplied by the filter. The Continuous Convolution Operator Tracker (C-COT) [6] uses the correlation filter and adopts an implicit interpolation model to pose the learning problem in the continuous spatial relation and thus obtains a continuous response function to achieve sub-pixel localization. Although C-COT won the championship in VOT2016, its performance is far from complying with real-time constraint. Therefore, in 2017, the Efficient Convolution Operators (ECO) [3] for tracking as an accelerated version of C-COT is published. It improves C-COT from three main aspects: the dimension of the original feature channel is reduced; the generation model is improved; the update mechanism is advanced.

Presently, multi-camera tracking applications mainly concentrate on pedestrian detection, traffic monitoring, smart rooms, etc. [2, 8]. In these applications, multiple targets are often tracked at the same time, and the perspectives do not or partially overlap between cameras in order to obtain a larger field of view.

The problem of coordinate conversion between two-dimensional point in camera pixel coordinate system and three-dimensional point rises. It is mentioned in the literature [13] that the traditional stereo dual-camera system requires the distance between two cameras within a certain range. Only in this way can the two simultaneously obtained images of the same scene have enough matching points that the depth information can be solved correctly and accurately. The second Kinect in this article is chosen to shoot at another angle in order to obtain more information. So, it is impossible to reconstruct the same scenario by simply using traditional binocular vision method. The problem of obtaining three-dimensional coordinates from two-dimensional images is considered in robotic grasping with a probabilistic model in [14]. In [14], two images of the same object are captured from different positions by the same camera to obtain the three-dimensional coordinates of grab point. The published error is within 4 cm. In this paper, considering that Kinect can get depth information, the probabilistic model is used to obtain the three-dimensional coordinates of the target point.

3   A Brief Description of FDSST

The target sample x consists of a d-dimensional feature vector $x(n) \in R^d$, at each location n in a rectangular domain. We denote the feature channel $l \in \{1, \ldots, d\}$ of x by x^l. The objective is to construct a correlation filter h consisting of one filter h^l per feature channel. This is achieved by minimizing the L^2 error of the correlation response compared to the desired correlation output g,

$$\epsilon = \left\| g - \sum_{l=1}^{d} h^l \odot x^l \right\|^2 + \lambda \|h^l\|^2. \tag{1}$$

Here, $\odot$ denotes circular correlation. The second term in (1) is a regularization with a weight parameter λ.

The filter that minimizes (1) is given by

$$H^l = \frac{\bar{G}X^l}{\sum_{k=1}^{d} \bar{X}^k X^k + \lambda}, l = 1, \ldots, d. \tag{2}$$

Here, the capital letters denote the discrete Fourier transform (DFT) of the corresponding quantities. The bar denotes complex conjugation.

The numerator A_t^l and denominator B_t^l of the filter H_t^l with a new sample x_t are defined as follows

$$A_t^l = (1 - \eta)A_{t-1}^l + \eta \bar{G} X_t^l, l = 1, \ldots, d \tag{3a}$$

$$B_t^l = (1 - \eta)B_{t-1}^l + \eta \sum_{k=1}^{d} \bar{X}_k^t X_k^t \tag{3b}$$

Here, the scalar η is a learning rate parameter. The DFT of the correlation scores y_t is computed in the frequency domain

$$Y_t = \frac{\sum_{l=1}^{d} \bar{A}_{t-1}^l Z_t^l}{B_{t-1} + \lambda}. \tag{4}$$

The test sample z_t is extracted using the same feature representation of training samples. The estimate of the current target state is obtained by finding the maximum correlation score.

Based on multi-channel discriminative correlation filters given above, fDSST learns separate discriminative correlation filters for translation and scale estimation and reduces the feature dimension using Principal Components Analysis (PCA).

4 Probabilistic Projection Model Between Two *Kinects*

4.1 Projection Theory and Coordinate System Conversion

An ideal imaging model for a camera is normally linear for both simplicity and efficiency. The principle of linear imaging is depicted in Fig. 1.

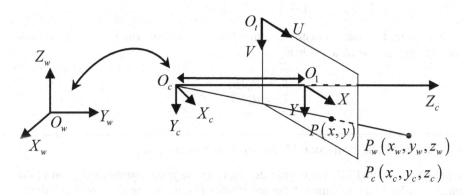

Fig. 1. Linear model of a camera

The target point $P_w(P_c)$, the point P on the image plane and the optical center of the camera O_c are collinear. An imaginary world coordinate system $O_w - X_w Y_w Z_w$ is used to describe the position information of objects in space. $O_c - X_c Y_c Z_c$ denotes the camera coordinate system. The optical center of the camera O_c is defined as the origin of the coordinate system. The distance from the optical center to the image plane is f, the focal length of the camera. The pixel coordinate system is expressed as $O_t - UV$. The upper left corner of the image is the origin and the basic unit of this coordinate system is pixel. Each image pixel is actually a small rectangle and its physical size is recorded as dx, dy. $O_1 - XY$ is the physical coordinate system which takes the center point of the image as the origin and millimeter as the basic unit. The coordinates of O_1 in the $O_t - UV$ coordinate system is (u_0, v_0). It is assumed that the coordinates of any spatial point in the world coordinate system and camera coordinate system can be respectively expressed as (x_w, y_w, z_w) and (x_c, y_c, z_c). The conversion between the coordinates of the same spatial point in the world coordinate system and the pixel coordinate system of the image can be derived [18]:

$$
z_c \begin{bmatrix} u \\ v \\ 1 \end{bmatrix} = \begin{bmatrix} f/dx & 0 & u_0 & 0 \\ 0 & f/dy & v_0 & 0 \\ 0 & 0 & 1 & 0 \end{bmatrix} \begin{bmatrix} x_c \\ y_c \\ z_c \\ 1 \end{bmatrix}
$$

$$
= \begin{bmatrix} f/dx & 0 & u_0 & 0 \\ 0 & f/dy & v_0 & 0 \\ 0 & 0 & 1 & 0 \end{bmatrix} \begin{bmatrix} R & T \\ 0^T & 1 \end{bmatrix} \begin{bmatrix} x_w \\ y_w \\ z_w \\ 1 \end{bmatrix}
\tag{5}
$$

For camera0, R_0, T_0 respectively represent the rotation matrix and translation vector of the camera coordinate system relative to the space coordinate system. And for camera1, R_1, T_1 represent the same parameters. Hence, we can get:

$$
\begin{bmatrix} x_{c1} \\ y_{c1} \\ z_{c1} \end{bmatrix} = R_0 \begin{bmatrix} x_w \\ y_w \\ z_w \end{bmatrix} + T_0 \qquad \begin{bmatrix} x_{c2} \\ y_{c2} \\ z_{c2} \end{bmatrix} = R_1 \begin{bmatrix} x_w \\ y_w \\ z_w \end{bmatrix} + T_1
\tag{6}
$$

Therefore, the rotation matrix and translation vector between two camera coordinate systems can be obtained by:

$$
R_c = R_0^{-1} R_1
$$
$$
T_c = R_0^{-1}(T_0 - T_1)
\tag{7}
$$

4.2   Probabilistic Projection Model for Two *Kinect* System

From Sects. 4.1 and 4.2, the coordinates (u, v) in the pixel coordinate system of the image can be easily obtained if the coordinates (x_w, y_w, z_w) in the world coordinate system of the correspondent spatial point are known. Since two *Kinects* are used as image sensors in this paper, RGB images and depth information can be attained at the same time which enables us to get the 3-D coordinates of certain point in the 2-D image. In this way, the coordinates of this 3-D point can be projected to the coordinates in the pixel coordinate system of any other calibrated camera.

Here, the problem is how to get proper and accurate information of the coordinates in the world coordinate system. Since the rectification between RGB and depth images from a *Kinect* usually leads to some non-numeric points in the rectified depth images, we apply a novel probabilistic model for the depth offered by depth image.

It is assumed that, even though error exists in the rectified RGB and depth images, the coordinates of depth value closer to the chosen RGB point (u, v) are more likely to be the true depth value of the point. Then the two-dimensional Gaussian distribution is used to represent the possibility of the depth value at certain positions to be the true depth value, which can be written in:

$$
\begin{aligned}
P(z(\hat{u}, \hat{v}) = 1|D) &= \left(2\pi\sigma_1\sigma_2\sqrt{1 - \rho^2}\right)^{-1} \\
&\exp\left[-\frac{1}{2(1 - \rho^2)}\left(\frac{(\hat{u} - u)^2}{\sigma_1^2} - \frac{2\rho(\hat{u} - u)(\hat{v} - v)}{\sigma_1\sigma_2} + \frac{(\hat{v} - v)^2}{\sigma_2^2}\right)\right],
\end{aligned}
\tag{8}
$$

where D denotes the depth image, $D(u, v)$ denotes the depth value directly get from the coordinates (u, v) in the depth image D, $\hat{u}, \hat{v}$ are random variables obeying two-dimensional normal distribution and can be expressed as:

$$
\hat{u}, \hat{v} \sim N\left(u, v, \sigma_1^2, \sigma_2^2, \rho\right).
\tag{9}
$$

$z(\hat{u}, \hat{v}) = 1$ denotes that $D(\hat{u}, \hat{v})$ is the true depth value of the point (u, v) in RGB image, and $z(\hat{u}, \hat{v}) = 0$ otherwise. Then the expectation of the true depth value of the point (u, v) in RGB image can be calculated in:

$$
E(D(u, v)) = \sum_{\hat{u}, \hat{v}} D(\hat{u}, \hat{v}) P(z(\hat{u}, \hat{v}) = 1|D).
\tag{10}
$$

Noted that, for certain coordinates $(\hat{u}, \hat{v})$, if the value $D(\hat{u}, \hat{v})$ equals 0 (out of *Kinect* detection range) or is non-numeric, we specially define

$$
P(z(\hat{u}, \hat{v}) = 1|D) = 0.
\tag{11}
$$

And this will result in

$$
\sum_{\hat{u}, \hat{v}} P(z(\hat{u}, \hat{v}) = 1|D) < 1
\tag{12}
$$

and the calculated depth will be smaller than the actual value.

We remedy this problem by changing the expectation equation like

$$E(D(u, v)) = \left(\sum_{\hat{u},\hat{v}} D(\hat{u}, \hat{v}) P(z(\hat{u}, \hat{v}) = 1|D) \right) \Big/ \sum_{\hat{u},\hat{v}} P(z(\hat{u}, \hat{v}) = 1|D) \qquad (13)$$

5   Multi-camera Object Tracking Framework

Our multi-camera object tracking method runs fDSST separately on each *Kinect*. The difference between traditional tracker and ours is that the multimodal target detection [15] is introduced as the criterion for judging whether the target is lost or not and when the projection process is needed. For example, when the camera0 finds that the ratios between multiple peaks to the highest peak of the correlation scores $y_{t,trans}$ are greater than a predefined threshold θ, the loss of the targeted object is inferred. Then, the coordinates $proj_t$ projected from the other camera (camera1) to the pixel coordinate system of camera0 is calculated. The algorithm will re-detect the response $yproj_{t,trans}$ at that point, compare its maximum with that of $y_{t,trans}$ and choose the higher one for the translation vector calculation. The original fDSST algorithm is followed subsequently to estimate the scale and update translation filter model and scale filter model.

6   Experimental Results

6.1   Experiments for Projection

Based on the theories in Sect. 4, MATLAB stereo calibration app is used to get inner parameters and inter parameters between two *Kinects*. To ensure the effectiveness and robustness of our projection method, experiment is conducted on 10 pairs of random matching points. Firstly, the actual coordinates of each pair of points are labelled manually. Then, the Euclidean distance between the actual coordinates and the calculated coordinates is used as error criterion. The results are compared with that of traditional projection methods. All specific data is shown in Table 1 and is in pixels.

From the table above, there are two non-numeric results represented by *NaN* after using traditional projection method. This is directly due to the non-numeric depth value at the point in Camera0. As for our probabilistic projection method, the problem of invalid depth value caused by rectification of *Kinect* is completely avoided. The projection result for every point is achieved successfully. In order to compare results quantitatively, the root mean square (RMS) of error, excluding the invalid results, of traditional projection method is 9.99 pixels while the correspondent one of our probabilistic method is 9.57 pixels. This proves that our method has a slight improvement in accuracy and is much more robust compared to the traditional projection method.

Since the distance between projection results and true positions of our method maintains within 15 pixels, it can certainly meet the tracking requirement according to the common size of target which is bigger than 40 * 40 pixels. With such acceptable error range, the projection result will be within the target window.

Table 1. Projection results of traditional method and ours

Coordinates get manually		Traditional projection results	Distance (error)	Probabilistic projection results	Distance(error) of our method
Camera0	Camera1				
(136, 246)	(385, 377)	NaN	NaN	(136, 241)	4.53
(147, 225)	(409, 418)	(139, 218)	9.92	(136, 218)	12.35
(144, 221)	(407, 428)	(130, 213)	15.69	(131, 213)	14.84
(142, 211)	(407, 438)	(126, 209)	15.57	(153, 206)	12.35
(405, 304)	(130, 295)	(400, 308)	6.36	(400, 307)	5.70
(121, 251)	(385, 379)	(122, 141)	10.11	(123, 241)	10.31
(188, 271)	(517, 345)	NaN	NaN	(184, 258)	12.98
(448, 238)	(191, 356)	(443, 241)	6.10	(443, 241)	6.10
(402, 305)	(133, 294)	(402, 307)	2.55	(402, 307)	2.55
(304, 416)	(115, 220)	(299, 416)	5.02	(299, 416)	5.02
RMS of distance (excluding data contains NaN)			9.99		9.57
RMS of distance (all data)			NaN		9.60

6.2 Benchmark Building and Evaluation

To validate the effectiveness of our proposed tracking method, a dataset including 4 pairs of video sequences is built by two *Kinect*s sensors. Each pair of sequence has two RGB videos and two sets of depth information. All target positions at each frame in RGB images are annotated using rectangles. The manual annotations are treated as the ground-truth to evaluate the methods performance. Each of the recorded video sequences faces several challenges such as occlusion, out-of-plane rotation, in-plane rotation, out-of-view, background clutter, deformation and scale variation. Some of the frames are illustrated in Fig. 2.

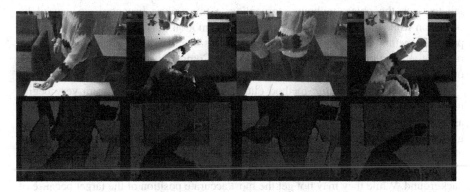

Fig. 2. Demonstration of video sequences in our datasets

The data were captured by two *Kinect* v1.0 cameras. The resolution of output RGB image is 480 * 640 pixels and the depth information is rectified to the same size as the RGB image. The frame rate is 25 fps.

All tracking parameters are set the same as in [7]. As for multimodal target detection, the parameter is set as [15].

Since this is a real-time tracking system, the comparison confined within the results of several algorithms with high speed like CN [4], KCF [9], CA-SAMF [11], CA -DCF [11] and fDSST [7].

Two tracking evaluation metrics, success rate and precision rate proposed in [16] are employed with one-pass evaluation (OPE). The success rate measures the intersection over union (IoU) between the ground-truth and tracking results. Area Under the Curve (AUC) of success plots is used to rank the trackers. The precision rate is defined as the distance error between the estimated target center and the ground-truth. Trackers are ranked in terms of the distance error at a threshold of 20 pixels.

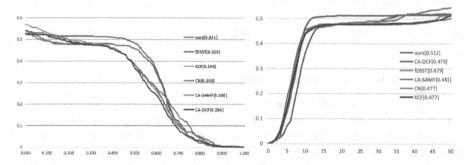

Fig. 3. The success rate plot and the precision plot

6.3   Empirical Results

Because of the challenging characteristics of our locally captured videos, all trackers fail to track the object without intervention. Some failure instances are caused by occlusion while others are mostly affected by fast motion. It is promising to see that the proposed method can alleviate these problems to some extent, reflected by the success rate plot and the precision plot shown in Fig. 3. Compared with all the other trackers, our tracker ranks the first place in both evaluation plots.

As for precision plot, our method outperforms other algorithms from very beginning. Among all algorithms for comparison, KCF is proposed earliest and is often used as a baseline. CN tracker puts the color information into consideration. When all trackers can catch up with the object, this tracker can easily figure out background and choose a better center of the target window. The CA-SAMF and CA-DCF use the context information as negative samples to cope with the challenge of cluttered background. While they may not get the most accurate position of the target because of the negative effect of certain context, they can get better tracking performance than KCF tracker overall. Our method is based on the fDSST algorithm. The fDSST is also a correlation filter tracker that especially joints a scale correlation filter with a translation filter. When the scale of the object changes, our method can change the window size for better adaptation under the incorporated background information. As a result, our method achieves better performance than the rest.

In the plot of success rate, our method outperforms significantly at the overlap rate of 0.5. This means that our method catches up with the object in more frames than other algorithms. This result also owes to the advantages of fDSST algorithms, since the scale space filter can improve the overlap effectively. And it is intuitive that the projection strategy assists in catching up with a fast moving object.

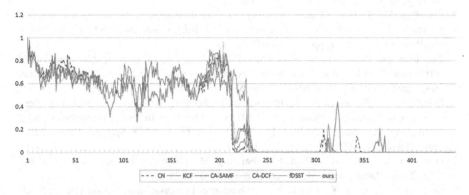

Fig. 4. Overlap curve of the sequence 'toy car' from camera0

In Fig. 4, the overlap curve of the sequence 'toy car' from camera0 is demonstrated. Near the 203rd frame, there is an obvious drop of overlap for all other algorithms, while an overlap of about 0.5 remains for the following 40 frames by using our method. The video is finally checked manually and we find that there is a frame where the object moves so fast and changes its appearance so rapidly at the same time, that none algorithm succeeds to catch up with it. The projected coordinates used in our method successfully update the model after the multimodal target detection works and finish the tracking task.

7   Conclusion and Discussion

In this paper, a novel probabilistic projection model for multi-camera object tracking based on two *Kinect*s is proposed. The multimodal target detection is combined with the multi-camera object tracking method and further fuses information from two *Kinect*s by projecting points between them. The probabilistic projection model achieves satisfactory experimental results with robustness and it can be further used in robotic vision and control to promote autonomy of robots or robotic systems. Experimental results also demonstrate that our method outperforms other algorithms and helps alleviate the problem of tracking during fast motion. However, there is still improvement to be done such as fusing the information from two *Kinect*s to predict out-of-view in the future work.

References

1. Bolme, D.S., Beveridge, J.R., Draper, B.A., Lui, Y.M.: Visual object tracking using adaptive correlation filters. In: 2010 IEEE Conference on Computer Vision and Pattern Recognition (CVPR), pp. 2544–2550. IEEE, June 2010
2. Chen, W., Cao, L., Chen, X., Huang, K.: A novel solution for multi-camera object tracking. In: 2014 IEEE International Conference on Image Processing (ICIP), pp. 2329–2333. IEEE, October 2014
3. Danelljan, M., Bhat, G., Khan, F.S., Felsberg, M.: ECO: efficient convolution operators for tracking. In: CVPR, vol. 1, no. 2, p. 7, July 2017
4. Danelljan, M., Shahbaz Khan, F., Felsberg, M., Van de Weijer, J.: Adaptive color attributes for real-time visual tracking. In: Proceedings of the IEEE Conference on Computer Vision and Pattern Recognition, pp. 1090–1097 (2014)
5. Danelljan, M., Hager, G., Shahbaz Khan, F., Felsberg, M.: Learning spatially regularized correlation filters for visual tracking. In: Proceedings of the IEEE International Conference on Computer Vision, pp. 4310–4318 (2015)
6. Danelljan, M., Robinson, A., Shahbaz Khan, F., Felsberg, M.: Beyond correlation filters: learning continuous convolution operators for visual tracking. In: Leibe, B., Matas, J., Sebe, N., Welling, M. (eds.) ECCV 2016. LNCS, vol. 9909, pp. 472–488. Springer, Cham (2016). https://doi.org/10.1007/978-3-319-46454-1_29
7. Danelljan, M., Häger, G., Khan, F.S., Felsberg, M.: Discriminative scale space tracking. IEEE Trans. Pattern Anal. Mach. Intell. 39(8), 1561–1575 (2017)
8. Dongyuan, G., Xifan, Y., Kainan, L.: Calibration of binocular stereo vision system. Mech. Des. Manufact. 6(6), 1–2 (2010)
9. Henriques, J.F., Caseiro, R., Martins, P., Batista, J.: High-speed tracking with kernelized correlation filters. IEEE Trans. Pattern Anal. Mach. Intell. 37(3), 583–596 (2015)
10. Henriques, J.F., Caseiro, R., Martins, P., Batista, J.: Exploiting the circulant structure of tracking-by-detection with kernels. In: Fitzgibbon, A., Lazebnik, S., Perona, P., Sato, Y., Schmid, C. (eds.) ECCV 2016. LNCS, vol. 7575, pp. 702–715. Springer, Heidelberg (2012). https://doi.org/10.1007/978-3-642-33765-9_50
11. Mueller, M., Smith, N., Ghanem, B.: Context-aware correlation filter tracking. In: Proceedings of the IEEE Conference on Computer Vision and Pattern Recognition (CVPR), vol. 2, no. 3, p. 6, July 2017
12. Nam, H., Baek, M., Han, B.: Modeling and propagating CNNs in a tree structure for visual tracking. arXiv preprint arXiv:1608.07242 (2016)
13. Saxena, A.: Monocular depth perception and robotic grasping of novel objects. Stanford university, Dept of Computer Science, CA (2009)
14. Saxena, A., Driemeyer, J., Ng, A.Y.: Robotic grasping of novel objects using vision. Int. J. Robot. Res. 27(2), 157–173 (2008)
15. Wang, M., Liu, Y., Huang, Z.: Large margin object tracking with circulant feature maps. In: Proceedings of the IEEE Conference on Computer Vision and Pattern Recognition, Honolulu, HI, USA, pp. 21–26, July 2017
16. Wu, Y., Lim, J., Yang, M.H.: Object tracking benchmark. IEEE Trans. Pattern Anal. Mach. Intell. 37(9), 1834–1848 (2015)
17. Zhang, Z., Xie, Y., Xing, F., McGough, M., Yang, L.: MDNet: a semantically and visually interpretable medical image diagnosis network. In: Proceedings of the IEEE Conference on Computer Vision and Pattern Recognition, pp. 6428–6436 (2017)
18. Zhang, Z.: A flexible new technique for camera calibration. IEEE Trans. Pattern Anal. Mach. Intell. 22(11), 1330–1334 (2000)

Soft Robotics, Sensing and Mobile Robots

Soft Fiber-Reinforced Pneumatic Actuator Design and Fabrication: Towards Robust, Soft Robotic Systems

Jan Fras$^{(\boxtimes)}$ and Kaspar Althoefer

Centre for Advanced Robotics @ Queen Mary (ARQ),
Faculty of Science and Engineering, Queen Mary University of London, London, UK
j.fras@qmul.ac.uk

Abstract. Soft robotics is a rapidly evolving, young research area. So far there are no well-established design standards nor fabrication procedures for soft robots. A number of research groups are working on soft robotics solutions independently and we can observe a range of designs realized in different ways. These soft robots are based on various actuation principles, are driven with various actuation media, and offer various actuation properties. Still, most of them require lots of manual effort and high manual fabrication skills from the person manufacturing these kinds of robots. A significant share of the proposed designs suffers from some imperfections that could be improved by simple design changes. In this work, we propose a number of design and fabrication rules for improving the performance and fabrication complexity of soft fiber-reinforced pneumatic actuators. The proposed design approach focuses on a circular geometry for the pressure chambers and applying a dense, fiber-based reinforcement. Such an approach allows for a more linear actuator response and reduced wear of the actuators, when compared to previous approaches. The proposed manufacturing procedure introduces the application of the reinforcement before the fabrication of the actuator body, significantly reducing the required fabrication effort and providing more consistent and more reliable results.

Keywords: Soft robotics · Soft pneumatic actuation · Soft actuation ·
Soft robotics manufacturing · Compliant robotics

1 Introduction

Soft robotics is a young and very promising research area. Soft robots are compliant, they can passively adapt to the environment and safely interact with fragile objects. In many cases, they also consist of fewer parts than traditional, rigid

This work was supported in part by the EPSRC in the framework of the NCNR (National Centre for Nuclear Robotics) project (EP/R02572X/1) and the Innovate UK funded and q-bot led project WormBot.

© Springer Nature Switzerland AG 2019
K. Althoefer et al. (Eds.): TAROS 2019, LNAI 11649, pp. 103–114, 2019.
https://doi.org/10.1007/978-3-030-23807-0_9

equivalents and provide very good power-to-weight and force-to-weight ratio [1]. They also promise an opportunity to simplify the control strateges when compared to traditional robots [2]. For those reasons they are considered to be suitable for many applications such as medical applications (minimal invasive surgery [3], laparoscopy [4], rehabilitation [5]) a human-robot cooperation [6,7], grasping [8] or prosthetics [9,10]. There are plenty of actuators that offer various actuation principles and motion types. They are fabricated using various materials and techniques. The design space of soft actuators is very broad and thus still not fully explored. Despite such a big interest in soft robotics, many pneumatic system designs are suboptimal and fabricated in an inefficient way.

In fact, design and manufacturing are big issues in soft robotics [11]. Due to the short history, there are no well-defined standards for soft robot designs yet. There are various designs of soft actuators and various manufacturing procedures [11]. Most techniques require a lot of manual operations and high manual skills from the person manufacturing such robots. The most commonly used technique is molding and usually consists of many molding steps to manufacture the device. In case any reinforcement is required, it is usually achieved requiring additional manual manufacturing steps.

Researchers explore additive techniques extensively as they would to minimize required labor and improve repeatability, reliability, and prototyping speed [12,13]. However, those techniques are still very limited regarding the material selection (in particular when different materials within the process are required) and struggle with the fabrication of airtight internal voids.

In this paper, we propose some general rules to be considered when designing new soft-robotics systems in order to make them more reliable, their actuation response more linear and fabrication more convenient. For the purpose of this paper, we will focus only on soft fiber-reinforced actuators driven with positive pneumatic pressure.

The paper is organized as follows: In Sect. 2 we discuss the general design rules that apply to fiber-based reinforcement Sect. 2.1 and the actuator geometry Sect. 2.2. In Sect. 3 we discuss the manufacturing of the proposed actuators with the focus on the reinforcement and the actuator body. In Sect. 4 we conclude the paper.

2   The Soft Actuator Design

There are various actuation types and each of them can be implemented by different actuator designs. The most basic actuation types are linear actuation (expansion, contraction), bending and twisting. The linear actuator design can be considered trivial since any airtight tube made of flexible material can be considered as a linear actuator. Adding a braided sheath converts it to a contracting McKibben pneumatic muscle [14]. Adding a fiber reinforcement perpendicular to its main axis makes it a linearly expanding actuator. Further addition of strain limiting layers or fibers at certain angles can convert it to a bending or twisting actuator. Bending and twisting motion can be also induced by the geometry of the actuator such as unsymmetrical actuation chambers or a curved, toroidal shape.

2.1   Reinforcement

In the case of positive-pressure-driven soft actuators, their deformation is caused by the internal pressure applied to a pressure chamber. The pressure acting on the internal chamber surfaces induces forces that stretch the device. Since a pressure inside a closed volume in a passive state can be considered to be constant, those forces are distributed equally in the whole actuation chamber volume. For that reason, the actuator tends to deform not only in the desired direction but in all the other directions as well. In many applications, such deformations are very undesired. Thus, pneumatic actuators often contain some reinforcement, some structures that are designed to amplify the desired motion and to limit any other deformation of the device. Those structures can be made of the same material the actuator is made of (e.g., bellows or groves) or different material (such as fibers, fabrics and tendons). In all those cases, the reinforcement limits the deformation in some direction while allowing it in the direction of actuation. In our work, we focus on fiber-based reinforcement which has a number of advantages. First of all, the fibers can have a very small diameter, so that they can be embedded into the device without greatly affecting its dimensions or geometry. They can also be very resilient allowing high pressure to be applied into the device and consequently to exert high external forces. Ideally flexible fibers cannot resist any forces in the radial direction but they do restrict elongation. Thanks to that, they do not affect the overall stiffness of the device, but only the stretch along the direction they are oriented. Fiber-based reinforcement can be described by various features such as the material used for it, its geometry in the chamber cross-section and its density along the primary axis (how close are the fibers each other). The material of the fiber does not affect the mechanics of the actuator that much, since we consider it to be ideally flexible, so let's discuss the other two features.

The Reinforcement Density. The fibers embedded into the silicone constrain the silicone deformation in the direction along the fiber. Since the silicone is flexible and stretchable, this effect is the strongest in the close neighborhood of the fiber and gets lower when moving away from the fiber. Consider a cylindrical actuator reinforced with circles made of a thread as depicted in Fig. 1.

Distances between the reinforcement rings grow when the actuator is pressurized. In case the initial reinforcement density is sparse (Fig. 1a) it will get even sparser during the actuation allowing the pressure to expand the chamber in between the reinforcement (ballooning). Making the reinforcement denser improves the situation, as smaller gaps between threads restrict the ballooning better. Ballooning is a problem, as this kind of inflation induces a nonlinear behavior in the actuator, leads to more intensive wear of the flexible material in the areas it expands more (balloons) and results in lower pressure resistance of the device.

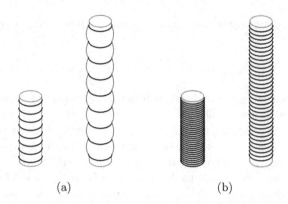

(a)   (b)

Fig. 1. Comparison of sparse and dense reinforcement applied to a linear actuator. Sparse reinforced actuator (a) expands between the reinforcing rings, while dense reinforced (b) does not.

Such a principle applies to all the expanding actuators including linear and rotational ones, see Fig. 2.

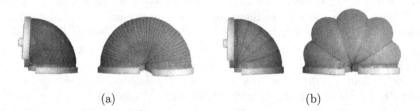

(a)   (b)

Fig. 2. Different angular densities of reinforcing fibers. Ballooning visible for the spare reinforcement. (a) dense reinforced actuator in passive state and actuated, (b) sparse reinforced actuator passive and actuated

On the other hand, the ballooning causes the actuation area to grow in parallel with the pressure and consequently to amplify the actuation response of the actuator. One can argue that this way we can eventually get an actuator that can generate higher forces and extend and bend more at the same input pressure. However, ballooning means the actuator expands its radial dimensions during the actuation. Thus, if the higher forces are required, a larger actuator can be used so that the higher force will be exerted while keeping the benefits of the dense reinforcement (linearity, reliability, durability).

An example of how the reinforcement density affects the actuation process is presented in Fig. 3.

The Reinforcement Pitch. Most commonly, the reinforcement of fiber-reinforced actuators is made with a single thread. This means that there are

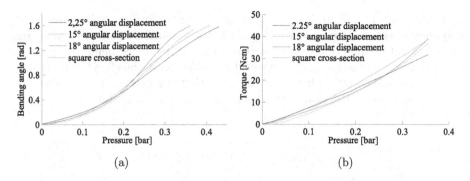

Fig. 3. The characteristics of a bending actuator for different reinforcement densities. (a) bending angle vs pressure, (b) generated torque vs pressure [15].

no individual rings, but subsequent periods of a helix made with a single thread. Thus the actual overall shape of the reinforcement is helical and the thread is not perpendicular to the actuator axis, but declined by some angle α, Fig. 4. It is important to note that value of angle α is not constant and changes while the actuator elongates.

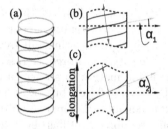

Fig. 4. The reinforcement in most fiber-reinforced actuators has a helical geometry. (a) The more spare the reinforcement is, the bigger value of the pitch angle (α). (b) The pitch angle determines the actuator behaviour. The deformation is constrained only in the direction of the fiber (red axis) and not affected in the perpendicular direction (blue axis). (c) The elongation causes the pitch angle to increase, so the effect increases as well. (Color figure online)

As already mentioned, the fibers can constrain only expansion in the direction parallel to them. Since they are angled, the tension they generate is not perpendicular to the actuation axis. In such a case, they not only constrain the radial expansion but also cause the actuator to twist, see Fig. 5. Consider an imaginary cut line along the actuator's pressure chamber. If the chamber is cut along this line and resulting membrane is put flat on a surface, it contains a set of straight sections of fibers parallel to each other. All of them are angled resulting from the helical shape of the reinforcement. Since only the expansion in the direction parallel to fibers is constrained, if a uniform stretching net force is applied to the membrane it would deform in a way it is no longer rectangular. The deformation direction will be perpendicular to the fibers, depicted as green arrow in Fig. 5. If the membrane is rolled again to create the chamber back and stitched along the cutting line, we will notice that the cutting line is no longer straight, and beside the elongation the actuator has twisted a bit.

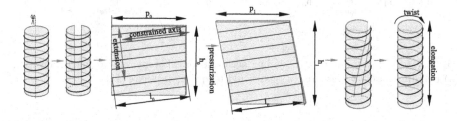

Fig. 5. Explanation for twisting motion resulting from angled fibers.

The relation of the elongation and twist of the device could be described by $sin(\alpha)$ and $cos(\alpha)$ functions of α angle. While the elongation of the actuator along its primary actuation axis is proportional to $cos(\alpha)$ function, its twist is proportional to $\frac{sin(\alpha)}{r}$, where r is radious of the actuator's chamber. It is important to notice that single helical reinforcement will never provide pure extension since α can not be zero. Some twisting will always appear. However, by increasing the reinforcement density we can reduce α so that $sin(\alpha) << cos(\alpha)$, and that way reduce the twisting motion to an acceptable level. In some cases twist might be a desired behavior [16–18], but often it is not, and require an additional helix of the reinforcement in the opposite direction to compensate [9, 19]. For that reason, the dense reinforcement has one more advantage to consider.

2.2   The Actuation Chamber Cross-Section Geometry

The actuation of soft actuators is based on the deformation of its soft body. For that reason, the cross-section shape of the actuator chamber can change during the actuation process. Since we consider fiber-reinforced actuators, the cross-section of the actuation chamber is constrained by fibers. That said, its perimeter length is constant and has the same value for passive and actuated state. Since the pressure inside the actuation chamber acts to increase the internal volume, the cross-section of the chamber will converge towards a shape that offers biggest area under the constant perimeter constrain. Any geometry of the pressure chamber cross-section will converge towards a circular shape when pressurized and the only geometry that will not change its shape is the circular one, see Fig. 6.

As a consequence of such deformation, the cross-section area as well as the centroid change, resulting in nonlinearity in the actuation process. Moreover, the

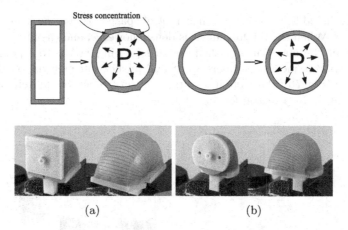

Fig. 6. Process of pressure chamber deformation during pressurization. (a) rectangular cross-section converges towards circular when pressurized, cross-section area grows, (b) circular cross-section does not change when pressurized, area remains constant.

device suffers from high strains in corners that in turn may result in fast wear of the material in those areas.

Even if the material wear is not a big issue, it is good to take it into account when designing a soft device. In some applications, the cross-section deformation might cause serious issues with regards to actuation and also sensing [20].

3   Fabrication

Most of the fabrication techniques for soft actuators reinforced with fibers require many manual operations. Manual operations are not desired because they are often a source of inconsistency and errors, as well as, labor is a very expensive factor in production. For that reason, we propose some improvements to reduce the manual work required to manufacture the device and to increase the process reliability.

3.1   The Reinforcement

Conceptually the simplest and the most popular way to reinforce a soft actuator with fibers is to create its body, and put the reinforcement on it afterward. This is, however, the most time and manual-work consuming approach. Moreover, applying the non-stretchable fiber on the soft body of the actuator causes internal tensions in the soft material and thus requires a lot of attention during the manufacturing process. The internal tensions are not a big issue for sparse reinforcements, but they became a real problem if the reinforcement has to be dense, Fig. 7. The tension required to wind the actuator with the fiber squeezes the soft body of the actuator and pushes the squeezed material to the sides. When the reinforcement is sparse this might not be considered as a significant problem as the additional material has a lot of space between the fibers to dissipate, Fig. 7a. When the reinforcement is dense, however, and the fibers are close to each other the material is pushed forward ((1) in Fig. 7b) to a point where the internal stress moves the fibers apart and pushes soft material out between them ((2) in Fig. 7b). This often results in inconsistency of the reinforcement and might likely be a reason for later failure.

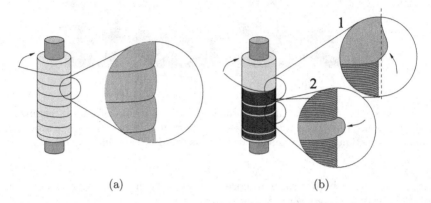

(a)   (b)

Fig. 7. Most commonly used technique: manual thread winding on the surface of soft actuator body. (Fig. 7a) spare reinforcement, pressed material dissipates between fibers, (Fig. 7b) dense reinforcement, pressed material is pushed in the direction of winding (1) which leads to potential inconsistencies in the reinforcement (2).

For that purpose, we propose to reverse this order and create the reinforcement first, before the soft acutor's body is made. For that purpose, a rigid moulding core can be used. Thanks to that there is no deformation induced by the fiber's tension. Using a rigid rod for that purpose allows also to automatize the process easily Fig. 8.

Such an approach is not limited to cylindrical actuation chambers. In [10, 21] we proposed a double-chamber conical actuator capable of varying the bending direction and in [15] we proposed a rotary actuation with toroidal actuation chamber. However, in case the actuator has axial symmetry, the reinforcement can be easily deployed by rotating the rod (Figs. 8a and b). In such a case, a screw gun or a dedicated winding machine can be used. Toroidal reinforcement (Fig. 8c), however, still needs to be made by hand.

3.2   The Soft Body of the Actuator

After the fibers are wound onto the rods, they are covered with silicone material and then removed. To protect the reinforcement structure and to make the removal easier, the employed cylindrical rods are split into three parts. The internal parts are being removed first (while the external parts are still attached to the reinforcement). After the first part is removed, the other two are getting lose

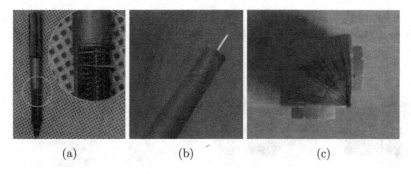

Fig. 8. The reinforcement created dedicated moulding cores. (a) three-part cylindrical rod, (b) conical core (single-part), (c) three-part toroidal core.

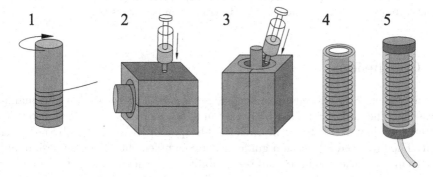

Fig. 9. The actuator fabrication stages. (1) reinforcement winding using a rigid rotating core, (2) external silicone layer casting, (3) internal silicone layer casting (preventing the reinforcement from being detached from the outer layer), (4) the actuation chamber ready, (5) chamber enclosure and pressure pipe attachment.

and can be removed without any problem. The same procedure can be applied to a bending actuator. Since the adhesion forces in case of silicone are low, and friction between fibers and the internal rod high, pulling it out at once could damage the reinforcement by dragging the threads out of the pressure chamber. This issue can be also solved by using some smooth rods (e.g., polished metallic rods) or conical rods (they can be easily removed by pulling out the wider end). Metallic rods are a good solution for cylindrical actuators having some standard dimensions. Other techniques, 3D printing in particular, allow for much more flexible designs like curved shapes, variable diameters etc. In the case of 3D printed parts splitting the core makes the fabrication process easier. After removing the internal molding cores used to shape the reinforcement, smaller core is inserted into the actuator and the volume between the fibers and the core is filled with new silicone material. The new silicone material creates the actual pressure chamber wall. After the material has cured, all the molded parts are removed and the actuator is closed on both ends by dip molding or by gluing on caps made form stiffer silicone. The manufacturing procedure is presented in Fig. 9 and photos showing subsequent stages of the actuator beingbr produced in Fig. 10.

(a)   (b)   (c)   (d)

Fig. 10. Fabrication steps: (a) - reinforcement, (b) - external layer, (c) - reinforcement attached to external layer exposed, (d) - internal chamber layers [22].

4   Conclusions

In this paper, we proposed some new rules for soft actuator design and manufacturing. The design rules are built assuming the more linear the actuation the better, but they also help to improve the life span of the actuators by reducing wear. The proposed fabrication guidelines are complementary to the design and help to increase the reliability and repeatability of the actuators, but also reduce the required manual work substantially. The points that need to be considered according to our experience and study are as follows:

1. Always using a circular cross-section will lead to
   (a) a more linear response
   (b) reduced wear and tear
2. Ensuring a dense fiber reinforcement will lead to
   (a) a more linear motion behaviour
   (b) reduced wear and tear
   (c) reduced twist while keeping simple design (single reinforcing helix)
3. Using rigid shafts for the fiber reinforcement manufacturing will achieve
   (a) a more reliable and predictable fabrication process
   (b) less manual effort

The described solutions address the issues we encountered in our research, but those issues are also widely noticeable in the majority of similar designs described in the literature.

References

1. Shapiro, Y., Wolf, A., Gabor, K.: Bi-bellows: pneumatic bending actuator. Sens. Actuators A: Phys. **167**(2), 484–494 (2011)
2. Althoefer, K: Neuro-fuzzy path planning for robotic manipulators (1996)
3. Konstantinova, J., Shafti, A., Althoefer, K.: Soft and Stiffness-Controllable Robotics Solutions for Minimally Invasive Surgery: The STIFF-FLOP Approach. River Publishers, Gistrup (2018). https://www.riverpublishers.com/book_details.php?book_id=493
4. Arezzo, A., et al.: Total mesorectal excision using a soft and flexible robotic arm: a feasibility study in cadaver models. Surg. Endosc. **31**, 264–273 (2016)
5. Stilli, A., et al.: AirExGlove–a novel pneumatic exoskeleton glove for adaptive hand rehabilitation in post-stroke patients. In: 2018 IEEE International Conference on Soft Robotics (RoboSoft), pp. 579–584. IEEE (2018)
6. Althoefer, K.: Antagonistic actuation and stiffness control in soft inflatable robots. Nat. Rev. Mater. **3**(6), 76 (2018)
7. Stilli, A., Wurdemann, H.A., Althoefer, K.: A novel concept for safe, stiffness-controllable robot links. Soft Robot. **4**(1), 16–22 (2017)
8. Ilievski, F., Mazzeo, A.D., Shepherd, R.F., Chen, X., Whitesides, G.M.: Soft robotics for chemists. Angew. Chem. **123**(8), 1930–1935 (2011)
9. Deimel, R., Brock, O.: A novel type of compliant and underactuated robotic hand for dexterous grasping. Int. J. Robot. Res. **35**(1–3), 161–185 (2016)
10. Fras, J., Althoefer, K.: Soft biomimetic prosthetic hand: design, manufacturing and preliminary examination. In: 2018 IEEE/RSJ International Conference on Intelligent Robots and Systems (IROS), pp. 1–6. IEEE (2018)
11. Schmitt, F., Piccin, O., Barbé, L., Bayle, B.: Soft robots manufacturing: a review. Front. Robot. AI **5**, 84 (2018)
12. Walker, S., Yirmibeşoğlu, O.D., Daalkhaijav, U., Mengüç, Y.: Additive manufacturing of soft robots. In: Robotic Systems and Autonomous Platforms, pp. 335–359. Woodhead Publishing (2019)
13. Wallin, T.J., Pikul, J., Shepherd, R.F.: 3D printing of soft robotic systems. Nat. Rev. Mater. 1 (2018)
14. Klute, G.K., Hannaford, B.: Fatigue characteristics of McKibben artificial muscle actuators. In: IROS (1998)
15. Fras, J., Noh, Y., Wurdemann, H., Althoefer, K.: Soft fluidic rotary actuator with improved actuation properties. In: International Conference on Intelligent Robots and Systems. IEEE (2017)
16. Galloway, K.C., Polygerinos, P., Walsh, C.J., Wood, R.J.: Mechanically programmable bend radius for fiber-reinforced soft actuators. In: 2013 16th International Conference on Advanced Robotics (ICAR), pp. 1–6. IEEE (2013)
17. Connolly, F., Polygerinos, P., Walsh, C.J., Bertoldi, K.: Mechanical programming of soft actuators by varying fiber angle. Soft Robot. **2**(1), 26–32 (2015)
18. Bishop-Moser, J., Krishnan, G., Kim, C., Kota, S.: Design of soft robotic actuators using fluid-filled fiber-reinforced elastomeric enclosures in parallel combinations. In: 2012 IEEE/RSJ International Conference on Intelligent Robots and Systems (IROS), pp. 4264–4269. IEEE (2012)
19. Polygerinos, P., et al.: Modeling of soft fiber-reinforced bending actuators. IEEE Trans. Robot. **31**(3), 778–789 (2015)
20. Fras, J., Czarnowski, J., Macias, M., Glowka, J., Cianchetti, M., Menciassi, A.: New STIFF-FLOP module construction idea for improved actuation and sensing. In: International Conference on Robotics and Automation, pp. 2901–2906. IEEE (2015)

21. Fras, J., Noh, Y., Macias, M., Wurdemann, H., Althoefer, K.: Bio-inspired octopus robot based on novel soft fluidic actuator. In: Submitted to International Conference on Robotics and Automation. IEEE (2018)
22. Fras, J., Macias, M., Noh, Y., Althoefer, K.: Fluidical bending actuator designed for soft octopus robot tentacle. In: 2018 IEEE International Conference on Soft Robotics (RoboSoft), pp. 253–257. IEEE (2018)

Ultrasound Feature Evaluation for Robustness to Sensor Shift in Ultrasound Sensor Based Hand Motion Recognition

Peter Boyd$^{(\boxtimes)}$, Yinfeng Fang, and Honghai Liu

School of Computing, University of Portsmouth, Portsmouth, UK
{peter.boyd,yinfeng.fang,honghai.liu}@port.ac.uk

Abstract. Pattern Recognition based approaches have offered great promise in the field of bio-signal controlled prosthesis. Traditionally Surface Electromyography based Approaches (SEMG) have been used to satisfy the purpose of providing Bio-Signal control in upper extremity Prosthesis. Although these methods have been shown to be robust, there still exists issues in performance within clinical environments. In recent years, Ultrasound signal based methods have seen growing interest within the field of motion Recognition, largely due to the increased resolution, deeper muscle observation, and reduced cross-talk that can be achieved in comparison to SEMG methods. However, the methods to be applied for hand Motion recognition are still only just beginning to be explored. In this paper, we shall investigate the applicability of SEMG feature extraction techniques to Ultrasound based hand motion recognition and the subsequent impact of Sensor shift on these features. The results of this study indicate that SEMG feature extraction techniques have excellent single location accuracy in Ultrasound based Hand motion recognition. However this paper more visibly presents the strong impact of Sensor Shift on A-Mode ultrasound based hand motion Recognition, and finally presents which feature extraction methods are most robust to this shift.

Keywords: Ultrasound · Hand gesture recognition ·
Feature extraction · Sensor shift · Prosthesis · Pattern recognition

1 Introduction

Bio-Signal controlled prosthesis are highly important to enabling amputees to be capable of mitigating the impact on their quality of life that comes with a lost limb [3]. Whereas early prosthesis had either limited or just no functionality, modern prosthesis have seen promising growth in providing a more intuitive control system for amputees. Generally speaking, a bio-signal controlled prosthesis attempts to relate a given set of bio-input to a set of anticipated motions. The

© Springer Nature Switzerland AG 2019
K. Althoefer et al. (Eds.): TAROS 2019, LNAI 11649, pp. 115–125, 2019.
https://doi.org/10.1007/978-3-030-23807-0_10

exact forms of bio-signal controlled upper limb prosthesis can be divided into two categories, conventional bio-signal prosthesis or pattern recognition based bio-Signal control strategies [16]. The most common form of these bio-signal controlled devices comes in the form of Electromyography (EMG) based bio-signal control devices. Traditionally conventional EMG controlled prosthesis followed an "on-off" switched control system, however newer conventional devices provide a more diverse series of control routines and inputs [15]. The benefit of these conventional approaches are that they are simple to implement, provide a desirable degree of robustness to transient changes in the bio-signal, and can satisfy the basic needs of an amputee for daily use. Conversely, conventional bio-signal controlled prosthesis hold limitations in several areas, such as having limited degrees of functionality and most importantly that their control scheme is unnatural in comparison to how a person would naturally move their original limb prior to amputation. Pattern Recognition based approaches, however, follow in the concept that an amputee may be able to voluntarily produce repeatable bio-signals that can be directly mapped to gestures that are best fitting to that bio-signal. Therefore, pattern recognition based approaches have seen considerable growth of interest in academia in recent years as they promise control schemes which are seemingly more natural to an amputee, whilst also providing a potentially larger pool of gestures that an amputee can perform therefore allowing a larger increase in quality of life, and finally this natural control scheme may aid in reducing the cognitive burden involved in the rehabilitative procedure of training the amputee with their new prosthesis.

1.1   Transient Changes

As with Conventional approaches, Pattern Recognition devices that utilize EMG have seen much popularity within academia, presently demonstrating highly promising results within laboratory environments. Unfortunately, EMG based pattern recognition approaches experience varying issues in their viability once applied to a clinical scenario. As for how such a dichotomy may occur a specific set of transient changes within Pattern Recognition based control systems have been cited in literature, these issues being electrode shift [19], crosstalk, fatigue [11], changes to skin conductivity, time [2,4,10], and concept drift.

1.2   Ultrasound

In an attempt to explore robust alternatives to SEMG motion recognition, researchers have in recent years began investigating the applicability of ultrasound sensors for the purpose of motion recognition [1,18]. With good promise being displayed in the topics of rehabilitative Human Machine Interaction [7]. Researchers have noted that the higher resolution of Ultrasound Signal and ability to observe deeper tissue than SEMG sensors as factors that could provide more robust control schemes [17]. The usage Ultrasound (US) imaging has long been used as a non invasive method for visualizing the inside of a body. The method of action for US Imaging, in its most simple form, is by projecting a beam of high frequency sound waves from a piezoelectric transducer, where the subsequent echoes of this sound wave can then be monitored for intensity and amount of time it took for the echo to return. This common usage of ultrasound for imaging in the medical field can be tied to the capability of the ultrasonic sound waves to penetrate soft tissues without harming them, a trait long previously recognised by [6]. Typically, Ultrasound methods used for hand motion recognition will either be the more traditional B-Mode Ultrasound, or the somewhat more compact but low resolution A-Mode Ultrasound.

1.3   Area of Focus - Electrode/Diode Shift

As with sEMG based hand motion recognition, ultrasound diode shift may drastically impact the quality of long term hand motion recognition. Frequently with sEMG devices, a small degree of electrode shift may have an insignificant impact on the classifiers performance. The likely reasoning for this being due to area of detection of sEMG electrodes to be shallow but across a larger area, frequently meaning that the main impact of electrode shift comes in the form of reduced amplitude of the targeted muscle and increased crosstalk form neighbouring muscles. It had also been observed that shift may impact SEMG signals dependent upon if the shift is perpendicular or parallel to the original location [9].

With a-mode ultrasound, the issue of shift manifests itself in a much more noticeable fashion. It could best be considered to be from the area targeted by a-mode ultrasound diodes to be deeper than sEMG electrodes but also much more concentrated, effectively removing much of the crosstalk but providing very different signals dependant upon the sensors location.

Although it is an easy argument to make that the quality of a-mode ultrasound will be affected heavily by ultrasound shift, it is important that we quantify just what degree of performance impact can be expected from such shift such that we may make progress towards counteracting shift.

In this paper, we will firstly define the problem of a-mode ultrasound diode shift and how this shift may manifest itself in the visible signal, secondly we will quantify the relationship between degrees of ultrasound diode shift across a targeted area of the forearm and degradation of classifier performance that comes with shift, we shall explore available feature extraction methods and feature sets.

Thirdly, the relative performance of these Feature sets shall be compared for their classification accuracy and rate of degradation across increasing shift.

2   Materials and Methods

2.1   Ultrasound Data Collection Device

The ultrasound data was collected through a 2 channel A-Mode Ultrasound device that collected 100 data points (or time dots) at a rate of 10MHZ. The device was placed on the muscle grouping above and below the wrist of the candidate. Transmission of Ultrasound data was performed via Ethernet to a windows based PC (Fig. 1).

Fig. 1. Ultrasound collection hardware

2.2 Representing Shift

In order to correctly model the degree of shift across the targeted muscle area, a 7 by 7 grid of 49 individual locations was marked on the top and bottom of the subjects forearm. This set location of space was chosen to simulate both the potential shift from extended daily use, and the expected shift from donning and doffing the ultrasound device.

2.3 Experimental Protocol

For this preliminary study, a single able bodied participant was used. The participant had prior experience with SEMG motion recognition. for each set of data collected, the participant would be advised to follow a set of hand motion gestures in sequence through on-screen guidance. After every set of motions was completed, both the upper and lower Ultrasound diode would be moved to a new location with ultrasound gel reapplied as necessary.

2.4 Motions

The motion collection scheme consisted of 6 gestures that involved either movement of the wrist or hand. The selected gestures were hand at rest, hand open, hand closed, wrist flexion, wrist extension, fine pinch. Each gesture was performed sequentially, for a period of 10 s per gesture before shifting to the next gesture. A period of 5 min was provided between locational shifts as to prevent fatigue.

The motion collection scheme consisted of several minor and major movements involving the hand or entire arm referred to as a primitive. For every collected dataset, a particular motion and its opposite would be performed sequentially, before a period of resting time. The allocated time per gesture was 5 s each, with a 10 s resting period. As each set of primitives were repeated 5 times, the resulting dataset would feature 110 s of data with 50 s of motion activity.

2.5 Data Pre-processing

All data processing was completed using Matlab r2017b. The pre processing for the ultrasound data firstly saw 6 s of stable motion data from each 10 s gesture performed, by removing 2 s from the beginning and end of each gesture. The intention of trimming using only the stable motion data is to the starting and ending 20 time points of each frame of data as the information carried here was not considered meaningful. A hilbert transform was subsequently applied onto the trimmed data and the envelope was extracted when viable for the chosen feature.

As the A-mode ultrasound data consists of a single frame every 100ms containing 960 time points, these time points indicating the muscle activity at a given depth from the US Diode. Presently, as there exists little comparative US feature selection strategies or comparisons. Therefore, traditional feature extraction methods for EMG data were to be modified to better exploit the generalizable traits of the data. The approach to feature extraction was to operate directly on the time points within each frame, as opposed to across multiple frames, using a 120 ms window and a 30 ms sliding window.

2.6 Data Processing

As mentioned in the pre-processing stage, few feature selection methods for A-Mode Ultrasound have been evaluated in literature. Therefore this paper shall explore the applicability of several TD-AR methods in both the no shift and the shift conditions.

To evaluate the quality of the feature sets, several simple features shall be selected, these being Root Mean Square (RMS), Auto Regressive Coefficients (AR), Waveform Transform (WL), Slope Sign Change (SSC), Mean + Standard Deviation (MSD), Zero Crossing (ZC), and Mean Absolute Value (MAV), all of these being traditional EMG feature extraction methods that had been implemented frequently in literature.

for classification, LDA, was used, due to this being suggested as a method that is robust to changes in input signal [10], alongside performing well during Ultrasound Hand Motion Recognition compared to methods such as Decision trees [14].

3   Methodology

During normal data collection from any bio-signal based system, the sensor is placed on the optimal location for any data to be collected. While this may provide the best exemplar of the expected bio-signal, it can be expected that any external sensor will shift from this location during daily use. Therefore, it was chosen to exploit the unforeseeable directionality of this diode shift by comparing the decreased performance of a trained classifier from the nominal training location in any given direction for every feature set. The working theory behind this selection is to provide the best characteristic of minor or major shift within a 360° field around the nominal location. For each location, a dataset was trained, and then tested against all neighbouring nodes. A benefit of this approach is that while there may be an individual subject the quantity of data and classifications for each individual location will bolster the potential for variability within the datasets.

4   Results

In Fig. 4, the outputs of a 10kfold loss method are demonstrated for each set of single Feature case, as an average of all 49 locational datasets. Generally, the performance of each method provides very good responses for when there is no shift in the Ultrasound sensor. However, once shift is applied, then the rate of accuracy for all cases begin to drop at a considerable rate, as shown in Fig. 2.

One noticeable change between the two charts is where Zero Crossing and Slope Sign change perform the worst under no shift, however, once shift is applied then both methods achieve not only a higher base accuracy, but also degrade at a similar but reduced rate in comparison to other methods (Fig. 3).

In Table 1, the spatial performance of all single features are displayed, alongside the top five of each increasingly large feature set upto size for features = 5, then the top two sets of six feature featuresets, and finally the featureset of all features together. The most visible trait of this table is that each subsequent set of combined features perform worse than the prior best performing features, such as SSC-ZC out performing the WL-SSC-ZC combination.

5   Discussion

In this study, several feature extraction methods were analysed to observe their robustness to Ultrasound Sensor Shift. The results of this study demonstrated that, while ultrasound based methods achieve good accuracy when kept on the nominal location, there is a significant impact on performance from shift, especially when larger than 4 mm shift. this would appear to be very much in-line with the findings of other researchers when experiencing transducer shift [5, 18], alongside similar reports being found in SEMG signal pattern recognition [20]. One likely factor into the heavier degrade in accuracy seen in this study is due to the nature of A-Mode Ultrasound having a deeper but much more concentrated

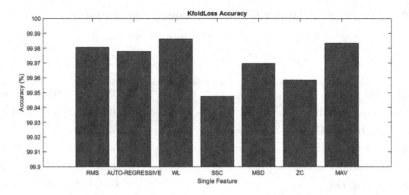

Fig. 2. Relative KfoldLoss Accuracy from each single Feature method

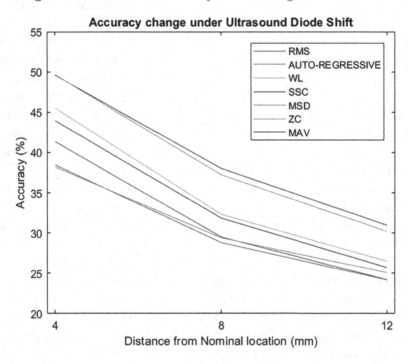

Fig. 3. Change in Accuracy under Ultrasound Sensor Shift conditions

section of the arm to observe, in a sense it could be considered that the resilience to crosstalk also makes Ultrasound methods less resilient to shift. Other factors that could potentially negatively impact the performance of a Ultrasound based method is that of the subject unconsciously moving their wrist, or fingers wither when performing a movement or by not fully returning to a rest state, as noted by Li [12]. Further to this, the grip strength used in a grasp may also deteriorate a classifier, as noted by Ortenzi et al. [14]. However, the most likely major factor

Table 1. Comparison of Feature Extraction techniques and Feature sets under sensor Shift

Feature	Accuracy		
	4 mm	8 mm	12 mm
Root Mean Square (RMS)	41.3502	29.4994	24.2456
AutoRegressive (AR)	38.4634	28.8036	24.2031
Waveform Length (WL)	45.5218	32.3189	26.5053
Slopesign Change (SSC)	49.5948	38.0151	30.9701
Mean + Standard Deviation (MSD)	38.2035	29.3982	25.1040
Zero Crossing (ZC)	49.6582	37.2260	30.2115
Mean Absolute Value (MAV)	43.9495	31.8411	27.7215
SSC-ZC	49.2386	37.2020	30.6760
WL-ZC	45.7314	32.4774	26.5321
WL-SSC	44.8713	32.3658	26.2964
ZC-MAV	44.1881	32.0853	26.0027
WL-MAV	43.9709	31.5118	28.9517
WL-SSC-ZC	44.8788	31.6372	25.9495
SSC-ZC-MAV	43.7783	31.6879	25.7942
WL-ZC-MAV	43.5127	31.1777	25.6881
WL-SSC-MAV	43.1884	31.3576	26.1230
WL-MSD-ZC	43.1755	31.5351	25.9677
SSC-MSD-ZC-MAV	42.2245	30.0888	25.3892
WL-MSD-ZC-MAV	42.0067	30.1947	24.7848
WL-SSC-MSD-ZC	41.9771	30.5604	25.4144
WL-SSC-MSD-MAV	41.9579	30.5913	25.0622
WL-SSC-ZC-MAV	41.4526	30.4854	25.6745
AUTO-REGRESSIVE-WL-SSC-ZC-MAV	42.6839	30.8301	25.3570
AUTO-REGRESSIVE-WL-SSC-MSD-ZC	42.3035	31.3956	25.6678
RMS-AUTO-REGRESSIVE-SSC-ZC-MAV	41.9753	30.3633	25.1596
AUTO-REGRESSIVE-SSC-MSD-ZC-MAV	41.9150	30.0390	24.9601
RMS-AUTO-REGRESSIVE-WL-SSC-ZC	41.8352	31.0312	25.4697
AUTO-REGRESSIVE-WL-SSC-MSD-ZC-MAV	43.7954	32.0128	26.3671
RMS-AUTO-REGRESSIVE-WL-SSC-MSD-ZC-MAV	43.7206	32.5627	26.7492

here is directly due to the manifestation of shift itself and therefore the focus is on what feature sets may be robust to this issue.

One notable trait of the results displayed here is that the multiple feature datasets all gradually performed worse as more features were added. This could imply a degree of over training is occurring from the single nominal location datasets. In all cases, Zero Crossing, Slope sign change, and Waveform Length, constituted the three main features in any strong dataset. Therefore, it could be described that these 3 features are far more robust to the occurrence of Sensor shift in Ultrasound hand, otion recognition. This could suggest that these methods are stronger at defining the spikes within the ultrasound signal, while other approaches are likely to smooth the signal and bring forward minor changes in signal that don't relate directly to expected signal. Moving forward, there could be great promise in combining these existing features with methods that promote retraining, or the construction of robust datasets that anticipate the impact of shift or other transient changes in signal [8,13].

A further consideration is that the results displayed here are on a two channel system, whilst prior studies used a 4 channel device. It is likely that a 4 channel device could only serve to further improve the accuracy demonstrated in this study.

6   Conclusion

In this paper, the robustness of traditional EMG feature extraction techniques were explored when applied to Ultrasound Sensor based Hand motion recognition. From the results of this study, there are two major conclusions. Firstly: the main feature Extraction methods demonstrated that the quality of Ultrasound based hand motion recognition is extremely high under no shift conditions. However, it can be recognised that Ultrasound sensor shift can significantly impact the quality of the classification result, especially at larger ranges.

Secondly, the results that are demonstrated in this paper indicate that combined feature sets seemingly do not perform as well as individual features. This could suggest that the matter comes to being related specifically to the representation of the ultrasound data, or potentially as a consequence of over training in the cases of combined feature sets.

The intent of this research was to explore the relative robustness of different Ultrasound feature extractions methods under the situation of sensor shift and to find a feature or set of features that can provide a meaningful representation of the Ultrasound Signal for hand motion recognition.

It is suggested that future directions in Ultrasound hand motion recognition is to investigate whether the inclusion of more channels when considering sensor shift may further improve the classification accuracy alongside the impact of larger arm motions. To expand the features tested here on other traditional feature selection methods. Further to this, to investigate training strategies that may improve the robustness to sensor shift in Ultrasound. Finally, it is suggested to further investigate the relative comparison of Ultrasound based hand Motion Recognition, in comparison to EMG when considering Long Term Use.

References

1. Akhlaghi, N., et al.: Real-time classification of hand motions using ultrasound imaging of forearm muscles. IEEE Trans. Biomed. Eng. (2016). https://doi.org/10.1109/TBME.2015.2498124
2. Amsuss, S., Paredes, L.P., Rudigkeit, N., Graimann, B., Herrmann, M.J., Farina, D.: Long term stability of surface EMG pattern classification for prosthetic control. In: Proceedings of the Annual International Conference of the IEEE Engineering in Medicine and Biology Society, EMBS, pp. 3622–3625 (2013). https://doi.org/10.1109/EMBC.2013.6610327
3. Biddiss, E., Chau, T.T.: Upper limb prosthesis use and abandonment: a survey of the last 25 years. Prosthet. Orthot. Int. **31**(3), 236–257 (2007). https://doi.org/10.1080/03093640600994581
4. Boyd, P., Fang, Y., Liu, H.: Preliminary results of EMG-based hand gestures for long term use. In: Huang, Y.A., Wu, H., Liu, H., Yin, Z. (eds.) ICIRA 2017. LNCS (LNAI), vol. 10464, pp. 98–108. Springer, Cham (2017). https://doi.org/10.1007/978-3-319-65298-6_10
5. Castellini, C., Passig, G., Zarka, E.: Using ultrasound images of the forearm to predict finger positions. IEEE Trans. Neural Syst. Rehabil. Eng. **20**(6), 788–797 (2012). https://doi.org/10.1109/TNSRE.2012.2207916
6. Donald, I., Macvicar, J., Brown, T.G.: Investigation of abdominal masses by pulsed ultrasound. Lancet (1958). https://doi.org/10.1016/S0140-6736(58)91905-6
7. González, D.S., Castellini, C.: A realistic implementation of ultrasound imaging as a human-machine interface for upper-limb amputees. Front. Neurorobotics (2013). https://doi.org/10.3389/fnbot.2013.00017
8. Hargrove, L., Englehart, K., Hudgins, B.: A training strategy to reduce classification degradation due to electrode displacements in pattern recognition based myoelectric control. Biomed. Sig. Process. Control. (2008). https://doi.org/10.1016/j.bspc.2007.11.005
9. He, J., Sheng, X., Zhu, X., Jiang, N.: Electrode density affects the robustness of myoelectric pattern recognition system with and without electrode shift. IEEE J. Biomed. Health Inform. (2019). https://doi.org/10.1109/JBHI.2018.2805760
10. Kaufmann, P., Englehart, K., Platzner, M.: Fluctuating EMG signals: investigating long-term effects of pattern matching algorithms. In: 2010 Annual International Conference of the IEEE Engineering in Medicine and Biology Society, EMBC 2010 (2010). https://doi.org/10.1109/IEMBS.2010.5627288
11. Lalitharatne, T.D., Hayashi, Y., Teramoto, K., Kiguchi, K.: Compensation of the effects of muscle fatigue on EMG-based control using fuzzy rules based scheme. In: Proceedings of the Annual International Conference of the IEEE Engineering in Medicine and Biology Society, EMBS, pp. 6949–6952 (2013). https://doi.org/10.1109/EMBC.2013.6611156
12. Li, Y., He, K., Sun, X., Liu, H.: Human-machine interface based on multi-channel single-element ultrasound transducers: a preliminary study. In: 2016 IEEE 18th International Conference on e-Health Networking, Applications and Services, Healthcom 2016 (2016). https://doi.org/10.1109/HealthCom.2016.7749483
13. Liu, J., Sheng, X., Zhang, D., Jiang, N., Zhu, X.: Towards zero retraining for myoelectric control based on common model component analysis. IEEE Trans. Neural Syst. Rehabil. Eng. (2016). https://doi.org/10.1109/TNSRE.2015.2420654

14. Ortenzi, V., Tarantino, S., Castellini, C., Cipriani, C.: Ultrasound imaging for hand prosthesis control: a comparative study of features and classification methods. In: IEEE International Conference on Rehabilitation Robotics (2015). https://doi.org/10.1109/ICORR.2015.7281166

15. Scheme, E., Englehart, K.: Electromyogram pattern recognition for control of powered upper-limb prostheses: state of the art and challenges for clinical use. J. Rehabil. Res. Dev. **48**(6), 643–660 (2011). https://doi.org/10.1682/JRRD.2010.09.0177. http://www.rehab.research.va.gov/jour/11/486/pdf/scheme486.pdf

16. Toledo, C., Simon, A., Muñoz, R., Vera, A., Leija, L., Hargrove, L.: A comparison of direct and pattern recognition control for a two degree-of-freedom above elbow virtual prosthesis. In: Proceedings of the Annual International Conference of the IEEE Engineering in Medicine and Biology Society, EMBS (2012). https://doi.org/10.1109/EMBC.2012.6346925

17. Yang, X., Li, Y., Fang, Y., Liu, H.: A preliminary study on the relationship between grip force and muscle thickness. In: International IEEE/EMBS Conference on Neural Engineering, NER, pp. 118–121 (2017). https://doi.org/10.1109/NER.2017.8008306

18. Yang, X., Sun, X., Zhou, D., Li, Y., Liu, H.: Towards wearable a-mode ultrasound sensing for real-time finger motion recognition. IEEE Trans. Neural Syst. Rehabil. Eng. (2018). https://doi.org/10.1109/TNSRE.2018.2829913

19. Young, A.J., Hargrove, L.J., Kuiken, T.: The effects of electrode size and orientation on the sensitivity of myoelectric pattern recognition systems to electrode shift. IEEE Trans. Biomed. Eng. **58**(9), 2537–2544 (2011). https://doi.org/10.1109/TBME.2011.2159216

20. Young, A.J., Hargrove, L.J., Kuiken, T.A.: Improving myoelectric pattern recognition robustness to electrode shift by changing interelectrode distance and electrode configuration. IEEE Trans. Biomed. Eng. (2012). https://doi.org/10.1109/TBME.2011.2177662

Light Intensity-Modulated Bending Sensor Fabrication and Performance Test for Shape Sensing

Faisal ALJaber[✉] and Kaspar Althoefer[✉]

Queen Mary University of London, Mile End Road, London E1 4NS, UK
{f.aljaber,k.althoefer}@qmul.ac.uk

Abstract. Notable advancements in shape sensing for flexible continuum robot arms can be observed. With a keen interest to develop surgical and diagnostic tools that can advance further and further into inaccessible spaces along tortuous pathways, such as the human body, a need for the precise determination of the robot's pose arises. Whilst there have been techniques developed that use external sensors to observe the advancing robot from the outside to determine its location and orientation in space, there is an observable trend towards using integrated, internal sensors to measure these positional parameters. Especially in the medical world with its tough requirements on robot size, e.g., catheter-type robots, most pose-sensing approaches to date make use of a technique called Fiber Bragg Grating (FBG). FBG sensors make use of fibers that are grated, and the amount of bending can be determined with an appropriate optical inter- rogator. Although these fiber sensors have been successfully employed to measure the deformation and through advanced signal processing the pose of continuum catheters, they have a major drawback which is their exorbitant cost. To address this issue a different design and fabrication process is proposed to produce an affordable shape sensor that is highly flexible and can detect bending. The method of operation involves a segmented flexible robot arm with three waveguides in a 120-degrees configuration. The segments are made of silicone elastomer with channels that encapsulate light propagating internally, with a photodiode and light-emitting diode (LED) embedded in each individual channel. The prototype was developed and characterized for strain, and bending response detection.

Keywords: Shape sensing · Optical fiber · Intensity modulated shape sensor · Soft robotics · Fiber Bragg Grating (FBG) · PDMS

1 Introduction

Modern minimally invasive surgical systems are now considered to be established alternatives to conventional open surgical intervention [35, 36]. MIS surgery is known for having many post-operative positive impacts on patients, such as reduced pain, blood loss, tissue trauma. Also, with the advancement of technology of MIS tech- niques, nowadays it is more likely to create more compact and highly flexible surgical instruments with high dexterity that can enhance the surgeon performance for better

© Springer Nature Switzerland AG 2019
K. Althoefer et al. (Eds.): TAROS 2019, LNAI 11649, pp. 126–137, 2019.
https://doi.org/10.1007/978-3-030-23807-0_11

results. However, the main drawbacks associated with flexible robotic surgical instruments is the lack of four main features, (1) accurate position feedback, (2) information about the interaction force between the instrument and the tissue, (3) degrees of freedom reduction and (4) limited access to the operational area [35].

In order to enable flexible MIS manipulators to possess an accurate steering, and to be able to obtain their position information about its shape in 3D environment is required. Different imaging techniques and shape reconstruction modalities were created to help identify the location and realize the shape of MIS flexible manipulators. These modalities and techniques are divided to two main categories. The first category are techniques allowing shape reconstruction by using imaging-based modalities, such as ultrasound, x-ray, computed tomography (CT) and magnetic resonance imaging (MRI). These imaging-based shape reconstruction techniques pose a lot of technical challenges. Ultrasound has low image resolution and tissue contrast, x-ray and CT will risk exposing the patients to high dosage of ionizing and radiation, and MRI has a low refresh rate which makes it a time-consuming process [3]. Moreover, most of these modalities require a large workspace, their inherent size characteristics limit their intraoperative implementation in operative theaters, and they are not cost efficient. The second category includes optical fibers utilizing FBG shape-based sensors and EM-tracker for shape reconstruction and bending profile estimation. Unlike the pervious imaging-based modalities, FBG sensors and EM-trackers are miniaturized shape sensors, they have small footprint and they can be easily coupled with any flexible surgical instrument, and they are suitable to be used in a confined workspace. Also, FBGs and other fiber-based approaches are well-known to be compatible with other magnetic or electrical shape reconstruction modalities.

Furthermore, both techniques are easy to be integrated into intraoperative procedures for their accessibility and free from line-of-sight restrictions [1]. However, both techniques have their own limitations and disadvantages. The EM-tracker technique is sensitive to distortions imposed by metallic objects and electrical/magnetic noise close to their field of generation. Its workspace is constrained by the field of generation produced by the EM tracker generator, and they tested to have better accuracy when used in combination with continuum robots with simplified design and computationally expensive modelling [1–5]. FBGs are well-known for being sensitive to both strain and temperature, and they measure mainly the axial strain. Moreover, FBG accuracy depends on the number of sensors, the placement position of the sensors along the instrument they are attached to, the manufacturing precision, the surrounding environment, and the stiffness of the instrument they are attached to. Finally, FBGs-based shape sensors tend to be very expensive which limits their use in general.

2 Background

Recent progress of soft robotics came as a result of the need of sophisticated robotic systems that are developed to have close interaction with human beings within a safe environment. There has been an extensive number of researches on creating optical fiber FBG-based sensors which are regarded to be a method suitable for shape deformation estimation and preferred to other approaches due to its electromagnetic interference immunity [19–21].

Besides their bio-compatibility, small size and, thus, suitability for various MIS applications, and compatibly with other magnetic or electrical systems. For instance, the early work by Park et al. who implemented FBG sensing in miniaturized-gauge MRI-compatible biopsy needle for real-time shape reconstruction of needle deflection profile [37]. Park continued to inspire other research groups adopting his triplet optical FBG-based sensor with 120-degrees configurations [37]. Henken used the configuration with different FBG sensors placement positions on a trocar needle for liver tumor ablation for planar 3D shape reconstruction [38].

However, FBG shape-based sensors pose a lot of challenges. These challenges include loss of strain inaccuracies due to the surrounding environments that can directly interfere with wavelength detection, calibration issues, reduction in reflected wavelength transfer, geometrical inaccuracies, and high cost of interrogator equipment limiting the technology's accessibility and real-life implementations.

More research focused on shape sensing and deflection estimation sensors based on the principle of light intensity modulation using optical fibers. For instance, Searle et al. designed a novel temperature independent soft optical sensor based on the principle of light intensity modulation as shown in Fig. 1. The purpose of designing the sensor is to measure the bending curvature of flexible MIS surgery manipulators for easy access to the desired operational targeted area [39].

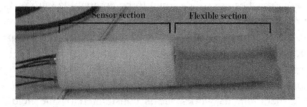

Fig. 1. Design by Searle et al. showing the sensor with both sections labeled [39].

The material selection and the components used in soft robots and sensors are different from those in conventional robots and sensors that are typically made of rigid components [6, 7]. The performance of sensors is considered generally to be one of the most essential elements in robotics and soft robotics. The fabrication of soft robots and associated sensors is largely based on a range of polymer materials, such as Polydimethylsiloxane (PDMS) and other types of commercialized silicone rubbers [25].

Nevertheless, one of the disadvantages of polymers is that they are not conductive; hence, integrated conductive media are required to communicate electrical signals along a soft material robot without compromising the flexibility and elasticity of the used rubber material. A most preferred conductive medium is based on liquid conductors due to their electrically-conductive property and high elasticity [8–10]. The liquid conductors can be easily sealed and encapsulated by closed microchannels inside a highly deformable soft sensor [25]. The encapsulated liquid inside the microchannels behaves like a sensing element by changing the resistance with respect to deformation of the sensor shape [11, 12]. For strain, pressure [9, 13], curvature and multi-axis shear forces detection many soft sensors developed utilize liquid metals [14, 15]. Non-metallic liquid conductors, such as ionic liquids were proposed as a biocompatible option; however, their limited conductivity has constrained their use in applications [16–18].

Despite the many advantages of liquid conductors, there are several drawbacks that they are suffer from when they are coupled with soft materials. Liquid conductors require high pressure injection when introduced to a microchannel with a very thin needle; this is due to the hydrophobic nature of polymers that is injected inside a narrow space. The air captured during fabrication inside the microchannels makes it very challenging to control the injection process. Therefore, the manufacturing of such sensors consisting of microchannels is complicated by the fact that appropriate sealing of the injection ports needs to be ensured. Also, there is the risk of a mechanical failure that might result in leakage, and in case of using liquid metal this could be harmful and toxic if getting in direct contact with a living organism [25].

As an alternative to the microfluidic-based sensing approach, this paper proposes a soft sensor with channels that can encapsulate optical fibers. These fibers are used to transfer light from an LED at one end to a photoreceiver on the other end; fiber bending leads to a change in light intensity which is being detected by the photoreceiver. The fabrication for the proposed sensor aims to ease the manufacturing complexity and operational risks without compromising the mechanical properties desired. The idea behind this sensor is to exploit the optical fiber light conducting principles to estimate bending. The contribution of the paper is to propose an approach that novelty is the easy fabrication process of the soft sensor, setup of the segmented sensor and the range of the miniaturized sizes that is provided by the fabrication process.

3   Design and Fabrication of Shape Sensor

3.1   The Fabrication of Soft Silicone Segments

PDMS is a commonly used polymer especially because of its transparency and optical characteristics compatibility [22–24]. Nevertheless, PDMS is also known for its relatively low elongation at breaking point which is considered to be one of its main limitations. Even though, the availability of highly stretchable commercialized elastomers is relatively high, it is difficult to find one with high optical transparency. Therefore, the challenge here was to create a design which addresses the balance between optical transparency and stretchability. The approach employed by Celeste et al. is based on creating a hybrid material by mixing PDMS and commercially available silicone gel (EcoFlex Gel, Smooth-On) [25]. The mixing ratio of the material created was 9 parts of optical transparent PDMS and 1 part of soft stretchable silicone gel [25]. As Celeste et al. report, their five-hour fabrication approach consists of a three-step process for creating the sensor. Firstly, two separate moulds are used to fabricate a semi-circular waveguide and the bottom layer of the sensor. Secondly, an LED and a photodiode are embedded at opposite ends before curing the waveguide. Then, the waveguide gets coated by a thin gold leaf layer after curing and the complete waveguide is then placed on top of the bottom layer. Lastly, more substrate of the 9:1 mixture of EcoFlex Gel and PDMS is poured to cover the waveguide and complete the sensor housing [25].

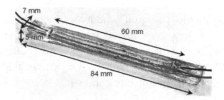

Fig. 2. Image shows the soft pressure, curvature, and strain sensor by Celeste et al. [25].

Although, Celeste et al. attempted to design and fabricate a highly flexible optical sensor based on waveguide technique for strain, pressure, and curvature measurements as Fig. 2 shows. This sensor potentially was developed as an alternative for other stretchable sensors for shape reconstruction which will impose any harm if it came in contact with any human being. And the sensor design suggested was an attempt to replace the highly stretchable conductive liquid sensors, too. It is noted by Celeste that, the liquid-based deflection sensors proposed are toxic in nature unless nonmetallic liquid is used which reduces conductivity significantly. In addition, there is always a risk of leakage which might harm the patient if used in MIS procedures. Furthermore, the complicated liquid sensor fabrication process is considered to be time consuming, particularly when it comes to injecting the liquid to the microchannels. However, the waveguide-based highly stretchable sensor suffers from several constraints, such as the sensor rectangular design shape and size makes it considerably large for MIS applications. Also, the thin gold layer which plays the role of the reflective interface is susceptible to microcracks allowing partial escape of the light resulting in light intensity reduction [25]. These microcracks created by stretching the sensor will be permanent making the gold coating unsustainable for long term usage of the sensor.

The mixture ratio of the materials used to create our proposed flexible soft arm is 1A:1B of two silicone rubber (Dragon Skin 10 Fast, Smooth-On) a soft silicone rubber (A) and fast cure silicone (B), respectively. The mixture ratio was achieved by using a volumetric plastic measuring cup and a digital scale to ensure equal added volume of both silicone rubber A, and B. 30 ml of each individual material is added, then a silicone thinner was added and the mixture stirred thoroughly before dispensing. The amount of silicone thinner added is 10% of the total amount of A + B added together (which is 6 ml). It is advisable for the silicone thinner not to exceed the recommended 10%. Table 1 below shows the properties of the mixture before and after adding the silicone thinner. Using the silicone thinner has some advantages, such as lower mixed viscosity of the created material which means fast de-air of the silicone while vacuuming. The silicone thinner helps the mixture to flow better over the details of the mold. Also, the life expectancy and working time is proportional to the silicone thinner applied. However, the tensile strength and the ultimate tear will be reduced proportionally to the amount of silicone thinner added.

Table 1. The silicone material mixture used properties before and after adding the silicone thinner.

Dragon skin 10 fast (A + B)	The hybrid mixture with 0% silicone thinner	The hybrid mixture with 10% silicone thinner
Shore A Hardness (ASTM D-2240)	10A	Decreases
Tensile Strength (ASTM D-412)	475 psi	Decreases
Elongation at Break % (ASTM D-412)	1000%	Increases
Tear Strength (Die B) (ASTM D-624)	102 pli	Decreases
Mixed Viscosity (A + B) (ASTM D-2393)	23000 cps	Decreases

3.2   Calibration

For us to be able to create the soft segments of the soft sensor molds were designed using computer-aided design software (SolidWorks). Five different molds were created with different diameters ranged between 3.2 cm to 7 mm, however only the segment with the largest diameter was used for this performance test. The mold has the following features as Fig. 4 shows: there are channels created to accommodate optical fibers, magnet attachments, and the center supporting tensile spring which have the following diameters 3.6 mm, 5 mm, and 4 mm, respectively. The molds are designed in a way to make it easy to extract them after the curing time has passed and easy to be reused. The silicone segments are disposable and their diameter differ individually as Fig. 5(a) shows. The calibration process was done by moving the three photodiodes that are used for the light intensity modulated sensors from the LEDs to known voltage interval to from 5 V when the distance is 0 cm and decreasing by 0.5 V to the least recorded voltage. The calibration was conducted four times and the resultant average distance, at each light intensity was selected as the function of the distance with respect to light intensity. Figure 3 shows the calibration results. It can be detected that the sensor has sensitive range between 4.58 cm 12 cm with corresponding light intensity between 4.5 V to 0.3 V when it starts to give one constant minimum value. The standard deviations of the averaged distance results are 4.91 cm, 4.95 cm, and 5.04 cm with corresponding standard error of 0.55 cm, 0.56 cm, and 0.57 cm. The calibration was done to the distance with respect to the light intensity to decide the proper length of one segment that will allow maximum bending and light intensity.

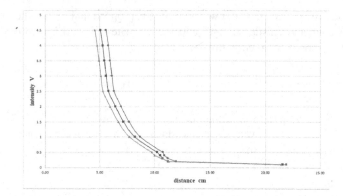

Fig. 3. The plot shows the calibration results for the three photodiodes used in the sensor over the range 0 to 22 cm.

Fig. 4. (a) Mold CAD design showing the columns that will create the channels. (b) Different dimensions of molds created. (c) Complete design of the mold with its parts diameters. (d) Length of the mold. (e) Inner part of the mold.

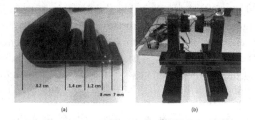

Fig. 5. (a) Soft silicone segments with different diameters. (b) Holder used to hole both the LED and to photodiode to decide the length of the silicone segment.

4   Concept

The principle of operation of our sensor depends on optical fibers since the sensor utilizes optical fibers to sense the change of shape of any flexible soft instrument that has the ability to bend. A single optical fiber consists of three main components: the core, the cladding, and the coating or buffer. Figure 4(a) shows the basic structure of an optical fiber. The core of an optical fiber is a cylinder-shaped rod made of dielectric material and is typically made of glass. Light beam propagates primarily along the core of the fiber [26].

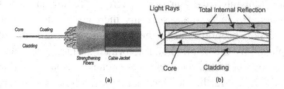

(a)   (b)

Fig. 6.   (a) Basic structure of an optical fiber. (b) Total internal reflection in an optical fiber [26].

The cladding layer consists of a dielectric material. The cladding is generally made of glass or plastic and its main functionality is to execute such tasks by limiting the loss of light from the core into the air, decreasing the scattering loss at the core surface, and preserving the fibers from absorbing the surface impurities [26, 27].

The optical fiber is coated by a layer of material applied to protect it from any external impact or any physical damage. Usually the material used as a coating is a type of plastic and the coating is elastic in nature to avoid abrasions of the core [26, 28–30]. Optical fibers achieve total internal reflection by using two different refractive indices between the waveguide and the outer cladding. At any angle of incidence that is greater than the critical angle, the light is totally reflected back into the glass medium (see Fig. 6(b)). The total reflection of the light back into the glass medium would happen if the angle of incidence is greater than the critical angle (see Fig. 6(b)) [26, 28–30].

4.1   Light Intensity Modulation

The sensor we are developing mainly based on the principle of light intensity modulation [31–33]. The intensity of the light emitted can possibly be modulated when an external force is exerted on the sensor designed. The measurements of the deformation were defined as the result of bending along each channel that occupies a fiber optic. For light detection and emission, a silicon PIN photodiode (OSRAM Opto Semiconductors, SFH 229) with a maximum wavelength sensitivity of 860 nm and maximum sensitivity of 1100 nm and a warm white color light-emitting diode (LED) (Hebei) were used, respectively. The surface mount of both LED and the photodiode is 3 mm facilitating a miniaturized sensor design. All photodiodes utilized in designing the sensor were operating in forward bias in which both the voltage signals output and the light intensity has a logarithmic relationship shown in the following equation [34]:

$$V = \frac{kT}{q}\left(\ln\frac{i}{i_s} + 1\right)$$ (1)

where V, k, T, q, i and i_s are the voltage output, Boltzman's constant, temperature, current, and saturation current, respectively. It is known to us that the current is linearly proportional to the light intensity. For our design of the soft silicon that goes under bending, the assumption can be made that any increase of the soft silicone structure deformation is inversely proportional to the light intensity, and that the ratio of the current can be replaced by the original and deformed surface areas ratio of the sensor. The assumption can be made that the surface area change is subjected to the change in length, the ratio is reduced further to that of lengths. The original length and length after deformation can be denoted by l_o and l, respectively. In addition, the expression $\frac{kT}{q}$ can be replaced by a single notation which is the initial voltage V_o for simplification. Finally, the theoretical model equation can be written as [34]:

$$V = V_o\left(\ln\frac{i}{i_s} + 1\right).$$ (2)

5   Results

The soft segment is tested by labeling each channel that contains an optical fiber and set between a photodiode from the bottom and an LED from the top end. The soft segment went under 90-degrees dynamic bending three times towards the direction of each channel along the x-y plane. The performance test was done as following: (1) the recording of the voltage output starts from the initial position at 0-degree (2) then it is bent gradually until it reaches 90-degrees (3) finally, the soft segment is released to it is initial position. Each experiment is repeated five times for 75 s which explains the behavior of the plots shown in Fig. 7(a), (b), and (c). All three plots show similar behavior to bending when an external force is applied with minor delays of the third photo-diode of plot (a) in Fig. 7 and the first photodiode on plot (b) when it is rested after bending.

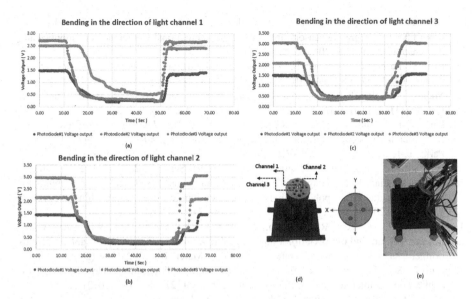

Fig. 7. (a), (b), and (c) is the voltage outputs of channels one, two, and three when the segment is bent. (d) Channels locations. (e) The soft segment is bent 90-degrees.

6 Conclusion

This design and fabrication of the soft silicone with channels that can contain optical fiber has the potential to test more than bending. We currently working on a simulation that can mimic the movement of the segment while goes under different type of deformations. Next, the sensor accuracy will put into test and it will be compared to similar sensors designed by other researchers.

Acknowledgment. The authors would like to thank each of Eng. Ahmed Al-Kuwari, Mr. Sunith Padinjarayil, and Sara Abazid for their help in 3D-printing, setting up the electrical circuit of the photodiode, and the calibration experiments.

References

1. Shi, C., Luo, X., Fukuda, T.: Shape sensing techniques for continuum robots in minimally invasive surgery: a survey. IEEE Trans. Biomed. Eng. **PP**(99) (2016)
2. Roesthuis, R.J., Kemp, M., van den Dobbelsteen, J.J.: Three-dimensional needle shape reconstruction using an array of fiber Bragg grating sensors. IEEE/ASME Trans. Mechatron. **19**(4), 1115–1126 (2013)
3. Roesthuis, R.J., Janssen, S., Misra, S.: On using an array of fiber Bragg grating sensors for closed-loop control of flexible minimally invasive surgical instruments. In: IEEE/RSJ International Conference on Intelligent Robots and Systems, Tokyo (2013)
4. Ryu, S.C., Dupont, P.E.: FBG-based shape sensing tubes for continuum robots. In: IEEE International Conference on Robotics and Automation (ICRA), Hong Kong (2014)

5. Abayazid, M., Kemp, M., Misra, S.: 3D flexible needle steering in soft-tissue phantoms using fiber Bragg grating sensors. In: 2013 IEEE International Conference on Robotics and Automation, Karlsruhe (2013)
6. Kim, S., Laschi, C., Trimmer, B.: Soft robotics: a bioinspired evolution in robotics. Trends Biotechnol. **31**(5), 287–294 (2013)
7. Majidi, C.: Soft robotics: a perspective–current trends and prospects for the future. Soft Robot. **1**(1), 5–11 (2014)
8. Park, Y.-L., Majidi, C., Kramer, R., Berard, P., Wood, R.J.: Hyperelastic pressure sensing with a liquid-embedded elastomer. J. Micromech. Microeng. **20**(12), 125029 (2010)
9. Park, Y.-L., Chen, B., Wood, R.J.: Design and fabrication of soft artificial skin using embedded microchannels and liquid conductors. IEEE Sens. J. **12**(8), 2711–2718 (2012)
10. Wu, C.-Y., Liao, W.H., Tung, Y.-C.: Integrated ionic liquid-based electrofluidic circuits for pressure sensing within polydimethylsiloxane microfluidic systems. Lab Chip **11**(207890), 1740–1746 (2011)
11. Dickey, M.D., Chiechi, R.C., Larsen, R.J., Weiss, E.A., Weitz, D.A., Whitesides, G.M.: Eutectic gallium-indium (EGaln): a liquid metal alloy for the formation of stable structures in microchannels at room temperature. Adv. Func. Mater. **18**, 1097–1104 (2008)
12. Liu, T., Sen, P., Kim, C.: Characterization of nontoxic liquid-metal alloy Galinstan for applications in microdevices. J. Microelectromech. Syst. **21**, 443–450 (2012)
13. Wong, R.P., Posner, J., Santos, V.: Flexible microfluidic normal force sensor skin for tactile feedback. Sens. Actuators A **179**, 62–69 (2012)
14. Vogt, D.M., Park, Y.-L., Wood, R.J.: Design and characterization of a soft multi-axis force sensor using embedded microfluidic channels. IEEE Sens. J. **13**(10), 4056–4064 (2013)
15. Majidi, C., Kramer, R., Wood, R.J.: A non-differential elastomer curvature sensor for softer-than-skin electronics. Smart Mater. Struct. **20**, 105017 (2011)
16. Visser, A., Bridges, N., Rogers, R.: Ionic Liquids: Science and Applications, vol. 1117. American Chemical Society, Washington, D.C. (2012)
17. Chossat, J.-B., Park, Y.-L., Wood, R.J., Duchaine, V.: A soft strain sensor based on ionic and metal liquids. IEEE Sens. J. **13**(9), 3405–3414 (2013)
18. Chossat, J.-B., Shin, H.-S., Park, Y.-L., Duchaine, V.: Design and manufacturing of soft tactile skin using an embedded ionic liquid and tomographic imaging. J. Mech. Robot. (2014)
19. Li, K., Chen, I.-M., Yeo, S.H., Lim, C.K.: Development of finger-motion capturing device based on optical linear encoder. J. Rehabil. Res. Dev. **48**(1), 69 (2011)
20. Kampmann, P., Kirchner, F.: Integration of fiber-optic sensor arrays into a multi-modal tactile sensor processing system for robotic end-effectors. Sensors **14**(4), 6854–6876 (2014)
21. Grillet, A., et al.: Optical fiber sensors embedded into medical textiles for healthcare monitoring. IEEE Sens. J. **8**(7), 1215–1222 (2008)
22. Kopetz, S., Cai, D., Rabe, E., Neyer, A.: PDMS-based optical waveguide layer for integration in electrical–optical circuit boards. AEU-Int. J. Electron. Commun. **61**(3), 163–167 (2007)
23. Chang-Yen, D., Eich, R., Gale, B.: A monolithic PDMS waveguide system fabricated using soft-lithography techniques. J. Lightwave Technol. **23**(6), 2088–2093 (2005)
24. Kee, J.S., Poenar, D.P., Neuzil, P., Yobas, L.: Monolithic integration of poly(dimethylsiloxane) waveguides and microfluidics for on-chip absorbance measurements. Sens. Actuators B **134**(2), 532–538 (2008)
25. To, C., Hellebrekers, T.L., Park, Y.-L.: Highly stretchable optical sensors for pressure, strain, and curvature measurement. In: IEEE/RSJ International Conference on Intelligent Robots and Systems (IROS), Hamburg (2015)
26. Fidanboylu, K.: Fiber optic sensors and their applications (2009)

27. Méndez, A.: Overview of fiber optic sensors for NDT applications. In: IV NDT Panamerican Conference, pp. 1–11 (2007)
28. Jones, D., Introduction to Fiber Optics. Naval Education and Training Professional Development and Technology Center (1998)
29. Jenny, R.: Fundemantals of Fiber Optics: An Introduction for Beginners. Volpi Manufacturing USA Co., New York (2000)
30. Tracey, P.M.: Intrinsic fiber-optic sensors. IEEE Trans. Ind. Appl. **27**, 1 (1991)
31. Polygerinos, P., Ataollahi, A., Schaeffter, T., Razavi, R., Seneviratne, L.D., Althoefer, K.: MRI-compatible intensity-modulated force sensor for cardiac catheterization procedures. IEEE Trans. Biomed. Eng. **58**(3), 721–726 (2011)
32. Polygerinos, P., Seneviratne, L.D., Althoefer, K.: Modeling of light intensity-modulated fiber-optic displacement sensors. IEEE Trans. Instrum. Meas. **60**(4), 1408–1415 (2011)
33. Puangmali, P., Althoefer, K., Seneviratne, L.D.: Mathematical modeling of intensity-modulated bent-tip optical fiber displacement sensors. IEEE Trans. Intrum. Meas. **59**(2), 283–291 (2010)
34. Fraden, J.: Handbook of Modern Sensors, 3rd edn. Springer, New York (2004)
35. Kuo, C.H., Dai, J.S.: Robotics for minimally invasive surgery: a historical review. In: Yan, H.S., Ceccarelli, M. (eds.) International Symposium on History of Machines and Mechanisms, pp. 337–354. Springer, Dordrecht (2009). https://doi.org/10.1007/978-1-4020-9485-9_24
36. Dogangil, G., Davies, B.L., Rodriguez y Baena, F.: A review of medical robotics for minimally invasive soft tissue surgery. Proc. Inst. Mech. Eng. Part H: J. Eng. Med. **224**(5), 653–679 (2010)
37. Park, Y.L., Elayaperumal, S., Daniel, B., Ryu, S.C., Shin, M., Savall, J., et al.: Real-time estimation of 3-D needle shape and deflection for MRI-guided interventions. IEEE ASME Trans. Mechatron. **15**, 906–915 (2010)
38. Henken, K., Van Gerwen, D., Dankelman, J., Van Den Dobbelsteen, J.: Accuracy of needle position measurements using fiber Bragg gratings. Minim. Invasive Ther. Allied Technol.: MITAT: Off. J. Soc. Minim. Invasive Ther. **21**, 408–414 (2012)
39. Searle, T.C., Althoefer, K., Seneviratne, L., Liu, H.: An optical curvature sensor for flexible manipulators. In: 2013 IEEE International Conference on Robotics and Automation (ICRA), 6–10 May 2013, pp. 4415–4420 (2013)

Designing Origami-Adapted Deployable Modules for Soft Continuum Arms

Ketao Zhang[(⊠)] and Kaspar Althoefer

Queen Mary University of London, Mile End, London E1 4NS, UK
{ketao.zhang,k.althoefer}@qmul.ac.uk

Abstract. Origami has several attractive attributes including deployability and portability which have been extensively adapted in designs of robotic devices. Drawing inspiration from foldable origami structures, this paper presents an engineering design process for fast making deployable modules of soft continuum arms. The process is illustrated with an example which adapts a modified accordion fold pattern to a lightweight deployable module. Kinematic models of the four-sided Accordion fold pattern is explored in terms of mechanism theory. Taking account of both the kinematic model and the materials selection, a 2D flat sheet model of the four-sided Accordion fold pattern is obtained for 3D printing. Following the design process, the deployable module is then fabricated by laminating 3D printed origami skeleton and flexible thermoplastic polyurethane (TPU) coated fabric. Preliminary tests of the prototype shown that the folding motion are enabled mainly by the flexible fabric between the gaps of thick panels of the origami skeleton and matches the kinematic analysis. The proposed approach has advantages of quick scaling dimensions, cost effective and fast fabricating thus allowing adaptive design according to specific demands of various tasks.

Keywords: Origami-folding · 3D printing · Deployable module

1 Introduction

Origami folding and sculpting techniques transform flat sheet materials such as paper and cardboard into three-dimensional objects following basic and compound folds [1]. With unravelled mathematical and geometrical principles in the attractive art of paper folding [2], artistic origami folding has been sources of inspiration for engineers making innovative machines towards a wide range of engineering applications, where foldability, deployability and portability are sought after. For instance, origami folding are widely adapted in the design of versatile gift boxes in the packaging industry [3]. Taking origami creases as compliant hinges, novel compliant mechanical systems were successfully developed [4,5]. Origami patterns were also adapted in designing thin-walled structures

This work was partially supported by research awards from the Engineering and Physical Sciences Research Council (EPSRC) under grant agreements EP/R02572X/1.

K. Althoefer et al. (Eds.): TAROS 2019, LNAI 11649, pp. 138–147, 2019.
https://doi.org/10.1007/978-3-030-23807-0_12

[6,7], where origami pattern guides deformation and allows energy absorption in crushing process.

By integrating various actuation technologies [8–10], passive origami structures have been adapted to active robotic systems, such as the crawling robot that folds itself from a flat sheet with embedded electronics [11], the self-foldable 3D robot functional for working and swimming [12], robot end-effector for medical devices [13] and self-locking robotic arm that can access confined spaces [14]. Of all these examples, the origami structures have been used as skeletons in place of the conventional mechanical systems composed of rigid links and kinematic pairs.

With recent advancements in materials particularly functional materials and soft filaments suitable with rapid additive manufacturing technologies, origami folds and structures have been adapted to designs of soft robots composed of compliant materials in parallel to the development of robotic systems employing rigid-foldable origami. Drawing inspiration from origami, a design method were developed for building multimaterial based machines and robots [15]. Using 3D printable soft materials (PolyJet^{TM}), a modular origami twisted tower was converted into a 3D printable model, leading to 3D printed semi-soft segments of a robotic manipulator [16]. In a similar way, a soft pneumatic actuator capable of extension and contraction was developed using elastomeric composite with embedded flexible sheets [8]. Most recently, soft and lightweight polymeric films including thermoplastic polyurethane (TPU) and polyethylene (PE) are used as air proof membrane of origami folding inspired soft machines. For example, a design and fabrication method was introduced to make low-cost fluid-driven artificial muscles which employ folded origami structure as skeleton and TPU film as skin [17]. A pneumatic soft robotic arm capable of a large extension and contraction ratio was developed by adapting a quadrilateral origami structure in the design of 3D printable origami exoskeletons of a pneumatic robot arm [18].

In this work, we propose an engineering design process for developing deployable modules of soft continuum arms by adapting foldable origami structures. A modified four-sided accordion fold pattern is taken as an example to demonstrate the presented process and a prototype is fabricated by laminating 3D printed TPU origami skeleton and TPU fabric skin as proof of concept of the deploayable module. The contribution of this work includes (1) engineering design process for origami-folding based deployable modules of soft continuum arms, and (2) a four-sided Accordion fold patterns based deployable module for soft continuum arm.

In the following sections, we first introduce the engineering design process for origami folding inspired deployable modules. Following this process, Sect. 3 presents the kinematic modelling and 3D printable design of a modified four-sided accordion fold pattern. Section 4 details the steps of fabricating the deployable module with 3D printed thick-panel origami skeleton. The paper is then concluded in Sect. 5.

2   The Engineering Design Process of Origami-Inspired Deployable Modules for Soft Continuum Arms

In the past decade, novel design and fabrication technologies of fully-integrated robotic mechanisms have been extensively investigated. Among the emerging technologies for fabricating multi-part and multi-material systems, the origami inspired techniques shed bright light, especially the design methodology and manufacturing process for constructing three-dimensional active structure from two-dimensional flat sheet model. In contrast to the traditionally multi-body systems with disjoint components, the origami-enabled mechanical systems have distinct deployability and foldability which are expected in various practical applications. In this section, we introduce an engineering design process for developing foldable origami structure based deployable modules of soft continuum arms by fusing geometric modelling, materials selection and additive manufacturing (Fig. 1).

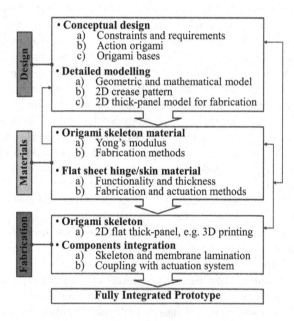

Fig. 1. The process for designing and fabricating foldable origami structure based deployable modules of soft continuum arms with multiple modules.

The design process starts from the conceptual design by defining the constraints and requirements for making an extensible continuum arm. The deployability requires the robot arm to be able to contract into a compact configuration thus adapt to confined space and to elongate in the axial direction thus enable an extended working space. A number of 3D origami structures, including the accordion [19,20], Kresling [19] and Tachi-Miura polyhedron [21], are foldable and match the requirements of extensible continuum arm. With consideration of the materials selection and possible fabrication techniques simultaneously, desired action origami are then selected from the foldable 3D origami structures.

With selected action origami in the conceptual design stage, the origami bases and their corresponding equivalent mechanisms are then extracted for exploiting the geometric and kinematic model in terms of theories of mechanisms. Based on the modelling, geometric parameters of the 2D crease pattern as well as the pre-fabrication flat sheet model are then defined with consideration of thickness of both the origami skeleton panels and thin sheet membranes Fig. 1.

The materials selection is a step bridging the design and fabrication steps. The material of origami skeleton is determined mainly based on the required softness (Young's Modulus in the range of 10^5–10^6 Pa) as well as available fabrication technologies. Further to the origami skeleton, the thin sheet membranes, which are used as flexible hinges or air-tight skin, are selected and in conjunction with fabrication approaches.

The final step is fabrication and integration of the components, including the arm and the actuation system. The origami skeletons are manufactured first using 3D printing and then combined with the thin sheet membrane through techniques including thermal laminating. The prototype is then completed by adding a actuation system which can be an external actuator (air pump and tendons, for example) or embedded actuators made from functional materials.

3   Origami Models of the Four-Sided Accordion Fold Pattern

In this section, we use the four-sided accordion fold pattern [20] as an example origami fold pattern for making a deployable module. The pattern is selected because its large ratio between the stowed and expanded configurations and square-shaped cross-section of the 3D bellow-like structure.

3.1   Kinematic Modelling of the Four-Sided Accordion Fold Pattern

The origami accordion and it's modified version (Fig. 2) can be produced by folding a piece of thin-sheet paper with 2D crease pattern in Fig. 2.

As illustrated in Fig. 2(a), the original accordion pattern consists of identical panels that are in the shape of isosceles trapezium. The origami base of the crease pattern is a symmetric Miura-ori vertex, a degree-4 single-vertex folds where four creases intersect at a same point symmetric with the two co-linear creases. The symmetric Miura-ori vertex folds are assembled with bilateral symmetry and any two adjacent miura-ori vertex folds in a row can be considered as a rectangular tile [2]. By adding fold lines along the vertices of the original accordion pattern based on the method of including additional fold lines [22], it obtains a modified crease pattern in Fig. 2(b), leading to increased expansion of the origami model [20].

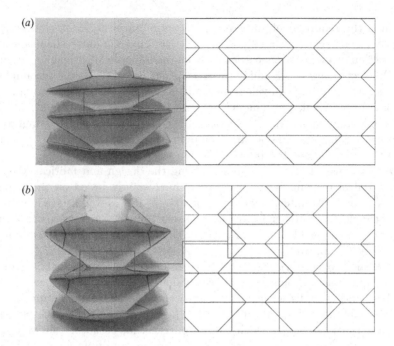

Fig. 2. The four-sided accordion fold pattern. (a) the original 2D crease pattern and 3D model, (b) the modified 2D crease pattern and corresponding 3D model.

Looking closely at the crease pattern of rectangular tile with two symmetric Miura-ori vertex in the accordion fold pattern, the kinematic equivalent of this crease pattern is an assembly of two spherical 4R linkages sharing a common revolute joint (Fig. 3(a)). The kinematic equivalent is a multi-loop linkage and has only one degree-of-freedom (DOF) as the two-spherical 4R linkages are rigidly combined. The multi-loop linkages in Fig. 3(a) is equivalent to a single loop 6R double-centered linkage (Fig. 3(b)). This can be proved by analyzing the geometric constraints of the two linkages. With consideration of the spherical motion at each vertex and the bilateral symmetry of the double-centered linkage, it revealed the linkage has three bifurcated motion branches with one DOF demonstrated by the distinct ways of folding [23].

The double-centered 6R linkage is a single loop mechanism that consists of six links. The product of the transform matrices is equal to the 4×4 unit matrix and the loop-closure equation [24] is expressed as

$$\mathbf{T}_{21}\mathbf{T}_{32}\cdots\mathbf{T}_{65}\mathbf{T}_{16} = \mathbf{I}_4 \tag{1}$$

in which $\mathbf{T}_{(i+1)i}$ is the transformation matrix between ith and $(i+1)$th coordinate frames.

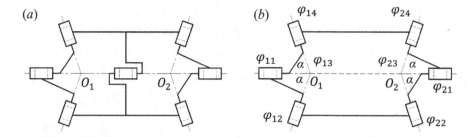

Fig. 3. Equivalent kinematic linkages of a rectangular tile crease pattern with two symmetric Miura-ori vertex folds. (a) a multi-loop linkage, (b) a 6R double-centered linkage.

Considering the bilateral symmetry and shared joint between two spherical centers O_1 and O_2, the relationship of the dihedral angles are given by

$$\varphi_{11} = \varphi_{13}, \varphi_{12} = \varphi_{14} \tag{2}$$

$$\varphi_{21} = \varphi_{23}, \varphi_{22} = \varphi_{24} \tag{3}$$

$$\varphi_{13} = \varphi_{23}, \varphi_{14} = \varphi_{24} \tag{4}$$

and

$$\tan\frac{\varphi_{11}}{2} = \frac{1}{\cos\alpha}\tan\frac{\varphi_{12}}{2}, \tan\frac{\varphi_{21}}{2} = \frac{1}{\cos\alpha}\tan\frac{\varphi_{22}}{2} \tag{5}$$

in which φ_{ij} are the dihedral angles that describe the folding of the origami corresponding to the linkage.

The relationship shows that the symmetric double-centered 6R linkage is flat-foldable. Hence, both the original multi-loop kinematic equivalent and the rectangular tile pattern are flat-foldable.

3.2   3D Printable Flat Sheet Model of the Origami Skeleton

Folding flat sheet material to a 3D origami model, the compliance of the thin sheet material allows deformation in the panels thus enable a fold pattern to move from a deployed state to a compact state even the pattern is not rigid-foldable. In contrast to the origami model made of thin sheet materials, thickness of panels of thick panel origami structures have to be accommodated to account for rigid-foldability [25].

For accommodating the thickness of panels during folding motion, both panel thickness t_p and membrane thickness t_s are taken into account in the design of the 3D printable flat sheet model of the origami skeleton. Following the panel-membrane model [22], the gaps corresponding to mountain and valley creases are calculated as $g_m = 2t_s$ and $g_v = 2t_p + 4t_s$, respectively.

The angle α measured between the adjacent mountain and valley creases is $45°$, which allows the dihedral angle φ_{i3} has a rotation range of $[0, 180°]$.

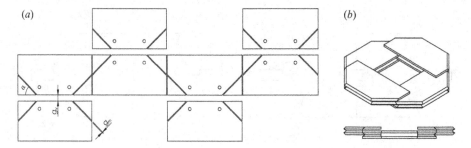

Fig. 4. The modified accordion pattern fold for a single module. (a) the model of the foldable skeleton with panel thickness t_p and membrane skin thickness t_s for 3D printing, (b) the folded compact configuration.

To make one module of the four-sided accordion fold pattern, at least four rectangular tile bases are required and jointed in a sequence as shown in Fig. 4. The kinematic equivalent of this assembly is a mechanism consists of four identical 1-DOF double-centered 6R linkages jointed to each other with rotary hinges, of which the axes are perpendicular to the collinear joint axes passing two spherical centers. Taking all the panels as rigid links, the mechanism is also a 1-DOF system during the folding process. When the dihedral angle φ_{i3} change from $0°$ of the configuration in Fig. 4(a) to $180°$, the mechanism reconfigures to a compact configuration in Fig. 4(b). In this flat-folded configuration, the height of the assembly is purely related to the thickness of the panels and the membrane.

4   Fabrication of the Deployable Module: Skeleton 3D Printing and Membrane Adhesion

With advancement of multi-material additive-manufacturing technologies particularly the 3D printing using soft materials, a number of cost effective approaches have been developed for making both rigid and soft robotic systems [26,27]. In this section, we presents the 3D printed origami skeleton using TPU filament and the fabrication of the deployable module by adhering the foldable skeleton to thin sheet TPU coated fabric.

We use a commercial 3D printer, the Ultimaker 3, with dual 0.4 mm nozzles to print the skeleton structure. The printable filaments including Nylon, ABS, PLA and TPU 95A are considered while all data sheets of materials show that TPU 95A is the only material with flexibility and resistant to wear and tear. The selection of materials for the membrane skin is concurrently considered together with materials for printing origami skeleton. Considering both mechanical properties and compatibility with other materials, a type of air tight TPU coated fabric is selected for the membrane skin.

With the flat sheet model illustrated in Fig. 4, samples of foldable skeleton (Fig. 5) were printed using Ultimaker TPU 95A. In the printing setting, the

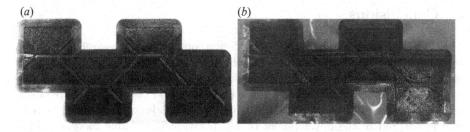

Fig. 5. Fabrication of the deployable module (a) 3D printed foldable skeleton using TPU 95A (black), (b) the laminated material in which the skeleton is adhered to the TPU coated fabric (green). (Color figure online)

adhesion layer is particularly used to maintain the gap assigned to mountain and valley creases thus the geometry of the pattern.

The 3D printed skeleton is then laminated to the TPU coated fabric using a steam iron for preliminary validation of the fabrication process. The welding temperature for laminating the skeleton and the TPU fabric is tested between 120 °C and 200 °C. To achieve best adhesion of the two components, the maximum temperature was used for the materials selected in this paper. Due to the high temperature, the TPU fabric was wrinkled slightly at the area without skeleton (Fig. 5(b)). The final step of the fabrication process is to seal the open creases thus form a four-sided accordion structure made of TPU fabric with 3D printed origami skeleton. As illustrated in Fig. 6(a), the module is in its fully deployed configuration due to the stiffness of the TPU fabric. Apply external force along the axis of the module, it can be passively folded into a partially folded configuration (Fig. 6(b)) and finally the near compact configuration (Fig. 6(c)). It needs to mention that the deformation that occurs in the panels of the compliant models and small motions at the flexible hinges make the module deployable.

Fig. 6. The prototype of the deployable module. (a) the fully deployed configuration, (b) the partially folded configuration, (c) the folded configuration (not flat due to the compliance of the fabric).

5   Conclusions

This paper presented an engineering design process for developing foldable origami based deployable modules of robotic devices with 3D printed origami skeletons. The proposed process concurrently combines conceptual design, detailed design, materials selection and 3D printing and thermal laminate based fabrication phases. Based on the design process, a modified accordion fold pattern is adapted in the development of a lightweight deployable module, which consists of 3D printing origami skeleton and thermoplastic polyurethane (TPU) coated fabric as flexible membrane. The preliminary inspection proves that the 3D printed foldable skeleton enables controllable motion of the deployable module as the foldable motion and compliance are enabled mainly by the flexible membrane between the gaps of origami skeletons panels. The proposed design and fabrication approach is beneficial to scalability of size thus adaptable to different working conditions. The combination of technologies including 3D printing using soft filament and thermal lamination provides a cost effective approach for making deployable soft devices based on additive manufacturing. Future work will focus on developed of a complete robotic arm a number of the deployable modules, integration of actuation system and motion control.

References

1. Kanade, T.: A theory of origami world. Artif. Intell. **13**(3), 279–311 (1980)
2. Lang, R.J.: Origami Design Secrets: Mathematical Methods for an Ancient Art. AK Peters/CRC Press, Natick (2011)
3. Dai, J.S., Jones, J.R.: Kinematics and mobility analysis of carton folds in packing manipulation based on the mechanism equivalent. Proc. Inst. Mech. Eng. Part C: J. Mech. Eng. Sci. **216**(10), 959–970 (2002)
4. Howell, L.L.: Compliant Mechanisms. Wiley, New York (2001)
5. Greenberg, H., Gong, M.L., Magleby, S.P., Howell, L.L.: Identifying links between origami and compliant mechanisms. Mech. Sci. **2**(2), 217–225 (2011)
6. Song, J., Chen, Y., Lu, G.: Axial crushing of thin-walled structures with origami patterns. Thin-Walled Struct. **54**, 65–71 (2012)
7. Ma, J., You, Z.: Energy absorption of thin-walled square tubes with a prefolded origami pattern–part i: geometry and numerical simulation. J. Appl. Mech. **81**(1), 011003 (2014)
8. Martinez, R.V., Fish, C.R., Chen, X., Whitesides, G.M.: Elastomeric origami: programmable paper-elastomer composites as pneumatic actuators. Adv. Funct. Mater. **22**(7), 1376–1384 (2012)
9. An, S.M., Ryu, J., Cho, M., Cho, K.J.: Engineering design framework for a shape memory alloy coil spring actuator using a static two-state model. Smart Mater. Struct. **21**(5), 055009 (2012)
10. Zhang, K., Qiu, C., Dai, J.S.: An extensible continuum robot with integrated origami parallel modules. J. Mech. Robot. **8**(3), 031010 (2016)
11. Felton, S., Tolley, M., Demaine, E., Rus, D., Wood, R.: A method for building self-folding machines. Science **345**(6197), 644–646 (2014)

12. Miyashita, S., Guitron, S., Ludersdorfer, M., Sung, C.R., Rus, D.: An untethered miniature origami robot that self-folds, walks, swims, and degrades. In: 2015 IEEE International Conference on Robotics and Automation (ICRA), pp. 1490–1496. IEEE (2015)

13. Salerno, M., Zhang, K., Menciassi, A., Dai, J.S.: A novel 4-DOF origami grasper with an SMA-actuation system for minimally invasive surgery. IEEE Trans. Robot. **32**(3), 484–498 (2016)

14. Kim, S.J., Lee, D.Y., Jung, G.P., Cho, K.J.: An origami-inspired, self-locking robotic arm that can be folded flat. Sci. Robot. **3**(16), eaar2915 (2018)

15. Zhakypov, Z., Paik, J.: Design methodology for constructing multimaterial origami robots and machines. IEEE Trans. Robot. **34**(1), 151–165 (2018)

16. Liu, T., Wang, Y., Lee, K.: Three-dimensional printable origami twisted tower: design, fabrication, and robot embodiment. IEEE Robot. Autom. Lett. **3**(1), 116–123 (2018)

17. Li, S., Vogt, D.M., Rus, D., Wood, R.J.: Fluid-driven origami-inspired artificial muscles. Proc. Natl. Acad. Sci. **114**(50), 13132–13137 (2017). https://doi.org/10.1073/pnas.1713450114

18. Zhang, K., Zhu, Y., Lou, C., Zheng, P., Kovač, M.: A design and fabrication approach for pneumatic soft robotic arms using 3D printed origami skeletons. In: The 2019 IEEE International Conference on Soft Robotics (RoboSoft 2019), pp. 1–7. IEEE (2019)

19. Guest, S.D., Pellegrino, S.: The folding of triangulated cylinders, part i: geometric considerations. J. Appl. Mech. **61**(4), 773–777 (1994)

20. Morgan, J., Magleby, S.P., Howell, L.L.: An approach to designing origami-adapted aerospace mechanisms. J. Mech. Des. **138**(5), 052301 (2016)

21. Tachi, T., Miura, K.: Rigid-foldable cylinders and cells. J. Int. Assoc. Shell Spat. Struct. **53**(4), 217–226 (2012)

22. Zirbel, S.A., et al.: Accommodating thickness in origami-based deployable arrays. J. Mech. Des. **135**(11), 111005 (2013)

23. Zhang, K., Dai, J.S.: Classification of origami-enabled foldable linkages and emerging applications. In: ASME 2013 International Design Engineering Technical Conferences and Computers and Information in Engineering Conference, p. V06BT07A024. American Society of Mechanical Engineers (2013)

24. Chen, Y., Feng, H., Ma, J., Peng, R., You, Z.: Symmetric waterbomb origami. Proc. R. Soc. A: Math. Phys. Eng. Sci. **472**(2190), 20150846 (2016)

25. Chen, Y., Peng, R., You, Z.: Origami of thick panels. Science **349**(6246), 396–400 (2015)

26. MacCurdy, R., Katzschmann, R., Kim, Y., Rus, D.: Printable hydraulics: a method for fabricating robots by 3D co-printing solids and liquids, pp. 3878–3885, May 2016. https://doi.org/10.1109/ICRA.2016.7487576

27. Zhang, K., et al.: Bioinspired design of a landing system with soft shock absorbers for autonomous aerial robots. J. Field Robot. https://doi.org/10.1002/rob.21840

A Debris Clearance Robot for Extreme Environments

Craig West[1], Farshad Arvin[2(✉)], Wei Cheah[2], Andrew West[2], Simon Watson[2], Manuel Giuliani[1], and Barry Lennox[2]

[1] Bristol Robotics Laboratory, University of the West of England, Bristol, UK
`craig.west@uwe.ac.uk`
[2] Robotics for Extreme Environments Lab at the School of Electrical and Electronic Engineering, The University of Manchester, Manchester, UK
{`farshad.arvin,barry.lennox`}`@manchester.ac.uk`

Abstract. The need for nuclear decommissioning is increasing globally, as power stations and other facilities utilising nuclear reaches the end of their operational life. Currently the majority of decommissioning tasks are carried out by workers in protective air fed suits, which is slow, expensive and dangerous. The work presented here is the early stages in the development of a flexible mobile manipulator platform, combining a Clearpath Husky, a Universal UR5 manipulator and various sensors. The system will be used for research specifically in the area of exploration of contaminated environments, map building to aid in task planning, and also to investigate manipulation for waste sorting. The aim is to develop a system that can, in the short term, be used in real world tasks but longer term function as a research platform to allow continued research and development. As well as developing a hardware platform, a detailed simulation model is also being developed to allow testing of algorithms in simulation before being deployed on hardware. The use of the simulation model for operator training is also an area that will be investigated in the future. This article focuses on the planned work for developing the system, as well as discussing the progress on the simulation model.

Keywords: Exploration · Autonomous · Extreme environments ·
Nuclear · Simulation · Mobile robots

1 Introduction

Nuclear decommissioning often involves working in areas contaminated with high levels of radiation, where human entry is only possible with the use of protective air fed suits. The use of air fed suits require a team of people to put on and take off, and following the use of the suit it becomes contaminated waste which

This work was supported by EPSRC RNE (No. EP/P01366X/1) project and UK Research and Innovation via the TORONE consortium (EP/P018505/1). The second author would like to thank EPSRC Impact Acceleration Account (EP/R511626/1).

© Springer Nature Switzerland AG 2019
K. Althoefer et al. (Eds.): TAROS 2019, LNAI 11649, pp. 148–159, 2019.
https://doi.org/10.1007/978-3-030-23807-0_13

needs to be disposed of accordingly. Besides being costly and time consuming, the working time for the operators wearing these protective suits are limited due to the radiation risk [1]. These are contributing factors to why nuclear decommissioning is expensive, slow and dangerous. Nonetheless, nuclear decommissioning remains a critical task that needs to be undertaken.

The need for decommissioning is in fact increasing as more facilities are approaching the end of their operational life. One such example is the Sellafield site in the UK, where the Thermal Oxide Reprocessing Plan (THORP) has been recently shut down, and the Magnox reprocessing plant is due for closure before 2020 [10]. These facilities potentially contain a variety of contaminated materials.

It is required that the contamination level of items in these areas is confidently identified so that the items can be processed and sorted accordingly. There are four levels of radiation contamination, High level, Intermediate level, low level, very low level [18] and each level requires different handling. For example very low level waste can be disposed of with normal rubbish, but low level waste needs to be stored in special near surface or below surface facilities. Therefore misclasifying waste has a significant impact on costs, also if the contamination level can not be confidently determined it has to be treated as higher level further impacting costs and time scales.

With this in mind, this work aims to develop a mobile manipulator platform for remote operation in these hazardous areas. By combining a mobile base with a manipulator, namely a Clearpath Husky robot [3] with a Universal Robots UR5 robot arm [17], a platform that can operate remotely, indoors, and perform a variety of useful tasks will be created.

Fig. 1. V-REP simulation of a Clearpath Husky robot with a UR5 robot arm mounted to it.

1.1   Robot Platform

The Husky was chosen for being a good compromise between its small size and maneuverability for operating in confined or cluttered spaces, whilst still large enough to mount a manipulator and other sensors. For example, its small size allows it to traverse through doorways, under tables, and also over small obstacles or uneven terrain that may be encountered in a nuclear facility. The Universal UR5 arm is compact enough to be mounted on the Husky (see Fig. 1) and has a payload of 5 kg, which is useful for real-world manipulation tasks. The manipulator is also widely supported manipulator and is available off-the-shelf in an integrated package with the Husky.

Applications for this system will range from visual inspection and mapping, to manipulation and waste sorting. This will give operators a view inside these hazardous facilities, some of which have not been entered for many years, allowing necessary tasks to be identified and a decommissioning plan to be constructed. The same system can be used for task such as moving and sorting waste material, or collecting samples. There is also the potential to fit specialist tools as the manipulator's end-effector, such as a saw for cutting large waste items to downsize it for storage. Although this has potential to cause other issues, such as creating contaminated dust, so is an area that would require further consideration.

1.2   Challenges

The challenges presented by these environments extend beyond the obvious radiation risks, and include:

- chemical hazards
- operating in confined spaces
- operating in potentially unknown environments as some facilities have been closed for many years
- communication challenges presented by thick steel re-enforced concrete walls
- materials may have perished over time for example metal rusting which may affect the handling of objects.

The dangers posed by these hazards can be minimized by the use of robotic systems instead as the environment is dangerous, unknown and potentially unpredictable. Even so, these environments do pose a challenge for robotic systems. Communication between robot and user is of utmost importance in the target deployment scenario. However, the work environment results in unreliable wireless communication. Hence, a tether is proposed in this work to allow communication between the operator and the robot. This also gives the advantage of extending operation time beyond the limited on-board battery. As such, part of this work is to develop a tether management system that will consider the tether during path planning and aim to avoid problems other tethered robots have faced. This is discussed below.

Another challenge that has to be considered with the deployment of robots in radiation contaminated environment is what happens to the robot post operation, or if it breaks. The robot will have become radiologically contaminated and thus requires a complete radiation cleanup which is very difficult and often deemed not worth the time and cost. More commonly, contaminated systems are disposed of which in turn creates more contaminated waste that needs to be disposed off. This forms part of the motivation for developing a flexible system that can perform a variety of tasks rather than a highly specialised robot for one particular task. A system that can operate for a prolonged period and perform a range of tasks could be very beneficial to the decommissioning industry.

With these considerations in mind, we chose to make use of proven off-the-shelf components to create the mobile manipulator platform, rather than an entirely bespoke solution. This approach will yield a reliable system which is of high importance for the target application. The system will also be modular, allowing parts such as sensors to be easily replaced if they get damaged. Although the replacement of parts requires human intervention, this approach is able to extend the lifetime of the system, reducing both cost and further contaminated waste.

2   Background

The use of mobile robots in the nuclear industry is not a new idea, [16] gives a detailed review of mobile robots deployed in the nuclear industry over the last few decades. Many robots used previously have been used in response to accidents such as at Chernobyl or Fukushima, with relatively few robots being used in decommissioning tasks. A similar platform to the one discussed here has also been developed by the Nuclear and Applied Robotics Group at the University of Texas at Austin, called Vaultbot [14]. Their system combines a Husky with dual UR5 manipulators. However their system required extensive modification of the Husky platform to allow two manipulators to be fitted, and being battery powered it has a short run time. In contrast our system requires almost no modification and so is kept modular and retains the mean time between failure (MTBF) of the off-the-shelf hardware. It will also utilise a tether with a novel tether management system, allowing extended periods of operation and maintain communication in environments where wireless communication is unreliable.

The main contributions of this work come from the combination of expertise from different UK Institutions to create:

- A reliable mobile platform with semi-autonomous grasping abilities
- A tether management system to prevent cable tangling with obstacles
- An intuitive user interface that is effective and simple to use, shared by the real hardware and simulation model
- An accurate simulation model, which somewhat uniquely, includes the tether in the model

The platform will be developed focusing on real world challenges but will also allow novel research into areas such as grasping, manipulation and human robot interfaces. The aim is to develop a system that in the short term can be deployed in the real world, and with minimal operator training be used by nuclear industry workers, whilst simultaneously in the longer term be used as a research platform to develop industry relevant functionality. Another benefit of using off-the-shelf components is that the platform can be replicated at each of the partner institutions, allowing research in different aspects to be carried out in parallel to each other.

As such the first iteration will use a direct teleoperation system for both the mobile base and the manipulator. This will allow the basic system to be assembled with the various sensors integrated and tested. Once the basic system is working other areas can be investigated such as semi-autonomous algorithms for both the mobile base and the manipulator as well as different user interfaces.

There is also scope to use the platform for further research into, for example, human factors experiments, studying the effects of different sensors on ease of tele-operation, or different input methods and levels of automation. This could involve carrying out a series of tests with different cameras attached, e.g. a fixed camera, fixed stereo cameras, pan-tilt camera system, fish eye or 360 camera, and also comparing between on screen images with the use of a VR headset. To investigate different input methods and levels of automation, a study comparing e.g. keyboard tele-operation, game pad control and point and click interactive target markers could also be carried out. These two areas overlap, as the control method has a direct impact on the information required by the operator.

A reliable communication link between a remote inspection robot and operators is invaluable. In nuclear environments, the thick concrete walls designed to shield against ionising radiation attenuate most radio signals as to become unusable, thus making wireless communications impractical in most cases.

A wired connection between the robot and operators offers a reliable and usable solution to the problem of data transfer. The major drawback is the additional weight, mechanical complexity, and the threat of a cable tether becoming tangled or caught on obstacles, incapacitating the robot. The latter ended remote robotic inspection operations of Unit 2 at the Fukushima Daiichi Nuclear Power Plant. The tether management system became jammed, immobilising the Quince 1 robot [9], resulting in loss of communications and the robot had to be abandoned [20]. Tether management for this robot was sited as the most significant problem faced for inspection of Unit 2 and 3.

Mechanical considerations can be made to try minimise tangling events, but robot path planning can play an important role in avoiding tether crossing and minimising cable length. Previous work on path planning of single tethered robots have concentrated on minimising cable length for a given goal position, with the tether fixed to a base position [19].

The majority of work on single tethered robot path planning has allowed for the robot to cross it's tether if it would result in the shortest path (so-called semi-planar, compared to purely planar where no crossing occurs) [2, 7, 8, 13, 19].

In real-world robotic deployment scenarios crossing of a communications cable could lead to wear and damage of the tether, as well as risk of tangling.

It is common for robots to utilise an occupancy grid [15] for obstacle mapping and path planning due to the ubiquity of the Robot Operating System (ROS) [12] and it's native navigation stack [6]. The solutions proposed in previous works require absolute knowledge of all obstacles, and the ability to describe them as a polygon with a centre [7]. As obstacles are typically identified as locations where an instrument such as lidar or depth camera has encountered an object, then marked on a costmap, it is not readily possible to fully identify and describe every distinct obstacle as required by these algorithms.

Existing algorithms further require full knowledge of an obstacle map to be able to compute possible paths, ultimately making requests for path planning quicker. This pre-computation can take tens of minutes [8], but in an unknown environment, an obstacle map may be updated on the order of every few seconds. Computation time of an hour before being able to make a path planning request is infeasible for every time the map is updated. Finally, these algorithms minimise path length of the tether, a consequence is that the tether comes into direct contact with obstacles, under the assumption the cable can be pulled taut. This acts to minimise cable length, however, in unstructured and cluttered nuclear environments, it would be an unacceptable risk to possibly move or topple an obstacle which may contain contaminated waste.

A path planner for a single tethered robot for unstructured nuclear environments would need to avoid direct contact of obstacles with the tether, forbid crossing of the tether at the expense of time or cable length, be able to adapt to changes in the obstacle map with minimal computational overhead, and cope with a gridded costmap representation of obstacles in the environment.

To test such a path planner, it is advantageous to use a robot simulation which can mimic not only robot motion, but most importantly the dynamics of the tether.

3 Simulation

Whilst the hardware is purchased and assembled to create the mobile manipulator, a simulation model has been created using the V-REP simulation software [4]. V-REP was chosen based on the recommendations of previous work by Pitonakova et al. [11], which compared the performance of different simulation environments. The Clearpath Husky model is not included in V-REP, however a CAD file of the complete Husky is available from Clearpath, and so this was used as a base to create the assembly for the simulation model. The finished model has a UR5 manipulator, which is readily available in V-REP, attached as shown in Fig. 1. Due to the detail in this model, particularly the geometry of the tyres, the physics based simulation runtime was very slow, and so a simplified version was also created as shown in Fig. 2. While this version has simplified geometry, properties such as mass and friction are maintained so the dynamic behaviour of the real system is still represented closely.

Both of these models can be integrated through V-REP with ROS, eliminating code porting issues between the real and simulated robot. This allows new algorithms to be quickly and safely developed in simulation before being deployed on the hardware. It also allows the possibility of operator training on a simulated robot, using the same control interface, before using the hardware. This could be particularly useful where following an exploration and mapping stage, the real environment can be simulated, allowing navigation or manipulation tasks to be evaluated prior to executing the same tasks in the real world.

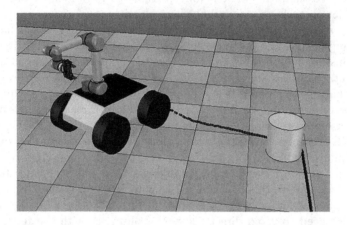

Fig. 2. Simplified model of Clearpath Husky in V-REP with UR5 mounted and power/communication tether attached.

3.1   Tether Simulation

As part of the simulation, a tether has also been created, shown in Fig. 2 (note that the tether can be added to the detailed model also). Again, V-REP does not include cables in the model library hence it has been developed from the ground up. The tether was created by forming a kinematic chain of small cylinders connected by joints. Each cylinder has physical properties such as mass and friction and each joint, as well as providing flexibility, acts as spring damper system. Tuning these parameters allowed realistic cable behaviour to be achieved as a result of the physics engine in V-REP, as illustrated in Fig. 3 where the cable can be seen sagging either side of the solid block and being pulled onto the motorized drum.

The tether is fixed to the rear of the platform and having both mass and friction acts realistically as it is dragged along the floor. To the authors current knowledge there are no examples of a tether being included in a mobile robot simulation, despite the impact it has on the path planning and the effect on dynamic properties from dragging a cable along the floor that can snag or interact with obstacles. Including the tether in the simulation also allows the tether management solution to be evaluated as it is developed, facilitating rapid and safe development.

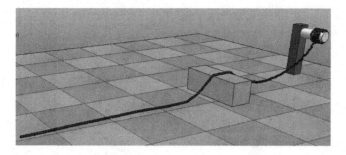

Fig. 3. Example from testing the cable, cable is wound onto a motorized drum whilst being dragged over block.

3.2   Hardware Configuration

During the development of the simulation model it became apparent that the placement of the manipulator has a noticeable effect on the performance of the system. Results of an initial investigation placing the manipulator at the front, middle and rear of the simulated Husky and monitoring the XY position of the robot when given identical motor inputs are shown in Fig. 4. This is an area that needs further investigation as the difference seems much larger than would be expected. It is assumed that the difference is caused by the change in the robot's centre of mass affecting traction. Results such as these show one of the benefits of simulation, these effects can be easily investigated by changing the robot configuration, which would be a significant undertaking with the real hardware.

To determine whether this difference is exaggerated in the simulation a test using the real Husky will be carried out when the hardware is available. The results shown here are with the manipulator static, so the manipulator moving whilst the base is moving would potentially have a large effect on performance. This may have an impact on the control of the system when objects are being carried, for example it may be required that the manipulator remains static whilst the base is moving, as such understanding if this is as noticeable on the real robot is important. On the other hand, using a SLAM algorithm and semi autonomous navigation may provide enough performance to mitigate the effect. Testing on the real hardware is necessary to better understand the issue and will also help to improve the simulation model, narrowing the reality gap.

Another area that is currently being investigated is what sensors are needed on the robot. It is desirable to keep the system as simple as possible whilst also making it capable enough to be easily controllable and with some semi-autonomous behaviours. It is anticipated that at a minimum a 2D Lidar, a camera and a radiation sensor will be needed. The 2D Lidar will allow SLAM (Simultaneous localisation and mapping) so that the environment can be navigated. A camera on the Husky will allow the operator to see what the robot can see, this is essential for tele-operation. Additionally using stereo or depth cameras would allow a 3D point cloud of the environment to be created which would aid planning of tasks and visualizing the area. It is also likely a second

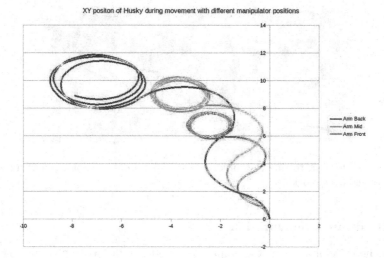

Fig. 4. Initial results showing XY position of the platform, with the same motor input, for 3 different manipulator mounting locations.

camera would be needed on the manipulator, to act as an eye in hand camera to allow grasping. A radiation sensor would allow both monitoring of the environment to identify radiation level and also aid in separating items into high and low level waste. Date from the radiation sensor could potentially be combined with a 3D point cloud, to give a 3D environment map showing areas of contamination. Having the detailed simulation model allows different configurations and positioning of sensors to be tested, this will give a greater level of confidence when assembling the hardware as we can test that one sensor placement doesn't occlude another and that all the desired sensors fit on the platform for example.

3.3   User Interface

The simulation model being integrated with ROS allows different combinations of sensors to be tested in simulated environment and the output to be displayed in RVIZ as it would be with real hardware sensors. This allows quickly testing different sensor combinations and seeing the output on the user interface before implementing with expensive hardware. An example of this is shown in Fig. 5, which shows the combined output of a simulated 2D Lidar and a low resolution depth camera (64 × 64 pixel) in a simulated corridor. The 2D Lidar data is used with a SLAM algorithm, currently GMapping [5], to produce a 2D map of the area and the depth camera creates a 3D point cloud. The investigation into different sensor combinations is ongoing, and more work is required to identify suitable sensors. A user study may be carried out to identify what data the operators want which can then help identify necessary sensors.

Using this simulation model and data from simulated sensors work has begun on looking at simple user interfaces for teleoperating the platform. This currently

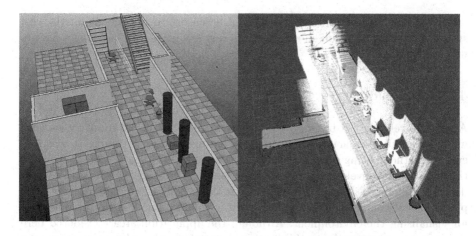

Fig. 5. (left) initial test scene created in VREP (right) Simulated 2D lidar and depth sensor data combined in Rviz. Created by the mobile platform moving in a straight line in a single direction in simulation.

has focused on getting the data from the simulated sensors published to ROS so it can be used and displayed elsewhere, and mimics the real system, for this purpose the output from a camera mounted on the front of the platform is shown alongside the map created from Lidar and 3D point cloud data, and the operator controls the platform using standard ROS keyboard teleoperation. An example of the current interface is shown in Fig. 6. This was mainly developed to test the integration of the simulation with ROS and is not intended as a final user interface. Using the simulation model different user interfaces can now be developed, using different combinations of simulated sensors. These can then be

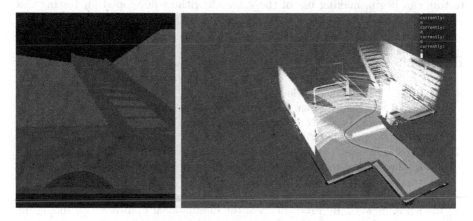

Fig. 6. Snapshot of user interface, showing view from front mounted camera on the left and generated 3D map to the right.

evaluated and inform the decision on which sensors to implement on the real system, which could result in a significant cost saving as only necessary sensors will need buying.

4   Conclusion

A need for reliable flexible robotic systems within the nuclear industry is clear, with the number of facilities requiring decommissioning continuing to rise and current methods being slow, expensive and dangerous. This paper has focused on the plans for the development of a mobile manipulator platform for use in nuclear decommissioning tasks, which is currently in the early stages of development. The platform will combine a mobile base with a manipulator and multiple sensors for visualising the environment. Although the application area considered here is a nuclear one, a flexible mobile manipulator platform could be used in many different areas and so this work could in the future be adapted to other areas.

Details of the simulation model, developed by the present author, are given and some initial results of testing the simulation presented, including a simulated tether and visualisation of combined sensor data. This model will allow testing of different sensor combinations in simulation so the right choice can be made when implemented on hardware, as well as testing of different user interfaces, new control algorithms and novel tether management and path planning systems. There is also potential to use the model for training of new operators as it will share a control interface with the hardware platform, and real environments can be recreated after being mapped in 3D.

Next steps include investigating tele-operation interfaces such as joystick or game-pad controllers and implementing one for the simulation model, this together with the sensor output will allow work on the user interface to begin. At the same time the hardware can be assembled to make the platform and testing can begin, making use of the same algorithms developed for testing the simulation model thanks to both systems using ROS.

References

1. Bayliss, C., Langley, K.: Nuclear Decommissioning, Waste Management, and Environmental Site Remediation. Elsevier, Amsterdam (2003)
2. Brass, P., Vigan, I., Xu, N.: Shortest path planning for a tethered robot. Comput. Geom. **48**(9), 732–742 (2015)
3. Clearpath Robots: Husky-unmanned ground vehicle (2013). https://www.clearpathrobotics.com/husky-unmanned-ground-vehicle-robot/. Accessed 14 Dec 2018
4. Rohmer, E., Singh, S.P.N., Freese, M.: V-REP: a versatile and scalable robot simulation framework. In: Proceedings of the International Conference on Intelligent Robots and Systems (IROS) (2013)
5. Grisetti, G., Stachniss, C., Burgard, W.: Improved techniques for grid mapping with rao-blackwellized particle filters. IEEE Trans. Robot. **23**(1), 34–46 (2007)

6. Guimarães, R.L., de Oliveira, A.S., Fabro, J.A., Becker, T., Brenner, V.A.: ROS navigation: concepts and tutorial. In: Koubaa, A. (ed.) Robot Operating System (ROS). SCI, vol. 625, pp. 121–160. Springer, Cham (2016). https://doi.org/10.1007/978-3-319-26054-9_6

7. Kim, S., Bhattacharya, S., Kumar, V.: Path planning for a tethered mobile robot. In: 2014 IEEE International Conference on Robotics and Automation (ICRA). IEEE (2014)

8. Kim, S., Likhachev, M.: Path planning for a tethered robot using multi-heuristic a* with topology-based heuristics. In: 2015 IEEE/RSJ International Conference on Intelligent Robots and Systems (IROS), pp. 4656–4663. IEEE (2015)

9. Nagatani, K., et al.: Redesign of rescue mobile robot quince. In: 2011 IEEE International Symposium on Safety, Security, and Rescue Robotics, pp. 13–18 (2011)

10. NDA and Innovate UK: Robots compete in nuclear decommissioning challenge, January 2018. https://www.gov.uk/government/news/robots-compete-in-nuclear-decommissioning-challenge. Accessed 10 Dec 2018

11. Pitonakova, L., Giuliani, M., Pipe, A., Winfield, A.: Feature and performance comparison of the V-REP, Gazebo and ARGoS robot simulators. In: Giuliani, M., Assaf, T., Giannaccini, M.E. (eds.) TAROS 2018. LNCS (LNAI), vol. 10965, pp. 357–368. Springer, Cham (2018). https://doi.org/10.1007/978-3-319-96728-8_30

12. Quigley, M., et al.: ROS: an open-source robot operating system. In: ICRA Workshop on Open Source Software (2009)

13. Salzman, O., Halperin, D.: Optimal motion planning for a tethered robot: efficient preprocessing for fast shortest paths queries. In: 2015 IEEE International Conference on Robotics and Automation (ICRA). IEEE (2015)

14. Sharp, A., Kruusamäe, K., Ebersole, B., Pryor, M.: Semiautonomous dual-arm mobile manipulator system with intuitive supervisory user interfaces. In: 2017 IEEE Workshop on Advanced Robotics and its Social Impacts (ARSO), pp. 1–6. IEEE (2017)

15. Thrun, S., Burgard, W., Fox, D.: Probabilistic Robotics (Intelligent Robotics and Autonomous Agents series). The MIT Press (2005)

16. Tsitsimpelis, I., Taylor, C.J., Lennox, B., Joyce, M.J.: A review of ground-based robotic systems for the characterization of nuclear environments. Prog. Nucl. Energy 111, 109–124 (2019)

17. Universal Robots: UR5 technical specifications (2014). https://www.universal-robots.com/media/50588/ur5_en.pdf. Accessed 14 Dec 2018

18. World Nuclear Association: Radioactive waste management, April 2018. http://www.world-nuclear.org/information-library/nuclear-fuel-cycle/nuclear-wastes/radioactive-waste-management.aspx

19. Xavier, P.: Shortest path planning for a tethered robot or an anchored cable. In: Proceedings 1999 IEEE International Conference on Robotics and Automation (Cat. No. 99CH36288C). IEEE (1999)

20. Yoshida, T., Nagatani, K., Tadokoro, S., Nishimura, T., Koyanagi, E.: Improvements to the rescue robot quince toward future indoor surveillance missions in the Fukushima Daiichi nuclear power plant. In: Yoshida, K., Tadokoro, S. (eds.) Field and Service Robotics. STAR, vol. 92, pp. 19–32. Springer, Heidelberg (2014). https://doi.org/10.1007/978-3-642-40686-7_2

Dynamic Response Characteristics in Variable Stiffness Soft Inflatable Links

Ahmad Ali, Kaspar Althoefer, and Jelizaveta Konstantinova[(✉)]

The Centre for Advanced Robotics @ Queen Mary (ARQ),
Queen Mary University of London, London, UK
{ahmad.w.ali, j.konstantinova}@qmul.ac.uk

Abstract. In soft robotics, there is the fundamental need to develop devices that are flexible and can change stiffness in order to work safely in the vicinity of humans. Moreover, these structures must be rigid enough to withstand the force application and accuracy in motion. To solve these issues, previous research proposed to add a compliance element between motor and load – Series Elastic Actuators (SEAs). This approach benefits from improved force control and shock tolerance due to the elasticity introduced at joint level. However, series compliance at the joint level comes at the cost of inferior position controllability and additional mechanical complexity. In this research, we move the elastic compliance to the link, and evaluate the characteristics of variable stiffness soft inflatable links. The detailed investigation of the dynamic behaviour of inflatable link takes into consideration different internal pressures and applied loads. Our results demonstrate that the use of soft inflatable links leads to good weight lifting capability whilst preserving compliance which is beneficial for safety critical applications.

Keywords: Dynamic response · Variable stiffness ·
Inflatable soft link · Human-robot interaction

1 Introduction

In the last few years, there has been a growing interest in the development of soft robots. Soft robots feature compliance as the fundamental property in their structure. Traditional industrial robots are made of rigid components that have a remarkable performance in position controllability, high speed precision and large force output [1]. However, in other scenarios such as when it is required to perform tasks in a complex and nonstationary environment, as well as working in shared space with the human workers, rigid-bodies robots have disadvantages due to the lack of compliance, elasticity and safety. The introduction of elasticity in the robotic systems enables them to store and release energy at the time of need. This paradigm shift was introduced with the works of Hogan et al. on impedance [2], and of Pratt and Williamson on the concept of Series Elastic Actuators (SEAs) [3]. Their concept introduces an elastic element with constant stiffness between the gear and the actuator output. SEA minimizes the potential of injury in case of any contact with the environment and enables robotic manipulators to exhibit compliance in safe mode [4]. SEAs provide

© Springer Nature Switzerland AG 2019
K. Althoefer et al. (Eds.): TAROS 2019, LNAI 11649, pp. 160–170, 2019.
https://doi.org/10.1007/978-3-030-23807-0_14

improvements for many realistic tasks such as shock tolerance, fidelity in force controllability and interaction with the environment. Recently some robotic devices, such
as Sawyer or Baxter, introduce the use of inherently compliant actuators based on the
concept of SEAs [5]. These commercially available robots are certified to work in the
vicinity of human workers, hence stretching the frontiers of robotic systems. Usually,
all SEAs are composed of a traditional electric motor in series with an elastic element
(typically a spring) that, in turn, is connected to a robotic link. However, numerous
expensive spring designs that are proposed in literature to realize the compact series
elastic actuator result in high cost [6]. Moreover, this concept requires additional
systems to modulate their stiffness in order to ensure shared autonomy factory environments with the human worker.

In recent years, research on soft robots has become very popular as such devices
provide solutions to the issues of elasticity, compliance and safety. Therefore, there is a
great potential for applications that require human-robot interaction in shared workspace. Soft robotic devices feature the inherit compliance over the whole structure
rather than only at their joints as it is the case for SEAs. The natural compliance
observed in biological organisms plays a central role in the exploration of novel soft
robotic designs: the dexterity of natural limbs such as the trunk of the elephant [7, 8],
the tentacle of the octopus [9] or the complex body motion of the snake [10, 11]. These
biological systems are rarely composed of rigid mechanical components, but they
generally make use of soft, elastic, and flexible materials in order to survive in complex
unstructured environment [12, 13]. Therefore, soft robots are often made from soft,
rubber or silicone-based polymers and fabrics that can enable complex body poses for
whole-body manipulation and articulated movements in constrained environment [14].

However, so far too little attention has been paid to consider robot links that can
change their stiffness to achieve compliance with the environment. The compliance in
the links support the idea of autonomous sharing of the robot working space with the
human workers. The inclusion of elasticity in the robotic link can replace the use of
high-cost components relating to the SEA with a single inexpensive component: an
inflatable, stiffness-controllable link made from low cost materials. Moreover, sensing
the force at the link level has more significant advantages over the force sensing
capability in a SEA which is at actuator level. Also, the robotic links with changing
stiffness can respond promptly to any contact (either a perturbation or required interaction) at the environment level.

Current studies of variable stiffness soft robots are scarce with regards to soft
inflatable links. Most collaborative robots are based on SEA implementations which
add more complex mechanism near the actuators at joint level [15]. Our simple soft-
link design provides a lightweight, low-cost solution with an opportunity to change
stiffness at the link level. A continuum silicon-based soft manipulator was suggested to
achieve change in stiffness via pneumatic pressure and tendons [16]. The experimental
results showed that actuation mechanisms with tendons considerably increase load
bearing capability. Although tendon-based solutions provide good control in position
and orientation of manipulator, it lacks stiffness controllability. A variable stiffness link
(VSL) concept was proposed with inherently elastic properties to work in a human-
robot friendly environment [14]. These links are made of a number of chambers
independently inflated in order to make them stiffer.

Although the soft robotic approach has been seen many optimized designs for inflatable links, there are a number of limitations that researchers in this field are trying to overcome. Due to the deformability of soft robots, the modelling and control is more complex in comparison with their rigid counterparts [17]. This directly relates to what is widely considered as one of the core challenges of soft robotics: the stiffening of soft structures [18]. In the search for the right trade-off between desired compliance and exertable force, researchers explore numerous approaches to enable on-demand stiffness tuning of soft robots [19]. In addition, lightweight elastic links have challenging position control. Therefore, in this paper we investigate the dynamic behavior of soft and inflatable links under applied load and for different levels of pressure. The experiments reported here were designed to access the practicalities of using lightweight, low-cost inflatable link instead of rigid-link by taking into account the vibration analysis. In this article, we propose and investigate the dynamic behavior of a variable stiffness link (VSL) that is composed of an inner inflatable circular chamber and an outer layer of soft material.

This paper is organized as follows. First, we present the design and fabrication of VSL in Sect. 2. The analytical modelling of the dynamic behavior for different pressure levels is presented in the Sect. 3. The description of experimental setup and results is presented Sect. 4. Section 5 concludes our work, discussing the results obtained in the experiments and highlighting the achievements in developing soft inflatable links.

2 Design and Fabrication of Variable Stiffness Links (VSLs)

In this section, we describe the general principles of the design of VSL. In addition, the fabrication method of VSLs for the evaluation studies of the dynamic response is presented. Previously, our group has presented the design of the variable stiffness link in [15]. In that work, silicone is chosen as the base material/layer where a plastic mesh (polypropylene) with diamond shaped texture is incorporated. The composite material of silicon and plastic mesh create an inflatable chamber for pneumatic pressure that can change its stiffness based on the internal pneumatic pressure. In addition, non-stretchable fabric material is used as an outer skin to constrain the expansion of the soft silicone. The outer skin plays an important role in the stiffening of link as it puts the boundary conditions to avoid any ballooning of the internal elastic chamber and holds up the maximum expansion allowing to increase the stiffness.

In this work, we focus on understanding the dynamic responses of the VSL, and, hence, we employ a similar design concept when manufacturing our VSL prototypes. The proposed inflatable link is composed of two main structural elements: a circular inner chamber to encapsulate the pneumatic pressure and an outer skin layer. The component details of the soft inflatable link are depicted in Fig. 1. The inner chamber is made from a circular-shaped butyl rubber. This material is airtight and typically used as an inner bladder for sports equipment, such as balls. Several types of the outer material were tested for the outer skin, such as ripstop fabric, neoprene, leather and polythene membrane. The outer layer is wrapped around the inner chamber and fixed at the both ends of the link to ensure airtightness. Hard 3D printed circular caps from lightweight plastic are used to plug the ends of link. In addition, the ends caps are padded with rubber, sealed with a silicone glue and clamped with metal rings. The air supply tube is fixed at one end of the link. Further on, air is used to inflate the tube and to increase its stiffness.

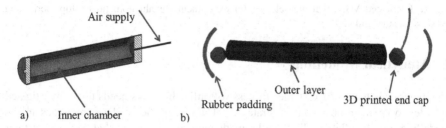

Fig. 1. Design concept of the variable stiffness link: (a) cross-section of the link showing the inner circular chamber; and (b) exploded view of the VSL, showing the main components of the outer layer, and the 3D printed end cups with the rubber paddings for air tightness.

In order to fabricate the inflatable link, an inner tube with a diameter of 38 mm and a length of 400 mm is selected. The outer skin of the link is fabricated from a rectangular sheet of material, including ripstop fabric and suede leather. The width of the sheet is 70 mm; which is shaped into a cylinder by wrapping the sheet around the circular end-caps. As a result, the fully inflated tube is 40 mm in diameter, and 400 mm in length.

2.1 Evaluation of the Material for the Outer Layer of VSL

Further on, it is required to evaluate the feasibility of the different materials for use in the outer layer of the link. Four links were fabricated and inflated to the maximum pressure of 43 psi. Further on, we discuss the mechanical properties observed for the selected materials. Neoprene layer creates a flexible, lightweight and air tight link. However, its highly elastic behavior leads to the ballooning of internal tube. In addition, the rapture of the link structure is observed for a pressure of about 20 psi. The polythene membrane is selected as a possible material for the outer skin of the inflatable link due its air tightness, and also because it is lightweight and low-cost. The link exhibits a considerable amount of stiffness when the pressure is applied. However, when the pressure exceeds 18 psi, wrinkling of the material is observed and there is the danger that the link material can rupture. Finally, both soft suede leather and ripstop fabric links were successfully tested and selected as a materials for the outer layer (Fig. 2). The results of the dynamic response testing are presented in Sect. 4.

Fig. 2. Fabricated VSLs that are selected for experimental evaluation: (a) ripstop fabric, and (b) suede leather links.

3 Analytical Modelling

The dynamic behavior of variable stiffness soft inflatable links needs to be investigated in order to create robust control strategies. Therefore, one of the core issues in the modelling of soft inflatable links is the mathematical framework that can predict their physical behavior. During the operation of the link, the inner circular chamber is equally inflated along the length of link. The air inside the tube is acting as a compressible fluid that can change the working pressure of the VSL. The impact of this working pressure creates a considerable amount of force on the surface of circular chamber, inflating the robotic link. The VSL is a continuous circular tube, and when it is inflated it can be approximated as a continuous elastic beam. The Pascal's law states that if there is an increase in pressure at any point in a confined fluid, an equal increase in force at every point in the container is realized. According to that, the inner pressure of the VSEL remains the same along the length of the link. Further on, the use of different pneumatic pressure can be used in changing and controlling the stiffness of the inflatable link.

The stiffness of the VSL is a result of the combined effects of the inertia and elastic properties of materials used for inner chamber and outer skin. The inertia of the soft inflatable link is compared to the change in the density of the air particles when the pneumatic pressure inside the inner chamber is changed. This can be expressed by the ideal gas Eq. (1) [20]:

$$PV = mRT, \tag{1}$$

where P is the maximum pressure inside the tube; V is the volume of the link at maximum inflation; R is the gas constant; m is the mass of air particles; and T is the temperature of the air particles. At the beginning of the operation, the pneumatic pressure is used to inflate the VSL (Fig. 3). Once the inner tube reaches its maximum expansion, i.e., the volume of the link becomes constant, the stiffness of the link increases. Hence, increasing the pneumatic pressure means that larger number of air mass is being accumulated inside the tube leading to higher stiffness of the VSL. The accumulated air mass (inertia) of the link becomes a function of supply pressure because all other physical quantities V, T, R, are constant except P and m. This shows that the stiffness is a function of number of air particles that lead to an increase in the inertia of the inflatable link. This variation in the inertial property makes the inflatable links suitable for applications that require stiffness controllability.

An inflatable link at the maximum pressure can be modelled as a horizontal cantilever beam fixed at one end. When the dynamic load is applied, the link goes into vibrations at its natural frequency. If the inner tube inside the link is packed densely with air mass through an increased pneumatic pressure, then the flexural rigidity is changed. This change in flexural properties of the inflatable link causes the natural frequency of the vibration to shift. When the inflatable link goes into free vibrations after the impact of point loading at the free end of the link, the equation of motion that describes its dynamic response assuming equally distributed gas molecules inside the chamber [21], is as follows:

$$\frac{d^2}{dx^2}\left\{EI(x)\frac{d^2Z(x)}{dx^2}\right\} = \omega^2 m(x)Z(x),$$ (2)

where, E is the modulus of elasticity of the beam material, I is the moment of inertia of the circular section of inflatable, $Z(x)$ is the displacement in z direction at distance x from the fixed end of the link, ω is the circular natural frequency, m is the mass per unit length: $m = \rho A(x)$. In this equation, ρ is the mass density of air particles, x is the distance measured from the fixed end of the link. The following boundary conditions can be considered in case the load is applied in the normal direction:

$$x = 0, \ Z(x) = 0, \ \frac{\partial Z(x)}{\partial(x)} = 0,$$ (3)

$$x = 1, \ \frac{\partial^2 Z(x)}{\partial(x^2)} = 0, \ \frac{\partial^3 Z(x)}{\partial(x^3)} = 0.$$ (4)

Each vibrating system (in our case – the inflatable link) exhibits its own natural frequency when it is deflected by an external forcing agent. The natural frequency of the system is defined as:

$$f = \frac{k_n^2}{2\pi L}\sqrt{\frac{EI}{\rho A}}.$$ (5)

Equation (5) demonstrates that a vibrating system gradually starts getting higher natural frequency if the Young's modulus is increased, e.g. by pneumatic pressure.

4   Evaluation of the Dynamic Response for VSL

4.1   Experimental Setup

The main focus of the experiments is to observe the dynamic response of the link when it is subject to impact loading. Moreover, employing the feature of variable stiffness, we are testing the impact of the internal pneumatic pressure. Based on the results obtained in Sect. 2.1, the dynamic responses of both suede leather and ripstop fabric links are tested. The experimental setting is shown in Fig. 3. The link is positioned horizontally, and the proximal end connected to the air supply is tightly fixed to avoid any displacement at the base. During the experiments, the stiffness of the VSL was increased from 6 psi to 24 psi at steps of 3 psi. Further on, the load was applied to the link for each pressure level. The load was increased from 1 N to 5 N at steps of 1 N. The load was attached via small thread at the suspended end of the VSL and, then, cut to observe the dynamic response of the link. Each experiment was repeated 3 times.

The dynamic response of the link is measured using an LIS344ALH 3-axis linear capacitive accelerometer. The acceleration measurement is recorded using a PicoScope 2000 oscilloscope with a measurement bandwidth of 25 MHz. The pressure control for the stiffness variability is implemented with SMC ITV electro-pneumatic pressure regulator. The control of the regulator was implemented using an Arduino Mega SDK board.

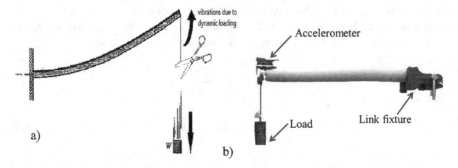

Fig. 3. Evaluation of the dynamic response of VSL: (a) sketch of the experimental procedure, and (b) suede leather link with the maximum weigh of 5 N applied.

4.2   Analysis of the Experimental Results

This section presents the analysis and evaluation of the experimental study presented above. The aim of the study is to understand the dynamic characteristics of the VSL during the application of load. In addition, the effect of the pressure level inside VSL is evaluated. The data was processed using MATLAB 2018b, and the statistical analysis was performed using R-statistical software. The significance level or the probability of rejecting the null hypothesis is defined as 0.05, with a confidence interval of 95%.

For the experimental evaluation, displacement and velocity data was obtained from the recorded acceleration using cumulative trapezoidal numerical integration. The sample response of the displacement pattern for the leather link during the application of a fixed load is shown in Fig. 4. It can be observed that the link displacement is following a vibration pattern that is settling down after a period of time.

To understand whether the settling time is changing for different pressures and applied load, the settling time was analyzed for both leather and fabric links and a different pressures. The mean settling time for the leather link is 1.164 s, with a

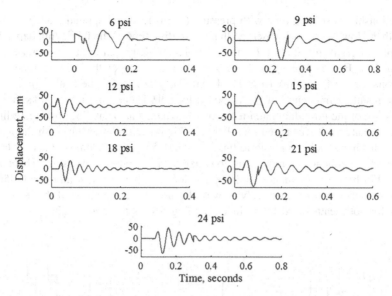

Fig. 4. Sample response for leather link for different internal pressures and an applied load of 3 N.

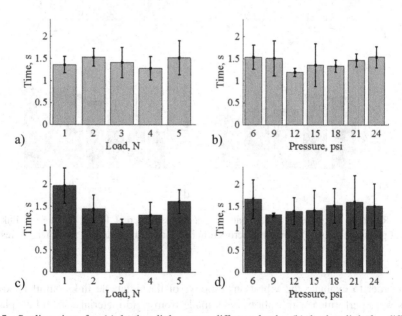

Fig. 5. Settling time for (a) leather link across different loads; (b) leather link for different pressure values; (c) fabric link across different loads; (d) fabric link for different pressure values.

standard deviation of 0.211 s (18%). In addition, similar values can be observed for the link made from fabric – we observe a mean settling time of 1.484 s, and a standard deviation of 0.275 s (18.5%). According to nonparametric Kruskal Wallis test, there is no relationship of settling time with pressure ($p = 0.153$) and applied load ($p = 0.472$) for leather. However, it was observed that the settling time of the fabric link depends on the applied weight ($p < 0.005$). It can be observed that the settling time decreases for a load of 3 N, Fig. 5. The applied pressure does not impact the settling time of the vibrations for the fabric link ($p = 0.904$), similarly as it is for the leather link.

The resultant frequency of the response for both leather and fabric links is evaluated, as one of the important parameters of the dynamic analysis (Fig. 6). According to statistical analysis, it was noted that there is a significant relationship with the applied pressure for both leather and fabric links ($p < 0.005$). As it is demonstrated in Fig. 6, the response frequency is increasing together with the internal pressure. There is no relationship between frequency and applied load; with $p = 0.158$ and $p = 0.056$ for leather and fabric links respectively. It was also noted that the range of the response is similar for both leather and fabric links, ranging from 4.5 Hz to 17 Hz.

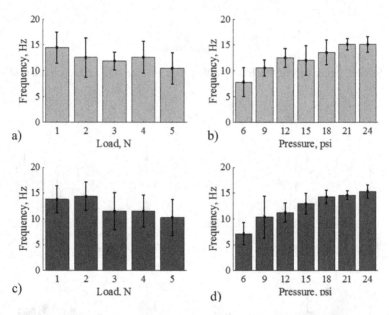

Fig. 6. Response frequency for (a) leather link across different loads; (b) leather link for different pressure levels; (c) fabric link across different loads; (d) fabric link for different pressure levels.

In order to evaluate the vibration response of the inflatable links, similar experiments were performed with hollow links made from rigid materials, including plastic and steel. Two rigid links comparable in dimensions with the inflatable links were selected to perform a comparative study (Fig. 7). The first link is a hollow steel tube with a wall thickness of 3 mm. The second link is made from rigid and lightweight PVC (polyvinyl chloride) with a wall thickness of 2 mm. The length and diameter of both links are 400 mm and 40 mm, respectively. Force stimuli ranging for 1 N to 20 N were applied to these links, as shown in Fig. 8. It was found that the average resultant

Fig. 7. Hard links for comparative study: (a) steel tube, and (b) PVC link.

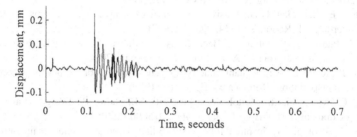

Fig. 8. Sample displacement response of the steel link; the applied force in the shown case is 20 N.

frequency of the response for steel and PVC links is 84.5 Hz with a standard deviation of 6.9 Hz and 79.8 Hz with a standard deviation of 3.6 Hz, respectively. It can be seen that the response frequency of rigid links is considerably higher than the response frequency of the inflatable ones.

5   Conclusions

In this paper we propose the initial evaluation of the dynamic response for variable stiffness links (VSLs). This knowledge can shed light on the dynamic behavior of soft and inflatable links. VSLs are capable of achieving stiffness modulation by varying the applied pneumatic pressure. The links benefit from the fact that they are lightweight and made of low-cost materials. It was found that the most suitable outer layer of the VSL is soft fabric or leather. However, the dynamic response characteristics, such as settling time can be influenced by the material of the outer layer. In future work, it is planned to perform additional dynamic studies and to develop control strategies, including those based on neuro-fuzzy paradigms [22], for the proposed variable stiffness link concept.

References

1. Siciliano, B., Khatib, O.: Handbook on Robotics. Springer, Heidelberg (2014)
2. Hogan, N.: Impedance control: an approach to manipulation: part III—applications. ASME. J. Dyn. Sys. Meas. Control. **107**(1), 17–24 (1985). https://doi.org/10.1115/1.3140701
3. Pratt, G., Williamson, M.: Series elastic actuators. In: Proceedings of the 1995 IEEE/RSJ International Conference Intelligent Robots and Systems Human Robot Interaction and Cooperative Robots, vol. 1, pp. 399–406 (1995)
4. Wolf, S., et al.: Variable stiffness actuators: review on design and components. IEEE/ASME Trans. Mechatron. **21**, 2418–2430 (2016)
5. Yang, C., Luo, J., Pan, Y., Liu, Z., Su, C.: Personalized variable gain control with tremor attenuation for robot teleoperation. IEEE Trans. Syst. Man Cybern.: Syst. **48**(10), 1759–1770 (2018). https://doi.org/10.1109/TSMC.2017.2694020
6. Colgate, J.E., Schenkel, G.G.: Passivity of a class of sampled-data systems: application to haptic interfaces. J. Robot. Syst. **14**, 37–47 (1997)
7. Yang, J., Pitarch, E.P., Potratz, J., Beck, S., Abdel-Malek, K.: Synthesis and analysis of a flexible elephant trunk robot". Adv. Robot. **20**, 631–659 (2006)
8. Cieślak, R., Morecki, A.: Elephant trunk type elastic manipulator - a tool for bulk and liquid materials transportation. Robotica **17**(1), 11–16 (1999)
9. Laschi, C., Mazzolai, B., Mattoli, V., Cianchetti, M., Dario, P.: Design of a biomimetic robotic octopus arm. Bioinspir. Biomim. **4**(1), 015006 (2009)
10. Hirose, S.: Biologically inspired robots: snake-like locomotors and manipulators. Appl. Mech. Rev. **48**(3), B27–B27 (1995)
11. Rollinson, D., et al.: Design and architecture of a series elastic snake robot. In: 2014 IEEE/RSJ International Conference on Intelligent Robots and Systems, IROS 2014, 14–18 September 2014, pp. 4630–4636 (2014)
12. Majidi, C.: Soft robotics: a perspective—current trends and prospects for the future. Soft Robot. **1**, 5–11 (2014)
13. Rus, D., Tolley, M.T.: Design, fabrication and control of soft robots. Nature **521**, 467 (2015)
14. Stilli, A., Grattarola, L., Feldmann, H., Wurdemann, H.A., Althoefer, K.: Variable stiffness link (VSL): toward inherently safe robotic manipulators. In: Proceedings - IEEE International Conference on Robotics and Automation (2017)
15. Stilli, A., Wurdemann, H.A., Althoefer, K.: A novel concept for safe, stiffness-controllable robot links. Soft Robot. **4**, 16–22 (2017)
16. Shiva, A., et al.: Tendon-based stiffening for a pneumatically actuated soft manipulator. IEEE Robot. Autom. Lett. **1**(2), 632–637 (2016)
17. Lipson, H.: Challenges and opportunities for design, simulation, and fabrication of soft robots. Soft Robot. **1**(1), 21–27 (2014)
18. Manti, M., Cacucciolo, V., Cianchetti, M.: Stiffening in soft robotics: a review of the state of the art. IEEE Robot. Autom. Mag. **23**, 93–106 (2016)
19. Blanc, L., Delchambre, A., Lambert, P.: Flexible medical devices: review of controllable stiffness solutions. In: Actuators (2017)
20. Atkin, P., Paula, J.: Physical Chemistry (2006)
21. Meirovitch, L.: Analytical Methods in Vibrations (1967)
22. Althoefer, K.: Neuro-fuzzy motion planning for robotic manipulators. Ph.D. thesis, King's College, London (1997)

Investigating Balance Control of a Hopping Bipedal Robot

Beichen Ding$^{(\boxtimes)}$, Andrew Plummer, and Pejman Iravani

Centre for Power Transmission and Motion Control,
Department of Mechanical Engineering, University of Bath, Bath, UK
b.ding@bath.ac.uk

Abstract. Legged robots are dynamic moving machines that are potentially able to traverse through rough terrain which is inaccessible for wheeled or tracked vehicles. For bipedal robots, balancing control while hopping/running is challenging, especially when the foot contact area is small. Servo hydraulics is highly suitable for robot leg actuation due to its high power density and good power-to-weight ratio. This paper presents a controller for a hydraulically actuated bipedal robot, the Bath Bipedal Hopper (BBH). The controller follows the well-established structure of the 'Three-part' control algorithm. The three parts are: hopping height control; longitudinal velocity control by changing the leg angle during the flight phase to place the foot in the desired position; and body attitude correction during the stance phase. Simulation results from a detailed non-linear model indicate that this controller can successfully balance the hydraulic robot while hopping with different longitudinal velocities.

Keywords: Bipedal hopping robot · Hydraulic actuation · Balancing controller

1 Introduction

Legged animals are found widely in the natural world, and many are highly effective at traversing rough terrain. Similarly, legged robots present themselves with potential advantages for easily travelling through rough terrain comparing with wheeled or tracked vehicles [1]. Some successfully developed legged moving machines are summarized in [2]. The study of mono-legged or bipedal hopping robot is a sustained interest that is motivated by human's desire to have a comprehensive understanding of this locomotion, which can also be expanded and applied to multi-legged robots. A springy leg interacting with a body mass is able to give a natural running/hopping frequency. Coil springs and compressed air are widely used to provide the required leg compliance. Servo hydraulics is highly suitable for robot leg actuation due to the high power density and quick system response. KenKen is a famous hopping robot with articulated type of leg, which takes advantage of coil spring accompanied by hydraulic actuation [3], which is shown in Fig. 1.

Maintaining balance is an important objective for dynamic robots while walking or running. For pseudo-static multi-legged robots, balance can be achieved by keeping the body CoG above the support region created by the feet, which is called 'Zero Moment

© Springer Nature Switzerland AG 2019
K. Althoefer et al. (Eds.): TAROS 2019, LNAI 11649, pp. 171–182, 2019.
https://doi.org/10.1007/978-3-030-23807-0_15

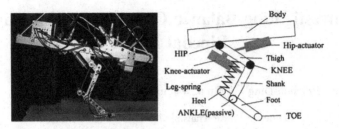

Fig. 1. Kenken: one-legged hopping robot.

Point' (ZMP) control [4]. The SILO4 robot and Asimo, as shown in Fig. 2, are successfully balanced using this method while walking.

However, balancing control becomes challenging for bipedal robots when the foot contact area is small. In 1986, Raibert developed a 'Three-part' control algorithm to explain the basic locomotion mechanism of a one-legged case [5], for which there is only one type of gait, namely hopping. The three controlled variables are: the hopping height, the horizontal velocity and the body attitude. In order to accomplish different control actions, a distinction between the flight phase and the stance phase is necessary. During the stance phase, the one-legged robot behaves as a spring loaded inverted pendulum (SLIP) with the foot pivoted on the ground. During stance, the robot can be balanced by controlling the body rotation angle, and the leg actuator is required to accomplish the hopping height control task. During the flight phase, the horizontal velocity control can be achieved by controlling the leg angle with respect to the CoG to place the foot at required position for the next touch-down.

Several dynamic running robots were built to test this control algorithm during 1980s and 1990s, which are introduced in [6]. This controller is also extended for multi-legged robots for control the body pitching and rolling [7].

A hydraulically actuated bipedal hopping robot, called the Bath Bipedal Hopper (BBH) has been developed at the University of Bath to study motion control of legged robots. In this paper, the 'Three-part' control algorithm is investigated for this robot via simulation. A detailed non-linear simulation model will be developed and the controller implementation is described in the following sections.

Fig. 2. SILO4: a quadruped walking robot; Asimo: a humanoid walking robot.

2 Description of the Bath Bipedal Hopper Robot

A sketch of the BBH is shown in Fig. 3. The BBH is a small-sized, hydraulically actuated bipedal hopping robot. The articulated type robot leg is composed of three links. The 1st link: a hydraulic actuator, named the leg actuator, is placed in parallel with the *'thigh'* to actuate the knee joint; the 2nd link: an extension coil spring is mounted in parallel with the *'shank'* to provide the required leg compliance; the 3rd link: a *'lower leg'* is used to connect the ankle joint and the heel joint.

The robot body is an aluminum frame for mounting the manifold, valves and PC-104 controller. A hip actuator is placed under the body to drive the hip joint. For the initial condition, the hip actuator position is controlled to give a 45° hip angle, plus the leg actuator is controlled to the mid-stroke, resulting in the body's CoM being aligned with the foot contact point, vertically. The main dimensional specifications of the BBH are summarized in Table 1.

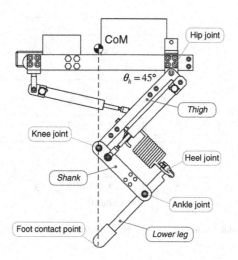

Fig. 3. Sketch of the BBH robot.

Table 1. Main dimensional specifications of the BBH robot.

Parameters	Symbol	Value	Unit
Height	H	552	mm
Length	L	400	mm
Width	W	315	mm
Weight	M	14.78	kg
Spring stiffness (physical)	K	9.62	N/mm

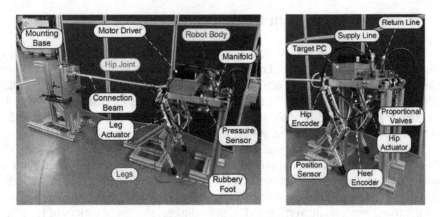

Fig. 4. The BBH robot (shown with mechanical constraint, left picture).

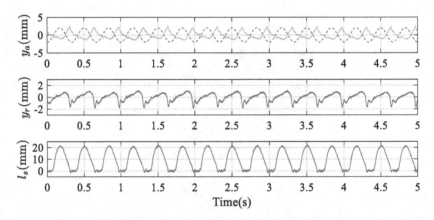

Fig. 5. Experimental results of using 3 Hz sinusoid signal to excite the leg actuator.

The test rig setup is shown in Fig. 4. A position transducer is place in parallel with each leg actuator to measure the piston position. A pressure sensor is used to measure the piston side pressure of the actuator. Additionally, an incremental encoder is added at the heel joint so that the spring displacement can be calculated using a kinematic transformation.

A primary bench test has been taken to validate the efficacy of the mechanical design of the robot. A sinusoid position signal (2 mm of the amplitude at 3 Hz frequency) is used to excite the leg actuator to achieve an open loop hopping. Additionally, the two leg actuator displacements are synchronized using a 'Modal Controller'. This controls the mean of the leg actuator positions and the corresponding difference, which are called the average position (y_a) and roll position (y_r), respectively. If the demand roll position is zero, the two leg actuators are synchronized. The consistent spring displacement, l_s, in Fig. 5 indicates that the robot is hopping, plus the roll position error is mainly caused by different friction applied at each foot, left and right.

3   Modelling

3.1   Hydraulic Model

The modelling follows well established procedures [8] accompanied by some findings from experiments. The hydraulic circuit is shown in Fig. 6.

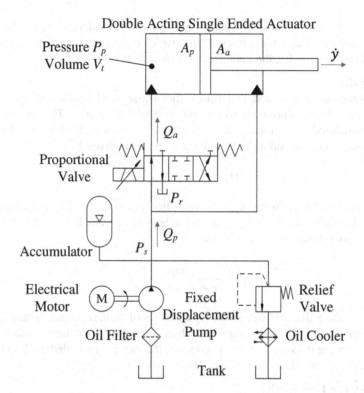

Fig. 6. Hydraulic circuit for one leg actuator.

Actuator Model

Assuming there is no internal or external leakage, the hydraulic actuator is modelled by:

$$P_p A_p - P_s A_a - F_f = F_h \tag{1}$$

$$Q_a = A_p \dot{y} + \frac{V_t}{B} \dot{P}_p \tag{2}$$

where A_a is the annulus area, F_h is the actuation force, F_f is the friction, Q_a is the piston side flow rate, V_t is the trapped oil volume and B is the bulk modulus of the oil.

Additionally, the friction force is modelled by:

$$F_s = f_v \dot{y} \tag{3}$$

$$F_f = \begin{cases} F_c & \text{for } F_s \geq F_c \\ F_s & \text{for } |F_s| < F_c \\ -F_c & \text{for } F_s \leq F_c \end{cases} \tag{4}$$

where F_c is the Coulomb friction force, and F_s is velocity-dependent friction at low velocity, introduced to avoid a discontinuity which can cause numerical issues during the simulation; f_v is a friction coefficient which is relatively large.

Valve Model

The proportional valve is modelled using orifice equation. Only one orifice equation is needed as the flow is only metered into one side of the actuator. The spool displacement is considered as a dimensionless variable which ranging from −1 to +1 with the closed position corresponding to 0. The valve model is given by:

$$Q_a = K_v X_v \sqrt{P_s - P_v} \tag{5}$$

where P_v is the outlet pressure, K_v is the valve flow coefficient and X_v is the normalized spool displacement. Additionally, a second-order transfer function is used to represent the valve spool dynamics, which is given by:

$$X_v = \frac{\omega_v^2}{s^2 + 2\xi_v \omega_v + \omega_v^2} \tilde{u}_c \tag{6}$$

where, $\tilde{u}_c$ is the valve driving signal, ω_v is the spool natural frequency and ξ_v is the spool damping ratio, which are empirical values determined from the manufacturer data sheet or experimental results. The hysteresis of the valve is modelled as 'backlash', as shown in Fig. 7, in which u_w is the dead-band width.

Hose Pressure Loss Model

The model of the pressure loss between the valve and the cylinder is given by:

$$Q_a = K_h \sqrt{P_p - P_v} \tag{7}$$

where K_h is the hose pressure loss factor, which is an empirical value.

The parameter values of the hydraulic models are provided in Table 2.

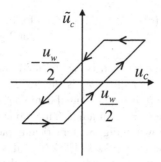

Fig. 7. Valve hysteresis.

Table 2. Parameter values of the hydraulic models.

Parameters	Symbol	Value	Unit
Supply pressure	P_s	160×10^5	Pa
Return pressure	P_r	0	Pa
Piston area	A_p	1.13×10^{-4}	m²
Annulus area	A_a	0.63×10^{-4}	m²
Valve flow coefficient	K_v	4.89×10^{-8}	m⁴/s/N$^{1/2}$
Valve spool natural frequency	ω_v	942.48	rad/s
Valve spool damping ratio	ξ_v	0.7	
Backlash deadband width	u_w	0.2	A
Coulomb friction (actuator piston)	F_f	105	N

3.2 Mechanical Model

The mechanical model of the BBH, which effectively is a planar robot, is built using SimMechanics®, a multi-body mechanical simulation tool in Simulink®. The mechanical properties of the rigid bodies are defined in Autodesk Inventor 2017®, then uploaded to SimMechanics® to create a 3D visualization.

A 'spring and damper force' block is used to represent the spring force between the connections on upper leg and lower leg. Modelling the ground contact is an important issue. The reaction force from the ground should support the robot vertically (y-axis) and prevent horizontal foot slip (z-axis) during the stance phase. Define the coordinate of the robot foot contact point is $(0, y_n, z_t)$ and the corresponding projection to the ground is $(0, y_n', z_n')$. The ground reaction force is modelled as a spring and damper both vertically and horizontally. The ground stiffness is relatively large so as not to significantly reduce the effective robot leg's stiffness. Thus, the vertical reaction force and the horizontal friction force are given by:

$$F_y = \begin{cases} -k_y\left(y_n - y_n'\right) - b_y\left(\dot{y}_n - \dot{y}_n'\right) & \text{for stance phase} \\ 0 & \text{for flight phase} \end{cases} \tag{8}$$

$$F_z = \begin{cases} -k_z(z_t - z_t') - b_z(\dot{z}_t - \dot{z}_t) & \text{for stance phase} \\ 0 & \text{for flight phase} \end{cases} \quad (9)$$

where F_y is the vertical reaction force, k_y is the ground normal spring stiffness and b_y is the ground normal damping coefficient. F_z is the horizontal friction force, k_z is the tangential spring stiffness and b_z is the tangential damping coefficient. Combining with the hydraulic models implemented in Simulink®, the top level of the simulation model and the 3D visualization is shown in Fig. 8. Numerical implementation is performed by a stiff/Mod. Rosenbrock solver (Simulink's ODE23s) with variable step size, which is a compromise between the computing speed and the simulation accuracy.

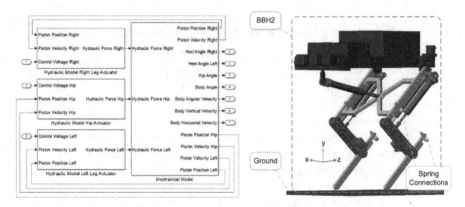

Fig. 8. Top level of the simulation model and 3D visualization.

4   Controller Implementation

To simplify the controller implementation, the distance between the body CoG and the foot is introduced as a '*virtual leg*'. The leg displacement is calculated using a kinematics transformation. Figure 9 is a simplified diagram of one hopping cycle.

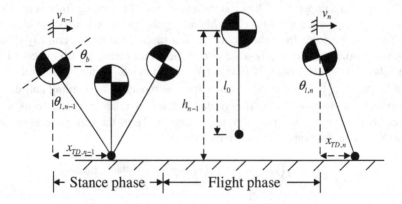

Fig. 9. Simplified diagram of one hopping cycle.

4.1   Control of the Hopping Height

Bhatti et al. developed a simple hopping height control technique for a planar robot travelling over discontinuous surfaces in [9]. The leg actuator demand velocity during the stance phase is derived using the achieved height of the previous hop, denoted $h_{n-1,a}$, and the desired height for the next hop, $h_{n,d}$, and is given by:

$$q_{n,d} = K_{h1}\sqrt{h_{n,d}} + K_{h2}\left(\sqrt{h_{n,d}} - \sqrt{h_{n-1,a}}\right) \tag{10}$$

where $q_{n,d}$ is the desired extension velocity of the leg, K_{h1} and K_{h2} are the controller gains. Integrating this desired velocity gives the demand position, which is common for servo-hydraulics system. Additionally, the virtual leg is controlled to return to mid-length during the flight phase to be ready for the next touch-down, plus the demand hopping height remains constant in this simulation, i.e. $h_{n,d} = 0.43$ m. The closed-loop leg length control is achieved using a PI controller:

$$u_c = K_p e + K_i \int edt \tag{11}$$

where K_p is the proportional gain, K_i is the integral gain and e is the leg position error.

4.2   Control of the Longitudinal Velocity

During the flight phase, the robot has a parabolic trajectory, thus moving the hip actuator results in different rotation angle for the body and legs due to the moment of inertia. The leg angle, θ_l, is controlled to place the foot on the ground at horizontal position, x_{TD}, relative to the body CoG, to achieve the required longitudinal velocity.

An appropriate leg angle for the next touch-down can be calculated from the previous hop. Thus, the foot placement at the previous touch-down, $x_{TD,n-1,a}$, is given by:

$$x_{TD,n-1,a} = \frac{1}{2} v_{n-1,a} T_{s,n-1,a} \tag{12}$$

where $v_{n-1,a}$ is the achieved body longitudinal velocity at previous touch-down and $T_{s,n-1,a}$ is the corresponding stance duration.

Thus the leg angle is given by:

$$\theta_{l,n-1,a} = \sin^{-1}\frac{x_{TD,n-1,a}}{l_0} \tag{13}$$

where $\theta_{l,n-1,a}$ is the achieved leg angle of the previous hop and l_0 is the nominal length of the virtual leg, which is 0.4 m.

According to small perturbation approximation, define:

$$\Delta\theta_l = K_l\left(v_{n,d} - v_{n-1,a}\right) \tag{14}$$

where $v_{n,d}$ is the desired body longitudinal velocity for the next touch-down, $\Delta\theta_l$ is the corresponding leg angle change and K_l is the feedback gain. Thus, the desired leg angle for the next touch-down, $\theta_{l,n,d}$, is given by:

$$\theta_{l,n,d} = \theta_{l,n-1} + \Delta\theta_l \tag{15}$$

If hip torque is the control variable, leg angle can be controlled in closed loop, thus:

$$\tau_l = K_{l1}\left(\theta_{l,n} - \theta_{l,n,d}\right) + K_{l2}\left(\dot{\theta}_{l,n}\right) \tag{16}$$

where τ_l is the control torque for the hip during flight phase, K_{l1} and K_{l2} are feedback gains, and $\theta_{l,n}$ is the actual leg angle.

4.3 Control of the Body Attitude

Controlling the leg angle during flight phase changes the body pitch angle, which can be corrected during the stance phase. It is assumed there is a sufficient friction at the ground to avoid the robot foot slipping. The body angle, θ_b, is controlled towards a horizontal position, i.e. $\theta_{b,d} = 0°$, using a simple servo given by:

$$\tau_b = K_{b1}\left(\theta_b - \theta_{b,d}\right) + K_{b2}\left(\dot{\theta}_b\right) \tag{17}$$

where τ_b is the control torque for the hip during stance phase, K_{b1} and K_{b2} are feedback gains, and $\theta_{b,d}$ is the desired body angle.

Table 3 shows the values of the controller gains and feedback gains used in this simulation.

Table 3. Controller and feedback gains.

Parameters	Value	Unit
K_{h1}	0.02	$m^{1/2}/s$
K_{h2}	1	$m^{1/2}/s$
K_{l1}	100	Nm/rad
K_{l2}	0.02	Nms/rad
K_{b1}	1×10^5	Nm/rad
K_{b2}	9×10^3	Nms/rad
K_p	320	1/m
K_i	100	1/(sm)

5 Simulation Results

Figure 10 shows the simulation results. The simulation starts with a free drop of the robot from a small initial body height. Note that y is the actual body height. The achieved hopping frequency is approximately 3 Hz and the hopping height controller is able to correct the robot motion within several hops when the longitudinal velocity, $\dot{x}$, is changing. The leg angle is adjusted by the controller to achieve different velocity demands. At $t = 6$, a sudden movement of the hip actuator is found due to a large step change of the velocity demand, so more hops are needed to allow the robot to gradually achieve the demand velocity. Between $t = 5$ and 10, the forward traveling speed is 0.24 m/s; between $t = 15$ and 20, the backward speed is 0.08 m/s; between $t = 20$ and 25, the backward speed is 0.15 m/s. The body angle is successfully controlled to maintain balance, not only when hopping on a spot, i.e. $\dot{x}(t) = 0$, but also to be balanced with different moving speed. The hip angle, θ_h, keeps adjusting associate with body balancing.

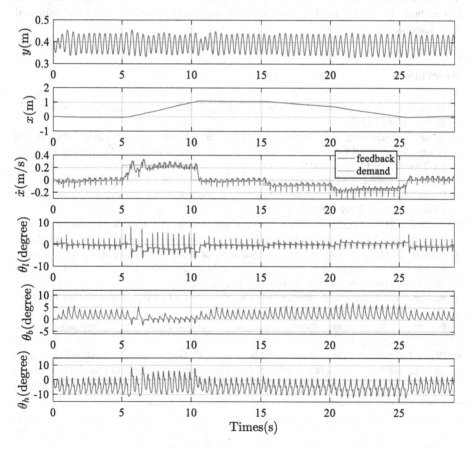

Fig. 10. Simulation results.

6 Conclusion

The investigation of the control of a bipedal robot while hopping is under taken in this paper. The bench test results indicate the efficacy of the mechanical design of the BBH robot. A detailed non-linear simulation model accompanied by physical empirical data is developed. The implemented controller is built according to the well-established 'Three-part' control algorithm. The hopping height is controlled using an adaptive controller; changing the leg angle during the flight phase to place the foot in the desired position is able to achieve longitudinal velocity control; the body attitude is controlled during the stance phase to maintain balance. The simulation results demonstrate that the controller can successfully balance the robot while hopping with different longitudinal velocities, e.g. traveling forward at 0.24 m/s, backward at 0.08 m/s or 0.15 m/s.

The practical implementation of this controller is challenging, mainly due to the performance of the sensors and signal processing, e.g. the direct measurement of the robot hopping height and longitudinal velocity requires sufficiently quick response and high measurement accuracy of the sensors. If necessary, state estimators or observers can be built, i.e. derive the hopping height or longitudinal velocity from the estimated state variables.

References

1. Sayyad, A., Seth, B., Seshu, P.: Single-legged hopping robotics research—a review. Robotica **25**(5), 587–613 (2007)
2. Bhatti, J., Plummer, A.R., Iravani, P., Ding, B.: A survey of dynamic robot legged locomotion. In: 2015 International Conference on Fluid Power and Mechatronics (FPM), pp. 770–775. IEEE, July 2015
3. Hyon, S.H., Mita, T.: Development of a biologically inspired hopping robot-"Kenken". In: Proceedings of the IEEE International Conference on IEEE Robotics and Automation, ICRA 2002, vol. 4, pp. 3984–3991, May 2002
4. Al-Shuka, H.F., Corves, B., Zhu, W.H., Vanderborght, B.: Multi-level control of zero-moment point-based humanoid biped robots: a review. Robotica **34**(11), 2440–2466 (2016)
5. Raibert, M.H.: Hopping in legged systems—modeling and simulation for the two-dimensional one-legged case. IEEE Trans. Syst. Man Cybern. **3**, 451–463 (1984)
6. MIT Leg Laboratory. http://www.ai.mit.edu/projects/leglab/
7. Raibert, M., Chepponis, M., Brown, H.B.J.R.: Running on four legs as though they were one. IEEE J. Robot. Autom. **2**(2), 70–82 (1986)
8. Plummer, A.R.: A detailed dynamic model of a six-axis shaking table. J. Earthquake Eng. **12**(4), 631–662 (2008)
9. Bhatti, J., Plummer, A.R., Sahinkaya, M.N., Iravani, P., Guglielmino, E., Caldwell, D.G.: Fast and adaptive hopping height control of single-legged robot. In: The 11th Biennial Conference on Engineering Systems Design and Analysis, pp. 303–309. American Society of Mechanical Engineers, July 2012

Continuous Motion Utilising Advanced Motions on a Hexapod

Wei Cheah[✉], Hassan Hakim Khalili, Simon Watson, Peter Green,
and Barry Lennox

School of Electrical and Electronic Engineering, University of Manchester,
Manchester M13 9PL, UK
wei.cheah@manchester.ac.uk
http://uomrobotics.com/

Abstract. This paper presents the interpolation of motion primitives
and the foothold planner for a hexapod which utilises advanced motions
to navigate through complex environments such as narrow pathways and
large holes which are surrounded by walls. Advanced motions are concerned with the use of vertical surfaces for footholds and currently consists of two motion primitives, wall and chimney walking aside from the
standard ground walking. Previous work have not considered in detail
the interpolation between the motion primitives for achieving continuous
motion. The transition routines and foothold planning for the interpolation between these motion primitives are generated using a heuristic
approach which ensures that the motion of the robot remains stable and
avoids both inter-leg collision and kinematic singularity. The motion plan
which includes the transition routines has been evaluated successfully in
a kinematic simulation on the Corin hexapod. The results show that
the robot was able to transition between the different motion primitives
required for navigating through the complex environment and that such
motions are realisable for hexapods.

Keywords: Advanced motions · Legged robots · Motion planning ·
Autonomous · Hexapods

1 Introduction

The research on legged robots has gained a huge traction since the 80's [17]
and has achieved much over recent years. This is made possible with technolog-
ical advancement in actuation, computer systems, sensors, and the decades of
research in this area. Another primary driving factor for this increase in interest
is the support of government bodies and industry through initiatives such as
competitions [10,14] or trials[1]. These initiatives have allowed the state-of-the-
art in legged robots to be driven forward to the extent that these robots are

---

[1] https://enrich.european-robotics.eu/.

This work was supported by the EPSRC Grant Nos. EP/R026084/1 and
EP/P01366X/1.

© Springer Nature Switzerland AG 2019
K. Althoefer et al. (Eds.): TAROS 2019, LNAI 11649, pp. 183–194, 2019.
https://doi.org/10.1007/978-3-030-23807-0_16

now competing on the same level as wheeled and tracked robots [9], and are also slowly becoming commercially available.

The locomotion of legged robots is generally dictated by the motion planner. Even though a large body of research in the area of motion planning for hexapods is available, there remains a gap in the literature on the use of vertical surfaces (wall) for foothold placement. Foothold contact on wall surfaces are required for navigating through complex environments with holes that are too large to step over and pathways that are narrower than the robot's footprint (see Fig. 1).

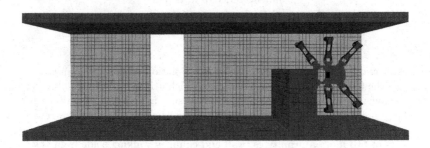

Fig. 1. Cluttered spaces with narrow pathway and large hole.

A grid-based motion planner has been proposed in [5] which uses the wall for foothold contact, allowing exploration in areas previously deemed inaccessible using the standard motion of ground walking (all footholds on the ground plane). However, the base trajectory of the planner is 2D and assumes instantaneous transition between different motion primitives. The contribution of this paper is to extend the dimensionality of the base trajectory and introduce transition routines, along with a refined foothold planner for achieving a smooth and continuous motion to reach the goal position.

The rest of this paper is organised as follows: Sect. 2 presents the background to this work. Section 3 details the transition routines while Sect. 4 details the foothold planner. Next, Sect. 5 presents the evaluation of the proposed motion plans on the Corin hexapod. Finally, Sect. 6 concludes the work and presents an outlook to future work.

2   Background

The work in [5] uses the notion of motion primitives where ground walking (all footholds are on the ground), wall walking (footholds on one side of the robot are on the wall while the other side are on the ground) and chimney walking (all footholds are on the wall) are each considered a motion primitive. The post-processing stage of the planner has been able to segment the path according to motion primitives and also identify instances where transition routines are required to change from one motion primitive to another.

The wall walking and transition achieved in [11] on an under-actuated hexapod with the aid of a semi-elliptical shell is inapplicable as the study here is concerned with a nominally-actuated hexapod. On the other hand, the chimney walking achieved in [6] starts and ends with the same motion hence the transition from ground to chimney walking was not considered.

The transition from the ground to wall surface and vice versa has been proposed for Wall Climbing Robot (WCR) to extend autonomous operations even when the gradient of the plane changes significantly e.g. ground-to-wall plane or vice versa. The transition routines generally constrain the robot's base to avoid collision with the environment [1,8,15] and may even lie outside the support polygon [12]. Following this, the robot's base path and footholds are selected either manually [8] or autonomously [1,15]. Common to these approaches is that the measure of stability using support polygon does not apply to such robots as they are able to adhere to the surfaces.

The foothold selection for grid-based planners generally uses the nominal position of each leg centred in a fixed area as the starting point [13,19]. At each new robot's base position, the foothold with the lowest cost is selected using a greedy search within the foothold area, biased towards the nominal position. However, this approach limits the distance travelled per gait cycle as the legs do not start nor continue in the gait position [17] and is further limited if the distance between the legs on the same side is small. The nominal position for each of the motion primitives used in advanced motions are very different and previous work have yet to address having a change in the nominal position.

What has not been considered is the transition between motion primitives for a nominally actuated robot that is unable to adhere to the surface - this in fact covers a wide range of legged robots. The foothold planner should be capable of selecting footholds on either the ground or wall surface depending on the motion primitive used while ensuring the robot's stability is retained and the legs does not reach singularity. Furthermore, the distance travelled per gait cycle should also be maximised as this indirectly optimizes the energy expenditure [3].

3   Transitions

This section details the transition routines for allowing a smooth and continuous motion from one motion primitive to another. There are altogether four types of transition routines: ground-to-wall, wall-to-ground, ground-to-chimney and chimney-to-ground. These can be paired to ground-wall and ground-chimney as the routines in each pair are simply the reverse of each other.

3.1   Ground-Chimney

The ground-to-chimney transition, w_{g-c}, starts at the last instance of ground walking, w_g, and ends with the segmented path for chimney walking, w_c. The routine first changes the robot from the hybrid to the rectangular stance (Fig. 2a–b) since the latter stance is used for w_c and allows equal lateral reach for all the legs compared to the hybrid stance. From this point on, the foothold planner will attempt to select wall footholds as the robot travels from its current position to the end of the segmented path. Since there is a possibility that not all the legs are able to satisfy w_c at the start of the segmented path, the foothold planner first search within the foothold area for w_c and if none exists, defaults to foothold area for w_g. This combination allows a gradual transition when the walls required for w_c does not extend past the entire length of the robot.

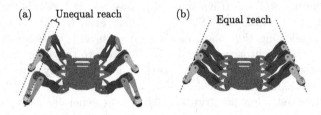

Fig. 2. Robot stance lateral reach for (a) hybrid (b) rectangular stance.

The transition from chimney-to-ground, w_{c-g}, simply takes the reverse of w_{g-c}. At the end of the segmented path, the foothold planner searches the foothold area for w_g and if no valid foothold exists, defaults to the foothold area for w_c. The motivation for this combination is similar to w_{g-c}. When all the legs have resumed ground contact, i.e. footholds exists within the leg area for w_g on all legs, the robot reverts back to the hybrid stance and resumes w_g. The hybrid stance is preferred for w_g as larger steps can be taken and yields a larger stability margin as well compared to the rectangular stance [18].

3.2   Ground-Wall

The ground-to-wall transition, w_{g-w}, has a prior step which modifies the goal pose for this transition and the subsequent wall walking, w_w, path segment. The most energy conserving pose for w_w is when the robot's base roll approaches 90° because the robot's centre of mass in this pose acts directly or close to leg's actuator in ground contact i.e. the moment arm distance is reduced thus reducing the torque requirement. For this purpose, the maximum base roll and the corresponding y-coordinate within the w_w path segment is used as the goal base roll and goal y-coordinate for the w_{g-w}. There is then no longitudinal motion from the robot during this transition. The starting position of the w_w path segment is then changed to be the same as the goal position of the transition.

This transition consists of three stages: (1) stance modification, (2) change in contact surface for legs on one side of the robot, and (3) moving to transition's goal pose. For wall-to-ground transition, w_{w-g}, the procedures of w_{g-w} are simply reversed.

The first stage is to modify the stance (Fig. 3a) and the motivation for this is similar to that in w_{g-c} and w_{c-g}. It should be noted that having an equal

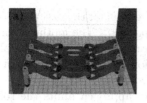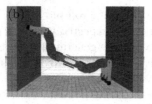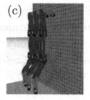

Fig. 3. Transition routine for ground-to-wall, stage (a) one (b) two (c) three.

reach for the legs on each side is vital especially when the robot attempts to travel through the minimum permissible pathway. In this scenario, the robot's lateral footprint needs to be minimised and is achieved using the combination of a rectangular stance, rolling its base by 90° and having the legs in ground contact only slightly further away from the robot's base position projected on the ground plane (see Fig. 3c). In such a configuration, the front and rear legs will not be able to reach the ground for contact if the hybrid stance is used.

The second stage changes the contact surface for one side of the legs to wall contact (Fig. 3b). The wave gait with a duty factor of 5/6 is used from this point on as it is the most stable motion [16]. This stage moves the robot to the configuration with the widest footprint achievable using wall walking.

The final stage (Fig. 3c) interpolates the robot's current base position to the goal position motivated by [1,15]. A combination of having the goal position ending at a suitable distance from the wall and using the interpolation using an ellipsoidal curve ensures that the robot's base is collision free. The robot's base angular rotation is interpolated linearly while its linear position is interpolated in an ellipsoidal manner. The base orientation, q_b, and linear position, x_b, interpolations are,

$$q_b(n) = q_{b,0} + n \cdot \frac{q_d}{n_s} \tag{1}$$

$$x_b(n) = x_{b,0} + \begin{bmatrix} 0 \\ 1 - \cos(q_r(n)) \\ \sin(q_r(n)) \end{bmatrix} \circ \frac{x_d}{n_s} \tag{2}$$

where $n = \{0, 1, \ldots, n_s\}$, n_s is the total number of discrete segments, $q_{b,0}, x_{b,0} \in \Re^3$ are the initial base orientation and position, $q_d, x_d \in \Re^3$ are the difference between the start and goal orientation and position respectively, q_r is the linearly interpolated base roll angle at instance n, and $(\circ)$ is the Schur product.

4   Foothold Planner

The corresponding Centre of Base (CoB) at each node of the segmented path and transition routines are interpolated using standard cubic spline technique [2]. The generated 6D trajectory is a continuous polynomial spline with the maximum linear and angular velocity defined according to the robot's actuation capability. The Euler angles using roll-pitch-yaw are used for the base orientation trajectory as the robot is not expected to rotate pass 90°. The foothold planner then selects footholds along the generated trajectory, constrained by the robot's kinematics and stability, as well as avoids collision with the environment and between its own legs.

As mentioned in Sect. 2, the nominal foothold approach limits the robot's base movement per gait cycle. This movement is further limited when the rectangular stance is used since the step size now needs to be even smaller to avoid inter-leg collision. To address this, the Anterior Extreme Position (AEP) and Posterior Extreme Position (PEP) are used here for selecting footholds along the base trajectory. Figure 4 shows the flow diagram of the foothold planner. Briefly, the robot's base is moved along the trajectory until one of the constraints (PEP, leg kinematic reach and stability margin) are violated or the gait phase has ended. This position is then used as the reference frame for identifying the next foothold location. The process is repeated until the goal is reached.

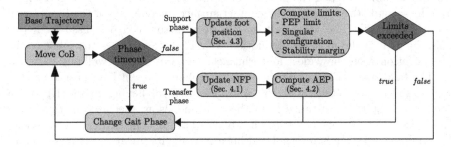

Fig. 4. Flow diagram for foothold planner.

4.1   Nominal Position

The Nominal Foothold Position (NFP), remains vital as the AEP and PEP are anchored to this position. The NFP for ground walking is similar to previous work in the literature [13], while for chimney walking the NFP simply is based on the rectangular stance and lies on the same plane as the robot's base. This section details the NFP for wall transition, illustrated in Fig. 5, where the z-axis of the world frame is assumed to be normal to the ground plane.

Ground Contact Leg Configuration. To achieve the configuration shown in Fig. 5a, where the tibia link is perpendicular to the ground plane, the height between the femur and tibia link, h_1, is

$$\boldsymbol{p}_{fem}^w = \boldsymbol{p}_b^w + {}^w\boldsymbol{p}_{fem}^b \tag{3}$$

$$h_1 = p_{fem}^w(z) - l_3. \tag{4}$$

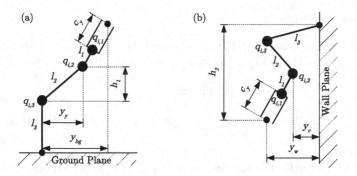

Fig. 5. Annotations for wall transition (a) leg in ground contact (b) leg in wall contact. $l_{1,2,3}$ is the coxa, femur and tibia link length respectively, $q_{i,1}, q_{i,2}, q_{i,3}$ is the coxa, femur and tibia joint for leg i. c_y is the fixed lateral distance from the robot's geometrical centre to the coxa joint.

where $p_b^w, {}^w p_{fem}^b \in \Re^3$ is the desired base pose and the vector from the robot's base to femur frame expressed in the world frame.

The lateral distance from the robot's base to the foot is

$$y_{bg} = \left[\sqrt{l_2^2 - h_1^2} + (c_y + l_1)cos(q_r) \right] \sin(q_i) \tag{5}$$

where q_r is the base roll angle, $i = \{1, 2, \dots, 6\}$ is the reference number for the legs[2], q_i is the rotation from base to leg i frame.

The NFP expressed in the base frame is

$$p_{i,nom}^b = R_b^w \left[d_{i,x}, y_{bg}, -p_b^w(z) \right]^{\mathsf{T}} \tag{6}$$

where $R_b^w \in SO(3)$ is the world to base rotation, $d_{i,x}$ is the fixed longitudinal distance from the robot's base to the respective coxa joint.

Wall Contact Leg Configuration. The only constraint for the leg in wall contact is that it should not collide with the walls on the opposite side during the transfer phase of wall walking. The foothold position selected as shown in Fig. 5b,

$$y_c = \left[y_w - (c_y + l_1) \cos(q_r) \right] \sin(q_i) \tag{7}$$

$$h_2 = \sqrt{l_3^2 - y_c^2} + 0.5l_2 + (c_y + l_1) \sin(q_r) \tag{8}$$

The NFP expressed in the base frame is

$$p_{i,nom}^b = R_b^w \left[d_{i,x}, y_w, h_2 \right]^{\mathsf{T}} \tag{9}$$

---

[2] The reference number are as follows: 1 – left front leg, 2 – left middle leg, 3 – left rear leg, 4 – right front leg, 5 – right middle leg, 6 – right rear leg.

4.2   Transfer Phase

To select footholds using the AEP for non-straight line motions requires the AEP to be a function of the heading direction. The heading direction is determined by

$$d_b = p_b^w(t) - p_b^w(t - t_{phase}) \qquad (10)$$

where $p_b^w(t)$ is the base position at the end of the support phase obtained from Sect. 4.3, and $p_b^w(t - t_{phase})$ is the base position at the start of the previous support phase.

The unit vector for the heading direction is then projected onto the surface normal the foothold is on so that the AEP will lie on the surface,

$$proj(d_b) = d_b - n_i \, (d_b \cdot n_i) \qquad (11)$$

$$d = \frac{proj(d_b)}{|proj(d_b)|} \qquad (12)$$

where $n_i \in \Re^3$ is the surface normal vector of the current foothold.

Finally, the AEP for the leg expressed in the base frame for a step size, S, is

$$^w p_{i,aep}^b = {}^w p_{i,nom}^b + d \cdot S/2, \qquad (13)$$

$$p_{i,aep}^b = R_w^b(t) \cdot {}^w p_{i,aep}^b \qquad (14)$$

4.3   Support Phase

To track the desired base pose at time instant t, the legs in the support phase would have to move in a direction opposite to the base trajectory. The new position of the robot's foot, i, with respect to the robot's base frame, $p_i^b \in \Re^3$, is described by

$$p_i^b(t) = p_w^b(t) \left[R_w^b(t) p_i^w \right] \qquad (15)$$

where $p_w^b(t) \in \Re^3$ is the desired base position, $R_w^b(t) \in SO(3)$ is the desired base orientation and $p_i^w \in \Re^3$ is the position of the current foothold expressed in the world frame.

The new position of p_i^b is then checked if it:

1. exceeds the PEP circular boundary of the step size centred at the leg's nominal position,

$$b_{pep} = \begin{cases} True, & \text{if } \left[\left({}^w p_{i,x}^{nom} \right)^2 + \left({}^w p_{i,y}^{nom} \right)^2 / (0.5S)^2 \right] > d_{pep} \\ False, & \text{otherwise.} \end{cases} \qquad (16)$$

where ${}^w p_{i,(x,y)}^{nom}$ is the distance between the nominal position and the current position in the x and y direction expressed in the world frame, d_{pep} is the boundary constant which determines how far the leg can exceed the boundary.

2. approach singular configuration,

$$b_{sing} = \begin{cases} True, & \text{if } \sqrt{\left(^w p_{i,y}^{fem}\right)^2 + \left(^w p_{i,z}^{fem}\right)^2} > d_{max}. \\ False, & \text{otherwise.} \end{cases} \tag{17}$$

where $^w p_{i,(y,z)}^{fem}$ is the distance between the femur joint and the foot expressed in the world frame, d_{max} is the maximum leg extension permitted for the leg's second and third link.

3. violates the robot's stability margin,

$$b_{sup} = \begin{cases} True, & \text{if } \boldsymbol{A}_{sp}\boldsymbol{p}_{cob} > \boldsymbol{b}_{sp}. \\ False, & \text{otherwise.} \end{cases} \tag{18}$$

where $\boldsymbol{A}_{sp}$ and $\boldsymbol{b}_{sp}$ are the linear constraints of the support polygon.

If any of the conditions are violated, the gait phase is terminated and $\boldsymbol{q}_b^w(t)$ is used as the reference position to determining the foothold position for the next leg in transfer phase.

5 Evaluation

The proposed motion planning framework has been verified in simulation on the Corin hexapod [4].

5.1 Simulation Setup

The environment is visualised in RViZ (Fig. 1) while the 2.5D grid map utilises the NetworkX package [7]. The map measures $2.52 \times 0.80\,\text{m}^2$ with a cell resolution of $0.03\,\text{m}$, roughly the size of Corin's foot. It consists of two challenging areas: a hole measuring $0.45 \times 0.69\,\text{m}^2$ and a narrow pathway of $0.30\,\text{m}$ width. The start and goal positions are located at opposite ends of the map. The Corin hexapod was used as the robot in this study [5].

5.2 Results and Discussion

The resulting grid map representation in Fig. 6 overlaid with both the path generated by the planner and the actual path following the introduction of the transition routines. The motion primitive for each segment of the path is also shown. All the transition routines proposed in Sect. 3 were required for completing this path. The actual path (blue) in Fig. 6 is very similar to the original where the only change is where wall walking starts and end. The w_{g-w} is immediately made to the most extreme position as discussed in Sect. 3.2.

A video[3] is available that shows Corin navigating the scenario. A set of stills from that video appears in Fig. 7. The three mechanisms employed for the

---

[3] https://youtu.be/Q1HQdX-92uE.

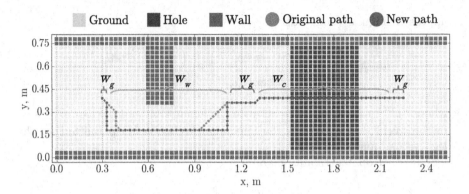

Fig. 6. Path generated by planner showing original and modified path. (Color figure online)

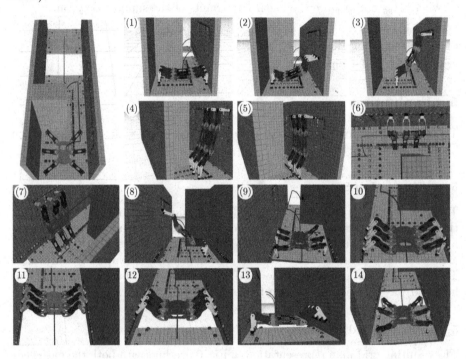

Fig. 7. Motion plan for the scenario and the sequence of stillshot numbered in sequence.

support phase may result in gait phases where the robot's CoB does not move. In such cases, the footholds for the legs in transfer phase are placed at the NFP instead since (12) resolves to zero. An example of this is during the w_{g-w}, the footholds on the ground surface are expected to move closer towards the wall

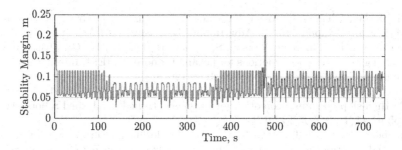

Fig. 8. Stability margin for entire motion remains within the support polygon.

starting from leg 3 (left rear) to leg 1 (left front). When the CoB is suspended, leg 2 is placed further away (NFP) from the wall compared to leg 3 (AEP).

Figure 8 shows that the kinematic stability margin (distance of the robot's CoB to the support polygon edge) for the entire motion. Although the stability was used as a criteria during the foothold planning (Sect. 4.3), this criteria was not called upon during the planning stage for this scenario as the transition routines and the gaits used are inherently stable.

6 Conclusion

This paper presented the motion plan (transition routines and the foothold planning) for achieving continuous motion using advanced motions. The proposed motion plan has been successfully executed in simulation on the Corin hexapod, navigating over areas previously deemed inaccessible, namely narrow pathways and large holes. The results support previous work and confirms the use of advanced motions as being feasible for hexapods. A limitation of this work is that the transitions are all on straight line paths and is not attempted in a corner.

Future work should consider optimising the motion plan to minimise criteria such as the travelling time and the number of steps required as these indirectly optimizes the energy consumption of the robot. Another area is to evaluate the full motion plan on the physical platform to identify potential limitations of the planner including the transition routines.

References

1. Alsalameh, A., Amin, S.H.M., Mamat, R.: Mechanical design of a quadruped robot for horizontal ground to vertical wall movement. In: TENCON Proceedings of Intelligent Systems and Technologies for the New Millennium, pp. 213–217 (2000)
2. Biagiotti, L., Melchiorri, C.: Trajectory Planning for Automatic Machines and Robots. Springer, Heidelberg (2009). https://doi.org/10.1007/978-3-540-85629-0
3. Bodrov, A., Cheah, W., Green, P., Watson, S., Apsley, J.: Joint space reference trajectory to reduce the energy consumption of a six-legged mobile robot. In: 25th International Workshop on Electric Drives (2018)

4. Cheah, W., Khalili, H., Arvin, F., Watson, S., Lennox, B., Green, P.: Advanced motions for hexapods. Int. J. Adv. Robot. Syst. **16**(2) (2019)
5. Cheah, W., Khalili, H.H., Watson, S., Green, P., Lennox, B.: Grid-based motion planning using advanced motions for hexapod robots. In: IEEE International Conference on Intelligent Robots and Systems (2018)
6. Focchi, M., del Prete, A., Havoutis, I., Featherstone, R., Caldwell, D.G., Semini, C.: High-slope terrain locomotion for torque-controlled quadruped robots. Auton. Robots **41**(1), 259–272 (2017)
7. Hagberg, A.A., Schult, D.A., Swart, P.J.: Exploring network structure, dynamics, and function using NetworkX. In: Proceedings of the 7th Python in Science Conference, pp. 11–16 (2008)
8. Henrey, M., Ahmed, A., Boscariol, P., Shannon, L., Menon, C.: Abigaille-III: a versatile, bioinspired hexapod for scaling smooth vertical surfaces. J. Bionic Eng. **11**(1), 1–17 (2014)
9. Hutter, M., et al.: ANYmal - toward legged robots for harsh environments. Adv. Robot. **31**(17), 918–931 (2017)
10. Kydd, K., Macrez, S., Pourcel, P.: Autonomous robot for gas and oil sites. In: SPE Offshore Europe Conference and Exhibition, pp. 1–10. Society of Petroleum Engineers (2015)
11. Li, C., Pullin, A.O., Haldane, D.W., Lam, H.K., Fearing, R.S., Full, R.J.: Terradynamically streamlined shapes in animals and robots enhance traversability through densely cluttered terrain. Bioinspiration and Biomim. **10**(4) (2015)
12. Loc, V.G., et al.: Sensing and gait planning of quadruped walking and climbing robot for traversing in complex environment. Robot. Auton. Syst. **58**(5), 666–675 (2010)
13. Petr, C., Faigl, J.: Foothold placement planning with a hexapod crawling robot. In: IEEE/RSJ International Conference on Intelligent Robots and Systems, pp. 4096–4101 (2017)
14. Pratt, G., Manzo, J.: The DARPA robotics challenge official website. IEEE Robot. Autom. Mag. **20**(june), 10–12 (2013)
15. Qian, J., Zhang, Z., Ma, L.: Gait programming for multi-legged robot climbing on walls and ceilings. In: Bioinspiration and Robotics Walking and Climbing Robots, pp. 147–170. IntechOpen (2017)
16. Song, S.-M., Waldron, K.J.: Machines that Walk: The Adaptive Suspension Vehicle. MIT Press, Cambridge (1989)
17. Waldron, K.J., Vohnout, V.J., Pery, A., Mcghee, R.B.: Configuration design of the adaptive suspension vehicle. Int. J. Robot. Res. **3**(2), 37–48 (1984)
18. Wang, Z.Y., Ding, X.L., Rovetta, A.: Analysis of typical locomotion of a symmetric hexapod robot. Robotica **28**(06), 893–907 (2010)
19. Winkler, A.W., Mastalli, C., Havoutis, I., Focchi, M., Caldwell, D.G., Semini, C.: Planning and execution of dynamic whole-body locomotion for a hydraulic quadruped on challenging terrain. In: IEEE International Conference on Robotics and Automation, pp. 5148–5154 (2015)

Robotic Learning, Mapping and Planning

Towards Adversarial Training for Mobile Robots

Todd Flyr[1(✉)] and Simon Parsons[2(✉)]

[1] Department of Computer Science, Graduate Center, City University of New York,
New York City, USA
`tflyr@gradcenter.cuny.edu`
[2] Department of Informatics, King's College London, London, UK
`simon.parsons@kcl.ac.uk`

Abstract. This paper reports some preliminary work on learning on a
physical robot. In particular, we report on an experiment to learn how to
strike a ball to hit a target on the ground. We compare learning based just
on previous trials with the robot with learning based on those trials plus
additional data learnt using a generative adversarial network (GAN).
We find that the additional data generated by the GAN improves the
performance of the robot.

1 Introduction

While machine learning as a field has advanced considerably in recent years
[9], there has yet been relatively little work using neural networks with mobile
robots. A significant reason for this is the fundamental difficulty of obtaining
a sufficiently large dataset to train a neural network for use in such devices.
Traditional techniques for training a neural network require a large corpus of
labeled training data [4,5]. Obtaining such a corpus generally requires thou-
sands to millions of trials and the additional human labor for labeling them. For
many machine learning tasks, such as image or speech recognition, large labeled
datasets are collaboratively created by various labs which are then shared online
for use by anyone wishing to train on them [5].

In mobile robotics, the use of large datasets is a challenge. It is difficult to
run a mobile robot in a complex task for enough trials to create such a dataset.
In addition, each trial can take a long time to complete. Devices embedded in
the real world must deal with a level of uncertainty that is difficult to recreate
without the experience of many real world trials. Lastly, mobile robots vary
considerably in their design and components, and the tasks they can complete
also vary greatly. Thus developing large collaborative datasets has not proved
to be practical.

Recent developments in adversarial learning offer a way to solve this problem.
Generative Adversarial Networks (GANs) [6], originally introduced for predictive
learning and generation of image and video data, can be configured to rely
on a much smaller corpus of labeled data than is normally needed for other

© Springer Nature Switzerland AG 2019
K. Althoefer et al. (Eds.): TAROS 2019, LNAI 11649, pp. 197–208, 2019.
https://doi.org/10.1007/978-3-030-23807-0_17

artificial neural network (ANN) training methods. This paper begins to explore how GANs might be used in the training of a controller for a mobile robot when only a small training dataset is available.

2   Related Work

Research into robot learning is extensive. Here we summarise only the most related elements. In [3] Bongard suggests that there are three aspects of adaptive evolution, the last, of which, *prospection*, is most relevant here. Prospection is the ability of an organism or robot to predict future actions, in particular the ability to mentally simulate the actions of future events that have never been previously encountered. Thus a robot equipped with prospection can then adapt to novel situations and can simulate itself to try to understand itself in more detail. Such a robot could rehearse novel actions that can enable it to recover in the face of degraded ability or partial injury or failure. A form of prospection is the ultimate aim of our work.

Pinto *et al.* [11] trained a convolutional neural network (CNN) on image data. However, instead of training images to labels, they trained the images to physical interactions with the robot. Specifically, they record grasping data, pushing data, poke data, and lastly what they label "identity vision", which is a variant of active vision [12]. This method for comprehending objects without labels is proposed as a form of unsupervised learning wherein a robot could be given objects and follow a routine of physical interactions with them to learn what they were in a more intimate way than images. Our work shares the underlying use of neural network methods and the combination of vision data and physical action.

In addition to a recurrent neural network, [8] use a GAN framework to improve on trajectory prediction models for navigating in a crowd with a reduced computational cost. Like the work reported here, [8] shows what can be achieved with a GAN architecture in a learning and simulation environment. Unlike this work, it does not use a physical robot.

Somewhat similar to [11] is the work of [10]. This work developed a method for training a large CNN combined with an autoencoder to learn from first person videos of humans doing a task that involves manipulating objects with their hands. Learning from a sequence of frames allows the network to predict the next frames (future regression) for up to 1–2 s. The robot equipped with the neural network can learn to clear space on a table to allow a person carrying a box towards the table to set down the box. The future prediction mechanism from [10] has subsequently been applied to a similar scenario to that in [11]. Here we have a robot engaging in learning in self simulation via a mechanism similar to the proposal in [3]. In [10] a turtlebot is trained to recognize and approach (or avoid) an object in a room by using a process described as a "dreaming model". The robot wanders randomly in the space taking pictures. Then a variational autoencoder with the prediction mechanism from [10] is used to produce sequences of images that are realistic for a path to the object, and a reinforcement learning algorithm learns the correct policies on them. This is done without any real-world trials, and so represents a form of imagining how to achieve a simple goal.

3   Background

A key component of the approach that we use in this paper is a Generative Adversarial Network. GANs are a relatively recent approach to machine learning [6]. They involve one network that is trained to deceive another network by mimicking a dataset:

> "We simultaneously train two models: a generative model G that captures the data distribution, and a discriminative model D that estimates the probability that a sample came from the training data rather than G. The training procedure for G is to maximize the probability of D making a mistake." [7]

In other words, GANs can be a means of generating data that mimics a dataset. Once the GAN is trained, the discriminator cannot tell the difference between real trial data and data from the generator. This means that GANs can potentially be used to increase the amount of data available for training another machine learning method. When that method is a neural network, which (as mentioned above) are typically data hungry, GANs can be used to boost a small dataset, that is unable to do a good job of training a neural network, into a larger dataset that is able to train a neural network well. That is exactly how we used a GAN in the work described here. In particular, we use a Wasserstein GAN (WGAN) [2]. WGANs are a variant of the original GAN, specifically designed to minimize "mode collapse" in which G repeatedly generates the same data accepted by D.

4   Experimental Setup

4.1   Overview

A Turtlebot was modified to strike a ball on the ground at a target inside an arena. This is intended to mimic the actions of a simple golf putt. If the hit ball reaches the target, then it is considered a successful shot or score. The overall aim of the work is for a robot to be able to learn a strategy for hitting the ball, compute a set of movements to line up the shot, hit the ball, and score. The experiment is to determine whether the robot will be able to learn this task with only a small number of trials, using adversarial learning techniques to create additional training data. The work reported here involved three sets of experimental trials. In the first set of trials, the robot was controlled by a simple rule-based system. This was intended to both provide a baseline set of results against which robot performance could be compared, and to provide some initial data for learning experiments. In the second set of trials, the robot was controlled

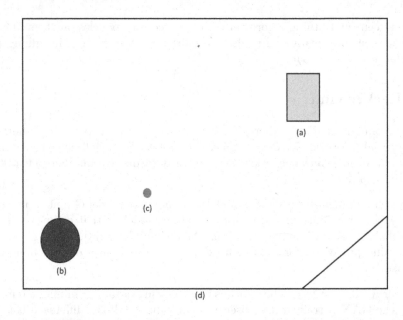

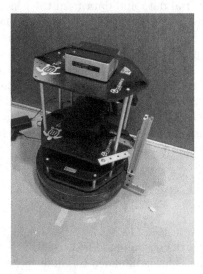

Fig. 1. The experimental setup. At the top is a diagrammatic view of the area (a) The target—a piece of colored paper. (b) The turtlebot with the putter head attached to the side. (c) The ball is placed in an initial position. The robot must locate the ball and the target and then properly position itself to line up the shot. (d) The arena walls. On the bottom left is a photograph of the arena. On the bottom right is a photograph of the modified Turtlebot. (Color figure online)

by a feed-forward neural network trained on the data from the rule-based trials. In the third set of trials, the robot was under the control of a neural network learnt from a combination of the data generated in the rule-based trials, and additional data generated by a GAN which was itself trained using data from the rule-based trials.

4.2 Physical Setup

A Turtlebot 2 (Kobuki base) running the Robot Operating System (ROS) was placed in a mapped fixed-sized arena of 2×3 m. The Turtlebot 2 comes equipped with a mounted Microsoft Kinect RGB-D sensor for 3D depth mapped vision/pointcloud generation. Attached to the left side of the Turtlebot is a small putter constructed from 80/20 aluminium. This putter has an approximately 6 cm head that is about 1 cm above the floor (see Fig. 1, bottom right). This putter is fixed to the robot and cannot swing independently of the robot base. There are no additional sensors for the putter. A colored sheet of paper representing a target is placed on the floor within view of the robot. A colored ball (pink, about 7 cm diameter) is also placed on the floor within view of the robot. The robot is running the ROS turtlebot navigation stack. It is also running the ROS package *cmvision_3d*, which performs color blob detection and combines it with depth data from the RGB-D sensor. This allows the robot to locate the ball and the target. The robot is placed in a marked, fixed initial position in the corner of the arena, as if in position to approach a putt (see Fig. 1).

4.3 Data and Training

As described above, data was collected during trials using a rule-based controller. This was then used to train two new controllers. One was a neural network learnt directly from data collected from the rule-based trials. The other was a neural network learnt from the same data augmented with data generated by a GAN (itself trained using data from the rule-based trials).

The data collected during the rule-based trials includes the following components. One is the target location (x, y) where x is the left/right distance and y is the depth of the arena. The coordinate for height, while available, is not needed for a flat target on the floor. The second component is the initial (x, y) position of the ball. The next component is the initial robot location and pose including the (x, y) position and a quaternion for its orientation. ROS uses quaternions for rotations as defined by its *tf* (transform) package. It is composed of (a, b, c, w) and encodes a rotation in three dimensional space [13]. All the coordinates are converted to the coordinates of the map via the ROS transform package. Thus we have a vector of:

$$\langle target(x, y), ball(x, y), robot\_initial\_pose(position(x, y), quaternion(a, b, c, w)) \rangle \quad (1)$$

available for training. The robot also tracks the ball when hit and records the closest approach to the centre of the target, recording the inverse, q, of the ball being the output $(1 - (\text{min distance of ball}))$ or $(1 - d_{min})$.

The neural network learnt directly from this data was a fully connected feed forward network with two hidden layers. The network topology was $7 \times 120 \times 84 \times 3$. Note that training only considered the yaw (rotation on the z-axis) of the robot. This makes the inputs

$$\langle target(x,y), ball(x,y), robot\_initial\_pose(position(x,y), yaw))\rangle \qquad (2)$$

and the outputs $\langle position(x,y), yaw\rangle$ which are converted into the robot final pose in ROS,

$$\langle position(x,y), quaternion(a,b,c,w)\rangle \qquad (3)$$

This is where the robot should be positioned in order to hit the ball to the target. The robot swing rotational distance and swing velocity are currently fixed. Once the neural network was trained, trials were carried out in which it controlled the robot by setting the target point at which the robot tried to strike the ball.

To augment the data from the rule-based trials, we used a GAN to mimic the trial data (which was then used to train a neural network with the same topology as before). The aim in doing so is that the discriminator, D, trains the generator to only generate input parameters and output trajectories that make sense in the context of the actual training corpus, and thus can eliminate nonsensical examples such as the ball going in the opposite direction from where it was hit. To train a GAN G (specifically a WGAN [2]), all of the data from the rule-based trials becomes outputs, as G is trying to simulate the entire system, and generators only accept noise as inputs by definition, thus seven inputs plus three outputs equals ten. The critic, D, accepts G's outputs and only outputs whether or not G looks like a genuine trial run.

We used a WGAN because it helps prevent mode collapse, where the GAN output would have zero variability in the generated trials. The GAN we used is a modification of the WGAN code from [1]. Those scripts are written in PyTorch, a python DSL (Domain Specific Language) built on the Torch libraries for machine learning. A separate script takes the dumped YAML from the ROS python scripts and creates and serializes a dataset for use by the PyTorch WGAN script. The data we used was a small corpus of 14 entries from the rule-based trials. In all of these the target was located in basically the same location. The GAN was trained to a loss on the critic of -0.000014 and on the generator to 0.010729 on a network of $8 \times 96 \times 106 \times 106 \times 106 \times 106 \times 96 \times 11$ in size for the generator and a critic of $11 \times 64 \times 74 \times 74 \times 74 \times 74 \times 64 \times 1$ over 6000 iterations of training. After some preliminary work, we added an additional output parameter to the generator to reinforce the importance of being close enough to actually hit the ball. If a ball was missed outright, it was set to zero and if it was close enough to hit, it was set to $+1$ for the trial. Hence the generator output and discriminator input size of eleven. This additional parameter is dropped when the feed-forward network (denoted MLP for "multi-layer perceptron") is trained.

4.4   Experimental Procedure

The following section describes how each experimental trial was performed.

The robot, ball, and target are placed in the arena, and the robot controller uses the RGB-D sensor to locate the ball and target via the *cmvision_3d* package. It then computes a location that will position the robot next to the ball with the putter aligned hit the ball to the target. This position is chosen so that base of the robot is in a location where the putter head is perpendicular to the target. Once this position is determined, the robot sets it as a navigation goal and moves to that location. When the navigation goal is reached, the robot rotates counterclockwise approximately a quarter turn, to prepare for the swing, and then swings the club by quickly executing a clockwise turn at a relatively high rate of rotational velocity. Upon completion of the swing the robot then quickly moves to the forward facing position in relation to the arena. After the ball is hit the robot attempts to track it via the RGB-D sensor. It then records all movement of the ball, whether it hits the target, and the closest approach to the centre of the target.

Note that ROS *tf* is used when the robot tracks the ball after it is hit (and while the robot may still be in motion) as it recovers from its swing to ensure that the ball is accurately tracked on the map. In practice this approach works quite well despite the fast rotational movement of the robot.

The key thing about the setup is that the experiments revolve around setting the location that the robot chooses to move to before beginning its "swing". This is the element that is computed by the rule-based system and the neural networks. All these calculations were based on the relative locations of target and ball, so represent general mechanisms for making this decision, although the results presented here were obtained from experiments in which the ball and target were always in the same place.

5   Experiments

5.1   Trials

As described above, we carried out three sets of trials. First, we ran 14 trials where the robot was under the control of the rule-based system. Second, we took the data recorded in these trials and used it to train a feed forward neural network (MLP) as described in Sect. 4.3. We then ran trials where the trained MLP determined the location to which the robot would move before attempting to hit the ball to the target. We carried out six trials, stopping when it became apparent that the robot would not approach the ball closely enough to ever strike it. (Recall that the sensors on the robot cannot detect the ball when the robot is close to it—the key skill that the robot is learning here is to pick a location from which to strike the ball from its initial observation of the ball.) Third, we used the GAN described in Sect. 4.3 to generate data based on the rule-based trials, and used this and the data from the rule-based trials to train another feed-forward neural network (denoted MLP/GAN). We then ran another 14 trials in which the MLP/GAN picked the location to which the robot would move.

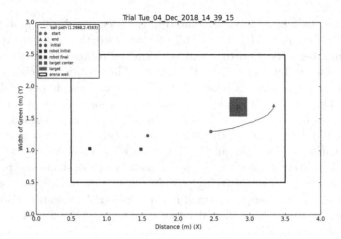

Fig. 2. A trial with the robot controlled by the MLP/GAN trained neural network. This glancing hit caused a spin resulting in the hook seen here and the closest approach was measured at 28.8 cm from the target centre. (Color figure online)

5.2 Results

We present results from all three sets of trials. As examples of what data was collected for each trial, see Fig. 2. This is data from a trial with the MLP/GAN, but the same data was collected for all trials. We have the initial and final positions of the robot (green and blue squares, respectively), the initial position of the ball (red circle), the target position (yellow-green square), and the tracked location of the ball. Since the ball is tracked by the robot, it is not tracked right from the point at which it is hit because it is within the minimum range of the RGB-D sensor. What is recorded are the earliest point at which the moving ball is observed (magenta circle), around 1 m from the robot, where the ball comes to rest (magenta triangle), and the track (blue line). From this we can compute the closest approach of the ball to the centre of the target.

Table 1 summarises the overall performance of the three controllers on the task at hand—hitting the ball to the target. Performance is measured by the closest approach of the ball to the centre of the target. The table includes data for all 14 trials of the rule-based system. In each of these trials the robot hit the ball, and, on average, hit it within 23 cm of the target centre. The data from the trials was subsequently used to train the MLP and MLP/GAN controllers, and the performance of the rule-based controller demonstrates that the dataset used to train the MLPs was of reasonable quality with examples of both of successful and failed shots (six hits and eight misses). The table includes data on six trials of the MLP controller. The robot hit the ball in none of these trials, so there was no "closest approach" data to collect. Since it became clear that this controller would not position the robot close enough to the ball to hit it, we abandoned these trials after the six failures. Finally, Table 1 includes data from 14 trials

Table 1. The closest approach of ball to target for each control system. Distances reported in X and Y directions and *Euclid*ian. Note that the target location bug requires occasional correction by 19 cm (the distance between the corner and the centre of the target). Items with a dash "-" indicate the robot did not get close enough to the ball to hit it. The MLP trials were abandoned after six trials when it became clear it was never going to get close enough to the ball to hit it. The average for the MLP/GAN includes the corrected values. In the rule-based system, trials 4, 7, 9–12 were recorded as hits, in general, any ball within about 18 cm of the target centre will be recorded by the robot as a hit. None of the MLP/GAN trials come that close.

Trial	Rule-based system			MLP			MLP/GAN			
	X	Y	Euclid	X	Y	Euclid	X	Y	Euclid	Corrected
1	0.0928	0.2346	0.2523	-	-	-	0.2164	0.4787	0.5252	
2	0.0308	0.3041	0.3057	-	-	-	0.5646	0.3243	0.6444	
3	0.0047	0.2769	0.2769	-	-	-	-	-	-	
4	0.0665	0.0521	0.0845	-	-	-	-	-	-	
5	0.1738	0.4496	0.4820	-	-	-	0.3099	0.2475	0.3966	
6	0.0539	0.2509	0.2566	-	-	-	-	-	-	
7	0.1467	0.0871	0.1706				-	-	-	
8	0.0444	0.2671	0.2708				0.0145	0.0135	0.0198	0.2098
9	0.1347	0.0742	0.1538				0.089	0.2739	0.288	
10	0.1346	0.0013	0.1346				0.0767	0.1716	0.188	0.378
11	0.0253	0.1649	0.1668				0.0004	0.4972	0.4953	
12	0.0084	0.0682	0.0687				-	-	-	
13	0.2099	0.2069	0.2947				0.4892	0.4299	0.6513	
14	0.0428	0.2611	0.2646				0.5131	0.3819	0.6166	
Average	0.0835	0.1928	0.2273				0.2526	0.3132	0.4672	

with the MLP/GAN controller. In nine of these the robot managed to hit the ball, and the closest approach data is provided for these trials.

Figure 3 gives plots of six trials of the MLP/GAN controller. As discussed in the caption of Fig. 3, note that a bug in the ball-tracking code means that in several of the trials, the closest approach was recorded incorrectly. As Fig. 3(c) shows, this led to data initially being recorded with a smaller "closest approach" than was actually the case. Table 1 gives the corrected data.

Because the MLP-controlled robot never hit the ball, Table 1 does not provide a quantitative comparison of the performance of the MLP and MLP/GAN controllers. To provide this, Tables 2 and 3 provide data on how close the MLP-controlled and MLP/GAN-controlled robots approached the ball.

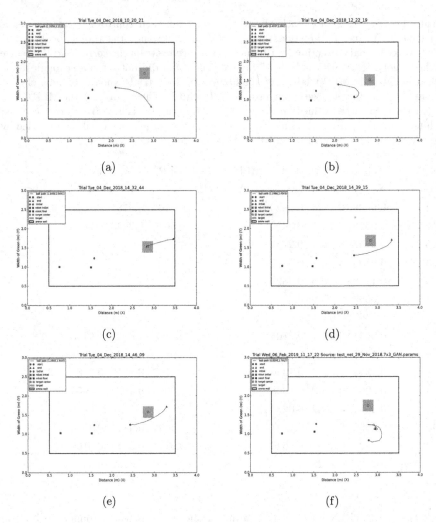

Fig. 3. Plots of putts with the robot under control of the MLP/GAN controller. Note that the robot position is consistently too far behind the ball to hit it effectively. (a) - A miss (Closest: 0.5252 m), (b) A glancing hit sent the ball spinning (Closest: 0.3966 m), (c) Target shift bug suggests a hit but it was not (Closest: 0.0198 m corrected in Table 3), (d) Close. (Closest: 0.288 m), (e) Close but not a hit (target shift bug) (Closest: 0.188 m corrected in Table 3), (f) A hard hook due to spin. (Closest: 0.4953 m)

5.3 Analysis

Comparing the MLP and the MLP/GAN, it is clear that the MLP/GAN has better performance. Not only did the MLP/GAN manage to hit the ball in a number of its trials, unlike the MLP, the MLP/GAN also approaches the ball more closely. The average distance of the MLP controlled robot was 14 cm from the X coordinate of the ball and 25 cm from the Y coordinate while the

Table 2. Summary of the six trials where the robot was controlled with the MLP that was trained on a dataset that consisted *only* of data from physical trials with the robot under control of the rule-based system.

Trial	Initial ball position		Final robot position		Robot distance from ball		
	X	Y	X	Y	X	Y	Euclidian
1	1.5811	1.2869	1.4499	1.021	0.1312	0.2661	0.2967
2	1.5821	1.2516	1.4529	1.0016	0.1292	0.2450	0.2813
3	1.5804	1.2722	1.4496	1.0395	0.1308	0.2327	0.2669
4	1.5565	1.2737	1.3996	1.0416	0.1569	0.2321	0.2801
5	1.5759	1.2439	1.4151	0.9737	0.1608	0.2702	0.3144
6	1.5754	1.2548	1.4422	0.9738	0.1332	0.2819	0.3110
Average					0.1403	0.2553	0.2914

Table 3. Summary of the six trials where the robot was controlled with the MLP that was trained on a dataset that consisted data from physical trials with the robot under control of the rule-based system augmented with GAN generated data.

Trial	Initial ball position		Final robot position		Robot distance from ball		
	X	Y	X	Y	X	Y	Euclidian
1	1.5588	1.2697	1.4643	1.0543	0.0945	0.2154	0.2352
2	1.6091	1.2413	1.5431	1.0365	0.0660	0.2048	0.2152
3	1.5804	1.1979	1.4607	0.9319	0.1197	0.2660	0.2917
4	1.5767	1.2362	1.4508	0.9860	0.1259	0.2502	0.2801
5	1.5691	1.236	1.4506	0.9854	0.1185	0.2506	0.2772
6	1.6021	1.2792	1.4798	1.0339	0.1223	0.2453	0.2741
Average					0.1062	0.2387	0.2623

MLP/GAN controlled robot approached within 11 cm (X) and 24 (Y) cm. The latter result is obviously correlated with the former since stopping too far away from the ball will mean that the robot cannot hit it. However, it is gratifying to see this so clearly in the data.

The robot controlled by the MLP/GAN failed to hit the ball to the target in 14 trials. It did, however, hit the ball in nine of those trials. As a result, there is "closest approach" data for the MLP/GAN, and this shows that the MLP/GAN controller does not perform as well as the rule based system. The average closest approach for the MLP/GAN is 47 cm, as opposed to 23 cm for the rule-based system. Examining the full set of plots of the trials (a subset of which are in Fig. 3), it seems that to hit the target it is necessary for the robot's final position to be facing the target before attempting its swing. The MLP/GAN was not as effective as the rule-based system at doing that. When the MLP/GAN-controlled robot hit the ball, it generally sent the ball straight ahead, as opposed to the angle necessary to hit the target. This misalignment resulted in the relatively high average closest approach. However, the best shots were within 20 cm. These shots tended to be glancing shots which put a slight counterclockwise spin on the ball, which hooked it towards the target (see Fig. 3(e)).

6   Conclusion

This preliminary work indicates that given a small dataset on which to train a neural network to control a robot, the performance of that network can be significantly improved by augmenting the dataset with the output of a GAN. This is possible given an initial training set with as few as 14 trials. While the performance of the neural network trained with data from the GAN does not outperform the system that generated the initial data, we have yet to make a serious attempt to achieve this. The performance of systems that make use of GANs in other domains suggest that they have the potential to further boost the performance of this system, and can make it more robust overall by generating data that is more varied than the original trial data, while still being realistic. Future work will examine if this is possible in our domain.

References

1. Arjovsky, M., Chintala, S., Bottou, L. https://github.com/martinarjovsky/WassersteinGAN (2017). Accessed 10 Jan 2019
2. Arjovsky, M., Chintala, S., Bottou, L.: Wasserstein GAN (2017). arXiv:1701.07875
3. Bongard, J.C.: Using robots to investigate the evolution of adaptive behavior. Curr. Opin. Behav. Sci. **6**, 168–173 (2015)
4. Coates, A., Baumstarck, P., Le, Q.V., Ng, A.Y.: Scalable learning for object detection with GPU hardware. In: IROS (2009)
5. Deng, J., Dong, W., Socher, R., Li, L., Li, K., Fei-Fei, L.: ImageNet: a large-scale hierarchical image database. In: CVPR (2009)
6. Goodfellow, I.J.: Generative adversarial networks. CoRR, arXiv:1701.00160 (2017)
7. Goodfellow, I.J., et al.: Generative adversarial nets. In: NIPS (2014)
8. Gupta, A., Johnson, J., Fei-Fei, L., Savarese, S., Alahi, A.: Social GAN: socially acceptable trajectories with generative adversarial networks. CoRR, arXiv:1803.10892 (2018)
9. LeCun, Y., Bengio, Y., Hinton, G.: Deep learning. Nature **521**, 436 (2015)
10. Lee, J., Ryoo, M.S.: Learning robot activities from first-person human videos using convolutional future regression. CoRR, arXiv:1703.01040 (2017)
11. Pinto, L., Gandhi, D., Han, Y., Park, Y.-L., Gupta, A.: The curious robot: learning visual representations via physical interactions. In: Leibe, B., Matas, J., Sebe, N., Welling, M. (eds.) ECCV 2016. LNCS, vol. 9906, pp. 3–18. Springer, Cham (2016). https://doi.org/10.1007/978-3-319-46475-6_1
12. Swain, M., Stricker, M.: Promising directions in active vision. Int. J. Comput. Vis. **11**, 109 (1993)
13. Zelenak, A.: TF2 ROS quaternion basics. http://wiki.ros.org/tf2/Tutorials/Quaternions (2019). Accessed 10 Jan 2019

Collaborative HRI and Machine Learning for Constructing Personalised Physical Exercise Databases

Daniel Delgado Bellamy$^{(\boxtimes)}$ and Praminda Caleb-Solly$^{(\boxtimes)}$

Bristol Robotics Laboratory, University of West England, Bristol, UK
{daniel.delgadobellamy,Praminda.Caleb-solly}@uwe.ac.uk

Abstract. Recent demographics indicate that we have a growing population of older adults with increasingly complex care-related needs, and a shrinking care workforce with limited resources to support them. As a result, there are a large number of research initiatives investigating the potential of intelligent robots in a domestic environment to augment the support care-givers can provide and improve older adults' well-being, particularly by motivating them in staying fit and healthy through exercise. In this paper, we propose a robot-based coaching system which encourages collaboration with the user to collect person-specific exercise-related movement data. The aim is to personalise the experience of exercise sessions and provide directed feedback to the user to help improve their performance. The way each individual user is likely to perform specific movements will be based on their personal ability and range of motion, and it is important for a coaching system to recognise the movements and map the feedback to the user accordingly. We show how a machine learning technique, a Nearest Neighbour classifier enhanced with a confidence metric, is used to build a personalised database of 3D skeletal tracking data. This approach, combined with collaborative Human-Robot Interaction to collect the data, could be used for robust and adaptable exercise performance tracking by a collaborative robot coach, using the information to provide personalised feedback.

Keywords: Human-Robot Interaction · Robot coaching · Assistive robots

1 Introduction

There is a growing need to support an ageing population who have a number of care-related needs (Park (2018), United Nations (2017) and Coombs (2017)) and in particular to help support them in keeping healthy and well for as long as possible. Technology offers a lot of potential to support people with a range of disabilities. Recent advancements in assistive robotics are showing how these technologies can help in a number of ways - from rehabilitation to social support and physical assistance. It is important for such technologies to be adaptable

© Springer Nature Switzerland AG 2019
K. Althoefer et al. (Eds.): TAROS 2019, LNAI 11649, pp. 209–220, 2019.
https://doi.org/10.1007/978-3-030-23807-0_18

and flexible to make them practical in the real world. This research investigates the use of machine vision and learning to enable collaborative human-robot interaction and personalisation in providing exercise coaching support.

The rapidly ageing population, and the variability of individual needs within this group, together with a growing shortage of carers with the skills to meet the needs of this section of the population, is exacerbated by the complexity of care needs in later life. These needs include support for activities of daily living, as well as support to maintain a healthy and active lifestyle Bianchi-Berthouze (2013).

There are already services which encourage people to engage in physical activities to ensure they can stay fit for as long as possible, however given the accessibility needs of older adults with ageing-related impairments, there are specific challenges which include difficulties in understanding technology, limited physical capacities, cognitive impairments or simply more varied physiological needs because of the wide range of ages (Burns (2016), Mitchell (2009), Sharkey and Sharkey (2012)), Ofcom (2017). As such, the monitoring, evaluation and continued support or treatment for specific conditions that are likely to change over time, becomes a complex process requiring particular consideration of the following:

1. "personalisation" of the support and/or treatment.
2. "interpretability" of the user's changing needs so that the system can adapt the support provided, and also enable specialists to improve or update the quality of services provided.

Focusing on the provision of programmes for physical activity or exercise, which delay or ameliorate the effect of ageing, can be an effective way of coping with the growing crisis. However, ensuring effective engagement with exercise regimes still requires considerable personalised assistance. For our study, we formulated the following research questions in considering a system where a socially assistive robot offers support for a physical exercise:

1. What type of information regarding the user's movements could be collected by the robot to provide personalised feedback and support successful human-robot interaction through physical exercise?
2. To what extent can information regarding the user's performance be used to develop a self-learning system enabling online evaluation?

2   Literature Review

Motivational roles in the context of supporting physical activity are commonly performed by professional therapists, as well as relatives or friends, however frequent access to professionals is limited due to lack of resources. Moreover, as people age, maintaining social and physical interaction may be more difficult due to limited mobility or energy, which is also why they might need a significant level of time and personalised attention. In the field of Assistive

Robotics, there are many initiatives that aim at consolidating a user database to develop assistive robotics systems which can enhance older people lives. These include projects such as Grow me up by Martins et al. (2015), ASTRO by Cavallo et al. (2013), Accompany by Saunders et al. (2013), MOBISERV by Nani et al. (2010), SRS by Pigini et al. (2012), CoSHE by Pham et al. (2018). While the approaches for creating user profiles used in these projects are promising, they have a lot of associated complexity and expense, with an emphasis on the technology rather than on the user or on improving the HRI. While the design of a "coach" robot can benefit from these studies, there is potential to introduce an approach which focuses on the development of an off-the-shelf intelligent application which enables personalisation of the system for carrying out exercise routines, in a collaborative manner.

In order to provide real-time feedback on physical activity it is important to be able to track the user's body position. Regarding the perception of the user's posture data, survey papers such as Poppe (2010), Krüger et al. (2007), Moeslund et al. (2006), Wang et al. (2003) have reviewed studies that focused on full-body movement recognition using cameras. Activities such as running, swimming, walking and others or specific actions such as waving, clapping or pointing could be detected with good levels of accuracy. In Lara et al. (2013) and Lo Presti and La Cascia (2016), the detection of links and joints was considered more efficient for more complex human action recognition.

With regards to the capture of the user posture data, the state-of-the-art approaches which use skeletal joint data normally train their algorithms using large data sets available online or collected specifically for the study as reviewed in Lara et al. (2013) and Lo Presti and La Cascia (2016). These databases are composed of people of different ages, sizes, constitutions and other traits, with people performing specific actions so that the algorithms can learn to extract the common pixel features from an image when the action performed. However, it is well-known that the collection of data sets is a time-consuming and complex task.

For providing support for exercise coaching, specific movements do not just need to be detected, but also evaluated with respect to the user's baseline performance in order to provide appropriate feedback and encouragement. Earlier research by Ros and Demiris (2013), already explored the idea of motivational feedback for children by using a dancing coach robot to boost their creativity. The research presented here goes beyond this, by considering additional feedback to ensure correct movement, as part of a coaching system.

A number of studies use supervised neural networks for learning postures and movements of vision-based data, however supervised learning methods such as neural networks may not be transparent for evaluation of the learning process and therefore are not very accessible for therapists or caregivers who might need to tune or modify the system. Alternative machine learning approaches used are clustering techniques, such as k-means, PCA and Self-Organising Maps. Recently, Maharani et al. (2018) used K-means clustering for hand gesture recognition.

From what we see in the literature, most of the approaches which could be relevant to our study do not facilitate ease of data collection and interpretability, which, for our application of providing coaching assistance to the user, are key to monitoring progress and learning how the performance of the user changes over time. We therefore investigated that a collaborative approach that could ease the gathering and labelling of data, enabling continuous learning and adaptation, and be developed as a re-usable module for different users.

While we have found some interesting coach robot deployments to encourage and engage older adults, none of them make it possible to give constructive feedback to the end-user to address their specific needs in terms of positional and posture correction, which is fundamental when delivering therapeutic coaching. We also found that due to different users having very specific movement characteristics, it is not practical to develop and deploy activity recognition algorithms which are more generic. As such, we propose the use of machine learning classifiers which could be developed in collaboration with a user to overcome the limitations of labelling and collecting large amounts of data, while still being able to provide feedback based on continuous evaluation of the user's performance.

3 Human-Robot Collaboration for Data Collection

Exercise coaches play the role of advisors, motivators, carers, teachers and learners. If we want a robot to develop these capacities we first have to build some prototype modules which constitute a robotic cognitive structure as shown in Fig. 1 on the left. Our system integrates an Astra ORBBEC camera and a Pepper robot in ROS where the systems blocks are organised as shown in Fig. 1 on the right.

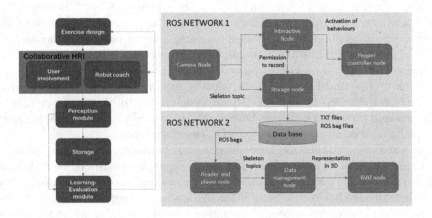

Fig. 1. System architecture

For our system, the chosen approach uses a learning by demonstration concept, meaning that the user can guide the robot in learning the different actions without the intervention of another human. If we want the user to collaborate with the robot, he or she first has to understand what the robot is asking, to be able to perform the expected exercise. Speech is one of the most common communication modality in Human-Human Interaction especially when a coach has to provide instructions. Moreover, speech can be supported by other expressive behaviours which correspond with human-like communication such as gestures or pictures. The Pepper NaoQi Software Development Kit (NaoQi SDK) provides multiple modules for social interaction from which we chose five as the most relevant to create a basic communicative robot coach, these included the voice module, animated speech gesticulation, visual display, people gaze tracking and Pepper modes control.

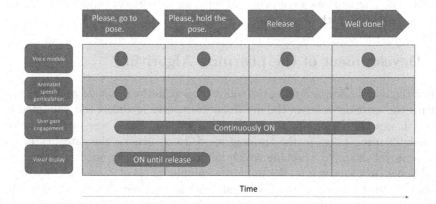

Fig. 2. Interaction sequence for data collection

The robot was thus programmed so that its complete performance comprises speaking and gesticulating in a timely manner while keeping eye contact with the user, see Fig. 2. Furthermore, at certain times, the robot was programmed to make use of its tablet to clarify what the user is expected to execute by displaying an image of each pose. The interaction sequence for collecting the data is shown in Fig. 3 where the robot announces each pose which the user has to perform and hold for a moment so that the robot can record the user joint positions for

Fig. 3. Real exercise application

that pose via the Orbbec camera. We prioritised the interaction structure over the sophistication of the modules as the goal is to have a functional system first. In the future, the specific poses, timing of the exercises and other factors which relate to the therapeutic aspects of the exercise will be fine tuned in consultation with experts in physiotherapy and psychology.

In terms of data collection, each session comprised the execution of 4 sets of poses with a break after the first two to let the user rest. The complete execution of the collaborative data collection session produced 4 sets of poses, each containing 6 iterations or repetitions of the three poses (a total of 24 samples per pose, $24 \times 3 = 72$) and 4 poses arbitrarily recorded at the beginning of the session for validation purposes also known as "rest poses". The total duration of the entire session lasted for around 30 min and we collected data from 10 participants. The participants were provided with an information sheet and consent form as part of the ethics process.

4   Development of the Learning Algorithm

When the user performs a pose, the robot saves it in the database and compares it with the existing poses in the database previously recorded and validated by a health expert. The robot then associates the perceived pose with the closest neighbouring poses in the training space to determine the category of the new pose, for example, checking which label occurs more frequently among the neighbours. In other words, the unknown sample labels are assessed by using a probability distribution of the Euclidean distance to their closest samples. This method is commonly known as K-Nearest Neighbours (KNNs) where K is the number of neighbours considered to classify the new sample. This is a supervised learning approach.

To test this classifier we separated the data of each participant into two sets: Training and Test sets. Every set comprised three different data subsets, one for each pose, which are randomised and evenly distributed to form the corresponding training or test set. While we uniformly randomised the samples, we kept an equal proportion of poses (Pose 1, 2 or 3) in each set to ensure that the sets were balanced.

As ultimately our aim is for the database to be dynamically generated, we also considered test and training set distributions, other than 50-50 proportion, for instance, 30-70; 20-80 or 10-90 of test and training sets respectively. We also evaluated the performance of the Nearest Neighbours algorithm for different numbers of neighbours. In this way we were able to empirically analyse the performance of the algorithm. In practise, we found that the distribution of the sets, as well as the number of neighbours, do not significantly affect the accuracy; finally adopting a 50-50 distribution for training and test sets as fixed parameters and considering K neighbours equal to the size of the training data set.

In total we collected 76 samples per participant (24 per pose and 4 rest poses) and each subject's samples were evaluated against his/her own data because we assume physical body sizes and the participant's interpretation of the exercise poses to be different so the learning has to be personalised as discussed in Sect. 2. As such we conducted a within-subjects analysis, rather than combine the data from all participants.

If we would be just using K-Nearest Neighbours every new sample will be classified within one of the three categories (Pose 1, 2 or 3) not really evaluating how well the pose was performed or if it was actually a totally different pose, for instance, the "rest pose" was recorded from the users when they were waiting for instructions from the robot. The key point about the Nearest Neighbours approach is how it uses distances to determine the label of a sample. However, if it is applied in early stages of data collection, the closest neighbours may be very distant samples due to the lack of alternatives or there might not be enough samples for each pose to generate a high confidence value. Hence, we thought of a variant of the nearest neighbours approach where we consider distance to the centroids for each pose cluster. This way, as long as some poses are created and labelled by an expert first, we can always access a relevant representation of the cluster and give a confidence level based on cluster membership. Figure 4 gives a simplified visual example of what we are trying to achieve.

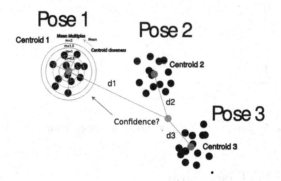

Fig. 4. Simplified confidence procedure

To evaluate the quality of the performance, we introduced a threshold for each segment to the cluster centroids. This threshold will act as a limit that will decide if the distance from the new pose to cluster centroid is close enough to assign the label of the cluster. This will produce different levels of confidence for the labels (Pose 1, Pose 2 and Pose 3) which can be tuned by defining a membership function. As we also need poses that do not represent either Pose 1, 2 and 3, we recorded the validation pose to test the case of a sample that does not belong to any label.

Figure 5 is a linear function based on a gradient towards the cluster centroid. The slope of the line will be represented by a multiple of the mean of the training set distribution, where m = 1 corresponds to the mean μ in metres, with reference to the centroid. We considered other options, such as the Gaussian function which could be one of the parameters to be tuned, to alter the system performance. Consequently, we chose this configuration from pilot experiments to produce a functional approach to evaluate our learning algorithm considering the whole training set for each evaluation (K = size(Training set)), however a future study on interaction enhancement will consider tuning aspects.

Ideally, for the participants' data sets, we can run different tests to detect which pose holds the higher level of confidence against the label that was set during the Collaborative Human-Robot interaction. We can thus analyse how to use these membership functions and thresholds to give feedback and improve the collaborative exercise session in a more robust way than nearest neighbours.

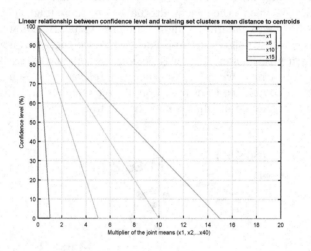

Fig. 5. Confidence (%) vs threshold (μ multiple) function

5   Results and Discussion

Using Nearest Neighbours we obtained an overall accuracy above 94% accuracy for most participants' individual assessments, as we expected. However, while the recognition accuracy was high, there is no information regarding how well the poses have been performed, they reflect how well the camera recorded the positions involving loss of skeletal tracking for the worst performing cases. Two participants obtained an accuracy of approximately 60% due to the emergence of two clusters for each pose when the participants started to lean forward as the exercise session progressed, see Sect. 5.2.

5.1   Classification and Identification of New Poses

On further analysis of the confidence versus threshold graphs, the most noticeable finding examining all the participants' results (example from participant

5 shown in Fig. 6) is that the highest confidence levels correspond to their correct classification from the collaborative interaction. Moreover, the validation samples or "rest poses" have the lowest confidence values. This was expected as the rest poses are very different from the other three poses but what is clear is that each pose lies within a distinct band of confidence levels. If we move along the horizontal axis (distance threshold), the discernment of the groups becomes clearer thus facilitating the decision making process. By setting a fixed threshold and a confidence limit we could give the user feedback based on how the robot assesses the performance. This is the basis of the information from which the robot can decide which engaging comments should be formulated ('Well done' or 'Try moving the arms a little bit upwards') or, further, enquire if the user is actually performing a new pose and classify it. For future research, designing questions that unequivocally expect a "label" as an answer are the best option to enrich the collaborative aspect of the Human-Robot Interaction. For example, "Is that a new pose?" or "How do you feel?" or "How do you call this pose?". The more specific the questions are, the more accurately the robot can evaluate the users' movement.

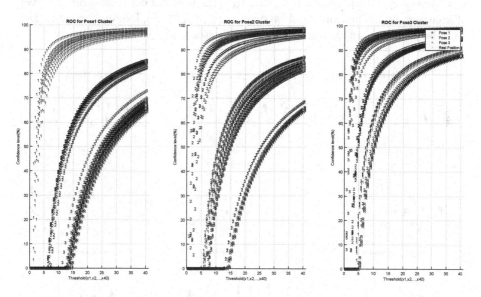

Fig. 6. Confidence vs threshold (μ multiple) graph example (Participant 5)

Furthermore, we think the data collection approach could be enhanced by applying other machine learning variants as part of online processing. For instance, genetic algorithms can be a more adaptable way to represent the user joint distances and configure the different parameters of the algorithm design such as thresholds, speech delays, number of nearest neighbours, etc. Alternatively, neural networks could be used to reinforce the users' database once it is large enough to be considered for these purposes, adding degrees of complexity for the learning.

5.2   Changes to User Posture over Time

For some participants we found that specific pose categories were represented by two clusters. Further examination of these showed that they had changed their body posture by tilting their spine forward during the exercise session. Participants 3, 6 and 8 present high standard deviation in the X-axis, with their confidence-threshold graphs showing two clusters in Fig. 7 where the doted pose is a reference pose extracted from all participants' pose 1 average. This could be an indicator to detect changes over time during the exercise session that could be used to detect bad posture habits, as well as fatigue and boredom.

An approach that can clearly detect subtle differences in the poses and flag them to the user can benefit older adults when individual people may have a different way of expressing their comfort levels. We propose that the use of time windows could be an efficient way to allow the user to respond to the robot when it requests a specific pose. If during that time the user did not meet a certain level of accuracy, an evaluation could be done in terms of pace, looking for anomalies and also enriching the variability of the exercises that can be performed.

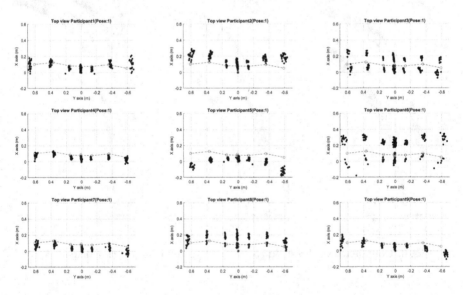

Fig. 7. Top view all participants performing Pose 1 to appreciate the presence of clusters.

6   Conclusion

Other researchers in this field have tried different approaches to designing a coach robot that can engage with older adults and create an entertaining system to support exercise. In general aspects, our approach has illustrated potential to give meaningful feedback based on confidence levels extracted from the machine learning algorithm, detecting how well a specific user is performing a pose with respect to their past performance or a reference performance (e.g. specified by a physiotherapist). Moreover, our approach can provide a history of the user's performance which is readable by non-experts, enabling further diagnosis and support by professionals. Our approach provides a framework for a customisable and evaluative coaching service which can be delivered by a socially assistive robot. It establishes the foundation of a system that would be more acceptable to users due to its ability to learn and respond to the user's specific movement characteristics. The next stage of this research is to test the system in a closed-loop manner, using the information regarding how well the user is performing a pose or exercise, to experiment with different ways this could be used to provide personalised feedback in an accessible manner to older adults.

References

Bianchi-Berthouze, N.: Understanding the role of body movement in player engagement. Hum.-Comput. Interact. **28**(1), 40–75 (2013)

Burns, A.: Old age psychiatrist newsletter of the old age faculty of the Royal College of Psychiatrists. Technical report. Royal College of Psychiatrists (2016)

Cavallo, F., et al.: On the design, development and experimentation of the ASTRO assistive robot integrated in smart environments. In: 2013 IEEE International Conference on Robotics and Automation, pp. 4310–4315. IEEE (2013)

Coombs, N.: Estimates of the very old (including centenarians) - Office for National Statistics. Technical report. Office of National Statistics (2017)

Krüger, V., Kragic, D., Ude, A., Geib, C.: The meaning of action: a review on action recognition and mapping. Adv. Robot. **21**(13), 1473–1501 (2007)

Lara, O.D., Labrador, M.A., et al.: A survey on human activity recognition using wearable sensors. IEEE Commun. Surv. Tutorials **15**(3), 1192–1209 (2013)

Lo Presti, L., La Cascia, M.: 3D skeleton-based human action classification: a survey. Pattern Recogn. **53**, 130–147 (2016)

Maharani, D.A., Fakhrurroja, H., Machbub, C.: Hand gesture recognition using k-means clustering and support vector machine. In: 2018 IEEE Symposium on Computer Applications Industrial Electronics (ISCAIE), pp. 1–6 (2018)

Martins, G., Santos, L., Dias, J.: The GrowMeUp project and the applicability of action recognition techniques. In: Third Workshop on Recognition and Action for Scene Understanding (REACTS) (2015). mrl.isr.uc.pt

Mitchell, M.: One voice: shaping our ageing society. Br. J. Community Nurs. **14**(6), 259–261 (2009)

Moeslund, T.B., Hilton, A., Krüger, V.: A survey of advances in vision-based human motion capture and analysis. Technical report (2006)

Nani, M., et al.: MOBISERV: an integrated intelligent home environment for the provision of health, nutrition and mobility services to the elderly (2010)

Ofcom: Television and audio-visual content - media consumption statistics. Technical report. Ofcom, London (2017)

Park, N.: Population estimates for the UK, England and Wales, Scotland and Northern Ireland - Office for National Statistics. Technical report. Office for National Statistics (UK) (2018)

Pham, M., Mengistu, Y., Do, H., Sheng, W.: Delivering home healthcare through a Cloud-based Smart Home Environment (CoSHE). Future Gener. Comput. Syst. **81**, 129–140 (2018)

Pigini, L., Facal, D., Garcia, A., Burmester, M., Andrich, R.: The proof of concept of a shadow robotic system for independent living at home. In: Miesenberger, K., Karshmer, A., Penaz, P., Zagler, W. (eds.) ICCHP 2012. LNCS, vol. 7382, pp. 634–641. Springer, Heidelberg (2012). https://doi.org/10.1007/978-3-642-31522-0_96

Poppe, R.: A survey on vision-based human action recognition. Image Vis. Comput. **28**(6), 976–990 (2010)

Ros, R., Demiris, Y.: Creative dance: an approach for social interaction between robots and children. In: Salah, A.A., Hung, H., Aran, O., Gunes, H. (eds.) HBU 2013. LNCS, vol. 8212, pp. 40–51. Springer, Cham (2013). https://doi.org/10.1007/978-3-319-02714-2_4

Saunders, J., Burke, N., Koay, K.L., Dautenhahn, K.: A user friendly robot architecture for re-ablement and co-learning in a sensorised home (2013). books.google.com

Sharkey, A., Sharkey, N.: Granny and the robots: ethical issues in robot care for the elderly. Ethics Inf. Technol. **14**(1), 27–40 (2012)

United Nations: World Population Prospects. Technical report. United Nations, New York (2017)

Wang, L., Hu, W., Tan, T.: Recent developments in human motion analysis. Pattern Recogn. **36**, 585–601 (2003)

ORB-SLAM-CNN: Lessons in Adding Semantic Map Construction to Feature-Based SLAM

Andrew M. Webb$^{(\boxtimes)}$ⓘ, Gavin Brown, and Mikel Luján

School of Computer Science, University of Manchester, Manchester, UK
{andrew.webb,gavin.brown,mikel.lujan}@manchester.ac.uk

Abstract. Recent work has integrated semantics into the 3D scene models produced by visual SLAM systems. Though these systems operate close to real time, there is lacking a study of the ways to achieve real-time performance by trading off between semantic model accuracy and computational requirements. ORB-SLAM2 provides good scene accuracy and real-time processing while not requiring GPUs [1]. Following a 'single view' approach of overlaying a dense semantic map over the sparse SLAM scene model, we explore a method for automatically tuning the parameters of the system such that it operates in real time while maximizing prediction accuracy and map density.

Keywords: Online parameter tuning · SLAM · Semantic segmentation

1 Introduction

We describe a method for associating semantic predictions with the 3D model of a sparse, feature-based SLAM system. We perform visual SLAM on the Scan-Net dataset [3] using ORB-SLAM2 [11], while passing each frame used by the SLAM system through a convolutional neural network for semantic segmentation, based on MobileNets [6]. The output of the neural network is at one eighth of the resolution of the input image in each dimension; we use the fully connected conditional random field (CRF) method of Krähenbühl and Koltun [7] to upsample and refine the segmentation images.

The predictions associated with each pixel in each inference frame are projected into the 3D scene; we do not fuse predictions from multiple views. We show that this method has the advantage that we can fit a simple model to predict the accuracy of the 3D map as a function of the system parameters. We use this model to automatically tune the parameters such that the system operates in real time on a given platform while maximizing performance metrics. The following sections describe the various components of the system. For evaluation, we have two metrics for accuracy. The overall accuracy measures the proportion of correctly labelled points. The per-class accuracy is the mean of the proportion of correctly labelled points for each class, and is sometimes more useful than the overall accuracy in an imbalanced dataset.

© Springer Nature Switzerland AG 2019
K. Althoefer et al. (Eds.): TAROS 2019, LNAI 11649, pp. 221–235, 2019.
https://doi.org/10.1007/978-3-030-23807-0_19

Finally, in the appendix we describe our experience combining predictions from multiple views in order to predict the labels of points in the 3D map. This technique does not work well in the sparse, feature-based setting, because it restricts predictions to object boundaries, which are harder to classify.

2   Related Work

In this section we describe other approaches for incorporating semantic predictions into the 3D model of a SLAM system. SemanticFusion [10] combines predictions from a convolutional neural network from multiple views, and associates them with a dense surfel based reconstruction produced by a SLAM system. Theirs was the first work to demonstrate, in real time, the use of pixel correspondences between frames from a SLAM system to fuse per-frame segmentations in order to produce an accurate 3D semantic map. McCormac et al. show that combining predictions from multiple views results in greater 3D semantic map accuracy when used in conjunction with a dense SLAM system, while our initial experiments (see Appendix) do not yield similar results for the case of an unmodified, sparse, feature-based SLAM system.

They use as their SLAM system ElasticFusion [16], which constructs a dense surfel-based model. One consequence is that, because they associate predictions with every surfel in the dense model, their Bayesian update step, which combines predictions from individual frames, takes almost as long as the forward pass of the CNN. In our work, we avoid combining predictions.

In order to achieve the real-time construction of a 3D semantic map, McCormac et al. reduce the image size fed into the neural network, to 224×224 or 320×240 depending on the network used, and perform the inference on a high end GPU (an Nvidia TITAN Black). In our system, the use of the efficient MobileNets networks reduces the computational cost of inference. This, and our use of parameters other than image resolution to reduce computational cost at the expense of accuracy, means we are able to run the system at real time at full VGA resolution on more moderate hardware. In our experiments, inference is performed on an Nvidia GTX 1050 (Notebook), with a peak power consumption of around 50 W, one fifth of that of the Titan Black.

As in our work, McCormac et al. use the CRF scheme of Krähenbühl and Koltun [7] to refine their segmentation map. However, they apply the CRF to the 3D surfel map, whereas we apply it to the 2D segmentation images before predictions are associated with the 3D model. We have not performed experiments to compare these two approaches.

Also related is the work of Pillai and Leonard, in which correspondences between frames, according to a SLAM system, are used to achieve strong object recognition performance [12]. As in our own work, they use ORB-SLAM to produce a sparse 3D map of the scene. In contrast to our work, the point cloud is clustered after points in low density regions are removed, and the clusters are taken to represent objects. Bounding boxes for each object are computed by projecting back down onto the keyframes, and a set of features are then computed for each object for each frame, and a linear classifier uses these features to predict the class of the object. As in SemanticFusion, a conditional independence assumption is used when combining the predictions from multiple frames.

This object recognition system is unable to perform in real-time, taking 1.6 s per keyframe—with approximately 1 s between keyframes with default ORB-SLAM2 settings on most datasets—to perform the feature extraction and encoding steps. However, unlike this work and SemanticFusion, the SLAM supported object recognition work is done without the use of a GPU. Another difference with our work is that we construct a 3D semantic map, with a different prediction associated with every point in the map but no notion of 'objects', whereas Pillai and Leonard perform object recognition.

Sünderhauf et al. combine predictions from multiple views by using a Bayesian filter method [14], assuming first order Markov properties. Vineet et al. use a voxel-based map representation, with voxel predictions being updated based on sequential single-view predictions [15]. Their update rules are designed to quickly correct map corruptions caused by moving objects within the scene.

Kundu et al. [8] and Li and Belaroussi [9] construct a 3D semantic map from monocular input, rather than the RGB-D input we use here. Kundu et al. use semantic cues to constrain the 3D structure of the scene in a voxel-based model. Li and Belaroussi use a scale-drift aware method that allows them to transition between indoor and outdoor scenes. Häne et al. [4] treat image segmentation and dense 3D (voxel-based) reconstruction as a joint inference problem, allowing each task to inform the other.

3   Configuring the Convolutional Neural Network

3.1   The ScanNet Dataset

The ScanNet dataset [3] consists of 1513 video sequences with 2.5 million frames. For each frame there is an RGB image, a depth image, and per-pixel labels with 1163 distinct object classes, which we can use to evaluate semantic segmentation accuracy. The dataset also contains the groundtruth for the camera trajectory for each scene, which can be used to evaluate the SLAM system.

We use the same train/validation/test split of the dataset as used in the classification tasks in the original ScanNet paper; we use 1045 of the scenes to train the neural network, 156 to tune the network hyperparameters and CRF parameters, and 312 to evaluate our system.

3.2   MobileNet Semantic Segmentation Network

We use a modified version of MobileNets [6] for semantic segmentation. We train the network on the twenty most common classes in the dataset, and merge some similar classes, such as 'chair' and 'office chair'., We reserve class zero for unlabelled pixels. We modified the network to take four input channels, so that the network takes the RGB-D images as input. The RGB and depth inputs are normalized such that values lie between −1 and 1.

We removed the average pooling layer and reduced the stride from 2 to 1 in two convolutional layers, so that the output is a low resolution semantic segmentation of the input image. We also modified some layers after the reduced stride layers to be atrous convolutions with a dilation of 2 to compensate for the reduced receptive field, as in the DeepLab system [2].

The MobileNets networks have two parameters to trade off accuracy and computation. In the MobileNets paper, lowering the input image resolution reduces the accuracy of the prediction. In our work, lowering the resolution lowers the output segmentation resolution. We control the input resolution with the *rescale factor* parameter r, which scales both the height and width. The MobileNets networks also have a *width multiplier* w, which controls the number of feature channels throughout the network. In this work we train two versions of the MobileNets, with width multiplier values of $w = 0.5$ and $w = 1.0$.

3.3   Conditional Random Field Post-processing

As in the work of Krähenbühl and Koltun, and in the DeepLab system [2], we apply bilinear upsampling and conditional random field (CRF) post-processing to the output of the network to obtain a segmentation the same size as the input image. The upsampled output is coarse, with smoothed edges and lacking fine detail. The CRF is used to refine the segmentation.

Fig. 1. Top left: a test image from ScanNet. Top right: ground truth labels. Bottom row: pre-CRF, then CRF-processed images with 3 and 5 iterations, in which the segmentation conforms more closely to the ground truth.

A CRF is a graphical model for expressing the posterior distribution over a collection of variables via the relative compatibilities of assignments to subsets of those variables. Here it is used to express a preference that pixels close to each other in the image and in colour-space should be labelled similarly. The effect is to assign more probability to segmentations that are smooth, without pixels that are assigned a different label to all of their neighbours, and to refine the edges in the segmentation to conform to sharp colour changes. An example of applying a dense CRF in this way is shown in Fig. 1.

The posterior of the CRF is approximated iteratively. We can vary the number of *CRF iterations I* in order to trade off accuracy against computational cost. A CRF can be implemented as a layer in a deep neural network [17], which would enable end-to-end training and would reduce CRF inference time. However, in this work we have used an available C++ implementation [7][1]. We first train the network and then separately fit the parameters of the CRF.

3.4   Training and Parameter Fitting

We use a cross entropy loss function with L2 regularization, and use batch normalization throughout the network. No loss is assigned for unlabelled pixels. We correct for class imbalance by making the per-class loss inversely proportional to the frequency of the class. Two modified MobileNets networks, with width multiplier parameters of 0.5 and 1.0, were trained for 85,000 and 165,000 iterations respectively using a batch size of 32 on a TITAN X (Pascal). Each batch was rescaled randomly between 0.25 and 1.0 times the original image size (in terms of area), and then cropped to a random 224×224 region.

We tune the hyperparameters—the learning rate and the L2 regularization parameter—by training until convergence ten times with randomly sampled hyperparameter settings, and choosing the settings that maximize the mean per-class accuracy on the validation set. To tune the CRF parameters, we randomly sample values 50 times, each time evaluating the post-CRF per-class accuracy on 312 images from the validation set—two images per scene.

Table 1. Overall/per-class accuracy (%) (with CRF iterations $I = 5$) on 312 images from validation and test sets.

(a) Width multiplier $w = 0.5$.

	Validation	Test
Pre-CRF	57.3 / 57.4	55.5 / 55.9
Post-CRF	58.2 / 59.0	56.6 / 56.3

(b) Width multiplier $w = 1.0$.

	Validation	Test
Pre-CRF	66.2 / 60.0	64.9 / 57.7
Post-CRF	67.4 / 60.7	65.9 / 58.4

Table 1 gives the accuracy of the two versions of the network on the frames of the ScanNet dataset, with width multipliers $w = 0.5$ and $w = 1.0$, before and after applying the CRF step (with iterations $I = 5$), on 312 images each of the validation and test sets. Figure 2 shows some example predictions made by the network with width multiplier $w = 1.0$ after applying the CRF.

4   Feature-Based SLAM: ORB-SLAM2

We use ORB-SLAM2 [11], a feature-based SLAM system that picks out a relatively small number of 'ORB features' in each frame. These features, also called

---

[1] We use **pydensecrf**, available at github.com/lucasb-eyer/pydensecrf.

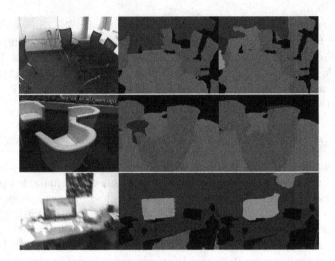

Fig. 2. Example images and predictions using width multiplier $w = 1.0$. Left: input images. Middle: ground truth labels. Right: predicted labels.

keypoints, are invariant to small changes in scale and rotation [13], and so corresponding features can be found between different frames. These correspondences are then used to jointly infer the trajectory of the camera and the positions of these points in 3D space. We will call the 3D points, which make up the model of the scene as constructed by ORB-SLAM2, MapPoints, in accordance with the terminology used in the ORB-SLAM2 source code.

4.1   Semantic Map Construction

We construct the 3D semantic map by projecting all predictions of the segmentation network into the 3D scene maintained by ORB-SLAM2. We can do this by using the SLAM system's prediction for the camera pose and the depth values from the depth camera. The result is that we overlay a dense or semi-dense semantic map on top of the sparse 3D model produced by the SLAM system.

Since the SLAM system does not know how pixels other than keypoints/features correspond to each other in different frames, we cannot combine predictions from multiple views; the role of the SLAM system in constructing the semantic map is restricted to estimating the current camera pose. The structure of the system in this 'single view' setting is shown in Fig. 3. For comparison, a feature-based 'multi-view' approach is described in the appendix.

5   Performance Models

In the single view setting, single-frame predictions are embedded directly into the 3D semantic map using the current estimate of the camera pose from the SLAM system and the depth channel of the images. If we assume that both are

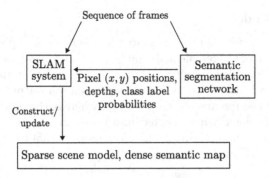

Fig. 3. Class label predictions from a deep network for semantic segmentation are passed to the SLAM system along with depth information. The SLAM system overlays this dense semantic map over its sparse 3D scene model.

accurate, then the accuracy of the single view 3D semantic map on a scene in the ScanNet dataset is the same as the accuracy of the semantic segmentation network averaged across the frames in that scene. This allows us to, unlike in the multiview setting described in the appendix, efficiently estimate the 3D semantic map accuracy by measuring the accuracy of the segmentation on a subset of frames.

The parameters listed in Sect. 5.1 affect the map accuracy, the map density, the inference time per frame, and the number of frames between inference frames. The key idea of this section is that we can fit an accuracy and a density model *offline* and then, on a given platform, or with a given new implementation of one of the components of the system, we can efficiently fit a timing model *online*. The three models—for the accuracy, density, and inference time—then allow us to choose parameter settings such that we can run the system in real time while maximizing the accuracy and density of the semantic map. The following sections describe the density, accuracy, and timing models used and the fitting process for the timing model.

5.1 Accuracy, Density, and Computation Trade Off Parameters

We have various means to reduce the amount of computation required at the cost of reducing the accuracy and density of the produced 3D semantic map. The MobileNets semantic segmentation network has a width multiplier w and input resolution rescale factor r parameters. As well as rescaling the input images, we can crop them using a *crop factor* c, feeding only a region of each frame to the segmentation network. Another possibility is to skip keyframes using a *skip factor* s, performing inference on one frame in every s.

We can also vary the number of *CRF iterations* I. The method used to compute the posterior of the CRF is iterative, with the approximation improving with the number of iterations. We vary the number of iterations between zero—leaving the network output unaltered—and five.

5.2   Density Model

The density of the semantic map, measured by the number of points in the map, is a simple function of the rescale and crop factors r and c and the skip parameter s; it is simply the number of individual pixel predictions that are projected into the map. The resolution of the semantic segmentation output scales with the square of each of the rescale and crop factors, whereas the number of inference frames with predictions being inserted into the map scales inversely with the skip parameter. The map density is therefore proportional to

$$f_{\text{density}}(r, c, s) = \frac{r^2 c^2}{s}.$$

5.3   Accuracy Model

We evaluate the accuracy of the 3D semantic map by projecting the predictions onto individual frames and comparing to the groundtruth. Therefore, the accuracy of the 3D map on a scene is the same as the accuracy of the semantic segmentation network averaged over frames in that scene. The accuracies (overall and per-class) of the semantic segmentation network are functions of the width multiplier w, the number of CRF iterations I—we have already seen the effect of these parameters on the accuracy of the segmentation network in Table 1—and possibly of the rescale and crop factors r and c. We express these as two functions $f_{\text{overall}}(w, I, r, c)$ and $f_{\text{per-class}}(w, I, r, c)$. We wish to fit offline two functions $\hat{f}_{\text{overall}}$ and $\hat{f}_{\text{per-class}}$ that will be used to estimate the accuracies for given parameter settings.

   We randomly sampled 3500 times from the joint parameter space, with $w \in \{0.5, 1.0\}$, $I \in \{0, 1, \ldots, 5\}$, and with r and c sampled uniformly from $[0.469, 1.0]$, rejecting the sample if $r \cdot c < 0.469$. This reflects the way that rescaling and cropping were performed during training, with the input image resolution always at least 224×224. For each setting of the parameters, we measure the overall and per-class accuracy on 32 random frames from the dataset.

   We found by inspection and by conditional mutual information measures that, conditional on the width multiplier and number of CRF iterations, the rescale and crop factors are not informative for predicting accuracy values[2]. Since the width multiplier and number of CRF iterations are discrete parameters with a small number of values—there are twelve combinations in total—we use the empirical mean overall and per-class accuracies for each parameter setting as our estimate for $\hat{f}_{\text{overall}}(w, I)$ and $\hat{f}_{\text{per-class}}(w, I)$. These estimates are shown in Fig. 4, along with their associated standard errors.

5.4   Timing Model

The inference time of the semantic segmentation network is a function of the width multiplier w and the rescale and crop factors r and c, with the rescale and

---

[2] To measure conditional mutual information, we used the *scikit-feature* feature selection library available at github.com/jundongl/scikit-feature.

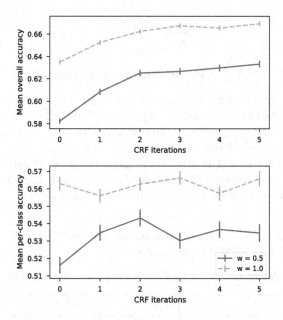

Fig. 4. Mean overall and per-class accuracies and standard errors. The mean values are used as a predictive model of the accuracy of the 3D semantic map as a function of the width multiplier and number of CRF iterations.

crop factors acting symmetrically to reduce the size of the input and subsequent layers in the network. We express the inference time as $f_{net}(w, rc)$. The inference time of the CRF step is a function of the number of CRF iterations I and the rescale and crop factors, expressed as $f_{CRF}(I, rc)$. We wish to fit online two functions $\hat{f}_{net}$ and $\hat{f}_{CRF}$ in order to estimate inference time when running the system on a new platform, or when we have new implementations of the components of the system. For example, we may have switched from running the neural network on a GPU to a CPU, or switched the CRF inference to a neural implementation.

We make the assumption that each of these functions can be approximated by a low order polynomial, with terms up to the second power in each variable. I.e., we assume that $f(x, y) \approx \{a_{ij}x^i y^j | (i, j) \in \{0, 1, 2\}^2\}$. We also know that we can set the CRF part of the timing model to zero if the number of CRF iterations is zero. We fit the timing models by expanding the independent variables out to the appropriate polynomial basis, and then use linear regression with a mean squared error loss function to fit the parameters.

Once the timing model has been fit, it is used to restrict the choice of parameters to those that will allow inference to be performed in real time. On the ScanNet dataset, ORB-SLAM2 selects a keyframe every 1040 ms on average. Since inference is performed on one in every s keyframes, where s is the skip parameter, we restrict ourselves to parameter settings where

$$\frac{\hat{f}_{net}(w, rc) + \hat{f}_{CRF}(I, rc)}{s} \leq 1040 \, \text{ms}.$$

5.5 Example Use of the Parameter Tuning Method

We collected timing information for 170 settings of the parameters with the semantic segmentation network running on an Nvidia GTX 1050 (Notebook) graphics card (GPU), and another 170 settings with the segmentation network running on an Intel i7-7700HQ (CPU). Table 2 shows the results of fitting the timing model to this data. The first column gives the range of values for inference time across the parameter settings sampled. The second column gives the root mean squared error (RMSE) for the predictive timing models.

Table 2. Range of times (ms) taken for neural network and CRF inference and RMSE of the corresponding predictive timing model.

<table>
<tr><td colspan="3">(a) CPU</td><td colspan="3">(b) GPU</td></tr>
<tr><td></td><td>Range</td><td>RMSE</td><td></td><td>Range</td><td>RMSE</td></tr>
<tr><td>Network inference time</td><td>33.3–82.2</td><td>4.0</td><td>Network inference time</td><td>91.8–627</td><td>7.2</td></tr>
<tr><td>CRF inference time</td><td>108–586</td><td>32</td><td>CRF inference time</td><td>124–1013</td><td>50</td></tr>
</table>

The final stage of the tuning tool is to take a large number of samples from the parameter space, and then exclude from consideration those that—according to the timing model—would result in slower than real time performance. We then select the Pareto front with respect to the semantic map accuracy and map density, according to the accuracy and density models. The resulting Pareto fronts in this case are shown in Fig. 5.

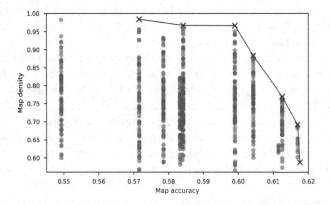

Fig. 5. Pareto front (red crosses) of accuracy and density. Each point (red or blue) is a setting of the parameters that allows the system to run in real time. (Color figure online)

6   Conclusions

ORB-SLAM2 provides good 3D model accuracy and real-time processing [1]. Following a 'single view' approach of overlaying a dense semantic map over the sparse SLAM scene model (ORB-SLAM), we explore a method for automatically tuning the parameters of the system such that it operates in real time while maximizing prediction accuracy and map density.

We can fit models of the semantic map accuracy and density offline, and efficiently fit an inference time model online on a given, new platform, or when we have new implementations of the system components. Given a platform on which ORB-SLAM2 runs in real time, this allows us to construct a 3D semantic map, also in real time, while maximizing map accuracy and density. There is room for the development of more sophisticated predictive accuracy and timing models.

Acknowledgements. The authors gratefully acknowledge the support of the EPSRC grants LAMBDA (EP/N035127/1), PAMELA (EP/K008730/1), and RAIN (EP/R026084/1).

A   Appendix: Multi-view Semantic Map Construction with Feature-Based SLAM

In this section we describe a multi-view approach to associating semantic predictions with the 3D scene model of ORB-SLAM2, by using the correspondence between keypoints in different frames recorded by the SLAM system to combine predictions. We show that this approach—similar to SemanticFusion [10]—has drawbacks when used with sparse, feature-based SLAM systems.

We have modified ORB-SLAM2 to, for each keyframe, pass the (x, y) positions of keypoints to the code implementing the segmentation network. The segmentation network performs inference on each keyframe, and passes the prediction probability vector for each keypoint back to ORB-SLAM2. ORB-SLAM2 then computes an aggregate prediction for each MapPoint by combining the predictions of the associated keypoints. This setup is illustrated in Fig. 6. The aggregate MapPoint prediction probabilities were computed by taking the element-wise product of the keypoint prediction probabilities and then renormalizing. This is like a *product of experts* in ensemble machine learning methods [5]. Other aggregation methods were tried, such as taking the arithmetic mean or a maximum vote, with similar results.

We report the accuracy of the segmentation network across all pixels and across all keypoints in the test set, and the accuracy of the 3D semantic map based on multi-view (aggregate) feature predictions. For each of these, we compute the 'overall accuracy', which is the total proportion of correctly classified pixels or MapPoints, and the 'per-class accuracy', which is the mean of the proportion of correctly classified pixels or MapPoints for each class.

These results are shown in Table 3. The first three rows show the accuracies computed for various settings of the parameters described in Sect. 5.1. The first

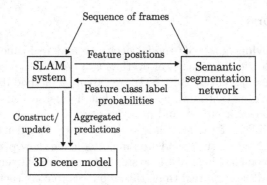

Fig. 6. Class label predictions from a deep network for semantic segmentation are made based on multiple views of the same objects and then associated with parts of the 3D model constructed by the SLAM system.

Table 3. Overall/per-class accuracy (%) of the semantic segmentation network averaged across pixels and features, and the accuracies of the multiview-constructed 3D semantic map. The 'full network' has width parameter $w = 1.0$ with CRF iterations $I = 5$. The 'no CRF' network is the same but with CRF iterations $I = 0$. The third row is the same as the 'full network' but with a width multiplier of $w = 0.5$. The final row results are for a modified version of ORB-SLAM2 which uses more keyframes.

	Accuracies (OP/PC) (%)		
	Per pixel	Per feature	Multiview
Full network	65.9/58.4	58.0/53.3	59.9/54.9
No CRF	64.9/57.7	53.4/51.1	55.9/53.1
$w = 0.5$	56.6/56.3	49.9/53.7	51.9/54.9
More frames	64.9/57.7	52.5/51.0	55.7/53.7

row gives the results for setting the parameters to maximize accuracy at the cost of increased computation; the full network is used, with width multiplier $w = 1.0$, there is no cropping, rescaling, or frame skipping, and we apply $I = 5$ CRF iterations. The second row shows the results with the same parameters, but without any CRF post-processing. For the third row the parameters are the same as the first, but with the 'half width' network, with $w = 0.5$.

The multi-view per-feature predictions consistently give a two to three percentage point improvement in accuracy over the per-frame per-feature accuracy; combining predictions does result in increased accuracy. This low improvement—compared to the three to seven percentage point improvement seen from multi-view predictions in SemanticFusion—seems to be due to low diversity amongst predictions based on multiple views; in cases where the multiview predictions are wrong, the corresponding pairwise single view predictions (i.e., the predictions being combined) are the same in approximately 75% of cases, and the KL-divergence of the pairwise prediction probabilities are low. These diversity measures are shown in Table 4. This low diversity may in turn be due to ORB features being invariant under only small changes in orientation and scale, so that the multiple views that are combined are very similar.

Another feature of the results is that restricting predictions to only keypoints—as we are required to in order to take advantage of ORB-SLAM2 to combine predictions from multiple views—results in a reduction in accuracy by around 3–6 percentage points compared to the accuracy measured over all pixels; this drop in accuracy more than compensates for the increase in accuracy that comes from combining predictions from multiple views. This may be because ORB features are likely to be found on corners and edges, and so may be likely to be found on the boundary between objects. These points will be harder to classify, and a lower accuracy will result if the segmentation edges do not align well with object edges. Some evidence is lent to this interpretation by the fact that the drop in accuracy when restricting predictions to keypoints is higher when no CRF iterations are applied, as seen in Table 3, and that the use of the CRF drastically reduces the KL-divergence between predictions associated with the same MapPoint, as shown in Table 4; the CRF, by aligning segmentation edges with object edges, has removed a major source of uncorrelated errors between predictions.

In the multiview setting, a surprisingly small number of observations/predictions are associated with each MapPoint; the mean number of observations per MapPoint is a little over four. It is possible to modify ORB-SLAM2 to create more keyframes per frame. The final row of Tables 3 and 4 give the results for a modified version of ORB-SLAM2, with a mean number of 7.0 observations per MapPoint. This modified version still shows only a small improvement in accuracy for multiview predictions over single view predictions.

Table 4. Mean number of observations/predictions per MapPoint. The second and third column show, in the case that the aggregate prediction for a MapPoint is wrong, the pairwise probability that two predictions agree and the pairwise KL-divergence between the prediction probabilities.

	Obs	Agreement	KL div.
With CRF	4.35	0.778	0.0375
Without CRF	4.34	0.754	0.337
More frames, no CRF	7.0	0.752	0.292

In this section, we have shown that the popular method of combining predictions from multiple views in conjunction with a SLAM system to build a 3D semantic map is not suitable in the sparse, feature-based SLAM setting. Restricting predictions to ORB-SLAM2 keypoints, as is required for the multiview approach, reduces the semantic map accuracy by more than the increase in accuracy from combining predictions from multiple views can compensate for, suggesting that multiview semantic map construction using a sparse, feature-based SLAM system is not viable if the features are likely to appear on object boundaries, as will often be the case. It may be possible to do multiview prediction with a feature-based SLAM system by modifying the features such that they are more likely to appear in object interiors, but this is likely to affect SLAM tracking performance.

References

1. Bodin, B., et al.: SLAMBench2: multi-objective head-to-head benchmarking for visual SLAM. In: 2018 IEEE International Conference on Robotics and Automation (ICRA), pp. 1–8 (2018)
2. Chen, L.C., Papandreou, G., Kokkinos, I., Murphy, K., Yuille, A.L.: Semantic image segmentation with deep convolutional nets and fully connected CRFs. In: ICLR (2015). http://arxiv.org/abs/1412.7062
3. Dai, A., Chang, A.X., Savva, M., Halber, M., Funkhouser, T., Nießner, M.: ScanNet: richly-annotated 3D reconstructions of indoor scenes. In: Proceedings of the Computer Vision and Pattern Recognition (CVPR). IEEE (2017)
4. Häne, C., Zach, C., Cohen, A., Angst, R., Pollefeys, M.: Joint 3D scene reconstruction and class segmentation. In: 2013 IEEE Conference on Computer Vision and Pattern Recognition, pp. 97–104, June 2013. https://doi.org/10.1109/CVPR.2013.20
5. Hinton, G.E.: Training products of experts by minimizing contrastive divergence. Neural Comput. **14**(8), 1771–1800 (2002). https://doi.org/10.1162/089976602760128018
6. Howard, A.G., et al.: MobileNets: efficient convolutional neural networks for mobile vision applications. CoRR abs/1704.04861 (2017). http://arxiv.org/abs/1704.04861
7. Krähenbühl, P., Koltun, V.: Efficient inference in fully connected CRFs with Gaussian edge potentials. In: Shawe-Taylor, J., Zemel, R.S., Bartlett, P.L., Pereira, F., Weinberger, K.Q. (eds.) Advances in Neural Information Processing Systems 24, pp. 109–117. Curran Associates, Inc. (2011). http://papers.nips.cc/paper/4296-efficient-inference-in-fully-connected-crfs-with-gaussian-edge-potentials.pdf
8. Kundu, A., Li, Y., Dellaert, F., Li, F., Rehg, J.M.: Joint semantic segmentation and 3D reconstruction from monocular video. In: Fleet, D., Pajdla, T., Schiele, B., Tuytelaars, T. (eds.) ECCV 2014. LNCS, vol. 8694, pp. 703–718. Springer, Cham (2014). https://doi.org/10.1007/978-3-319-10599-4_45
9. Li, X., Belaroussi, R.: Semi-dense 3D semantic mapping from monocular SLAM. CoRR abs/1611.04144 (2016). http://arxiv.org/abs/1611.04144
10. McCormac, J., Handa, A., Davison, A.J., Leutenegger, S.: SemanticFusion: dense 3D semantic mapping with convolutional neural networks. In: 2017 IEEE International Conference on Robotics and Automation (ICRA), pp. 4628–4635 (2017)
11. Mur-Artal, R., Tardós, J.D.: ORB-SLAM2: an open-source SLAM system for monocular, stereo and RGB-D cameras. IEEE Trans. Robot. **33**(5), 1255–1262 (2017). https://doi.org/10.1109/TRO.2017.2705103
12. Pillai, S., Leonard, J.: Monocular SLAM supported object recognition. In: Proceedings of Robotics: Science and Systems (RSS), Rome, Italy, July 2015
13. Rublee, E., Rabaud, V., Konolige, K., Bradski, G.: ORB: an efficient alternative to SIFT or SURF. In: 2011 IEEE International Conference on Computer Vision (ICCV), pp. 2564–2571. IEEE (2011)

14. Sünderhauf, N., et al.: Place categorization and semantic mapping on a mobile robot. In: IEEE International Conference on Robotics and Automation (ICRA 2016), Stockholm, Sweden. IEEE, May 2016

15. Vineet, V., et al.: Incremental dense semantic stereo fusion for large-scale semantic scene reconstruction. In: 2015 IEEE International Conference on Robotics and Automation (ICRA), pp. 75–82, May 2015. https://doi.org/10.1109/ICRA.2015. 7138983

16. Whelan, T., Leutenegger, S., Moreno, R.S., Glocker, B., Davison, A.: ElasticFusion: dense SLAM without a pose graph. In: Proceedings of Robotics: Science and Systems, Rome, Italy, July 2015. https://doi.org/10.15607/RSS.2015.XI.001

17. Zheng, S., et al.: Conditional random fields as recurrent neural networks. In: ICCV, pp. 1529–1537 (2015)

Probabilistic Planning for Robotics with ROSPlan

Gerard Canal[1]([⊠]), Michael Cashmore[2], Senka Krivić[2], Guillem Alenyà[1], Daniele Magazzeni[2], and Carme Torras[1]

[1] Institut de Robòtica i Informàtica Industrial, CSIC-UPC, Barcelona, Spain
{gcanal,galenya,torras}@iri.upc.edu
[2] Department of Computer Science, King's College London, London, UK
{michael.cashmore,senka.krivic,daniele.magazzeni}@kcl.ac.uk

Abstract. Probabilistic planning is very useful for handling uncertainty in planning tasks to be carried out by robots. ROSPlan is a framework for task planning in the Robot Operating System (ROS), but until now it has not been possible to use probabilistic planners within the framework. This systems paper presents a standardized integration of probabilistic planners into ROSPlan that allows for reasoning with non-deterministic effects and is agnostic to the probabilistic planner used. We instantiate the framework in a system for the case of a mobile robot performing tasks indoors, where probabilistic plans are generated and executed by the PROST planner. We evaluate the effectiveness of the proposed approach in a real-world robotic scenario.

1 Introduction

Planning for robotics means planning in dynamic and uncertain domains, in which the outcomes of actions can have a reasonable chance of failure, or non-deterministic effects, for example in complex manipulation tasks and navigation in crowded spaces. Probabilistic planning is an approach to plan under uncertainty, commonly meaning planning with probabilistic action effects. A probabilistic planner tries to maximize the probability of success of a plan.

In many domains it is possible to ignore the probabilistic nature of the environment by generating deterministic plans, and replanning when they fail during execution. However, for some problems it is advantageous to consider the probabilities: for example when there is more than one path to the goal and those paths

This work has been supported by the ERC project Clothilde (ERC-2016-ADG-741930), the HuMoUR project (Spanish Ministry of Science and Innovation TIN2017-90086-R) and by the Spanish State Research Agency through the María de Maeztu Seal of Excellence to IRI (MDM-2016-0656). G. Canal is also supported by the Spanish Ministry of Education, Culture and Sport by the FPU15/00504 doctoral grant and the mobility grant EST17/00371. The research from KCL was partly supported by Korea Evaluation Institute of Industrial Technology (KEIT) funded by the Ministry of Trade, Industry & Energy (MOTIE) (No. 1415158956).

© Springer Nature Switzerland AG 2019
K. Althoefer et al. (Eds.): TAROS 2019, LNAI 11649, pp. 236–250, 2019.
https://doi.org/10.1007/978-3-030-23807-0_20

Fig. 1. The scenario in which we test the proposed system is an office environment. A mobile robot, the TurtleBot 2 (https://www.turtlebot.com/) is used for the print-fetching service. When the robot gets a request for fetching prints, it decides from which printer to collect them. Since it is not equipped with an arm, it asks a random nearby person to put prints on it, and delivers them to the user.

have different associated rewards and probabilities of success, or the state-space includes dead-end states. Given different paths to a goal, the paths with higher associated rewards might counterintuitively be those that are longer, or otherwise the cost structure might be far from obvious. These kinds of problems are termed *probabilistically interesting* [20]. Robotics domains are often probabilistically interesting. For example, an autonomous robot in a dynamic environment can easily move into a state from which it does not have the capability to recover by itself, requiring human intervention. Therefore, robots are often expected to follow the slower, safer paths to the goal to avoid failure. However, by reasoning over the probabilities during planning, more efficient solutions can be found.

The Relational Dynamic Influence Diagram Language (RDDL) is a stochastic domain description language for probabilistic planning. The International Probabilistic Planning Competition (IPPC) uses RDDL [25] for probabilistic planning problems. RDDL is well-suited to describing probabilistically interesting problems, using a dynamic Bayes net formalism [8], as opposed to the effects-based (P)PDDL. Subsequently, both the first and second-place entries in the 2012 IPPC were planners that actively reasoned with probabilities: PROST [16], used in our experiments; and Glutton [17].

The ROSPlan framework [6] provides a standard approach for planning in the Robot Operating System (ROS). Until now, one drawback of ROSPlan is that it has been limited to deterministic and contingent planning, using PDDL2.1 [9], and is not suitable for probabilistic planning. The main contributions of this paper are: *(i)* A standardized integration of RDDL and ROSPlan, enabling the straightforward application of the probabilistic planning in robotic domains using ROS. *(ii)* A demonstration of a mobile robot autonomously generating and executing probabilistic plans using this integration in an extensible RDDL domain. We extend ROSPlan to handle RDDL semantics, produce RDDL problem instances, and interface with any RDDL planner that can be used with the RDDLSim server used in the IPPC. In addition, we extend the action interface of ROSPlan, which handles the execution of discrete actions, to reason with non-deterministic effects. To enable distinction between deterministic and non-deterministic effects, we identify two kinds of propositions: *sensed*, whose truth value can be sensed by the agent during execution, and so can be included within a probabilistic effect; and *non-sensed*, which can only produce deterministic effects.[1]

We test the system in a mobile robot scenario and define a challenging *print-fetching* domain where the robot is used as a service robot for fetching printed documents in an office (Fig. 1). Human-robot interaction supplements the lack of manipulation abilities of the used robot, thus allowing it to perform this task. A real-world evaluation is carried out in an environment with high uncertainty.

2   Related Work

There are numerous approaches addressing uncertainty in the planning and execution process e.g. conformant planning [26], contingent planning [2] or replanning [29]. Other approaches use machine-learning techniques to decrease uncertainty in the planning problem, e.g. [7] learn probabilistic action models and [18] remove uncertainty in state prior to planning by making predictions based on initially known data. Also, there is work on building architectures that involve reactive components to cope with uncertainties in robotics domains [15]. ROSPlan has been used to perform planning for control of multiple-robot systems running with ROS [4,6]. However, all of these works focus on purely deterministic planning.

Furthermore, probabilistic planning is a standard approach for planning with uncertainty in robotics. An overview of approaches to probabilistic planning is provided in [10]. The most common approach to planning with uncertainties in robotics is modelling the task as a Markov Decision Problem (MDP), optionally a partially-observable MDP (POMDP). In contrast to deterministic planning, notably the PDDL2.1 [9] formalism used so far with ROSPlan [6], robotics scenarios must often cope with exogenous and uncontrollable events [22], which can be easily modelled as POMDPs [21]. Solutions to the MDPs for robotics can form policies with finite horizon [3], adopt a satisficing approach [19], or maximize the probability of reaching a goal state [23]. RDDL [25] is well-suited for modelling problems of this kind. It is a dynamic Bayes net formalism, allowing for unrestricted concurrency. This is an essential component in robotics applications, in which the agent must execute the plan in a physical environment. For example, in multi-robot navigation scenarios in which motion is stochastic from the perspective of the planning model.

Atrash and Koenig [1] note that POMDP planning policy graph solutions are similar to the finite-state machines normally used for control. As a result, it has been applied successfully in many robotic use cases featuring uncertainty, such as robotic exploration missions [27]; or those with action outcomes that are inherently non-deterministic, such as manipulation problems [14], human-robot interaction [12] and physically assistive robotics [5]. The office setting is a common environment for autonomous service robots, and can exhibit these

---

[1] The source code of the elements described in this paper can be found in the main ROSPlan repository https://github.com/KCL-Planning/ROSPlan.

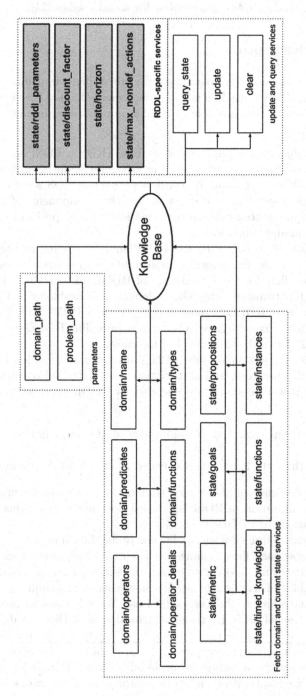

Fig. 2. ROSPlan's Knowledge Base interface. The RDDL services are highlighted.

kinds of uncertainty. Examples are collaborative robots servicing human indoor environments [28] and an office-guide robot for social studies [24].

3   System Description

In order to include the ability of planning with probabilistic domains within the ROSPlan framework, we have designed and implemented a new Knowledge Base and problem generator that are able to handle probabilistic planning problems written in RDDL.

RDDL Knowledge Base. The Knowledge Base (KB) in ROSPlan stores the current model of the environment. It is an interface for updating and fetching a PDDL model in ROS, and primarily consists of a set of ROS services forming this interface. These services are used by many other components of ROSPlan, most of which require state or domain information, such as problem generation and plan execution and validation.

The integration of RDDL with the ROSPlan KB adheres to the existing interface for two reasons: to preserve compatibility with systems already using ROSPlan, and to allow for the interchange of RDDL and PDDL KBs. Therefore, the RDDL KB translates the RDDL domain and problems to PDDL-like structures. Given that RDDL is more expressive than PDDL, the RDDL KB also extends the interface with new ROS services providing RDDL-specific functionality. Figure 2 shows the extended KB interface.

To process the RDDL domain into a PDDL-like structure, action-fluents are mapped to PDDL operators, and state-action constraints (also called action-preconditions in newer versions) are encoded as PDDL preconditions in the following way:

1. The constraints are searched to find those of the form *action-fluent* $\rightarrow$ (*formula*).
2. When found, the right hand side is encoded as an action precondition.

We assume the *formula* only includes conjunctions of state fluents. This is due to a current limitation of ROSPlan, which does not support quantified or disjunctive conditions in PDDL.

Action effects are obtained from conditional probability functions (*cpfs*). This block describes how each fluent changes at each time step, determined by the current state and actions. In order to obtain the effects of an operator, the *cpfs* block is processed for each action fluent. As a new feature, probabilistic effects are also considered and added to the Knowledge Base. We only consider probabilistic effects to be of the RDDL's Bernoulli distribution and Discrete distribution types. Stochastic effects are processed in a similar way to non-probabilistic ones, but when the result of the *cpf* expression is probabilistic, the effect is added to a new effect list with an associated probability formula. In order to provide information on exogenous effects, a new operator named *exogenous* is created. This operator has as its effects all the exogenous effects that may happen but are not related to any specific action-fluent. Effects of this kind are otherwise considered in the same way as the effects of other operators. Finally, the reward function is fully instantiated and represented as a PDDL metric function, with the metric set to be maximized. In the case where there is a state-fluent named "goal", its expression from the *cpfs* block will be included as the PDDL goal.

Although some assumptions are made, such as the conjunctive-only preconditions, it should be noted that these assumptions apply only to the RDDL domain file, which will not be modified when loaded into the KB. Instead, it is passed entirely to the planner. Therefore, although some elements of the domain may be unknown by the KB, the problem is entirely captured, and the planner will still provide correct plans.

Problem Generation. The ROSPlan Problem Interface node is used to generate a problem instance. It fetches the domain details and current state through service calls to a Knowledge Base node and publishes a PDDL problem instance as a string, or writes it to file. To be able to use a planner with a RDDL input, a RDDL Problem interface has been implemented.

The generation of the RDDL problem requires checking operator effects to find which predicates change due to some operators (the state fluents) and which are static for the planning problem (called non-fluents). Additionally, the planning horizon and the discount factor are set by default, or from RDDL-specific services in the KB. A feature of this approach is that as the KB interface is common for both RDDL and PDDL, ROSPlan can generate problems independently of the which KB is used. Thus, a RDDL instance file can be generated from a PDDL instance and vice versa. The requirement is that that both domains share the same structure (i.e., operators and predicates). Therefore, it is now very simple to have both deterministic and probabilistic planners running together, for example, for plan checking and validation or in a planning system composed of both stochastic and deterministic planners.

4   Online Planning and Execution with RDDL Planners

ROSPlan provides two plan dispatchers: the simple plan dispatcher for non-temporal, sequential plans, and the Esterel plan dispatcher for temporal plans with concurrency. Both dispatchers require as input a complete plan produced offline. For stochastic plan execution with RDDL, a third plan dispatcher was designed and implemented that allows the use of online planners (Fig. 3: Nodes *Planner Interface* and *RDDL Plan Dispatch*). The online plan dispatcher interleaves plan execution and computation, removing the need of computing an offline plan and replanning when an action fails.

The online dispatcher uses the RDDL Client/Server protocol, also used by the competition server for the IPPC. In each round, the dispatcher obtains the world's state from the Knowledge Base and sends it to the planner, which returns the actions to be executed in the next time step. This process is repeated until the planner has reached the horizon defined in the instance file, in which case the planning process can be repeated when the task is not yet finished. With

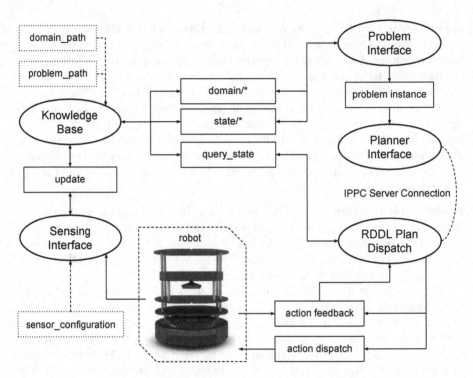

Fig. 3. The system architecture used in our scenario. ROS nodes are represented by ovals, and implement the ROSPlan interfaces. Message and service topics are represented by solid boxes, parameters by dotted boxes.

this dispatcher, any RDDL planner that uses the RDDL Client/Server protocol can be used with ROSPlan with no extra effort.

4.1   Action Execution with Non-deterministic Effects

A robotic system interacting with the real world must keep the symbolic state of the task up to date, based on its sensory inputs. This means updating the Knowledge Base at a fixed rate such that the state is updated before each action is planned and executed. This is crucial in probabilistic planning, as with non-deterministic action outcomes it is not possible to assume that the effects of each action can be applied to the state. Instead, sensing is required to determine which outcome occurred. Therefore, we implemented a new sensing interface (Fig. 3: *Sensing Interface*) that allows the definition of "sensed predicates and functions", which are those whose values are obtained from sensor data.

The sensing interface automatically obtains the sensor data, processes it based on a minimal code definition, and updates the Knowledge Base accordingly at a fixed rate. At the same time, the KB is updated to include the information regarding which propositions are sensed or not, such that effects on the sensed propositions are not automatically applied when an action is executed. The sensed predicates are defined in a configuration file in which is specified: (1) the predicate label; (2) the parameters of the predicate which can be instantiated, and those which are fixed; (3) the sensor containing the required data, expressed as a ROS topic or service; (4) the message type of the data; (5) a single line of code whose result will be the value assigned to the predicate in the KB. Here we show an example of this configuration for a predicate:

```
1. docked:
2.    - params kenny
3.    - /mobile_base/sensors/core
4.    - kobuki_msgs/SensorState
5.    - msg.charger != msg.DISCHARGING
```

This configuration shows (line 1) the name of the predicate, *docked*; (line 2) that the single parameter of the predicate is fixed, so that this configuration is sensing the value of the proposition (docked kenny); (lines 3 and 4) the ROS topic to which the sensing interface will subscribe and the message type; and (line 5) a single line of code that returns a Boolean result to be assigned to the proposition.

If a more complex processing needs to be done, the interface can be linked with another file containing the implementation for each predicate, in which any kind of program can be defined in order to process the sensor data.

5   Example System and Scenario

We have used the RDDL nodes in our example scenario, using the system architecture shown in Fig. 3. In this system, the RDDL Knowledge Base loads the RDDL domain and initial state. The Problem Interface requests the domain and state information to generate a RDDL problem instance. The Planner Interface and RDDL Plan Dispatch communicate through the IPPC server interface, as described above, suggesting and dispatching actions. The sensing interface is also being used to instantiate the predicates based on sensor data and update the state accordingly.

To demonstrate the effectiveness of the developed framework, we have tested it in a scenario in which a mobile robot fetches printed documents in a large office building. This scenario involves a high degree of uncertainty, since the environment is dynamic and humans can obstruct the corridors and printers. The scenario also involves human-robot interaction, which is intrinsically uncertain.

Scenario Description. The robot operates in a single-floor office environment with 16 offices shown in Fig. 4. There are three printers distributed along the corridor. The robot can trigger printing on any of these printers when a request is made. Since the mobile robot is not equipped with an arm, the robot can request human assistance to place the papers onto its tray. There are many employees working in this area, and the corridor is usually dynamic. The robot relies on the fact that someone will pass by and assist the robot upon request. However, it can happen that there is no one at the printer and the robot has to wait or go to another printer. Once the documents are on the carrier, the robot brings them to the person who made request. It is important to note that printers can be occupied, in which case the robot will have to wait. Moreover, the robot will know whether there is somebody there to assist or if the printer is busy until it has arrived to the printer. Figure 1 shows an example of the scenario.

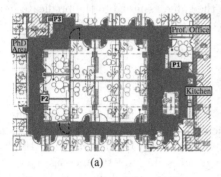 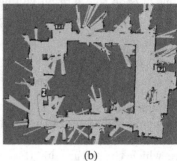

(a)   (b)

Fig. 4. (a) The layout of office environment where the robot is operating. The corridor is marked with the green color and printers are marked with yellow boxes. The orange boxes denote potential goal destinations. (b) A screenshot of the visualization tool RViz taken while performing experiments. It shows the map of the corridor and a green line indicating the robot's current path. (Color figure online)

This scenario could be well-suited to be modeled as a Partially Observable Markov Decision Process (POMDP), as there are fluents that cannot be known until observed, such as the presence or absence of people near the printer. Also, it could be modeled as an Stochastic Shortest Path (SSP) problem, given that the scenario is goal-oriented in that the robot has to deliver the printed papers to a specific location. However, given the lack of available out-of-the-box solvers for both POMDPs and SSPs, we have modeled the problem as an MDP where a positive reward is given only once the goal is reached.

5.1 Print-Fetching Domain

In order to run the scenario on both PDDL and RDDL planners, a domain model has to be written in each language[2]. Care must be taken to ensure that the state transition in both domains remains identical, with the exception of probabilistic effects. While the RDDLSim software used to run the IPPC includes an automatic translation from RDDL to a subset of PPDDL, to properly determinize the domain we performed this translation by hand. In future work we intend to investigate the prospect of using the Knowledge Base to perform this determinization automatically.

RDDL Domain Description. The print-fetching domain in RDDL is made of seven action fluents: one for moving (*goto_waypoint*), two actions for interacting

---

[2] Both PDDL and RDDL domains can be found here: https://github.com/m312z/KCL-Turtlebot/tree/master/domains.

Table 1. Prior probabilities of events in the experimental setup. The same values are used in the problem definition of RDDL.

Printer	Events	Probability of the event
P1	Occupancy	0.5
P1	Nearby person	0.9
P2	Occupancy	0.2
P2	Nearby person	0.4
P3	Occupancy	0.8
P3	Nearby person	0.5

Table 2. Experimental setups. For each setup and planning approach we run 5 tests.

Experiments	Start position	Delivery goal	Printer	Printers occupancy	Nearby person
1	Prof. office	PhD area	P1	Free	Yes
			P2	Free	No
			P3	Free	No
2	PhD area	Kitchen	P1	Free	Yes
			P2	Free	Yes
			P3	Busy	Yes
3	Docking station	Prof. office	P1	Busy	Yes
			P2	Free	No
			P3	Busy	Yes

with the user and asking him/her to load or take the printed papers, two for waiting for the user to do it, and the ones for docking and undocking the robot to the charging station. A fluent named *goal* is used to specify the goal condition, such that the final reward is given only once the goal is reached, thus simulating a goal-oriented MDP. In the print-fetching domain the goal is to deliver the printed papers to a specific location. The domain has two stochastic fluents, both sampled from a Bernoulli distribution. One represents whether there is somebody to help the robot in one location, and the second specifies whether a printer is being used or not, being the parameter of the Bernoulli distribution dependant on the location. Finally, the reward function provides a positive reward when the goal is reached and the robot is docked, and then some penalizations, considered as costs, for moving (weighted by the distance of the moving action), waiting in a printer where there is nobody to help, and waiting in a printer which is busy.

6   Experiments

In our experiments we used a mobile robot (TurtleBot 2). The robot is equipped with a Kinect sensor which is used for both mapping and navigation [11]. Experiments were run in a real-world office environment where people were performing their regular daily activities. Therefore, corridors were crowded and the robot had to avoid obstacles while performing the task. All actions used in the scenario were implemented, apart for the detection of paper placement and human presence perception, which were simulated. An implementation of these actions is not in the scope of this paper.

We tested the system architecture shown in Fig. 3 using the probabilistic planner PROST [16] and compared with the default ROSPlan system using the PDDL 2.1 planner Metric-FF [13]. The goal for both planners is to deliver the printed papers in the shortest time. There were two sources of uncertainty in the scenario whose prior probabilities were modeled in the RDDL domain: (1) the presence of people near the printer and (2) the occupancy of the printer. The values are given in Table 1. When using the deterministic planner (Metric-FF), the system replanned in the case of an action failure.

6.1 Results

We performed three different real-world robotic experiments which represented three situations obtained by sampling the events of person near the printer and occupancy of the printer. These experiments are described in Table 2. For each experiment we applied both planning approaches in five executions. A fourth experiment has been simulated.

As a measure of effectiveness we compare total time of execution, time of planning and robot travel distance. To measure execution time, we measure from the start of planning until the robot completes the task. To measure planning time: (1) in the case of Metric-FF replanning can be performed several times, so the total planning time is the sum of these planning episodes; (2) in the case of PROST, planning is performed before each action is taken so total planning time is the sum of the time to produce each action. The travel distance is the length of the path that the robot traveled.

The results of all three experiments are shown in Fig. 5. Experiment 1 demonstrates the advantage of probabilistic planning. In this set up, the robot can only succeed in printer $P1$, though when only the traveled distance is considered, $P3$ would be the best option. In order to minimize the expected duration of the plan, the Metric-FF planner chose to visit printers $P2$ and $P3$ without taking probabilities of events into account. As these printers were empty, the plan execution failed and replanning was performed both times, to finally succeed when visiting $P1$. On average, the Metric-FF planner had to replan 4 times in each test run of this experiment. In contrast, the probabilistic approach attempted to use printer $P1$ first[3].

Experiment 2 shows a simple case where conditions are optimal for a deterministic planner (no unexpected effects). In this case, $P1$ and $P2$ are the best option to select. As expected, the Metric-FF planner did not have to replan at all, as the best solution was the one selected in the first attempt. Therefore, it exhibits a shorter planning and execution time than the probabilistic planning approach. The distance is still approximately the same, because only in one case did PROST not find the optimal solution.

Experiment 3 shows a case where the available printers are busy, therefore forcing the robot to either wait for the printer to become available or to try another printer. In this case, we simulate the printer to be busy for one action execution. Therefore the printer will become available if the robot waits until a timeout and checks again, or if the robot goes to another location and comes back to a visited printer which was busy. The observed behavior for the deterministic planner in this case was to visit the closest printer $P1$, which was busy, then

---

[3] A video demonstration of this setup can be found in https://youtu.be/aozTz4Ex7PI.

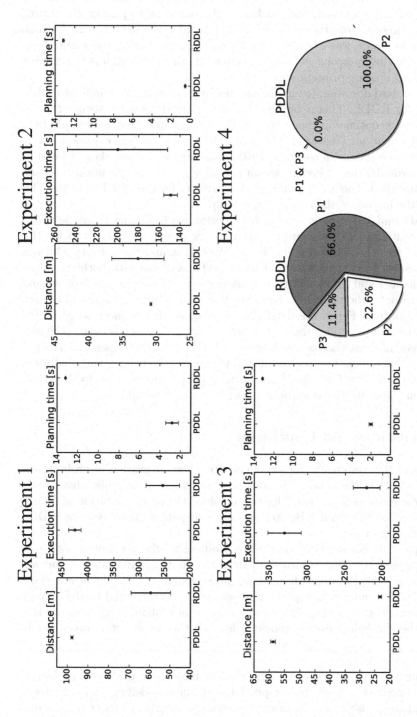

Fig. 5. Experimental results, showing mean values with standard deviations of the robot travel distance, test execution time and planning time for the first 3 experiments. In each experiment, 5 tests were performed for each approach. In Experiment 4, 500 tests were made in simulation. Experimental results show the distribution of the first printer selected across all plans and planner.

visit printer $P2$, which was empty, the printer $P3$, which is also busy, to finally succeed at $P1$. In contrast, the stochastic planner went to printer $P1$, waited for it until timeout, and then waited again, obtaining the papers in this second step. This behavior was obtained due to the planner having the certainty of eventually having someone to help at printer $P1$, though there was uncertainty of succeeding if other printers were visited.

The standard deviation (σ) in distance and execution time is small for PDDL, and large for RDDL. This is because the deterministic planner always chooses the plan that is optimal in time and distance, and in fact the σ comes only from real-world execution. The variance seen in PDDL is due to the navigation system and person interaction. In contrast, PROST produces different plans depending upon the probabilities of events, which can vary greatly in execution time and distance travelled. The σ in planning time is greater for the PDDL planner. This is due to the impact of the replanning attempts.

A final simulated experiment has been performed to further show the effects of the probabilities in the planning scenario we proposed. The setup for this experiment was the robot starting at the *PhD Area*, and the delivery goal was the *Professor's office*. For this experiment, 500 executions with both the deterministic planner and the stochastic one are carried out, and we take into account only the action of the plan that shows the first chosen printer. As it can be seen in the results from Fig. 5, the deterministic planner always chose to go to $P2$, which is the one providing shortest travel distance. In contrast, the stochastic planner has different choices, leading to a distribution that resembles the one shown in Table 1, selecting to visit most of the times $P1$, then $P2$ and finally $P3$. Therefore, given that $P2$ is less likely to have people around to help the robot, the deterministic planner is more prone to fail in such setup.

7   Discussions and Conclusions

The focus of this systems paper was to describe the integration of probabilistic planning into ROSPlan, and to demonstrate the execution of probabilistic plans in real-time robotics scenarios. This has involved the implementation of RDDL models into the ROSPlan KB, and an online dispatcher that uses the RDDL Client/Server protocol.

This paper is not intended to make a comparison of deterministic vs. probabilistic approaches. Our experiments show that both approaches have advantages, and a more thorough discussion can be found in [20]. There are many factors that determine which planning approach is better-suited to the domain and problem. For example, whether the domain is probabilistically interesting and whether probabilities are known. Also, whether or not it is necessary to have an optimal plan, or that from a given initial state the same plan is always generated for execution.

Although the use of a probabilistic planner may result in shorter paths and faster plan execution, from the perspective of domain modelling we found it was more intuitive to use an action-oriented language. Another element to take into account is that, while the handling of uncertainties by means of probabilistic planning can be useful in robotics and real-world scenarios, those probabilities must be coherent with the real-world. Such probabilities are often hard to obtain or estimate, and will usually need some kind of learning or adaptation to the real world.

As a contribution of this work, it is possible to combine both of these approaches in ROSPlan. By integrating RDDL into the ROSPlan framework, it is now straightforward to use both PDDL and RDDL planners in a single system. This means a robotic task can be divided into subtasks, in which some are probabilistic and the others deterministic. Moreover, as the online dispatcher conforms to the RDDL Client/Server protocol used in the IPPC, a wide choice of probabilistic planners is made available.

References

1. Atrash, A., Koenig, S.: Probabilistic planning for behavior-based robots. In: FLAIRS, pp. 531–535 (2001)
2. Bonasso, R.P., Firby, R.J., Gat, E., Kortenkamp, D., Miller, D.P., Slack, M.G.: Experiences with an architecture for intelligent, reactive agents. J. Exp. Theor. Artif. Intell. **9**(2–3), 237–256 (1997)
3. Boutilier, C., Dean, T., Hanks, S.: Decision-theoretic planning: structural assumptions and computational leverage. J. Artif. Intell. Res. **11**, 1–94 (1999)
4. Buksz, R.D., Cashmore, M., Krarup, B., Magazzeni, D., Ridder, B.C.: Strategic-tactical planning for autonomous underwater vehicles over long horizons. In: IROS (2018)
5. Canal, G., Alenyà, G., Torras, C.: Adapting robot task planning to user preferences: an assistive shoe dressing example. Auton. Robots 1–14 (2018). https://doi.org/10.1007/s10514-018-9737-2
6. Cashmore, M., et al.: ROSPlan: planning in the robot operating system. In: ICAPS (2015)
7. Celorrio, S.J., Fernández, F., Borrajo, D.: The PELA architecture: integrating planning and learning to improve execution. In: AAAI (2008)
8. Dean, T., Kanazawa, K.: A model for reasoning about persistence and causation. Comput. Intell. **5**(2), 142–150 (1989)
9. Fox, M., Long, D.: PDDL2.1: an extension to PDDL for expressing temporal planning domains. J. Artif. Intell. Res. **20**, 61–124 (2003)
10. Ghallab, M., Nau, D., Traverso, P.: Automated Planning: Theory and Practice. Elsevier, Amsterdam (2004)
11. Grisetti, G., Stachniss, C., Burgard, W.: Improved techniques for grid mapping with rao-blackwellized particle filters. IEEE Trans. Robot. **23**(1), 34–46 (2007)
12. Hoey, J., Von Bertoldi, A., Poupart, P., Mihailidis, A.: Assisting persons with dementia during handwashing using a partially observable Markov decision process. Vis. Syst. **65**, 66 (2007)
13. Hoffmann, J.: The Metric-FF planning system: translating "ignoring delete lists" to numeric state variables. J. Artif. Intell. Res. **20**, 291–341 (2003)
14. Hsiao, K., Kaelbling, L.P., Lozano-Perez, T.: Grasping POMDPs. In: ICRA (2007)
15. Iocchi, L., Jeanpierre, L., Lázaro, M.T., Mouaddib, A.I.: A practical framework for robust decision-theoretic planning and execution for service robots. In: ICAPS, pp. 486–494 (2016)

16. Keller, T., Eyerich, P.: PROST: probabilistic planning based on UCT. In: ICAPS (2012)
17. Kolobov, A., Dai, P., Mausam, M., Weld, D.S.: Reverse iterative deepening for finite-horizon MDPs with large branching factors. In: ICAPS (2012)
18. Krivic, S., Cashmore, M., Magazzeni, D., Ridder, B., Szedmak, S., Piater, J.: Decreasing uncertainty in planning with state prediction. In: IJCAI, pp. 2032–2038, August 2017
19. Kushmerick, N., Hanks, S., Weld, D.S.: An algorithm for probabilistic planning. Artif. Intell. **76**(1–2), 239–286 (1995)
20. Little, I., Thiebaux, S.: Probabilistic planning vs replanning. In: ICAPS Workshop on Planning Competitions: Past, Present, and Future (2007)
21. Littman, M.L.: Markov games as a framework for multi-agent reinforcement learning. In: ICML, pp. 157–163 (1994)
22. Martínez, D., Alenyà, G., Ribeiro, T., Inoue, K., Torras, C.: Relational reinforcement learning for planning with exogenous effects. J. Mach. Learn. Res. **18**(1), 2689–2732 (2017)
23. Martínez, D., Alenyà, G., Torras, C.: Relational reinforcement learning with guided demonstrations. Artif. Intell. **247**, 295–312 (2017)
24. Pacchierotti, E., Christensen, H.I., Jensfelt, P.: Design of an office-guide robot for social interaction studies. In: IROS, pp. 4965–4970 (2006)
25. Sanner, S.: Relational dynamic influence diagram language (RDDL): language description (2010, unpublished manuscript)
26. Smith, B.D., Rajan, K., Muscettola, N.: Knowledge acquisition for the onboard planner of an autonomous spacecraft. In: Plaza, E., Benjamins, R. (eds.) EKAW 1997. LNCS, vol. 1319, pp. 253–268. Springer, Heidelberg (1997). https://doi.org/10.1007/BFb0026790
27. Smith, T., Simmons, R.: Probabilistic planning for robotic exploration. Ph.D. thesis, Carnegie Mellon University, The Robotics Institute (2007)
28. Veloso, M., et al.: Cobots: collaborative robots servicing multi-floor buildings. In: IROS, pp. 5446–5447 (2012)
29. Yoon, S.W., Fern, A., Givan, R.: FF-Replan: a baseline for probabilistic planning. In: ICAPS, pp. 352–359 (2007)

Coverage Path Planning for Large-Scale Aerial Mapping

Nasser Gyagenda[1(✉)], Ahmad Kamal Nasir[2], Hubert Roth[1],
and Vadim Zhmud[3]

[1] Department of Computer Science and Electrical Engineering,
University of Siegen, Siegen, Germany
{nasser.gyagenda, hubert.roth}@uni-siegen.de
[2] School of Science and Engineering,
Lahore University of Management Sciences, Lahore, Pakistan
ahmad.kamal@lums.edu.pk
[3] Department of Automation, Novosibirsk State Technical University,
Novosibirsk, Russia
oao_nips@bk.ru

Abstract. Aerial coverage path planning is a type of path planning where the sensor footprint covers all accessible parts of the area of interest. This type of path planning finds application in precision agriculture, precision forestry and service robots. Limited endurance of micro aerial vehicles has limited their operations to small areas coverable in a single flight. New application domains like geological survey cover vast areas exceeding endurances of most modern aerial platforms and the available path planners do not address coverage of such areas. This paper presents an approach for generating coverage paths for large-scale aerial mapping. The planner applies voronoi partitioning to decompose large areas into manageable cells. Then generates boustrophedon paths to cover each cell. The proposed planner is incorporated into Mission Planner. Software in the loop simulation results have ascertained the feasibility and completeness of the generated paths, even with multiple micro aerial platforms.

Keywords: Aerial coverage path planning · Voronoi partitioning

1 Introduction

Coverage path planning (CPP) is a type of path planning where the generated trajectory ensures the robot footprint covers all open spaces in the area of interest (AOI). It is key to autonomous robotics and differs from start-to-goal path planning where a path from a start point to a goal is sought. These path planners find application in mobile ground robotics like vacuum cleaning, lawn mowing, security and surveillance, deicing of airports, and harvesting or seeding, among others, and mobile aerial robotics like crop sensing, geological documentation, urban planning, wetland management, search and rescue, land-use monitoring, mapping and remote sensing among others.

Literature has many elegant solutions to the coverage problem. Unfortunately, most of these solutions are specific to mobile ground robotic applications and do not scale

© Springer Nature Switzerland AG 2019
K. Althoefer et al. (Eds.): TAROS 2019, LNAI 11649, pp. 251–262, 2019.
https://doi.org/10.1007/978-3-030-23807-0_21

optimally to aerial robotics. This limited generalizability together with advances in aerial robotics and remote sensing have fueled intense research in the field of aerial coverage path planning (ACPP).

According to PwC global report [1] on commercial applications of unmanned aerial vehicle technology, the two leading industries, infrastructure and agriculture, account for more than a half of the global market share Fig. 1. Clearly, all involved industrial application are large-scale and coverage in nature.

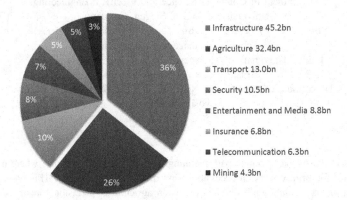

Fig. 1. Predicted market value for UAV powered industrial solutions in US dollars [1]

These applications call for close proximity flights to the subject of interest, which favors micro aerial vehicles (MAVs) as opposed to medium and large size vehicles. Unfortunately, large coverage industrial applications oftentimes exceed the coverage capability of most modern MAVs. Luckily, dropping prices have enabled acquisition of multiple platforms, whose aggregate capability can easily satisfy most of the large-scale coverage applications. It should be noted that even with a single platform and a path planner, multiple flights can be systematically conducted in a short period of time, owing to maneuverability and low operating costs of these aerial platforms.

To harness the cumulative power in numbers, partitioning schemes are necessary for partitioning of large areas into manageable portions and assigning them to a fleet of aerial platforms or flying them with one platform multiple times. To this point, we are not aware of any coverage path planning methods capable of planning paths for large areas exceeding the coverage capability of modern MAVs.

The problem overview is as follows, given a large-scale input area (impossible to cover in one flight), partition it into manageable subareas coverable by a multirotor MAV with limited endurance in multiple flights or a fleet of multirotor MAVs, and then plan trajectories to cover each subarea whilst adhering to coverage requirements.

We propose an approach that partitions large input areas into manageable cells with respect to endurance and flight speed, then plans coverage paths and assigns each cell to the most suitable MAV (with minimum coverage time).

The planner is applicable to a single platform, homogeneous (similar endurance and camera properties) and heterogeneous (varying endurance and camera properties) multirotor fleets. Furthermore, it guarantees complete coverage and resolution constraints.

Guarantee of coverage is through exact cellular decomposition of the input area, and designing paths that ensure coverage of each cell. This work strives to achieve a good enough result but does not guarantee optimality.

2 Related Work

Generally, coverage path planning (CPP) considers four main set of factors, environmental, robot, actuator/sensor and algorithmic factors. Table 1 highlights the properties underlying each of the factors. Literature contains CPP algorithms based on permutations of these properties. We refer readers to a survey of coverage path planning in robotics [2] for a comprehensive characterization of the different approaches.

Two CPP surveys [2, 3] spread over a decade apart report the most influential approaches up until 2013. Surveys [3] and [2] have 0% and <5% mention of ACPP respectively. This could have been a consequence of the under-developed state of unmanned aerial technology. The recent past has seen a surge in ACPP research works, but mostly for fixed-wing type MAVs. Next, we cover some of the influential works.

Table 1. Classification factors of coverage path planners

Component	Property
Environment	Static/dynamic, 2D/3D/2.5D, non-differentiable, size
Robot	Aerial/ground/amphibian, holonomic/non-holonomic, finite energy storage/infinite energy storage, single/multiple robots
Actuator/Sensor	Footprint shape, mounting (Gimbal or no gimbal)
Algorithm	Offline/online, optimality, completeness, complexity
Optimization objective	Number of turns, path length, time-to-completion, area-per-distance travelled, energy

To cover concave polygonal areas, the authors of [4] proposed four convex decomposition strategies that yield minimum polygon altitude sub-regions. The decomposition works by drawing edges at concave vertices oriented to yield minimum width sum convex polygons. Entire adjacent cells with similar directions are then combined into one cell to shorten coverage paths. The resulting cells are then transformed into a minimum traversal undirected graph on which the minimum weight path to all cells is generated. Individual cells are covered with boustrophedon paths.

Interesting work from marine robotics in [5] proposed a coverage method for seabed using autonomous underwater vehicles (AUVs). K-means clustering segments the area into a user-defined number of sub-regions within predefined depth ranges. Morse exact cellular decomposition is applied to each cluster. Morse decomposition applies a Morse function contour at critical points to divide the clusters further into cells. Therefore, the number of cells depends on the number of critical points contained within a cluster, which may result into impractically small cells. The cells form an adjacency graph, where traveling-salesman algorithm plans a path to all cells. Each cell is covered using boustrophedon sweep lines oriented perpendicular to surface gradient.

A spiral-like method proposed in [6] plans paths for a fleet of heterogeneous unmanned aerial systems (UASs). The area is decomposed into triangular cells whose size depend on the sensor field of view (FOV) and platform orientation. The cells are transformed into an undirected graph whose vertices are assigned costs with the highest cost at the root (border) and lowest at the leaves (center). Based on cost, a path is generated from the border covering the entire area. Lloyd iterations and valley sensitivity settings were applied to improve the path.

An application specific, complete coverage yet non-optimal algorithm in [7], decomposes the area into triangular cells using Constrained Delaunay Triangulation (CDT). It starts by assigning each platform an initial cell at the border from which all the other cells are visited in a spiral-like pattern depending on their depth cost. This work assumes the starting point to lie within the area of interest.

To address endurance limitations, some researchers have adopted energy minimization objectives to maximize coverage per battery charge. In [8], a digital elevation model combined with a power consumption model created an energy consumption map, from which genetic algorithms generated an optimal coverage path. Although the generated path is complete, it is highly convoluted and self-intersecting. The approach in [9] generates a minimum energy complete coverage path using an energy model derived from real measurements with resolution constraints. Here an active gimbal stabilized camera is used, hence, the assumption of camera-ground parallelism. For coverage, boustrophedon motion pattern is applied with flight lines oriented parallel to the longest borderline. This approach performs poorly for areas with more than four edges, especially when the longest side is nearly parallel to the minor axis of variation of vertices.

Decomposition is a key step in most coverage approaches and one popular form of decomposition is grid-based decomposition. In [10], a gradient ascending algorithm tracks wavefront gradients on a grid-map selecting a sequence of waypoints that completely covers the area of interest while minimizing completion time. In case of multiple waypoints with similar potentials, a backtracker keeps record of these waypoints.

The work presented in [11], implemented the dual of Delaunay Triangulation, voronoi partitioning to partition the overlapping workspace of manipulator robots into appropriate cells. A coverage path plan for each is then generated covering its specific area plus the overlapping portion closest to it. We share the choice of partitioning algorithm with this work, but differ in the way voronoi sites are treated. In our case, the sites are user inputs whereas in [11] the site locations are the optimization variables. Most usage of voronoi diagrams have been centered around generating paths through narrow operating regions [12].

For complete coverage, spiral and boustrophedon trajectories are the most commonly used flight trajectories for both fixed-wing and multirotor micro aerial vehicles. An empirical performance assessment based on three metrics: energy, time and distance showed that spiral trajectories were more suitable for fixed wing platforms, whereas boustrophedon trajectories for multirotor platforms [13]. Based on this conclusion, boustrophedon trajectories are applied in our work for partition coverage.

The path planner describes in this paper involves techniques like home point-based area decomposition as opposed to number of platforms, and path generation and path splitting constrained by map resolution and platform endurance. The flexible placement of home points ensures accessibility to all areas whereas path splitting ensured complete coverage of even large cells. This level of flexibility, which is key to handling of large-scale areas, lacks in most of the available path planners.

3   Aerial Coverage

Aerial maps support many data–driven processes. Satellites and manned airplanes have for long been the main techniques for capturing raw aerial data. As depicted in Table 2, these techniques exhibit low revisit cycles and generate low-resolution maps compared to MAVs. Thus, MAVs provide a great alternative to satellite and manned mapping, but their sensors have a limited field of view that is compensated for by capturing numerous geo-referenced images at spatially distributed points within the input area. The images are then stitched together to generate an orthorectified mosaic. Here, the challenge is generating a path to all imaging geo-locations for completeness.

Table 2. Comparison of MAV and satellite remote sensing solutions

System	Repeat cycle	GSD (m)
SPOT (Commercial satellites)	26 days	2.5, 10, 20
LANDSAT 1-7	16 days	30, 60
Sentinel-2	10 days	10, 20, 30
Sentinel-2 (two satellite constellation)	5 days	10, 20, 30
MODIS	1–2 days	250, 500, 1000
SPOT 6-7 (Commercial satellites)	1 day	1.5
Micro aerial vehicles (MAVs)	<1 day	0.01–0.1

3.1   Mapping Process

We adopted a mapping process consisting of three sub-steps, input area preparation, area partitioning and coverage path planning. The input area is defined by a set of mouse selected unordered geo-coordinates from a customized interactive digital map in Ardupilot Mission Planner software by Michael Oborne. The input area can be convex, concave or complex in geometry. Operations on complex and nonconvex polygons for tasks of aerial coverage add unnecessary levels of complexity.

Since mapping sensors have a nonzero footprint, a collage of such footprints automatically converts complex polygons into nonconvex ones as illustrated in Figs. 2 and 3. Interesting for aerial mapping is moving the imaging sensor to all geo-locations regardless of the overall area geometry. This reduces the problem to visiting a set of waypoints as opposed to planning at the geometric level. This transformed problem is solvable as a graph traversal problem or like in our case, with boustrophedon coverage paths. Next, we look at input area preparation.

Input Area Preparation
Using the abundant arithmetic tools necessitated projecting the coordinates into a planar space, this transformation and its inverse are implemented using Lambert azimuthal equal area projection [14]. Counter clockwise coordinates sorting done in the

polar space simplifies complex input areas to convex or concave areas. For concave areas, a convex approximation is determined using the Quickhull algorithm [15].

Area Partitioning

Comparison of the input area to the platform's endurance determines the need for partitioning. The conditions for partitioning are expressed as follows,

$$\frac{D_{BB}}{60 \cdot v_N} > T_E \text{ AND } T_C > T_E \tag{1}$$

where D_{BB} is perimeter of the oriented bounding box around the area of interest (m), v_N is ground speed (m/s), T_E is endurance (min) and T_C is coverage time (min).

After ascertaining the necessity for partitioning, we then determine the number of partitions n_P. A partition is approximated by an oriented bounding box of area A_N.

$$n_P = \frac{A_T}{A_N} = \frac{16A_T}{D_N^2}, \; n_P \in \mathbf{Z} \tag{2}$$

where A_T is area of interest, A_N is the maximum area associated with endurance T_E, i.e. the perimeter of A_N is equal to the nominal coverage distance D_N of a quadcopter.

Since the area is too huge to survey from the current home point, n_P new home points (discarding the original home point) are needed. These are the sites upon which voronoi partitioning is based. Voronoi cells are generated based on Euclidean distance and voronoi sites. Then, the final partitions are the regions of intersection between voronoi cells and or input area. The result is an exact cellular decomposition where,

$$AOI = \sum_{i=1}^{n_P} P_i \tag{3}$$

where P_i is the area of partition i. It should be noted that site placement plays a key role in partitioning. For better results, the sites should be distributed spatially evenly within and or around the area of interest. Most optimal locations for sites are near vertices of the intersection between bounding box and convex hull. If only $T_C > T_E$ is true in Eq. 1, no area partitioning is necessary, but path splitting.

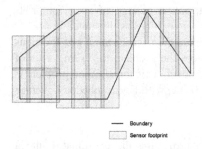

Fig. 2. Complex area of interest covered with sensor footprints

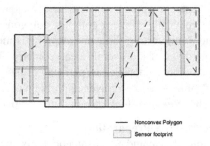

Fig. 3. Complex AOI automatically transformed into a non-convex polygon by sensor footprint coverage

Coverage Path Planning

Before planning the actual path, let us look at optimal travel orientation determination and system specifications, as they are key to quality path plans.

Optimal Travel Lines Orientation

The choice of sweep direction greatly influences the number of turns and number of traversal lines and coverage distance [9, 16, 17]. The number of turns is proportional to number of traversal lines. Therefore, minimizing number of turns minimizes coverage distance, number of images and completion time.

Approaches for flight line heading determination include orientation of longest edge of input polygon [9, 17], longest edge of an axis aligned minimum area-bounding box, longest edge of an oriented minimum area bounding box and principal direction of variation of convex hull vertices. Aligning flight lines parallel to the longest edge of an oriented minimum area bounding box is the only method proven to yield optimal number of turns [16]. We empirically ascertained this optimality assertion by monitoring the variations in coverage path length with respect to path orientation. Figure 5 shows distance variation as the coverage path in Fig. 4 is rotated through 180°. Such characteristic is typical of a diameter function with global minima corresponding to optimal flight lines orientation.

Specifications Elicitation

The following parameters constitute the independent variables for analysis:

- Camera parameters: focal length f, pixel pitch p, pixel count ($m \times n$ pixels) and shutter speed, T_S
- Quadrotor specifications: ground nominal speed v_N, endurance T_E
- Mission specifications: an interactive digital map, desired ground sample distance (GSD), forward overlap f_{OVLP} and side overlap s_{OVLP}, area of interest AOI.

From the above independent variables, dependent variables are derived as follow:

(a) Flight height

$$AGL = \frac{GSD * f}{p} \tag{4}$$

(b) Image footprint/ground coverage/image size on the ground is the actual area on the ground captured in an image.

$$D_w \times D_h = GSD \cdot m \times GSD \cdot n = GSD \cdot (m \times n) \tag{5}$$

(c) Side gain, s_{gain} and forward gain, f_{gain}

$$s_{gain} = D_w \cdot \frac{(100 - s_{OVLP})}{100}, \ f_{gain} = D_h \cdot \frac{(100 - f_{OVLP})}{100} \tag{6}$$

(d) Number of images per flight line (*NIM*) and number of flight lines (*NFL*)

$$NIM = NFL + ceil\left(\sum_{i=1}^{NFL} \frac{l_i}{f_{gain}}\right) \text{ and } NFL = ceil\left(\frac{b}{s_{gain}} + 1\right) \tag{7}$$

where b is the diameter of convex hull and l_i is the length of flight line i

(e) Camera trigger time T_T is given by the expression,

$$T_T = \frac{f_{gain}}{v_N}, \text{ subject to } T_T > T_S \tag{8}$$

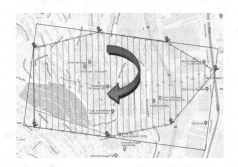

Fig. 4. Sample cell with coverage paths

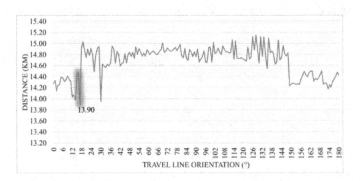

Fig. 5. Distance variation as a function of path orientation. Critical point occurs at 13.90 km

To guarantee adjacency and stereoscopic coverage, images are captured with overlapping fields of view. Near vertical photos for aerial map generation overlap along direction of flight (forward overlap) and between adjacent flight lines (side overlap).

Spatial resolution determines not only image quality, but also the amount of imagery data needed for map generation. The amount of imagery data scales exponentially with ground spatial resolution [18, 19], as indicated in Fig. 6. The dependence of GSD on AGL and camera properties introduces a level of flexibility in terms of hardware selection, as the required map quality is achievable through strategic selection of camera properties and flight height. Flight altitude is upper bounded by air traffic regulations, which for North Rhine-Westphalia in Germany is limited to 100 m [20].

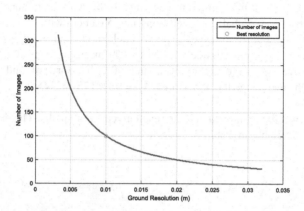

Fig. 6. Number of images scales exponentially with ground resolution. Results are based on a Sony NEX-5 camera with 25 mm focal length, 5.07 μm pixel pitch and 4595 × 3056 pixel count

Coverage Path

We generate coverage paths for each cell as a series of parallel flight lines oriented towards the optimal travel direction. The generated coverage path may exceed the nominal endurance of available aerial platforms, in which case a splitter function automatically divides the area further into manageable paths. All planned paths are cyclic in nature. This approach is generalizable to multiple homogeneous MAVs with no modification whatsoever. Heterogeneous fleets require systematic scheduling.

Heterogeneous MAVs

Path planning for fleets of heterogeneous quadrotors is not as trivial as planning for a single or homogenous fleet. To accommodate the variation in platform capabilities, the previous planning steps are modified as follows:

Partitioning decision is based on minimum coverage quadrotor, Eq. 9. This ensures accessibility to even the furthest imaging points by all aerial platform.

$$\frac{D_{BB}}{60 \cdot v_{N,Emin}} > T_{Emin} \tag{9}$$

where T_{Emin} and $v_{N,Emin}$ are endurance and velocity of minimum coverage quadcopter. For the definitions of other parameters see Eq. 1.

For each platform i, a coverage path is planned on each cell j, resulting in coverage time $T_{C,ij}$ and number of flights $n_{F,j}$. A scheduler then allocates cells to available quadrotors with priority given to high endurance quadrotors and longest coverage time cells.

4 Simulation Results

The approach presented in this paper has been incorporate into the C# based Ardupilot Mission Planner to take advantage of the abundant functions available, and tested with software in the loop (SITL) simulator. In the following test, we used DJI Matrice 100 (M100) quadcopter with endurance $T_E = 20$ min and nominal (minimum camera vibration) speed $v_N = 5$ m/s, microdrones md4-1000 with endurance 45 min and nominal speed 6 m/s, a gimbal stabilized Sony nex-5 camera with focal length 25 mm, image size of 4595×3056 pixels, pixel pitch = 5.07 μm and sensor size of 23.5×15.6 mm. The flight altitude was set to 100 m, giving a ground resolution of 2.03 cm. The overlaps were set to 50% and 60% for forward and side overlap respectively. On analyzing, the input area $A_T = 9838175$ m^2, $D_{BB} = 12.6$ km, partitions $n_P = 5$.

Figure 7 shows the input area and the resultant coverage paths. The details for each of the cells are available in Table 3.

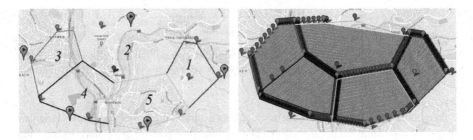

Fig. 7. (left) Input area partitioned into five cells according to the big green home points. (right) complete coverage paths for the five cells (Color figure online)

Table 3. Results of AOI partitioning

Cells	Cell 1	Cell 2	Cell 3	Cell 4	Cell 5
Area (m^2)	1372337	2895632	1339350	1996098	2235851
Perimeter (m)	4500	5000	3900	4700	4800
Path length (m)	61660	123220	60160	86900	93520
T_C (min) M100/n_F	256/13	513/26	250/13	362/19	389/20
T_C (min) md4-1000/n_F	214/5	421/10	208/5	301/7	324/8

For the homogeneous case, only M100 was considered. Since the cell coverage paths exceeded the platform endurance, the paths were automatically split into segments matching quadrotor's nominal coverage, which was 6000 m and output as waypoint files. The individual mission files have been tested on SITL simulator.

For the heterogeneous case, M100 and md4-1000 were considered. Each platform planned a coverage path for each cell. The resulting completion times are tabulated in

Table 3. The cells were then scheduled on the quadrotors with priority given to high coverage quadrotors and longest completion time cells. Cells 2, 1, 3 were assigned to md4-1000 and 4, 5 to M100. The total completion time and total number of flights are 843 min and 20, 751 min and 39 for md4-1000 and M100 respectively.

5 Conclusion and Future Work

This paper has described and tested an offline large-scale aerial path planner that breaks endurance barriers on the deployment of MAVs for large-scale mapping applications. The planner uses voronoi exact cellular decomposition to partition large input areas into manageable cells. The approach is applicable to tasks involving a single MAV, heterogeneous and a homogeneous fleet of MAVs.

The planner accounts for location of home points, map resolution and multirotor capabilities in the process of planning coverage paths. The resulting plans can support decision-making processes, ensure recoverability of platforms and mission success.

SITL simulation tests conducted ascertained the feasibility and deploy-ability of the conceptualized method. Assumptions of perfect waypoint tracking, constant endurance and zero influence of environmental factors like wind on endurance do not hold in the real world and may lead to performance degradation in the field.

Regarding future work, further improvements on Mission Planner will be conducted to allow simultaneous tracking of multiple MAVs. Home points optimization will be incorporated to minimize user inputs and improve coverage performance. Last but not least, terrain effect on the performance of MAVs and map quality will be studied.

References

1. PricewaterhouseCoopers, Clarity from above. PwC global report on the commercial applications of drone technology. https://www.pwc.pl/clarityfromabove. Accessed 09 Feb 2019
2. Galceran, E., Carreras, M.: A survey on coverage path planning for robotics. Robot. Auton. Syst. **61**, 1258–1276 (2013)
3. Choset, H.: Coverage for robotics – a survey of recent results. Ann. Math. Artif. Intell. **31**, 113–126 (2001)
4. Jiao, Y.-S., Wang, X.-M., Chen, H., Li, Y.: Research on the coverage path planning of UAVs for polygon areas. In: Proceedings of the 2010 5th IEEE Conference on Industrial Electronics and Applications, Taichung, Taiwan, 15–17 June 2010, pp. 1467–1472 (2010)
5. Galceran, E., Carreras, M.: Efficient seabed coverage path planning for ASVs and AUVs. In: IEEE/RSJ International Conference on Intelligent Robots and Systems (IROS), Vilamoura-Algarve, Portugal, 7–12 October 2012, pp. 88–93 (2012)
6. Balampanis, F., Maza, I., Ollero, A.: Spiral-like coverage path planning for multiple heterogeneous UAS operating in coastal regions. In: 2017 International Conference on Unmanned Aircraft Systems (ICUAS 2017), Miami Marriott Biscayne Bay, Miami, FL, USA, 13–16 June 2017, pp. 617–624 (2017)

7. Balampanis, F., Maza, I., Ollero, A.: Area decomposition, partition and coverage with multiple remotely piloted aircraft systems operating in coastal regions. In: 2016 International Conference on Unmanned Aircraft Systems (ICUAS 2016), Key Bridge Marriott, Arlington, VA, USA, 7–10 June 2016, pp. 275–283 (2016)

8. Wang, X., Sun, T., Li, D.: Energy-optimal coverage path planning on topographic map for environment survey with unmanned aerial vehicles. Electron. Lett. **52**(9), 699–701 (2016)

9. Di Franco, C., Buttazzo, G.: Coverage path planning for UAVs photogrammetry with energy and resolution constraints. J. Intell. Robot. Syst. **83**(3–4), 445–462 (2016)

10. Nam, L.H., Huang, L., Li, X.J., Xu, J.F.: An approach for coverage path planning for UAVs. In: 2016 IEEE 14th International Workshop on Advanced Motion Control (AMC), Auckland, New Zealand, 22–24 April 2016, pp. 411–416 (2016)

11. Hassan, M., Liu, D., Huang, S., Dissanayake, G.: Task oriented area partitioning and allocation for optimal operation of multiple industrial robots in unstructured environments. https://opus.lib.uts.edu.au/bitstream/10453/33422/5/ICARCV2014.pdf

12. Kurabayashi, D., Ota, J., Arai, T., Yoshida, E.: Cooperative sweeping by multiple mobile robots. In: Proceedings of IEEE International Conference on Robotics and Automation, Minneapolis, MN, USA, April 1996, pp. 1744–1749 (1996)

13. Mora, A., Vemprala, S., Carrio, A., Saripalli, S.: Flight performance assessment of land surveying trajectories for multiple UAV platforms. In: 2015 Workshop on Research, Education and Development of Unmanned Aerial Systems (RED-UAS), Cancun, Mexico, November 2015, pp. 1–7 (2015)

14. Snyder, J.: Map projections-a working manual. U S Govt. Printing Office (1983). [Place of publication not identified]

15. Barber, C.B., Dobkin, D.P., Huhdanpaa, H.: The quickhull algorithm for convex hulls. ACM Trans. Math. Softw. **22**(4), 469–483 (1996)

16. Huang, W.H.: Optimal line-sweep-based decompositions for coverage algorithms. In: 2001 IEEE International Conference on Robotics and Automation, Seoul, South Korea, pp. 27–32 (2001)

17. Di Franco, C., Buttazzo, G.: Energy-aware coverage path planning of UAVs. In: 2015 IEEE International Conference on Autonomous Robot Systems and Competitions (ICARSC 2015), Vila Real, Portugal, 8–10 April 2015, pp. 111–117 (2015)

18. Matese, A., et al.: Intercomparison of UAV, aircraft and satellite remote sensing platforms for precision viticulture. Remote Sens. **7**(3), 2971–2990 (2015)

19. Volkmann, W.: Small unmanned aerial system mapping versus conventional methods (en): CTA. https://cgspace.cgiar.org/bitstream/10568/90130/3/1987_PDF.pdf

20. Bundesministerium für Verkehr und digitale Infrastruktur, Verordnung zur Regelung des Betriebs von unbemannten Fluggeräten. https://www.bmvi.de/SharedDocs/DE/Anlage/LF/verordnung-zur-regelung-des-betriebs-von-unbemannten-fluggeraeten.pdf?__blob=publicationFile. Accessed 02 June 2018

Self-organized Collective Motion
with a Simulated Real Robot Swarm

Mohsen Raoufi[1], Ali Emre Turgut[2], and Farshad Arvin[3(✉)]

[1] Department of Aerospace Engineering, Sharif University of Technology,
Tehran, Iran
`mohsen_raoufi@ae.sharif.edu`
[2] Mechanical Engineering Department, Middle East Technical University,
06800 Ankara, Turkey
`aturgut@metu.edu.tr`
[3] School of Electrical and Electronic Engineering, The University of Manchester,
Manchester M13 9PL, UK
`farshad.arvin@manchester.ac.uk`

Abstract. Collective motion is one of the most fascinating phenomena observed in nature. In the last decade, it aroused so much attention in physics, control and robotics fields. In particular, many studies have been done in swarm robotics related to collective motion, also called flocking. In most of these studies, robots use orientation and proximity of their neighbors to achieve collective motion. In such an approach, one of the biggest problems is to measure orientation information using on-board sensors. In most of the studies, this information is either simulated or implemented using communication. In this paper, we implemented a fully autonomous coordinated motion without alignment using very simple Mona robots. We used an approach based on Active Elastic Sheet (AES) method. We modified the method and added the capability to enable the swarm to move toward a desired direction and rotate about an arbitrary point. The parameters of the modified method are optimized using TCACS optimization algorithm. We tested our approach in different settings using Matlab and Webots.

Keywords: Swarm robotics · Collective motion ·
Coordinated motion · Flocking · Self-organized

1 Introduction

Collective motion (CM) is an eye-catching demonstration of a more broad phenomenon called collective behaviour [22]. CM is observed in diverse domains such as: physics [11], chemistry [12], from micro-size creatures such as bacteria colonies [20], cells [1], macro-molecules [18] to handful macro-size examples of fish [24], birds [4,5], even humans [15] and to non-living systems [21]. The principle feature of CM is that each individual agent behaves based on the interaction

This work was supported by EPSRC Impact Acceleration Account (EP/R511626/1).

K. Althoefer et al. (Eds.): TAROS 2019, LNAI 11649, pp. 263–274, 2019.
https://doi.org/10.1007/978-3-030-23807-0_22

between its neighbors; resulting in polarized motion of the group. This interaction might be either simple (attraction/repulsion) or complex (combinations of simple interactions) [23].

In most of the works on CM, agents use both orientation and proximity information of their neighbors [6,8]. In contrast to these works, some works introduced methods that do not rely on this information. An individual-based model is defined in [17], where the interaction between neighbor agents is defined only by escape-pursuit behavior. In [9], inelastic collisions between isotropic agents, and in [13] a pairwise repulsive force between deformable, self-propelled particles are introduced as interaction mechanism regardless of the orientation of neighbors. These methods leave an indirect effect on individual agents, and as a result, enable them to establish aligning interaction in an effective, implicit manner. By so doing, not only the swarm achieves CM, but also the reduced dynamics reaches consensus in the heading direction of agents. An example of this implicit aligning is [7], in which, Ferrante et al. identified a new elasticity-based approach for achieving collective motion and illustrated the behavior by introducing an Active Elastic Sheet (AES) model. In their proposed model, the motion of an individual is determined by only attraction-repulsion forces. This feature is very useful in practical cases, such as a swarm of robots in which a specific robot have not any information of its neighbors' orientation [3].

In this paper, we improve the AES model presented in [7], and optimize some of the parameters of the proposed algorithm using a heuristic optimization algorithm. To illustrate the improved performance of the model, various simulations with different assumptions are performed. In addition, some simulations are conducted in Webots [14] using the model of Mona robot [2]. Finally, We implement the AES model on a swarm of simulated real Mona robots for the first time. To the best of our knowledge, this is the first implementation of fully autonomous CM using such a simple robotic platform without alignment information.

This paper is organized as follows: in the Sect. 2, we introduce the concept of AES mechanism to achieve CM, and the modifications are addressed there. Then, the optimization algorithm is discussed and the objective function is defined in Sect. 3. We mention the settings of simulations in the Sect. 4. In Sect. 5, the results are shown and we discuss them. Section 6 closes the paper with a conclusion about the current work.

2   Collective Motion Control

In this section, the dynamic model of AES along with some modifications is presented. The model is derived based on a simple two-dimensional active elastic sheet mechanism [7]. After defining the basic mechanism, the numerical dynamics of particles and modifications will be elaborated upon.

2.1   Active Elastic Sheet Model and Numerical Dynamics

Each agent i out of N agents, is affected by the attraction-repulsion force of its neighbors. This force will leave an effect on both the linear velocity $\dot{x}_i$ and the

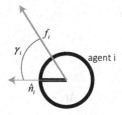

Fig. 1. The angle between force and heading vectors

rotational velocity $\dot{\theta}_i$ of the agent. This effect is formulated in continuous-time form as:

$$\dot{x}_i(t) = \left\{ v_0(t) + \alpha \left[\left(f_i(t) + D_r \hat{\xi}_r(t) \right) \cdot \hat{n}_i(t) \right] \right\} \hat{n}_i(t) \tag{1}$$

$$\dot{\theta}_i(t) = \beta \left\{ \left[f_i(t) + D_r \hat{\xi}_r(t) \right] \cdot \hat{n}_i^\perp(t) \right\} + D_\theta \xi_\theta(t) \tag{2}$$

where, v_0 is the forward biasing speed, and parameters α and β are the inverse transitional and rotational coefficients, respectively. The unit vector $\hat{n}_i(t)$ is the heading vector which is parallel to the heading direction of agent i, and $\hat{n}_i^\perp(t)$ is perpendicular to it.

$$\hat{n}_i(t) = \begin{bmatrix} \cos(\theta_i(t)) \\ \sin(\theta_i(t)) \end{bmatrix} \tag{3}$$

The term $f_i \cdot \hat{n}_i^\perp$ of Eq. (2) indicates that the angle between force and heading vectors (γ_i) defines the rotation speed of the agent (Fig. 1). So, the rotation speed will be zero if two vectors f_i and $\hat{n}_i$ are parallel (i.e. f_i and $\hat{n}_i^\perp$ are perpendicular.)

Agents are subject to measurement and actuation noises $D_r \hat{\xi}_r(t)$ and $D_\theta \xi_\theta(t)$; in which, $\hat{\xi}_r(t)$ is a randomly oriented unit vector and $\xi_\theta(t)$ is a random variable with standard normal distribution. D_r and D_θ are noise strength coefficients. Inducing total force vector $f_i(t)$ over agent i at time t can be calculated by the summation of linear spring-like forces, which link agent i to its interacting neighbor j, member of set S_i:

$$f_i(t) = \sum_{j \in S_i} -\frac{k}{l_{ij}} \left(\|r_{ij}(t)\| - l_{ij} \right) \frac{r_{ij}(t)}{\|r_{ij}(t)\|} \tag{4}$$

$$r_{ij}(t) = x_j(t) - x_i(t) \tag{5}$$

l_{ij} is equilibrium distance (or alternatively called natural length) of the spring that links agent i and j. In order to simulate the model, we need to numerically integrate the dynamic equations of motion. Integrating Eqs. (1) and (2) using Euler method at time step t, results in the governing discrete-time kinematic equations of each particle which is expressed by the following equations:

$$x_i^{t+1} = x_i^t + \left\{ v_0 \hat{n}_i^t + \alpha \left[\left(f_i^t + \frac{D_r}{\sqrt{\Delta t}} \hat{\xi}_r^t \right) . \hat{n}_i^t \right] \hat{n}_i^t \right\} \Delta t \tag{6}$$

$$\theta_i^{t+1} = \theta_i^t + \left\{ \beta \left[\left(f_i^t + \frac{D_r}{\sqrt{\Delta t}} \hat{\xi}_r^t \right) . \hat{n}_i^{\perp,t} \right] + \frac{D_\theta}{\sqrt{\Delta t}} \xi_\theta^t \right\} \Delta t \tag{7}$$

here, x_i^t and θ_i^t are the position and orientation of agent i at step time t, respectively, and Δt is the numerical time-step interval of integration. It is noteworthy that the velocity vector in Eq. (1) points parallel to the heading of the agent which means it is assumed that each agent can only turn, and move forward/backward. Modeling agents with 2 degrees of freedom provides many advantages to robotic applications in which the robots are not able to move omnidirectionally, e.g. Mona [2] robot.

2.2 Modifications to AES

In this section, we present some modifications to AES model, which result in collective linear and rotational motion of swarm. Firstly, we add a stimulating force to compel the swarm to move toward a specific direction. This modification leads to faster convergence of collective motion. Furthermore, the desired direction of swarm movement is also achievable by such modification. To model this auxiliary inducing force, at a certain time, we simply added the auxiliary force $f_{aux,\,l}$ to the induced force of Eq. (4). This force is parallel to the desired velocity unit vector $\hat{v}_d$ and its magnitude is defined by a weighting parameter w_l as follows:

$$f_{aux,\,l} = w_l \hat{v}_d \tag{8}$$

The second modification enables the swarm to rotate collectively by adding another auxiliary force. This force is also related to another desired linear velocity which itself is proportional to the rate of rotation. According to the kinematics of 2D rotation, the linear speed of each agent is proportional to its distance with respect to the center of rotation x_c. Thus, pointed in the following equation, the linear velocity of rotation v_r is related to r_{ic}, the position vector of agent i w.r.t. the center of rotation, and ω is the rate of rotation. $r_{ic,x}$ and $r_{ic,y}$ are the x- and y-component of r_{ic}.

$$v_r = \omega \begin{bmatrix} r_{ic,y} \\ -r_{ic,x} \end{bmatrix} \tag{9}$$

$$r_{ic} = x_i - x_c \tag{10}$$

Rotation center x_c is an arbitrary point, yet it is common to consider it on the center of swarm. Hence, same as the previous approach, we calculated the modified force for rotation by the following equation:

$$f_{aux,\,r} = w_r v_r \tag{11}$$

where, w_r is the weighting parameter of induced force for swarm rotation. It is worth mentioning that $f_{aux, r}$ should be calculated for each agent, but $f_{aux, l}$ is a universal force and is same for all agents. The linearity feature of the aforementioned phenomena enables us to add both terms together and form the total auxiliary force, which still satisfies both motions. So, the final modified inducing force is:

$$f = f_{neighbors} + f_{aux, l} + f_{aux, r} \qquad (12)$$

$f_{neighbors}$ is exactly the same as Eq. (4), but we added the subscript to show that this is the force which is defined by the influence of interacting neighbors.

2.3   Degree of Alignment

Since the symmetry is a principal feature for achieving flocking behavior, a criteria is introduced to measure it. This metric is defined by a specific system variable, called the degree of alignment. One of the most common, and widely used definition is represented in [23]. In this case the variable ψ is the average normalized velocity vectors:

$$\psi = \frac{1}{N v_0} \left\| \sum_{i=1}^{N} v_i \right\| \qquad (13)$$

where N is the total number of the agents, v_0 is the average absolute velocity, and v_i is the velocity vector of the agent i. However, in methods with 2-DoF agents, like AES, as previously mentioned, the velocity vector is parallel to the heading direction. So, the degree of alignment of the system is defined as [7]:

$$\psi = \frac{1}{N} \left\| \sum_{i=1}^{N} \hat{n}_i \right\| \qquad (14)$$

Because our purpose is to simulate the AES method on robots, we added another criterion which is defined from a control viewpoint. In this respect, the alignment of each particle ψ_i is defined by its desired direction of movement, i.e. an agent is called aligned when its orientation is parallel to its desired direction of motion. Referred to Fig. 1, the alignment is defined by the angle γ_i as follows:

$$\psi_i = |cos(\gamma_i)| = \left| \frac{f_i \cdot \hat{n}_i}{\|f_i\|} \right| \qquad (15)$$

In this definition, ψ_i is between zero (agent's orientation is perpendicular to the force, $\gamma_i = \pi/2$) and one (agent is directed toward the force, $\gamma_i = 0$ or $\gamma_i = \pi$). Note that, as the norm of the unit vector $\hat{n}_i$ is equal to one, it is eliminated from the denominator. Therefore, the degree of system alignment is calculated by the following equation:

$$\psi = \frac{1}{N} \left\| \sum_{i=1}^{N} \psi_i \right\| \qquad (16)$$

Mathematically, the value of this variable is between zero (asymmetric, disordered, random orientation) and one (fully symmetric orientation).

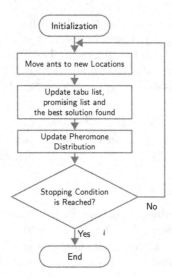

Fig. 2. General flowchart of TCACS

3   Optimization

In this section, the parameter optimization of the algorithm will be introduced. For so doing, we utilized a heuristic optimization algorithm called Tabu Continuous Ant Colony System (TCACS) [10]. TCACS combines two algorithms: Continuous Ant Colony System (CACS) [16], and Tabu Search (TS) [19]. We will mention a brief description of the algorithm in the next subsection. Our aim is to find the optimal decision parameters for AES model with a specific setup configuration. The decision parameters to be tuned are α, β, and k.

3.1   TCACS Optimization Algorithm

The structure of the algorithm is very similar to CACS; however, the advantages of tabu concept are also added. Borrowing the concept of tabu balls (meta-spherical shapes in the decision-space), prevents the ants choosing their destination within the tabu regions. The flowchart of TCACS is illustrated in Fig. 2.

In this paper, we considered the parameters of TCACS as $N_{ants} = 15$, $\gamma = 0.5$, $m = 2$ (which are number of ants, weighting factor, and PCA factor, respectively) and used Roulette as the weighting strategy.

3.2   Objective Function

One of the most important steps in optimization is the definition of objective function, which can leave a considerable effect on the performance of the algorithm to solve the problem. Various objective functions can stand as candidates, depending on what the aim of the problem is and which conditions needs to be satisfied. In case of collective motion using the modified AES method, we have two main objectives:

- To minimize the total induced force, which, generally speaking, means that agents are at their ideal position according to the elastic force of the sheet. Satisfying this objective will result in maintaining the shape of swarm same as its natural shape.
- To maximize the rate of convergence, which will be reached when the orientation of agents are about the same as the desired ones. To fulfill this objective, the optimization algorithm will try to maximize the degree of system alignment.

Although the defined problem is multi-objective, we combine both previous functions, multiplied by their weights, into a single objective function. This will help us to simplify and solve the parameter tuning problem in a more straight-forward manner.

It is notable that the system is subject to noise; consequently, the objective function gets stochastic, and it is necessary to reduce the effect of noise on it, otherwise, the performance of optimization will be reduced. Therefore, we calculate the average of multiple Monte Carlo simulations as the output of the objective function. With this in mind, the objective function is as follows:

$$J = \frac{1}{N_{MC}} \sum_{m=1}^{N_{MC}} \left\{ \sum_{t=0}^{t_f} \left[w_1 \left(\sum_{i=1}^{N} \|\boldsymbol{f}_i^t\| \right) + w_2 \psi^t \right] \right\} \qquad (17)$$

In which, the first term of the RHS is calculated by Eq. (12), and the second term by Eq. (16). Additionally, N_{MC} is the number of Monte Carlo simulations which is set to 10, and t_f is the final time of simulation. Considering the fact that the first objective is a minimization problem, and the second objective is a maximization problem, we determined w_1 (the weighting parameter of the first function) positive and w_2 negative. As the result, the optimization can be alternatively called minimization, and the objective function is a *cost* function. Determining the value of weighting parameters depends mainly on the purpose of the optimization, however, a common initial setting is normalizing the order of each term; so, we considered them as $w_1 = 1/N$, and $w_2 = -1$.

4   Experimental Setup

To model Mona robot [2] in Webots, we assembled different parts including upper and lower boards, motors, and wheels which is shown in Fig. 3-b. A population of 100 Monas, where presented in the simulations and each one has its own specific ID in order for the *supervisor* to recognize them in the simulation world-model, and calculate the adequate displacement of linear and rotational motion. Besides the simulations in Webots, we also conducted some simulations in Matlab to check the modifications and to run optimization programs. In this paper, we represented three different setups for simulations in both Webots and Matlab, which will be described in the following subsections.

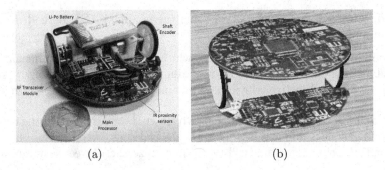

Fig. 3. (a) Mona, an open-source miniature mobile robot developed for swarm robotic applications and (b) Mona model in Webots.

4.1   Setup 1: Linear Motion

The first simulation is executed to prove the linear motion of swarm is achievable thanks to the first modification. The configuration of this setup is similar to Table 1, but the rate of rotation is set to zero, $\omega = 0$. The result of this Matlab simulation is illustrated in the first row of Fig. 5.

4.2   Setup 2: Rotational Motion

Similarly, the second modification is verified by another simulation, in which the setting makes the swarm rotate about its center. The setting of Table 1 is analogous to the current setting, yet the desired linear speed is set to zero, $\|\hat{v}_d = 0\|$. The second row of Fig. 5 represents a time lapse of this simulation in Matlab.

4.3   Setup 3: Combination of Linear and Rotational Motion

This simulation is conducted in Webots. We considered the robots as independent particles, each of which is determined by its orientation and position in the xy-plane. In this paper, a *supervisor* code is programmed to calculate the position and orientation of robots and dictate them to the corresponding agent. In other words, it is assumed that the controller of robots are ideal and the desired states of robots which supervisor calculates, is the same as the actual state of robots.

The settings of this simulation is placed at Table 1. By defining such settings, we expect the swarm to rotate about its center while moving collectively toward the west direction. To depict the result of the simulation, we saved a log file from Webots, and then plot the position and rotation of each robots in Matlab, results of which are placed in the third row of Fig. 5.

Table 1. AES simulation settings

Parameter	Description	Value
v_0	Absolute linear velocity of each agent	$0.05\,[\text{m/s}]$
t_f	Final time of simulation	$30\,[\text{s}]$
N	Number of agents	$10*10$
d_{init}	Initial distance between two side-by-side agents	$0.2\,[\text{m}]$
$\hat{v}_d$	Desired linear velocity unit vector	$[-1.0, 0.0]^T\,[\text{m/s}]$
w_l	Weight for desired linear velocity	0.8
ω	Desired rate of rotation	$0.7\,[\text{rad/s}]$
w_r	Weight for desired rotational velocity	1
D_r	Strength coefficient of measurement noise	0.5
D_θ	Strength coefficient of actuation noise	0.02

5   Results and Discussion

Applying TCACS optimization algorithm on the previously defined problem provided us the tuned parameter of the algorithm for a specific setting of simulation. The setting was considered as Table 1. In the optimization, the maximum number of function evaluations was limited to 300. Finally, the optimized parameters achieved as $\alpha^* = 0.066$, $\beta^* = 0.97$, and $k^* = 1.28$. The shape of swarm was considered as a square with 10 rows and 10 columns of agents.

In order to show the effect of optimized parameters on the performance of flocking, we investigated those objectives with both the optimized and non-optimized set of parameters. Figure 4-b shows the significant improvements, in comparison with the default parameters Fig. 4-a, which is achieved by optimized parameters. As it is shown, the rate of convergence is increased, so the CM achieved faster. Besides, the total force of the network is decreased, meaning that the shape of the swarm is maintained better.

We also studied the effect of objective weights w_1, and w_2 on the optimized parameters. Since the behavior of swarm varies for each obtained parameters, we defined two more different weight sets to show the effect of different weights on swarm behavior:

- More emphasis on the first objective, $w_1 = 10/N$, $w_2 = -1$ (Fig. 4-c)
- More emphasis on the second objective, $w_1 = 1/N$, $w_2 = -10$ (Fig. 4-d).

As we expected, the former setting resulted in the more reduction of total force, and the latter one, increased the rate of convergence of alignment, yet made the system more sensitive to noise (the effect of which is shown on the fluctuating behavior of force on Fig. 4-d). The first row of Fig. 5 proves that the initially perturbed formation of the swarm is eliminated, then the collective motion of swarm is achieved. The inducing linear force caused the swarm to move toward the west direction, as it was expected by $\hat{v}_d$. Due to the robustness of AES to

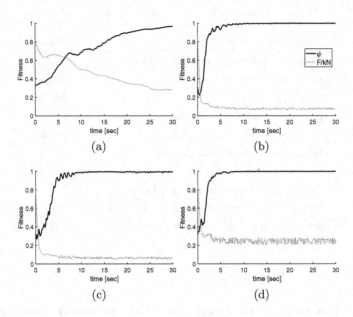

Fig. 4. Effect of Parameter optimization, and Weights on CM: (a) Default parameters, (b) optimized parameters, (c) optimized parameters with emphasis on force objective, (d) optimized parameters with emphasis on alignment objective

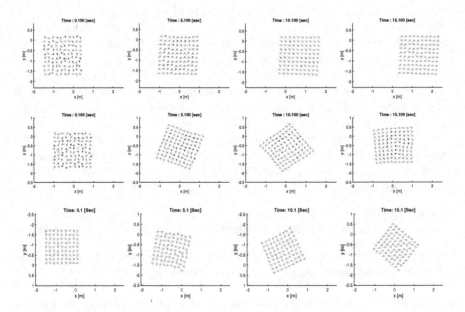

Fig. 5. Simulation results: First row: Pure linear motion in Matlab, Second row: Pure rotational motion in Matlab, Third row: Linear+rotational motion in Webots

noises, noises were not effective enough to prevent the swarm from flocking. The time history of the second row, for rotational motion, proves that the second modification is verified, similarly. In this simulation, the swarm rotates about its center and maintain its shape, meanwhile.

The third row shows that the combination of linear and rotational motions made the swarm to move toward the desired direction, and in the mean time, rotate about its center. The same optimized parameters were used for this simulation, in Webots, proving that similar settings results in similar behavior in Matlab and Webots.

6   Conclusion

We have addressed the parameter optimization and Webots simulations of AES model, which is an elasticity-based approach for achieving CM. Some of its advantages such as not relying on exchanging orientation information, and assuming 2-DoF agents attracted our attention. So, considering our robotic case, we added some modifications helping the swarm of robots to move toward the desired direction and turn about an arbitrary rotation center point. In addition, a new criterion for measuring the alignment of the swarm is defined based on the desired direction of motion.

Utilizing TCACS optimization algorithm, we tuned the parameter of AES model for a specific setup containing combination of linear and rotational motion of swarm. The effect of optimization on the behavior of CM, such as increasing the rate of convergence and decreasing the total force, has been shown. Various weighting strategies for optimization has been studied, too.

Finally, three different scenarios have been conducted in Matlab and Webots. For this end, we have designed a CAD model of Mona robot in Webots and have simulated a supervised program to control agents. The results proved that our modifications are applicable and the optimized parameters improved the performance of the AES mechanism.

References

1. Arboleda-Estudillo, Y., Krieg, M., Stühmer, J., Licata, N.A., Muller, D.J., Heisenberg, C.P.: Movement directionality in collective migration of germ layer progenitors. Curr. Biol. **20**(2), 161–169 (2010)
2. Arvin, F., Espinosa, J., Bird, B., West, A., Watson, S., Lennox, B.: Mona: an affordable open-source mobile robot for education and research. J. Intell. Robot. Syst. **94**, 761–775 (2018)
3. Arvin, F., Turgut, A.E., Krajník, T., Yue, S.: Investigation of cue-based aggregation in static and dynamic environments with a mobile robot swarm. Adapt. Behav. **24**(2), 102–118 (2016)
4. Bajec, I.L., Heppner, F.H.: Organized flight in birds. Anim. Behav. **78**(4), 777–789 (2009)
5. Ballerini, M., et al.: Interaction ruling animal collective behavior depends on topological rather than metric distance: evidence from a field study. Proc. Natl. Acad. Sci. **105**(4), 1232–1237 (2008)

6. Couzin, I.D., Krause, J., James, R., Ruxton, G.D., Franks, N.R.: Collective memory and spatial sorting in animal groups. J. Theoret. Biol. **218**(1), 1–11 (2002)

7. Ferrante, E., Turgut, A.E., Dorigo, M., Huepe, C.: Collective motion dynamics of active solids and active crystals. New J. Phys. **15**(9), 095011 (2013)

8. Grégoire, G., Chaté, H.: Onset of collective and cohesive motion. Phys. Rev. Lett. **92**(2), 025702 (2004)

9. Grossman, D., Aranson, I., Jacob, E.B.: Emergence of agent swarm migration and vortex formation through inelastic collisions. New J. Phys. **10**(2), 023036 (2008)

10. Karimi, A., Nobahari, H., Siarry, P.: Continuous ant colony system and tabu search algorithms hybridized for global minimization of continuous multi-minima functions. Comput. Optim. Appl. **45**(3), 639–661 (2010)

11. Kudrolli, A., Lumay, G., Volfson, D., Tsimring, L.S.: Swarming and swirling in self-propelled polar granular rods. Phys. Rev. Lett. **100**(5), 058001 (2008)

12. Lewandowski, J.R., Sein, J., Blackledge, M., Emsley, L.: Anisotropic collective motion contributes to nuclear spin relaxation in crystalline proteins. J. Am. Chem. Soc. **132**(4), 1246–1248 (2009)

13. Menzel, A.M., Ohta, T.: Soft deformable self-propelled particles. EPL (Europhys. Lett.) **99**(5), 58001 (2012)

14. Michel, O.: Cyberbotics Ltd. Webots^{TM}: professional mobile robot simulation. Int. J. Adv. Robot. Syst. **1**(1), 5 (2004)

15. Moussaïd, M., Helbing, D., Theraulaz, G.: How simple rules determine pedestrian behavior and crowd disasters. Proc. Natl. Acad. Sci. **108**(17), 6884–6888 (2011)

16. Pourtakdoust, S.H., Nobahari, H.: An extension of ant colony system to continuous optimization problems. In: Dorigo, M., Birattari, M., Blum, C., Gambardella, L.M., Mondada, F., Stützle, T. (eds.) ANTS 2004. LNCS, vol. 3172, pp. 294–301. Springer, Heidelberg (2004). https://doi.org/10.1007/978-3-540-28646-2_27

17. Romanczuk, P., Couzin, I.D., Schimansky-Geier, L.: Collective motion due to individual escape and pursuit response. Phys. Rev. Lett. **102**(1), 010602 (2009)

18. Schaller, V., Weber, C., Semmrich, C., Frey, E., Bausch, A.R.: Polar patterns of driven filaments. Nature **467**(7311), 73 (2010)

19. Siarry, P., Berthiau, G.: Fitting of tabu search to optimize functions of continuous variables. Int. J. Numer. Methods Eng. **40**(13), 2449–2457 (1997)

20. Sokolov, A., Aranson, I.S., Kessler, J.O., Goldstein, R.E.: Concentration dependence of the collective dynamics of swimming bacteria. Phys. Rev. Lett. **98**(15), 158102 (2007)

21. Suematsu, N.J., Nakata, S., Awazu, A., Nishimori, H.: Collective behavior of inanimate boats. Phys. Rev. E **81**(5), 056210 (2010)

22. Vicsek, T.: Fluctuations and Scaling in Biology. Oxford University Press, New York (2001)

23. Vicsek, T., Zafeiris, A.: Collective motion. Phys. Rep. **517**(3–4), 71–140 (2012)

24. Ward, A.J., Sumpter, D.J., Couzin, I.D., Hart, P.J., Krause, J.: Quorum decision-making facilitates information transfer in fish shoals. Proc. Natl. Acad. Sci. **105**(19), 6948–6953 (2008)

Contact Planning for the ANYmal Quadruped Robot Using an Acyclic Reachability-Based Planner

Mathieu Geisert[1]([✉]), Thomas Yates[1], Asil Orgen[2], Pierre Fernbach[3], and Ioannis Havoutis[1]

[1] Oxford Robotics Institute, University of Oxford, Oxford, UK
mathieu@robots.ox.ac.uk
[2] Faculty of Engineering and Natural Sciences, Sabanci University, Istanbul, Turkey
[3] Laboratoire d'Analyse et d'Architecture Système, CNRS, Toulouse, France

Abstract. Despite the great progress in quadrupedal robotics during the last decade, selecting good contacts (footholds) in highly uneven and cluttered environments still remains an open challenge. This paper builds upon a state-of-the-art approach, already successfully used for humanoid robots, and applies it to our robotic platform; the quadruped robot ANYmal. The proposed algorithm decouples the problem into two subproblems: first a guide trajectory for the robot is generated, then contacts are created along this trajectory. Both subproblems rely on approximations and heuristics that need to be tuned. The main contribution of this work is to explain how this algorithm has been retuned to work with ANYmal and to show the relevance of the approach with a variety of tests in realistic dynamic simulations.

Keywords: Motion planning · Contact planning · Legged robotics · Quadruped robots

1 Introduction

Many quadruped robots have shown great control capabilities while moving on difficult terrains such as grass, ice or stairs. However, many examples mostly rely on the intrinsic robustness of quadruped robots and reactive locomotion approaches based on body velocity estimation, to reject unpredicted perturbations. Navigating through highly uneven and cluttered environments, often with only a small set of potential footholds, is still an open problem. Some of the most impressive results on the problem come from the DARPA Learning Locomotion

This research is supported by the UKRI and EPSRC (EP/R026084/1, EP/R026173/1, EP/S002383/1) and the EU H2020 project MEMMO (780684) and project THING (780883). This work has been conducted as part of ANYmal Research, a community to advance legged robotics.

© Springer Nature Switzerland AG 2019
K. Althoefer et al. (Eds.): TAROS 2019, LNAI 11649, pp. 275–287, 2019.
https://doi.org/10.1007/978-3-030-23807-0_23

project using the LittleDog robot [1]. This small quadruped was able to navigate through terrains with rocks of a size comparable to its body. However, such performance has still to be reproduced on bigger quadruped robot platforms.

In this paper, we present an approach to automatically compute a contact plan on challenging and uneven terrains. This is only the first step towards our goal to build a generic framework, that can produce consistently good plans for most environments that a quadruped robot can encounter. However, this is an important step since several papers have shown that once a feasible footstep plan has been generated, a stable Whole-Body trajectory can be computed in real-time [2,3].

1.1 Related Work

Planning contacts is a difficult problem as the algorithm needs to simultaneously take into account the capabilities of the robot (kinematics and dynamics) and the shape of the terrain (non-smooth and cluttered). On one hand, the non-continuity and non-convexity resulting from uneven terrain and obstacles make the problem difficult to solve using optimization techniques. On the other hand, the number of degrees of freedom and the contact constraints make the problem difficult to solve with sampling-based methods. Moreover, checking for collisions between the robot and the environment make this problem even more difficult to solve fast enough to result in a reactive motion planner.

For simple cases like flat terrains, optimization techniques are able to correctly solve, simultaneously, the motion of the main body of the robot and its footstep placements [4,5]. Using more complex models and solvers, the problem can be reformulated to solve motion on other terrains [6,7]. However, this algorithm is doomed to fall into local minima, e.g. ignoring intermediate steps on stairs or trying to jump over impassable obstacles. Such behaviors can be reduced by first relaxing the complementary constraint of contacts then slowly converging back to the initial problem [8–10]. Alternatively, one can decompose the non-smooth terrain into different convex and even patches, and rely on Mixed-Integer Programming to find the best patches for each footstep [11,12]. However the computation time of those approaches make them difficult to use on a real robot. Overall, optimization techniques are not well suited for collisions and all of the presented approaches ignore this problem.

Another common approach is to rely on Graph Search [13–15]. The space of possible footsteps is discrete and actions are selected using graph search algorithms, such as A*. However, such approaches quickly become too computationally expensive when solving for a large number of footsteps and/or considering the movement of the main body.

A final set of methods are based on machine learning. Approaches based on supervised learning [12,16] take the foosteps generated by a planner, or from motion capture as an input, so the resulting plan will be efficient/feasible only if the initial planner or the motions captured correspond to the capabilities of the robot. Reinforcement learning has shown more and more impressive results during the last few years [17,18] but, as of yet, the results are limited to either

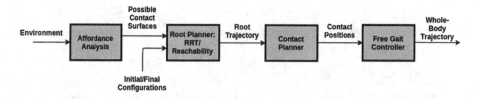

Fig. 1. The steps of the acyclic reachability-based planner.

flat ground or to behaviors that are unsuitable for real robot hardware on other terrains.

In this paper, we apply the work of Steve Tonneau et al. [19] on our robotic platform, ANYmal [20], and explain some of the adjustments that need to be done to successfully compute feasible contact plans.

The next Section describes in more detail the decomposition of the contact planning problem and the different algorithms used to solve it. Section 3 discusses the different adaptations and tuning that were necessary to compute more realistic contact plans and Sect. 4 shows the resulting contact plans and the tests of those trajectories in a physically realistic simulation environment.

2   Planner Description

Figure 1 shows the general structure of the pipeline used to generate a whole-body trajectory. First, an algorithm analyses the environment to extract the set of possible contact surfaces. The planning problem is then decomposed into two subproblems, as described in [19]; the algorithm searches for a trajectory of the main body of the robot, then contacts are created along this trajectory. This decomposition allows for a considerable reduction in problem complexity, as after the trajectory for the main body is found each limb is considered separately. The following Sections explain these different blocks in more detail.

2.1   Foothold Affordances

As a first step, the algorithm analyses the entire environment model to find which surfaces can be used to generate contacts. In this case, we consider the surfaces on which the robot can push. The criteria used to select whether a surface can be a contact surface are its inclination with respect to the vertical axis and the minimum size of the affordance.

Moreover, affordance analysis is used to avoid selecting contact points too close to an edge, to avoid the foot slipping and falling. Figure 6d shows an example of possible contact surfaces after such affordance analysis.

2.2   Root Planner

A guide path for the main body of the robot is generated, in which static equilibrium is feasible. Some previous works have sampled for static equilibriums

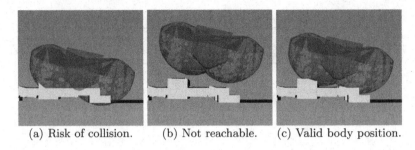

(a) Risk of collision.   (b) Not reachable.   (c) Valid body position.

Fig. 2. The reachability condition is met by the figure on the right, and not by the other two. The root (red) is free from colliding with the environment geometry while the reachable space of the limbs (green) intersect the environment, meaning that contact can be created. (Color figure online)

feasibility at intervals along the guide path [21]. However this is a very taxing process, so equilibrium feasibility is in this part approximated by contact reachability. This maintains the low problem dimensionality and minimises computation time.

A root configuration is said to be *contact reachable* if the environment intersects with the limb workspace and not the main body. If the main body intersects the environment, this implies collision, but if the environment does not intersect with the limb workspace then the robot cannot reach the environment to create contact. Therefore the region between these extremes, in which contact can be created without the body colliding, is considered to meet the reachability condition. Figure 2 shows several examples where only the last one is considered a valid body position.

A root path is then planned using an optimised Bi-RRT algorithm, propagating a random tree from both the start and goal positions to rapidly generate a complete trajectory, with sub-trajectories being validated by the reachability condition. In addition, planing of the root trajectory is done in both position and velocity spaces, i.e. kinodynamic planing, as explained in [22].

2.3 Contact Planner

Given an initial whole-body configuration and a root trajectory, a sequence of whole-body configurations following this trajectory is computed, each separated by one step, to finish at the goal configuration. A step is defined as the breaking of one contact with the environment, followed by the creation of another contact for the same limb. This means that for each configuration, all 4 legs are in contact, which in turn means the current approach is limited to walking gaits, that can potentially be acyclic.

Selection of the Stepping Leg. The root trajectory is first discretized into equidistant intervals. On each interval, an inverse kinematic algorithm moves the

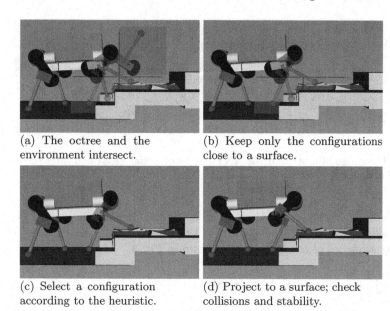

(a) The octree and the environment intersect.

(b) Keep only the configurations close to a surface.

(c) Select a configuration according to the heuristic.

(d) Project to a surface; check collisions and stability.

Fig. 3. Generation of a new contact.

root of the robot while trying to maintain the contacts. If it succeeds without collision, all contacts are maintained. If one contact cannot be maintained, the corresponding leg will be the stepping leg. If several contacts need to be broken, the interval is further subdivided so that only one contact will have to change.

On flat terrains, this algorithm will naturally result in a cyclic gait. However on more difficult terrains, where the footsteps can have different lengths or parts of the environment interfere with the movements of the robot, the algorithm is able to adapt and generate acyclic motions.

Contact Generation. Once the stepping leg is selected, the algorithm needs to project the corresponding foot to the new contact location. To reduce the computation time and select both the most suitable contact location and leg configuration, a database of leg configurations is used.

Offline, a database of random configurations is generated and stored in an octree data structure according to the foot position. Online, this octree is intersected with the environment to retrieve a set of leg configurations close to contact. Then, one of these configurations is selected (using a user-defined heuristic) to be projected into contact.

If the projection of the leg succeeds and the resulting whole-body configuration is statically stable and without collision, the configuration is kept and the algorithm continues to the next step. If not, the next (according to the heuristic) leg configurations are tested until a valid whole-body configuration is found.

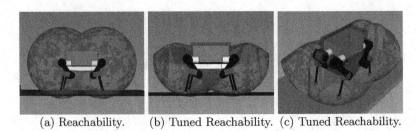

(a) Reachability.   (b) Tuned Reachability. (c) Tuned Reachability.

Fig. 4. The range of motion of the ANYmal robot before (left) and after (centre and right) retuning.

Moreover, we check that there exist a feasible dynamic transition between each configuration using the algorithm presented in [23]. An example of the resulting sequence of configuration is shown in Fig. 3.

3   Adjustments to ANYmal

The algorithm is able to generate contact plans for any robot morphology on different terrain, nonetheless it relies on different user inputs that need to be adjusted for the robot at hand. These user inputs are mainly the shapes (range of motions and non-collision with the main body) and the heuristics used to select between leg configurations in the octree. The next sections present how these inputs have been adjusted to generate more realistic contact plans for the ANYmal quadruped robot.

3.1   Adjusting the Shapes for the Root Planner

The ranges of motion for each limb are generated by sampling random configurations. Only configurations in the range of the motor are sampled and configurations that result in self-collision are rejected. The position of the feet are saved, then ROMs are generated by constructing the convex hull of those foot positions.

While this approach is valid for robots where the range of motion is limited enough to actually correspond to possible contact positions, ANYmal's joints allow 360° rotations in both directions. To avoid the robot attempting to walk upside-down (technically possible, but not suitable) and to avoid the robot walking with large steps that could generate high torques at the hips, the range of the joints are limited and the range of motion is reduced by a factor of 0.85. Figure 4 shows the different range of motions, before and after retuning.

Moreover, if the main body is close to the ground, the torques in the legs become prohibitively large and the space where the legs can feasibly make contact without colliding with the main body is greatly reduced. Therefore, a shape corresponding to the non-collision constraint is added close to the ground, as shown in Fig. 4(b) and (c). This 'V' shape is used to allow smooth trajectories on terrains like stairs.

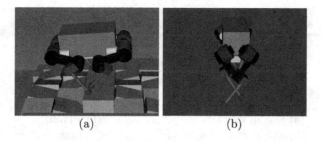

(a)   (b)

Fig. 5. Examples of instability due to poor heuristics. On the left, the hind legs' reference position is too far forward under a forward motion. On the right, the legs' reference position is too far over in the direction of lateral motion.

3.2 Heuristics for Selecting the Leg Configurations in the Octree

Each sample of the leg configuration is scored based on two sets of heuristics. The first uses all available offline parameters, to perform as much calculation as possible ahead of time and reduce the required online computation.

In our case, this part is computed as a weighted distance (in configuration space) between the sample configuration and the standard standing configuration of the robot. This cost is used so the robot keeps a relatively constant configuration and avoids the motors making 360° rotations or constantly switching between "X" and "O" configurations.

The second set of heuristics uses parameters that can only be determined online, such as environment slope and the robot's direction of motion. Samples close to the reference position are favoured to increase controllability, stability and maintain motion towards the goal. This reference position is set as the position of the foot for a reference limb configuration and a main body position at time $t + \Delta t$. Δt must then be adjusted to avoid the support polygon becoming too small as in Fig. 5a or to prevent limbs being placed far across from the body and overlapping other legs as in Fig. 5b.

4 Results

This Section shows the results obtained with the contact planner and the experiments in physically realistic simulation, using the Gazebo simulator. All trajectories shown are obtained using the open source planner HPP and its implementation of the reachability-based planner [24, 25].

For the set of weights, parameters and shapes used in this work please refer to https://github.com/Mathieu-Geisert/hpp-rbprm and https://github.com/Mathieu-Geisert/hpp-rbprm-corba under branch "anymal."

The pipeline presented in this paper is tested on terrains of progressively varying difficulty:

- Flat floor.
- Terrains with small height variation and obstacles like Fig. 6a.

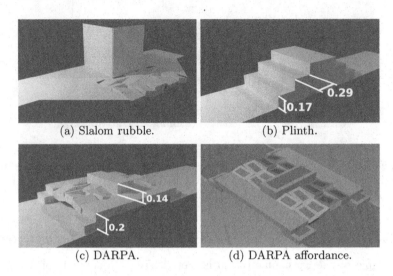

(a) Slalom rubble.   (b) Plinth.

(c) DARPA.   (d) DARPA affordance.

Fig. 6. Samples of test environments.

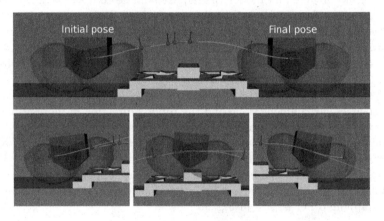

Fig. 7. Top: the trajectory of the main body of the robot computed by the kinodynamic planner. Bottom: the reachability condition at several configurations.

- Flat surfaces but with large height variation like the stairs in Fig. 6b.
- Non-flat surfaces with large height variation like the rubble terrain from the DARPA Robotics Challenge final in 2015 shown in Fig. 6c.

4.1   Generation of the Contact Plan

The guide path planner has proven very robust, and has given trajectories for the root to follow in all tested environments, including the DARPA rubble terrain challenge. In comparison with the previous version of the algorithm that was

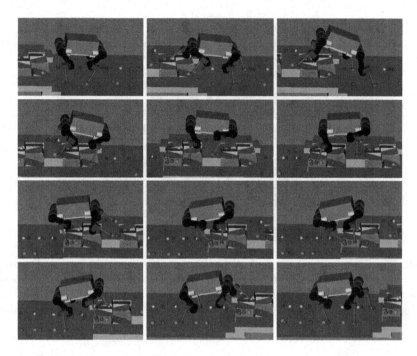

Fig. 8. Contact plan over the DARPA environment, top to bottom and left to right, ANYmal is walking to the left. Each coloured ball represents a planned footstep, where each colour corresponds to a different leg. (Color figure online)

not based on kinodynamic planning, the generated trajectories are smooth and have no sudden change of direction. An example of root trajectory is shown in Fig. 7. This smoothness allow us to use the motion of the root for the heuristic of the contact planner.

The contact planner implemented has been very effective at producing a set of footsteps in which static equilibrium is feasible. For each environment yet tested, the computation time can vary between each test but the planner always produces contacts that follow the guide path while avoiding collision and statically unstable configuration. This suggests that the reachability condition is a reasonable approximation to have static equilibrium for a quadruped robot. Figure 8 shows an example of sequence of configuration generated by the planner.

Table 1 shows the computation time for each algorithm of the planner. For those tests, an important factor that influence the computation time is the size of the boxes of the octree and the number of generated samples for each limb. In those examples, we use $1\,cm^3$ boxes populated with 50000 samples. The generation of this octree takes about 5.4 s, but for an real usage on the robot, this octree would only need to be constructed once.

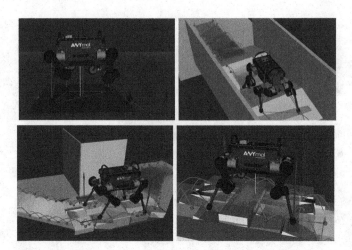

Fig. 9. The ANYmal in dynamical simulation for different environments. Footsteps appear as red spheres while red curves represent the interpolated foot trajectories between consecutive footsteps. (Color figure online)

4.2 Tests in Simulation

As shown on Fig. 9, once a contact plan is generated we can use the Free Gait controller [26] of the ANYmal to generate the corresponding trajectory for the whole-body. Trajectories are simulated in the Gazebo simulator, which includes constraints such as contacts, velocity and torque limits, that have not been explicitly addressed thus far in the planning pipeline.

Table 1 shows the rate of success for the ANYmal to execute the contact plan. The rate of success is high on simple terrains – and most failures come from the fact the robot does not take into account the environment when computing the leg trajectories – but it quickly decreases on more complex terrains.

Table 1. Mean computation times and success in dynamic simulation, evaluated over 20 runs for each environment.

Environments	Affordance	Root	Contact (Number of steps)	Success
Flat ground (5 m)	1.36 ms	0.54 s	3.30 s (62.2)	20/20
Slalom debris	8.85 ms	0.82 s	5.48 s (79.1)	18/20
Plinth	2.27 ms	1.26 s	4.26 s (59.8)	12/20
DARPA	25.4 ms	2.18 s	8.94 s (29.9)	7/20

An important part of the failures comes from too high torques. Even if the shape of the range of motion was scaled down in the root planner, the contact planner can keep a contacts until it becomes unreachable. However, in the environment with height variation, the torque limits are reached much sooner than the reachability limits.

Another part of the failures comes from a too small support polygon. Although the algorithm used to check stability is able to give us a robustness score, this score reflects the margins between the contact forces and their friction cones and not the margin with respect to the support polygon.

A video showing the trajectories presented in this paper is available via https://youtu.be/X78Y9oZvGHY.

5   Conclusion

We demonstrated how the HPP planning pipeline can be adapted to automatically generate trajectories for our ANYmal quadruped robot, on a variety of challenging terrains. We showed that the generated motion plans can be validated on a physically realistic simulation, and outlined the challenges that can cause execution to fail. The generation of the full contact plan on average takes less than 7 s for approximately 50 steps on an environment with many surfaces, on commodity hardware. This makes this algorithm a suitable choice for online replanning in a receding horizon manner.

However, the success rate in dynamic simulation is still too low to allow for unsupervised deployment on the real robot. This problem is primarily a result of the controller. The controller used to generate the whole-body motion and control the center-of-mass motion is too restrictive and sometimes fails to find a trajectory to link the sequence of static configurations. More specifically, the controller only computes quasi-static trajectories that often reach the limit of the support polygon or that generate high torques. Using a more advanced controller, with a prediction horizon [2,3], would allow us to compute dynamic motions of the CoM and result to more robust execution of the contact plans.

In future work, we aim to use this planning pipeline on the real ANYmal quadruped robot in a set of benchmark examples similar to the environments presented in this work.

References

1. Kalakrishnan, M., Buchli, J., Pastor, P., Mistry, M., Schaal, S.: Learning, planning, and control for quadruped locomotion over challenging terrain. Int. J. Robot. Res. **30**, 236–258 (2010)
2. Carpentier, J., Mansard, N.: Multi-contact locomotion of legged robots. IEEE Trans. Robot. **34**, 1441–1460 (2018)
3. Ponton, B., Herzog, A., Schaal, S., Righetti, L.: A convex model of momentum dynamics for multi-contact motion generation. In: IEEE-RAS International Conference on Humanoid Robots (2016)
4. Herdt, A., Diedam, H., Wieber, P.B., Dimitrov, D., Mombaur, K., Diehl, M.: Online walking motion generation with automatic foot step placement. Adv. Robot. **24**, 719–737 (2010)
5. Naveau, M., Kudruss, M., Stasse, O., Kirches, C., Mombaur, K., Soures, P.: A reactive walking pattern generator based on nonlinear model predictive control. IEEE Robot. Autom. Lett. **2**, 10–17 (2016)

6. Mastalli, C., et al.: Trajectory and foothold optimization using low-dimensional models for rough terrain locomotion. In: IEEE-RAS International Conference on Robotics and Automation (2017)
7. Winkler, A., Bellicoso, D., Hutter, M., Buchli, J.: Gait and trajectory optimization for legged systems through phase-based end-effector parameterization. IEEE Robot. Autom. Lett. **3**, 1560–1567 (2018)
8. Mastalli, C., Havoutis, I., Focchi, M., Caldwell, D.G., Semini, C.: Hierarchical planning of dynamic movements without scheduled contact sequences. In: IEEE-RAS International Conference on Robotics and Automation (2016)
9. Posa, M., Kuindersma, S., Tedrake, R.: Optimization and stabilization of trajectories for constrained dynamical systems. In: IEEE/RAS International Conference on Robotics and Automation (2016)
10. Mordatch, I., Todorov, E., Popović, Z.: Discovery of complex behaviors through contact-invariant optimization. ACM Trans. Graph. **31**, 43 (2012)
11. Deits, R., Tedrake, R.: Footstep planning on uneven terrain with mixed-integer convex optimization. In: IEEE-RAS International Conference on Humanoid Robots (2014)
12. Aceituno Cabezas, B., et al.: Simultaneous contact, gait and motion planning for robust multi-legged locomotion via mixed-integer convex optimization. IEEE Robot. Autom. Lett. **3**, 2531–2538 (2018)
13. Kuffner, J., Nishiwaki, K., Kagami, S., Inaba, M., Inoue, H.: Footstep planning among obstacles for biped robots. In: IEEE/RSJ International Conference on Intelligent Robots and Systems (2001)
14. Perrin, N., Stasse, O., Lamiraux, F., Yoshida, E.: Humanoid motion generation and swept volumes: theoretical bounds for safe steps. Adv. Robot. **27**, 1045–1058 (2013)
15. Winkler, A., Mastalli, C., Havoutis, I., Focchi, M., Caldwell, D., Semini, C.: Planning and execution of dynamic whole-body locomotion for a hydraulic quadruped on challenging terrain. In: IEEE-RAS International Conference on Robotics and Automation (2015)
16. Holden, D., Komura, T., Saito, J.: Phase-functioned neural networks for character control. ACM Trans. Graph. **36**, 42 (2017)
17. DeepMind: Producing flexible behaviours in simulated environments (2017). https://deepmind.com/blog/producing-flexible-behaviours-simulated-environments/
18. Hwangbo, J., et al.: Learning agile and dynamic motor skills for legged robots. Sci. Robot. **4**(26) (2019). https://doi.org/10.1126/scirobotics.aau5872
19. Tonneau, S., Del Prete, A., Pettré, J., Park, C., Manocha, D., Mansard, N.: An efficient acyclic contact planner for multiped robots. IEEE Trans. Robot. **34**, 586–601 (2018)
20. Hutter, M., et al.: Anymal - a highly mobile and dynamic quadrupedal robot. In: IEEE/RSJ International Conference on Intelligent Robots and Systems (2016)
21. Bouyarmane, K., Escande, A., Lamiraux, F., Kheddar, A.: Potential field guide for humanoid multicontacts acyclic motion planning. In: IEEE International Conference on Robotics and Automation (2009)
22. Fernbach, P., Tonneau, S., Del Prete, A., Taïx, M.: A Kinodynamic steering-method for legged multi-contact locomotion. In: IEEE/RSJ International Conference on Intelligent Robots and Systems (2017)

23. Fernbach, P., Tonneau, S., Taïx, M.: CROC: Convex Resolution Of Centroidal dynamics trajectories to provide a feasibility criterion for the multi contact planning problem. In: IEEE/RSJ International Conference on Intelligent Robots and Systems (2018)

24. Mirabel, J., et al.: HPP: a new software for constrained motion planning. In: IEEE/RJS International Conference on Intelligent Robots and Systems (2016)

25. LAAS-CNRS: Humanoid Path Planner (2018). https://humanoid-path-planner.github.io/hpp-doc/download.html?branch=rbprm

26. Fankhauser, P., Bellicoso, D., Gehring, C., Dube, R., Gawel, A., Hutter, M.: Free gait an architecture for the versatile control of legged robots. In: IEEE-RAS International Conference on Humanoid Robots (2016)

Multi-robot Multi-goal Motion Planning with Time and Resources

Stefan Edelkamp$^{(\boxtimes)}$ and Junho Lee

Department of Informatics, King's College London, London, UK
{stefan.edelkamp,junho.lee}@kcl.ac.uk

Abstract. This paper addresses multi-robot multi-goal motion planning with temporal and resources constraints. It solves the vehicle routing problem for mobile robots that operate according to their system dynamics, and which have to visit a number of waypoints scattered in a two-dimensional map environment with obstacles, while satisfying time window and capacity constraints. We compute the shortest path distances between each pair of waypoints in advance, and Monte-Carlo search plans the vehicles' tour through adaptation of a rollout policy, while adding the constraints to its optimization objective. Macro actions enable the vehicles to run in real-time with best actions being distributed to the individual controllers. We analyze how the simulation is affected by varying parameters such as the number of vehicles.

1 Introduction

In recent years, the vast use of logistics has led to a decline in costs, and research on the vehicle routing problem (VRP) has been actively conducted with minimizing the travel distance of the vehicles, while making the loading capacity-efficient (Lenstra and Kan 1981). In order to reduce costs further, it is important to establish and operate an appropriate shipping policy to minimize the total distance of the vehicle, reduce the number of vehicles, and maximize the load of each vehicle. Therefore, each vehicle avoids revisiting the same waypoint, and a delivery plan is established. Instead of finding the VRP's optimal solution, known as NP-hard, fast approximate solutions are found through heuristic methods.

In companies such as Amazon a fleet of robots deliver shelves automatically to the picking stations within a warehouse. Visiting multiple desired destinations in an environment with obstacles requires to find fairly distributed, non-colliding routes plans. It is also important to steer each robot in real-time. Since these robots are executed in a discrete environment such as a grid (Kasurien 2017), they are efficient and easy to handle in areas such as small warehouses, however, this approach is limited when the environment becomes larger, the robot execution model more complex, and the diversity of the work to perform increases. Therefore, there is a need for a method to navigate a mobile robot in a continuous environment that can cover the dynamics of a real robot. Planning motions of multiple agents in real-time in a indoor environment with obstacles is as important as mapping and localization. Implementing a controller for the robots is one

© Springer Nature Switzerland AG 2019
K. Althoefer et al. (Eds.): TAROS 2019, LNAI 11649, pp. 288–299, 2019.
https://doi.org/10.1007/978-3-030-23807-0_24

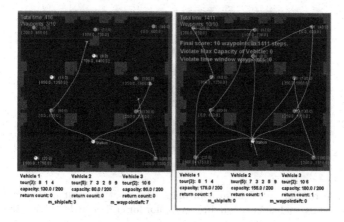

Fig. 1. Snapshots of one simulation for solving the physical vehicle routing problem: three mobile robots move in an environment with obstacles, visiting all the waypoints, subject to given capacity and time window constraints; intermediate situation (left), final result (right). Below the simulation we find information on the vehicles, tours and waypoints visited so far; blue color: waypoint has been visited, green color: time window is open, white color: time window is not yet open. (Color figure online)

solution to the above problem. In order to solve and simulate these problems, this paper introduces and studies the physical vehicle routing problem (PVRP) considering not only existing time windows, capacity constraints and travel but also parameters like the speed, direction, and collision of the robot.

For this purpose, we extend solutions to the known physical traveling salesman problem (PTSP), where several waypoints have to be visited by one mobile robot in a most efficient tour (Perez et al. 2012). For PVRP, we study refined scenarios with several robots by extending environments of the PTSP. In other words, PVRP is the real-time motion planning variant of the classic vehicle routing problem (VRP) in operation research. As such, each of the vehicles in the PVRP travels along the waypoints, starting from and ending at a common depot. This simulation includes physical motion components such as position, direction, and speed acting on the vehicle (see Fig. 1) The aim is to visit all waypoints as quickly as possible, subject to the given constraint.

2   Background Theories

As usual in sampling-based motion planning we assume a general vehicle model, that is defined by simulation of control actions a to robotic states s in a small period of time δ_t such that for the next state s' we have $s' = simulate(s, a, \delta_t)$.

Definition 1. *Given an autonomous vehicle model defined by its simulation semantics for a fleet of k robots operating with capacity restrictions in the environment in form of world $\mathcal{W}$ of connected regions $\mathcal{R}$, obstacles $\mathcal{O}$, and goals $\mathcal{G}$ with items attached to time windows $t_g = [l_g, r_g]$ as well as load w_g*

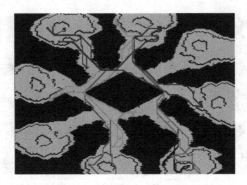

Fig. 2. Vehicle routing problem in a bitmap. Traces of shortest paths for tours of a VRP solution are visualized using a different color for each vehicle. (Color figure online)

for each item to pickup at $g \in \mathcal{G}$, and travel cost $c_{r,r'}$ for each pair of connected regions $r, r' \in \mathcal{R}$, the task is to follow a valid collision-free temporal trajectories $\psi^i = (\psi_1^i, \ldots, \psi_{l_i}^i)$, determining the control actions of every robot i, $i \in \{1, \ldots, k\}$, that in combination visit all the goals, collect all the items, start from and return to the depot, while satisfying all the time windows and capacity constraints.

Vehicle Routing. The vehicle routing problem was first posed by Dantzig and Ramser (1959) as the problem of allocating and routing the vehicle to collect and distribute goods and services to geographically dispersed customers. The goal of such VRP is to minimize operating costs in accordance with basic policies such as the number of vehicles, loading capacity, and time window (Takes and Kosters 2010). Figure 2 illustrates the vehicle routing problem in a bitmap.

VRPs experienced in real applications are challenging as they may involve many constraints. including vehicle capacity, delivery time (time windows), combined pick-up and deliveries, contributing to the importance of demand, service time, and so on. We look at capacitated vehicle routing problem (CVRP) and vehicle routing problem with time window (VRPTW), referring to the limited load of vehicles and the imposed service time constraints. By a reduction to the TSP, VRPs cannot be solved in polynomial time, urging algorithms to find approximate solutions using heuristics (Lenstra and Kan 1981).

The CVRP is a vehicle routing problem that includes a capacity of vehicles and load to be picked-up at each location (Adewumi and Adeleke 2018). Because each vehicle has a limit on the total load it can carry, an optimized plan varies depending on the item weight at each location and the cost of visiting. If the vehicle is making delivery services, the total amount the vehicles can carry may increase or decrease depending on their route. In a typical CVRP, vehicles visit each customer exactly once, and start and finish their trips from the central depot (Laporte 1992). The objective of this problem is to minimize the sum of the vehicle fleet travel time, and the total demand for goods on the route should not exceed the vehicle's maximum capacity. That is, the solution is feasible only if the total quantity of weights of items on the path is less than the maximum capacity of the vehicle.

The CVRP has been solved using branch-and-bound (Toth and Vigo 2002), and with heuristic methods such as ant colony (Mazzeo and Loiseau 2004), simulated annealing (Gendreau et al. 2006), and tabu search (Bortfeldt 2012).

In the classic VRPTW, a planner provides each vehicle a tour, taking into account the time to be serviced (Adewumi and Adeleke 2018). The goal of this problem is to minimize the amount of time it takes for the vehicle to reach all customers plus the waiting time it takes for the customer to get serviced. Also, if the vehicle arrives before the lower end of the time window, the vehicle must wait until the customer is ready, and if the upper end is exceeded, the service will not be executed or penalized (Koskosidis et al. 1992). Again, in such typical VRPTWs, tours of all vehicles start and finish at the depot. Homberger and Gehring (2005) solved the VRPTW with a central depot using an evolution strategy and tabu search, Another solution methods solved the problem with iterative localized optimization (Ursani et al. 2011).

Navigation and Search. Navigation is one of the topics that is being actively researched by many commercial companies and encompass areas such as logistics, automatic guided vehicles, and mobile robots (Barshan and Durrant-Whyte 1993). The planning task is reaching all waypoints while avoiding collisions with the obstacles.

In a directed and weighted graph (without negative edge weights) the algorithm of Dijkstra (1959) finds the shortest distances from one start node to all other nodes. This algorithm has been extensively been extended (e.g., to Johnson's or the A* algorithm), and is used in many fields (Reddy 2013). The shortest-path travel from one item location to the next is subproblem of finding the tour with lowest possible cost, hence, many calls to the algorithm of Dijkstra can be posed to solve the VRP. We use the algorithm to precompute accurate shortest-path distances.

Theorem 1. *The efforts to compute the shortest path distance matrix for solving the VRP with n waypoints in a graph with v nodes and e edges is bounded by $O(n(v \log v + e))$. In an octile grid imposed by the input bitmap with obstacles with v free cells the running time can be improved to $O(nv)$.*

Proof. The time complexity is dominated by solving the all-pair shortest path problem for the VRP. Using Fibonacci heaps, one call to Dijkstra's algorithm takes $O(v \log v + e)$. For n calls, we get the stated result. In the octile grid structure we have $e = O(v)$. By using a bucket-based priority queue, logarithmic access can be avoided, such that the running time improves to $O(nv)$.   □

Nested Monte-Carlo Search. Sometimes hardly any refined lower bound heuristic is available for exploring problems with huge and complex state spaces. Nested Monte-Carlo search (NMCS) by Cazenave (2009) is an advanced randomized search algorithm, combining reinforcement learning with random simulations/rollouts. For the VRP a rollout results in an assignment of tours to all

Algorithm NRPA
Input: recursion l, policy pol
Output: best $score$ and TSP $tour$
if $l = 0$
  $n \leftarrow root()$, $j \leftarrow 0$, $tour \leftarrow []$
  while children of $n > 0$ **do**
    $tour[j] \leftarrow$ child i with prob. $e^{pol[n,i]}$
    $n \leftarrow tour[j]$; $j \leftarrow j + 1$
  return $(score(n), tour)$
$best \leftarrow \infty$
for N iterations **do**
  $(res, new) \leftarrow$ NRPA$(l - 1, pol)$
  if $res < best$
    $best \leftarrow result$; $tour \leftarrow new$
    $pol \leftarrow$ Adapt(pol, seq)
return $(best, tour)$

Algorithm Adapt
Input: policy pol, TSP $tour$
Output: updated policy pol'
$n \leftarrow root()$, $pol' \leftarrow pol$
for $j = 0, \ldots, length(tour) - 1$ **do**
  $pol'[n, tour[j]] = pol'[n, tour[j]] + 1$
  $z \leftarrow \sum_i e^{pol[n,i]}$
  for children i of n **do**
    $pol'[n, i] \leftarrow pol'[n, i] - e^{pol[n,i]}/z$
  $n \leftarrow tour[play]$
return pol'

Fig. 3. Nested rollout search with policy adaption for the TSP.

vehicles, scoring a linear combination of total travel cost and number of constraint violations. When the NMCS is started, the simulations themselves are nested, applying actions to generate the children of the current state according to the given search level. The basic algorithm is as follows. (a) in a level, the action with the highest score is selected. (b) all actions of the previously selected state are determined and the simulation for the next action is executed. (c) The best state is backed up and changes the likelihood for selecting the successors to the above level. These steps are repeated until the search finishes or time is up.

Nested Rollout with Policy Adaptation. NMCS-based nested rollout policy adaptation (NRPA) was proposed by Rosin (2011) as a way to use gradient ascent rather than navigating the tree directly. The algorithm consists of three elements: the policy, the rollout, and the policy adaptation. The algorithm (see Fig. 3) starts with nested level l which is defined by a user and performs a sequential call to $l-1$, $l-2$, and if they reach the lowest recursion level, the rollout (simulation) occurs. Iterations correspond to the recursion width and helps replacing the best solution found.

An important principle of NRPA is to bias rollouts through learning by weighting possible actions. The weights for the actions are updated in each step of the algorithm to prioritize the movements of the best routing sequence found. In addition, each simulation state is coded differently to prevent the policy of the simulation state from affecting the selection of subsequent simulation state steps. The choices of the simulation steps are random, but the probability is not the same in each step. This differs from the NMCS. Policy adaptation adds value to the action of the best sequence and decreases the weight of other possible actions by an amount proportional to their weight.

Scenario and Framework. We have two different scenario modes: the capacitated VRP (CVRP) with a capacity of vehicle and time windows, and VRP with time window (VRPTW) with only time window added. The objective of both PVRP variants is to complete the tour at the lowest cost while satisfying constraints. In VRP mode the cost includes the time steps consumed by all vehicles wrt. capacity constraints of each vehicle, and time windows in each city.

Our routing framework was initially developed for the WCCI 2012 PTSP competition (Perez et al. 2012). One spaceship has to visit each waypoint. The program itself runs largely on two separate threads: the game thread and the controller thread. This will deal with the controller's response time, demanding that an action is executed at every 40ms. When the game starts, the controller is initialized and the distances for the TSP solver are set. The PTSP framework provides bitmap environments, containing various information, such as the location of each waypoint and the starting position of the spaceship.

The physics (speed and rotation) of the vehicles are also relevant, where velocity is expressed as a vector changed according to acceleration or collision. For realistic implementations, when the spaceship is not accelerated, the friction coefficient decelerates the ship. It is set to $\pi/60$ radian for the rotation phase and to 0 for no rotation. For the update of the spaceship we have

$$d_{t+1} = \begin{pmatrix} \cos\alpha & -\sin\alpha \\ \sin\alpha & \cos\alpha \end{pmatrix} d_t$$

$$v_{t+1} = (v_t + (d_{t+1}F_tK))L$$

$$p_{t+1} = p_t + v_{t+1}$$

where d_t is orientation (direction) at time step t, α is the current heading of the spaceship in angular representation, v_t is velocity at time step t, p_t is position of the ship at time step t, L is the friction factor, K is an acceleration constant, and F_t the force applied to in time step t.

The framework discretizes the continuous action space of the vehicles. Their controllers have to select actions to reach all waypoints quickly, while avoiding obstacles. This problem is solved by generating in a tree. The tree consists of nodes representing the state of the vehicle and edges corresponding to actions. Macro actions increase the ability to execute actions more quickly and reduce the size of the state space. Setting parameter T properly is a trade-off between the granularity of paths and the forward planning potential for tree search. Decreasing T makes it easier to alter the route, especially when the vehicle is near to an obstacle, but the controller performance may be affected.

NMCS views the VRP as a variant of the TSP. Through simulating future states, the route with better score will be searched more intensively, so that after many iterations the best action will be returned (Perez et al. 2014).

In PCVRP mode (see Fig. 4), there is only a demand and service time associated with a waypoint but not a time window. When planning a route for each vehicle in a PCVRP, we calculate the distance traveled, the overall simulation time, the service time, and the demand of each waypoint on the individual tours. The tours continue even if the maximum capacity of the vehicle is exceeded, but

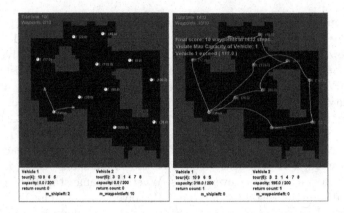

Fig. 4. PCVRP simulation: two snapshots of robots moving in environment with obstacles, visiting all the given waypoints, s.t. capacity constraints.

the color of the vehicle is changed to inform the user of the violation, and this violation is printed with vehicle ID after the simulation terminates. With a common rule, all vehicles must return to the station (depot) after the tour and wait near the waypoint for the service time to complete the visit each waypoint.

In PVRP mode (Fig. 1), we also have time windows to be met at each waypoint. If the current time does not satisfy the ready time, the waypoint is not opened. That is, when the vehicle reaches the waypoint, it cannot start being serviced and waits around the waypoint. If the current time of the simulation exceeds the ready time, the waypoint opens and the color changes to green. In this case, the item for the vehicle that has the corresponding waypoint on its tour becomes consumable, and the service starts when it is reached. In the case of finishing time, if the vehicle can not reach a waypoint within the finishing time, its color will turn yellow as an expression of the violation and after visiting, yellow changes to magenta. Waypoints with constraints that have not been violated, are displayed in blue. The remaining rules match the ones in the PCVRP.

3   Experiments

For the experiments we chose PTSP maps as well as one Solomon benchmark[1]. As system infrastructure we had Windows 8.1 K; Java 1.8.0_144; ran on Intel Core i7-4710HQ @ 2.5 GHz. Depending on the search parameters, and number of vehicles, the routes vary considerably. The formation of obstacles and map size also affect the results. We have selected the following four configurations for the simulation. Figure 5 show the results of each configuration: (1) Mode: PVRPTW map 2, vehicles: 3; (2) Mode: PVRPTW map 9, vehicles: 4 (3) Mode: PVRPTW map 25, vehicles: 3 (4) Mode: PCVRP map r202, vehicles: 10.

---

[1] For videos see https://youtu.be/uDNpEHILV6M https://youtu.be/BsoyyihVsHs https://youtu.be/my5zIDsTeiU https://youtu.be/KLzlfSoiCZU https://youtu.be/RNuh5vMgsXw https://youtu.be/9k86S8g4sNk https://youtu.be/mDR7tZ_YQm4.

Configuration	Time Step		Computation Time (s)		VRP Time (ms)		Graph Time (ms)		Score
	Average	Standard Deviation	Average	Standard Deviation	Average	Standard Deviation	Average	Standard Deviation	
1	1529.85	51.078	37.75	1.118	70.3	1.08	1217.85	21.731	2808
2	1517.1	90.277	54.3	3.341	78.2	3.664	1490.7	45.722	4360
3	2336.35	382.402	66.05	4.860	275.9	3.416	3093.5	177.718	106016
4	16315.9	1090.154	1616.8	150.46	15524.	812.195	38434.7	1691.147	2539883

Fig. 5. Performance results of simulation on different maps. Level: 2, number of iteration: 100, controller time: 20 ms.

Number of Vehicles. Few vehicles tend to violate capacity limits and time windows, while many waste resources. Thus, we tested how varying the fleet size affects the solution of the PVRP. Figure 6 shows the results of both modes. The number of time steps decreases as the number of vehicles increases, especially for the PCVRP with no time windows. Keeping the search parameters constant, more vehicles slow down tour planning, because all controllers ran in one thread, s.t. the performance decreases every time one is added.

Recursion Depth. More iterations and a larger recursion depth generate more search nodes in the NRPA recursion tree, and generally yields better routes. Figure 7 shows the impact of the different search levels on the results of PVRP simulation in a selected environment. We see that the level affects the tour generation of the vehicles. A tour with a lower score relates to a more efficient tour in terms of fewer time steps and constraint violations. E.g., for level 1, the third vehicle violates the capacity limitation, even though the vehicle capacity total is greater than the total of item weight. This is because the number of nodes being evaluated is too small, and results in a poor distribution of tours. While the solving time of the VRP reduces, this solution leads to a longer simulation.

Recursion Width. Figure 8 shows the effects of changing the NRPA iteration parameter in the above environment. As expected, changing the level and the iteration parameters influence outcome of the search. The plot shows the time steps and computation time wrt. the number of iterations. As N is raised, planning time increases, but for the simulation outcome there is no large difference. When the level is 2, more than 50 iterations yield fewer violations. This indicates that even though plans are better, one can obtain worse results. For $N = 10$, a capacity violation occurs due to low number of rollouts.

Macro Action Length. The macro-action parameter T plays an important role in selecting the steering the vehicle. Well chosen, it avoids hitting obstacles with smooth vehicle movements. Figure 9 visualizes the results. The relation between this parameter T (investigated for values 2, 6, and 12) and the time steps as well as the computation time is shown. Using an appropriate macro-action length ($T = 6$), the computation was fast. If T was too large (e.g., $T = 12$), it became

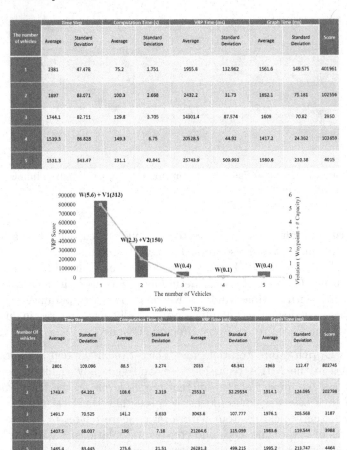

The number of vehicles	Time Step		Computation Time (s)		VRP Time (ms)		Graph Time (ms)		Score
	Average	Standard Deviation	Average	Standard Deviation	Average	Standard Deviation	Average	Standard Deviation	
1	2381	47.478	75.2	1.751	1955.8	132.962	1561.6	149.575	401961
2	1897	83.071	100.3	2.668	2432.2	31.73	1652.1	75.181	102556
3	1744.1	82.711	129.8	3.705	14301.4	87.574	1609	70.82	2950
4	1539.3	86.828	149.3	6.75	20528.5	44.92	1417.2	24.362	103659
5	1531.3	543.47	231.1	42.841	25743.9	509.993	1580.6	230.38	4015

Number Of vehicles	Time Step		Computation Time (s)		VRP Time (ms)		Graph Time (ms)		Score
	Average	Standard Deviation	Average	Standard Deviation	Average	Standard Deviation	Average	Standard Deviation	
1	2801	109.096	88.5	3.274	2033	48.341	1963	112.47	802745
2	1743.4	64.201	108.6	2.319	2553.1	32.29534	1914.1	124.095	202798
3	1491.7	70.525	141.2	5.633	3043.6	107.777	1976.1	205.568	3187
4	1407.5	68.037	196	7.18	21264.6	115.059	1983.6	119.544	3988
5	1465.4	83.445	275.6	21.51	26281.3	499.215	1995.2	213.747	4464

Fig. 6. Influence of number of vehicles (top: without time windows, middle bottom: with time windows, Mode: PCVRP/PVRPTW Map: 1, level: 4, 25 iterations, $T = 6$, controller time: 40 ms.

difficult to alter direction because the search considers a too narrow range of actions. Thus, when the vehicle bumps in an obstacle, getting out took a lot of time. On the other hand, if T was too small (e.g., $T = 2$), the steering direction oscillated, causing several changes in speed. Likewise, in proximity to an obstacle, it was difficult to locate the desired target. This also explains the large standard deviation for $T = 12$.

Inter-Vehicle Collision. We implemented an algorithm to resolve conflicts of inter-colliding vehicles as follows. After solving the VRP, the according shortest paths are first reconstructed and visualized in the map (see Fig. 2). We then take two colliding vehicles at a time and apply dynamic programming (similar to Wagner-Fischer and Smith-Waterman algorithm) to determine the minimal number of waiting steps to avoid collisions. After solving this approximate string

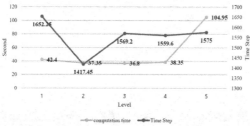

Level	Time Step		Computation Time (s)		VRP Time (ms)		Graph Time (ms)		Score
	Average	Standard Deviation	Average	Standard Deviation	Average	Standard Deviation	Average	Standard Deviation	
1	1652.25	48.45	42.4	1.095	5.35	1.386	1381	19.813	403912
2	1417.45	55.97	37.35	1.225	10.8	0.615	1368	12.032	203410
3	1569.2	94.09	36.8	1.105	119.15	1.182	1380	13.430	3187
4	1559.6	62.74	38.35	1.308	2806	11.394	1387	18.068	3187
5	1575	113.7	104.95	2.394	68866	322.393	1402	21.807	3187

Fig. 7. Influence of recursion level. Mode: PVRPTW, map 1, number of vehicles: 3 25 iterations, $T = 6$, controller time: 20 ms.

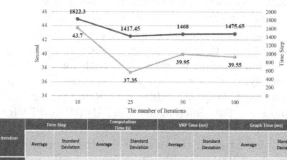

Iteration	Time Step		Computation Time (s)		VRP Time (ms)		Graph Time (ms)		Score
	Average	Standard Deviation	Average	Standard Deviation	Average	Standard Deviation	Average	Standard Deviation	
10	1822.3	63.742	43.7	1.559	8.55	1.605	1658.1	118.351	304159
25	1417.45	55.971	37.35	1.225	10.8	0.615	1368.45	12.032	203410
50	1468	48.142	39.95	1.356	27.25	2.613	1872.75	113.632	3485
100	1475.65	89.979	39.55	1.82	77.6	3.118	1880.35	91.827	3489

Fig. 8. Influence of number of iterations, Mode: PVRPTW, map 1, number of vehicle: 3 level: 2, macro-action T: 6, controller time: 20 ms.

matching problem to optimally resolve the collision the next conflict vehicle pair is chosen (at random) until there is no conflict pair left. Special care is needed at the depot, given that all vehicles initially collide. The solutions worked well in all considered benchmarks, but there are pathological cases, on which the algorithm fails to resolve all the conflicts.

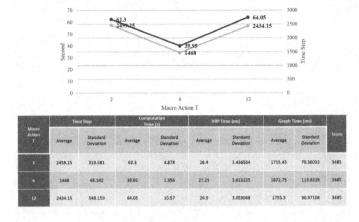

Fig. 9. Influence of macro length. Mode: PVRPTW map: 1, number of vehicles: 3, level: 2, the number of iteration: 50, controller time: 20 ms.

4   Discussion

Autonomous robots are becoming more and more capable to execute complex tasks in the intra-logistics domain. As an example, current technology is capable to automate item-specific picking of individual objects in warehouse shelves[2]. While with this technology, individual objects can be identified and localized, securely grasped and finally placed precisely at their destination, the temporal task-motion planning problem to generate a path for the robot to execute a long-term plan satisfying time windows and resources constraints, however, has not been solved satisfactorily. We address PVRPs that extend VRPs with real-time robotic motions. Two different modes (PCVRP and PVRPTW), were considered, and implementation extended the PTSP framework.

The simulation was tested on the basis of varying several parameters: the number of vehicles, the NRPA algorithm's recursion level, its number of iterations, and the macro action length. The results show that a large number of vehicles can make better tours with reducing violations, but resources can be wasted and be inefficient in terms of cost. Also, more vehicles significantly increase the computation time. The parameters level and iteration increase the number of searches and help planning before starting the tour in real time. Macro parameters are also identified to affect real-time operation.

References

Adewumi, A.O., Adeleke, O.J.: A survey of recent advances in vehicle routing problems. Int. J. Syst. Assur. Eng. Manag. **9**(1), 155–172 (2018)

Barshan, B., Durrant-Whyte, H.F.: An inertial navigation system for a mobile robot. In: Proceedings of the 1993 IEEE/RSJ International Conference on Intelligent Robots and Systems (IROS), vol. 3, pp. 2243–2248 (1993)

---

[2] https://www.magazino.eu/toru-cube/?lang=en.

Bortfeldt, A.: A hybrid algorithm for the capacitated vehicle routing problem with three-dimensional loading constraints. Comput. Oper. Res. **39**(9), 2248–2257 (2012)

Cazenave, T.: Nested Monte-Carlo search. In: IJCAI, vol. 9, pp. 456–461, July 2009

Dantzig, G.B., Ramser, J.H.: The truck dispatching problem. Manag. Sci. **6**(1), 80–91 (1959)

Dijkstra, E.W.: A note on two problems in connexion with graphs. Numer. Math. **1**(1), 269–271 (1959)

Edelkamp, S., Greulich, C.: Solving physical traveling salesman problems with policy adaptation. In: IEEE Conference on Computational Intelligence and Games (CIG), pp. 1–8, August 2014

Gendreau, M., Iori, M., Laporte, G., Martello, S.: A tabu search algorithm for a routing and container loading problem. Transp. Sci. **40**(3), 342–350 (2006)

Homberger, J., Gehring, H.: A two-phase hybrid metaheuristic for the vehicle routing problem with time windows. EJOR **162**(1), 220–238 (2005)

Jozefowiez, N., Semet, F., Talbi, E.G.: Multi-objective vehicle routing problems. EJOR **189**(2), 293–309 (2008)

Koskosidis, Y.A., Powell, W.B., Solomon, M.M.: An optimization-based heuristic for vehicle routing and scheduling with soft time window constraints. Transp. Sci. **26**(2), 69–85 (1992)

Laporte, G.: The vehicle routing problem: an overview of exact and approximate algorithms. Eur. J. Oper. Res. **59**(3), 345–358 (1992)

Lenstra, J.K., Kan, A.R.: Complexity of vehicle routing and scheduling problems. Networks **11**(2), 221–227 (1981)

Mazzeo, S., Loiseau, I.: An ant colony algorithm for the capacitated vehicle routing. Electron. Notes Discret. Math. **18**, 181–186 (2004)

Perez, D., et al.: Solving the physical traveling salesman problem: tree search and macro actions. IEEE Trans. CI AI Games **6**(1), 31–45 (2014)

Perez, D., Rohlfshagen, P., Lucas, S.M.: The physical travelling salesman problem: WCCI 2012 competition. In: 2012 IEEE Evolutionary Computation (CEC), pp. 1–8, June 2012

Reddy, H.: PATH FINDING-Dijkstra's and A* algorithm's. Int. J. IT Eng. 1–15 (2013)

Rosin, C.D.: Nested rollout policy adaptation for Monte Carlo tree search. In: IJCAI, pp. 649–654, July 2011

Takes, F., Kosters, W.A.: Applying Monte Carlo techniques to the capacitated vehicle routing problem. In: BNAIC (2010)

Toth, P., Vigo, D.: Branch-and-bound algorithms for the capacitated VRP. In: The Vehicle Routing Problem, pp. 29–51. SIAM (2002)

Ursani, Z., Essam, D., Cornforth, D., Stocker, R.: Localized genetic algorithm for vehicle routing problem with time windows. Appl. Soft Comput. **11**(8), 5375–5390 (2011)

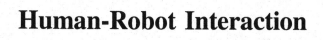

Human-Robot Interaction

instruMentor: An Interactive Robot for Musical Instrument Tutoring

Shreyus Bagga, Benedikt Maurer, Tom Miller, Luke Quinlan, Lorenzo Silvestri, Dan Wells, Rebecka Winqvist, Mark Zolotas$^{(\boxtimes)}$ ⬤, and Yiannis Demiris ⬤

Personal Robotics Lab, Department of Electrical and Electronic Engineering, Imperial College London, Exhibition Road, London SW7 2BT, UK
{mark.zolotas12,y.demiris}@imperial.ac.uk
http://www.imperial.ac.uk/personal-robotics

Abstract. Musical instrument education has typically faced challenges in providing students with a cost-efficient and long-term solution for personalised tutoring. To address these challenges, we propose a musical instrument tutor robot for students learning the recorder, called instru-Mentor. Equipped with robotic hands and a multimodal interface, the robot interacts with users by playing the recorder and demonstrating in real-time the proper handling of the instrument. A pilot study was conducted to investigate the effectiveness of a robot tutor for instrument learning. Experimental results suggest that instruMentor is successful at teaching the recorder and is positively appreciated by users, showing promise for the future coupling of music tutoring and social robots.

Keywords: Music tutoring · Human-robot interaction · User engagement

1 Introduction

A recent study conducted by the Associated Board of the Royal Schools of Music (ABRSM) showed a significant increase in children claiming to know how to play an instrument, from 41% in 1999 to 76% in 2014, as well as a greater diversity in instruments played [1]. Influential role models and new technology are two of the main factors believed to have driven this increase – the former by inspiring young learners to pick up an instrument, while the latter enables children to engage with and create their own music.

Despite these positive outcomes, there remains a prominent gap between students from different socio-economic backgrounds

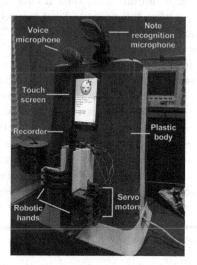

Fig. 1. instruMentor and its main components.

K. Althoefer et al. (Eds.): TAROS 2019, LNAI 11649, pp. 303–315, 2019.
https://doi.org/10.1007/978-3-030-23807-0_25

and their accessibility to music lessons. Demographic variables, such as parents' education and family income, can dictate whether a child will take music lessons, with higher socio-economic status indicating a greater likelihood for musical education [3,12]. Likewise, the duration of music training has been positively associated with better socio-economic status [2,3].

In addition to the economic variables, a multitude of other factors can affect how long a student continues to pursue music lessons. For instance, negative personality traits [3], poor parental support [4] and a music academy or teacher that does not encourage lifelong instrument learning [7] are some of the main reasons for a student quitting or losing interest in their instrument.

With the aim of leveraging advances in technology to address the long-term challenges of learning an instrument, we introduce *instruMentor* (see Fig. 1), an interactive robot and musical instrument tutor[1]. The robot is designed to replicate the style of a human instrument tutor by delivering lessons, answering questions and demonstrating proper playing technique. To evaluate the effectiveness of instruMentor as a musical tutoring system, a pilot study is conducted in which participants imitate the robot at playing the recorder. It is envisioned that users will demonstrate improved musical ability and levels of engagement through learning by imitation.

2   Related Work

A wide range of musical tutoring technologies have stemmed from the field of human-computer interaction. For instance, software tools have previously been developed to extract metrics on the performance of musical instruments, such as the saxophone [10] or recorder [13]. Such tools offer students with an automated means of evaluating their ability in real-time.

Other technologies have focused more on identifying ways to motivate students into long-term instrument playing. Games and multimedia interfaces that actively engage students during the interaction have previously proven to be effective in enhancing musical practice on both an individual [9] and classroom [6] basis. In general, the objective of most of these computer interfaces is to foster a user-centred environment that assists students in their daily practice.

Another progressive domain of research addressing this objective in instrument tutoring is human-robot musical collaboration. Many social robots have been designed with an anthropomorphic appearance to play physical instruments for the purpose of collaboration or instruction [5,14,15]. One advantage of these platforms over multimedia interfaces is that they can demonstrate the actual playing style of an instrument to students, thus allowing them to learn by imitation. Moreover, collaborative musical robots have also been integrated with frameworks to adapt to the user's capabilities or tastes during the interaction, hence providing a personalised user experience [11].

---

[1] A supplementary video is available at: http://www.imperial.ac.uk/personal-robo tics/videos.

(b) CAD software model of the hands.

(a) 3D-printed hands holding a recorder.

Fig. 2. Robotic hands.

From these studies, we stipulate that robots equipped with interactive features and appropriate physical characteristics are a promising approach to long-term personalised instrument tutoring. As a result, instruMentor has been designed to fit these criteria in two ways: it has an anthropomorphic appearance to mimic that of a human recorder player, and it also adapts its user interface to match the student's instrumental ability.

3   Robot Architecture

In this section, we present the main components and features of the instruMentor architecture, for which an illustration is provided in Fig. 1.

To provide the best possible learning experience, instruMentor uses the technique of learning by imitation. In this setting, the objective is to engage users into intuitively imitating the motion of the robot, thereby learning the correct movements and hand positions. However, this technique can only guarantee success if the robot closely matches that of a human expert musician. Therefore, we developed the robot's physical appearance, morphology and actions with great care for how students could feasibly perceive instruMentor as a recorder tutor.

3.1   Physical Appearance

A vital element of instruMentor is its robotic hands, as they give the robot its anthropomorphic appearance and allow physical demonstrations of how to hold and play a recorder. Figure 2 demonstrates the resulting prototype of the motorised hands alongside their CAD software model.

These 3D-printed hands are formed of three major components: a base recorder mount, finger attachments and servo motors. The base mount serves the

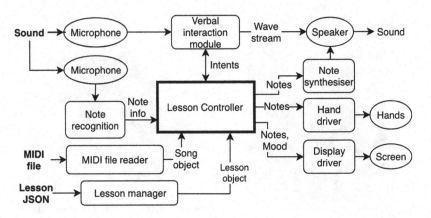

Fig. 3. System diagram illustrating the interaction between individual modules.

purpose of holding the recorder and acts as glue for all other operational parts of the robot. 3D-Printed fingers were also included to provide instruMentor with human-like hands that can realistically imitate recorder playing. Using finger templates from InMoov[2], each finger was printed and then assembled before being correctly attached to the base. Finally, seven servo-motors were used to actuate the fingers, with each individual finger covering a corresponding hole in the recorder. Each finger also has a piece of tight string running inside it, such that motor rotation varies the tension in the string. This rotational motion results in the closing or opening of a finger, much like tendons in a human hand.

Another crucial design choice for instruMentor's external appearance was to keep it as minimal as possible, so as to reduce the cognitive load on the end-user during music instruction [8]. To achieve this, no text or images were printed on the robot exterior and only components essential to the robot-user interaction were visible (*i.e.* the microphones, display and robotic hands). Every other component was hidden within the enclosure (*i.e.* the speaker, Raspberry Pi, servo-motor controllers, audio controllers, power adapters and wiring).

3.2   Software and Hardware Design

The core computational unit of the robotic architecture is a Raspberry Pi Model 3B+ with an add-on touch screen display. In order to directly control all the servo-motors, an Adafruit 16-Channel PWM Servo expansion board was interfaced with the Rasperry Pi. Two microphones are also attached to instruMentor, one for the vocal interaction with the user and the other for musical note recognition. Both microphones were selected to be unidirectional facing towards the user, such that noise in the surroundings is heavily reduced.

Figure 3 demonstrates an overview of the system and its constituent modules, which are described in the following:

---

[2] Assembly of the "Finger Starter": http://inmoov.fr/finger-starter.

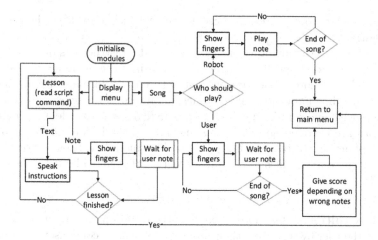

Fig. 4. Lesson controller flow diagram. Yellow boxes indicate branching dependent on user input, while blue boxes represent steady states, green boxes show processes and the red box terminates/resets control flow. (Color figure online)

Lesson Controller: This is the central module responsible for running and coordinating the interactions between all other system modules. Each of these modules runs in separate threads for continuous parallel operation. To communicate between the different threads, a number of interaction-specific events are defined and triggered to execute a set of instructions relevant to that detected event. For example, an event is configured for whenever the user wants to exit a lesson/song, which is either triggered via the touch display or saying "Stop Lesson/Song".

Figure 4 demonstrates a flow diagram of the different events and the corresponding actions taken when these events are triggered. In particular, the diagram provides a reference on how user input (yellow diamond-shaped boxes) triggers different interactions with instruMentor.

MIDI File Reader: This module generates songs from MIDI files, a widely standardised file format containing information regarding the notes, pitch and other musical properties of audio data. The reader decodes MIDI files and renders them into individual .wav files for each note using a C library, *FluidSynth*. Output audio files are created in the synthesis style of a recorder by passing SoundFont file representations of the corresponding note into the decoding function. During this process, information regarding songs and individual notes is also extracted from the MIDI files.

Lesson Manager: instruMentor makes available two different modes of learning to accommodate students of different ability. Beginner students are greeted with a set of introductory lessons designed to teach students the basics of playing the recorder. Once the student has gained a working knowledge of the instrument, they can move onto a more advanced mode in which they learn how to play actual songs.

The content of the introductory lessons includes instructions on how to hold the recorder, correctly position fingers and blow into the openings to transition between different notes. Each lesson is structured and formatted following the advice of an online published guide for classroom recorder teachers[3]. It combines visual cues with auditory instructions to mimic real teacher-student interactions.

Lessons are encoded as JSON files and inform the lesson controller on the sequence of actions to take during a lesson. This module is thus responsible for converting these JSON files into a data structure that is readable by the central controller.

Note Recognition: This module extracts the duration and frequency of notes played by the user by recording their input sound using a condenser microphone. The key objective of this module is to detect the duration of every note, as well as determine its fundamental frequency.

Note duration is established using a sequence of spectral analysis techniques. A chunk of audio data comprised of 4800 samples is first recorded and then processed using an adapted version of an open-source spectral analyser[4]. Once the spectrum of each chunk is computed using an onset function, a bandpass filter is applied to only preserve the bandwidth of interest. Comparing each received band of the power spectrum to prior ones results in the power flux, which is used to determine the start time of a note. Similarly, an offset function is used to evaluate when the level of the power spectrum falls below 90% and hence establishes the note's end. It is worth noting that short notes with a duration of less than 50 ms are ignored, hence minimising detection errors caused by clapping or similar sounds.

For each recognised note, this module also performs a set of steps to detect its frequency. As harmonics are dominant in the spectrum of the input audio chunks, the frequency of maximal power is searched in the cepstrum to detect the fundamental frequency over its fifth and octave. A linear filter is also applied to boost low frequency notes. The identified fundamental frequency of the tone is then converted into a MIDI value and a pitch accuracy, representing the displacement concerning the expected note.

Verbal Interaction: All verbal communication between the user and instru-Mentor is handled by this module. In order to establish natural conversation with users, Text-to-Speech (TTS) and Speech-to-Text (STT) functionality were required, as well as a versatile dialogue manager.

Conversation possibilities range from asking and answering questions to making requests and administering instructions. By utilising the online STT engine,

---

[3] "Let's Make Music: Classroom recorder course", available at: http://classroom recorder.com.

[4] https://github.com/aniawsz/rtmonoaudio2midi.

Google Web Speech, any recorded voice input could be interpreted as text. A suitable response is then formulated by first parsing through conversation flow dictionaries to search for keywords and subsequently responding using the online TTS engine, *Google Text to Speech*. In the event of poor or no internet connection, offline STT and TTS engines, *PocketSphinx* and *eSpeak*, are used instead.

All conversation flow relies on a conversation map to formulate a response to the user. The map includes multiple dictionaries corresponding to different types of conversations (*e.g.* responding to instructions from the user or casual conversation about the weather). Specific keywords are mapped to lists of suitable responses, where each response is randomly selected to be spoken whenever a keyword is recognised. The benefits of this approach are that the user can speak naturally and take part in a diverse dialogue with instruMentor.

Display Driver: The display driver runs the Raspberry Pi's touch display and provides a user interface for students. It is built using *Tkinter*, where each section and screen of the interface is a separate "frame". A simple switch function is utilised to alternate between these frames.

Note Synthesiser: This module enables instruMentor to play sounds from the recorder. Whenever a new song is selected by a user, the .wav files output by the MIDI file reader are sent to the Raspberry Pi's native audio player. As songs are decomposed into multiple individual .wav files, they can be played back in any order, allowing students to skip and replay notes if requested.

Hand Driver: This module abstracts away the details of the PWM motor control and individual motor calibration. It provides a simple interface to the lesson controller, wherein a target MIDI note is selected and the robotic hands automatically move into place to play that note. For motor control, the Adafruit PCA9685 Python library[5] is utilised to manipulate the individual PWM channels.

3.3 User Interface

Students can interact with instruMentor in two ways: either by verbal instruction or via the touch display. On start up, the robot will make a simple greeting and instruct users on how to initialise conversation. At the same time, a list of lessons and songs will be displayed on the touch screen for users to scroll through (see Fig. 5a). Depending on whether a lesson or a song is selected by the user, instruMentor will act accordingly.

Whenever a lesson is selected, a "nerd face" emoji is displayed to indicate teaching. A set of verbal instructions are then provided and instruMentor begins to play a section of notes to demonstrate correct fingering. After the robot plays a section of notes, it will then wait for the student to play that same section. As

---

[5] https://github.com/adafruit/Adafruit_Python_PCA9685.

Twinkle Twinkle Little Star
Game of Thrones
Mary Had A Little Lamb
Jingle Bells
All Star
C
Hot Cross Buns
London Bridge

(a) Main menu interface.

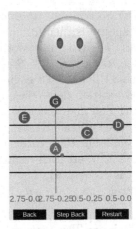

(b) Music page interface.

Fig. 5. User interface of instruMentor's touch display. (Color figure online)

the lesson progresses, instruMentor tells the user helpful tips on how to improve their playing ability. Upon completion of a lesson, feedback on the student's performance is presented both vocally and visually.

For songs, a user is presented with the option to select the song in different behaviour modes. In *"Play at your own pace"* mode, a stave of notes will be displayed on the music page and users can play without instruMentor's continuous involvement (see Fig. 5b). Red notes indicate the current note to play (with small red circles to indicate that the thumb is pressed down) and green notes indicate which note the user is currently playing. In *"Play along"* mode, a similar interface is loaded but now instruMentor plays as well, with its robotic hands moving to finger the notes. A final mode option is to *"Listen"*, which involves instruMentor playing by itself and simultaneously voicing trivia or information about the song. As with lessons, instruMentors presents feedback to users on their playing technique after each song is completed.

A final notable feature of the touch display interface is the inclusion of emojis. Numerous emojis were deployed onto the system as a way of improving the user's experience. For instance, different types of "smiley" faces are presented depending on how a student is currently performing at playing a song. These characteristics of instruMentor communicate a sense of personality and are particularly relevant in appealing to younger audiences.

4   Experimental Design

A pilot study was conducted to investigate the effectiveness of utilising human-robot interaction for musical instrument tutoring. The purpose of this study was to identify whether subjects perceived instruMentor as a useful tool for instrument learning, as well as highlight which of its behaviour modes or features were most beneficial to the teaching process.

We invited a total of 11 university students (aged 18–25) who had varying levels of experience at playing the recorder. The independent (predictor) variables being tested are the mode of teaching and the robot's features, whilst the dependent variable is the quality of user experience based on subjective feedback.

The experimental protocol for assessing instruMentor's effectiveness at tutoring the recorder is as follows. Each subject was first introduced to the robot with a brief explanation on the purpose of the experiment and the features available. Users did not require any specific calibration, but were allowed to familiarise themselves with the system and its interface before they were requested to try out a number of lessons. After completing various lessons, users were then asked to "play along" with instruMentor for a simple song. Finally, subjects were instructed to explore the song section of the interface and attempt to play longer, more complex songs, both in the *"Play along"* and *"Play at your own pace"* behaviour modes.

Subjects were also encouraged to explore the verbal interaction capabilities of the robot during their trial. This would involve users asking for advice on how to play specific notes, or requesting that the robot demonstrate how to play a particular section of a song.

In order to assess the relative importance of each feature of instruMentor, trials were split into fractions of time intervals. Therefore, a segment of time per user was spent without any verbal instruction, another segment without use of the touch display and the remaining segment with all features enabled. At the end of each experiment, subjects were asked to fill out a survey detailing their experiences with instruMentor, as well as provide any additional comments or suggestions. An entire experiment run took approximately 10–15 min.

5   Results and Discussion

Survey feedback on the different features and modes is illustrated in Fig. 6. In order to evaluate how significant preference was for one mode or feature over the others, we perform the non-parametric Kruskal-Wallis test. If statistical significance was found, then pairwise evaluations were further tested using the Mann-Whitney U-test. However, it is worth noting that the data collected is not representative of the entire population of potential users. Some indications of this include the similar experience levels (with most subjects highly inexperienced), the narrow age group, and the small sample size of 11 people.

With regard to the usefulness of the different behaviour modes (*lessons, playing along* and at *own pace*), we report no statistical significance between the user ratings. Although all instruMentor modes of tutoring were positively appreciated, there is a trend for higher ratings allocated to the *"Play at your own pace"* mode. A notable comment made by subjects that could explain this discrepancy

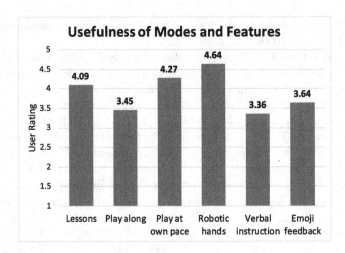

Fig. 6. Average user rating for the different behaviour modes and features of instru-Mentor ($1 = low$, $5 = high$).

is how it was difficult to *"Play along"*, as users often found that they had to stop playing and look down to imitate the correct position before resuming play. One suggestion made was to relocate the hands to the top of the robot and the microphones to the bottom, such that the hands are visible at all times.

Comparing how useful subjects found the different features of instruMentor (*hands*, *verbal interaction* and *emojis*), user ratings are deemed to be statistically different ($p \approx 0.0158$) according to the Kruskal-Wallis test. Further pairwise comparisons using the Mann-Whitney U-test show a statistical difference between the *hands* and the *verbal interaction* ($p \approx 0.00318$), but not between the *hands* and *emojis* ($p \approx 0.0767$). In spite of these findings, the feedback of users and general trend in the data strongly suggest that the robotic hands are the most critical aspect of instruMentor. This is further exemplified by Fig. 7, which shows the most favoured aspect of instruMentor chosen by participants. Likewise, nine of the 11 participants selected *hands* as the characteristic with the most beneficial impact on the instrument learning experience.

Finally, Fig. 8 summarises the overall experience users had with instruMentor during their recorder learning trials. With mean ratings of 3.91 for improvements in recorder playing confidence, 4.36 for a positive experience and 3.64 on hopeful outlooks for the future, instruMentor has proven to be a promising approach to musical instrument tutoring. Overall, our findings are an encouraging validation that the technique of learning by imitation of the robotic hands can be an effective method of teaching the recorder to students.

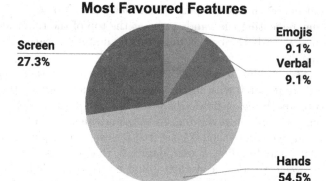

Fig. 7. Most preferred aspect of instruMentor.

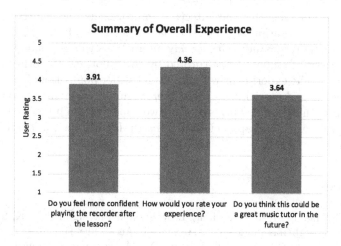

Fig. 8. Average user rating of the overall musical instrument tutoring experience with instruMentor ($1 = low$, $5 = high$).

6   Conclusions and Future Work

A few positive outcomes have been identified from the deployment of instruMentor in this pilot study on recorder tutoring. First and foremost, the experimental results strongly suggested that integrating robotic hands into the architecture was the most useful feature and aided in the imitation learning process. Furthermore, the majority of users reported an improvement in their confidence and ability to play a recorder by the end of a lesson. In addition to these results, a number of potential improvements were raised in this study and thus motivate a few areas for future work.

From the feedback of subjects in the pilot study, a couple of hardware extensions could be made to instruMentor. The robotic hands should first be extended to include a physical thumb and thereby avoid the need to bloat the user interface with additional detail on how to play individual notes. Moreover, many users pointed out that relocating the hands to be at the top of the robot and moving the microphones towards the base could ease the imitation learning experience during real-time demonstrations.

Building a user model of each student over time is another fundamental direction for future research with instruMentor. One way in which this could be approached is by recording visual feeds of the student playing their instrument and storing this data for later reviewing. At the same time, this video feed and the general performance of users should be scored for every song played. By storing performance data and building a user database that carries across aggregate information between sessions, a student could easily track their improvement over time. This would also provide more opportunities for advancing the human-robot interaction, such as commenting on score improvements or recommending songs based on user ability and tastes.

After incorporating these architecture improvements into instruMentor, a final route for exploration will be to expand the scope of this pilot study. In particular, a long-term study with weekly interactions will be conducted for two separate streams of students, one tutored by the robot and the other by a professional tutor. The experiment will also target wider population demographics, such as children and participants with different initial experience at playing the recorder. From this extended investigation, we hope to glean further insights into both the effectiveness and appreciation of instruMentor as a musical instrument tutor.

References

1. ABRSM: Making Music - Teaching, Learning and Playing in the UK, September 2014. https://gb.abrsm.org/en/making-music. Accessed 8 Feb 2019
2. Corrigall, K., Schellenberg, E.G., Misura, N.: Music training, cognition, and personality. Front. Psychol. **4**, 222 (2013). https://doi.org/10.3389/fpsyg.2013.00222
3. Corrigall, K.A., Schellenberg, E.G.: Predicting who takes music lessons: parent and child characteristics. Front. Psychol. **6**, 282 (2015). https://doi.org/10.3389/fpsyg.2015.00282
4. Creech, A.: Learning a musical instrument: the case for parental support. Music Educ. Res. **12**(1), 13–32 (2010). https://doi.org/10.1080/14613800903569237
5. Crick, C., Munz, M., Scassellati, B.: Synchronization in social tasks: robotic drumming. In: ROMAN 2006 - The 15th IEEE International Symposium on Robot and Human Interactive Communication, pp. 97–102, September 2006. https://doi.org/10.1109/ROMAN.2006.314401
6. Ferrari, L., Addessi, A.R.: A new way to play music together: the continuator in the classroom. Int. J. Music Educ. **32**(2), 171–184 (2014). https://doi.org/10.1177/0255761413504706
7. Myers, D., Bowles, C., Dabback, W.: Music learning as a lifespan endeavor. In: Community Music Today, pp. 133–150 (2013)
8. Owens, P., Sweller, J.: Cognitive load theory and music instruction. Educ. Psychol. **28**(1), 29–45 (2008). https://doi.org/10.1080/01443410701369146

9. Percival, G., Wang, Y., Tzanetakis, G.: Effective use of multimedia for computer-assisted musical instrument tutoring. In: Proceedings of the International Workshop on Educational Multimedia and Multimedia Education, EMME 2007, pp. 67–76. ACM, New York (2007). https://doi.org/10.1145/1290144.1290156

10. Robine, M., Percival, G., Lagrange, M.: Analysis of saxophone performance for computer-assisted tutoring. In: Proceedings of the International Computer Music Conference, ICMC 2007, pp. 381–384 (2007)

11. Sarabia, M., Lee, K., Demiris, Y.: Towards a synchronised grammars framework for adaptive musical human-robot collaboration. In: 2015 24th IEEE International Symposium on Robot and Human Interactive Communication (RO-MAN), pp. 715–721, August 2015. https://doi.org/10.1109/ROMAN.2015.7333649

12. Schellenberg, E.G.: Examining the association between music lessons and intelligence. Br. J. Psychol. **102**(3), 283–302 (2011). https://doi.org/10.1111/j.2044-8295.2010.02000.x

13. Schoonderwaldt, E., Askenfelt, A., Hansen, K.F.: Design and implementation of automatic evaluation of recorder performance in IMUTUS. In: Proceedings of the International Computer Music Conference (ICMC), pp. 97–103 (2005)

14. Solis, J., Taniguchi, K., Ninomiya, T., Yamamoto, T., Takanishi, A.: The Waseda flutist robot No. 4 refined IV: enhancing the sound clarity and the articulation between notes by improving the design of the lips and tonguing mechanisms. In: 2007 IEEE/RSJ International Conference on Intelligent Robots and Systems, pp. 2041–2046, October 2007. https://doi.org/10.1109/IROS.2007.4399081

15. Solis, J., Ninomiya, T., Petersen, K., Takeuchi, M., Takanishi, A.: Development of the anthropomorphic saxophonist robot WAS-1: mechanical design of the simulated organs and implementation of air pressure feedback control. Adv. Robot. **24**(5–6), 629–650 (2010). https://doi.org/10.1163/016918610X493516

Position and Velocity Control for Telemanipulation with Interoperability Protocol

Bukeikhan Omarali[1,2(✉)], Francesca Palermo[1], Maurizio Valle[2],
Stefan Poslad[1], Kaspar Althoefer[1,3], and Ildar Farkhatdinov[1,4]

[1] School of Electronic Engineering and Computer Science,
Queen Mary University of London, London, UK
{b.omarali,i.farkhatdinov}@qmul.ac.uk
[2] University of Genoa, Genoa, Italy
[3] School of Engineering and Material Sciences,
Queen Mary University of London, London, UK
[4] Department of Bioengineering,
Imperial College of Science, Technology and Medicine, London, UK

Abstract. In this paper we describe how a generic interoperability telerobotics protocol can be applied for master-slave robotic systems operating in position-position, position-speed and hybrid control modes. The interoperability protocol allows robust and efficient data exchange for teleoperation systems, however it was not shown how it can fit switching position and rate control modes. Here we propose the general framework of hybrid position and rate control modes with interoperability protocol. Furthermore, we demonstrate experimentally that the framework is suitable for robotics teleoperation systems in which a human-operator can switch between position-position and position-speed master and slave robots' workspace mapping.

Keywords: Teleoperation · Control · Protocol

1 Introduction

Robotic teleoperation is used for remote tasks that cannot be automated or carried out directly by a human. These tasks are often complex, unstructured, and require human judgment, knowledge and skills. They are also associated with environments that are either unreachable or too dangerous for direct human presence. Hence, teleoperation is used in underwater exploration [13], surgical robotics, and training [9,16], nuclear waste management [14,18], and other applications. In these scenarios, a human-operator controls the movements of the slave robot through manipulating a master robot.

© Springer Nature Switzerland AG 2019
K. Althoefer et al. (Eds.): TAROS 2019, LNAI 11649, pp. 316–324, 2019.
https://doi.org/10.1007/978-3-030-23807-0_26

Several types of haptic master devices have been commercially available to be used as master robots, e.g. Geomagic Touch[1], Omega[2], Virtuose[3]. All these devices have different features, workspaces, and degrees of freedom. Mapping correctly the master's movements and workspace to the slave's task space is crucial for efficient and safe teleoperation. In certain applications the master's workspace can be ten times smaller than the slave robot's operational space [2,19]. This may lead to difficulties in achieving successful task completion. Therefore, in position-position teleoperation control mode, the effective workspace of the slave robot is reduced to that of the master.

Appropriate master-slave robot workspace mapping requires the application of scalable position control gains [5,15] or implementation of rate (speed) control modes [17], or hybrid approaches when switching between position and rate control mapping is employed depending on the task [1]. It should however be noted that, if precise manipulation is required, motion up-scaling should not be chosen for control, as all manipulation errors will be magnified leading to decreased control accuracy [10].

In this work we demonstrate how the hybrid position/speed mapping approach is applied to a master-slave telemanipulation system. Implementation of hybrid mapping approaches to master-slave manipulators is not novel, however previous implementations [6,7] were not based on standard teleoperation protocols which provide a universal approach to exchange the kinematic data between the master and slave stations. Here we show how previously proposed universal teleoperation protocol, the Interoperable Teleoperation Protocol (ITP) [12], can be combined with a hybrid position and rate control approach in a teleoperation system. In order to accomplish this task, a unilateral teleoperated system is implemented which consists of a Geomagic Touch as the master device and a Franka Emika's Panda as the slave robot.

The structure of the paper is as follows. The general description of the proposed hybrid control integration with the ITP is given is Sect. 2. The description of the experimental setup used for validation of the proposed hybrid control is given in Sect. 3. Experimental validation is presented in Sect. 4. The conclusions and future work are given in Sect. 5.

2   Teleoperation Protocol and Control

Hybrid position-position and position-speed control strategies were initially proposed for mobile robot teleoperation [3,7] and later applied to master-slave manipulators [1]. Position-position control was utilized for precise manipulations while position-rate mode was useful for relatively large movements. Therefore, the entirety of the slave robot's workspace can be used. Meanwhile, integrating the ITP with hybrid control allows deploying the proposed control scheme on any couple of master-slave devices.

---

[1] https://uk.3dsystems.com/haptics-devices/touch.

[2] https://cs.stanford.edu/people/conti/omega.html.

[3] https://www.haption.com/en/products-en/virtuose-6d-en.html.

2.1 Interoperability Protocol

The ITP [12] was introduced to enable easy and stable communication between master and slave robots with different type of kinematics, workspaces, and hardware architecture. Key point of the protocol was using integer values to transfer required kinematic data with minimal loss and errors. The original ITP packet consists of following:

- **unsigned int** *sequence*
- **unsigned int** *pactyp*
- **unsigned int** *version*
- **int** *delx*
- **int** *dely*
- **int** *delz*
- **int** *delyaw*
- **int** *delpitch*
- **int** *delroll*
- **int** *buttonstate*
- **int** *grasp*
- **int** *surgeon mode*
- **int** *checksum*

Importantly, sending position commands from the master to the slave robot is implemented through velocity information exchange. The velocities are encoded through incremental displacements expressed as integers (which normally correspond to incremental encoders digital measurements) to avoid any workspace configuration mismatch. We used this protocol to send master's linear velocities (as *delx, dely, delz* in micrometers) and angular velocities (*delyaw, delpitch, delroll* in microradians). Furthermore, the *buttonstate* was used to communicate the master devices switches states. The *buttonstate* is used to communicate the desired mapping mode, explained in more detail in the next section. It should be noted that *pactyp, version, grasp* and *surgeon mode* are not currently utilized in our implementation.

2.2 Hybrid Control

Let a robot's end effector Cartesian state be defined by $[x, v]^T$, where x is the vector of position and orientation, meanwhile the v is the vector of linear and angular velocities. The slave's and the master's dynamics (f_s and f_m, respectively) can be described as:

$$v_s = f_s(x_s, u_s, F_{external}), \tag{1}$$
$$v_m = f_m(x_m, u_m, F_{operator}), \tag{2}$$

where the slave's variables are denoted with a subscript "s", whereas master's variables are denoted with a subscript "m". Inputs u and F correspond to robot control forces and human-operator/environment forces, respectively.

The hybrid bilateral control [4] of the slave is performed with:

$$u_s = \begin{bmatrix} (m-1)(m-2)/2 & 0 & 0 \\ 0 & -m(m-2) & 0 \\ 0 & 0 & m(m-1)/2 \end{bmatrix} \begin{bmatrix} C_p(x_s, v_s, v_m) \\ C_v(v_s, v_m) \\ C_d(x_s, v_s) \end{bmatrix}, \quad (3)$$

where $m = 0, 1, 2$ is the control mode, obtained from the ITP's *buttonstate*. C_p, C_v, C_d are position-position, position-rate, and decoupled control functions. Hence, if $m = 0$ the position-position mapping is used, if $m = 1$ the position-rate mapping is used, and if $m = 2$ the decoupled mode is used.

A simple case for position-position control in a unilateral teleoperation architecture can be expressed with linear tracking controllers as:

$$C_p = P_s^p(\alpha x_m - x_s) - D_s^p v_s, \quad (4)$$

where P, D are control gains, the latter acting as a damper. Note that here and further superscripts "p" and "v" are used to denote variables that belong to position-position and position-rate mapping respectively. The scaling factor α is generally set in the interval of $1 \geq \alpha > 0$. If $\alpha = 1$ the displacement is mapped one-to-one, which is the most intuitive for the operator. Reducing the α results in a higher mapping resolution that provides the operator with a finer motion accuracy. Setting the α higher than 1 is ill advised, since it would magnify the operator's manipulation inaccuracies.

Applying the ITP requires time integration of the reference master and slave position signals on both sides:

$$C_p = P_s^p(\alpha \int v_m dt + x_{s,o} - x_s) - D_s^p v_s, \quad (5)$$

where $x_{s,o}$ is the initial position of the slave robot.

Similarly, the velocity (rate) mode control for master-slave teleoperation can be expressed as:

$$C_v = P_s^v(\beta \int v_m dt - v_s) - D_s^v \dot{v}_s, \quad (6)$$

where β is the scaling factor. Unlike the α the value of the β is chosen heuristically depending on the master and slave robot's workspace dimensions and kinematic constraints.

Additionally, we introduce the decoupled mode, which is used by the human-operator to reset the master robot coordinate frame to zero when the limit of the master's workspace is reached. Hence, the goal of the decoupled control function C_d is to decelerate the robot to and maintain zero Cartesian velocity until switched to another control mode.

3   Implementation

The experimental setup used to test the feasibility of the proposed hybrid control is a single master/single slave unilateral system. The control and communication

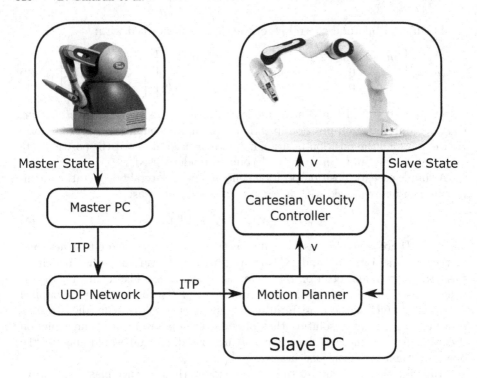

Fig. 1. The experimental setup's control and communication scheme

scheme is illustrated in Fig. 1. The experimental environment is shown in Fig. 2. The master-slave communication is maintained via UDP. It is assumed that the communication delay is zero, hence the system is considered passive.

The master robot used in the setup is the 3D Systems' Touch - 6 DoF haptic device with 2 buttons on the stylus type end-effector. The Open Haptics library [11], running on the master Ubuntu PC, allows reading the device's data such as: buttons' state, transform, individual joint positions, Cartesian forces, etc. The displacement and orientation change necessary for the ITP are extracted from the transform at 1 kHz. It should be noted that the resulting signal is extremely noisy, so it is passed through a low-pass filter.

In addition to displacements, buttons' state is also recorded and included in the ITP. These two button states are used to switch modes. By default the decoupled mode is used and the operator needs to hold a button on the master robot's stylus in order to engage another mode. Furthermore in the position-velocity mode, a deadzone is implemented around the master robot's end-effector zero position. Hence, the operator needs to move outside the deadzone in order to initiate the motion.

The slave robot is the Franka Emika's Panda - 6DOF serial manipulator. The robot is controlled using *franka_ros* [8] ROS Kinectic wrapper of the *libfranka* library running on a slave Ubuntu PC. The *franka_ros* allows the robot to be con-

Fig. 2. The experimental setup: slave PC, master and slave robots

trolled in joint or Cartesian space. These control interfaces require the controller node to run at 1 kHz signal turn around rate, which includes script execution time, communication with the robot, and any routines executed in the robot's control box.

The slave controller uses the Cartesian velocity interface as it is the most suitable for integration with the ITP protocol. The Cartesian velocity interface utilizes the native Inverse Kinematics (IK) solver and takes v as input. Hence the input u_s from Eq. (3) is set as reference v_s. The native IK solver requires the reference motion to comply with a number of constraints such as: limits on maximum linear and angular velocity, acceleration, and jerk.

The slave controller is split into two ROS nodes: the motion planner and the Cartesian velocity controller. This is done to ensure that the Cartesian velocity controller maintains sub-1ms execution time, meanwhile the motion planner does all the heavy lifting. The motion planner receives and parses the master's data as well as the slave robot's state from the *franka_state* rostopic. Further, the motion planner runs the controller described by Eq. (3), which is implemented as optimal control problem using the Sequential Least Square Quadratic Programming (SLSQP) solver using the *scipy* package. The SLSQP solver finds velocities that ensure accurate tracking whilst complying with the robot's Cartesian velocity, acceleration, and jerk constraints. The SLSQP is a rather computationally costly solver, therefore it is scheduled at 100 Hz and the resulting v_s are passed to the Cartesian velocity controller. The Cartesian velocity controller extrapolates command velocities and passes them on to the robot.

4 Validation

The position-position to decoupled mode transition is shown in Fig. 3. In this sample the master was moved a certain distance in position-position mode, followed by switching to the decoupled mode and bringing the master back to initial position. This motion was executed multiple times. The switches between coupled and decoupled modes are denoted with vertical dashed lines. It can be seen that the slave robot repeats the motion when in position-position mode and remains stationary in the decoupled mode. The small kink in the velocity plot, that occur after switching to the decoupled mode, is caused by SLSQP solver rapidly bringing the robot to a halt and compensating for master-slave position mismatch. Meanwhile, the small kink after switching to the position-position mode is likely to be caused by unconscious displacement of the master end-effector by the operator, when pressing mode switch button.

Similarly, the position-velocity to position-position mode transition is shown in Fig. 4. Here, it can be seen that the slave robot's velocity mirrors the master's displacement, if the latter exceeds the position-velocity deadzone denoted by horizontal dotted lines. Next, the mapping is switched to position-position mode, in which the slave robot copies the master's displacement.

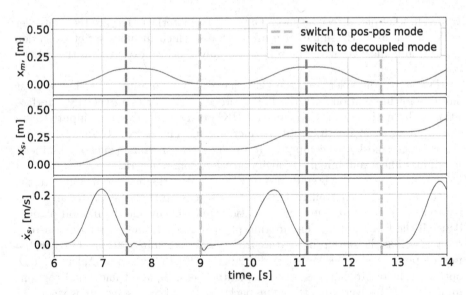

Fig. 3. Switching from position-position to decoupled mode. Dashed lines show when the switch have occurred.

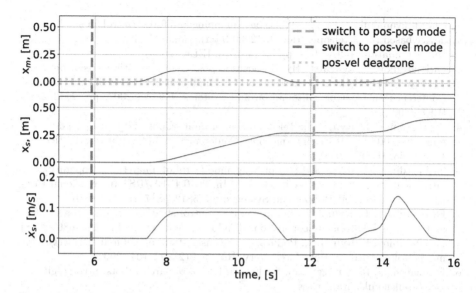

Fig. 4. Switching from position-position to position-velocity mode. Vertical dashed lines show when the switch have occurred. Horizontal dotted line show the deadzone.

5   Conclusion

In this paper we present a method for integration of hybrid position and velocity control with the ITP. The proposed hybrid mapping strategy allows to utilize the entirety of the slave's workspace in teleoperation setups, where the slave's workspace is larger than that of the master. The position-rate control can be used for large motions, meanwhile the position-position control can be used for fine manipulations. The proposed strategy is compatible with the ITP protocol by design. Therefore, it can be used with any couple of master-slave robots.

The validation has been performed on a unilateral teleoperation setup with Franka Emika's Panda robot as slave and 3D Systems' Touch haptic device as the master robot. Results show the satisfactory compatibility of the hybrid control scheme with the ITP.

The future work will be dedicated to extending the proposed mapping method to bilateral control. This will require reducing the lag caused by filtering and enforcing hard real-time constraints on the communication network as well as the motion planner.

Acknowledgments. This work is funded by the EPSRC NCNR hub EP/R02572X/1 and QMUL-Genova University PhD Program.

References

1. Bu, W., Liu, G., Liu, C.: Rate-position-point hybrid control mode for teleoperation with force feedback. In: 2016 ICARM, pp. 420–425 (2016)

2. Chotiprayanakul, P., Liu, D.: Workspace mapping and force control for small haptic device based robot teleoperation. In: 2009 International Conference on Information and Automation, ICIA 2009, pp. 1613–1618. IEEE (2009)

3. Farkhatdinov, I., Ryu, J.H.: Hybrid position-position and position-speed command strategy for the bilateral teleoperation of a mobile robot. In: 2007 International Conference on Control, Automation and Systems, ICCAS 2007, pp. 2442–2447. IEEE (2007)

4. Farkhatdinov, I., Ryu, J.H.: Teleoperation of multi-robot and multi-property systems. In: 2008 6th IEEE International Conference on Industrial Informatics, pp. 1453–1458. IEEE (2008)

5. Farkhatdinov, I., Ryu, J.H.: Improving mobile robot bilateral teleoperation by introducing variable force feedback gain. In: 2010 IEEE/RSJ International Conference on Intelligent Robots and Systems, pp. 5812–5817. IEEE (2010)

6. Farkhatdinov, I., Ryu, J.H., Poduraev, J.: Control strategies and feedback information in mobile robot teleoperation. IFAC Proc. Vol. **41**(2), 14681–14686 (2008)

7. Farkhatdinov, I., Ryu, J.H., Poduraev, J.: A user study of command strategies for mobile robot teleoperation. Intell. Serv. Robot. **2**(2), 95–104 (2009)

8. FrankaEmika: ROS integration for Franka Emika research robots. https://github.com/frankaemika/franka_ros

9. Ghorbanian, A., Rezaei, S., Khoogar, A., Zareinejad, M., Baghestan, K.: A novel control framework for nonlinear time-delayed dual-master/single-slave teleoperation. ISA Trans. **52**(2), 268–277 (2013)

10. Hokayem, P.F., Spong, M.W.: Bilateral teleoperation: an historical survey. Automatica **42**(12), 2035–2057 (2006)

11. Itkowitz, B., Handley, J., Zhu, W.: The OpenHaptics™ toolkit: a library for adding 3D Touch™ navigation and haptics to graphics applications. In: WHC 2005, pp. 590–591 (2005)

12. King, H.H., et al.: Plugfest 2009: global interoperability in telerobotics and telemedicine. In: ICRA 2010, pp. 1733–1738. IEEE (2010)

13. Lin, Q., Kuo, C.: On applying virtual reality to underwater robot tele-operation and pilot training. Int. J. Virtual Reality (IJVR) **5**(1), 71–91 (2015)

14. Manocha, K.A., Pernalete, N., Dubey, R.V.: Variable position mapping based assistance in teleoperation for nuclear cleanup. In: 2001 Proceedings of the IEEE International Conference on Robotics and Automation, ICRA 2001, vol. 1, pp. 374–379. IEEE (2001)

15. Namerikawa, T., Kawada, H.: Symmetric impedance matched teleoperation with position tracking. In: 2006 45th IEEE Conference on Decision and Control, pp. 4496–4501. IEEE (2006)

16. Okamura, A.M.: Methods for haptic feedback in teleoperated robot-assisted surgery. Ind. Robot Int. J. **31**(6), 499–508 (2004)

17. Park, S., Seo, C., Kim, J.P., Ryu, J.: Robustly stable rate-mode bilateral teleoperation using an energy-bounding approach. Mechatronics **21**(1), 176–184 (2011)

18. Pruks, V., Farkhatdinov, I., Ryu, J.-H.: Preliminary study on real-time interactive virtual fixture generation method for shared teleoperation in unstructured environments. In: Prattichizzo, D., Shinoda, H., Tan, H.Z., Ruffaldi, E., Frisoli, A. (eds.) EuroHaptics 2018. LNCS, vol. 10894, pp. 648–659. Springer, Cham (2018). https://doi.org/10.1007/978-3-319-93399-3_55

19. Zinn, M., Khatib, O., Roth, B., Salisbury, J.K.: Large workspace haptic devices-a new actuation approach. In: 2008 Symposium on Haptic Interfaces for Virtual Environment and Teleoperator Systems. HAPTICS 2008, pp. 185–192. IEEE (2008)

Intrinsically Motivated Autonomy in Human-Robot Interaction: Human Perception of Predictive Information in Robots

Marcus M. Scheunemann[1]([⊠]) [iD], Christoph Salge[1] [iD],
and Kerstin Dautenhahn[1,2] [iD]

[1] University of Hertfordshire, Hertfordshire AL10 9AB, UK
marcus@mms.ai
[2] University of Waterloo, Waterloo N2L 3G1, Canada
https://mms.ai/sHRI

Abstract. In this paper we present a fully autonomous and intrinsically motivated robot usable for HRI experiments. We argue that an intrinsically motivated approach based on the Predictive Information formalism, like the one presented here, could provide us with a pathway towards autonomous robot behaviour generation, that is capable of producing behaviour interesting enough for sustaining the interaction with humans and without the need for a human operator in the loop. We present a possible reactive baseline behaviour for comparison for future research. Participants perceive the baseline and the adaptive, intrinsically motivated behaviour differently. In our exploratory study we see evidence that participants perceive an intrinsically motivated robot as less intelligent than the reactive baseline behaviour. We argue that is mostly due to the high adaptation rate chosen and the design of the environment. However, we also see that the adaptive robot is perceived as more warm, a factor which carries more weight in interpersonal interaction than competence.

Keywords: Robotics · Sustained interaction ·
Human-robot interaction · Autonomous human-robot interaction ·
Robot behaviour · Cognitive robotics · Robot control ·
Autonomous robots · Intrinsic motivation · Predictive information ·
Information theory

1 Introduction

Why use autonomous robots for human-robot interaction (HRI) experimentation [12] instead of teleoperation by human experimenters or scripted behaviour? Scripting reduces the adaptability of the robot to novel situations, limiting the range and flexibility of interaction scenarios. Teleoperation offers more flexibility,

C. Salge—Funded by Marie Sklodowska-Curie grant INTERCOGAM (705643).

K. Althoefer et al. (Eds.): TAROS 2019, LNAI 11649, pp. 325–337, 2019.
https://doi.org/10.1007/978-3-030-23807-0_27

but has problems with scalability, introduction of human bias, and experimenters struggling with acting from the robot's perspective [1]. In contrast, autonomous robots could realise experiments where they freely interact with humans in real environments. Here we want to introduce some exploratory experiments with an intrinsically motivated robot as a pathway towards realising autonomous robots that are interesting to interact with.

This paper is motivated by the authors' work with a spherical robot [22] (similar to Fig. 1) and children. The children's interaction patterns were usually very diverse, making a general, pre-scripted robot behaviour for a group of children hard to achieve. Without human interaction or without remotely controlling the robot, the behaviour of the robot was limited, leading to the children losing interest in the robot. While it would be trivial to have a self-controlled robot that exhibits some form of behaviour, the hard question is: What kind of behaviour makes a robot interesting to interact with? We assume that robots are more interesting to interact with if they have perceived agency, allowing the human interaction partner to assign motivations to the robot, support or hinder its goals, or even sympathise with its "joy" when achieving a goal. Once we identify something as an agent, we are likely to direct our attention towards that agent, trying to understand its goals, intentions and behaviour. This interest is, if not synonymous with engagement, a step towards more engagement with the agent. While the simple act of moving [8] or the look of a robot's "head" [5] can change a human's perception of the robots, e.g., animacy, the behaviour also needs an observable goal-directedness [11]. We think that behaviour based on actual intrinsic motivation [18] would be a good candidate to create a consistent perception of a robot's motivation. We think that this enables the possibility of eventually sustaining the interaction with a fully autonomous robot.

In psychology, intrinsic motivation is defined as doing an activity for its inherent satisfaction rather than for some separable consequence or reward [9, 20]. The concept has been linked to the idea of autonomy and agency [19], and intrinsic motivations are alternatively defined as those motivations that are an integral, non-instrumental, non-optional part of an agent [17]. The recent interest in computational approaches to intrinsic motivations [18] gives us a rich assortment of formalisms to consider. Most of them have a set of common properties, such as semantic independence, universality and sensitivity in regards to embodiment, and a high degree of robustness. They are usually used to answer questions, such as what is a good general heuristic (i.e. motivation function) if my robot knows nothing about the world or even its own morphology? Ideas such as curiosity or self-maintenance are turned into AI formalism that enhance model learning and were generally used to enhance AI and robot performance [4]. More relevant to our approach, recent work in the HCI domain of games used intrinsically motivated agents to generate more interesting, self-learning agents [16], or to create believable, generic antagonists [13] and companions [14].

2   Predictive Information

The Intrinsic Motivation used to generate the robot's behaviour in our study is the Predictive Information (PI) formalism, closely following the implementation of Martius et al. [15]. A formal introduction of the measures is omitted due to space constraints. Conceptually, the measure falls into a family of learning rules related to the reduction of the time prediction error in the perception-action loop of the robot. The book Playful Machines [10] offers a good introduction. The book also shows how these approaches can be computed from a robot's perspective alone, and the zoo of different robots and their behaviours presented within shows how behaviour resulting from the different formalisms is sensitive towards the agent's specific embodiment.

Predictive Information [2] derives a specific learning rule, that aims to maximise the mutual information between a robot's past and future sensor states. The relevant literature argues that this produces exploratory behaviour sensitive to the robot's embodiment. The derivation from information theory also offers an intuitive interpretation of the robot's adaptation towards being able to reliably predict its own future from its past, while enriching the diversity of its experiences. The approach we use here [15] works by updating the internal neural networks of the robot, one that generates behaviour from sensor input, and the other predicting the futures states. The continuous adaptation, aimed at improving the time-local Predictive Information, moves the robot through a range of behavioural regimes. Importantly, the changes in behaviour are partially triggered by the interaction with the environment, as mediated through the robot's embodiment. The rate at which those internal neural networks are updated is the one model parameter which we will change between experiments.

To the best of our knowledge, this is the first experiment that uses Predictive Information in the context of HRI, and evaluates how the behaviour based on this intrinsic motivation is perceived by participants.

3   Study Design and Procedure

The challenge in designing this study is that this work is, as far as we know, the first HRI experiment of a robot using Predictive Information. Consequently, we lack an existing baseline for comparison.

3.1   Baseline Behaviour

We considered the following four alternative means of behaviour-generation for serving as a baseline: (1) human remotely controls the robot, (2) random behaviour and (3) pre-adapted reactive behaviour.

Ideally, we want to see how the algorithm compares to a human remotely controlling the robot. However, human controlled behaviour has a high degree of variance, dependent on the particular human controller. Furthermore, it is unclear how much access the human controller should have to environmental information. If the human can directly observe the participants, it could obtain much more information than the robot, giving it an unfair advantage in creating behaviour responsive to the participant. If we limit the human controller to only the robots' sensors, then the human controller would likely struggle to make sense of this limited input, potentially being unable to control the robot at all.

The problem with using random behaviour as a baseline is that "randomness" actually has a set of parameters that need to be chosen, like how often do values change, or is it the change of value or the value that is being randomised. PI does not show a real pattern of behaviour switches we could use for the timing of changing speed, heading and/or the overall behaviour. We performed some preliminary trials with random values, but were quickly facing the question of a fair baseline behaviour again. Having the experimenter choose these values leads to basically designing a certain kind of behaviour (chosen from a whole range of behaviours), which makes it problematic as a baseline.

We decided to use a pre-adapted reactive behaviour. The pre-adaptation is done with the very same PI implementation and parameters, using the same sensors as the robot will use during the experiments. In absence of an established existing baseline behaviour, we also compare between the participant's expectations, the reactive behaviour and a robot utilising PI. We will discuss the chosen conditions in more detail in Sect. 3.4.

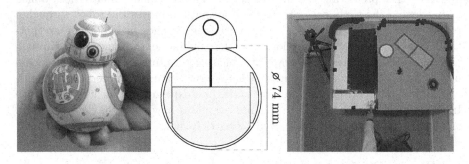

Fig. 1. Left: the used robot platform BB8 from Sphero. Middle: A 2-D cross-sectional view of the robot. A two-wheel vehicle, kept in position by a heavy weight, moves the sphere when driving. A magnet attached to the vehicle keeps the head on top of the sphere facing in moving direction. Right: the environment the robot explores during the trials from a birds eye perspective. The white area is paper, the black is foam material and the beige coloured area is wood. At the top of the foam material is a hill area and a pit in the lower part. The bottom edge does not have a wall, forcing the participant to interact with the robot. (Color figure online)

3.2 Robot, Environment and Tasks

We want a very simplistic platform with a few degrees of freedom for focusing on the effects induced by Predictive Information. However, for rich behaviour, the robot also has to offer some sensor capabilities. We chose the off-the-shelf spherical robot from the company Sphero, specifically, the BB8 platform as depicted in Fig. 1(left). We chose this version of Sphero because of the advantages the head offered. A magnet keeps the head in driving direction, which gives the user a sense of the robot's direction. This, and the fact that many people know the robot from movies, provides a better impression of a robot than using a white Sphero. The robot weighs 168 g. It has a 75 MHz ARM Cortex M4 on board powered by two 350 mAh LiPo batteries. The robot has a two-wheel electric vehicle inside the spherical shell, as depicted in the cross-sectional view of the robot in the middle of Fig. 1. This is kept in position by a heavy weight, which is made out of the coil for power inductive charging. A connection of a magnet to the vehicle keeps the attached head in position.

There are two ways of controlling the robot. The vehicle inside the robot has two servos. You can either control the speed and direction of each servo directly or you can use Sphero in "balancing mode". In this mode the in-built controller tries keeping the robot upright and listens to speed and heading commands. The direct control mode offers a wide range of possible behaviours, e.g. turning on the spot or more wobbly locomotion. We decided however to use the balanced mode, again, for the sake of simplicity.

The BB8 can stream sensor information. It offers readings of a 3-DOF accelerometer, a 3-DOF gyroscope and the current servo position and servo speed. It also offers IMU readings in quaternions or euclidean angles[1]. The JavaScript API for BB8 has been unsupported since 2016-05-11 and we decided for developing a custom API which is based on C++ and is available from [21]. Figure 1(right) shows the experimental environment. Two tables form the space where the robot can move around. The area is 180×120 cm in size. It is open to one side where the participant is supposed to stand and interact with the robot. In Fig. 1 you can see a participant nudging the robot. The surface of the table differs in friction and height. The black foam area has a hill (top) and a pit (bottom). Additionally, the black area and the white paper area is softer and has higher friction compared to the wooden part.

The participants' task is to observe the robot and understand whether it has a strategy for exploring the environment. We wanted to encourage the participants to interact with the robot. Therefore, we kept one side open so participants had to interact actively with the robot to prevent it from falling off the table. We hoped this enforcement of interaction would provide the participants with a better understanding of the robot's capabilities and behavioural richness. The robot itself has no pre-coded task.

3.3   Groups and Conditions

We decided for two different conditions:

REA (**reactive**): participants interact for approximately 10 min with a reactive robot and are asked about what they have seen.

---

[1] We found that the roll angle readings of the IMU are faulty.

ADA (**adaptive**): same as *REA*, but the robot is continuously adapting, based on maximisation of Predictive Information as a motivation to interact with its environment.

The adaptive robot in the *ADA* condition realises behaviour motivated by maximising predictive information, and it continuously updates its internal networks based on that gradient during the experiment. The reactive robot in the *REA* condition starts with the same networks as the adaptive one (based on pre-trial adaptation), which determines how it reacts to sensor input, but it does not further update its internal network during the experiment.

We assign participants into two groups: (A) *ADA* → *REA* and (B) *REA* → *ADA*. The order of *REA* and *ADA* is randomly assigned, but balanced over the number of participants. The starting configuration for both conditions (*REA* and *ADA*) was generated in two steps. Firstly, we conducted three trials with the robot for 5 min in the previously described environment. At the end of each trial, we saved the robot's network configuration. In a second step we randomly choose one of these network configurations as the starting configuration.

The PI formalism allows for having different levels of adaptivity to changing environments and new stimuli. The update rate for *ADA* was determined empirically. We noticed that the robot can get caught in the pit we mentioned earlier. If the robot gets caught in the pit, it would need to adapt to leave and continue exploration. The *ADA* adaptation rate was set so that the robot would change its behaviour and leave the pit in less than 20 s. As we will discuss later, we hypothesised that a high adaptation rate yields a higher perceived intelligence, as the robot would continuously adapt to new stimuli and change the way it would react to certain inputs.

3.4   Robot's Behaviour

The chosen sensors will determine the behaviour to a large extent, as Predictive Information tries to excite sensor input. For example, if you decide to only use the IMU reading of the yaw angle speed, the robot only needs to adapt its heading in order to excite the sensor. It won't generate any rolling movement. Empirically, we decided for the pitch and roll angles, the x and y component of the accelerometer, as well as the z component of the gyrometer as sensor input.

The aforementioned strategy for using a fixed network for the reactive robot yields a somewhat predictable behaviour for the condition *REA*. The robot prefers left turns in light of environmental perturbations or human interaction, i.e. if it hits a wall, it will almost always turn left. Its major trajectory is that of circling in different radii. With this in mind, we assumed that the same arguments as discussed in Sect. 3.1 may hold true and people get bored very quickly. However, almost all participants did not recognise the mentioned pattern. Videos for both conditions are available from [21].

The adaptive robot starts with the same network configuration. We chose a very high update rate for its model, as discussed in Sect. 3.1. Its trajectory has a tendency of being straight, if it reaches an obstacle it adapts its heading to be able to continue moving in another direction. However, as soon as a participant interacts with the robot, it is not trivial to understand what the robot will do next to increase sensory stimuli.

3.5   Goals and Hypotheses

This paper aims to answer the research questions: (1) Is an adaptive robot perceived as more competent/intelligent and animal-like than the reactive robot? and (2) do the reactive and the adaptive robot have distinguishable behaviours? We formulate the following null hypotheses for further investigation:

$H_0(1)$ The reactive and the adaptive robot's strategy is described the same.
$H_0(2)$ The median change for the GodSpeed's factor Animacy is zero.
$H_0(3)$ The median change for the RoSAS' factor Competence is zero.
$H_0(4)$ The median change for the GodSpeed's factor Perceived Intelligence is zero.

3.6   Measures

We decide to use two standardised questionnaires to compare results with other studies: the GodSpeed scale [3], which been widely used in many experiments, and the Robotic Social Attributes Scale (RoSAS) [6], which is relatively new and has seen little use in HRI so far.

GodSpeed uses a 5-point semantic differential scale and investigates for the factors Anthropomorphism, Animacy, Likeability, Perceived Intelligence and Perceived Safety. The authors of RoSAS do not recommend a specific scale, but recommend having a neutral value, e.g. uneven number of Likert elements. We decided to use a 7-Likert scale. It tests for the factors Warmth, Competence and Discomfort. Although we are mostly interested in the factors Animacy, Perceived Intelligence, Competence and Warmth, we use all the provided items of both scales. This is done to hide the questionnaire intention and to check for other effects in later research. We will show results for the additional factors Anthropomorphism, Likeability, Perceived Safety and Discomfort for completeness purposes, but we will not discuss them in detail in this paper due to space constraints.

We use these scales for the questionnaires after each condition and we ask two open ended questions in addition: (1) "Can you describe the different behaviours of the robot? Did the robot have any particular strategy for exploring?" and (2) "What were the best and/or worst aspects of the robot's behaviour?".

3.7   Methodology

Participants are welcomed to the experimental room, they are handed an information sheet and are asked to sign an informed consent form. Then the environment and the robot is presented and briefly described. Participants are informed that the robot's aim is to explore the environment. They are asked to observe whether the robot follows a particular strategy to do so, and if they can identify any specific behaviour. They are also asked to prevent the robot from rolling over the open edge. They are shown how to use the hand as a "wall" or nudge the robot to prevent it from falling off the side of the arena that is not enclosed by a wall, or to illicit new behaviour through interaction. Participants then fill in the pre-questionnaire. This gathers information regarding their sex, age and background. Next, the two conditions are presented to the participants on a randomised order. Each lasts approximately 10 min. They fill in two post-questionnaire containing the two scales and the two additional questions discussed earlier in Sect. 3.6. The entire experiment takes 40 to 50 min.

3.8 Sample

We recruited 16 participants (5 female; 11 male) mostly from university staff and students, between the ages of 23 and 60 years ($M = 33.4$). The participants mostly have a background in Computer Science and where asked about how familiar they are with interacting with robots, programming robots and the chosen robot platform. A 5-point Likert scale was chosen with the value 1 for "not familiar" and 5 for "very familiar". The self-assessed experience for interacting with robots was an average 4.3. The average familiarity with programming robots was 3.8 and the experience with the chosen robot platform was rated an average of 1.9. The selection of this group was on purpose, as it was assumed that this group have a more realistic view on robot's capabilities in general. However, all participants were naïve with regards to the purpose of the experiment.

The study is ethically approved by the Health, Science, Engineering & Technology ECDA with protocol number aCOM/PGR/UH/03018. The anonymity and confidentiality of the individual data is guaranteed.

4 Results

Firstly, we conducted *Shapiro-Wilk normality test* of residuals for all factors to understand whether the data is normally distributed. The smallest test result was found for the factor Perceived Safety ($W = .97, p = .17$), indicating that the H_0-hypothesis (i.e., the data is not normally distributed) can be rejected, hence we can expect the data to be normally distributed and parametric tests can be applied. However, normality tests have little power to detect modest deviations from a normal distribution on small sample sets. We therefore decided to focus on non-parametric tests to analyse the questionnaire data, as these tests are more robust for small sample sizes.

For each factor, we investigate whether there is any interaction between the order and the condition. In case of interaction effects (i.e. order and condition) between these factors, investigating the main effects independently would be incomplete or even misleading.

Our study can be expressed as a F1 LD F1 Model with one within factor (condition) and one between factor (order). A non-parametric ANOVA-type test shows that there is no interaction between the condition and the order ($p > .05$).

Participants were not explicitly asked for differences in the seen behaviour. However, we looked into the answers of the open ended questions to see if they spotted and named differences. All participants answered them, however, answers differed in detail and length. Firstly, we checked whether participants described the behaviour and/or exploring strategy differently to the first interaction. 14 participants described the behaviour and or strategy different to the first one. Mostly, it was pointed out that one robot follows the edges more than the other or that one robot tried to leave the arena more often. In addition, we checked whether the participants used terms like "less", "compared to" or "this one" for directly addressing changes to the first session after the second session. 8 out of 16 participants did so.

One participant mentioned being "unsure, if something was fundamentally different" but described the robots differently. We conclude to reject hypothesis $H_0(1)$ and accept the alternative hypothesis that participants were able to distinguish between the behaviours.

Table 1. Wilcoxon Signed Rank Test results between REA and ADA

Factor	95% confidence interval		p	r
	Lower bound	Upper bound		
Anthropomorphism	−0.3	0.4	0.916	0.037
Animacy	−0.25	0.333	0.69	0.141
Likeability	−0.3	0.4	0.726	0.124
Perceived intelligence	−0.2	0.8	0.244	0.412
Perceived safety	−0.667	0.667	0.444	0.271
Warmth	−0.667	0.167	0.366	0.32
Competence	−0.583	0.5	0.798	0.09
Discomfort	−0.833	0.083	0.141	0.52

The effect size r is a robust measure for small sample sizes present in this study. The underlying effect is either small ($r = .10$), medium ($r = .30$) or large ($r = .50$) [7]. Table 1 shows the p-values and effect sizes r for all factors computed with the Wilcoxon Signed Rank Test. It can be seen that there is no statistical significance for any factor.

For the factor Animacy there is only a small effect and thus we accept the hypothesis $H_0(2)$, i.e., there is no change for the factor Animacy between both conditions. The factor competence doesn't show any effect between the conditions and we accept the null hypothesis $H_0(3)$ too.

The Godspeed factor Perceived Intelligence, on the other hand, has a medium effect. We thus can reject the hypothesis $H_0(4)$. From the confidence interval we infer that this effect is in favour for the REA condition.

Interestingly, there is a medium effect for Warmth ($r > 0.32$) and a large effect for Discomfort ($r > 0.52$). Both factors are from the RoSA scale and both are in favour for ADA.

5 Discussion

It is promising that participants could see differences in the behaviour of the reactive and the adaptive behaviour. One concern with choosing a very simplistic platform is that the magnitude of behaviour differences can be very low. However, to our surprise, the perception of the robot's competence and its animal-likeness was not (significantly) increased for the adaptive robot (ADA) compared to the reactive one (REA). We think this is due to the experimental design. Having the robot adaptive enough to leave the pit quickly was not as exciting for the participants as for us, and the quick adaptation needed to achieve this made the robot too unpredictable. Some participants even preferred the reactive behaviour because of its predictable and stable pattern. Only two participants mentioned in the open ended questions that the reactive robot's trajectory was mostly circling. We assume that a lower update rate for the adaptive robot will make a difference here and we will address this in another study. What also plays in favour for the reactive robot was the fact that it only rarely approaches the edge not enclosed by a wall, i.e., where the robot could fall off the table. The circling pattern makes it seem to be more alert for some participants, which in turn may have influenced their rating. Initially, we thought that people would feel that the robot tries to approach them rather than trying to fall off the table. However, only one participant mentioned "it may have sought attention". We designed the interaction at the edge so the participants could experience the adaptation of the robot to interaction. However, the steady, stable behaviour of the reactive robot was preferred by participants, as it seemed easier to keep the robot from rolling over. This is because the reactive robot approaches the edge less, and the robot's reactions were more predictive. These may all be reasons for the higher score of Perceived Intelligence for the reactive robot. We also have to rethink the initial hypothesis altogether. At the end of the day, the adaptive robot is exploring its sensor space. There is no goal other than exploring, making it more likely that the adaptive robot is indeed perceived as less competent and intelligent.

We assume a different experiment introduction could have also made a difference already. Rather than saying "also, your task is to prevent the robot from falling off the table", we could have said that "we did not enclose the edge by a wall, so you can better interact with the robot when it is seeking attention, but please take care it is not rolling over the edge". However, this would have induced a bias towards the robot's capabilities. We think we rather need to redesign the environment for future experiments.

Although the results are not overwhelmingly convincing for Predictive Information at first glance, they have to be interpreted in the context of their novelty. Additionally, the unexpected medium effect for Warmth is promising. The factor is created from the items Happy, Feeling, Social, Organic, Compassionate and

Emotional and it carries more weight in interpersonal interaction than Competence [6].

6 Conclusion and Future Work

In this work we used a minimal robot platform with only proprioceptive sensors updating the PI model. This makes it hard for the model to infer whether perturbations are induced by, e.g., a participant's hand or an obstacle like a wall. In other words, adaptivity to the environment and participants is limited by design. In addition, 4 participants mentioned in their open ended answers that they did not see the robot having any "memory" of previous obstacles or explored areas. We want to address this with feeding other sensors into the model in future work. One option is an odometry encoder providing the robot with information about its position in the environment. Another option is using a previously developed proximity sensor for mobile robots for sensing interacting humans [22]. Both these sensors will be investigated to see whether they enhance the behaviour and make it more adaptive and interesting for HRI experiments.

One contribution of this work is the presented baseline behaviour for PI. The experiment shows that the reactive robot, based on a pre-trial adaptation of its networks configurations with PI, is a good enough candidate. Future experiments can be conducted with a baseline behaviour, which is pre-adapted for the very same sensors and the very same environment as the comparing adaptive PI behaviour. It can be said that the capacity of the robot to leave the pit was not a driving factor for participants when judging the robot's competence positively. Again, the update rate allowing for that skill may have made the adaptive robot appear unnecessarily random. Further studies are needed for finding a good update rate for the robot.

The medium effect for Warmth for the adaptive robot is very promising. In a next step, we want to redesign the experimental setting, as the enforced interaction supposingly has a negative effect. Rather then enforcing the interaction with the robot, we want to implement a more game-like scenario which allows for the participants to interact when they feel the need or the joy to do so, rather than having to interact without them knowing when it is "intended" by the robot. That way we can investigate if the effect for Warmth is indeed caused by the interaction with the intrinsically motivated robot.

References

1. Adamides, G., Christou, G., Katsanos, C., Xenos, M., Hadzilacos, T.: Usability guidelines for the design of robot teleoperation: a taxonomy. IEEE Trans. Hum.-Mach. Syst. 45(2), 256–262 (2015). https://doi.org/10.1109/THMS.2014.2371048
2. Ay, N., Bertschinger, N., Der, R., Güttler, F., Olbrich, E.: Predictive information and explorative behavior of autonomous robots. Eur. Phys. J. B 63(3), 329–339 (2008). https://doi.org/10.1140/epjb/e2008-00175-0

3. Bartneck, C., Kulić, D., Croft, E., Zoghbi, S.: Measurement Instruments for the anthropomorphism, animacy, likeability, perceived intelligence, and perceived safety of robots. Int. J. Soc. Robot. **1**(1), 71–81 (2009). https://doi.org/10.1007/s12369-008-0001-3

4. Barto, A.G.: Intrinsic motivation and reinforcement learning. In: Baldassarre, G., Mirolli, M. (eds.) Intrinsically Motivated Learning in Natural and Artificial Systems, pp. 17–47. Springer, Heidelberg (2013). https://doi.org/10.1007/978-3-642-32375-1_2

5. Blow, M., Dautenhahn, K., Appleby, A., Nehaniv, C.L., Lee, D.C.: Perception of robot smiles and dimensions for human-robot interaction design. In: ROMAN 2006 - The 15th IEEE International Symposium on Robot and Human Interactive Communication, pp. 469–474, September 2006. https://doi.org/10.1109/ROMAN.2006.314372

6. Carpinella, C.M., Wyman, A.B., Perez, M.A., Stroessner, S.J.: The robotic social attributes scale (RoSAS): development and validation. In: Proceedings of the 2017 ACM/IEEE International Conference on Human-Robot Interaction HRI 2017, pp. 254–262. ACM, New York (2017). https://doi.org/10.1145/2909824.3020208

7. Cohen, J.: A power primer. Psychol. Bull. **112**(1), 155–159 (1992)

8. Dautenhahn, K.: I could be you: the phenomenological dimension of social understanding. Cybern. Syst. **28**(5), 417–453 (1997). https://doi.org/10.1080/019697297126074

9. Deci, E., Ryan, R.M.: Intrinsic Motivation and Self-Determination in Human Behavior. Springer, New York (1985)

10. Der, R., Martius, G.: The Playful Machine: Theoretical Foundation and Practical Realization of Self-Organizing Robots, Cognitive Systems Monographs, vol. 15. Springer, Berlin (2012). https://doi.org/10.1007/978-3-642-20253-7

11. Fukuda, H., Ueda, K.: Interaction with a moving object affects one's perception of its animacy. Int. J. Soc. Robot. **2**(2), 187–193 (2010). https://doi.org/10.1007/s12369-010-0045-z

12. Goodrich, M.A., Schultz, A.C.: Human-robot interaction: a survey. Found. Trends Hum.-Comput. Interact. **1**(3), 203–275 (2008). https://doi.org/10.1561/1100000005

13. Guckelsberger, C., Salge, C., Togelius, J.: New and surprising ways to be mean. In: 2018 IEEE Conference on Computational Intelligence and Games (CIG), pp. 1–8 (2018). https://doi.org/10.1109/CIG.2018.8490453

14. Guckelsberger, C., Salge, C., Colton, S.: Intrinsically motivated general companion NPCs via coupled empowerment maximisation. In: 2016 IEEE Conference on Computational Intelligence and Games (CIG), pp. 150–157, September 2016. https://doi.org/10.1109/CIG.2016.7860406

15. Martius, G., Der, R., Ay, N.: Information driven self-organization of complex robotic behaviors. PLoS one **8**(5), 1–14 (2013). https://doi.org/10.1371/journal.pone.0063400

16. Merrick, K.E., Maher, M.L.: Motivated Reinforcement Learning. Curious Characters for Multiuser Games, 1st edn. Springer, Heidelberg (2009)

17. Oudeyer, P.Y., Kaplan, F.: How can we define intrinsic motivation? In: Proceedings of the 8th International Conference on Epigenetic Robotics: Modeling Cognitive Development in Robotic Systems. Lund University Cognitive Studies, Lund. LUCS, Brighton (2008)

18. Oudeyer, P.Y., Kaplan, F.: What is intrinsic motivation? A typology of computational approaches. Front. Neurorobotics **1**, 6 (2009). https://doi.org/10.3389/neuro.12.006.2007

19. Ryan, R.M.: Agency and organization: Intrinsic motivation, autonomy, and the self in psychological development. Nebraska Symposium on Motivation, vol. 40, pp. 1–56 (1993). Nebraska Symposium on Motivation
20. Ryan, R.M., Deci, E.L.: Intrinsic and extrinsic motivations: classic definitions and new directions. Contemp. Educ. Psychol. **25**(1), 54–67 (2000). https://doi.org/10.1006/ceps.1999.1020
21. Scheunemann, M.M.: Intrinsically motivated autonomy in human-robot interaction: human perception of predictive information in robots (2019). https://mms.ai/TAROS2019-supplementary/. Supplementary material
22. Scheunemann, M.M., Dautenhahn, K., Salem, M., Robins, B.: Utilizing bluetooth low energy to recognize proximity, touch and humans. In: 2016 25th IEEE International Symposium on Robot and Human Interactive Communication (RO-MAN), pp. 362–367. IEEE, August 2016. https://doi.org/10.1109/ROMAN.2016.7745156

Modeling and Control of Ankle Actuation Platform for Human-Robot Interaction

Ata Otaran$^{(\boxtimes)}$ and Ildar Farkhatdinov

School of Electronic Engineering and Computer Science,
Queen Mary University of London, London, UK
{a.otaran,i.farkhatdinov}@qmul.ac.uk

Abstract. We present the design of a one-degree-of-freedom ankle actuation platform for human-robot interaction. The platform is actuated with a DC motor through a capstan drive mechanism. The results for platform dynamics identification including friction characterisation are presented. Control experiments demonstrate that a linear regulator with gravity compensation can be used to control the inclination of the platform efficiently.

Keywords: Haptic interfaces · Lower limb · Control

1 Introduction

Most of the haptic devices used in telerobotics or virtual reality (VR) are used to apply force or tactile feedback on a user's upper limbs. However, in many haptic applications, providing feedback to the lower limb can be useful and efficient. In this paper, we describe a robotic interface to provide force feedback through ankle actuation. There have been various ankle actuation platforms developed previously for neuromotor rehabilitation, as ankle health is crucial for the mobility of individuals. Normally robotic ankle rehabilitation devices comprise several degrees-of-freedom (DoF). A widely known rehabilitation system, Rutgers Ankle [6], used a Stewart platform equipped with a single force sensor under the foot. Reducing the mechanics of the Stewart platform to 3-DoF versions led to the development of a 3SPS/S and a 3-RSS/S type parallel mechanisms [2] and in [9] respectively. An Agile Eye type 3-DOF spherical parallel mechanism was used in [10]. In [11] and [12], authors presented impedance type rehabilitation devices for characterizing the ankle impedance to obtain valuable insight into post-stroke recovery in patients. Assist-On Ankle [3] made use of Bowden cable based series elastic actuated parallel mechanism that can align with the subject ankle axis and deliver plantar flexion/dorsiflexion and pronation/supination exercises. As can be inferred from the examples parallel mechanisms are ideal for ankle joint actuation as the addition of DoF does not result in a vastly increased device inertia due to having grounded motors and the ankle joint does not require a large workspace. Relatively simpler ankle tilt platforms were also used in VR

© Springer Nature Switzerland AG 2019
K. Althoefer et al. (Eds.): TAROS 2019, LNAI 11649, pp. 338–348, 2019.
https://doi.org/10.1007/978-3-030-23807-0_28

based studies like serious games [7] for rehabilitation or studying human postural control [1].

In this paper, we present the development of an ankle actuation interface for human-robot interaction research. In particular, we plan to use the proposed interface for emulation of movement sensation in virtual reality and telerobotics applications. As the single DOF, we selected plantar flexion and dorsiflexion movements as forwards and backwards is the primary axis of movement used in daily life. We decided to employ an impedance type interface with a back-driveable actuator that can also apply high enough ankle torque. Addition of a compliant force sensor would decrease the available control bandwidth. Using high quality force sensing will increase the cost of the device. Although it is not desirable to apply large amplitude and high frequency signals to the users to avoid human reflexes, we would like to be able to apply high frequency and low amplitude feedback to be able to account for smaller bumps in the terrain. Ability to apply feedback in a wide range of amplitudes and frequencies not only helps display a variety of feedback but it may also help superimpose different types of information in the feedback such as guidance and performance indication purposes. In order to single out forces applied by a human, a disturbance observer based force estimation method will be utilized [8].

This paper elaborates on the design and modeling stages that come before the implementation of the envisioned reaction torque observer implementation. Section 2 explains design of the proposed interface. A dynamic model including inertia and friction characterization and preliminary control performance evaluation of the device are provided in Sect. 3 which describes gravity compensation, angular orientation control, and friction compensation. Section 4 summarizes the project and discusses potential future improvements.

2   Mechanical Design Description

This section explains how mechanical components are put together for the construction of the initial iteration of the experiment setup. Figure 1 shows the prototype designed to be used in the initial experiments. The device is composed of four main mechanical assemblies: the base, the tilting platform, the motor and the capstan transmission. These main parts are explained in detail below.

The **base** supports the stability of the whole system and constrains the motion of the platform to one revolute DoF. The lower part of the base is made of aluminum sigma profiles. Sigma profiles are arranged to cover a large area for the stability of the base during operation. The vertical stands, made of 10 mm thick aluminum are attached to the base to support the rotation of the tilt platform.

The **tilt platform** is composed of two shafts, two quarter circular aluminum pieces (pulleys), four pieces of aluminum sigma profiles, a wooden plate, capstan mounting units and basic mechanical connection parts. The shafts and double bearings on the base provide the necessary constraint for a single DoF rotational motion around the ankle axes. Pulleys connect the shafts with the plate and are actuated by the motor using capstan transmission.

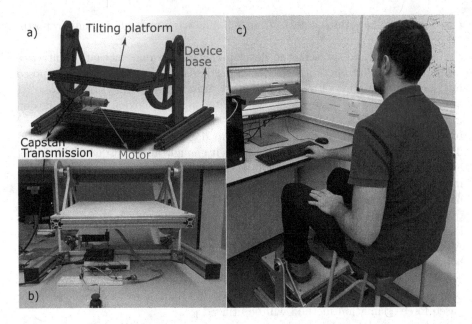

Fig. 1. (a) A computer aided design image of the device (b) image of the device along with the electronic components after construction (c) image of a user utilizing the device with a sample VR application instance.

Capstan drive, is used to transmit the motion of the motor to the tilt platform. One end of the capstan cable is mounted on the side of the pulley and the other one is mounted underneath one of the sigma profiles of the plate assembly. The latter end of the cable is connected to a spring which can alleviate a sudden rise of tensile stress on the cable. The spring is chosen to be stiff enough to avoid introducing additional vibration in the working bandwidth of the device. An additional sliding mechanism was installed to control the cable tension.

The **motor assembly** is composed of a geared DC motor with encoder (Maxon RE30, gear ratio 1:14), aluminium attachment elements fixed to the base and the driving pinion. The capstan is revolved around the pinion 5 times in order to avoid slipping under high torques. The properties of the motor and the gear are selected such that high enough torques at the ankle can be generated and, at the same time, the device is backdrivable enough for reliable impedance type operation.

3 Modeling and Control

In order to achieve a high operation performance with the platform, its dynamics were modeled and relevant control was developed. Figure 2 presents the dynamic model of the system which includes the DC-motor with gear, the cable transmission and the tilting platform. The parameters of the model are described in

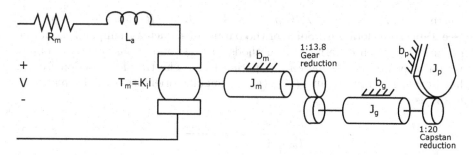

Fig. 2. Dynamic model of the bodies and transmission systems involved in the ankle tilt platform

Table 1 and many of them can be obtained from the DC-motor's datasheet and CAD design of the platform.

Table 1. Ankle platform characteristic parameters

J_a – inertia of the motor	33.5 gr-cm^2
J_g – inertia of the gearhead	0.8 gr-cm^2
J_p – inertia of the ankle platform	0.0717 kg-m^2
J_{eq} – equivalent inertia at motor end	42.92 g-cm^2
r_g – gearhead reduction ratio	13.8:1
r_c – capstan reduction ratio	20:1
L – motor inductance	0.119 mH
R – motor resistance	0.611 Ohm
K_i – motor torque constant	25.9 mN-m/A
K_b – motor speed constant	369 rpm/V
τ_m – mechanical time constant	3.05 ms
T_m – motor nominal torque	85.6 mN-m
w_m – motor nominal speed	8050 rpm
T_{ankle} – ankle axis nominal torque	23.6 N-m
w_{ankle} – ankle axis nominal speed	175 r/s
θ_{lim} – workspace limits	$\pm 43^\circ$

We describe the dynamics with the following transfer functions. The control voltage $V(S)$ (reference voltage for current control) to angular orientation of the platform, $\theta_m(s)$ transfer function is described as follows:

$$\frac{s\theta_m(s)}{V(s)} = \frac{K_i/R}{J_{eq}s + b_{eq}} \qquad (1)$$

where $J_{eq} = J_m + J_g/r_g^2 + J_p/(r_g r_c)^2$ and $b_{eq} = K_i K_b/R + b_m + b_g/r_g + b_c/r_g r_c$ (see Table 1 for notation). Some of the parameters, such as damping, should be estimated through experimental methods such as motor spin down and observation of pendulum oscillation dissipation tests. The transfer function from a human ankle torque input, $T_{ankle}(s)$, to angular orientation of the platform, $\theta_m(s)$, is

$$\frac{s\theta_m(s)}{T_{ankle}(s)} = \frac{-1/(r_g r_c)}{Js + b}. \tag{2}$$

The designed platform can be modelled as a linear system and therefore we utilize a PID regulator with gravity compensation to control the angular orientation of the ankle platform. Initially, the parameters of the PID regulator were selected based on the linear model of the system to achieve a critically damped response without taking into account the user's ankle dynamics. Since user's feet will be a big consideration in the selection of the parameters, a more reliable model-based feedback control scheme will be developed in parallel to the performance evaluation trials with different users.

3.1   Gravity Compensation

Since the centre of gravity of the system is not aligned with the axis of rotation the gravity compensation control was introduced in addition to the PID regulator. For the gravity compensation a simplified model of the device was used as shown in Fig. 3. The location of the COM was retrieved from the CAD model.

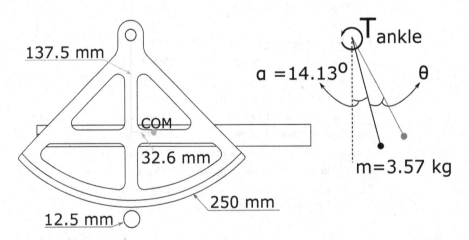

Fig. 3. Simplified model of the device. Due to the extra space in the front the center of mass is shifted towards the longer side of the plate.

To compensate for gravity, the torques induced around the axis of revolution due to the load should be provided by the actuator in a feed-forward manner.

Equation 3 is the required calculation for the feedforward gravity compensation signal:

$$T_{gravity} = mgl\sin(\theta + \alpha) \tag{3}$$

where θ is the tilt angle of the plate and α is the angle between the axis that is orthogonal to the plate and the shortest line from the COM to the axis of rotation as seen in Fig. 3. The DC-motor current required for gravity compensation is calculated as:

$$i_m = \frac{mgl\sin(\theta + \alpha)}{K_i r_g r_c} \tag{4}$$

The general system equation can be rewritten as:

$$T_{motor} + T_{human} = J_{eq}\ddot{\theta} + b_{eq}\dot{\theta} + G(\theta) \tag{5}$$

$$T_{motor} = K_p(\theta_{des} - \theta) + K_d(\dot{\theta}_{des} - \dot{\theta}) + G(\theta) \tag{6}$$

Elimination of gravity terms and separating the θ terms on the left hand side would result in:

$$J_{eq}\ddot{\theta} + b_{eq}\dot{\theta} + K_d\dot{\theta} + K_p\theta = K_d\dot{\theta}_{des} + K_p\theta_{des} + T_{human} \tag{7}$$

$$\frac{\theta(s)}{\theta_{des}(s)} = \frac{K_d s + Kp}{J_{eq}s^2 + (b + K_d)s + Kp} \tag{8}$$

$$\frac{\theta(s)}{T_m(s)} = \frac{1}{J_{eq}s^2 + (b + K_d)s + Kp} \tag{9}$$

The designed PID and gravity compensation controllers were used together to evaluate performance of the ankle platform.

3.2   Performance Evaluation

A set of control tests were performed to evaluate and analyze the performance of the designed ankle actuation platform. First, the designed PID regulator was tested. The results are shown in Fig. 4. The test showed that in all cases the platform reached the reference orientation within 300 ms which is sufficient for our study. To find suitable controller gains we first used the PD-regulator. Initially, the PD-gains were calculated from the platform's dynamics to achieve a critically damped response while assuming that the system does not have internal damping and gravity is perfectly compensated. Afterwards, the PID terms were further tuned to reduce the rise time and overshoot. The reason behind relatively slow response for the 5° set-point and high steady state error for 15° point is suspected to be the high static friction. To tackle this, a saturation was implemented on the error accumulation rate so that the increased integral gain would not be as effective in the increase of overshoot. The saturation limits the error at the maximum covered distance at each period by the device. A chirp reference tracking test was also performed to collect data on the position control

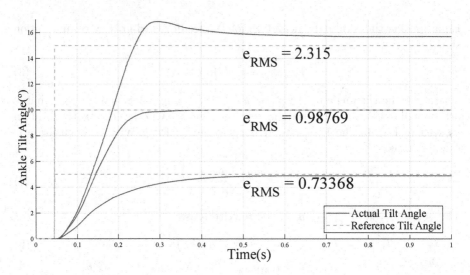

Fig. 4. Set-point reference tracking

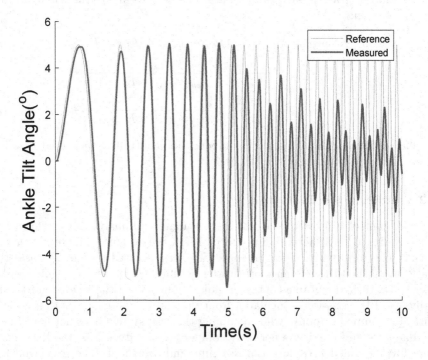

Fig. 5. Chirp reference tracking

bandwidth. The amplitude of the sinusoidal signal was set to be 5° and the frequency of the signal was linearly increased from 0.2 Hz to 5 Hz over the course of 10 s. The results shown in Fig. 5 suggest that the system can be used with good position tracking at frequencies up to 3 Hz.

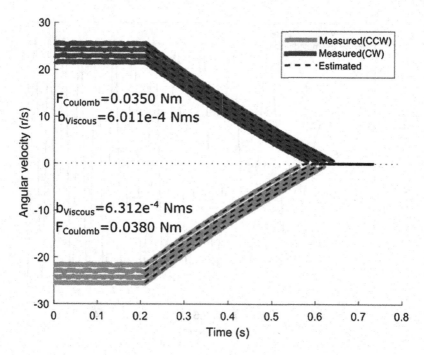

Fig. 6. Motor spin-down test starting from various velocities. The Coulomb and viscous friction are characterized separately for clockwise and counterclockwise cases.

3.3 Friction Modeling

This section elaborates on the modeling of the friction of the device which will be required for an accurate means of torque estimation with our impedance type device. As can be seen in the definitions of J_{eq} and b_{eq}, the motor inertia and friction constitute a large part of the effective inertia at the ankle joint after multiplication with the gear ratios. For this reason, the motor was separately modeled for friction and inertia. Two tests were employed for this. Since there will not be multiple inertia or viscous friction terms, the apparent inertia and viscous friction coefficient on the output shaft of the motor will be referred to as J and b.

The friction model we have used includes the components below:

– Static friction (T_{sf}): Friction threshold to overcome stiction.
– Coulomb friction $(T_{cf}\,sign(\dot{\theta}))$: Constant torque acting on the opposite direction of the movement.
– Stribeck effect $(T_{sf} = (T_{sf} - T_{cf})e^{-(\dot{\theta}/w_s)^{\sigma}})$: Friction that is effective after the beginning of sliding and exponentially decays with increase in velocity.
– Viscous friction $(T_{vf} = b\dot{\theta})$: Torque acting on the opposite direction of the movement, proportional to the velocity.

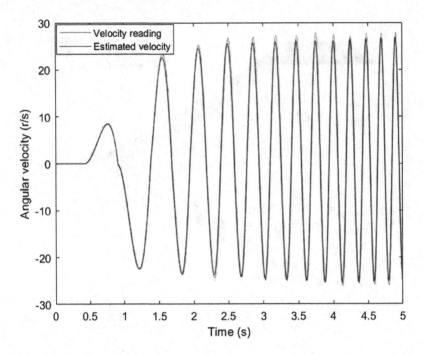

Fig. 7. Angular velocity vs. time graph generated with open loop torque sinusoidal input with linearly increasing frequency and amplitude

Motor Spin-Down Test: The motor is velocity controlled at different speeds and the torque input is suddenly cut. At high velocities only coulomb friction and viscous friction are effective, enabling an easier identification. The motor spins down until it stops. For speeds that are not close to zero, the equations are as follows.

$$J\ddot{\theta} + b\dot{\theta} = T_{cf} \tag{10}$$

$$Js\dot{\theta} - J\dot{\theta}(0)b\dot{\theta}(s) = T_{cf}/s \tag{11}$$

$$\dot{\theta}(s) = \frac{J\dot{\theta}(0)}{Js + b} + \frac{T_{cf}}{s(Js + b)} \tag{12}$$

$$\dot{\theta} = (\dot{\theta}(0) - \frac{T_{cf}t}{J}) * e^{-b/J} \tag{13}$$

Figure 6 demonstrates data retrieved from spindown tests carried out at 4 distinct speeds. The characterization of the inertia, coulomb friction and viscous friction are performed using this data.

Open Loop Chirp Torque Test: The motor spin-down test only supplies the ratios, T_{cf}/J and b/J, as there we primarily investigate the part where the input torque is zero. For this second test an open loop input signal is applied to the system and the output is recorded. Using the transfer functions between the angular

Table 2. Ankle platform characteristic parameters

Parameter	Description	Value	Unit
J	Inertia of the motor with gear and pinion	7.540e$^-$4	kg-m^2
b	Viscous friction coefficient (CW)	6.312e$^-$4	Nms
	Viscous friction coefficient (CCW)	6.011e$^-$4	Nms
T_{cf}	Coulomb force (CW)	0.0350	Nm
	Coulomb force (CCW)	0.0380	Nm
w_s	Stribeck velocity	3.2	r/s
T_{sf}	Static friction	0.045	Nm

velocity and the torque input along with the known ratios between T_{cf}, b and J parameters reliable estimates could be achieved as demonstrated in Fig. 7. Table 2 lists the resulting friction parameters estimation with the tests.

4   Conclusion

We have presented the design and preliminary modeling of a single DoF impedance type haptic interface for interactively actuating the ankle of a subject. The developed linear control with gravity and friction compensation allowed to achieve high performance movement response. The device was deliberately designed to be simple so that it is easier to augment it with further functionality useful for virtual reality and mobile robot teleoperation [5]. The system is currently being testing to investigate various aspects of self-motion perception [4] and spatial orientation in virtual reality.

Acknowledgments. This work was funded by the UK EPSRC grant EP/R02572X/1 (NCNR). Ata Otaran was funded by Queen May University of London Ph.D. scholarship.

References

1. Buettner, D., Dalin, D., Wiesmeier, I.K., Maurer, C.: Virtual balancing for studying and training postural control. Front. Neurosci. **11**, 531 (2017)
2. Dai, J.S., Zhao, T., Nester, C.: Sprained ankle physiotherapy based mechanism synthesis and stiffness analysis of a robotic rehabilitation device. Auton. Robots **16**(2), 207–218 (2004)
3. Erdogan, A., Celebi, B., Satici, A.C., Patoglu, V.: Assiston-ankle: a reconfigurable ankle exoskeleton with series-elastic actuation. Auton. Robots **41**(3), 743–758 (2017)
4. Farkhatdinov, I., Ouarti, N., Hayward, V.: Vibrotactile inputs to the feet can modulate vection. In: 2013 World Haptics Conference (WHC), pp. 677–681 (2013)
5. Farkhatdinov, I., Ryu, J.H., Poduraev, J.: A user study of command strategies for mobile robot teleoperation. Intell. Serv. Robot. **2**(2), 95–104 (2009)

6. Girone, M., Burdea, G., Bouzit, M.: The rutgers ankle orthopedic rehabilitation interface. In: Proceedings of ASME Haptics Symposium, vol. 67, pp. 305–312 (1999)
7. Goncalves, A.C.B.F., dos Santos, W.M., Consoni, L.J., Siqueira, A.A.G.: Serious games for assessment and rehabilitation of ankle movements. In: 2014 IEEE 3rd International Conference on Serious Games and Applications for Health (SeGAH), pp. 1–6, May 2014
8. Gupta, A., O'Malley, M.K.: Disturbance-observer-based force stimation for haptic feedback. J. Dyn. Syst. Measur. Control **133** (2010)
9. Liu, G., Gao, J., Yue, H., Zhang, X., Lu, G.: Design and kinematics analysis of parallel robots for ankle rehabilitation. In: 2006 IEEE/RSJ International Conference on Intelligent Robots and Systems, pp. 253–258, October 2006
10. Malosio, M., Negri, S.P., Pedrocchi, N., Vicentini, F., Caimmi, M., Molinari Tosatti, L.: A spherical parallel three degrees-of-freedom robot for ankle-foot neuro-rehabilitation. In: 2012 Annual International Conference of the IEEE Engineering in Medicine and Biology Society, pp. 3356–3359, August 2012
11. Roy, A., et al.: Measurement of human ankle stiffness using the anklebot. In: 2007 IEEE 10th International Conference on Rehabilitation Robotics, pp. 356–363, June 2007
12. Satici, A.C., Erdogan, A., Patoglu, V.: Design of a reconfigurable ankle rehabilitation robot and its use for the estimation of the ankle impedance. In: 2009 IEEE International Conference on Rehabilitation Robotics, pp. 257–264, June 2009

Investigating the Effects of Social Interactive Behaviours of a Robot on People's Trust During a Navigation Task

Alessandra Rossi[1]([⊠]), Fernando Garcia[2], Arturo Cruz Maya[2], Kerstin Dautenhahn[1,3], Kheng Lee Koay[1], Michael L. Walters[1], and Amit K. Pandey[2]

[1] University of Hertfordshire, College Lane, Hatfield, UK
{a.rossi,k.l.koay,m.l.walters}@herts.ac.uk
[2] SoftBank Robotics Europe, Paris, France
{ferran.garcia,arturo.cruzmaya,akpandey}@softbankrobotics.com
[3] University of Waterloo, Waterloo, ON, Canada
kerstin.dautenhahn@uwaterloo.ca

Abstract. Identifying the roles and the specific social behaviours that evoke human trust towards robots is key for user acceptance. Specially, while performing tasks in the real world, such as navigation or guidance, the predictability of robot motion and predictions of user intentions facilitate interaction. We present a user study in which a humanoid-robot guided participants around a human populated environment, avoiding collisions while following a socially acceptable trajectory. We investigated which behaviours performed by a humanoid robot during a guidance task exhibited better social acceptance by people, and how robot behaviours influence their trust in a robot to safely complete a guiding task. We concluded that in general, people prefer and trust a robot that exhibits social behaviours such as talking and maintaining an appropriate safe distance from obstacles.

Keywords: Human-robot interaction · Social robotics · Robot companion · Trust in robots · Robot social navigation

1 Introduction

Service robots are now being used in human-oriented environments, such as airports, hospitals, schools, commercial centres and homes [5,32]. In particular, during the last few years, research communities have been aiming at building robot companions that will assist people in their daily activities [4,6,8]. This involves robots that are able to share the same physical space and to engage in social interactions with human users. Moreover, people need to accept robots' presence in these contexts [17] and to trust that robots will look after their

© Springer Nature Switzerland AG 2019
K. Althoefer et al. (Eds.): TAROS 2019, LNAI 11649, pp. 349–361, 2019.
https://doi.org/10.1007/978-3-030-23807-0_29

safety [33]. When developing robots to work in human populated environments, an important aspect is to integrate strategies that allow robots to move around people in a safe and socially acceptable way. However, this raises new challenges in terms of defining safe robot navigation and natural and trusted Human-Robot interactions (HRI) [25]. Autonomous robots elicit certain expectations from the general public. One of the basic capabilities that they should possess is to be able to navigate safely in crowded environments, predicting the actions of others and acting accordingly. Several research studies have proposed different strategies for social acceptable movements for robots in complex environments where human users' presence and activities are unpredictable [29]. Classical robot navigation approaches to people tend to focus on efficiency during the path planning and execution; variables such as path length, clearance and smoothness are used to quantitatively evaluate performance [38], specially in cluttered environments. In contrast, more recent studies have also focused on robot socially-aware navigation, in which a robot can adapt its behaviour by estimating how its position affects the quality of interaction. This is by introducing social concepts, such as social distance or proxemics [21,26], in order to encode social conventions within robot navigation planners. Implementation and evaluation of the social component of these systems requires user studies in order to identify the most acceptable robot social behaviours in order to facilitate tasks such as guidance or human compliant navigation. Unfortunately, the scarce amount of detectable information under these circumstances increases the difficulty in evaluating human robot interactions. Resulting implementations are usually based on social conventions, essentially mimicking human-human interactions [14]. However, the study by Desai et al. [16] shows discrepancies between human-human and robot-human interactions. Therefore, evaluation of robot behaviours must be based on the acquisition of the desired response, natural acceptance and trust from humans.

This work investigated human users' responses to robot behaviours to enhance their acceptance and trust of a robot. In particular, we were interested in investigating people's trust in a robot which is able to complete safely a navigation task. Namely, the robot guiding them in both wide and narrow spaces, such as doors or corridors, in a human-populated environment. We were also interested in collecting people's preferences and perceptions of the social behaviours exhibited by the robot during the navigation task.

2   Research Questions

This research has been guided by the following Research Questions (R):

- **R1** Do human users trust a robot to be able to complete the task of guiding them from one point to another in a cluttered environment?
- **R2** Do people trust a robot to be able to guide them in narrow spaces, such as a door or corridor?
- **R3** What kind of robot behaviours do people prefer. A robot that behaves more like a tool or as a social entity?
- **R4** Which social behaviours should a robot exhibit during a navigation task according to human users' preferences?

3   Related Works

In this Section, we provide an overview of current research in the area of social robot navigation, with a particular focus on the development of trust in these particular human-robot interactions.

3.1   Robot Guide in Social Scenarios

Initial attempts to propose interactive guiding robots are presented by Burgard et al. [5] with a robot in the role of a museum guide. However, the focus of the work was the navigation performance with little consideration of the social aspects of the interaction. More recent experiments have studied associated social qualities such as people-aware navigation for goal oriented behaviour considering users [31]. Specifically, Pacchierotti et al. [28] used a multi-module path planner that focused on accompanying and manoeuvrering between groups and freezing when a safe trajectory is not feasible. Feil-Seifer and Matarić [11] proposed a Gaussian Mixture Model which is used to slow down or stop the robot when the human partner does not follow the robot's pace. However, such methodologies deviate from the expected behaviour of human beings, and exhibit a low degree of proactivity and social-awareness. More recent work [13], proposes a method that constantly monitors the user being guided, in order to proactively offer help. A Situation Assessment component of the system gathers spatial information in order to make decisions using a planning framework based on hierarchical MOMPDs (Mixed Observability Markov Decision Processes). Proactive change of speed is achieved by constantly monitoring the user where only the back of the robot is shown to the user. This necessarily limits any type of interaction during the navigation. However, in the study by Ferrer et al. [12], the guiding task is accomplished by the human and robot walking side by side. In this case, the platform is attracted to the user using the concept of a robot-person force implemented with an Extended-SFM (Social Force Model). Zhang et al. [40] went one step further by introducing a planner based on Artificial Potential Fields that includes the guided subjects and sub-goal location inside an office hallway. The guided person is represented as an attractive or repulsive potential field. In this manner, the authors not only achieve velocity adaptation to the guided person, but also a change of behaviour from guiding to following in the case that a person deviates from the original path.

3.2   Trust in Social Navigation

Several previous studies define the concept of trust in Human-Human, Human-Computer and Human-Robot Interactions. Although multiple definitions exist, we have adopted one of the first definitions of trust [10]. There is a convergent tendency [39] towards using this definition "Trust can be defined as the attitude that an agent will help achieve an individual's goals in a situation characterised by uncertainty and vulnerability" [22, p. 51]. Enhancing people's appropriate level of trust of the robot in a successful Human-Robot Interaction can be a challenge [15]. In particular, human trust during robot guidance tasks has not been studied in depth.

Wang et al. [37] proposed a trust-based real-time framework to switch between autonomous and manual motion planning. This achieved a trade off between task safety and efficiency. Therefore, the goal satisfaction was guaranteed by using a human-in-the-loop, which provided a quantitative trust measurement. In [35] task guidance is provided in a collaborative part assembly scenario, while measuring participants' perceived robot competence, safety, trustworthiness and the impact of participants' personality traits in their perceptions. The presence of faults had a limited effect on the participants' perception of the robot which can be mitigated by applying robot transparency in the decision process [36]. Such results were corroborated in [24], where a robot platform was used as a navigational system to guide participants through a sign-posted maze. This indicated that users generally trust directions given by the robot more than their own judgment.

Hancock et al. [18] showed that robot performance had the greatest association with trust. Specifically, early decreases in reliability, negatively impacted on real-time trust differently than later reductions in reliability [9]. However, that does not necessary mean that there is necessarily an effect on participants' willingness to cooperate with an unreliable robot, as indicated by Salem et al. [34]. Other studies [32] show that participants' personality traits will also affect users' perceptions of the robot and their interactions.

4   Approach

This Section describes the approach used to identify people's preferences for a social robot navigation task. In this study we used the robot Pepper developed by SoftBank Robotics, which in particular, is designed for safe HRIs [30].

4.1   Experimental Design

The participants were each asked to follow the robot and adapt their behaviours to the robot's behaviours. We used a within-subject, counterbalanced, repeated measures experimental design. In order to test our research questions, each experiment was executed under 3 different conditions when the robot encountered people on its path towards the destination: a control condition **C1**: the robot stops and waits to have a clear path; condition **C2**: the robot performs simple obstacle avoidance while continuing moving; and **C3**: the robot uses social behaviours to communicate and interact with participants (see Sect. 4.2).

We asked two actors to block the robot that guided the participants in the experimental environment (see Fig. 1).

In order to analyse the interactions between the human participants and the robot, we asked the participants to complete questionnaires.

4.2   Experimental Procedure

Participants were asked to imagine that they were in a shopping mall which they were not familiar with. The robot called "Jax" would help them to find the Information Centre. We told participants that they were free to position themselves next to, or behind the robot, according to their preference for following the robot. Participants completed a pre-experimental questionnaire to collect their experiences with robots and their perceptions of generic robots. Participants were presented with the same navigation task three times. All participants started their interaction with a control condition (**C1**). Then, they were tested with the social (**C3**) and non social (**C2**) conditions in a randomised order. During **C1**, Jax stopped when it encountered two people talking to each other and blocking the robot's way (see Fig. 1a). When the two people cleared away from the robot's path, it then proceeded with its navigation. Once at the destination, the robot stopped. The experimenter informed the participants they had reached the Information Centre. At the end of the trial, participants completed a second questionnaire to collect their perceptions of Jax and their self-confidence.

During **C2**, the robot did not exhibit any social behaviours, but it avoided the actors by moving according to the social norm of passing a person by maintaining position on the right side [19] and performing a simple obstacle-avoidance technique (see Fig. 1b). Once at the destination, the robot just stopped. At the end of the trial, participants were asked to answer the same questions as in the second questionnaire. In conditions **C1** and **C2**, the robot moved at a constant velocity of 1 m/s.

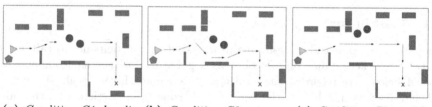

(a) *Condition C1: baseline* (b) *Condition C2: non so-* (c) *Condition C3: social*
                                            cial

Fig. 1. The robot's navigation behaviours. (a) The robot stops and wait for people to move away from its path; (b) the robot avoids the people on its path; and (c) the robot asks the people to let it pass, and when they clear the way, it continues its navigation. Participants are represented by the hexagon, and the robot by the triangle. The robot moves following the arrows until it reaches the destination, represented by an X. Obstacles are squares and rectangles. The two actors are represented by two circles.

In condition **C3**, the robot faced the participant and invited her to follow it to the Information Centre. It slowly increased and decreased the velocity, depending on whether the navigation was on a straight path, doing a turn or approaching an obstacle. Its velocity varied between 0 m/s to 1 m/s. It slowed down until it stopped when it detected people on its path (see Fig. 1c), while changing the colour of its shoulder LEDS to catch the participant's attention. It gently asked the two actors to let them pass saying "Excuse me, I would like to pass", and it thanked them once it had passed by. The robot continued its guidance task after gesturing with its arm for the participant to proceed. When it arrived at the destination, the robot verbally informed the participant while turning towards her. At the end of the trial, participants were asked to answer the same questions as in the second questionnaire and another small questionnaire about their preferred social cues.

At the end of the three conditions, participants were asked to complete a final questionnaire about their perception of the robot, their emotional state and preferences for Jax's behaviours.

5 Results

We collected data from 12 participants. However, since it was important to test participants' trust of the robot and not of the human operator, at the end of the final questionnaire we asked participants if they believed the robot was behaving autonomously. We decided to exclude two participants who did not believe this. We analysed responses from the remaining participants (5 men and 5 women), aged between 22 to 40 years old [mean age 27.7, std. dev. 5.59]. All participants were PhD students, researchers and administration staff members at SoftBank Robotics Europe in Paris, France.

5.1 Trust in Jax

As part of the pre-study questionnaire we asked the participants to rate levels of trust and acceptance of the robot as a guide in different environments, as shown below. We recorded their ratings on a 7-point Likert Scale [1 = not at all and 7 = very much]. At the end of each condition, participants were also given the same questionnaire. However, in these latter questionnaires we referred specifically to **Jax** instead of **a robot**. We asked participants to answer the following questions which were repeated specifically referring to Jax after each trial:

- Would you feel comfortable having **a robot** as a guide in a public environment, for example a museum, an airport or a shopping mall?
- Would you trust **a robot** to guide you safely in a public environment?
- Would you trust **a robot** to be able to navigate safely in narrow environments, such as a door or corridor?

We used Friedman tests to analyse the significant differences between three dimensions, which were the three different conditions participants' were tested with. We found that their perceptions of being comfortable in having the robot guiding participants was rated differently ($\chi^2(3) = 11.20, p = 0.011$) for the different conditions. Similarly, a Friedman test indicated that there is a statistically significant difference in participants' trust in the robot to guide them both in public ($\chi^2(3) = 7.405, p < 0.05$) and narrow ($\chi^2(3) = 17.28, p < 0.01$) spaces for these conditions.

In particular, a Wilcoxon Signed-Ranks test indicated that participants felt more comfortable ($z = -2.4, p < 0.01$) after condition **C3** (mean rank = 4) then after condition **C2** (mean rank = 0). Similarly, they felt more comfortable ($z = -2.81, p < 0.01$) after condition **C3** (mean rank = 5) than after condition **C1** (mean rank = 0).

Participants trusted the robot to be able to guide them more ($z = -1.86, p = 0.03$) when tested with condition **C3** (mean rank = 5) than their initial belief (mean rank = 4.43). While we did not find any statistically significant difference between the other conditions.

There are no other statistically significant differences between the conditions participants were tested with, but their initial trust towards a generic robot changed after their interactions with Jax. We found that they did not trust a generic robot to be able to guide them through narrow spaces more than the robot Jax respectively in **C1** ($z = -2.7, p = 0.004$), **C2** ($z = -2.539, p < 0.01$) and **C3** ($z = -2.682, p < 0.01$) conditions.

5.2 Participants' Self Confidence

After each trial, participants' self-confidence was rated with the following questions: (1) I believe I could have found the way on my own; (2) I believe I could have found a faster way on my own; (3) I believe I could have found a safer way on my own. We did not find any statistically significant differences in people's perception of self confidence in finding the destination on their own, in a faster or safer way or, depending the different conditions.

5.3 Previous Experiences with Robots

As part of the pre-experiment questionnaire, we were also interested in participants' previous experiences with robots. We used a 7-point Likert Scale where 1 corresponds to "not at all" and 7 corresponds to "very much". In particular, we asked participants about previous experience: (1) Do you have any experience interacting with robots? (2) Please, specify what kind of experience you have with robots (if any) [as a participant in an other experiment, observer, developer, researcher]. (3) Which robots? (if any).

Participants had previous experience with robots (min = 2, max = 7, mean 5, std. dev. 1.82). Participants with previous experiences with robots were (a) participant in previous studies = 30%, (b) developer = 40%, (c) observer = 50%, (d) researcher = 40%. In particular, 9 from 10 participants had previous experiences with a Pepper robot.

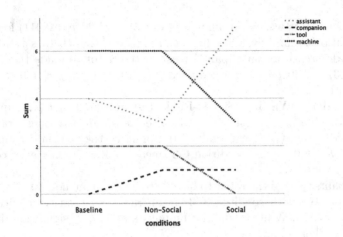

Fig. 2. Participants' perception of the robot's role after the conditions.

5.4 Role of the Robot

After each trial, we asked the participants to choose a role perceived as suitable for robots from the following: (1) friend; (2) butler; (3) companion; (4) pet; (5) assistant; (6) machine; (7) tool; or (8) other. These robot roles were chosen according to previous studies conducted by Dautenhahn et al. [6,7] and Ljungblad et al. [23].

Figure 2 shows that participants' ratings varied based on the different conditions. We observe that their perception of the robot as assistant and machine drastically changed. People perceived the robot more as an assistant and less as machine when it exhibited social behaviours. Figure 2 also highlights that there was a small variance in the perception of the robot as tool and companion when comparing these conditions. Participants considered a social robot less as a tool, while they considered a robot that is not social or does use simple obstacle avoidance techniques less as a companion.

5.5 Godspeed Questionnaire

At the end of all trials, we were also interested in evaluating the perceptions of the participants after their interactions with Jax. We used the Godspeed questionnaire [2] to evaluate the perception of the robot using a set of semantic differential scales. We tested the internal consistency of the subscales using Cronbach's alpha test. The high Cronbach's α is 0.930 which suggested that we could proceed by treating the data as interval scales [2].

The effects of the conditions on participants' ratings along the Goodspeed questionnaire's dimensions were assessed using an ANOVA test. We found a significant effect for stagnant ($p < 0.01, F = 20.00$), inert ($p < 0.01, F = 13.18$), dislike ($p = 0.03, F = 6.40$), unpleasant ($p < 0.01, F = 30.97$) and awful ($p = 0.01, F = 10.57$) dimensions. The results of the ANOVA test highlighted also that participants' mean ratings were higher when they were tested with conditions in the following order: **C1** (baseline), **C2** (non social robot) and **C3** (social robot). We also observed that participants tested with **C1**, **C2** and **C3** conditions' order felt more anxious ($p < 0.01, F = 13.91$) and agitated ($p = 0.02, F = 4.00$).

From these results, we tend to believe that people's perception of the robot is mostly formed at the beginning of the interaction with a non-social robot. Indeed these findings might be also in line with other studies [32, 39]. Similarly, we also hypothesise that participants' emotional state was affected by their very first interaction. However, we do not have enough information to corroborate our beliefs. Further studies are planned which will involve a larger pool of participants, and hopefully they will help to clarify this effect when comparing people's emotional state before and after the interactions with the robot. This is of particular interest because people's negative emotional state might affect their trust [27]. For example, anxiety, which is characterised as a low certainty emotion, might have affected negatively their trust in Jax.

5.6   Preferred Behaviour by Participants

We asked the participants to choose the robot behaviour they preferred or considered most necessary during a guidance task from the following: (1) the robot waited to have a clear path (Baseline) and the robot exhibited social behaviours (e.g. talking, changing velocity, using lights, etc.); (2) the robot waited to have clear path (Baseline) and the robot avoided people without any social behaviour; (3) the robot exhibited social behaviours (e.g. talking, changing velocity, using lights, etc.) and the robot avoided the people without any social behaviour.

All participants considered it necessary to have a social robot as a guide compared to both non-social behaviours and the baseline. They did not have specific preferences when asked to choose between a robot without social behaviours (50%) and a robot that waits to have clear path before continuing its navigation (50%).

5.7   Social Behaviours Preferred by Participants

As part of the questionnaire completed by participants after the condition in which the robot showed social behaviours, we asked them to select the specific behaviours they preferred during the guiding task with the robot. These were: speech; coloured lights; maintaining an appropriate distance from obstacles, humans or objects; approaching obstacles at an appropriate velocity, humans or objects, and narrow places; gesture; head and body orientation; or write down any social cues not included in the previous ones. These social cues were chosen according to [3], suggesting that naturalistic social interaction in robots can be designed through five main methods of non-facial and non-verbal affective expression: body movement, posture, orientation, color, and sound. Others [1, 20] have also studied participants' preferences based on the robot's type, size, proximity, and behaviour. One participant did not answer the question, the remaining participants unanimously preferred a robot that is able to talk. Other preferences were for a robot that is able: to maintain the appropriate distance from obstacles (55.5%), to use gestures to communicate (33.3%), and approach obstacles and narrow places at an appropriate velocity (22.2%).

5.8 General Observation

We told participants that they were free to follow the robot by positioning themselves as they preferred. During the **C3** condition, all participants chose to be behind the robot on its right side, while during the other conditions only 7 made the same choice. In **C1** and **C2** conditions, 2 participants were on the front-right side of the robot, which incidentally was perceived as too slow. One participant preferred to walk on the right side of the robot with his arm on the robot's shoulder. After the study, he did not give any specific justification for his behaviour besides feeling more comfortable that way.

6 Conclusions and Future Works

In this study we investigated people's trust in the capabilities of a robot to guide them in a cluttered environment, including passing through narrow spaces. We compared people's perception of trust in the robot after three different conditions in which the robot was behaving differently. We found that participants felt more comfortable to follow a social robot, and that the social robot gained participants' trust which they did not have before interacting with it. We also observed that people's expectations for a robot to be able to guide them in narrow spaces were significantly lower compared to their perceptions after their interactions with the real robot.

We were also interested in what kind of robot behaviours people preferred for a guidance task. For example, would they prefer a robot behaving more like a tool or a social entity? We observed that they perceived the robot more as an assistant and less as a machine when it behaved in a social manner. In particular, they preferred a social robot that communicates using speech and maintains an appropriate distance from obstacles.

The results of this study showed that in general people preferred and trusted an interactive sociable robot more. However, we are aware of limitations to this study. For example, further investigations will also investigate the development of trust in more complex navigation scenarios.

Acknowledgment. This project has received funding from the European Union's Horizon 2020 research and innovation programme under the Marie Sklodowska-Curie grant agreement No 642667 (Safety Enables Cooperation in Uncertain Robotic Environments - SECURE) and the Industrial Leadership Agreement (ICT) No. 779942 (Safe Robot Navigation in Dense Crowds - CROWDBOT).

References

1. Bainbridge, W.A., Hart, J.W., Kim, E.S., Scassellati, B.: The benefits of interactions with physically present robots over video-displayed agents. Int. J. Soc. Robot. **3**(1), 41–52 (2011)
2. Bartneck, C., Kulić, D., Croft, E., Zoghbi, S.: Measurement instruments for the anthropomorphism, animacy, likeability, perceived intelligence, and perceived safety of robots. Int. J. Soc. Robot. **1**(1), 71–81 (2009)
3. Bethel, C., Murphy, R.: Survey of non-facial/non-verbal affective expressions for appearance-constrained robots. Syst. Man Cybern. Part C (Appl. Rev.) **38**(1), 83–92 (2008)
4. Breazeal, C., Dautenhahn, K., Kanda, T.: Social Robotics, pp. 1935–1972. Springer, Cham (2016)
5. Burgard, W., et al.: Experiences with an interactive museum tour-guide robot. Artif. Intell. **114**(1–2), 3–55 (1999)
6. Dautenhahn, K., Woods, S., Kaouri, C., Walters, M., Koay, K., Werry, I.: What is a robot companion - friend, assistant or butler? pp. 1488–1493 (2005)
7. Dautenhahn, K.: Roles and functions of robots in human society: implications from research in autism therapy. Robotica **21**(4), 443–452 (2003)
8. Dautenhahn, K., Campbell, A., Syrdal, D.S.: Does anyone want to talk to me?: Reflections on the use of assistance and companion robots in care homes. In: Proceedings of 4th International Symposium on New Frontiers in Human-Robot Interaction. The Society for the Study of Artificial Intelligence and the Simulation of Behaviour (AISB) (2015)
9. Desai, M., Kaniarasu, P., Medvedev, M., Steinfeld, A., Yanco, H.: Impact of robot failures and feedback on real-time trust. In: Proceedings of the 8th ACM/IEEE International Conference on Human-Robot Interaction, pp. 251–258. IEEE Press (2013)
10. Deutsch, M.: Trust and suspicion. J. Conflict Resolut. **2**(4), 265–279 (1958)
11. Feil-Seifer, D., Matarić, M.: People-aware navigation for goal-oriented behavior involving a human partner. In: 2011 IEEE International Conference on Development and Learning (ICDL), vol. 2, pp. 1–6. IEEE (2011)
12. Ferrer, G., Garrell, A., Sanfeliu, A.: Robot companion: a social-force based approach with human awareness-navigation in crowded environments. In: 2013 IEEE/RSJ International Conference on Intelligent Robots and Systems (IROS), pp. 1688–1694. IEEE (2013)
13. Fiore, M., Khambhaita, H., Milliez, G., Alami, R.: An adaptive and proactive human-aware robot guide. Social Robotics. LNCS (LNAI), vol. 9388, pp. 194–203. Springer, Cham (2015). https://doi.org/10.1007/978-3-319-25554-5_20
14. Fong, T., Nourbakhsh, I., Dautenhahn, K.: A survey of socially interactive robots. Robot. Auton. Syst. **42**(3–4), 143–166 (2003)
15. Freedy, A., DeVisser, E., Weltman, G., Coeyman, N.: Measurement of trust in human-robot collaboration. In: International Symposium on Collaborative Technologies and Systems, 2007. CTS 2007, pp. 106–114. IEEE (2007)
16. de Graaf, M., Malle, B.F.: People's judgments of human and robot behaviors: A robust set of behaviors and some discrepancies. In: Companion of the 2018 ACM/IEEE International Conference on Human-Robot Interaction, pp. 97–98. ACM (2018)
17. de Graaf, M.M., Ben Allouch, S., van Dijk, J.A.: Why would I use this in my home? A model of domestic social robot acceptance. Hum.-Comput. Interact. **34**(2), 115–173 (2019)

18. Hancock, P.A., Billings, D.R., Schaefer, K.E., Chen, J.Y., De Visser, E.J., Parasuraman, R.: A meta-analysis of factors affecting trust in human-robot interaction. Hum. Factors **53**(5), 517–527 (2011)

19. Kirby, R., Simmons, R., Forlizzi, J.: Companion: a constraint optimizing method for person-acceptable navigation. In: IEEE International Symposium on Robot and Human Interactive Communication (RO-MAN), pp. 607–612, September 2009

20. Koay, K.L., Syrdal, D.S., Walters, M.L., Dautenhahn, K.: Living with robots: investigating the habituation effect in participants' preferences during a longitudinal human-robot interaction study. In: Proceedings - IEEE International Workshop on Robot and Human Interactive Communication, pp. 564–569 (2007)

21. Koay, K.L., Syrdal, D., Bormann, R., Saunders, J., Walters, M.L., Dautenhahn, K.: Initial design, implementation and technical evaluation of a context-aware proxemics planner for a social robot. In: Kheddar, A., et al. (eds.) ICSR 2017. LNCS, vol. 10652, pp. 12–22. Springer, Cham (2017). https://doi.org/10.1007/978-3-319-70022-9_2

22. Lee, J.D., See, K.A.: Trust in automation: designing for appropriate reliance. Hum. Factors: J. Hum. Factors Ergon. Soc. **46**(1), 50–80 (2004)

23. Ljungblad, S., Kotrbova, J., Jacobsson, M., Cramer, H., Niechwiadowicz, K.: Hospital robot at work: Something alien or an intelligent colleague? In: Proceedings of the ACM 2012 Conference on Computer Supported Cooperative Work, CSCW 2012, pp. 177–186. ACM, New York (2012)

24. Mason, E., Nagabandi, A., Steinfeld, A., Bruggeman, C.: Trust during robot-assisted navigation. In: 2013 AAAI Spring Symposium Series (2013)

25. Mitka, E., Gasteratos, A., Kyriakoulis, N., Mouroutsos, S.G.: Safety certification requirements for domestic robots. Safety Sci. **50**(9), 1888–1897 (2012)

26. Mumm, J., Mutlu, B.: Human-robot proxemics: physical and psychological distancing in human-robot interaction. In: Proceedings of the 6th International Conference on Human-Robot Interaction, pp. 331–338. ACM (2011)

27. Myers, C.D., Tingley, D.: The influence of emotion on trust. Polit. Anal. **24**(4), 492–500 (2017). https://doi.org/10.1093/pan/mpw026

28. Pacchierotti, E., Christensen, H.I., Jensfelt, P.: Design of an office-guide robot for social interaction studies. In: 2006 IEEE/RSJ International Conference on Intelligent Robots and Systems, pp. 4965–4970. IEEE (2006)

29. Pacchierotti, E., Christensen, H.I., Jensfelt, P.: Embodied social interaction for service robots in hallway environments. In: Corke, P., Sukkariah, S. (eds.) Field and Service Robotics. STAR, vol. 25, pp. 293–304. Springer, Berlin (2006). https://doi.org/10.1007/978-3-540-33453-8_25

30. Pandey, A., Gelin, R.: A mass-produced sociable humanoid robot: pepper: the first machine of its kind. In: IEEE Robotics Automation Magazine, p. 1 (2018)

31. Rios-Martinez, J., Spalanzani, A., Laugier, C.: From proxemics theory to socially-aware navigation: a survey. Int. J. Soc. Robot. **7**(2), 137–153 (2015)

32. Rossi, A., Dautenhahn, K., Koay, K., Walters, M.L.: The impact of peoples' personal dispositions and personalities on their trust of robots in an emergency scenario **9**(1), 137–154 (2018). https://doi.org/10.1515/pjbr-2018-0010

33. Rossi, A., Dautenhahn, K., Koay, K.L., Saunders, J.: Investigating human perceptions of trust in robots for safe HRI in home environments. In: Proceedings of the Companion of the 2017 ACM/IEEE International Conference on Human-Robot Interaction HRI 2017, pp. 375–376. ACM, New York (2017)

34. Salem, M., Lakatos, G., Amirabdollahian, F., Dautenhahn, K.: Would you trust a (faulty) robot? Effects of error, task type and personality on human-robot cooperation and trust. In: Proceedings of the Tenth Annual ACM/IEEE International Conference on Human-Robot Interaction, pp. 141–148. ACM (2015)

35. Sarkar, S., Araiza-Illan, D., Eder, K.: Effects of faults, experience, and personality on trust in a robot co-worker. arXiv preprint arXiv:1703.02335 (2017)

36. Wang, N., Pynadath, D.V., Hill, S.G., Ground, A.P.: Building trust in a human-robot team with automatically generated explanations. In: Proceedings of the Interservice/Industry Training, Simulation and Education Conference (I/ITSEC), vol. 15315, pp. 1–12 (2015)

37. Wang, Y., Humphrey, L.R., Liao, Z., Zheng, H.: Trust-based multi-robot symbolic motion planning with a human-in-the-loop. arXiv preprint arXiv:1808.05120 (2018)

38. Youakim, D., Ridao, P.: Motion planning survey for autonomous mobile manipulators underwater manipulator case study. Robot. Auton. Syst. **107**, 20–44 (2018)

39. Yu, K., Berkovsky, S., Taib, R., Conway, D., Zhou, J., Chen, F.: User trust dynamics: an investigation driven by differences in system performance, vol. 126745, pp. 307–317. ACM (2017)

40. Zhang, B., Nakamura, T., Kaneko, M.: A framework for adaptive motion control of autonomous sociable guide robot. IEEJ Trans. Electr. Electron. Eng. **11**(6), 786–795 (2016)

A Dataset for Action Recognition in the Wild

Alexander Gabriel[(✉)], Serhan Coşar, Nicola Bellotto, and Paul Baxter

Lincoln Centre For Autonomous Systems (L-CAS),
University of Lincoln, Lincoln, UK
{agabriel,scosar,nbellotto,pbaxter}@lincoln.ac.uk
https://lcas.lincoln.ac.uk

Abstract. The development of autonomous robots for agriculture depends on a successful approach to recognize user needs as well as datasets reflecting the characteristics of the domain. Available datasets for 3D Action Recognition generally feature controlled lighting and framing while recording subjects from the front. They mostly reflect good recording conditions and therefore fail to account for the highly variable conditions the robot would have to work with in the field, e.g. when providing in-field logistic support for human fruit pickers as in our scenario. Existing work on Intention Recognition mostly labels plans or actions as intentions, but neither of those fully capture the extend of human intent. In this work, we argue for a holistic view on human Intention Recognition and propose a set of recording conditions, gestures and behaviors that better reflect the environment and conditions an agricultural robot might find itself in. We demonstrate the utility of the dataset by means of evaluating two human detection methods: bounding boxes and skeleton extraction.

Keywords: Agricultural robotics · Dataset ·
Human-robot interaction · Intention recognition · Action Recognition

1 Introduction

An agricultural robot has to co-operate with human field workers efficiently, comfortably, and safely. To perform in this setting, the robot needs to understand the intentions behind worker behaviour and basic communication: with a desire to maintain reliability in challenging environments, gestures form an ideal medium.

Developing an Intention Recognition (IR) system for an autonomous, agricultural robot, requires a dataset relevant to task and domain. The agricultural setting differs substantially from the settings present in many existing datasets

Supported by the RASberry project (https://rasberryproject.com), and the CTP for Fruit Crop Research (www.ctp-fcr.org).

and the disambiguation challenges inherent to IR suggest a selection of behaviors, which includes actions that cannot be uniquely matched to an intention without taking into account additional information. This takes the task beyond Action Recognition (AR).

Existing datasets for 3D AR are often recorded under optimized lighting conditions, exhibit few if any artifacts, and show the subject well framed and conveniently oriented. An autonomous robot operating around the year in a field cannot rely on such consistent conditions and so our algorithms must be able to perform well in a less-optimized environment. The dataset we present in this work models such suboptimal conditions. Recordings at multiple distances, a natural background, changing weather, and a variety of clothing styles combine to model a wide range of detection challenges.

The term *intention* is used in various ways throughout the literature, which can be characterized in three main groups. In the first, an intention is synonymous with an action i.e., a series of movements with an atomic purpose like e.g. picking up a glass or turning right [7,27]. In the second, an intention is synonymous with a wish [23] or demand [22], command [13], intended meaning [5,26], goal [11,12,23], plan [16,23], or a goal-plan pair [14], where a plan is a series of actions that changes the state of the environment to a goal state. In the third group, an intention is the meaning [8] of, explanation [28] for, or idea [32] behind an action, plan or utterance.

We see our work as consistent with this third group. Our position is that intentions are not Actions, and that they can neither be observed directly nor unequivocally inferred from movement. The same movement might be performed with different intents, e.g. someone might rub their hands to either warm or clean them or to put on some lotion. The same intent might also lead to different movements being performed, e.g. two people congratulating each other might fist-bump, high-five, or shake hands.

Fig. 1. Left: robot (SAGA Robotics Thorvald II) in front of our poly-tunnels. **Middle:** sensor setup used in the recording. **Right:** robot collecting crates of fruit. **Bottom:** experimental setup: an actor performing actions and behaviors at various distances from the robot.

Intentions can also not be directly equated to Plans or Goals, as doing this disregards the possibility that the same Plan could be followed to the same Goal in service of different higher-level intentions. Taking into account contextual information should enable an understanding of other agents that surpasses Plan or Goal Recognition. We call the task of discerning intentions in the face of these ambiguities *Intention Recognition*.

The dataset we propose contains behaviors that exhibit these ambiguities, e.g. the act of pointing at something is inherently ambiguous in terms of intent. Although it is clear, that the pointing individual wants to draw attention to something in some direction, both the specific target as well as the reason for why they want to draw attention to it might be far from obvious.

The main contributions of this work are twofold. Firstly, we provide a new dataset for outdoor people and action detection[1], which is recorded by a robot in a setting consistent with our agricultural target domain (see Fig. 1). Secondly, we propose a methodology for the creation of such datasets, which takes into account the specific features of robot, task, and environment.

In Sect. 2 we will give an overview of related work before introducing the dataset in Sect. 3 and demonstrating two applications in Sect. 4.

2   Related Work

Existing datasets for AR come in basically two varieties: smaller, purposefully recorded datasets featuring good framing, lighting and often multiple sensors on the one side and significantly larger datasets, collected from YouTube and therefore limited to 2D video, but featuring a large variety of recording conditions, subjects, and action classes on the other side. Tables 1 and 2 give an overview of popular datasets. *Classes* gives the number of different action classes a dataset consists of, *Reps* refers to the number of samples collected per class and subject.

Popular datasets for AR from 3D joints or depth video all fall into the first category. Action classes found in this category mostly consist of basic movement, basic interaction with objects [30,31] (picking up, dropping, tossing) and people [4,33] (hugging, kissing, shaking hands, punching, kicking) but also include domain specific classes, e.g. personal hygiene [24], eating/drinking [24], donning/doffing clothes and accessories [24,29], office-style interactions (reading, writing, using laptops, phones) [24], and Wii-like menu navigation and gaming [3,9,19]. The action topic has a significant influence on the subset of actions covered by a dataset. Sensor data provided usually includes 2–3 takes of RGB+D video and 3D-joint positions as produced by the Microsoft Kinect v1 or v2, the NTU RGB+D [24] dataset additionally provides infrared video. A few datasets in this class (e.g. NTU RGB+D [24], Northwestern-UCLA [29]) feature simultaneous recordings from multiple viewpoints.

Although most of the work in this area has focussed on full-body skeletons and various human activities, there are also datasets with a special focus on

---

[1] The dataset is available upon request at https://lcas.lincoln.ac.uk/wp/research/data-sets-software/outdoor-action-intention-recognition-dataset-rasberry/.

Table 1. Overview of 3D AR Datasets

Dataset	Classes	Subjects	Reps	Topics
MSR Action 3D [19]	20	10	2–3	Gaming, general movement
MSR DailyActivity [30]	16	16	2	General movement, object interaction
MSR Gesture 3D [18]	12	10	2–3	Sign language symbols
MSRC-12 Kinect [9]	12	30	4–5	Gaming
SBU dataset [33]	8	21 pairs	1–2	Human and item interaction
UTKinect-Action [31]	10	10	2	General movement, object interaction
Northwestern-UCLA [29]	10	10	4–5	Clothes, general movement, objects
UTD-MHAD [3]	27	8	4	Wii-like menu navigation, gaming
L-CAS 3D Social [4]	8	10 pairs	1	Social interaction
NTU RGB+D [24]	60	40	2	Clothes, food, general movement, gestures, human interaction, hygiene

Table 2. Overview of 2D AR Datasets

Dataset	Classes	Samples	Topics
HMDB-51 [17]	51	6,849 videos	Face actions, human interaction, general movement, sports
UCF-101 [25]	101	13,320 videos	Cooking, hobby, hygiene, housework, sports, musical instruments
MPII Human Pose [1]	410	25,000 images	Hobby, household, hygiene, occupations, musical instruments, sports, transportation
Sports-1M [15]	487	1,133,158 videos	Sports

communicative gestures like we require for our use case. Examples of this are the MSR Gesture 3D [18] dataset, which provides 12 categories of gestures from the American Sign Language (ASL), and the MSRC-12 Kinect [9] dataset, which consists of 12 gestures for interaction with a video game console.

In the pursuit of high-quality data, work in this category generally has tried to optimize recording conditions like the background, illumination, location, and the distance to the subject. This leads to 3D-joint trajectories close to the actual movement but limits the transferability of algorithmic results to settings like ours, which differ significantly from these optimized conditions.

The second group of datasets was created for AR from 2D videos, generally using Deep Neural Networks. As they don't require multimodal data, researchers can make use of publicly available video sources like YouTube and therefore achieve a much wider variety of subjects and recording conditions, as well as larger numbers of samples. Subjects in these datasets are recorded at different distances and angles, as well as under a great variety of lighting conditions. The datasets additionally feature a generally larger number of action classes (51–487).

Samples of general movement and human interaction can be found in the HMDB-51 [17] dataset. More specialized action classes like occupations, hobbies, personal hygiene, playing a wide variety of musical instruments, or using various kinds of transport—all can be found in the MPII Human Pose [1] and UCF-101 [25] datasets where the former focusses on good framing in a mix of outdoor and indoor environments and features special face-related actions (e.g. smiling, smoking, talking, chewing), while the latter sports big variation in recording conditions. Even more specialized is the Sports-1M [15] dataset, featuring 487 different classes of sportive activities.

Despite the wide variety of action classes in 2D AR datasets, there are still no action classes fitting the agricultural domain and the limitation to 2D data is a definite downside in a setting where changing illumination, weather and background make the combination of multiple different sensors highly beneficial.

3   The Dataset

The construction of the dataset was guided by two principles. First, a set of discrete actions was chosen to be consistent with the purpose and application domain of the dataset. This incorporated both actions directly related to the activities undertaken by human fruit-pickers and actions with communicative and interactive intent relevant to the domain. The robot needs to interpret both types correctly: activities (such as walking and crate manipulation) are important clues as to the state of human co-workers, gestures (to ensure robot approach and retreat for example) may be interpreted as commands. Consistent with the definition of intentions we have committed to above, these gestures (in particular pointing) do not necessarily correspond to a unique underlying intention.

Second, a structure for the recording process was established, such that a range of aspects could be systematically characterized. This included the use of multiple subjects performing the same set of actions over the same defined set of distances from the recording robot.

The application of these two principles provides a dataset creation methodology that produced an annotated set of ground-truthed, discrete actions, relevant to the agricultural application domain. The dataset can form the basis for evaluation and testing of human and action/intention recognition algorithms, as we demonstrate below.

3.1   Features

The dataset was recorded on a piece of grassland, under varying lighting conditions (sunny, cloudy, morning to afternoon) and at distances ranging from 5 m to 50 m. The robot used for recording was equipped with a range of sensors that produced data for the dataset, including RGB+D and thermal images,

Fig. 2. Examples of varying light and weather conditions during the recording of the dataset (top). And an indication of resolution of a human at increasing distance from the camera, highlighting the human detection problem over longer distances (bottom).

and 3D LIDAR. We recorded 10 actors, performing every activity once at each distance. All participants provided written informed consent, with followed ethical approval from the University of Lincoln College of Science Research Ethics Committee (approval ID: CoSREC459). Behaviors were performed facing away from the robot, facing to the side and towards the robot for a basic coverage of different directions. A list of activities can be found in Table 3. An overview of distances is shown in Fig. 2. After recording, each frame up to 25 m distance was labeled with distance, actor ID, action and the direction the actor was facing. Labeling at further distances was hampered due to the actor being too small in the frame (see Fig. 2).

Gestures and Activities. Being able to detect different behaviors allows the robot to learn a model of the activities of each individual worker which allows it to predict the timing of future support requests. We chose a range of behaviors observable from human fruit-pickers at work, and a set of gestures we deem helpful for basic communication over distances between 10 and 50 m. To be able to direct the robot's attention to the worker in need of support, we selected a waving and a pointing gesture. For comfortable and efficient loading of the robot, we want to direct it to a preferred stopping distance. To this end, we selected the beckoning, stop and shoo gestures. For basic feedback purposes, we further included a thumbs-up/down gesture and a variant using the lower arm instead of the thumb, which should be easier to detect at greater distances.

The choice of activities is inspired by our application, the collection of fruit crates from human field workers and transportation of said crates to a cooling facility outside the field. The most common activities in this domain are (besides the picking of berries) walking and turning around, crouching down, and standing up—each of these activities occurs with free hands and while carrying a crate.

Table 3 shows the average duration for each action and behavior, as well as their descriptions. The individual actions have relatively short (<4 s) durations and many of them (such as waving, shooing or the 'come here' gesture) consist

Table 3. Table: characteristics of the set of actions. **Images:** example gestures recorded with RGB (left) and thermal (right) cameras.

Activity	Duration [s]	Description
wave	3.73	With the upper arm
come	2.20	stretched out to the
stop	2.25	side or front,
shoo	2.22	the subject performs
thumb up	1.71	the respective motion
thumb down	1.90	with their hand.
arm up	1.92	
arm down	2.09	
point 0°	1.92	The subject stretches
point 45°	1.91	their upper arm
point 90°	2.00	out to the front
point 135°	1.82	with fist clenched
point 180°	1.81	except for the
point 225°	1.88	index finger which
point 270°	1.99	is also outstretched.
point 315°	1.63	
crate up side	1.30	The subject is standing up
crate down side	1.21	or crouching down while
crate up toward	1.11	holding a crate. They are
crate down toward	1.34	facing either away or
crate up away	1.29	towards the camera,
crate down away	1.83	or to the side.
walk away	3.20	
walk away (crate)	2.20	

of many, much shorter, movements. A system running motion-based AR on this dataset will have to perform at a challengingly high framerate in order to capture these movements.

3.2   Characteristics

Recording the dataset outside, resulted in a number of characteristics differentiating it from indoor datasets. Outside, the robot and its sensors are subjected to influences from the environment in a variety of ways. In sunny weather, the robot accumulates heat due to the sun's radiation. Insects are then attracted to this new heat source and while buzzing around the robot, fly across the field of view of its sensors (see Fig. 3). This results in artifacts that might influence detection algorithms.

But there is not only sunny weather, our recording encompasses stable sunny and cloudy conditions as well as rapidly changing cloud cover (see Fig. 2). These influence brightness, hue, saturation as well as the harshness of shadows present in RGB video recordings. Another weather factor is wind, which will distort the recorded body shape either due to its effect on loose clothing or hair. Higher wind

Fig. 3. Occlusions due to environmental conditions; in this case flies close to the robot.

speeds than those present during our recordings can force humans to adapt their movement to the horizontal force being applied to them and thus significantly changes movement patterns.

Range further has a significant influence on the performance of detection algorithms, since subjects further away are captured at a lower resolution (see Fig. 2). To capture this effect we recorded data from 5 m to 50 m, which reduces the number of pixels per subject by the square of the magnification factor.

For the characterization we combined the hand-gesture classes (wave, come, stop, shoo, thumb-up, thumb-down) into a single class (hand_gesture), as the skeleton models we use do not support explicit hand detection. Detection of individual fingers at longer distances is ultimately complicated by limited sensor resolution.

While the dataset does not contain occlusions from objects in the environment, it does contain self-occlusions and those due to the presence of the crate. As this does not entirely reflect the nature of agricultural environments (where plants and other agricultural equipment may reduce visibility), this is an area for addressing in further data collection efforts.

4   Applications

In order to demonstrate the utility of our dataset, we use it to evaluate two methods for human detection: bounding boxes, and skeleton extraction. In both cases, established algorithms are applied to RGB images from the dataset, with performance evaluated. The systematic recording methodology used facilitates a rigorous characterization of performance in both cases.

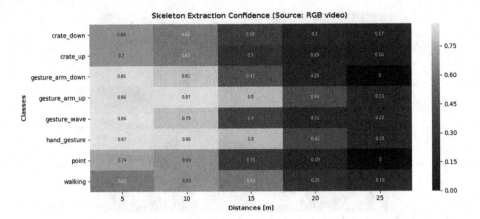

Fig. 4. Average Skeleton detection confidence from ZED RGB+D camera sensor (single RGB video) source on the right. Distances on the X-axis from 5 m to 25 m, confidence values ranging from 0 to 1. Notable here is the expected loss of extraction confidence with increasing distance. For a more detailed analysis and comparison to skeletons extracted from thermal false-color video, refer to [10].

4.1   Skeleton Extraction

We tested extracting 2D skeletons from RGB images[2], up to 25 m. The skeletons were extracted using a deep-learning based multi-person skeleton extractor called OpenPose [2].

The average confidence score for skeleton extraction shown in Fig. 4 are averages over the confidence scores produced by OpenPose for each skeleton over the duration of an action at various distances. OpenPose returns confidence scores between 0 and 1.

The data shows significantly better skeleton extraction for action classes where the actor is facing the camera (wave, hand and arm gestures) compared to classes where the actor is facing to the side or away (crate actions, pointing) for a part of the sample set. This results from self-occlusion of the further body side occurring in the side views and self-occlusion of the arms when the actor is performing some action while facing away from the camera. As expected, the extraction confidence progressively diminishes with distance, as the number of pixels covering the subject grows smaller (see Fig. 2).

4.2   Bounding Box Fitting

We have also tested extracting 2D bounding boxes from RGB images to identify humans. We used a deep-learning-based single-shot object detector called YOLOv3 [21]. The detector is run using the pre-trained model for the COCO dataset [20].

---

[2] As well as false-color thermal images. For results on these, and a more detailed comparison with the RGB results, see [10].

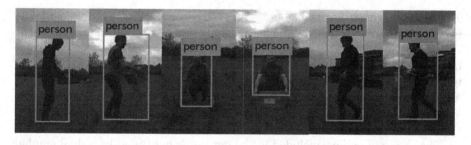

Fig. 5. Examples of person detection whilst performing actions with crates, using the YOLOv3 algorithm.

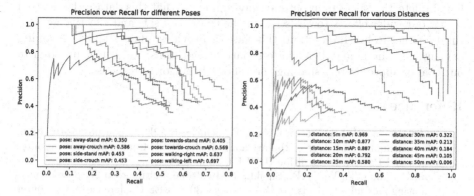

Fig. 6. Precision-Recall curves of person detector for various poses and distances.

Figure 5 shows some examples of person detection using YOLOv3. We evaluated the performance of the person detector by running on 800 annotated images from the dataset (see Sect. 3). Following the PASCAL Visual Object Classes Challenge [6], the precision and recall rates are calculated by assuming a correct detection, if the area of overlap a_o between the predicted bounding box B_p and ground truth bounding box B_{gt} exceeds 50%.

Figure 6 presents the Precision-Recall curves for various poses and distances, respectively. We can see that person detection works best when people walk laterally. The worst performance is obtained when people face away from the robot. We can also see that after 25 m, the algorithm fails to detect people, highlighting an area for prospective improvement in outdoor environments.

5   Conclusion

Our case studies (see Sect. 4) show that bounding box extraction is less susceptible to large distances compared to skeleton extraction but ultimately fails as well. It performs best when the subject is walking laterally and worst when the subject is standing. Subject orientation does not have an influence on the performance of bounding box extraction, it does however affect skeleton extraction.

This is to be expected as facing away from the camera occludes individual joints for the gestures and behaviors we have chosen. For a more detailed analysis of the skeleton extraction and a comparison with skeletons extracted from false-color images recorded by a thermal camera, see [10]. The results of our experiments together suggest that the use of multiple different sensors has the potential to achieve more robust detection performance over a greater variety of conditions. This demonstrates the utility of the systematic approach to the dataset creation that we have employed here.

The choice of actions included in the dataset is motivated by a dual emphasis on AR and IR (hence the hand-gestures, pointing, etc.) and the agricultural context (hence the crate actions). While in this paper we have focused on the human detection aspects in outdoor environments, that this dataset lends itself to, for our wider efforts towards IR (in the context of safe and effective agricultural Human-Robot Interaction) this dataset provides a first step to the ability of characterizing human behavior estimation algorithms, and brings us closer to our goal of appropriately shaping the robot's behavior in response.

References

1. Andriluka, M., Pishchulin, L., Gehler, P., Schiele, B.: 2D human pose estimation: new benchmark and state of the art analysis. In: IEEE Conference on Computer Vision and Pattern Recognition (CVPR), June 2014
2. Cao, Z., Simon, T., Wei, S.E., Sheikh, Y.: Realtime multi-person 2D pose estimation using part affinity fields. In: Proceedings - 30th IEEE Conference on Computer Vision and Pattern Recognition 2017, pp. 1302–1310, January 2017
3. Chen, C., Jafari, R., Kehtarnavaz, N.: UTD-MHAD: a multimodal dataset for human action recognition utilizing a depth camera and a wearable inertial sensor. In: Proceedings of the IEEE International Conference on Image Processing, pp. 168–172, September 2015
4. Coppola, C., Faria, D., Nunes, U., Bellotto, N.: Social activity recognition based on probabilistic merging of skeleton features with proximity priors from RGB-D data. In: Proceedings of IEEE/RSJ International Conference on Intelligent Robots and Systems, pp. 5055–5061 (2016)
5. Elzer, S., Carberry, S., Zukerman, I., Chester, D., Green, N., Demir, S.: A probabilistic framework for recognizing intention in information graphics. In: Proceedings of the International Joint Conference on Artificial Intelligence, pp. 1042–1047 (2005)
6. Everingham, M., Eslami, S.M.A., Van Gool, L., Williams, C.K.I., Winn, J., Zisserman, A.: The pascal visual object classes challenge: a retrospective. Int. J. Comput. Vis. 111(1), 98–136 (2015)
7. Fernandez, V., Balaguer, C., Blanco, D., Salichs, M.A.: Active human-mobile manipulator cooperation through intention recognition. In: Proceedings of the 2001 IEEE International Conference on Robotics and Automation, pp. 2668–2673 (2001)
8. Fleischman, M., Roy, D.: Why verbs are harder to learn than nouns: initial insights from a computational model of intention recognition in situated word learning. In: Proceedings of the Annual Meeting of the Cognitive Science Society (2005)
9. Fothergill, S., Mentis, H., Kohli, P., Nowozin, S.: Instructing people for training gestural interactive systems. In: Proceedings of the SIGCHI Conference on Human Factors in Computing Systems, CHI 2012, pp. 1737–1746. ACM, New York (2012)

10. Gabriel, A., Bellotto, N., Baxter, P.: Towards a dataset of activities for action recognition on open fields. In: Proceedings of the UKRAS 2019 Conference on Embedded Intelligence (2019, to be published)

11. Giersich, M., Kirste, T.: Effects of agendas on model-based intention inference of cooperative teams. In: Proceedings of the International Conference on Collaborative Computing: Networking, Applications and Worksharing, pp. 456–463 (2007)

12. Haigh, K.Z., Geib, C.W., Miller, C.A., Phelps, J., Wagner, T.: Agents for recognizing and responding to the behaviour of an elder. In: Proceedings of the AAAI-02 Workshop Automation as Caregiver, pp. 31–38 (2002)

13. Iba, S., Paredis, C.J.J., Khosla, P.K.: Intention aware interactive multi-modal robot programming. In: Proceedings of the 2003 IEEE/RSJ International Conference on Intelligent Robots and Systems (2003)

14. Kanno, T., Nakata, K., Furuta, K.: A method for team intention inference. Int. J. Hum.-Comput. Stud. **58**(4), 393–413 (2003)

15. Karpathy, A., Toderici, G., Shetty, S., Leung, T., Sukthankar, R., Fei-Fei, L.: Large-scale video classification with convolutional neural networks. In: CVPR (2014)

16. Kiefer, P., Stein, K.: A framework for mobile intention recognition in spatially structured environments. In: Proceedings of the 2008 Workshop on Behaviour Monitoring and Interpretation, pp. 28–41 (2008)

17. Kuehne, H., Jhuang, H., Garrote, E., Poggio, T., Serre, T.: HMDB: a large video database for human motion recognition. In: Proceedings of the International Conference on Computer Vision (ICCV) (2011)

18. Kurakin, A., Zhang, Z., Liu, Z.: A real time system for dynamic hand gesture recognition with a depth sensor. In: 2012 Proceedings of the 20th European Signal Processing Conference (EUSIPCO), pp. 1975–1979. IEEE (2012)

19. Li, W., Zhang, Z., Liu, Z.: Action recognition based on a bag of 3D points. In: 2010 IEEE Computer Society Conference on Computer Vision and Pattern Recognition - Workshops, pp. 9–14, June 2010

20. Lin, T.-Y., et al.: Microsoft COCO: common objects in context. In: Fleet, D., Pajdla, T., Schiele, B., Tuytelaars, T. (eds.) ECCV 2014. LNCS, vol. 8693, pp. 740–755. Springer, Cham (2014). https://doi.org/10.1007/978-3-319-10602-1_48

21. Redmon, J., Farhadi, A.: Yolov3: an incremental improvement. arXiv (2018)

22. Schrempf, O.C., Hanebeck, U.D.: A generic model for estimating user intentions in human-robot cooperation. In: Proceedings of the 2nd International Conference on Informatics in Control, Automation and Robotics, vol. 3, pp. 251–256 (2005)

23. Schrempf, O.C., Schmid, A.J., Hanebeck, U.D., Wörn, H.: A Novel Approach To Proactive Human-Robot Cooperation. In: Proceedings of the IEEE International Workshop on Robot and Human Interactive Communication, pp. 555–560 (2005)

24. Shahroudy, A., Liu, J., Ng, T.T., Wang, G.: NTU RGB+D: a large scale dataset for 3D human activity analysis. In: Proceedings of the IEEE Conference on Computer Vision and Pattern Recognition, pp. 1010–1019 (2016)

25. Soomro, K., Zamir, A.R., Shah, M.: UCF101: a dataset of 101 human actions classes from videos in the wild, November 2012

26. Sykes, E.R., Franek, F.: Inside the Java intelligent tutoring system prototype: parsing student code submissions with intent recognition edward. In: Proceedings of the 2004 International Conference on Computers and Advanced Technology in Education, pp. 613–618 (2004)

27. Tahboub, K.: Intention recognition of a human commanding a mobile robot. In: Proceedings of the 2004 IEEE Conference on Cybernetics and Intelligent Systems, vol. 2, pp. 896–901 (2004)

28. Tahboub, K.A.: Intelligent human-machine interaction based on dynamic bayesian networks probabilistic intention recognition. J. Intell. Robot. Syst.: Theory Appl. **45**(1), 31–52 (2006)
29. Wang, J., Nie, X., Xia, Y., Wu, Y., Zhu, S.: Cross-view action modeling, learning, and recognition. In: 2014 IEEE Conference on Computer Vision and Pattern Recognition, pp. 2649–2656, June 2014
30. Wang, J., Liu, Z., Wu, Y., Yuan, J.: Mining actionlet ensemble for action recognition with depth cameras. In: 2012 IEEE Conference on Computer Vision and Pattern Recognition, pp. 1290–1297. IEEE (2012)
31. Xia, L., Chen, C., Aggarwal, J.K.: View invariant human action recognition using histograms of 3D joints. In: 2012 IEEE Computer Society Conference on Computer Vision and Pattern Recognition Workshops, pp. 20–27, June 2012
32. Youn, S., Oh, K.: Intention recognition using a graph representation. Int. J. Appl. Sci. Eng. Technol. **4**(1), 13–18 (2007)
33. Yun, K., Honorio, J., Chattopadhyay, D., Berg, T.L., Samaras, D.: Two-person interaction detection using body-pose features and multiple instance learning. In: 2012 IEEE Computer Society Conference on Computer Vision and Pattern Recognition Workshops (CVPRW). IEEE (2012)

Feel It on Your Fingers: Dataglove with Vibrotactile Feedback for Virtual Reality and Telerobotics

Burathat Junput, Xuyi Wei, and Lorenzo Jamone[✉]

ARQ (Advanced Robotics at Queen Mary), School of Electronic Engineering
and Computer Science, Queen Mary University of London, London, UK
b.junput@se15.qmul.ac.uk, x.wei@se16.qmul.ac.uk,
l.jamone@qmul.ac.uk

Abstract. With the rise of Virtual Reality (VR) applications it is interesting to see how immersion can be improved, especially by providing haptic feedback on the user hands, using affordable technologies. Indeed, while several commercial products exist that can be used as input devices (i.e. from the user to the virtual reality), such as data gloves or optical trackers, solutions for effective feedback (i.e. from the virtual reality to the user) are still lacking, especially at low prices. We describe here the design and realization of an affordable data glove to provide vibrotactile feedback to human users using small vibrating motors, and we report preliminary user studies to prove its effectiveness; interestingly, combined with a commercially available optical tracker (i.e. Leap Motion) to be used as input device, the data glove can be used in a wide range of Virtual Reality and Telerobotics applications. User studies include (i) rendering a feedback to multiple fingers at the same time, and recording how many stimuli the users could correctly differentiate, and (ii) simulating the stiffness of a virtual object, and testing through a Just Noticeable Difference (JND) experiment whether participants could differentiate two objects chosen among 20 pairs of objects with varying stiffness. It was found that participants (i) can easily detect simultaneous feedback on up to two fingers, but struggle to precisely localize feedback on more than three fingers, and they (ii) can differentiate virtual objects of different stiffness by virtually "squeezing" them, up to a certain JND.

Keywords: Vibrotactile feedback · Data glove · Vibration frequency · JND · Positional difference · Frequency mappings · Stiffness · Telerobotics

1 Introduction

Humans are capable of experiencing the world through five senses: sight, smell, taste, hearing and touch. Machines which interact with humans can also experience or act upon the world via these senses as well, however, much of the electronic machines developed during the 20th century lent itself to only two of these senses: visual and audio interactions [1, 2]. It is only recently with the rise in virtual reality (VR) technology where the touch aspect (i.e. haptic feedback) has begun to be of interest to consumers [3]. Haptic feedback is the application of the sensation of touch on a human

© Springer Nature Switzerland AG 2019
K. Althoefer et al. (Eds.): TAROS 2019, LNAI 11649, pp. 375–385, 2019.
https://doi.org/10.1007/978-3-030-23807-0_31

via a force feedback [4] and it is imperative for immersive telerobotic operations in virtual or physical reality [5]. The use of haptic feedback in systems can range from audio-visual editing, multimedia publishing, vehicular operations, control rooms etc. [6]. In terms of telerobotic operations within virtual reality (VR), the inclusion of tactile perception summed with the innate kinaesthetic perception of VR creates a more immersive environment, attributed to the multi-dimensional information relayed to users [4].

The use of vibrotactile feedback on finger tips have been investigated extensively for almost half a decade now [7]. Generally the investigation of the vibrations are to do with how we distinguish between vibrations and how we perceive them. Currently the controllers used to simulate human hands in VR do not lend themselves very well to immersion, as an example the controllers for an Oculus Rift simply have triggers on them for grabbing and releasing objects [8]. This does not fully represent the complexity and versatility of the human hand as it cannot vary the force at which we can grip objects nor does it allow the possibility of simulating the 'feel' of the object [9]. There are wearable data gloves out on the market which can interface with VR technology, however, these devices are quite expensive and they do not have readily available user studies so their reliability for immersion is uncertain [10]. Therefore this project will propose a cheaper alternative made from readily available commercial products and incorporate a user study on vibrotactile feedback.

2   State of the Art

Reports investigating the application of vibrotactile feedback on finger tips have existed for almost 50 years [7], however, as technology improves, the conclusions drawn from the experimentation setup of earlier reports may not reflect the trends found in more recent experiments. In addition to this the experimental setups are not set up for a more compact use and although they are generally quite similar [7, 11–15], they are not the same as there are varying factors between them which could affect results across various papers e.g. angle of the finger, proportion of fingertip placed on surface, age etc. [12]. Due to the large size of the technology it may be noted that the conclusions drawn from the experiments may not translate to a portable device. One way in which vibrotactile feedback can help in immersion is to replicate the sensation of touching an object. When using a finger to scan a surface distinctions can be made between textures of the surface as vibrations are produced on the surface of the skin and travel through mechanoreceptors [15].

The Meissner and Pacinian Corpuscles are the mechanoreceptors in the fingertips which are responsible for the ability to distinguish between vibrations. The Pacinian corpuscles are responsible for detecting high frequencies above 40 Hz [16] whereas the Meissner corpuscles can detect low frequencies with a maximum peak of 200 Hz [17]. Due to the overlap in frequency ranges between the two corpuscles it could suggest that there is an obtrusive relationship between the two which may affect a participant's ability to distinguish between frequencies, furthermore it suggests that the coding of the two mechanoreceptors may be different [11].

3   Hardware/Software Architecture

3.1   Dataglove System Design

The data glove is made using the LilyPad system [18], a set of Arduino-type micro-controllers used in development of interactive wearable systems. Vibrotactile feedback is provided to the fingertips via a set of six vibe boards (max frequency of 250 Hz) sewn to a Simblee BLE board [19] with conductive thread and a coin cell battery holder to power the board if used wirelessly. Since the LiyPad has a Bluetooth chip, an attempt was made to enable wireless communications between the data glove and computer connected to another Bluetooth LilyPad along the serial port. It was discovered that Arduino-Arduino Bluetooth communication was not useful as the range to connect was very short and communication was not always stable (Fig. 1).

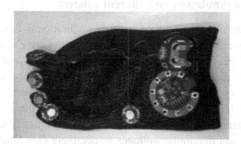

Fig. 1. The completed data glove, with five vibe-motors on the fingertips (left) and one on the side of the palm (bottom center), Simblee board (bottom right) and battery holder (top right).

3.2   Virtual Reality – Object Stiffness Design

The data glove is tracked in real time in a 3D space via a Leap Motion Controller [20] and displayed in virtual reality on a computer. A virtual object is simulated as a spring between the index finger and the thumb. By definition of Hook's law if the displacement between thumb and index finger were to decrease, the force, or in this case the frequency, would increase. Figure 2 displays the human-machine interaction system. A computational node based on the ROS architecture is used to determine the distance between the index finger and thumb and send that data to the data glove. There are 5 distances/ranges which will cause the vibes to change frequency: greater than 75 mm, 75–60 mm, 60–45 mm, 45–30 mm and less than 30 mm; frequencies are mapped to these ranges which increase as the distance gets smaller.

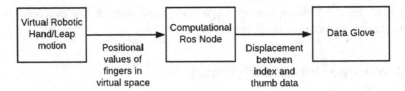

Fig. 2. Human-machine interaction system design

4 Experimental Design

In order to test the effectiveness of the dataglove two usability tests (user studies) were conducted. The first test would be to determine how users perceive stimulus on different fingers. The second test would be to determine the JND of virtual objects with different "stiffness". Before the experiment were conducted we obtained official approval (reference code #1833) from the Queen Mary Research Ethics Committee (QMREC), because of human participants being involved.

4.1 Simultaneous Stimulation on Different Fingers

This test was to determine how users perceive vibrational feedback and how the number of active vibrating motors would influence the user's ability to locate the position of the feedback. There were 10 participants in total, 6 female and 4 male, ages 23–29 and were all students of Queen Mary University of London.

There were two key factors in this test: the level of frequency and the number of simultaneous stimuli (i.e. quantity of stimuli) provided to the user. Each factor was tested at several different levels. The vibe motors a frequency range of 130 Hz to 230 Hz at minimum and maximum voltages respectively (1.8 V and 3.6 V) according to the vibe motor data sheet. As such four different levels of frequency with an increment of 30 were set. For each level of frequency, different number of fingers were given feedback in a random combination and order. The configuration of frequency is displayed in Table 1. Once participants agreed to take part in the experiment they were asked to wear the dataglove appropriately and rest their right arm and hand comfortably on the desk. Noise cancelling headphones were provided to eliminate the sounds from the motor.

Vibrational feedback of the motors was controlled via a separate mobile application developed for the Simblee BLE board. Participants were asked to be seated opposite the examiner and should not see the mobile phone interface. The participants were then allowed a pre-experiment section which allowed them to adapt to the glove. They would feel the different frequencies on each finger. The formal test then begins. At each frequency level, different number of stimuli were provided to the participant in incremental order. First, only one motor would be active at a time and the five motors were turned on once each in a random order. Second, two motors were turned on together, according to Table 1, there are 10 possible combinations in this situation. To prevent the user from being tired of a tedious experimental process, only 5 random combinations were tested. Similarly for the combinations of three and four motors only

5 random combinations were chosen. Finally, all the motors corresponding to the five fingers were turned on together at once. Whenever there was a new active vibrating motor, participants would tell the experimenter which finger or fingers had an active motor. Participants were allowed to take a one-minute break before each frequency test. The whole procedure lasted about 20 min.

Table 1. Configuration of frequency and amount of stimulus

Frequency	Amount of stimulus	Possible combinations
230	1	T; I; M; R; L
200	2	T and I; T and M; T and R; T and L; I and M; I and R; I and L; M and R; M and L; R and L
170	3	T, I and M; T, I and R; T, I and L; T, M and R; T, M and L; T, R and L; I, M and R; I, M and L; I, R and L; M, R and L
140	4	T, I, M and R; T, I, M and L; T, I, R and L; T, M, R and L; I, M, R and L
140	5	T, I, M, R and L

Note: The capital characters T, I, M, R and L represent thumb, index finger, middle finger, ring finger and little finger respectively

4.2 Simulation of the Stiffness of a Virtual Object

Another user study was designed to determine what were the minimum changes to the "stiffness" of virtual objects i.e. the frequencies mapped to the ranges, such that the user can distinguish between two virtual objects (i.e. which one is harder/softer?).

A just noticeable difference (JND) experiment would therefore be appropriate to determine the minimum amount of changes required for it to be noticeable. The following table is a list of suggested mappings of frequencies for the object based upon 5 distinguishable frequencies (0, 140, 170, 200, 230).

With each mapping from the table, one of the ranges in the frequency scale increments by one discrete level of frequency. As an example, going from mapping 1 to mapping 2 means an increment of 1 frequency level as the range of 45–30 is increased to 170 in mapping 2 and going from mapping 1 to mapping 4 means an increase of 3 frequency levels as 60–45, 45–50 and 30 > is incremented by 1 level each. For ease of understanding, the increase in frequency levels will simply be referred to as positional differences (Table 2).

Table 2. Table of suggested mapping of frequencies

Distance (mm)	Map 1 (Hz)	Map 2 (Hz)	Map 3 (Hz)	Map 4 (Hz)	Map 5 (Hz)	Map 6 (Hz)	Map 7 (Hz)	Map 8 (Hz)	Map 9 (Hz)	Map 10 (Hz)
>75	0	0	0	0	0	0	0	0	0	0
75–60	140	140	140	140	170	170	170	170	200	200
60–45	140	140	140	170	170	170	170	200	200	200
45–30	140	170	170	170	170	200	200	200	200	230
30>	170	170	200	200	200	200	230	230	230	230

The proposed setup for the JND experiment was for users to compare 20 randomly chosen pairs of mappings from the table and asked which object they felt was more 'stiff'. The stiffer object in this case being the one with the higher mapping. Since this experiment required a right hand to conduct it was necessary for participants to have control over their right hand. There were 10 participants in total, students and lecturers from the university aged 20–36, were asked to read the information sheet and given a quick reiteration of the experiment by the investigator. Once the participants confirmed they understood what the experiment would be and how the data would be analysed, they were then given a consent form to sign. After this procedure had concluded the experiment began. The experiment was conducted on a laptop PC as this experiment could be conducted anywhere which suited the schedule of participants. Manual switching of the objects was required by the investigator, however, participants were free to move onto the next object or pair whenever they wished, in addition to this they could switch between either object in a pair if they wished to feel the first one again. No time limit was set for this experiment in order for participants to proceed at their own pace although on average the experiment would take anywhere between 20–35 min. If the participant wished to take a small break they were free to do so and resume the experiment after. Participants were given the option to view the hand in 3D space using the visualiser and the distance between the fingers was also given to them. Initially the experiment was to be conducted using the index finger and thumb, however, the participants made note that the index finger was not particularly consistent at vibrating. The index finger was then switched to the middle finger which made the vibrations more consistent as well as making pinching the object feel "more natural" according to the participants.

5 Results and Discussion

5.1 Detection of Feedback on Multiple Fingers

In Experiment 1, participants need to judge which finger or fingers were receiving the vibrational feedback at different vibration frequency levels. To evaluate if the two factors, vibration frequency and the amount of vibration feedback stimulus, had an influence on the perception of the feedback independently, we calculated the judgement accuracy of participants overall on different frequency and stimulus numbers separately. The results of groups and the mean value of the judgement accuracy of each group are shown in Figs. 4 and 5. A one-way analysis of variance (ANOVA) method was used to determine whether there are statistically significant differences among those groups. This process was conducted twice as any significant difference in either factors should be determined (Fig. 3).

Fig. 3. Participant during the second test

As it can be seen in Fig. 4, the average frequencies show a slight declining tendency, which means as the frequency decreases, the judgement accuracy slowly falls down. However, this difference turned out not to be significant, $F = 0.212$, $p = 0.886$ (5% significance level was used in this case). Thus, the level of frequency does not affect participants' perception of positions of stimulus on the dataglove. The standard deviation value at all five frequency levels are relatively stable but quite large, which indicates that the accuracies under different stimulus quantities differ greatly from each other.

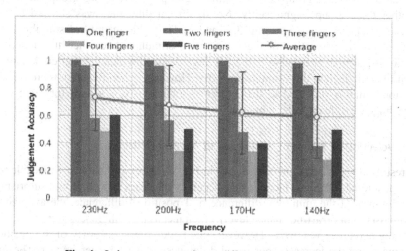

Fig. 4. Judgement accuracies at different frequency levels

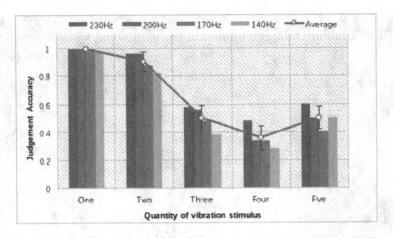

Fig. 5. Judgement accuracies with different number of simultaneous stimuli

Figure 5 illustrates the perception accuracy when subjects received the vibration feedback on different fingers at the same time. As shown in the figure, perception accuracy fluctuates among different groups widely. When there was only one stimulus provided to subjects, the perception accuracies at all frequency levels were showed to be as high as nearly 1, which means almost all participants could tell which finger was feeling the feedback correctly. When there were two stimuli provided to subjects, the average accuracy shows a minor decrease to be 0.905. However, the accuracy sharply goes down to 0.5 or less when the stimulus is provided to 3 fingers or more.

To compare them more precisely, a series of pairwise comparisons were conducted between these groups. The result shows that there was no significant difference between one-stimulus group and two-stimuli group, yet these two groups differ from the other three groups significantly. No significant difference was showed between pairwise comparison among group 3, 4 and 5. Thus, the quantity of stimulus has an influence on the perception of the positions of stimulus. And when the quantity of stimulus is less than or equal to 2, there is large probability that the user could perceive which finger is feeling the stimulus correctly. However, when there are more than two vibration stimulus provided to the wearer simultaneously, it's hard for them to tell which fingers are feeling the vibration

5.2   Detection of Different Stiffnesses of Virtual Objects

The results of the experiment can be seen in Fig. 6. The results show a noticeable trend as the positional difference increases the accuracy increases as well. It was surprising to note that even at the minimum difference of 1 positional difference, the average was still almost 0.5 or 50% (the chance level) which means that differences were most likely not being perceived very well. However, this is the lowest accuracy of the positional differences and the increased positional differences make a bigger impact. The minimum JND is 0.8 which means that the minimum positional difference for a user to notice is 3 positional difference. This could be attributed to the fact that there are 5 ranges where the frequency can change, if the majority (3/5) of the ranges were different from the previous object then it was a lot easier to notice. Therefore it could be concluded that if there is a majority difference in ranges when comparing two objects then it is easier to determine which object was stiffer than the other. From the testing it was found that the synchronisation of the vibes on the middle finger and the thumb were not always consistent which made the testing of the experiment difficult for some of the participants. This also means that the experiment was not without errors. Other errors found in the experiment could be the inaccuracy of the leap motion in response to the amount of IR light in a room leading to incorrect ranges given to users.

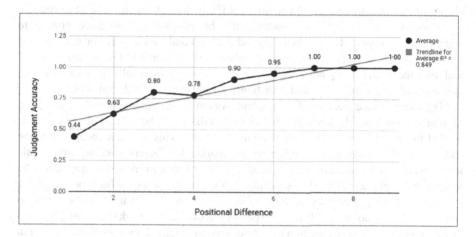

Fig. 6. JND results of the experiment

Other observations include the conductive thread coming loose after vibes had been running for long periods of time. If the user moved their fingers together too quickly, they would skip ranges and thus skip frequency ranges.

Advantages of this feature include the fact that it is also very easy to implement. The majority of the code used to run the feature e.g. the leap motion was already readily available as a package on the site. Although the simulation was not always synchronised the participants made note that it did mimic resistance well.

Improvements to this include rewiring the conductive thread to the vibes and ensure that the thread will not come loose. The synchronisation issue could be fixed by using timestamps and delays to ensure that the changes are processed and not skipped. It is also necessary to repeat the experiment in case the synchronisation issue was a significant factor in affecting the results. In addition to this the experiment should be conducted only in rooms with low levels of IR light to limit the amount affecting the leap motion. In future experiments it might also be of significance to the user if there was a 3D model of the object for them to visualise, it is possible that the 3D visualiser of the hand and the numerical value of the distance between the fingers was not enough to help the user determine the stiffness.

6 Conclusions

Our tests have highlighted some of the features and limitations of the proposed system. Our results show that when the number of simultaneous stimuli on the fingertips was less than 3 most participants could correctly perceive which finger was receiving the feedback; however, with 3 or more stimuli, the perception accuracy decreases sharply. Interestingly, there was no significant difference among groups with different vibration frequency levels. The simulation of stiffness of virtual objects was implemented with success; we verified that a minimum positional difference of 3 in the frequency was necessary for a user to just notice the difference i.e. the majority of the frequencies when comparing objects of varying stiffness should be different if any differences are to be observed.

However, there were small issues with the components we have chosen to implement our system; the Simblee LilyPad is cheap and excellent for broadcasting to multiple users, however, the quality is not always guaranteed and thus consumers may find that the features do not meet the expected level, especially in terms of data synchronisation on the board and data transmission with the BLE protocol.

The approximate cost of the complete system is less than 250 GBP: the Leap Motion is commercially available for about 80 GBP, and the cost of all components needed to assemble the data glove is about 150 GBP. This is much cheaper than the cheapest available systems available on the market for fingers tracking with haptic feedback. Although we have not yet compared our solution to any existing product, the features we implemented work sufficiently well to provide some useful haptic feedback to users, and the preliminary findings of our user tests can be used in the future to compare this technology with more expensive systems, and to drive development in this area. In the next future we aim to test our system in telerobotics applications, and in particular for robot learning by human demonstration. A robotic hand equipped with tactile/force sensors on the fingertips (such as [21] or [22]) can be remotely controlled by the human user to haptically "explore" an object, i.e. to touch different parts of the object while receiving the vibrotactile feedback when contacts are experienced, with the final objective of finding good grasp configurations for the robotic hand; interestingly, the human demonstrations (or, "suggestions") can complement automatic search algorithms, e.g. they can be used as priors for a Bayesian Optimization search [23, 24].

Acknowledgments. This work was partially supported by the EPSRC UK: project NCNR, EP/R02572X/1, and project MAN³, EP/S00453X/1.

References

1. Pantic, M., Rothkrantz, L.J.: Toward an affect-sensitive multimodal human-computer interaction. Proc. IEEE **91**(9), 1370–1390 (2003)
2. Zeng, Z., Pantic, M., Roisman, G.I., Huang, T.S.: A survey of affect recognition methods: audio, visual, and spontaneous expressions. IEEE Trans. Pattern Anal. Mach. Intell. **31**(1), 39–58 (2009)
3. Parsons, S., Cobb, S.: State-of-the-art of virtual reality technologies for children on the autism spectrum. Eur. J. Spec. Needs Educ. **26**(3), 355–366 (2011)

4. Zilles, C.B., Salisbury, J.K.: A constraint-based god-object method for haptic display. In: Proceedings 1995 IEEE/RSJ International Conference on Intelligent Robots and Systems. Human Robot Interaction and Cooperative Robots, vol. 3, pp. 146–151 (1995)

5. Stone, R.J.: Haptic feedback: a brief history from telepresence to virtual reality. In: Brewster, S., Murray-Smith, R. (eds.) Haptic HCI 2000. LNCS, vol. 2058, pp. 1–16. Springer, Heidelberg (2001). https://doi.org/10.1007/3-540-44589-7_1

6. Hayward, V., Astley, O.R., Cruz-Hernandez, M., Grant, D., Robles-De-La-Torre, G.: Haptic interfaces and devices. Sens. Rev. **24**(1), 16–29 (2004)

7. Stevens, S.S.: Tactile vibration: dynamics of sensory intensity. J. Exp. Psychol. **57**(4), 210–218 (1959)

8. Desai, P.R., Desai, P.N., Ajmera, K.D., Mehta, K.: A review paper on oculus rift-a virtual reality headset. arXiv preprint arXiv:1408.1173 (2014)

9. Tan, C.T., Leong, T.W., Shen, S., Dubravs, C., Si, C.: Exploring gameplay experiences on the oculus rift. In: Proceedings of the 2015 Annual Symposium on Computer-Human Interaction in Play, pp. 253–263 (2015)

10. Burdea, G.C.: Haptics issues in virtual environments. In: Proceedings Computer Graphics International 2000, pp. 295–302 (2000)

11. Pongrac, H.: Vibrotactile perception: examining the coding of vibrations and the just noticeable difference under various conditions. Multimed. Syst. **13**(4), 297–307 (2007)

12. Hatzfeld, C., Cao, S., Kupnik, M., Werthschützky, R.: Vibrotactile force perception - absolute and differential thresholds and external influences. IEEE Trans. Haptics **9**(4), 586–597 (2016)

13. Culbertson, H., Unwin, J., Kuchenbecker, K.J.: Modeling and rendering realistic textures from unconstrained tool-surface interactions. IEEE Trans. Haptics **7**(3), 381–393 (2014)

14. Hollins, M., Bensmaïa, S.J.: The coding of roughness. Can. J. Exp. Psychol./Revue canadienne de psychologie experimentale **61**(3), 184 (2007)

15. Bensmaïa, S.J., Hollins, M.: The vibrations of texture. Somatosens. Mot. Res. **20**(1), 33–43 (2003)

16. Bolanowski, S.J., Verillo, R.T., Gescheider, G.A., Checkosky, C.M.: Four channels mediate the mechanical aspects of touch. J. Acoust. Soc. Am. **84**(5), 1680–1694 (1988)

17. Kontarinis, D.A., Howe, R.D.: Tactile display of vibratory information in teleoperation and virtual environments. Presence Teleoperators Virtual Environ. **4**(4), 387–402 (1995)

18. Buechley, L., Eisenberg, M., Catchen, J., Crockett, A.: The LilyPad Arduino: using computational textiles to investigate engagement, aesthetics, and diversity in computer science education. In: Proceedings of the SIGCHI Conference on Human Factors in Computing Systems, pp. 423–432 (2008)

19. Freeman, C.W.: Bluetooth low energy platform with simblee (2016)

20. Weichert, F., Bachmann, D., Rudak, B., Fisseler, D.: Analysis of the accuracy and robustness of the leap motion controller. Sensors **13**(5), 6380–6393 (2013)

21. Paulino, T., et al.: Low-cost 3-axis soft tactile sensors for the human-friendly robot Vizzy. In: IEEE-RAS ICRA (2017)

22. Tomo, T.P., et al.: Covering a robot fingertip with uSkin: a soft electronic skin with distributed 3-axis force sensitive elements for robot hands. IEEE Robot. Autom. Lett. **3**(1), 124–131 (2018)

23. Nogueira, J., Martinez-Cantin, R., Bernardino, A., Jamone, L.: Unscented Bayesian optimization for safe robot grasping. In: IEEE-RSJ IROS (2016)

24. Castanheira, J., Vicente, P., Martinez-Cantin, R., Jamone, L., Bernardino, A.: Finding safe 3D robot grasps through efficient haptic exploration with unscented Bayesian optimization and collision penalty. In: IEEE-RSJ IROS (2018)

Virtual Reality Simulator for Medical Auscultation Training

Luis Andrés Puértolas Bálint[1](✉), Luis Humberto Perez Macías[2](✉), and Kaspar Althoefer[1](✉)

[1] Queen Mary University of London, London, UK
{l.a.puertolasbalint,k.althoefer}@qmul.ac.uk
[2] Benemérita Universidad Autónoma de Puebla, Puebla, Mexico
luis_cat_@hotmail.com

Abstract. According to the Oxford English dictionary, auscultation is "the action of listening to sounds from the heart, lungs, or other organs, typically with a stethoscope, as a part of medical diagnosis." In this work, we describe a medical simulator that includes audio, visual, pseudo-haptic, and spatial elements for training medical students in auscultation. In our training simulator, the user is fully immersed in a virtual reality (VR) environment. A typical hospital bedside scenario was recreated, and the users can see their own body and the patient increase immersion. External tracking devices are used to acquire the user's movements and map them into the VR environment. The main idea behind this work is for the user to associate the heart and lung sounds, as heard through the stethoscope with the corresponding health-related problems. Several sound parameters including the volume, give information about the type and severity of the disease. Our simulator can reproduce sounds belonging to the heart and lungs. Through the proposed VR-based training, the medical student ideally will learn to relate sounds to illnesses in a realistic setting, accelerating the learning process.

Keywords: Auscultation · Pseudo-haptic · Virtual reality · Simulator · Medical · Heart · Lungs · Pulmonary

1 Introduction

We are currently experiencing a virtual reality (VR) boom in the medical industry. VR is still not capable of addressing all aspects of medical training. However, it has been shown to work very well in some cases. This is the case in problems such as phobia treatment [1] to surgical training [2]. In this work, a different approach based on VR for the training of medical students in auscultation is proposed. Keeping a view on affordability, so that the proposed medical training can be applied widely. VR development software is becoming more sophisticated [3]. Lower hardware prices and greater software functionality is leading to a point where VR training makes both practical and economic sense. This rapidly changing landscape has encouraged the development of training simulators that take advantage of the latest technologies. Programming VR has recently become accessible. While in not such a distant past,

© Springer Nature Switzerland AG 2019
K. Althoefer et al. (Eds.): TAROS 2019, LNAI 11649, pp. 386–398, 2019.
https://doi.org/10.1007/978-3-030-23807-0_32

graphics engines were restricted to game developing. Graphics engines are now being used in serious simulations such as industry 4.0 [4] and robotics [5]. The available VR development tools have reached the maturity of allowing a single programmer or a small team of programmers to create a medical simulator in a short period. External medical input is also needed.

Since we aim to have a high degree of realism of the experienced motions and interactions in a simulator, it is essential to model the simulator's physics as accurately as possible. Since we want to obtain results quickly (but also accurately), we use an existing graphics engine that allows the rapid creation of realistic simulation environments. Modern graphics engines have the option to simulate a wide range of physical properties that happen. This allows VR developers to generate VR environments that ensure realistic motion of objects, (including visualization and tracking of human limbs) and the appropriate physical interaction between these objects (including collisions). Today, two graphics engines, Unreal and Unity, arguably dominate the market and are used by most developers. In this work, Unity is used. Through its asset store, Unity also allows us to incorporate portions of code and 3D models made by the community of VR software developers, into the application that is being programmed. This speeds up the development process considerably. We incorporated some valuable prefabricated Unity assets, including a hospital room [6], an accurate anatomic model to be used as a patient [7], and a sophisticated medic avatar [8]. The acquired Unity models were slightly modified using Autodesk's Fusion 360. These changes include the clothing of the medic's and the patient's avatars inside Unity.

To maximize realism and minimize the cost of the simulator, we emphasize on the accurate modeling of natural human motion. Realistic collision and the visualization of the user's whole body in VR was one of the top priorities in the design of the simulator. It is crucial for us to appropriately model the user's hands and strive for realistic interaction with other objects in the environment. This includes avoiding the penetration of one object with another. For this auscultation simulator, much effort was put into acquiring our sound base, ensuring the highest possible level of realism. Some current auscultation simulators employ mannequins [9, 10], while others achieve VR auscultation using a head-mounted display [11]. These systems provide useful training tools for medical students. After careful consideration, the conclusion that mannequins are not necessary was reached. They are too expensive for widespread application, and virtual objects can do this in a better way.

To enhance immersion, aspects from the area of pseudo-haptics were incorporated. The use of the physics capabilities of our graphics engine, to detect collisions between the user's simulated hands and solid objects was also implemented. Upon collision, the realistic computation of expectable behavior of the hand is experienced. This way, it is tricking the mind into believing that there is actual resistance to the user's hands. Enhancing immersion in VR is very important, with other researchers coming to similar conclusions [12–14].

This paper is organized as follows. Section 1 provides an overview of how auscultation learning is currently studied. In Sect. 2 (Methods and Materials), we present our VR-based simulator for the training of medical students. In Sect. 3 (Pilot study), we investigate the capabilities of the simulator. Section 5 concludes our paper.

2 Background in Auscultation Training

Medical students usually learn auscultation through audio clips, graphs, and textbooks with images. In some training sessions, the medical professors knock on a table twice. The sound intensity and speed of the knocks are varied to emulate heartbeats caused by a health problem. Currently, medical students learn about auscultation in their study program. It is known that health problems that happen in specific organs affect the way the body sounds. Several health issues can be detected by hearing these sounds. Experienced medics can identify the differences between healthy sounds and those that are altered because of a health-related problem. They also view images showing the correct placement of the stethoscope on the patient. Learning in this way is protracted. Students find it difficult to fuse the different elements of auscultation into one whole understanding of the process. For example, it is difficult to understand which sound relates to which position of the stethoscope on the patient's body. Here, we create a more natural way of linking the placement of the stethoscope to the sounds and the associated illness. All this happens in a realistic environment, also incorporating the student's limbs' movements, visual impressions as well as the connected sounds. Because medics are separated in different knowledge areas, they will often only study a small part of the full spectrum of auscultation. This will make them likely to miss out on learning several sounds whose interpretation would help them diagnose a broader range of diseases.

We could only find two basic VR auscultation simulators currently being available [9, 11, 18]. Other auscultation simulators make use of mannequins and stethoscopes; employing mannequins increases the costs of such systems.

On the back, the six top auscultation points are P1–P6 where "P" stands for "pulmonary" and the two lower points are B1–B2, where "B" stands for "base" (see Fig. 1 (right)) (Fig. 2).

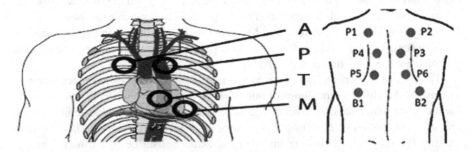

Fig. 1. (Left) Auscultation points on the chest. We can see the aortic (A), pulmonary (P), tricuspid (T), and mitral (M) valves auscultation points [15]. (Right) Auscultation points on the back of the patient. Adapted from Altan et al. [16]. If the stethoscope is not placed on these points, no relevant sounds will be heard, neither on the real patient nor our simulator.

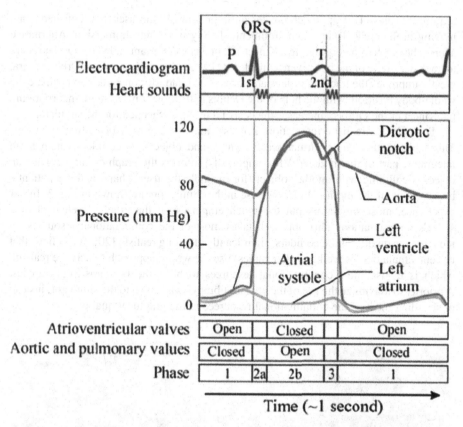

Fig. 2. During the learning of auscultation, students make use of tables and graphs like the one shown here [17]. These graphs are used to give a visual representation of the sounds that one is expected to hear during auscultation. These graphs mostly represent the first heartbeat, the second heartbeat, the sound intensity, and the timing between these two. Additional information in the form of textual descriptions (including sound amplitude, frequency, and type of disease) is usually provided.

3   Proposed Methods and Materials

The proposed simulator was created using the Unity graphics engine, making use of its physics simulation capabilities. Employing the assets from the Unity store, we download a realistic 3D environment resembling a standard hospital room. This is a place where auscultation is likely to happen. Our VR simulator requires users to have a commercially-available head-mounted display (HMD), compatible with Unity. From all the choices available at the time, the Oculus Rift was chosen in the end. This is because it is arguably the most comfortable, and less heavy HMD currently available.

To enhance immersion, the whole user's body movement was incorporated into the simulator. To capture the user's whole-body movement, a Leap Motion tracking system is attached to the HMD. The Leap Motion tracking system uses a camera system to observe its environment. It can extract the hands' and forearms' positions, and motions from the acquired images. This approach creates an impression in the user that their hands are moving in the created virtual environment, sharply increasing immersion. Alternative approaches such as incorporating a Kinect V2, or a newer variant called the Orbbec Astra to track the whole of the body were considered [19]. Adding a Kinect or an Orbbec Astra, greatly improves the tracking of legs and arms. The Leap Motion alone can estimate the whole-body position, with the help of the Oculus Rift's positional system. Incorporating the Kinect or the Orbbec, increases the cost and the space needed for the simulator.

To achieve a realistic interaction, it is essential to have realistic virtual collisions. This includes the whole virtual scene, actors, and objects. A collider (which is an integrative part of the modeled VR components) informs the graphics engine when an object is colliding with another object (for example the user's hand and the patient's body). Some of the mesh colliders we use in the simulation are shown in Fig. 3. In our experience, most simulators put too much emphasis on the graphical element of a scene's representation. This approach takes most of the computational resources by reducing the quality of the colliders, significantly affecting realism [20]. We believe that current simulators (as well as video games) use the wrong approach to achieve realism, which is to use most computational resources to have the best possible graphics. A priority to maximize the use of the physics libraries was given to the simulator, instead of spending most of the computational resources in the graphical quality.

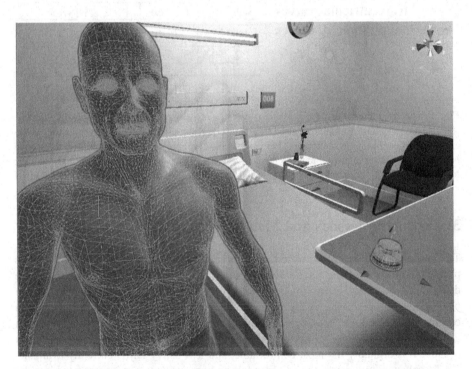

Fig. 3. Image of the proposed simulator, with a patient inside a standard hospital room. On the desk, we can see a wireless stethoscope. We added the most sophisticated colliders available, which are the mesh colliders (shown in green colour) to increase the realism of physical interaction in the simulator. This is how we create the illusion of touch or pseudo-haptics [21]. (Color figure online)

Using the Leap Motion tracking system and the described mesh colliders, the physical interaction of the user with objects in the VR environment was achieved. This means that the users can use their hands to grab the stethoscope. The described features have been made available by the "Humanoid Control Plus" asset from the Unity Store. Since the simulator was developed using a potent laptop, we changed the colliders from cylindrical to mesh colliders [20]. Work is being done to improve the grasping of objects by using particles with Nvidia's FleX plugin [22], which is a state-of-the-art

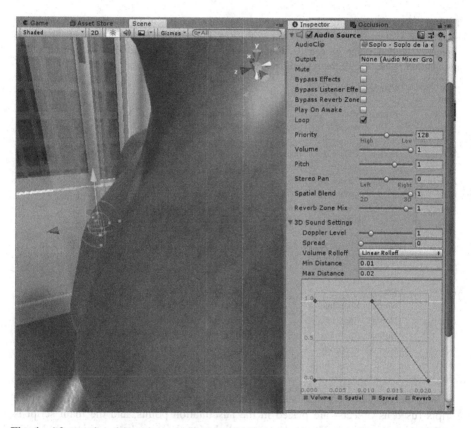

Fig. 4. After setting the scene, we add an audio listener and several audio sources [23]. The audio listener is usually positioned in the head of the character, centrally between the character's ears. We can define the audio listener as the ears of the simulation. As in the real world, the simulator provides sounds that are louder the closer we are to the sound source. However, if we find ourselves far enough, we will not hear that audio source. The scene contains only one audio listener, which is the stethoscope. Each of our 12 auscultation areas has audio sources, whose main parts are two spheres and with the respective audio clips that can happen in those places. We can see in this figure that there are several options to configure an audio source. The most important part is the volumetric sound consisting of two spheres. As we can see in the graph, the minimum distance is formed by a sphere of 0.01 distance units. A sphere of distance units forms the maximum distance on which the sound will propagate. A unit in Unity corresponds to one meter in the real world. This means that if the audio source (stethoscope) goes through the volume formed between these two spheres, the audio will play. These volumes were tuned until we could replicate a realistic experience in auscultation.

physics library that can be obtained as a Unity asset. This asset seems to work by detecting whether a hand is closed, and an object is near enough this hand to be grasped. With the FleX plugin which is part of Nvidia's PhysX [22], we can add particles, friction, stiction, stiffness, clothes, fluids, and other characteristics to make the simulator more realistic (Fig. 4).

A table with health-related problems with their own sound (see Table 1). Our has an unknown number of possible states.

Table 1. Overview relating auscultation points to diagnosis. It is noted that the sound amplitude is an essential element when distinguishing diseases. In the feasibility study, presented here, we explore a limited range of sounds. Future work will aim at considering the impact of all auscultation points for all the related heart diseases.

Auscultation point	Diagnostic							Sound %
Mitral	Normal	Mitral stenosis	Mitral insufficiency	Acute mitral insufficiency	Chronic mitral insufficiency	Mitral valve prolapses	Austin flint murmur	100
Tricuspid	Normal	Tricuspid stenosis	Tricuspid insufficiency	-	-	-	-	100
Pulmonary valve	Normal	Pulmonary stenosis	Pulmonary insufficiency	-	-	-	-	100
Aortic	Normal	Aortic stenosis	Aortic insufficiency	Acute aortic insufficiency	Severe acute aortic insufficiency	-	-	100
P1	Normal	-	-	Pleural rub	-	Sibilance	-	30
P2	Normal	-	-	Pleural rub	-	Sibilance	-	30
P3	Normal	-	-	Pleural rub	Crepitations	Sibilance	-	30
P4	Normal	-	-	Pleural rub	Crepitations	Sibilance	-	30
P5	Normal	Rhonchus	-	Pleural rub	Crepitations	Sibilance	-	30
P6	Normal	Rhonchus	-	Pleural rub	Crepitations	Sibilance	-	70
B1	Normal	Rhonchus	-	Pleural rub	Crepitations	Sibilance	-	70
B2	Normal	Rhonchus	-	Pleural rub	Crepitations	Sibilance	-	100

With the use of object-oriented programming, we coded 13 scripts. The first twelve scripts (used as objects) are placed in the auscultation points, and the main script is placed inside the patient. The twelve scripts linked to the auscultation points, make use of one method for each possible sound that we considered for so far (shown in Table 1). Every time the simulator runs, a feasible random health problem is created. The main script (inside the patient) oversees the task of generating a random health-related issue in the patient for the user to experience during the VR auscultation. Another option is to have a completely healthy patient can learn to identify them. Future work will explore cases of combined diseases, and the full use of our 23-sound database. Although this will be more challenging for the user, it will add more realism and has the potential to prepare medical students who use the simulator for real-life situations in a better way. Further study will also extend to other diseases in the thoracic area, beyond the set of illnesses discussed here. We will also explore how many combinations can happen; it is possible that they are more than previously thought. To further improve the simulator, more diverse models are needed, simulating different genders, differently sized people and people from different ages. Other aspects could also be considered, such as incorporating sounds from valve prostheses, pacemakers, stents and other types of implants routinely used on patients nowadays, and, hence, necessary to be included in medical training. Another critical aspect of future work will be to carry studies involving medical professionals and medical students (Figs. 5 and 6).

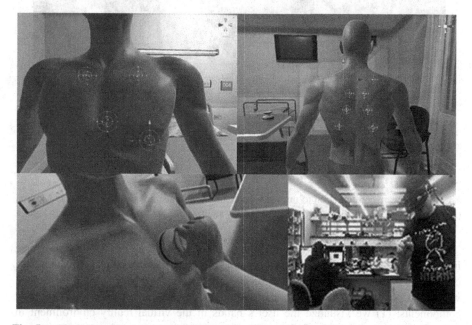

Fig. 5. (Top) Our VR patient with 12 auscultation points. Each auscultation point has two spheres. The inner sphere is where the sound experienced is the loudest. Moving from away from the inner sphere, the sound intensity linearly decreases coming to zero at the outer border of the bigger sphere. The three-dimensional spatial sound was also incorporated. (Bottom left) HMD image showing the user-held stethoscope on the chest of the patient. Because of the colliders integrated with the body and the stethoscope, the stethoscope will not penetrate through the body and create the illusion of resistance – this effect is called pseudo-haptics. (Bottom right) We see the user closing his hand to grab the stethoscope and moving it around to auscultate the patient.

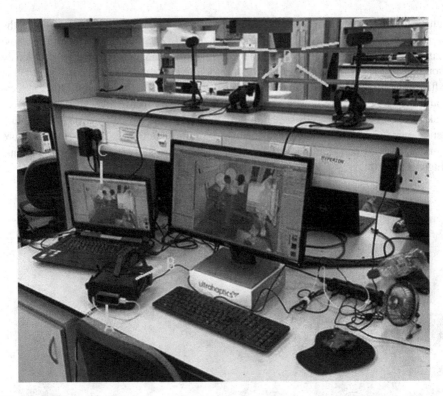

Fig. 6. Hardware configuration to run the auscultation training simulator. (A) The Leap Motion. (B) The Head Mounted Display with its controllers and tracking stations. (C) A VR ready laptop.

It is essential for a training simulator to be as realistic as possible to maximize immersion and training outcomes. At the same time, our research aims to create a low-cost solution of a trainer so that medical students across the world can be trained without incurring high costs. To increase immersion, we make use of two important components: (1) we visualize the user's hands in the virtual reality environment in order for the user to get the feeling of being part of the presented environment, and (2) through the use of colliders on visualized objects we ensure that objects including the user's hands properly collide with each other and cannot penetrate each other. The visualization of the user's hands is achieved using a Leap Motion sensor mounted at the front of the HMD. Using the output from the Leap Motion sensor, the user's hands can be registered with the environment and the virtual objects within.

The colliders that are integrated with the VR objects ensure that the user's hands cannot move through objects. For the user, this creates the feeling that objects actually have density. This is an aspect of pseudo-haptics whereby the human mind is tricked to haptically experience a physical interaction even though there is no actual interaction between the user and the environment. In our experience, pseudo-haptics has shown to improve immersion significantly. Pseudo-haptics have, for example, shown that users can be tricked to believe in resistive forces when pressing down the piston of a syringe solely through appropriately manipulated visual feedback. Using pseudo-haptics, as done here, noticeably increases the feeling in the user to be part of the presented reality and is likely to enhance the training performance.

4 Pilot Study

There is an unknown amount of realistic possible combinations. To reduce this combination, we ran a pseudo-random test. We first took 228 random samples (with python, as it proved too difficult to do it in C#). From this sample and to the best of our knowledge, table 3 was created. We debugged the code by reviewing 40 pseudo-random samples (C#) repeatedly until the resulting combinations were 100% accurate (Fig. 7 and Table 2).

Table 2. Our findings from a sample size of 228. This table remains the current standard we consider for measuring the combinations. From up to down, the algorithm has to choose one sound from each row. If the first sound picked is gray, it must go with other gray colours. The same applies to the black colour. The white can always happen in almost any possible combination.

Auscultation point	Diagnostic							Sound %
Mitral	Normal	*Mitral stenosis*	Mitral insufficiency	*Acute mitral insufficiency*	Chronic mitral insufficiency	Mitral valve prolapses;	**Austin flint murmur**	100
Tricuspid	Normal	Tricuspid stenosis	Tricuspid insufficiency	-·	-	-	-	100
Pulmonary valve	Normal	Pulmonary stenosis	Pulmonary insufficiency	-	-	-	-	100
Aortic	Normal	Aortic stenosis	Aortic insufficiency	Acute aortic insufficiency	**Severe acute aortic insufficiency**	-	-	100
P1	Normal	-	-	Pleural rub	-	Sibilance	-	30
P2	Normal	-	-	Pleural rub	-	Sibilance	-	30
P3	Normal	-	-	Pleural rub	*Crepitations*	Sibilance	-	30
P4	Normal	-	-	Pleural rub	*Crepitations*	Sibilance	-	30
P5	Normal	Rhonchus	-	Pleural rub	*Crepitations*	Sibilance	-	30
P6	Normal	Rhonchus	-	Pleural rub	*Crepitations*	Sibilance	-	70
B1	Normal	Rhonchus	-	Pleural rub	*Crepitations*	Sibilance	-	70
B2	Normal	Rhonchus	-	Pleural rub	*Crepitations*	Sibilance	-	100

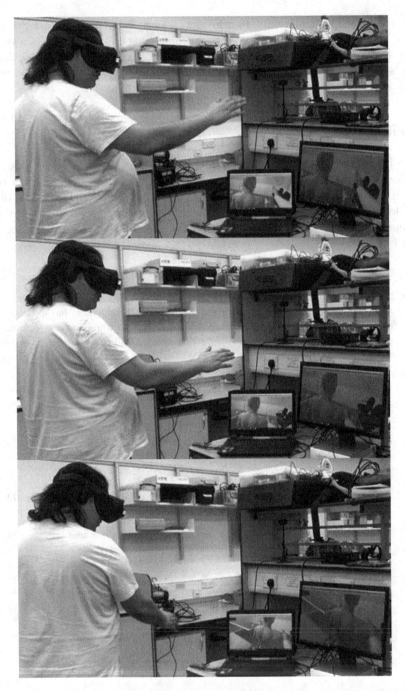

Fig. 7. From top to bottom. The first image shows no contact with the patient. The second image shows contact with the patient, where the real world and the virtual one overlap in both spaces, and there is contact with the patient's collider. The third image shows the pseudo-haptic effect, where the overlap is no longer existent. However, the third image tricks the mind of the user (medic) into thinking his hand is in the position of the virtual space, thanks to the complex colliders.

5 Conclusions

A virtual reality simulator for auscultation training of medical students was successfully programmed. Our work suggests there is potential for learning auscultation with an immersive VR environment. Accurately linking the sounds that the user can hear when using the simulator, to the diseases that produce these sounds in patients. This concept can reproduce the sounds of a range of diseases in the thorax and use an estimate to modulate their volume depending on the placement of the stethoscope. Through the inclusion of colliders and pseudo-haptics principles, we were able to achieve a good level of immersion and feel of physical interaction with the simulated environment, while keeping costs and hardware complexity low. Four medics from different fields and levels of education were consulted for this research, one of them a co-author of this document.

Acknowledgment. This work was supported by BALTECH Pty Ltd (Ballarat Technologies), CONACYT and Queen Mary University of London.

References

1. Cruz, M., Amann, E.: Virtual reality and tactile augmentation in the treatment of spider phobia: a case report. In: Capital Without Borders: Challenges to Development, vol. 35, pp. 39–52 (2010)
2. Aggarwal, R., et al.: Virtual reality simulation training can improve technical skills during laparoscopic salpingectomy for ectopic pregnancy. BJOG: Int. J. Obstet. Gynaecol. **113**, 1382–1387 (2006)
3. Wang, M., Reid, D.: Virtual reality in pediatric neurorehabilitation: attention deficit hyperactivity disorder, autism and cerebral palsy. Neuroepidemiology **36**, 2–18 (2011)
4. Pierdicca, R., Frontoni, E., Pollini, R., Trani, M., Verdini, L.: The use of augmented reality glasses for the application in industry 4.0. In: De Paolis, L.T., Bourdot, P., Mongelli, A. (eds.) AVR 2017. LNCS, vol. 10324, pp. 389–401. Springer, Cham (2017). https://doi.org/10.1007/978-3-319-60922-5_30
5. Erez, T., Tassa, Y., Todorov, E.: Simulation tools for model-based robotics: comparison of Bullet, Havok, MuJoCo, ODE and PhysX. In: 2015 IEEE International Conference on Robotics and Automation (ICRA), pp. 4397–4404 (2015)
6. Hospital Room - Asset Store. https://assetstore.unity.com/packages/3d/props/interior/hospital-room-57399
7. Anatomic Pack - Asset Store. https://assetstore.unity.com/packages/3d/props/anatomic-pack-79612
8. Humanoid Control Plus - Asset Store. https://assetstore.unity.com/packages/tools/animation/humanoid-control-plus-104965
9. Takashina, T., Masuzawa, T., Fukui, Y.: A new cardiac auscultation simulator. Clin. Cardiol. **13**, 869–872 (1990)
10. Kagaya, Y., Tabata, M., Arata, Y.: Variation in effectiveness of a cardiac auscultation training class with a cardiology patient simulator among heart sounds and murmurs. J. Cardiol. **70**, 192–198 (2017)

11. Vargas-Orjuela, M., Uribe-Quevedo, A., Rojas, D., Kapralos, B., Perez-Gutierrez, B.: A mobile immersive virtual reality cardiac auscultation app. In: 2017 IEEE 6th Global Conference on Consumer Electronics, GCCE 2017, pp. 1–2, January 2017

12. Gruchalla, K.: Immersive well-path editing: investigating the added value of immersion. In: Proceedings - Virtual Reality Annual International Symposium, pp. 157–164 (2004)

13. Stengel, M., Grogorick, S., Eisemann, M., Eisemann, E., Magnor, M.A.: An affordable solution for binocular eye tracking and calibration in head-mounted displays. In: Proceedings of the 23rd ACM International Conference on Multimedia - MM 2015, pp. 15–24 (2015)

14. Bowman, D.A., Mcmahan, R.P., Virginia Tech: Virtual reality - how much immersion is enough. Computer 40, 36–43 (2007)

15. Bhoi, A.K., Sherpa, K.S., Khandelwal, B.: Multidimensional analytical study of heart sounds: a review. Int. J. Bioautomat. 19, 351–376 (2015)

16. Altan, G., Kutlu, Y., Pekmezci, A.Ö., Nural, S.: Deep learning with 3D-second order difference plot on respiratory sounds. Biomed. Sig. Process. Control 45, 58–69 (2018)

17. Israel, S.A., Irvine, J.M.: Heartbeat biometrics: a sensing system perspective. Int. J. Cogn. Biom. 1, 39 (2012)

18. Abbas, A., Fahim, A.: An automated computerized auscultation and diagnostic system for pulmonary diseases. J. Med. Syst. 34, 1149–1155 (2010)

19. Călin, A.D., Coroiu, A.: Interchangeability of Kinect and Orbbec sensors for gesture recognition. In: Proceedings - 2018 IEEE 14th International Conference on Intelligent Computer Communication and Processing, ICCP 2018, pp. 309–315 (2018)

20. Matsas, E., Vosniakos, G.C.: Design of a virtual reality training system for human–robot collaboration in manufacturing tasks. Int. J. Interact. Des. Manuf. 11, 139–153 (2017)

21. Andrés, L., Bálint, P., Althoefer, K.: Medical virtual reality palpation training using ultrasound based haptics and image processing. In: CRAS (2018)

22. Macklin, M., Müller, M., Chentanez, N., Kim, T.-Y.: Unified particle physics for real-time applications. ACM Trans. Graph. 33, 1–12 (2014)

23. Unity - Scripting API: AudioSource. https://docs.unity3d.com/ScriptReference/AudioSource.html

Robotic Systems and Applications

Note on Geometric and Exponential Expressions of Screw Displacement

Guowu Wei[1]([✉]), Anthony H. Jones[1], and Lei Ren[2]

[1] School of Computing, Science and Engineering, University of Salford,
Salford M5 4WT, UK
{g.wei,a.h.jones}@salford.ac.uk
[2] School of Mechanical, Aerospace and Civil Engineering,
The University of Manchester, Manchester M13 9PL, UK
lei.ren@manchester.ac.uk

Abstract. This paper provides a comprehensive note on screw displacement. Expressions of screw displacement, including the Rodrigues' formulae for rotation and general spatial displacement, are derived in details with geometric approach, transform operator and matrix exponential method. The geometric approach provides better physical insights and the exponential method demonstrates elegant and rigours mathematical perception. Application of the screw displacement is illustrated by the development of a RSCR-mechanism based landing gear.

Keywords: Screw displacement · Rodrigues formula · Landing gear

1 Introduction

Chasles' theorem states that the general spatial displacement of a rigid body is a translation plus a rotation, a stronger form of the theorem states that regardless of how a rigid body is displaced from one location to anther, the displacement can be regarded as a rotation and a translation along some axis; such a combination of translation and rotation is called a screw displacement [1]. There are mainly two approaches to derive the screw displacement, one is through geometric and vector interpretation, and the other is through exponential derivation. In text books [1–7] and literature [8–12], to mention but a few; derivation of screw displacement was either presented in geometric form or exponential approach, but not both. To provide better overview of the screw displacement, this paper presents the detailed derivation of screw displacement using geometric method, transform operator and matrix exponential formulae. The aim of this paper is to provide a comprehensive note on screw displacement for the researchers in the fields of mechanisms and robotics. Application of the screw displacement is demonstrated by the development of a RSCR-mechanism based landing gear.

© Springer Nature Switzerland AG 2019
K. Althoefer et al. (Eds.): TAROS 2019, LNAI 11649, pp. 401–412, 2019.
https://doi.org/10.1007/978-3-030-23807-0_33

2   Geometric Expression of Screw Displacement

2.1   Geometric Derivation of Rodrigues Formula for Rotation

In this section a description of the orientation of a rigid body in terms of a rotation about a general screw axis is presented. As shown in Fig. 1, let a moving rigid body B rotate an angle θ about an axis $\boldsymbol{\omega}$ passing through the origin of a reference frame $\{A\}$. The first position of a point P of the rigid body B is denoted by vector $\boldsymbol{r}_1 = \overline{OP_1}$ and the second position is denoted by vector $\boldsymbol{r}_2 = \overline{OP_2^r}$. The direction of rotation is given by vector $\boldsymbol{\omega}(\omega_1, \omega_2, \omega_3)$.

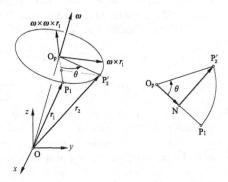

Fig. 1. Geometric derivation of Rodrigues rotation formula

Referring to Fig. 1, vector $\boldsymbol{r}_1$ can be decomposed into components parallel and perpendicular, respectively, to the rotation axis $\boldsymbol{\omega}$ as: $\boldsymbol{r}_1 = \boldsymbol{r}_\parallel + \boldsymbol{r}_\perp$; from Fig. 1 $\boldsymbol{r}_\parallel$ can be obtained as $\boldsymbol{r}_\parallel = (\boldsymbol{r}_1 \cdot \boldsymbol{\omega})\,\boldsymbol{\omega}$, and $r_\perp$ can be expressed as $\boldsymbol{r}_\perp = -\boldsymbol{\omega} \times (\boldsymbol{\omega} \times \boldsymbol{r}_1)$, yielding

$$\boldsymbol{r}_1 = (\boldsymbol{r}_1 \cdot \boldsymbol{\omega})\,\boldsymbol{\omega} - \boldsymbol{\omega} \times (\boldsymbol{\omega} \times \boldsymbol{r}_1) \tag{1}$$

When rigid body B is rotated by θ about axis $\boldsymbol{\omega}$ to the second position P_2^r, the parallel component is unaffected by the rotation and from Fig. 1, it has $\boldsymbol{r}_2 = \overline{OP_2^r} = \overline{OO_p} + \overline{O_pN} + \overline{NP_2^r}$, which can be written as

$$\boldsymbol{r}_2 = (\boldsymbol{r}_1 \cdot \boldsymbol{\omega})\,\boldsymbol{\omega} - \boldsymbol{\omega} \times (\boldsymbol{\omega} \times \boldsymbol{r}_1) \cos\theta + \boldsymbol{\omega} \times \boldsymbol{r}_1 \sin\theta \tag{2}$$

Considering that $\boldsymbol{\omega} \times (\boldsymbol{\omega} \times \boldsymbol{r}_1) = (\boldsymbol{\omega} \cdot \boldsymbol{r}_1)\,\boldsymbol{\omega} - (\boldsymbol{\omega} \cdot \boldsymbol{\omega})\,\boldsymbol{r}_1 = (\boldsymbol{r}_1 \cdot \boldsymbol{\omega})\,\boldsymbol{\omega} - \boldsymbol{r}_1$, it has $(\boldsymbol{r}_1 \cdot \boldsymbol{\omega})\,\boldsymbol{\omega} = \boldsymbol{r}_1 + \boldsymbol{\omega} \times (\boldsymbol{\omega} \times \boldsymbol{r}_1)$ such that Eq. (2) can be rearranged as

$$\boldsymbol{r}_2 = \boldsymbol{r}_1 + \boldsymbol{\omega} \times \boldsymbol{r}_1 \sin\theta + \boldsymbol{\omega} \times (\boldsymbol{\omega} \times \boldsymbol{r}_1)(1 - \cos\theta) \tag{3}$$

Let $[\boldsymbol{\omega}]$ be the 3×3 skew-symmetric representation of vector $\boldsymbol{\omega}$, Eq. (3) can be written as

$$\begin{aligned}
\boldsymbol{r}_2 &= \boldsymbol{r}_1 + \sin\theta\,[\boldsymbol{\omega}]\,\boldsymbol{r}_1 + (1 - \cos\theta)\,[\boldsymbol{\omega}]^2\,\boldsymbol{r}_1 \\
&= \left(\mathbf{I} + \sin\theta\,[\boldsymbol{\omega}] + (1 - \cos\theta)\,[\boldsymbol{\omega}]^2\right)\boldsymbol{r}_1 \\
&= \mathbf{R}\boldsymbol{r}_1
\end{aligned} \tag{4}$$

where $\mathbf{R}$ stands for a 3×3 rotation matrix as

$$\mathbf{R} = \begin{bmatrix} r_{11} & r_{12} & r_{13} \\ r_{21} & r_{22} & r_{23} \\ r_{31} & r_{32} & r_{33} \end{bmatrix}.$$

Equation (4) is known as Rodrigues' formula for rotation of an arbitrary axis passing through the origin of a reference frame. The elements for matrix $\mathbf{R}$ is given as: $r_{11} = \cos\theta + w_1^2 (1 - \cos\theta)$, $r_{12} = w_1 w_2 (1 - \cos\theta) - w_3 \sin\theta$, $r_{13} = w_1 w_3 (1 - \cos\theta) + w_2 \sin\theta$, $r_{21} = w_2 w_1 (1 - \cos\theta) + w_3 \sin\theta$, $r_{22} = \cos\theta + w_2^2 (1 - \cos\theta)$, $r_{23} = w_2 w_3 (1 - \cos\theta) - w_1 \sin\theta$, $r_{31} = w_3 w_1 (1 - \cos\theta) - w_2 \sin\theta$, $r_{32} = w_3 w_2 (1 - \cos) + w_1 \sin\theta$, $r_{33} = \cos\theta + w_3^2 (1 - \cos\theta)$.

Equation (4) is also called the *screw axis representation* of the rotation of a rigid body. This representation uses four parameters: three associated with the direction of the screw and one associated with the angle of rotation. However, only two of the three parameters associated with the direction of the screw axis are independent since they must satisfy the condition of a unit vector, i.e. $\boldsymbol{\omega}^T \boldsymbol{\omega} = 1$.

Hence, given the screw axis and angle of rotation, we can compute the elements of the rotation matrix from Eq. (4). On the other hand, given a rotation matrix, we can compute the screw axis and the angle of rotation. The angle of rotation is obtained by summing the diagonal elements of the rotation matrix in Eq. (4), leading to

$$\theta = \cos^{-1}\left(\frac{\text{tr}\mathbf{R} - 1}{2}\right) \tag{5}$$

where $\text{tr}\mathbf{R} = r_{11} + r_{22} + r_{33} = 1 + 2\cos\theta$.

The direction of the screw axis is obtained by taking the differences between each pair of two opposing off-diagonal elements:

$$w_x = \frac{r_{32} - r_{23}}{2\sin\theta}$$

$$w_y = \frac{r_{13} - r_{31}}{2\sin\theta}$$

$$w_z = \frac{r_{21} - r_{12}}{2\sin\theta} \tag{6}$$

which can also be obtained from the following skew-symmetric matrix as

$$[\boldsymbol{\omega}] = \begin{bmatrix} 0 & -w_z & w_y \\ w_z & 0 & -w_x \\ -w_y & w_x & 0 \end{bmatrix} = \frac{1}{2\sin\theta}\left(\mathbf{R} - \mathbf{R}^T\right) \tag{7}$$

From Eqs. (5) and (6) it appears that there are two solutions of the screw axis, one being the negative of the other. In reality, these two solutions represent the same screw since a $-\theta$ rotation about the $-\boldsymbol{\omega}$ axis produces the same result as a $+\theta$ rotation about the $\boldsymbol{\omega}$ axis.

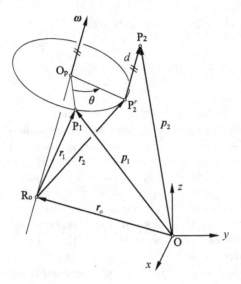

Fig. 2. Vector diagram of a general spatial displacement

2.2 Rodrigues' Formula for General Spatial Displacement

Figure 2 shows a point P that is displaced from a first position P_1 to a second position P_2 by a rotation of θ about a screw axis ω followed by a translation of d along the same axis. The rotation takes P from P_1 to P_2^r, and the translation takes P from P_2^r to P_2. In the figure, $\omega = [\omega_x, \omega_y, \omega_z]^T$ denotes a unit vector along the direction of the screw axis, and $r_o = [r_{ox}, r_{oy}, r_{oz}]^T$ denotes the position vector of a point lying on the screw axis. The rotation angle θ and the translational distance d are termed the screw parameters. The screw axis together with the screw parameters completely define the general displacement of a rigid body. Note that for a general displacement of a rigid body, the screw axis does not necessarily pass through the origin of the fixed frame. The displacement equation due to a rotation about an axis passing through the origin was derived in 2.1. Hence one only needs to consider the fact that the screw axis does not pass through the origin and add the contribution due to a translation along the screw axis. Referring to Fig. 2, there exist

$$r_1 = p_1 - r_o \tag{8}$$
$$r_2 = p_2 - r_o - d\omega \tag{9}$$

Substituting Eqs. (8) and (9) into (4), it has

$$p_2 = Rp_1 + (I - R)\, r_o + d\omega \tag{10}$$

Equation (10) is known as *Rodrigues' formula* for the general spatial displacement of a rigid body. Replacing p_1 by ^Bp and p_2 by ^Ap and defining

$^A q = (\mathbf{I} - \mathbf{R})\, \mathbf{r}_o + d\boldsymbol{\omega}$, it yields

$$^A p = {}_B^A\mathbf{R}\, {}^B p + {}^A q \tag{11}$$

where the elements of the rotation matrix ${}_B^A\mathbf{R}$, i.e. r_{ij} are the same as those in Eq. (4), and the position of the origin, $^A q$, of the moving frame is can be derived as

$$q_x = d\omega_1 - r_{ox}(r_{11} - 1) - r_{oy}r_{12} - r_{oz}r_{13}$$
$$q_y = d\omega_2 - r_{oy}r_{21} - r_{oy}(r_{22} - 1) - r_{oz}r_{23}$$
$$q_x = d\omega_3 - r_{ox}r_{31} - r_{oy}r_{32} - r_{oz}(r_{33} - 1) \tag{12}$$

Equation (11) can be written as a homogeneous transformation form as

$$^A p = {}_B^A\mathbf{T}\, {}^B p = \begin{bmatrix} {}_B^A\mathbf{R} & {}^A q \\ \mathbf{0} & 1 \end{bmatrix}\, {}^B p \tag{13}$$

This representation of a spatial displacement requires eight parameters: three associated with the direction of the screw axis, three associated with the location of the screw axis, one associated with the rotation angle, and one associated with the translational distance. However, only two of the three parameters associated with the direction of the screw axis are independent since they must satisfy the condition of a unit vector:

$$\boldsymbol{\omega}^T \boldsymbol{\omega} = 1 \tag{14}$$

Similarly, only two of the three parameters associated with the location of the screw axis are independent, since $\mathbf{r}_o$ can be any point on the screw axis. For convenience, one may choose $\mathbf{r}_o$ to be normal to the screw axis such that

$$\mathbf{r}_o^T \boldsymbol{\omega} = 0 \tag{15}$$

Given the screw axis and screw parameters, one can compute the elements of the transformation matrix by Eq. (13). On the other hand, given the spatial displacement of a rigid body in terms of a rotation matrix, ${}_B^A\mathbf{R}$, and a translation vector, $^A q$, we can compute the angle of rotation based on Eq. (5), the direction of the screw axis based on Eqs. (6) and (7), and the translational distance is calculated by

$$d = {}^A q^T \boldsymbol{\omega} \tag{16}$$

In addition, the screw axis location can be obtained by solving any two of the three equations in Eq. (12) together with Eq. (15). Since these equations are linear, there exists one solution corresponding to each solution set of $\boldsymbol{\omega}$, θ, and d.

From the derivation above, it appears that there are two solutions of the screw axis, one being the negative of the other. In reality, these two solutions represent the same screw, since a $-\theta$ rotation about and a $-d$ translation along the $-(\boldsymbol{\omega}, \mathbf{r}_o)$ screw axis produces the same result as a $+\theta$ rotation about and a $+d$ translation along the $+(\boldsymbol{\omega}, \mathbf{r}_o)$ screw axis.

In the case of pure rotation, i.e., $d = 0$, thus Eq. (10) becomes

$$\boldsymbol{p}_2 = \mathbf{R}\boldsymbol{p}_1 + (\mathbf{I} - \mathbf{R})\,\boldsymbol{r}_o \qquad (17)$$

Further, another interpretation for the above derivation can be obtained through transform operator [13] as follows; which has been revealed in [4]. Chasles' theorem states that all proper rigid body motions in 3-dimensional space, with the exception of pure translation, are equivalent to a screw motion, that is, a rotation about a line together with a translation along the line. Referring to Fig. 2, in the case that the line passes through the origin of the reference frame, the screw motion can be expressed as

$$\begin{bmatrix} {}^A\boldsymbol{p} \\ 1 \end{bmatrix} = \begin{bmatrix} {}^A_B\mathbf{R} & d\boldsymbol{\omega} \\ \boldsymbol{0} & 1 \end{bmatrix} \begin{bmatrix} {}^B\boldsymbol{p} \\ 1 \end{bmatrix} \qquad (18)$$

More generally, in the case that the axis of the screw motion does not pass through the origin of the reference frame, as indicated in Fig. 2; let r_o be the position vector of an arbitrary point on the axis, using transform operator [13], one can obtain the matrix representing such a screw motion by translating the screw axis back to the origin, performing the screw motion about the screw axis passing through the origin, and consequently translating the screw axis back to its original position; and this process can be expressed as

$$\begin{bmatrix} {}^A\boldsymbol{p} \\ 1 \end{bmatrix} = \begin{bmatrix} \mathbf{I}_3 & \boldsymbol{r}_o \\ 0 & 1 \end{bmatrix} \begin{bmatrix} {}^A_B\mathbf{R} & d\boldsymbol{\omega} \\ \boldsymbol{0} & 1 \end{bmatrix} \begin{bmatrix} \mathbf{I}_3 & -\boldsymbol{r}_o \\ 0 & 1 \end{bmatrix} \begin{bmatrix} {}^B\boldsymbol{p} \\ 1 \end{bmatrix}$$
$$= \begin{bmatrix} {}^A_B\mathbf{R} & (\mathbf{I}_3 - {}^A_B\mathbf{R})\,\boldsymbol{r}_o + d\boldsymbol{\omega} \\ 0 & 1 \end{bmatrix} \begin{bmatrix} {}^B\boldsymbol{p} \\ 1 \end{bmatrix} \qquad (19)$$

the result in Eq. (19) is exactly the same as the results obtained in Eq. (13).

3   Exponential Derivation of Screw Displacement

3.1   Exponential Coordinates for Rotation

Every rotation of a rigid body corresponds to some $\mathbf{R} \in SO(3)$, and referring to Fig. 1 $\mathbf{R}$ can be expressed as a function of $\boldsymbol{\omega}$ and θ.

To motivate the derivation, Consider the velocity of a point P attached to the rotating body, if the body rotates at constant unit velocity about the axis $\boldsymbol{\omega}$, velocity of the point $\dot{\boldsymbol{p}}$ can be written as

$$\dot{\boldsymbol{p}}\,(t) = \boldsymbol{\omega} \times \boldsymbol{p}\,(t) = [\boldsymbol{\omega}]\,\boldsymbol{p}\,(t) \qquad (20)$$

Which is a time-invariant linear differential equation which can be integrated, leading to

$$\boldsymbol{p}\,(t) = e^{[\boldsymbol{\omega}]t}\boldsymbol{p}\,(0) \qquad (21)$$

where $\boldsymbol{p}(0)$ is the initial ($t = 0$) position of the point and $e^{[\boldsymbol{\omega}]t}$ is the matrix exponential as

$$e^{[\boldsymbol{\omega}]t} = \mathbf{I} + [\boldsymbol{\omega}]\,t + [\boldsymbol{\omega}]^2\,\frac{t^2}{2!} + [\boldsymbol{\omega}]^3\,\frac{t^3}{3!} + \cdots \qquad (22)$$

If the rigid body rotates about the axis $\boldsymbol{\omega}$ at unit velocity for θ units of time, the net rotation can be expressed as

$$\mathbf{R}\left(\boldsymbol{\omega},\, \theta\right) = e^{[\boldsymbol{\omega}]\theta} \tag{23}$$

From its definition, it is easy to find that the matrix $[\boldsymbol{\omega}]$ is a skew-symmetric matrix, i.e., it satisfies $[\boldsymbol{\omega}]^T = -[\boldsymbol{\omega}]$. The vector space of all 3×3 skew matrices is denoted $so(3)$ and more generally the space of $n \times n$ skew-symmetric matrices is $so\,(n) = \{\mathbf{S} \in \mathbb{R}^{n \times n} : \mathbf{S}^T = -\mathbf{S}\}$.

It is convenient to represent a skew-symmetric matrix as the product of a unit skew-symmetric matrix and a real number. Given a matrix $[\boldsymbol{\omega}] \in so(3)$, $\|\,[\boldsymbol{\omega}]\,\| = 1$, and a real number $\theta \in \mathbb{R}$, the exponential of $[\boldsymbol{\omega}]\,\theta$ can be written as

$$\exp\left([\boldsymbol{\omega}]\,\theta\right) = e^{[\boldsymbol{\omega}]\theta} = \mathbf{I} + \theta\,[\boldsymbol{\omega}] + \frac{\theta^2}{2!}\,[\boldsymbol{\omega}]^2 + \frac{\theta^3}{3!}\,[\boldsymbol{\omega}]^3 + \cdots \tag{24}$$

Equation (24) is an infinite series. To obtain a closed-form expression for $\exp\left([\boldsymbol{\omega}]\,\theta\right)$, using the formulas for powers of $[\boldsymbol{a}]$ that $[\boldsymbol{a}]^2 = \boldsymbol{a}\boldsymbol{a}^T - \|\boldsymbol{a}\|^2\mathbf{I}$ and $[\boldsymbol{a}]^3 = -\|\boldsymbol{a}\|^2\,[\boldsymbol{a}]$, and considering that $[\boldsymbol{a}] = [\boldsymbol{\omega}]\,\theta$ and $\|\boldsymbol{\omega}\| = 1$, Eq. (24) can be written as

$$
\begin{aligned}
e^{[\boldsymbol{\omega}]\theta} &= \mathbf{I} + \theta\,[\boldsymbol{\omega}] + \frac{\theta^2}{2!}\,[\boldsymbol{\omega}]^2 - \frac{\theta^3}{3!}\,[\boldsymbol{\omega}] - \frac{\theta^4}{4!}\,[\boldsymbol{\omega}]^2 + \frac{\theta^5}{5!}\,[\boldsymbol{\omega}] + \frac{\theta^6}{6!}\,[\boldsymbol{\omega}]^2 - \frac{\theta^7}{7!}\,[\boldsymbol{\omega}] - \frac{\theta^8}{8!}\,[\boldsymbol{\omega}]^2 + \frac{\theta^9}{9!}\,[\boldsymbol{\omega}] + \cdots \\
&= \mathbf{I} + \left(\theta - \frac{\theta^3}{3!} + \frac{\theta^5}{5!} - \frac{\theta^7}{7!} + \frac{\theta^9}{9!} - \cdots\right)[\boldsymbol{\omega}] + \left(\frac{\theta^2}{2!} - \frac{\theta^4}{4!} + \frac{\theta^6}{6!} - \frac{\theta^8}{8!} + \cdots\right)[\boldsymbol{\omega}]^2
\end{aligned} \tag{25}
$$

Taylor's series for sine and cosine functions give that $\sin\theta = \theta - \frac{\theta^3}{3!} + \frac{\theta^5}{5!} - \frac{\theta^7}{7!} + \frac{\theta^9}{9!} - \cdots$, and $\cos\theta = 1 - \frac{\theta^2}{2!} + \frac{\theta^4}{4!} - \frac{\theta^6}{6!} + \frac{\theta^8}{8!} - \cdots$. Using these, Eq. (25) can be rearranged as

$$
\begin{aligned}
e^{[\boldsymbol{\omega}]\theta} &= \mathbf{I} + \sin\theta\,[\boldsymbol{\omega}] + (1 - \cos\theta)\,[\boldsymbol{\omega}]^2 \\
&= \cos\theta\mathbf{I} + \sin\theta\,[\boldsymbol{\omega}] + (1 - \cos\theta)\,\boldsymbol{\omega}\boldsymbol{\omega}^T
\end{aligned} \tag{26}
$$

and thus

$$
\begin{aligned}
\mathbf{R}\left([\boldsymbol{\omega}],\, \theta\right) = e^{[\boldsymbol{\omega}]\theta} &= \mathbf{I} + \sin\theta\,[\boldsymbol{\omega}] + (1 - \cos\theta)\,[\boldsymbol{\omega}]^2 \\
&= \cos\theta\mathbf{I} + \sin\theta\,[\boldsymbol{\omega}] + (1 - \cos\theta)\,\boldsymbol{\omega}\boldsymbol{\omega}^T
\end{aligned} \tag{27}
$$

where the relation $[\boldsymbol{\omega}]^2 = \boldsymbol{\omega}\boldsymbol{\omega}^T - \|\boldsymbol{\omega}\|^2\mathbf{I}$ is used. Equation (27) is the same as the rotation matrix that is obtained in Eq. (4) based on the geometric expression. Hence the elements for $\mathbf{R}\left([\boldsymbol{\omega}],\, \theta\right) = e^{[\boldsymbol{\omega}]\theta}$ are of the same as those in Eq. (4). Further, the quantity $e^{[\boldsymbol{\omega}]\theta}\boldsymbol{p}$ has the effect of rotating $\boldsymbol{p} \in \mathbb{R}^3$ about the fixed-frame axis $\boldsymbol{\omega}$ by an angle θ.

3.2   Exponential Coordinates for Spatial Rigid-Body Motion

The expression of the exponential coordinates for rotation introduced in 3.1 for $SO(3)$ can be generalized to the Euclidean group, $SE(3)$.

Referring to Fig. 2, consider a rigid body motion which consists of rotation about an axis $\boldsymbol{\omega}$ in space through an angle of θ radians, followed by translation along the same axis by an amount d. Such a motion is called a screw motion, since it is reminiscent of the motion of a screw, in so far as a screw rotates and translates about the same axis. By this analogy, the pitch of the screw is defined as the ratio of translation to rotation, $h = d/\theta$, assuming that $\theta \neq 0$. Thus, the net translational motion after rotating by θ radians is $h\theta$.

As aforementioned, the axis of rotation is $\boldsymbol{\omega} \in \mathbb{R}^3$, $\|\boldsymbol{\omega}\| = 1$, and $\boldsymbol{r}_o \in \mathbb{R}^3$ is the vector for a point R_o on the axis. Assuming that the rigid body rotates about $\boldsymbol{\omega}$ with angular velocity $\dot{\theta}\boldsymbol{\omega}$ together with a translational velocity $d\boldsymbol{\omega} = h\dot{\theta}\boldsymbol{\omega}$, then the velocity of the tip point, $\boldsymbol{p}(t)$, is

$$\dot{\boldsymbol{p}}(t) = \boldsymbol{\omega} \times (\boldsymbol{p}(t) - \boldsymbol{r}_o) + h\boldsymbol{\omega} \tag{28}$$

This equation can be conveniently converted into homogeneous coordinates by defining a 4×4 matrix $[\boldsymbol{S}]$ as

$$[\boldsymbol{S}] = \begin{bmatrix} [\boldsymbol{\omega}] & \boldsymbol{v} \\ \boldsymbol{0} & 0 \end{bmatrix} \tag{29}$$

with $\boldsymbol{v} = -\boldsymbol{\omega} \times \boldsymbol{r}_o + h\boldsymbol{\omega}$. Using Eq. (29), Eq. (28) can be rewritten in the homogeneous form as

$$\begin{bmatrix} \dot{\boldsymbol{p}} \\ 0 \end{bmatrix} = \begin{bmatrix} [\boldsymbol{\omega}] & \boldsymbol{v} \\ \boldsymbol{0} & 0 \end{bmatrix} \begin{bmatrix} \boldsymbol{p} \\ 1 \end{bmatrix} = [\boldsymbol{S}] \begin{bmatrix} \boldsymbol{p} \\ 1 \end{bmatrix} \tag{30}$$

That is

$$\dot{\bar{\boldsymbol{p}}} = [\boldsymbol{S}] \, \bar{\boldsymbol{p}} \tag{31}$$

The solution of the differential equation in Eq. (31) is given by

$$\bar{\boldsymbol{p}}(t) = e^{[\boldsymbol{S}]t} \bar{\boldsymbol{p}}(0) \tag{32}$$

where $e^{[\boldsymbol{S}]t}$ is the matrix exponential of the 4×4 matrix $[\boldsymbol{S}]\,t$, defined by

$$e^{[\boldsymbol{S}]t} = \mathbf{I} + [\boldsymbol{S}]\,t + \frac{([\boldsymbol{S}]\,t)^2}{2!} + \frac{([\boldsymbol{S}]\,t)^3}{3!} + \cdots \tag{33}$$

If the body rotates about the axis $\boldsymbol{\omega}$ at unit velocity for θ units of time, then the net transformation is given by

$$\mathbf{T} = e^{[\boldsymbol{S}]\theta} = \mathbf{I} + [\boldsymbol{S}]\,\theta + [\boldsymbol{S}]^2 \frac{\theta^2}{2!} + [\boldsymbol{S}]^3 \frac{\theta^3}{3!} + \cdots \tag{34}$$

where, $[\boldsymbol{S}]^2 = \begin{bmatrix} [\boldsymbol{\omega}]^2 & \boldsymbol{v} \\ \boldsymbol{0} & 0 \end{bmatrix}$, $[\boldsymbol{S}]^3 = \begin{bmatrix} [\boldsymbol{\omega}]^3 & [\boldsymbol{\omega}]^2 \boldsymbol{v} \\ \boldsymbol{0} & 0 \end{bmatrix}$, $[\boldsymbol{S}]^4 = \begin{bmatrix} [\boldsymbol{\omega}]^4 & [\boldsymbol{\omega}]^3 \boldsymbol{v} \\ \boldsymbol{0} & 0 \end{bmatrix}$, $\cdots$. Such that Eq. (34) becomes

$$\mathbf{T} = e^{[\boldsymbol{S}]\theta} = \begin{bmatrix} e^{[\boldsymbol{\omega}]\theta} & \mathbf{Q}(\theta)\,\boldsymbol{v} \\ \boldsymbol{0} & 1 \end{bmatrix} \tag{35}$$

with $\mathbf{Q}(\theta) = \mathbf{I}\theta + [\boldsymbol{\omega}]\frac{\theta^2}{2!} + [\boldsymbol{\omega}]^2\frac{\theta^3}{3!} + \cdots$; and using the identity $[\boldsymbol{\omega}]^3 = -[\boldsymbol{\omega}]$, $\mathbf{Q}(\theta)$ can be simplified to

$$\mathbf{Q}(\theta) = \mathbf{I}\theta + [\boldsymbol{\omega}]\frac{\theta^2}{2!} + [\boldsymbol{\omega}]^2\frac{\theta^3}{3!} + \cdots$$

$$= \mathbf{I}\theta + \left(\frac{\theta^2}{2!} - \frac{\theta^4}{4!} + \frac{\theta^6}{6!} - \cdots\right)[\boldsymbol{\omega}] + \left(\frac{\theta^3}{3!} - \frac{\theta^5}{5!} + \frac{\theta^7}{7!} - \cdots\right)[\boldsymbol{\omega}]^2$$

$$= \mathbf{I}\theta + (1 - \cos\theta)[\boldsymbol{\omega}] + (\theta - \sin\theta)[\boldsymbol{\omega}]^2 \tag{36}$$

Hence, considering that $v = -\boldsymbol{\omega} \times \mathbf{r}_o + h\boldsymbol{\omega}$, $\mathbf{Q}(\theta)v$ can be derived as following by using the identities that $[\boldsymbol{\omega}]^2\boldsymbol{\omega} = \mathbf{0}$ and $[\boldsymbol{\omega}]^3 = -[\boldsymbol{\omega}]$ as follows,

$$\mathbf{Q}(\theta)v = (\mathbf{I}\theta + (1 - \cos\theta)[\boldsymbol{\omega}] + (\theta - \sin\theta)[\boldsymbol{\omega}]^2)(-\boldsymbol{\omega} \times \mathbf{r}_o + h\boldsymbol{\omega})$$

$$= \mathbf{I}\theta(-\boldsymbol{\omega} \times \mathbf{r}_o + h\boldsymbol{\omega}) + (1 - \cos\theta)[\boldsymbol{\omega}](-\boldsymbol{\omega} \times \mathbf{r}_o + h\boldsymbol{\omega}) + (\theta - \sin\theta)[\boldsymbol{\omega}]^2(-\boldsymbol{\omega} \times \mathbf{r}_o + h\boldsymbol{\omega})$$

$$= -[\boldsymbol{\omega}]\mathbf{r}_o\theta + h\theta\boldsymbol{\omega} - (1 - \cos\theta)[\boldsymbol{\omega}]^2\mathbf{r}_o + 0 + (\theta - \sin\theta)[\boldsymbol{\omega}]\mathbf{r}_o + 0$$

$$= h\theta\boldsymbol{\omega} - (1 - \cos\theta)[\boldsymbol{\omega}]^2\mathbf{r}_o - \sin\theta[\boldsymbol{\omega}]\mathbf{r}_o$$

$$= \left(\mathbf{I} - e^{[\boldsymbol{\omega}]\theta}\right)\mathbf{r}_o + h\theta\boldsymbol{\omega} = (\mathbf{I} - \mathbf{R})\mathbf{r}_o + d\boldsymbol{\omega} \tag{37}$$

which is the same as $^A\mathbf{q}$ that is obtained in Eqs. (10) and (11). Substituting Eq. (37) into Eq. (35), it yields

$$\mathbf{T} = e^{[S]\theta} = \begin{bmatrix} e^{[\boldsymbol{\omega}]\theta} & \mathbf{Q}(\theta)v \\ \mathbf{0} & 1 \end{bmatrix} = \begin{bmatrix} e^{[\boldsymbol{\omega}]\theta} & (\mathbf{I} - e^{[\boldsymbol{\omega}]\theta})\mathbf{r}_o + h\theta\boldsymbol{\omega} \\ \mathbf{0} & 1 \end{bmatrix} = \begin{bmatrix} e^{[\boldsymbol{\omega}]\theta} & (\mathbf{I} - \mathbf{R})\mathbf{r}_o + d\boldsymbol{\omega} \\ \mathbf{0} & 1 \end{bmatrix}$$

$$\tag{38}$$

Further, considering that $\boldsymbol{\omega}^T v = \boldsymbol{\omega}^T(-\boldsymbol{\omega} \times \mathbf{r}_o) + h\boldsymbol{\omega}^T\boldsymbol{\omega}$ such that $h = \boldsymbol{\omega}^T v$, and $\mathbf{r}_o = \boldsymbol{\omega} \times v$, Eq. (38) can also be written as

$$\mathbf{T} = e^{[S]\theta} = \begin{bmatrix} e^{[\boldsymbol{\omega}]\theta} & (\mathbf{I} - e^{[\boldsymbol{\omega}]\theta})(\boldsymbol{\omega} \times v) + \boldsymbol{\omega}\boldsymbol{\omega}^T v\theta \\ \mathbf{0} & 1 \end{bmatrix} = \begin{bmatrix} e^{[\boldsymbol{\omega}]\theta} & [(\mathbf{I} - e^{[\boldsymbol{\omega}]\theta})[\boldsymbol{\omega}] + \boldsymbol{\omega}\boldsymbol{\omega}^T\theta]v \\ \mathbf{0} & 1 \end{bmatrix}$$

$$\tag{39}$$

which is the same as the one obtained in Ref. [2].

In the case of pure translation which complies with $\|\boldsymbol{\omega}\| = 0$, and $\|v\| = 1$, it has

$$[S] = \begin{bmatrix} \mathbf{0} & v \\ \mathbf{0} & 0 \end{bmatrix} \tag{40}$$

which leads to $\mathbf{R} = e^{[\boldsymbol{\omega}]\theta} = \mathbf{I}$, and $\mathbf{Q}(\theta) = \mathbf{I}\theta$ where $\theta = d$ is the amount of translation, such that

$$\mathbf{T} = e^{[S]\theta} = \begin{bmatrix} \mathbf{I} & d\mathbf{v} \\ \mathbf{0} & 1 \end{bmatrix} \tag{41}$$

In the case that $h = d = 0$ and $\|\boldsymbol{\omega}\| = 1$, which corresponds to the pure rotational motion, Eqs. (38) and (39) become

$$\mathbf{T} = e^{[S]\theta} = \begin{bmatrix} e^{[\boldsymbol{\omega}]\theta} & (\mathbf{I} - e^{[\boldsymbol{\omega}]\theta})\mathbf{r}_o \\ \mathbf{0} & 1 \end{bmatrix} = \begin{bmatrix} e^{[\boldsymbol{\omega}]\theta} & (\mathbf{I} - e^{[\boldsymbol{\omega}]\theta})(\boldsymbol{\omega} \times v) \\ \mathbf{0} & 1 \end{bmatrix} \tag{42}$$

where $\mathbf{r}_o$ is the vector for a point on the screw axis as shown in Fig. 2.

From the above derivations, we explicitly indicated that the geometric and exponential expressions of screw displacement lead to exactly the same results; with the geometric approach providing better physical insights and the exponential method demonstrating elegant and rigours mathematical perception. The screw displacement derived above provides background for kinematics investigation through transform operator approach [13], which also coined as POE (product of exponentials) approach [2], involving only one reference coordinate system and one tool coordinate system. The POE method is different from the traditional Denavit-Hartenberg method [14] which is based on transform mapping among $n + 1$ different coordinate systems with n being the number of links in a robotic manipulator.

4   Application of Screw Displacement in Landing Gear Design

Landing gear is an important system in aircraft design and different mechanisms have been used in the design of landing gears. For landing gear design, the mechanisms used need to be simple so as to reduce component failure and hence increase robustness of the system. As shown in Fig. 3, a RSCR (Here, R stands for revolute joint, S represents spherical joint and C denotes cylindrical joint.) mechanism is proposed in the design of a landing gear system. It is expected that the mechanism can locate the wheel at position 1 (see Fig. 3(a)) for storage during the flight mode, and place the wheel to position 2 (see Fig. 3(b)) to execute the landing task.

In this design, a revolute joint is to be fabricated on the fixed frame such that by rotating the wheel supporter about it, the wheel can reach both positions 1 and 2. Thus, identifying the direction of revolute joint A, $\boldsymbol{\omega}$ (see Fig. 3(a)) in the fixed frame is crucial for the design and fabrication of the fixed frame, and the Rodrigues formula for rotation derived in Sects. 2.1 and 3.1 can be applied to solve this problem.

Referring to Fig. 3, a reference coordinate frame $O\text{-}XYZ$ is established at the fixed frame and a body coordinate frame $o\text{-}xyz$ is attached to the wheel. At position 1, the wheel is parallel to the XY-plane of the reference frame and at position 2, the wheel is parallel to the XZ-plane. Based on transform mapping [13], the rotation of coordinate frame $o\text{-}xyz$ from position 1 to position 2 with respect to the reference frame $O\text{-}XYZ$ can be expressed with direction cosines as

$$
{}_{2}^{1}\mathbf{R} = \begin{bmatrix} \boldsymbol{X} \cdot \boldsymbol{x} & \boldsymbol{X} \cdot \boldsymbol{y} & \boldsymbol{X} \cdot \boldsymbol{z} \\ \boldsymbol{Y} \cdot \boldsymbol{x} & \boldsymbol{Y} \cdot \boldsymbol{y} & \boldsymbol{Y} \cdot \boldsymbol{z} \\ \boldsymbol{Z} \cdot \boldsymbol{x} & \boldsymbol{Z} \cdot \boldsymbol{y} & \boldsymbol{Z} \cdot \boldsymbol{z} \end{bmatrix} = \begin{bmatrix} 0 & -1 & 0 \\ 0 & 0 & 1 \\ -1 & 0 & 0 \end{bmatrix} \tag{43}
$$

According to Eq. (23), it has ${}_{2}^{1}\mathbf{R} = \mathbf{R}\,(\boldsymbol{\omega}, \theta)$, such that using Eqs. (5) and (7), rotation angle θ and direction vector $\boldsymbol{\omega}$ indicated in Fig. 3(a) can be calculated as

$$
\theta = \cos^{-1}\left(\frac{\mathrm{tr}\,{}_{2}^{1}\mathbf{R} - 1}{2}\right) = \cos^{-1}\left(\frac{0 - 1}{2}\right) = 120° \tag{44}
$$

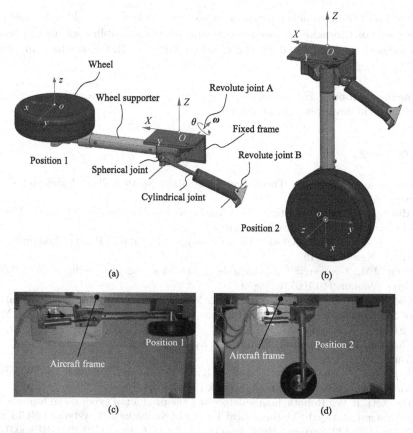

Fig. 3. Design and prototype of a RSCR-mechanism based landing gear

and

$$[\boldsymbol{\omega}] = \begin{bmatrix} 0 & -\omega_z & \omega_y \\ \omega_z & 0 & -\omega_x \\ -\omega_y & \omega_x & 0 \end{bmatrix} = \frac{1}{2\sin\theta}\left(\tfrac{1}{2}\mathbf{R} - \tfrac{1}{2}\mathbf{R}^T\right) = \frac{\sqrt{3}}{3}\begin{bmatrix} 0 & -1 & 1 \\ 1 & 0 & 1 \\ -1 & -1 & 0 \end{bmatrix} \quad (45)$$

Hence, the direction vector of revolute joint A is $\boldsymbol{\omega} = \left[-\frac{\sqrt{3}}{3}, \frac{\sqrt{3}}{3}, \frac{\sqrt{3}}{3}\right]$.

With the direction of the revolute joint A as shown in Figs. 3(a) and (b) obtained above, a RSCR-mechanism based landing gear was designed and a prototype of the proposed landing gear was developed and tested as illustrated in Figs. 3(c) and (d); where the C joint is a driving joint. This landing gear can be used for the design of small scale aircraft and UAV.

5   Conclusions

This paper presented the detailed derivations of screw displacement with geometric method, transfer operator and matrix exponential formula. The paper gathered all the approaches together as so to provide a comprehensive note for researchers in the fields of mechanisms and robotics. Application of the screw displacement was indicated by the development of a RSCR-mechanism based landing gear.

Acknowledgement. The authors wish to thank Mr Stefan Kenway for his valuable contribution in developing the prototype.

References

1. Bottema, O., Roth, B.: Theoretical Kinematics. North Holland Publishing Company, Amsterdam (1979)
2. Murray, R.M., Li, Z., Sastry, S.S.: A Mathematical Introduction to Robotic Manipulation. CRC Press, Boca Raton (1994)
3. Tsai, L.-W.: Robot Analysis : the Mechanics of Serial and Parallel Manipulators. Wiley, New York (1999)
4. Selig, J.M.: Geometric Fundamentals of Robotics, 2nd edn. Springer, NY (2005). https://doi.org/10.1007/b138859
5. Uicker, J.J., Sheth, P.N., Ravani, B.: Matrix Methods in the Design Analysis of Mechanisms and Multibody Systems. Cambridge University Press, New York (2013)
6. Shabana, A.A.: Dynamics of Multibody Systems. Cambridge University Press, New York (2013)
7. Lynch, K.M., Park, F.C.: Modern Robotics: Mechanics, Planning, and Control. Cambridge University Press, New York (2017)
8. Brockett, R.W.: Robotic manipulators and the product of exponential formula. In: Fuhrmann, P.A. (ed.) Mathematical Theory of Networks and Systems. LNCIS, vol. 58, pp. 120–129. Springer, Heidelberg (1984). https://doi.org/10.1007/BFb0031048
9. Park, F.C., Eobrow, J.E., Ploen, S.R.: A lie group formulation of robot dynamics. Int. J. Robot. Res. **14**(6), 609–618 (1995)
10. Gallier, J., Xu, D.: Computing exponential of skew-symmetric matrices and logarithms of orthogonal matrices. Int. J. Robot. Autom. **17**(4), 1–11 (2002)
11. Dai, J.S.: Finite displacement screw operators with embedded chalses' motion. J. Mech. Robot. Trans. ASME **44**, 041002 (2012)
12. Dai, J.S.: Euler-Rodrigues formula variations, quaternion conjugation and intrinsic connections. Mech. Mach. Theory **92**, 144–152 (2015)
13. Craig, J.J.: Introduction to Robotics: Mechanics and Control, 3rd edn. Pearson Education Inc., Upper Saddle River (2005)
14. Denavit, J., Hartenberg, R.S.: A kinematic notation for lower pair mechanisms based on matrices. ASME J. Appl. Mech **77**, 215–221 (1955)

A Modular 3D-Printed Inverted Pendulum

Ian S. Howard$^{(\boxtimes)}$

Centre for Robotics and Neural Systems, University of Plymouth,
Plymouth PL4 8AA, UK
ian.howard@plymouth.ac.uk

Abstract. Here we describe a simple modular 3D-printed design for an inverted pendulum system that is driven using a stepper motor operated by a microcontroller. The design consists of a stainless-steel pole that acts as the pendulum, which is pivoted at one end and attached to a cart. Although in its inverted configuration the pendulum is unstable without suitable control, if the cart travels backwards and forwards appropriately it is possible to balance the pole and keep it upright. The pendulum is intended for use as a research and teaching tool in the fields of control engineering and human sensori-motor control. We demonstrate operation of the design by implementing an observer-based state feedback controller, with augmented positional state of the cart and integral action, that can balance the pole in its unstable configuration and also maintains the cart at its starting position. When the controller is running, the pendulum can resist small disturbances to the pole, and it is possible to balance objects on its endpoint.

1 Introduction

Balancing an inverted pendulum is a classical problem in the field of control engineering. It is a task often used to demonstrate that it is possible to stabilize a system that is otherwise unstable without control and as such provides a test bed for control research, e.g. [1]. The inverted pendulum paradigm has also been adopted to investigate human balancing [2–4] as well as a model for human walking [5].

Inverted pendulums that are used to investigate control generally consists of a rod that acts as the pendulum, which is pivoted at one end and attached to a cart. In a linear inverted pendulum design, the cart can move along a linear track. Although many inverted pendulum designs and their variants exist (e.g. [6, 7]), very few are widely available. Thus, a major consideration of the current design was to ensure it would easy to construct using standard components and 3D printed parts, so other potential users can build their own pendulum units. To support this goal, the design has been made freely available for download (see Results and conclusions section).

2 Inverted Pendulum Components

To ensure the pendulum system easy use and transport, an important design consideration was to make the unit a manageable size (e.g. only about 1 m long), as well as being self-contained and be easy to program. The latter was the motivation to base the

© Springer Nature Switzerland AG 2019
K. Althoefer et al. (Eds.): TAROS 2019, LNAI 11649, pp. 413–424, 2019.
https://doi.org/10.1007/978-3-030-23807-0_34

control on an Arduino microcontroller, since they are widely available. Here we adopt a modular approach to design, so that the system can be updated and expanded in the future. The system is comprised of several 3D printed parts, which are illustrated in Fig. 1. These are mounted on 20 mm aluminum profile that forms the main structural support for the system.

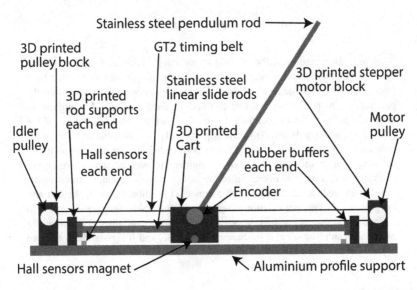

Fig. 1. Schematic of the modular inverted pendulum design, illustrating its main components.

To provide a low friction track, 16 mm diameter stainless steel rods are attached to the profile frame on supports by means of standard aluminum clamps and 3D printed mounting blocks. The large diameter rods were needed to ensure minimal bending due to load of the cart whilst the pendulum rod was swung around. At the end of each track rod section, a protective rubber grommet was used to damp any collisions that may occur between the cart and the end support blocks. Hall effect limit-switch sensors were also located on the frame, to deactivate the motor drive system when the cart reached the end of its travel. A neodymium magnet mounted at the base of the cart provides the necessary switching signal to achieve this.

The cart runs along the two track rods on linear ball bearings to keep friction to a low level. The pendulum element itself is a 600 mm long × 8 mm diameter stainless steel rod section, with an optional 3D printed end piece, so item can be balanced on it. It is attached to a rotary shaft mounted in the cart. An important design requirement here was to ensure the pendulum rod could swings freely through 360° and clear the profile frame structure. The shaft is supported by two sets of ball bearing and its far end is coupled to an incremental encoder. A unit with 2000 pulses per revolution was found suitable.

Fig. 2. Pendulum drive motor and cart mechanism. The drive pulley attached to the stepper motor can be seen on the right and the attachment clamp for the pendulum rod can be seen on the left.

The cart is pulled along its rails by means of a GT2 timing belt, which is attached to the cart using a simple toothed clamp. A tooth GT2 pulley is mounted on the motor to engage the belt. At the opposing end of the frame, a mounting block holds another GT2 pulley so that the belt loops over the length of the track and back and can therefore be used to pull the cart in both directions. Ball bearing were used in the passive pulley to ensure all moving parts could rotate with high precision and with little frictional resistance despite high belt tension.

The motor drive component consists of a 3D printed base located in-between the profile rails, which supports a 2A 1.8° per step standard NEMA23 industrial standard stepper motor attached by means of a standard NEMA23 angle bracket. The motor was driven using a Pololu A4988- type stepper driver. This implements intelligent current control up to 2A. The stepping mode is set via control pins – and in our application we made use of 4x micro stepping. The A4988 operates using a simple step and direction control interface. To operate a stepper motor using this controller, appropriately control pulses (1 pulse per micro step) and direction signals (so motor turns in desired direction) need to be sent to the driver. Overall the motor achieved a maximum cart speed of 0.6 ms^{-1}. We note a slow speed is desirable in many educational settings, since, it reduces the chance of operator (student) injury from the mechanism's moving parts.

The pendulum controller was implemented using an Arduino Mega 2560 R3 microcontroller because it meets the design requirements. Two digital input that support interrupts were needed to support the Hall sensors and another two for the incremental encoder, giving four in total. We note that the Mega has 6 Digital I/O Pins which support interrupts, whereas the cheaper Arduino Uno only supports 2. The Arduino Mega also has considerably more memory than the Uno and therefore this platform will also support future development of more memory-demanding software. It also offers the possibility of extending the current design to a dual pendulum system, since an additional encoder can be accommodated. The main pendulum application was programmed in Arduino-style C-code. Library functions to realize stepper motor velocity operation and state feedback control were written in C++. The system was run from a 20 v 2 A power supply. A close up of the cart and motor drive assemble is shown in in Fig. 2.

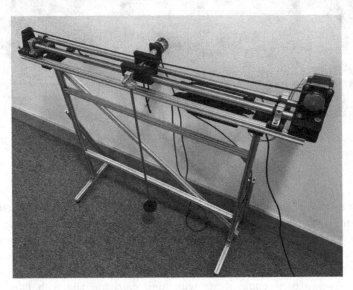

Fig. 3. Pendulum system mounted on its aluminum profile stand. This provides a convenient and elegant means of support and allows the pendulum to rotate freely and avoid collisions.

The main track holders, motor drive and end pulley support are all separately attached to the aluminum profile sections with T-nuts, so they can be easily removed and adjusted. This attachment methods also facilitates tensioning the drive belt, since the T-nuts can be loosened, and the motor block slid along the profile until desired tension is achieved. The modular construction ensures that the parts of the inverted pendulum system are easy to change and also upgraded with future designs, if so desired. This is particularly useful in teaching scenarios because different tasks can then be given to different groups of students with only minor modifications to the apparatus. For example, the pole rod can easily be changed with one on a different length. Similarly, the stepper motor unit could be exchanged for a drive unit employing a faster torque-controlled brushless DC motor, enabling the use of force control instead of velocity control and supporting one-shot swing-up operation in reinforcement learning experiments.

The mounting blocks and pendulum cart were designed using AutoCAD Fusion 360. This was subsequently used to generate STL format files and the mechanical parts were manufactured in PLA using a Flash forge Creator Pro 3D printer. We note that higher impact materials such as nylon would greatly improve the robustness of the design, but PLA has also proved to be an adequate choice.

During operation, the inverted pendulum unit requires mounting at a suitable height off the ground, so that so that the rod can swing freely. A custom-made support stand made out of 20 mm aluminum profile was therefore constructed to mount the pendulum system. This provided a strong but light weight construction that can be easily transported. It consists of two aluminum profile pillars. These are filled at their base with cross member section attached with feet. At the top they are capped with 3D printed support sections that fit in between the aluminum frame of the pendulum structure. Diagonal aluminum profile sections are also used to brace the structure to increase its stiffness. An assembled pendulum on its stand is shown in Fig. 3.

3 State Space Analysis of the Pendulum

To demonstrate operation of the inverted pendulum and provide a useful basis for experiments and demonstrations of control, here we implement observed-based state feedback control with augmented positional state (of cart) and integral action [8]. The non-linear differential equation describing the inverted pendulum kinematics is given by

$$(I + ml^2)\frac{d^2\theta}{dt^2} + \mu\frac{d\theta}{dt} = mgl\sin\theta + ml\frac{d^2x_P}{dt^2}\cos\theta \tag{1}$$

This expression can be linearized around the unstable equilibria of the pendulum to give the linearized differential equation describing an inverted pendulum kinematics, which is given by

$$(I + ml^2)\frac{d^2\theta}{dt^2} + \mu\frac{d\theta}{dt} = mgl\theta + ml\frac{d^2x_P}{dt^2} \tag{2}$$

Where: The angle to the vertical is denoted by θ, the coefficient of viscosity is denoted by μ, mass of the pendulum is denoted by m, moment of inertial of the rod about its center of mass is I, length to the center of mass is denoted by l and the displacement of the cart is given by x_p. We note that this kinematic description is sufficient to derive control, provided we use cart acceleration or velocity as the control input. Velocity control of the cart was chosen here over acceleration control because of the relative ease of implementing velocity control using a stepper motor. This can be achieved with a simple function that uses a timer to generates pulses at a frequency corresponding to the desired rotational speed of the motor. Writing the differential equation describing the inverted pendulum with the highest state related term on the LHS be have

$$\Rightarrow \frac{d^2\theta}{dt^2} = -\frac{\mu}{(I + ml^2)}\frac{d\theta}{dt} + \frac{mgl}{(I + ml^2)}\theta + \frac{ml}{(I + ml^2)}\frac{d^2x_P}{dt^2} \tag{3}$$

Since we wish to stabilize the pendulum using velocity control, we first write the acceleration control term on the RHS as

$$\frac{d^2x_P}{dt^2} = \frac{dv_c}{dt} \tag{4}$$

We now let the constant terms be represented by coefficients as follows:

$$a_1 = \frac{\mu}{(I + ml^2)} \tag{5}$$

$$a_2 = \frac{-mgl}{(I + ml^2)} \tag{6}$$

$$b_0 = \frac{ml}{(I + ml^2)} \tag{7}$$

We let the constant terms be represented by coefficients terms, leading to the equation for dynamics

$$\frac{d^2\theta}{dt^2} = -a_1 \frac{d\theta}{dt} - a_2\theta + b_0 \frac{dv_c}{dt} \tag{8}$$

We now choose the state variables

$$x_1 = \theta \tag{9}$$

$$x_2 = \frac{d\theta}{dt} - b_0 v_c \tag{10}$$

$$\Rightarrow \frac{d\theta}{dt} = x_2 + b_0 v_c \tag{11}$$

The choice of x_1 is clear since it is simply pendulum angle θ. However, we note that the choice of x_2 is not simply angular velocity. It also includes a term made to cancel-out the time differential of control velocity term, as will shortly become apparent. Differentiating the state x_1 with respect to time we get:

$$\Rightarrow \dot{x}_1 = \frac{d\theta}{dt} \tag{12}$$

Representing this in terms of the control and the state x_2:

$$\Rightarrow \dot{x}_1 = x_2 + b_0 v_c \tag{13}$$

$$\Rightarrow \dot{x}_2 = \frac{d^2\theta}{dt^2} - b_0 \frac{dv_c}{dt} \tag{14}$$

$$\Rightarrow \frac{d^2\theta}{dt^2} = \dot{x}_2 + b_0 \frac{dv_c}{dt} \tag{15}$$

Substituting the terms into Eq. (8)

$$\Rightarrow \dot{x}_2 + b_0 \frac{dv_c}{dt} = -a_1(x_2 + b_0 v_c) - a_2 x_1 + b_0 \frac{dv_c}{dt} \tag{16}$$

Cancelling terms and re-arranging this leads to

$$\Rightarrow \dot{x}_2 = -a_1 x_2 - a_2 x_1 - a_1 b_0 v_c \tag{17}$$

Rewriting Eqs. (13) and (17) in state space matrix notation we see that

$$\dot{x}_1 = 0x_1 + 1x_2 + b_0 v_c \tag{18}$$

$$\dot{x}_2 = -a_2 x_1 - a_1 x_2 - a_1 b_0 v_c \tag{19}$$

Writing equations in matrix format we therefore have

$$\Rightarrow \begin{bmatrix} \dot{x}_1 \\ \dot{x}_2 \end{bmatrix} = \begin{bmatrix} 0 & 1 \\ -a_2 & -a_1 \end{bmatrix} \begin{bmatrix} x_1 \\ x_2 \end{bmatrix} + \begin{bmatrix} b_0 \\ -a_1 b_0 \end{bmatrix} v_c \tag{20}$$

$$\Rightarrow y = \begin{bmatrix} 1 & 0 \end{bmatrix} \begin{bmatrix} x_1 \\ x_2 \end{bmatrix} \tag{21}$$

4 Observer to Estimate State

We use a Luenberger observer to estimate the full inverted pendulum system state by using the state space a model of the plant. This is captured by the matrices A and B given in Eq. (20), and a correction term arising from the measured output. We note that this is necessary since the state x_2 is not available for measurement in our implementation. The observer generates the state estimate according to the dynamical equation:

$$\dot{\hat{X}} = A\hat{X} + BU + L(Y - C\hat{X}) \tag{22}$$

The observer gain vector L needs to be found such that the eigenvalue solutions λ to the characteristic equation for its error dynamics all have suitable negative real values:

$$|(A - LC - \lambda I)| = 0 \tag{23}$$

Here we choose observer correction gain L using Matlab (The MathWorks Inc., Natick, MA, USA) by means of pole placement using the place command, with poles set to $[-20 \; -24]$. The values were found by experimentation.

5   Augmenting Positional State and Adding Integral Action

It is possible to build a controller just using feedback of the 2-dimensional state derived from the observer in Eq. (22). However, in practice we want to control cart position as well as pendulum angle, since otherwise the cart has no reason to stop moving or remain at a given location. To control cart position too, we add a third state x_3 to represent cart position. In the current pendulum design, there are two options to obtain cart position. We can either integrate the velocity control signal or we can count the pulses sent to the stepper motor and scale the count appropriately. In our analysis, here we demonstrate the former approach.

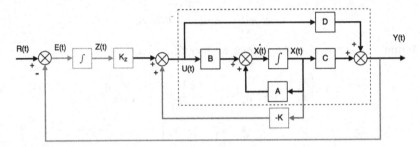

Fig. 4. Adding integral feedback using an integrator to reduce zero steady state error. The output from the plant is compared against a reference input (in our case zero). The resulting error is then integrated and weighted by the integral gain and added to the state feedback.

To use to the control signal in this way to estimate cart position, we note that differential of x_3 is simply given by the input velocity control signal. Therefore, we can write:

$$\begin{bmatrix} \dot{x}_1 \\ \dot{x}_2 \\ \dot{x}_3 \end{bmatrix} = \begin{bmatrix} 0 & 1 & 0 \\ -a_2 & -a_1 & 0 \\ 0 & 0 & 0 \end{bmatrix} \begin{bmatrix} x_1 \\ x_2 \\ x_3 \end{bmatrix} + \begin{bmatrix} b_0 \\ -a_1 b_0 \\ 1 \end{bmatrix} v_c \tag{24}$$

$$y = \begin{bmatrix} 1 & 0 & 0 \end{bmatrix} \begin{bmatrix} x_1 \\ x_2 \\ x_3 \end{bmatrix} \tag{25}$$

Integral action for a general system is illustrated in Fig. 4 and it provides an effective means to reduce steady state error for a state space controller. To reduce steady state positional error of the pendulum cart location, we also add an additional state within our controller that computes the integral of the positional error. To implement integral action, we further augment the pendulum system matrices given in Eq. (24) by adding a fourth state x_4 to represent integrated cart position error. This formulation assumes that our reference input is zero.

$$
\begin{bmatrix} \dot{x}_1 \\ \dot{x}_2 \\ \dot{x}_3 \\ \dot{x}_4 \end{bmatrix} = \begin{bmatrix} 0 & 1 & 0 & 0 \\ -a_2 & -a_1 & 0 & 0 \\ 0 & 0 & 0 & 0 \\ 0 & 0 & 1 & 0 \end{bmatrix} \begin{bmatrix} x_1 \\ x_2 \\ x_3 \\ x_4 \end{bmatrix} + \begin{bmatrix} b_0 \\ -a_1 b_0 \\ 1 \\ 0 \end{bmatrix} v_c
\tag{26}
$$

$$
y = \begin{bmatrix} 1 & 0 & 0 & 0 \end{bmatrix} \begin{bmatrix} x_1 \\ x_2 \\ x_3 \\ x_4 \end{bmatrix}
\tag{27}
$$

6 State Feedback Control

Finally, we design the feedback gain vector K needed to implement full feedback state control in the full state vector as given in Eq. (26), although we use estimates of states x_1 and x_2 obtained from the Luenberger observer, i.e. xhat$_1$ and xhat$_2$. The eigenvalues λ of the state feedback control system are found by solving its characteristic equation

$$
|(A - BK - \lambda I)| = 0
\tag{28}
$$

We can thus influence the location of eigenvalues of the system by changing gain matrix K. We determine K using pole placements using the Matlab place command, with poles set to $[-8.8 \; -9.6 \; -10.4 \; -1.6]$. The feedback gains were also found using a process of experimentation. We note that the observer poles were deliberately selected to be more aggressive than those used for the feedback controller, to ensure faster settling of its state estimate. The structure of the observer-based controller is illustrated in Fig. 5.

7 Pseudocode and Arduino Implementation

After the system matrices for the system, and the observer and controller gains L and K were calculated, they were tested using a Matlab simulation that made use of a non-linear simulation of the inverted pendulum, based on Eq. (1). Simulations (Fig. 6) indicated that with appropriate pole placement, the design was able to resist small velocity disturbances to the balanced pole (modeled as small non-zero initial rod velocity) and maintain the cart at its origin. Importantly this was achieved when cart velocity was limited to the maximum cart speed that could be achieved by the stepper motor. We then implemented the observer-based real-time controller using an Arduino Mega. Figure 7 shows the controller unit with its lid removed. This controller case was 3D printed and attaches to the pendulum frame with T-nuts. We note that the fan was essential in this design to prevent the stepper driver from overheating. The control processing was carried out in a poll loop. Its operation involves reading the encoder to determine pendulum angle, calculating the velocity control signal and using it to generate an output pulse train to drive the stepper motor in. State updates were performed using Euler integration [9].

Pseudo-code for the main controller loop operation is as follows:

loop

    Calculate time since last update
    Read the pendulum angle
    Compute control u using full state $[xhat_1\ xhat_2\ x_3\ x_4]^T$
    Calculate observer correction term using encoder position
    Update observer state estimates $[xhat_1\ xhat_2]^T$
    Use control velocity from input to update cart position x_3
    Update integral action positional error state x_4
    Generate stepper velocity drive pulses from u

End

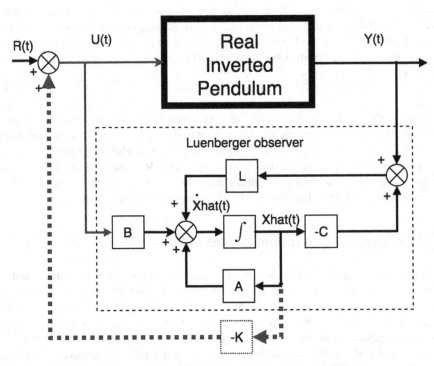

Fig. 5. State feedback control using a Luenberger observer to estimate pendulum state. We only have access to the output angle of the real pendulum Y(t), which is shown in the upper part of the diagram, and not all of its states. The observer, shown in the lower part of the diagram, is simply a model of the real inverted pendulum dynamics and generates a state estimate Xhat, which is used to provide state feedback. The output angle from the pendulum encoder is represented by Y (t), and this signal is only used to correct the state estimate.

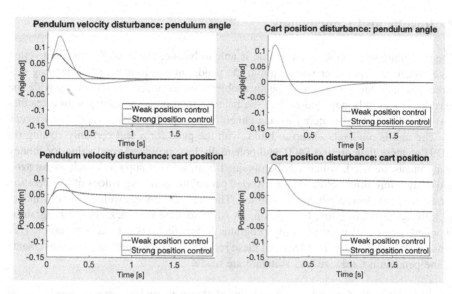

Fig. 6. Simulation of the pendulum system in Matlab showing effect of weak (poles at $[-8.8 \ -9.6 \ -0.016 \ -0.008]$; blue line) and strong control of cart position (poles at $[-8.8 \ -9.6 \ -0.016 \ -4.0]$; red line). Left panels shown the response to an initial perturbation of pendulum rod angular velocity (a simulated tap of the rod). Right panels shown the response to an initial displacement of pendulum cart position from its origin. In both cases the pendulum angle stabilizes to zero. However, it can be seen that when poles relating to cart position and its integral error are weak (close to zero), cart position is barely compensated. (Color figure online)

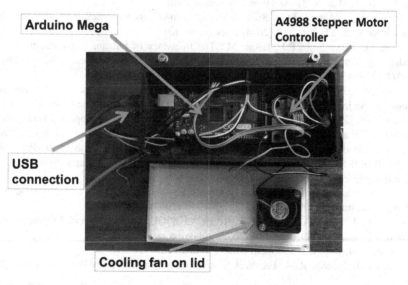

Fig. 7. Arduino Mega-based stepper motor controller unit using am A4988 stepper driver.

8 Results and Conclusions

The pendulum operated effectively and is able to balance the pendulum in its inverted state. When the controller was running, the pendulum could resist small tapping disturbances and it was possible to balance objects on its endpoint. Indeed, provide the encoder is precisely adjusted so that the balance state precisely aligns with a reading corresponding to 0°, balancing is maintained for many 10 s of minutes (if not longer).

The unit is relatively cheap to build, with the parts for a unit certainly costing (in 2019) no more than around £400, and potentially less, provided good value-for-money components are used, which can be obtained from internet suppliers such as Amazon and eBay. More information on the inverted pendulum including videos of its operation are available at Howardlab.com/pendulum. The design is freely available for download, as well as the list of parts. In addition, an Arduino state feedback control program is supplied, as well as a set of utility programs to test the encoder, stepper motor, Hall sensors and menu control system. All these resources will be updated as improvements to the pendulum hardware and software are made.

Acknowledgments. Two 3rd year University of Plymouth student projects, undertaken by Jacob Threadgould and Daniel Hunt, influenced and contributed to the inverted pendulum design presented here. We thank Phil Culverhouse and two anonymous reviewers for commenting on an earlier version of the manuscript.

References

1. Anderson, C.W.: Learning to control an inverted pendulum using neural networks. IEEE Control Syst. Mag. **9**, 31–37 (1989). cs.colostate.edu
2. Cabrera, J.L., Milton, J.G.: Stick balancing: on-off intermittency and survival times. Nonlinear Stud. **11**, 305–318 (2004) researchgate.net
3. Loram, I.D., Gawthrop, P.J., Lakie, M.: The frequency of human, manual adjustments in balancing an inverted pendulum is constrained by intrinsic physiological factors. J. Physiol. **577**(1), 417–432 (2006)
4. Franklin, S., Cesonis, J., Franklin, D.W.: Influence of visual feedback on the sensorimotor control of an inverted pendulum. Presented at the 2018 40th Annual International Conference of the IEEE Engineering in Medicine and Biology Society (EMBC), pp. 5170–5173 (2018)
5. Kajita, S., Kanehiro, F., Kaneko, K., Yokoi, K., Hirukawa, H.: The 3D linear inverted pendulum mode: a simple modeling for a biped walking pattern generation. In: Proceedings 2001 IEEE/RSJ International Conference on Intelligent Robots and Systems (2001). ieeexplore.ieee.org
6. Awtar, S., et al.: Inverted pendulum systems: rotary and arm-driven - a mechatronic system design case study. Mechatronics **12**(2), 357–370 (2002)
7. Grasser, F., D'arrigo, A., Colombi, S., Rufer, A.C.: JOE: a mobile, inverted pendulum. IEEE Trans. Ind. Electron. **49**, 107–114 (2002). robonz.com
8. Dorf, R.C., Bishop, R.H.: Modern control systems (2011)
9. Aström, K.J., Murray, R.M.: Feedback Systems. Princeton University Press, Princeton (2010)

A Geometric Dynamics Algorithm
for Serially Linked Robots

Mohammad Safeea[1,2] (ID), Pedro Neto[1(✉)] (ID), and Richard Béarée[2] (ID)

[1] Department of Mechanical Engineering, University of Coimbra, Coimbra, Portugal
ms@uc.pt, pedro.neto@dem.uc.pt
[2] Arts et Métiers, LISPEN, Lille, France
richard.bearee@ensam.eu

Abstract. This study introduces the Geometric Dynamics Algorithm
(GDA) for representing the dynamics of serially linked robots. GDA is
non-symbolic, preserves simple formulation, and is convenient for numerical implementation. GDA-based algorithms are deduced for efficient calculation of various dynamic quantities including (1) joint space inertia
matrix (JSIM) (2) Coriolis matrix (3) centrifugal matrix (4) and the time
derivative of JSIM. The proposed algorithms were analyzed in terms of
their computational complexity. Results compare favorably with other
methods.

Keywords: Dynamics · Serially linked robots ·
Geometric dynamic algorithm

1 Introduction

Inverse dynamics equation of robots is a complex multi-variable function of its
joints torques velocities accelerations and positions. The joint space formulation
of this equation is:

$$\boldsymbol{\tau} = \mathbf{A}(\boldsymbol{q})\ddot{\boldsymbol{q}} + \mathbf{B}(\boldsymbol{q}, \dot{\boldsymbol{q}})\dot{\boldsymbol{q}} + \boldsymbol{g} \tag{1}$$

Where $\boldsymbol{\tau}$ is the vector of robot's joints torques, $\boldsymbol{q}$ is the vector of joints positions,
$\dot{\boldsymbol{q}}$ is the vector of joints angular velocities, $\ddot{\boldsymbol{q}}$ is the vector of joints angular
accelerations, $\mathbf{A}(\boldsymbol{q})$ is the joint space inertia matrix of the robot, $\mathbf{B}(\boldsymbol{q}, \dot{\boldsymbol{q}})$ is the
joint space Coriolis matrix of the robot, and $\boldsymbol{g}$ is the vector of joint's torques
due to gravity.

One of the earliest methods used to deduce the equations of robot dynamics
is based on Lagrangian formulation. This method is well described in the literature [13]. However, the method requires partial differentiation, usually done
off-line on a computer using a symbolic math software [11]. In addition, for robots
with high degrees of freedom (high DOF) the generated equations are enormous
resulting in slow execution [9]. The formulation of robot-specific dynamics using
Kane's equations is in [8], the authors demonstrated the methodology for deducing dynamics equations of a robot by hand. Newton-Euler recursive method is

© Springer Nature Switzerland AG 2019
K. Althoefer et al. (Eds.): TAROS 2019, LNAI 11649, pp. 425–435, 2019.
https://doi.org/10.1007/978-3-030-23807-0_35

described in [10]. It includes forward propagation for calculating links acceler-ations followed by a backward propagation for calculating joints torques. The method is very efficient for calculating the torques vector. However, the calcu-lations are carried out implicitly such that the dynamic matrices (inertia, Cori-olis, centrifugal) cannot be retrieved directly. Composite Rigid Body Algorithm (CRBA) [7] is an efficient method for calculating the mass matrix of robots. Though, it can not be used for calculating other dynamic matrices. Calculating Coriolis matrix is important for control applications, for example in passivity-based control as noted in [5]. In [4], the Coriolis matrix was used for calculating collision detection signal. In that study the Coriolis matrix transpose appears in the term $\mathbf{B}^{\mathrm{T}}(\boldsymbol{q}, \dot{\boldsymbol{q}})\dot{\boldsymbol{q}}$ of equation (22), as such Coriolis matrix has to be cal-culated explicitly in real time for performing real time reaction control. Coriolis matrix can be deduced in a symbolic form by utilizing Euler-Lagrange formu-lation through partial differentiation and by utilizing Christoffel symbol of the first kind.

In this study we propose a novel method for representing the dynamics of robots. In our method, the dynamics quantities are calculated as contributions of frames' effects in what we call the frame injection effect. In such a case, the dynamics of each link is described using a separate equation linear in $\ddot{\boldsymbol{q}}$, expressed in a mathematical formulation resembling the manipulator's inverse dynamics equation. This facilitates (as shown later) the process of calculating: joint space inertia matrix (JSIM), Coriolis matrix, centrifugal matrix, and the time derivative of JSIM, (TD-JSIM), for serially linked robots. Accompanying code for various algorithms described in this article is available publicly in the repository [1].

2   Theory and Principals

The proposed algorithm depends on what we call the frame injection effect, introduced in our previous work [12]. Each frame j attached to joint j transfers to link i a linear acceleration into its center of mass $\ddot{\boldsymbol{p}}_{\mathrm{C}ij}$ and an inertial moment around its center of mass $\boldsymbol{\mu}_{\mathrm{C}ij}$, Fig. 1(a). This transfer is due to the rotational effect of joint j around its axes of rotation, or the z axis of frame j according to modified Denavit Hartenberg (MDH) designation. This cause and effect rela-tionship between frame j and link i is referred to by the subscript ij in $\ddot{\boldsymbol{p}}_{\mathrm{C}ij}$ and $\boldsymbol{\mu}_{\mathrm{C}ij}$, while the C in the subscript is used to refer to the mass center of link i, the same subscript notation will hold throughout this paper for denoting frame-link interaction of cause-and-effect unless stated otherwise.

2.1   Link's Acceleration Due to the Single-Frame Rotation

It can be proved that each frame j transfers to the center of mass of link i three acceleration vectors tangential ($\ddot{\boldsymbol{p}}_{\mathrm{C}ij}^{\tau}$), normal ($\ddot{\boldsymbol{p}}_{\mathrm{C}ij}^{n}$) and Coriolis ($\ddot{\boldsymbol{p}}_{\mathrm{C}ij}^{cor}$). The first of which is shown in Fig. 1(b), it is due to the angular acceleration of frame j, and it can be calculated from:

$$\ddot{\boldsymbol{p}}_{\mathrm{C}ij}^{\tau} = \boldsymbol{\varepsilon}_j \times \boldsymbol{p}_{\mathrm{C}ij} \tag{2}$$

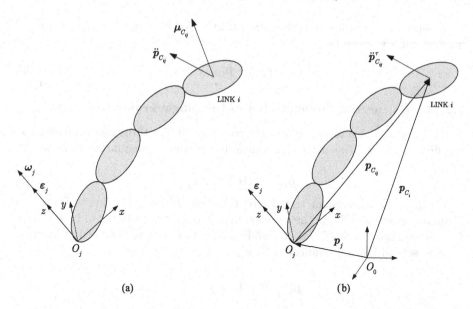

Fig. 1. (a) Inertial moment and linear acceleration transferred to link i by frame j. (b) Tangential acceleration of center of mass of link i transferred by frame j.

Where p_{Cij} is the vector connecting the origin of frame j and the center of mass of link i, $\times$ is the cross product, and ε_j is the angular acceleration of link j:

$$\varepsilon_j = \ddot{q}_j k_j \tag{3}$$

Where k_j is the unit vector associated with the z axis of joint j, and $\ddot{q}_j$ is the angular acceleration of that joint. The normal acceleration is shown in Fig. 2(a), and it is given by:

$$\ddot{p}^n_{Cij} = \omega_j \times (\omega_j \times p_{Cij}) \tag{4}$$

Where ω_j is the angular velocity of link j due to the rotation of joint j:

$$\omega_j = \dot{q}_j k_j \tag{5}$$

Thus, we can rewrite the equation of the normal acceleration:

$$\ddot{p}^n_{Cij} = k_j \times (k_j \times p_{Cij}) \dot{q}_j^2 \tag{6}$$

Coriolis acceleration $\ddot{p}^{cor}_{Cij}$ is shown in Fig. 2(b), it can be calculated from:

$$\ddot{p}^{cor}_{Cij} = 2\omega_j \times v^r_{Cij} \tag{7}$$

Where v^r_{Cij} is the velocity transferred to the center of mass of link i from frames $j+1$ up to frame i, and the superscript r is to denote that this is a relative velocity. v^r_{Cij} can be calculated from:

$$v^r_{Cij} = \sum_{k=j+1}^{i} \omega_k \times p_{Cik} \tag{8}$$

As such the total linear acceleration transferred by frame j to the center of mass of link i is given by:

$$\ddot{p}_{Cij} = \ddot{p}_{Cij}^{\tau} + \ddot{p}_{Cij}^{n} + \ddot{p}_{Cij}^{cor} \tag{9}$$

2.2   Link's Inertial Moment Due to the Single-Frame Rotation

It can be proved that each frame j will transfer to link i three inertial moments, the first of the inertial moments transferred is due to angular acceleration of frame j:

$$\boldsymbol{\mu}_{Cij}^{\tau} = (\mathbf{R}_i \mathbf{I}_i^i \mathbf{R}_i^{\mathsf{T}}) \boldsymbol{\varepsilon}_j \tag{10}$$

Where $\boldsymbol{\mu}_{Cij}^{\tau}$ is the moment transferred by frame j into link i due to frame's j angular acceleration, $\mathbf{R}_i$ is the rotation matrix of frame i relative to base frame, $\mathbf{I}_i^i$ is the inertial tensor of link i around its center of mass represented in frame i.

The second inertial moment $\boldsymbol{\mu}_{Cij}^{n}$ is due to centrifugal effect:

$$\boldsymbol{\mu}_{Cij}^{n} = \frac{1}{2}(\mathbf{L}_i \boldsymbol{\omega}_j) \times \boldsymbol{\omega}_j \tag{11}$$

Where $\mathbf{L}_i$ is a 3×3 matrix that is calculated from:

$$\mathbf{L}_i = \mathbf{R}_i (\mathrm{tr}(\mathbf{I}_i^i)\mathbf{1}_3 - 2\mathbf{I}_i^i)\mathbf{R}_i^{\mathsf{T}} \tag{12}$$

Where the subscript in $\mathbf{L}_i$ is to notate that the matrix calculated pertains to link i, $\mathrm{tr}(\mathbf{I}_i^i)$ is the trace of the inertial tensor, and $\mathbf{1}_3$ is the identity matrix.

The third inertial moment $\boldsymbol{\mu}_{Cij}^{cor}$ is due to Coriolis effect:

$$\boldsymbol{\mu}_{Cij}^{cor} = (\mathbf{L}_i \boldsymbol{\omega}_j) \times \boldsymbol{\omega}_{ij}^{r} \tag{13}$$

Where $\boldsymbol{\omega}_{ij}^{r}$ can be calculated from:

$$\boldsymbol{\omega}_{ij}^{r} = \sum_{k=j+1}^{i} \boldsymbol{\omega}_k \tag{14}$$

Thus, the total inertial moment transferred to link i around its center of mass due to the rotational effect of frames j is given by:

$$\boldsymbol{\mu}_{Cij} = \boldsymbol{\mu}_{Cij}^{\tau} + \boldsymbol{\mu}_{Cij}^{n} + \boldsymbol{\mu}_{Cij}^{cor} \tag{15}$$

2.3   Dynamical Representation of a Single-Link

Each link i can be represented dynamically by an equivalent acceleration of its center of mass $\ddot{p}_{Ci}$ and an inertial moment around its center of mass $\boldsymbol{\mu}_{Ci}$ Fig. 3(a). Where $\ddot{p}_{Ci}$ is given by:

$$\ddot{p}_{Ci} = \sum_{j=1}^{i} \ddot{p}_{Cij} \tag{16}$$

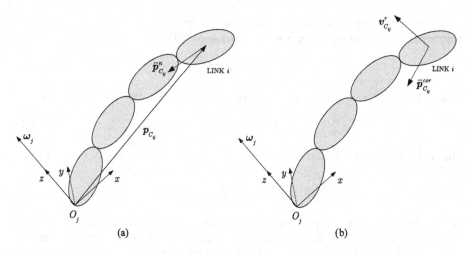

Fig. 2. (a) Normal acceleration of center of mass of link i transferred by frame j. (b) Coriolis acceleration of center of mass of link i transferred by frame j.

Or by substituting $\ddot{\boldsymbol{p}}_{Cij}$ with its value from (9) we get:

$$\ddot{\boldsymbol{p}}_{Ci} = \sum_{j=1}^{i} \ddot{\boldsymbol{p}}_{Cij}^{\tau} + \ddot{\boldsymbol{p}}_{Cij}^{n} + \ddot{\boldsymbol{p}}_{Cij}^{cor} \tag{17}$$

From the previous equation we notice that the total acceleration of the center of mass of link i can be rewritten in a form similar to the equation of inverse dynamics by using a matrix vector notation as in the following:

$$\ddot{\boldsymbol{p}}_{Ci} = \mathbf{C}_i \ddot{\boldsymbol{q}} + \mathbf{D}_i \dot{\boldsymbol{q}} \tag{18}$$

Where $\mathbf{C}_i$ is $3 \times n$ matrix and the jth column vector of this matrix is given by:

$$\mathrm{col}_j(\mathbf{C}_i) = \frac{\ddot{\boldsymbol{p}}_{Cij}^{\tau}}{\ddot{q}_j} = \boldsymbol{k}_j \times \boldsymbol{p}_{Cij} \tag{19}$$

The subscript i attached to the matrix $\mathbf{C}_i$ is used to notate that the matrix pertains to link i. The robot's links has n of $\mathbf{C}$ matrices each pertains to one link. $\mathbf{D}_i$ is also a $3 \times n$ matrix, and the subscript i in $\mathbf{D}_i$ is used as before. $\mathbf{D}_i$ columns can be calculated from:

$$\mathrm{col}_j(\mathbf{D}_i) = \boldsymbol{k}_j \times (\boldsymbol{k}_j \times \boldsymbol{p}_{Cij})\dot{q}_j + 2\boldsymbol{k}_j \times \boldsymbol{v}_{Cij}^r \tag{20}$$

Using the same reasoning μ_{Ci} can be calculated:

$$\mu_{Ci} = \sum_{j=1}^{i} \mu_{Cij}^{\tau} + \mu_{Cij}^{n} + \mu_{Cij}^{cor} \tag{21}$$

Again we notice that the contribution of $\ddot{q}$ to the inertial moment is associated only with $\boldsymbol{\mu}_{Cij}^{\tau}$. Consequently, we can rearrange (21):

$$\boldsymbol{\mu}_{Ci} = \mathbf{U}_i \ddot{q} + \mathbf{V}_i \dot{q} \tag{22}$$

Where $\mathbf{U}_i$ is a $3 \times n$ matrix, each column vector of this matrix is given by:

$$\mathrm{col}_j(\mathbf{U}_i) = (\mathbf{R}_i \mathbf{I}_i^i \mathbf{R}_i^{\mathrm{T}}) \boldsymbol{k}_j \tag{23}$$

Similarly, $\mathbf{V}_i$ is a $3 \times n$ matrix, each column vector of this matrix is given by:

$$\mathrm{col}_j(\mathbf{V}_i) = \frac{1}{2}(\mathbf{L}_i \boldsymbol{\omega}_j) \times \boldsymbol{k}_j + (\mathbf{L}_i \boldsymbol{k}_j) \times \boldsymbol{\omega}_{ij}^{\tau} \tag{24}$$

As a result, each link is represented by a linear acceleration of its center of mass, and an inertial moment around its center of mass. Their mathematical equation is linearized in $\ddot{q}$ and $\dot{q}$, resembling the manipulator's inverse dynamics equation.

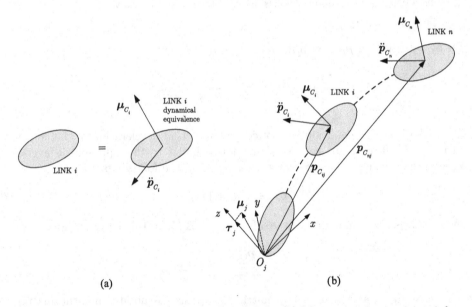

(a)   (b)

Fig. 3. (a) Dynamical representation of each link. (b) Moment acting on joint j due to robot's motion.

2.4   Moment Acting on a Joint Due to Robot Dynamics

From Fig. 3(b), the total moment $\boldsymbol{\mu}_j$ acting on joint j is:

$$\boldsymbol{\mu}_j = \sum_{i=j}^{n} \boldsymbol{\mu}_{Ci} + m_i \boldsymbol{p}_{Cij} \times \ddot{\boldsymbol{p}}_{Ci} \tag{25}$$

Which can be rearranged in a form resembling the inverse dynamics equation:

$$\boldsymbol{\mu}_j = \mathbf{G}_j \ddot{\boldsymbol{q}} + \mathbf{H}_j \dot{\boldsymbol{q}} \tag{26}$$

Where $\mathbf{G}_j$ is $3 \times n$ matrix, each column k of this matrix is given by:

$$\mathrm{col}_k(\mathbf{G}_j) = \sum_{i=j}^{n} \mathrm{col}_k(\mathbf{U}_i) + m_i \boldsymbol{p}_{Cij} \times \mathrm{col}_k(\mathbf{C}_i) \tag{27}$$

In a similar way, each column k of matrix $\mathbf{H}_j$ can be calculated from:

$$\mathrm{col}_k(\mathbf{H}_j) = \sum_{i=j}^{n} \mathrm{col}_k(\mathbf{V}_i) + m_i \boldsymbol{p}_{Cij} \times \mathrm{col}_k(\mathbf{D}_i) \tag{28}$$

Subscript j in $\mathbf{H}_j$ and $\mathbf{G}_j$ is to denote that these matrices are associated with joint j.

2.5 Robot's Dynamics, Joint Space Inertia Matrix, Coriolis and Centrifugal Matrices

The torque acting on joint k due to robot dynamics is calculated from projecting $\boldsymbol{\mu}_k$, derived in the previous section, onto the z axis of joint k as in the following:

$$\tau_k = \boldsymbol{k}_k^{\mathrm{T}} \boldsymbol{\mu}_k \tag{29}$$

If we designate the inertial matrix by the symbol $\mathbf{A}$, then each row k of it, $\mathrm{col}_k(\mathbf{A}^{\mathrm{T}})$, is calculated from:

$$\mathrm{col}_k(\mathbf{A}^{\mathrm{T}}) = \boldsymbol{k}_k^{\mathrm{T}} \mathbf{G}_k \tag{30}$$

Using the same notion, each row k of Coriolis matrix $\mathbf{B}$, or $\mathrm{col}_k(\mathbf{B}^{\mathrm{T}})$ can be calculated from:

$$\mathrm{col}_k(\mathbf{B}^{\mathrm{T}}) = \boldsymbol{k}_k^{\mathrm{T}} \mathbf{H}_k \tag{31}$$

Thus, the inverse dynamics equation of the robot defined by the inertial matrix $\mathbf{A}(\boldsymbol{q})$ and Coriolis matrix $\mathbf{B}(\boldsymbol{q}, \dot{\boldsymbol{q}})$, has been derived.

Using the same principals developed in this section the joint space centrifugal matrix can be calculated, this is done by considering only the terms resulting from Centrifugal accelerations during the calculation of matrices $\mathbf{D}_i$, $\mathbf{V}_i$ and $\mathbf{H}_j$.

2.6 Geometrical Calculation of the Time Derivative of Inertia Matrix

The time derivative of JSIM shows up as a by-product when calculating the time derivative of the generalized momentum in [4], which has applications in collision detection, while as noted in [5] the author had to change the formulation of the equation describing the rate of change of the generalized momentum in order to avoid the numerical differentiation of JSIM since calculating it numerically introduces errors which destroy its symmetric property. In this section we describe the methodology for deducing an efficient and fast algorithm of $O(n^2)$ for calculating TD-JSIM on the bases of the frame injection principal. The proposed algorithm was implemented in MATLAB® and the computational cost of this algorithm is presented in operation count section of this paper.

It has been shown previously in (30) that each row of JSIM is given by:

$$\text{col}_k(\mathbf{A}^T) = \mathbf{k}_k^T \mathbf{G}_k$$

Thus, the time derivative of matrix $\mathbf{A}$ is calculated:

$$\text{col}_k(\dot{\mathbf{A}}^T) = \dot{\mathbf{k}}_k^T \mathbf{G}_k + \mathbf{k}_k^T \dot{\mathbf{G}}_k \tag{32}$$

Since $\mathbf{k}_k^T$ is of a constant magnitude then its time derivative is given by:

$$\dot{\mathbf{k}}_k^T = (\boldsymbol{\omega}_k^0 \times \mathbf{k}_k)^T \tag{33}$$

Where $\boldsymbol{\omega}_k^0$ is the angular velocity of frame k. Since that the derivative of matrix $\mathbf{G}_k$ can be defined by the derivative of its columns then by considering (27), each column of $\dot{\mathbf{G}}_k$ is calculated from:

$$\text{col}_j(\dot{\mathbf{G}}_k) = \sum_{i=k}^{n} \text{col}_j(\dot{\mathbf{U}}_i) + m_i \dot{\mathbf{p}}_{Cik} \times \text{col}_j(\mathbf{C}_i)$$

$$+ m_i \mathbf{p}_{Cik} \times \text{col}_j(\dot{\mathbf{C}}_i) \tag{34}$$

While it can be shown that the derivative terms inside the summation of the previous equation are equal to:

$$\text{col}_j(\dot{\mathbf{U}}_i) = \boldsymbol{\omega}_i^0 \times (\mathbf{R}_i \mathbf{I}_i^i \mathbf{R}_i^T \mathbf{k}_j) - (\mathbf{R}_i \mathbf{I}_i^i \mathbf{R}_i^T)((\boldsymbol{\omega}_i^0 - \boldsymbol{\omega}_j^0) \times \mathbf{k}_j) \tag{35}$$

And:

$$\dot{\mathbf{p}}_{Cik} = \mathbf{v}_{Ci} - \mathbf{v}_k \tag{36}$$

Where $\mathbf{v}_{Ci}$ is the linear velocity of the center of mass of link i and $\mathbf{v}_k$ is the linear velocity of origin of frame k.

$$\text{col}_j(\dot{\mathbf{C}}_i) = (\boldsymbol{\omega}_j^0 \times \mathbf{k}_j) \times \mathbf{p}_{Cij} + \mathbf{k}_j \times (\mathbf{v}_{Ci} - \mathbf{v}_j) \tag{37}$$

Thus the TD-JSIM can be calculated. Using MATLAB®, the equations of this section were implemented in an efficient $O(n^2)$ algorithm for calculating TD-JSIM available in [1]. We also want to mention here that with slight modification of the algorithm proposed, the term $\mathbf{C}^T(\mathbf{q}, \dot{\mathbf{q}})\dot{\mathbf{q}}$ in equation (22) of [4] can be calculated numerically and efficiently from the relation

$$\mathbf{C}^T(\mathbf{q}, \dot{\mathbf{q}})\dot{\mathbf{q}} = \dot{\mathbf{A}}\dot{\mathbf{q}} - \mathbf{b}$$

Where $\mathbf{b}$ is the Coriolis vector. This calculation can be done efficiently, by taking an advantage of the fact that several parameters of robot dynamics are calculated at the same time when $\dot{\mathbf{A}}$ is being calculated, thus $\mathbf{b}$ can be calculated as a by-product while calculating $\dot{\mathbf{A}}$, the cost analysis of the proposed algorithms is described in operation count section.

3   Implementation and Results

To assess the performance of GDA, a comparison with well established algorithms was performed. While Robotics Toolbox for MATLAB® (RTB) [2], CRBA algorithm by Featherstone [6] and the symbolic-numeric method in [14], were used for comparison, we want to mention here that after a lengthy search for robotics toolboxes, RTB, is the only toolbox that we could find on MATLAB® that can calculate Coriolis matrix numerically.

Accompanying MATLAB® code is provided in the repository [1], where we developed the following functions:

1- GetMassMatrixGDA: calculates joint space inertia matrix.
2- GetCoriolisMatrixGDA: calculates joint space Coriolis matrix.
3- GetCentrifugalMatrixGDA: calculates joint space centrifugal matrix.
4- GetDerivativeOfMassMatrixGDA: calculates the time derivative of JSIM.
5- GetCTdqGDA: calculates the time derivative of JSIM, Coriolis vector, and $\mathbf{C}^{\mathrm{T}}(\boldsymbol{q}, \dot{\boldsymbol{q}})\dot{\boldsymbol{q}}$ as described before.

The repository also contains a detailed breakdown on the computational complexity for the implemented algorithms, or the number of floating point operations, additions and multiplications, as a function of the number of DOF of the robot. Table 1 shows a summary, for comparison the table lists also the computational complexity of the other algorithms. For constructing joint space inertia and Coriolis matrices, RTB invokes several calls of the efficient recursive Newton-Euler, as described in [3]. As such RTB constructs JSIM column by column. This is done by assigning a unity value to only one element of joint's acceleration vector, while assigning zeros to remaining elements, joints velocities and gravity term, then recursion is performed, and the associated column vector of the inertia matrix is calculated. The same procedure is repeated for all of JSIM columns, and since that the computational complexity of recursive Newton-Euler is $O(n)$ and that constructing the inertia matrix requires n recursions, then the total computational complexity of the algorithm is of $O(n^2)$. For calculating Coriolis matrix RTB uses the same methodology it applies for calculating JSIM, that is by performing several recursions, at each recursion the angular accelerations and gravity term are set to zero, while one of the possible combinations of $(\dot{q}_i, \dot{q}_j)$ is utilized, as such RTB invokes $n^2/2$ recursions, and the total computational complexity is of $O(n^3)$.

Table 1 also shows that the Composite Rigid Body Algorithm (CRBA) is more efficient in calculating the mass matrix. In contrast, the proposed method can be used to calculate the inertia matrix, Coriolis matrix, Centrifugal matrix, and TD-JSIM matrix with computational complexity of $O(n^2)$. An added advantage of GDA is that when the aforementioned matrices are being evaluated robot dynamics represented by inertial moments and accelerations of the links are being calculated as a by-product of the computations.

Table 1. Operation count for proposed method and other methods, m stands for multiplication and a for addition.

Method	Matrix	Cost
GDA	JSIM	$(18n^2 + 49n)m + (16n^2 + 37n - 3)a$
GDA	Coriolis	$(36n^2 + 49n - 3)m + (34.5n^2 + 32.5n - 6)a$
GDA	Centrifugal	$(15n^2 + 58n)m + (13.5n^2 + 39.5n - 3)a$
GDA	TD-JSIM	$(46.5n^2 + 124.5n - 36)m + (51.5n^2 + 117.5n - 41)a$
CRBA	JSIM	$(10n^2 + 22n - 32)m + (6n^2 + 37n - 43)a$
Symbolic-Numeric	JSIM-Coriolis	$(\frac{3}{2}n^3 + \frac{35}{2}n^2 + 9n - 16)m + (\frac{7}{6}n^3 + \frac{23}{2}n^2 + \frac{64}{3}n - 28)a$
RTB	JSIM	$O(n^2)$
RTB	Coriolis	$O(n^3)$

4 Conclusion

In this paper we proposed a novel algorithm for representing the dynamics of serially linked robots and calculating its joint space inertia matrix, Coriolis matrix, centrifugal matrix, and the time derivative of joint space inertia matrix. In addition we described the frame injection principal. A comparison between the proposed algorithm against other well established algorithms was made, the performance of the proposed algorithm was discussed in operation count section of this paper. We perceive that GDA's way of representing robot dynamics in a mathematical form resembling the equation of the inverse dynamics as intuitive, simple and easy to implement. It's remarkable efficiency is reflected by the $O(n^2)$ algorithm deduced for calculating the time derivative of joint space inertia matrix. By using this methodology other parameters of robot dynamics can be calculated efficiently in a like manner to what had been presented in this paper.

Acknowledgments. This research was partially supported by Portugal 2020 project DM4Manufacturing POCI-01-0145-FEDER-016418 by UE/FEDER through the program COMPETE 2020, and the Portuguese Foundation for Science and Technology (FCT) SFRH/BD/131091/2017 and COBOTIS (PTDC/EME- EME/32595/2017).

References

1. Matlab code for GDA. https://github.com/Modi1987/The-Geometric-Dynamics-Algorithm-GDA-/
2. Corke, P.: Robotics, Vision and Control: Fundamental Algorithms in MATLAB, vol. 73. Springer, Heidelberg (2011)
3. Corke, P.I., et al.: A computer tool for simulation and analysis: the robotics toolbox for matlab. In: Proceedings of National Conference on Australian Robot Association, pp. 319–330 (1995)
4. De Luca, A., Albu-Schaffer, A., Haddadin, S., Hirzinger, G.: Collision detection and safe reaction with the DLR-III lightweight manipulator arm. In: 2006 IEEE/RSJ International Conference on Intelligent Robots and Systems, pp. 1623–1630. IEEE (2006)

5. De Luca, A., Ferrajoli, L.: A modified Newton-Euler method for dynamic computations in robot fault detection and control. In: IEEE International Conference on Robotics and Automation, 2009, ICRA 2009, pp. 3359–3364. IEEE (2009)
6. Featherstone, R.: Spatial vectors and rigid-body dynamics. http://royfeatherstone.org/spatial/
7. Featherstone, R.: Rigid Body Dynamics Algorithms. Springer, Heidelberg (2014)
8. Kane, T.R., Levinson, D.A.: The use of Kane's dynamical equations in robotics. Int. J. Robot. Res. **2**(3), 3–21 (1983)
9. Khalil, W.: Dynamic modeling of robots using recursive Newton-Euler techniques. In: ICINCO2010 (2010)
10. Luh, J.Y., Walker, M.W., Paul, R.P.: On-line computational scheme for mechanical manipulators. J. Dyn. Syst. Meas. Control **102**(2), 69–76 (1980)
11. Neuman, C.P., Murray, J.J.: Symbolically efficient formulations for computational robot dynamics. J. Robot. Syst. **4**(6), 743–769 (1987)
12. Safeea, M., Bearee, R., Neto, P.: Reducing the computational complexity of mass-matrix calculation for high DOF robots. In: 2018 IEEE/RSJ International Conference on Intelligent Robots and Systems (IROS). pp. 5614–5619 (2018). https://doi.org/10.1109/IROS.2018.8593775
13. Sciavicco, L., Siciliano, B., Villani, L.: Lagrange and Newton-Euler dynamic modeling of a gear-driven robot manipulator with inclusion of motor inertia effects. Adv. Robot. **10**(3), 317–334 (1995)
14. Vukobratović, M., Li, S.G., Kirćanski, N.: An efficient procedure for generating dynamic manipulator models. Robotica **3**(03), 147–152 (1985)

Full-Rotation Singularity-Safe Workspace for Kinematically Redundant Parallel Robots

Yat Hei Cheung[1], Nicholas Baron[2(✉)], and Nicolas Rojas[1]

[1] Dyson School of Design Engineering, Imperial College London, London, UK
{yat.cheung16,n.rojas}@imperial.ac.uk
[2] School of Engineering and Informatics, University of Sussex, Brighton, UK
n.baron@sussex.ac.uk

Abstract. This paper introduces and computes a novel type of workspace for kinematically redundant parallel robots that defines the region in which the end-effector can make full rotations without coming close to singular configurations; it departs from the traditional full-rotation dexterous workspace, which considers full rotations without encountering singularities but does not take into account the performance problems resulting from closeness to these locations. Kinematically redundant architectures have the advantage of being able to be reconfigured without changing the pose of the end-effector, thus being capable of avoiding singularities and being suitable for applications where high dexterity is required. Knowing the workspace of these robots in which the end-effector is able to complete full, smooth rotations is a key design aspect to improve performance; however, since this singularity-safe workspace is generally small, or even non-existent, in most parallel manipulators, its characterisation and calculation have not received attention in the literature. The proposed workspace for kinematically redundant robots is introduced using a planar parallel architecture as a case study; the formulation works by treating the manipulator as two halves, calculating the full-rotation workspace of the end-effector for each half whilst ensuring singularity conditions are not approached or met, and then finding the intersection of both regions. The method is demonstrated on two example robot instances, and a numerical analysis is also carried out as a comparison.

Keywords: Singularity-safe workspace · Parallel robots ·
Kinematically redundant robots · Full-rotation

1 Introduction

Parallel robots are used in many different applications due to their high speed, accuracy and payload-to-weight ratio. However, they generally suffer from restricted workspaces and limited rotational capabilities. One of the main reasons

© Springer Nature Switzerland AG 2019
K. Althoefer et al. (Eds.): TAROS 2019, LNAI 11649, pp. 436–447, 2019.
https://doi.org/10.1007/978-3-030-23807-0_36

for these drawbacks is the existence of singularities in their workspaces—these are problematic configurations in which the total degrees of freedom of the robot changes, leading to a deterioration in its performance. A strategy to avoid singularities in the workspace of a parallel robot is to use kinematically redundant architectures; which have more actuators than required by the task workspace, but all of these are required to be in operation in order for the robot mechanism to be rigid [1,2,9]. The additional degrees of freedom indeed allows singularities to be avoided without changing the pose of the end-effector.

An important aspect of the design of parallel robot manipulators is the calculation of their workspaces. Multiple types of workspaces have been proposed in the literature, each of which are important for different potential applications [7]. Despite this, a workspace which defines the region in which the end-effector is ensured full, smooth rotations (i.e. full rotatability far from singularities) has not received attention in the literature, partly due to the limited rotational capabilities of most parallel robots. In [6], the author presents a full rotation workspace that is singularity free; however, this workspace only describes the region in which the robot avoids directly being in a singular configuration, but does not take into account cases where the robot is very close to one. This is an important limitation as the performance of a manipulator deteriorates significantly as the robot nears a singularity.

In this paper, a novel workspace is proposed for kinematically redundant architectures which ensures the robot is able to complete full rotations without coming close to a singularity; this characteristic implies that smooth trajectories of the end-effector can be reliably achieved anywhere within the workspace. The formulation of the workspace utilises the kinematically redundant architecture in order to guarantee that singularities are never encountered, but without needlessly reducing the size of the workspace. The method of calculating this workspace is formulated for a case study architecture; namely, a kinematically redundant planar parallel manipulator first proposed in [4]. The presented method consists of treating this mechanism as two 'halves', and the workspace in which the end-effector can complete full rotations is determined for each half whilst ensuring the conditions for being in a singularity are not approached. The intersection between the two regions is then computed to obtain the total full-rotation singularity-safe workspace. The method is carried out on two example robot instances, along with a numerical analysis to act as a comparison.

The paper is structured as follows. In Sect. 2, the proposed workspace is discussed and the case study architecture is described, as are the geometric conditions in which the robot is in a singularity. Section 3 presents the algorithms used to compute the boundaries of the workspace and the method of calculating the resulting area. In Sect. 4, the full-rotation singularity-safe workspaces of two example mechanisms are computed. We conclude in Sect. 5.

2   Kinematically Redundant Planar Parallel Robots

Kinematically redundant parallel robots are useful mechanisms for applications where high dexterity is required. When designing these devices, it is important to

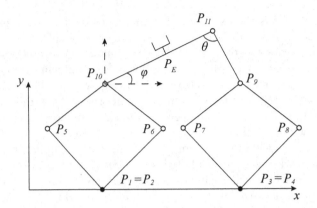

Fig. 1. The kinematically redundant planar parallel architecture used to computed the full-rotation singularity-safe workspace.

know the region where the end-effector can achieve full, smooth rotations; however, workspaces that fit this description remain elusive in the current literature. Herein, this workspace is introduced, and its computation utilises the additional degrees of freedom of the kinematically redundant architecture in order to avoid singularities without over-constraining the size of the workspace.

A method to calculate the full-rotation singularity-safe workspace is exemplified in this paper using the kinematically redundant planar parallel robot proposed in [4], with the actuation scheme of the robot using $\underline{R}RR$ legs instead of $R\underline{P}R$ kinematic chains. In this notation, R denotes a passive revolute joint, $\underline{P}$ denotes an actuated prismatic joint, and $\underline{R}$ denotes an actuated revolute joint. The kinematic architecture and notation of this robot mechanism is displayed in Fig. 1. The mechanism consists of a moving platform connected to the base via four $\underline{R}RR$ legs and an additional, or redundant, link. Two of the legs are joined to the platform via a revolute joint whose centre is P_{10} and to the base with revolute joints whose centres are P_1 and P_2. The other two legs are similarly joined to the base, joint centres P_3 and P_4, and are joined to the redundant link via a revolute joint whose centre is P_9. The redundant link is then connected to the platform via a revolute joint whose centre is P_{11}. Additionally, two extra conditions have been imposed which both increase the workspace of each pair of legs and simplify the following calculations. These are that the positions of the base joints P_1 and P_2 are coincident, as are P_3 and P_4, and that the lengths of the links in each pair of legs are equal.

The kinematic redundancy of the robot means that there is an infinite number of solutions to the inverse kinematics problem. This is because for any given pose of the moving platform, there is an infinite range of possible orientations that the redundant link can occupy and still produce a feasible configuration of the robot. This means that it is possible to control the orientation of this link in order to move further away from singularities. From here in, the term singularity refers to the direct kinematic singularity of planar parallel robots; a configuration where

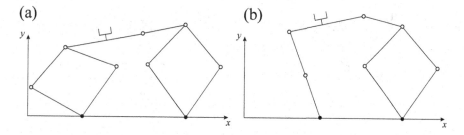

Fig. 2. The two singularity conditions. In (a), this is due to the collinearity between the moving platform and the redundant link. In (b), it is due to the collinearity between the distal links.

the total number of degrees of freedom of the mechanism increases, resulting in a loss of control of the robot.

For the architecture displayed in Fig. 1, there are two geometric conditions that result in the robot being in a singular configuration, which are shown in Fig. 2. The first condition is when two of the distal links of the legs become collinear, either due to the legs being at full extension or being oriented in the same manner. The second condition is when the redundant link becomes collinear with the moving platform.

A problem for parallel robots is that in addition to the the failure of the system when the mechanism is directly in a singularity, the performance of the robot also deteriorates as such a configuration is neared [8]. Therefore, as well as defining the geometric conditions where the robot is directly in a singularity, it is useful to define a region around this condition where the performance of the robot is likely to deteriorate. Here, since both singularity conditions are the collinearity of two links, the circumstance can be safely avoided by the introduction of a variable, γ, that defines the minimum angle between them, the maximum angle is then given by $\pi - \gamma$, such that

$$\gamma < \angle(\overrightarrow{P_i P_k}, \overrightarrow{P_j P_k}) < \pi - \gamma$$

where P_i, P_j, and P_k are replaced by P_5, P_6, P_{10}; P_7, P_8, P_9; and P_9, P_{10}, P_{11}.

If $\gamma = 0$, then the resulting workspace will not be singularity free, and if $\gamma = \pi/2$, then the workspace area shrinks to zero, because the legs would be constrained to a single length. In [4], the authors recommend that in order to compute the workspace of the mechanism, θ, the angle formed by points P_9, P_{10}, and P_{11}, should be set to $\pi/2$. The redundant link and the moving platform are then treated as one link, which allows straightforward methods of workspace calculation developed for non-redundant RRR mechanisms to be applied [3,5]. However, this needlessly reduces the workspace as it limits one degree of freedom of the robot.

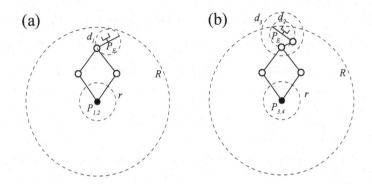

Fig. 3. Diagrams of the 'left' and 'right' sides of the robot. Each diagram shows the maximum and minimum reach of the legs. For the 'left' side, the circle of radius d_1 around P_E denotes the trajectory of P_{10} that must be feasible in order for full rotatability to be ensured. For the 'right' side, the radius of the equivalent P_9 trajectory can vary between d_2 and d_3.

3   Full-Rotation Singularity-Safe Workspace—A Case Study

In this section, the method of calculating the full-rotation singularity-safe workspace of the architecture in Fig. 1 is presented. Given the conditions that the lengths of the links in the legs are equal and that the base joints of each pair of legs are coincident, the workspaces of the end joints of each pair of legs, namely P_9 and P_{10}, can be described by the position of the coincident base joints and two radii, R and r, which denote the maximum and minimum reach of each pair of legs before the angle between the distal links becomes less than γ or greater than $\pi - \gamma$.

After setting the condition which ensures the distal links of the legs do not become close to being collinear, the aim is to find the region in which the end-effector, P_E, has full rotatability without the angle between the redundant link and the platform either becoming less than γ or greater than $\pi - \gamma$. This is done by considering, according to the notation of Fig. 1, the kinematic chain formed by legs 1 (P_1, P_5, P_{10}) and 2 (P_2, P_6, P_{10}) and the link from P_{10} to the end-effector P_E, then performing a similar analysis by considering the kinematic chain formed by legs 3 (P_3, P_7, P_9) and 4 (P_4, P_8, P_9) and the links connecting P_9 and P_E, and then finding the intersection of these regions. These two regions, illustrated in Fig. 3, will be referred to as the 'left' and 'right' side of the robot, respectively. The workspace of each side of the mechanism can consist of up to two regions, an outer annular and an inner circular region, and therefore each workspace is defined by the radii of three boundaries.

Algorithm 1. Workspace Boundaries of Left Side of Robot

1: **procedure** LEFT SIDE WORKSPACE BOUNDARIES (l_1, d_1, γ)
2:     $R \leftarrow (2l_1)cos(\frac{\gamma}{2})$
3:     $r \leftarrow (2l_1)cos(\frac{\pi - \gamma}{2})$
4:     **if** $d_1 > R$ **then**
5:         $B_{L1} = 0$
6:     **else**
7:         **if** $R - 2d_1 \geq r$ or $R - 2d_1 \leq -r$ **then**
8:             $B_{L1} = R - d_1$
9:         **else if** $d_1 > r$ **then**
10:            $B_{L1} = d_1 - r$
11:        **else**
12:            $B_{L1} = 0$
13:     **if** $d_1 \leq r$ **then**
14:         **if** $2d_1 \leq R - r$ **then**
15:             $B_{L2} = r + d_1$
16:         **else**
17:             $B_{L1} = 0$
18:     **else**
19:         The workspace divides into an inner circle and an outer annular region.
20:         **if** $2d_1 < r + R$ **then**
21:             $B_{L3} = d_1 - r$
22:         **else**
23:             $B_{L1} = 0$
24:         **if** $2d_1 \leq R - r$ **then**
25:             $B_{L2} = r + d_1$
26:         **else**
27:             $B_{L1} = 0$

3.1 Left Side of Robot

Firstly, let's start with the left side of the robot; Algorithm 1 is used to compute the radii of the boundaries which define the workspace; B_{L1} and B_{L2} denote the radii of the outer and inner boundaries of the annular region, respectively, and B_{L3} denotes the radius of the boundary of the inner circle (this equals zero if this region does not exist).

Here the algorithm is described, with the aid of Fig. 4. The logic of the algorithm is to find the most extreme feasible position of the end-effector, with respect to P_1, before P_{10} is unable to complete a circular trajectory of radius d_1 around it. The inputs to the algorithm are the leg link length, l_1, the distance between P_{10} and P_E, d_1, and γ. Firstly, the maximum and minimum leg extensions are calculated. If the maximum leg extension, R, is less than d_1, then there is no workspace. This is because in order for full rotation of the end-effector to be possible, P_{10} has to be able to follow a circular trajectory of radius d_1 around the end-effector, and at the same time, P_{10} must be within the workspace of the leg (within the circles defined by radii R and r) at all points of the trajectory.

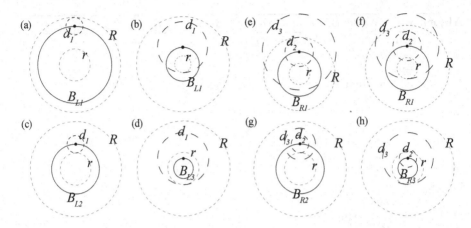

Fig. 4. A demonstration of multiple steps in the algorithms used to compute the workspaces of the left and right sides of the robot. Each of the circular boundaries of radius r, R, B_{Li} and B_{Ri} are centred around the base joint. The circles of radius d_1, d_2, and d_3 are centred around the end-effector when its position lies on the boundary B_{Li} or B_{Ri}.

Therefore if $d_1 > R$, no end-effector position exists where all P_{10} positions are possible. If $d_1 \leq R$, there may be a workspace possible.

If a circle of radius d_1 can be drawn which touches the circle of radius R without moving outside it, and which does not enter the void circular region defined by radius r, the radius of the outer boundary, B_{L1}, is given by $R - d_1$, see Fig. 4(a). If it does enter the void circle (that whose radius is r), then an additional condition needs to be checked. If $d_1 > r$, then $B_{L,1}$ equals $d_1 - r$, because the end-effector position has to be moved inwards until the circle of radius d_1 is able to clear the void circle, see Fig. 4(b). If $d_1 < r$, then there is no workspace because no matter how far inward the end-effector is moved, it will never be able to clear the void circle.

The next stage is to compute B_{L2} and B_{L3}. Firstly, if $d_1 < r$ the workspace consists of a single region. If twice the distance d_1 is less than the difference between R and r, then the minimum boundary B_{L2} equals $r + d_1$, because this is the furthest the end-effector can be moved inward until the circle of radius d_1 would move into the void circle, see Fig. 4(c). If twice the distance d_1 is greater than the difference between R and r, then there is no workspace because there is no place either between the circles defined by R and r, or within the void circle, where the end-effector can lie without the circle of radius d_1 passing outside the maximum leg extension, or into the void circle.

If $d_1 > r$, the workspace splits into an inner circle and an outer annular region. If $2d_1 < r + R$, then B_{L3} equals $d_1 - r$ because this is the furthest the end-effector can move out from the centre until the circle of radius d_1 moves into the void circle, see Fig. 4(d), otherwise there is no workspace. Like before, if $2d_1 < R - r$, then B_{L2} equals $r + d_1$, else there is no workspace.

Algorithm 2. Workspace Boundaries of Right Side of Robot

1: **procedure** RIGHT SIDE WORKSPACE BOUNDARIES $(l_2, d_{9,11}, d_{11,e}, \gamma)$

2:     $R \leftarrow (2l_2)cos(\frac{\gamma}{2})$

3:     $r \leftarrow (2l_2)cos(\frac{\pi - \gamma}{2})$

4:     $d_2 = \sqrt{d_{9,11}^2 + d_{11,e}^2 - 2d_{11,e}d_{9,11}cos(\gamma)}$

5:     $d_3 = \sqrt{d_{9,11}^2 + d_{11,e}^2 - 2d_{11,e}d_{9,11}cos(\pi - \gamma)}$

6:     **if** $d_2 > R$ **then**

7:         There is no workspace.

8:         $B_{R1} = 0$

9:     **else**

10:         **if** $2d_2 \leq r - R$ **then**

11:             $B_{R1} = R - d_2$

12:             $B_{R2} = r + d_2$

13:         **else**

14:             **if** $d_2 + d_3 < R + r$ **then**

15:                 **if** $d_3 < r$ **then**

16:                     $B_{R1} = 0$

17:                 **else**

18:                     $B_{R1} = d_3 - r$

19:             **else**

20:                 $B_{R1} = R - d_2$

21:         **if** $d_3 < r$ **then**

22:             **if** $2d_2 \leq R - r$ **then**

23:                 $B_{R2} = r + d_2$

24:             **else**

25:                 $B_{R1} = 0$

26:                 $B_{R2} = 0$

27:         **else**

28:             **if** $d_2 + d_3 > R + r$ **then**

29:                 $B_{R3} = R - d_2$

30:             **else**

31:                 $B_{R3} = d_3 - r$

3.2   Right Side of Robot

For the right side of the robot; Algorithm 2 is used to compute the radii of the boundaries which define the workspace; similar to before, B_{R1} and B_{R2} denote the radii of the outer and inner boundaries of the annular region, respectively, and B_{R3} denotes the radius of the boundary of the inner circle.

The logic of the algorithm is to find the most extreme feasible position of the end-effector before P_9 is unable to complete a circular trajectory of a radius between d_2 and d_3 around it. The inputs to the algorithm are the leg link length, l_2, the distance between P_9 and P_{11}, $d_{9,11}$, the distance between P_{11} and P_E, $d_{11,e}$, and γ. Again, the first step is the maximum and minimum leg extensions. The maximum and minimum distances between the end-effector and P_9, d_3 and d_2, are then calculated by considering the maximum and minimum allowed angles between the moving platform and the redundant link. The algorithm follows a similar logic to Algorithm 1; for brevity, the steps which are similar to those used there are not described in detail, and the remaining steps are described with the aid of Fig. 4.

Firstly, if the maximum leg extension is less than d_2, $R < d_2$, then there is no workspace. Otherwise, if a circle of radius d_2 can be drawn which fits between the circles defined by R and r, then $B_{R,1}$ is given by $R - d_2$ and B_{R2} is set at an initial value of $r + d_2$. Otherwise, additional conditions need to be checked. If $R - d_2 - d_3 \leq -r$, then the outer boundary is given by $R - d_2$; this is because if the circle of radius d_2 passes through the void circle but the circle of radius d_3 does not, then the outer boundary, B_{R1}, is given by moving the end-effector as close as possible to the outer leg boundary before part of the circle of radius d_2 moves outside the circle defined by R, see Fig. 4(e). However, if $R - d_2 - d_3$ is greater than $-r$, another condition needs to be checked. If $r > d_3$, there is no workspace because no matter how much the end-effector is moved towards the centre, any trajectory of P_9 around the end-effector will always pass through the void circle. On the other hand, if $r < d_3$ the maximum boundary equals $d_3 - r$; this is because now the end-effector can be moved toward the centre until d_3 can reach the other side of the void circle, see Fig. 4(f).

Next, radii B_{R2} and B_{R3} are calculated. The first condition to be checked is if $d_3 < r$; if so, the workspace is given by at most a single region. If $2d_2$ is greater than the difference between the circles defined by R and r, there is no workspace, otherwise the inner boundary of the annular region, B_{R2}, is given by $r + d_2$; this is because the end-effector cannot be moved into the void circle because d_3 is too small for P_9 to escape from it, therefore the end-effector has to be moved toward the void circle until the circle defined by d_2 touches the void circle, see Fig. 4(g).

If $d_3 > r$, the workspace splits into an outer annular region and an inner circular region. If $d_3 - r$ is greater than $R - d_2$ then B_{R3} is set to $R - d_2$; this is because otherwise P_9 would not always remain within the circle defined by R. If $d_3 - r$ is less than or equal to $R - d_2$, then B_{R3} equals $d_3 - r$; this is because this is the furthest the end-effector can be moved away from the centre before the circle of radius d_3 passes through the void circle, see Fig. 4(h). The last step is to make sure B_{R2} is greater than B_{R3}, if it is not, then there is no void workspace within the outer boundary and both are made equal to zero.

3.3   Workspace Intersection

Using Algorithms 1 and 2, a maximum of 6 boundary circles are formulated: $B_{L1}, B_{L2}, B_{L3}, B_{R1}, B_{R2}$ and B_{R3}. The total workspace is then given by the intersection of these regions. As B_{L1}, B_{L3}, B_{R1} and B_{R3} are bounding workspaces, their intersection regions are addition operations to the robot's workspace, whereas B_{L2} and B_{R2} are boundaries of void spaces, hence their intersection regions are subtraction operations to the robot's workspace. Given $B_{L1} \geq B_{L2} \geq B_{L3}$ and $B_{R1} \geq B_{R2} \geq B_{R3}$, there are a few workspace regions,

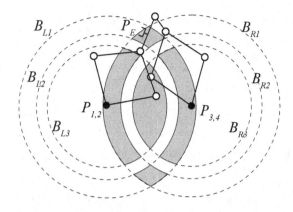

Fig. 5. Diagram showing five different workspace regions.

with C_i representing the circular region bounded by B_i:

$$W_1 = C_{L1} \cap C_{R1} - C_{L1} \cap C_{R2} - C_{L2} \cap C_{R1}$$
$$W_2 = C_{L3} \cap C_{R1} - C_{L3} \cap C_{R2}$$
$$W_3 = C_{L1} \cap C_{R3} - C_{L2} \cap C_{R3}$$
$$W_4 = C_{L3} \cap C_{R3}$$

In the cases where $C_{L3} \subseteq C_{R1}$, W_2 and W_4 are completely contained within W_1; and if $C_{R3} \subseteq C_{L1}$, W_3 and W_4 are completely contained within W_1. However it must be noted that W_1 can be divided into two symmetric regions by C_{L2} and C_{R2}. This happens when there are intersections between the boundaries B_{L1} and B_{R2}, B_{L2} and B_{R1}, and B_{L2} and B_{R2}. Hence there is a maximum of 5 full-rotation dexterous workspace, as show in Fig. 5. When computing the numerical area of W_1, the area of $C_{L2} \cap C_{R2}$ should also be added, otherwise this area would effectively be subtracted twice.

This simplifies the workspace calculation into the areas of intersection between multiple pairs of circles, as shown in Fig. 6. The intersection region is formed by two segments, each bounded by an arc from one of the circles and the line, L, which passes through the two intersection points I_1 and I_2.

The centres of the circles, P_1 and P_3, are known, and the positions of the points of intersection between the circles, I_1 and I_2, and their angles in relation to the circle centres, $\angle(\overrightarrow{P_1 I_1}, \overrightarrow{P_1 I_2})$ and $\angle(\overrightarrow{P_3 I_1}, \overrightarrow{P_3 I_2})$, are computed using simple algebra. In order to calculate the area of the segment bounded by line L and the circle centred at P_1, two vectors need to be formulated: v_1, the vector from P_3 to P_1; and v_2, the vector from P_3 to either I_1 or I_2. If the scalar projection of v_2 onto v_1, given by $(v_1 \cdot v_2)/|v_1|$, is smaller than $|v_1|$, the area of the segment is given by the area of the sector bounded by the arc between I_1 and I_2 centred at P_1 minus the area of the triangle with vertices I_1, I_2 and P_1. However if that is not true, such as the case shown in Fig. 6(b), a different method is needed. The area of the segment equals the area of the sector of the reflex angle, given by

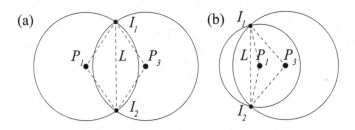

Fig. 6. The two different cases of circle intersections.

$2\pi - \angle(\overrightarrow{P_1 I_1}, \overrightarrow{P_1 I_2})$, plus the area of the triangle formed by the three points. The same method can be carried out when calculating the segment area bounded by line L and the circle centred at P_3, by swapping P_1 and P_3.

4   Numerical Example

In this section, the method of workspace calculation is carried out on two example mechanisms, the results of which are shown in Fig. 7. For each example, a numerical analysis has been carried out, the results of which are superimposed over their respective diagrams, as an independent verification of the workspace boundaries. The dimensions and safe zone of the first mechanism are as follows: $l_1 = 2$, $l_2 = 2$, $\gamma = \pi/6$, $d_1 = 1$, $d_{11,e} = 1$, $d_{9,11} = 1$, $P_1 = (0,0)^T$, and $P_3 = (2,0)^T$. After applying Algorithms 1 and 2, the following boundary radii were obtained: $B_{L1} = 2.86$, $B_{L2} = 2.04$, $B_{L3} = 0$, $B_{R1} = 3.35$, $B_{R2} = 1.55$, and $B_{R3} = 0.90$. As shown in Fig. 7(a), three distinct workspace areas are formed, the two largest each have an area of 2.06. In the second example, the mechanism has the following values: $l_1 = 2$, $l_2 = 2$, $\gamma = \pi/9$, $d_1 = 0.5$, $d_{11,e} = 0.5$, $d_{9,11} = 0.5$, $P_1 = (0,0)^T$, and $P_3 = (2,0)^T$. The calculated boundary radii are: $B_{L1} = 3.44$, $B_{L2} = 1.19$, $B_{L3} = 0$, $B_{R1} = 3.77$, $B_{R2} = 0.87$, and $B_{R3} = 0.29$. In this case, the result is a single workspace which has an area of 19.60 [Fig. 7(b)].

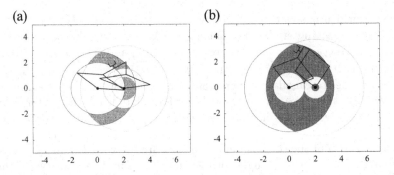

Fig. 7. The workspace boundaries of two robot instances, supported by a numerical workspace analysis.

5   Conclusion

This paper introduces a novel type of workspace for kinematically redundant parallel robots, which describes the area in which the robot's end-effector can complete full rotations without coming close to singularities. The workspace calculation takes advantage of the additional degrees of freedom of the kinematically redundant architecture in order to determine the region where singularities are safely avoided, but at the same time without needlessly constraining the size of the workspace. The method of calculating the workspace is carried out on a case study kinematically redundant planar parallel architecture. The algorithms used to compute the boundaries of the workspace are presented, as is the method of finding the resulting workspace area. Finally, the method is carried out numerically on a couple of example mechanisms. The proposed geometric method is straightforward in its implementation, and the resulting workspace is useful for a mechanism where high dexterity and reliability are important factors. Future work may include generalising the method to other architectures, and the determination of the singularity-safe maximal workspace.

References

1. Baron, N., Philippides, A., Rojas, N.: A novel kinematically redundant planar parallel robot manipulator with full rotatability. ASME J. Mech. Robot. **11**(1), 011008 (2019)
2. Ebrahimi, I., Carretero, J.A., Boudreau, R.: A family of kinematically redundant planar parallel manipulators. ASME J. Mech. Des. **130**(6), 062306 (2008)
3. Gallant, A., Boudreau, R., Gallant, M.: Geometric determination of the dexterous workspace of n-RRRR and n-RRPR manipulators. Mech. Mach. Theory **51**, 159–171 (2012)
4. Gosselin, C., Laliberté, T., Veillette, A.: Singularity-free kinematically redundant planar parallel mechanisms with unlimited rotational capability. IEEE Trans. Robot. **31**, 457–467 (2015)
5. Gosselin, C., Angeles, J.: The optimum kinematic design of a spherical three-degree-of-freedom parallel manipulator. ASME J. Mech. Trans. Autom. Des. **111**(2), 202–207 (1989)
6. Kumar, V.: Characterization of workspaces of parallel manipulators. ASME J. Mech. Des. **114**(3), 368–375 (1992)
7. Merlet, J.P., Gosselin, C.M., Mouly, N.: Workspaces of planar parallel manipulators. Mech. Mach. Theory **33**(1–2), 7–20 (1998)
8. Reveles, D., Wenger, P., et al.: Trajectory planning of kinematically redundant parallel manipulators by using multiple working modes. Mech. Mach. Theory **98**, 216–230 (2016)
9. Schreiber, L.T., Gosselin, C.: Kinematically redundant planar parallel mechanisms: kinematics, workspace and trajectory planning. Mech. Mach. Theory **119**, 91–105 (2018)

Model-Based 3D Point Cloud Segmentation for Automated Selective Broccoli Harvesting

Hector A. Montes[(✉)], Grzegorz Cielniak, and Tom Duckett

School of Computer Science, University of Lincoln,
Brayford Pool, Lincoln LN6 7TS, UK
{hmontes,GCielniak,tduckett}@lincoln.ac.uk

Abstract. In this paper we address the topic of feature matching in 3D point cloud data for accurate object segmentation. We present a matching method based on local features that operates on 3D point clouds to separate crops of broccoli heads from their background. Our method outperforms recent methods based on 2D standard segmentation techniques as well as clustering spatial distances. We have implemented our approach and present experiments on datasets collected in cultivated broccoli fields, in which we analyse performance and capabilities of the system as a point feature-based segmentation method.

1 Introduction

Segmentation of 3D objects in noisy and cluttered scenes is a highly relevant problem. Given a 3D point cloud produced by a depth sensor observing a 3D scene, the goal is to separate objects of interest in the foreground from other elements in the background. This has been extensively investigated in various research fields, such as computer vision, robotics, and pattern matching [4]. In this paper, we focus on 3D point clouds obtained with a structured light 3D camera and favourably compare our results to previously published experiments where sets of points where extracted based on the local proximity of the points. Our approach to this problem uses 3D classification based on point-to-point matching of estimated local 3D features. These features capture information of the local geometry of each point and are compared to the features of its surrounding points.

The objective of the work reported in this paper is to research 3D imaging methods to accurately segment and identify broccoli plants in the field. The ability to separate parts into different sets of sensor readings is an important task towards this goal. This research is focused on the broccoli head segmentation problem as a first step towards size estimation of each broccoli crop in order to establish whether or not it is suitable for cutting. This research contributions of this paper are as follows:

This research has been supported by the UK Agriculture and Horticulture Development Board (AHDB), https://ahdb.org.uk.

K. Althoefer et al. (Eds.): TAROS 2019, LNAI 11649, pp. 448–459, 2019.
https://doi.org/10.1007/978-3-030-23807-0_37

- a 3D point cloud segmentation method based on local surface features;
- an extensive evaluation of the method on datasets of broccoli plants from two different countries under real-world field conditions;
- comparisons to state of the art methods based on standard image segmentation and 3D spatial distances.

The paper starts with a brief contextual introduction of automated solutions for broccoli harvesting as well as a concise review of related work in Sect. 2. Section 3 describes the methodology and the data acquisition, while Sect. 4 describes the experimental results along with the evaluation metrics used to assess the overall performance. Section 5 concludes the paper.

2   Harvesting Broccoli Crops

Broccoli is a vegetable in the cabbage family that belongs to the *Brassica Oleracea* plant species. The interest in its cultivation has grown in recent years due to genetic improvement programmes developed in several countries and the healthy compounds contained in the crop that have increased its consumption [8]. A consequence of the methods used to breed broccoli is that the heads grow at different rates. This makes them difficult to harvest. Moreover, almost all broccoli is currently harvested by hand, relying on visual grading of size to estimate whether a head can be cut [9]. As a result, only around 50% of broccoli heads can be harvested economically.

Two approaches can be readily compared when harvesting crops, namely, slaughter harvesting, i.e. cutting everything in one pass, and selective harvesting, i.e. cutting each crop plant individually [2]. Slaughter harvesting is not a productive option as it potentially produces large quantities of unmarketable broccoli heads, whereas selective harvesting presents its own challenges as it relies on a subjective assessment by each person cutting the broccoli as to which head is ready. Additionally, labour has become increasingly scarce and more expensive due to a variety of factors ranging from political pressures to migration dynamics [2].

The goal of growing fresh fruit and vegetables is to keep the quality high while minimising costs. It is therefore desirable to find a method to harvest more frequently, more quickly, more accurately, with less waste, and that reduces labour and overall operation costs [1]. Thus, developing an automated method for selective harvesting capable of accurately identifying and separating broccoli crops from the background would help to increase productivity and to better control production costs.

2.1   Related Work

Automated harvesting systems usually consist of three independent systems: a recognition system to identify and locate the product, a picking system to perform grasping and cutting operations, and a navigation system to allow the robot to move around the cultivated crop plants [2]. One major challenge in autonomous harvesting is the recognition and segmentation of the crop from the rest of the plant. One of the first and common approaches has been to detect crops using 2D images. This can be promptly perceived in the wealth of techniques based on computer vision available in the literature [2,6,14]. For the particular case of broccoli, some approaches have used colour images to separate the broccoli head from the soil and other plant parts. We address the most relevant work below.

Ramirez [10] developed an algorithm to locate the broccoli head within an image of an entire broccoli plant. To locate the head, the method first finds the leaf stems using a threshold, a Canny edge detector, and a Hough transform to extract geometric features that approximate lines that can be fitted to the stems. Then the broccoli head can be located based on contrast texture analysis at the intersection of the stems. The method also determined the maturity of the crop using statistical texture analysis. Tu *et al.* [13] published results of a method to grade broccoli heads. The goal was to assess the quality decay of the harvested crop based on a set of colour and shape parameters. The system determined the area and roundness as the shape parameters and extracted the colour features using standard vision techniques. The resultant quality of the broccoli head was then decided by a neural network classifier.

More recently, Blok *et al.* [3] presented a method for detecting and sizing broccoli heads based on computer vision techniques. The method segmented an image based on texture and colour of the broccoli head buds. Firstly, the contrast of the image was enhanced to emphasise high frequency areas, followed by a series of filters and several morphological operations to fine-tune the image. Then, pixel connectivity was used to generate connected green-coloured components. Lastly, a shape-based feature selection on the connected area was conducted to separate small non-connecting components from the foreground. The segmented heads were sized using circle templates, and the mean image processing time took a little less than 300 ms. The system was part of a prototype harvesting device attached to a modified tractor and was tested in cultivated broccoli fields reaching an accuracy of 94%. Kusumam *et al.* [7] documented a system for detecting and locating mature broccoli heads in cluttered outdoor field conditions based on depth images acquired by a low-cost RGBD sensor. The paper evaluates a combination of Viewpoint Feature Histograms (VFH), a Support Vector Machines (SVM) classifier, and a temporal filter to track the detected heads. Their results showed a precision rate of 95.2% and 84.5% on datasets collected from fields in the UK and Spain, respectively.

Although 2D imagery is clearly important, this paper focuses on effective 3D depth features. Our primary goal is to design algorithms that reliably extract segments of the crop plants of interest. Our method captures and classifies the sensed information based on the local geometry of the points by analysing the relationship of the individual feature of each point and the features of the points in its vicinity. Such analysis exhibits a more discriminative power than an inspection based only on the Euclidean proximity of the cloud points. Nevertheless, 2D

Fig. 1. Top: Data acquisition with the 3D sensor mounted at the rear of the tractor. The sensor is fixed inside a purpose-built "black box" enclosure to block direct sunlight and other external incidences. Bottom: 3D point cloud images of broccoli plants (far left) are analysed offline based on local angular features (middle frames) to segment broccoli heads (far right).

features would be an interesting addition to 3D data worth studying in future work.

3   Methodology

3.1   Point Cloud Data Acquisition

The 3D point cloud data for our experiments were captured in outdoor fields under different weather conditions using the well-known Kinect 2 sensor (1920×1080 px RGB, and 512×424 px depth resolution). The sensor was fixed inside a specially constructed enclosure to block direct sunlight and to protect the equipment during rainy conditions. The point cloud data was collected with the camera enclosure mounted on the rear of a tractor, as shown in Fig. 1.

3.2   Model-Based 3D Point Cloud Segmentation

Two approaches are common in 3D object segmentation methods. In the first approach, the scene is segmented into smaller regions and global features are computed for each segment. These features are then matched to the descriptors of a model. In contrast, local methods commonly select a list of appropriate points, often referred to as interest points or key points, and extract a set of features in the vicinity of those points. The points are then matched to a model

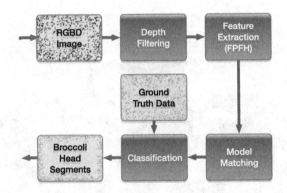

Fig. 2. 3D point cloud segmentation pipeline. The frames of 3D point cloud data are first filtered by depth. Then features are extracted from each point and matched to the reference models. The points are then classified using a decision function. The points with the same target class are grouped to form the final segments.

and the correspondences are grouped according to the geometry of the model. This paper applies a local recognition method for segmenting broccoli heads in sets of 3D point cloud images collected in planted broccoli fields. The method we present processes the depth data in a pipeline of four stages: point cloud depth filtering, feature extraction, model matching, and classification, as shown in Fig. 2.

The point cloud data captured by the sensor is first filtered to remove visible parts of the soil and other noisy points that are too distant from the surface of the scene. Feature descriptors are then computed in the remaining points and matched with the model references to finally determine if the points belong to a broccoli head. We use the algorithms available as part of the PCL C++ library [5] for processing point clouds.

Depth Filtering. Depth filtering of the soil and other distant points is achieved through a simple depth range thresholding of the input point cloud. The points that lie outside the desired range are simply discarded. The depth threshold is defined to be of 1 m and is based on the distance of the sensor to the ground measured during data collection.

Feature Extraction. We use a set of local 3D feature descriptors that are extracted for individual input points. Local descriptors are often used for object recognition and image registration. Even though descriptors have no notion of what object the points belong to, they do describe the local geometry around that point. Every feature descriptor should be discriminative with respect to the two given reference models, i.e., broccoli and non-broccoli points. To this end, we use the Fast Point Feature Histogram (FPFH) descriptor introduced by Rusu *et al.* [11].

Fast Point Feature Histogram (FPFH). We briefly summarize here the structure of the FPFH descriptor. The interested reader is referred to [11] for extended details on the descriptor and a discussion on its relevant properties.

The FPFH captures information of the local geometry of the points by analysing the difference between the directions of the normals in its surrounding area. The distribution of the surface normal directions should encode the underlying geometry of the broccoli heads and be discriminative compared to other elements in the scene. The FPFH derives from a more computationally expensive descriptor called Point Feature Histogram (PFH) [11]. To calculate the FPFH, the algorithm pairs the current point $\mathbf{pt}$ to all the points $\mathbf{qs}_i \mid i \in \{1, 2, ..., K\}$ in the vicinity of size K, and for each pair $\langle \mathbf{pt}, \mathbf{qs} \rangle$, a fixed coordinate frame is computed from their normals $\hat{\mathbf{n}}_t$ and $\hat{\mathbf{n}}_s$. The direction differences between the normals can then be encoded into three angular variables between the normal and the three axes of the fixed frame. The three angular variables are defined as follows:

$$\mathbf{v} = \hat{\mathbf{n}}_s \times \frac{\mathbf{pt} - \mathbf{ps}}{\|\mathbf{pt} - \mathbf{ps}\|} \qquad \mathbf{w} = \hat{\mathbf{n}}_s \times \mathbf{v}$$
$$\alpha = \mathbf{v} \cdot \hat{\mathbf{n}}_t$$
$$\varphi = \frac{\hat{\mathbf{n}}_s \cdot (\mathbf{pt} - \mathbf{ps})}{d}$$
$$\theta = \arctan\left(\mathbf{w} \cdot \hat{\mathbf{n}}_t, \mathbf{u} \cdot \hat{\mathbf{n}}_t\right)$$

where d is the Euclidean distance between the two points $\mathbf{ps}$ and $\mathbf{pt}$. These three variables $\langle \alpha, \varphi, \theta \rangle$ are then binned into a histogram when all pairs of points have been computed. The histograms of the neighbours are merged with the current point histogram, weighted according to their distances. The final FPFH descriptor is the concatenation of the histograms of each angular variable.

Classification. To compare two FPFH descriptors, we use a fast but effective measure between the descriptors of two points: the histogram intersection. Given a query point and its corresponding histogram H (its descriptor), and a reference histogram h calculated from the descriptors of sets of known models, the histogram intersection is defined as:

$$d_{INT}(H, h) = \sum_{i=1}^{n} min(H_i, h_i)$$

where n is the number of histogram bins. For the histogram intersection, higher values are better. After the intersections are calculated between the query and the reference descriptors, the difference between both intersections is used to make a choice as to which model is the best match and provides the final classification score. This score is computed with point-to-point correspondences obtained by matching local descriptors of feature points to a set of known reference models. Consecutive cloud points with similar high score are part of the same point cloud segment.

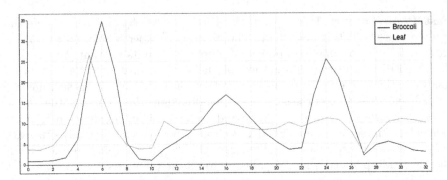

Fig. 3. Histograms of the reference models used in our algorithm. A FPFH descriptor is computed for each data point averaged over a set of ground truth samples. The descriptor is then matched to both reference models and the difference provides the final classification score.

Reference Models. We construct models for the 3D point cloud objects that we are interested in. The reference models are two FPFH descriptors calculated from the histograms of sets of known models. These models are sets of selected 3D points that are already labelled to be part of either a broccoli head or a leaf (although labelled as leaf, the points also include other elements in the scene that are not part of a broccoli head). Figure 3 shows a plot of the FPFH reference descriptors selected for our experiments. These two descriptors suffice for our segmentation purposes as the angular distributions of a broccoli head is most relevant for the classification and segmentation tasks.

4   Experimental Results

The experimental evaluation aims to determine the overall performance and the accuracy of the method. To evaluate our results, we use sets of the same point cloud dataset used in the experiments reported by Kusumam *et al.* [7].

To evaluate our system, we collected ground truth information to test the quality of the segmentation method. We manually labelled selected 3D point clouds using a software tool that we have designed especially for this task. This was an offline manual processing which was carried out independently from both the datasets collected and the segmentation process itself. We used subsets of two datasets collected in fields in the UK and one more set collected in a field in Fuente Alamo di Murcia, Spain, which we refer to simply as the UK and FA sets. All three sets consisted of point cloud sequences of 300 frames each. We particularly highlight the results on challenging frames where those experiments produced either *under-segmentation*, i.e., some of the target broccoli heads were missed, or *over-segmentation*, i.e., the extracted segments were larger that the broccoli heads seen in the scene frame. A sample of these two cases is shown in Fig. 4.

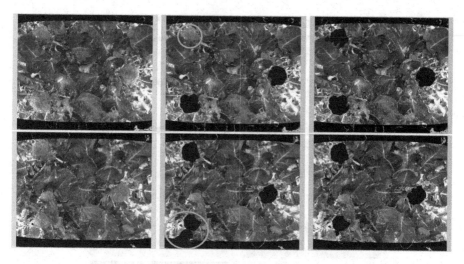

Fig. 4. Two segmentation samples on different frames. First column: The original frame. Center column: circled in green, under segmented (missed one head) and over segmented objects (not only the head) using the Euclidean Clustering method from [7]. Right column: Samples of our model-based segmentation method. (Color figure online)

The frames of a 3D point cloud are first filtered by depth and the FPFH descriptors are computed for each point and then matched to the reference models. These initial steps already show the areas of the point cloud that are more likely to contain broccoli heads. This allows to classify every point using a simple decision function that takes the current point matching score and determines the best label class. A function that examines nearby points of the same class forms the final segments and helps to eliminate false positives. An illustration of the broccoli segmentation steps is shown in Fig. 5.

4.1   Classifier Evaluation

We evaluated the classifier of the 3D system pipeline for segmenting broccoli heads using individual FPFH descriptors. For each point in the current frame a classification score is produced. If the point is part of a broccoli head, according to the ground truth data, it is labelled as a positive sample, otherwise it is labelled negative. The resulting sample sets are highly unbalanced, i.e. there is a significant difference in the number of positive and negative samples. In this case, the negatives notably outnumber the positives as large portions of each point cloud frame are from leaves, soil or other elements.

Classification results were evaluated using precision-recall (PR) curves, as they provide a more accurate interpretation of a classifier performance on unbalanced samples [12]. Precision represents the ratio of true positive detections to the total number of positive detections (true and false), whereas recall is the ratio of true positive detections to the total number of both true positive and

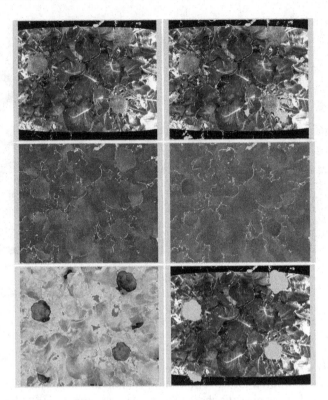

Fig. 5. Broccoli segmentation steps. Top row: The original frame on the left, and after being depth filtered on the right. Middle row: matched points of broccoli heads shown in bright green on the left, and other points shown on the right. Bottom row: The difference between the two reference models shown in contrasting colours on the left and, on the right, the extracted segments in red. (Color figure online)

false negative detections. The precision and recall values are computed over a range of discrimination threshold values across the classification scores. Figure 6 shows the performance evaluation on a PR plot on the set of classified points. The plot shows the average precision results on the scores computed for every point.

The results show a precision rate of 95.59%, 95.56%, and 88.17% on the UK and FA datasets examined by our model-based method, versus a precision rate of 93.05%, 93.29%, and 80.73% in the results published in [7]. Originally the EC method was applied on clusters of points and VFH global features were extracted. The PR plot shows the performance of the same method reflected on all the points that form the same clusters.

Similarly, the results show a precision rate of 92.22% on the datasets examined by our model-based method, versus a precision rate of 73.20% for the results published in [7]. This experiments show the classification performance of the segmented points for *under-segmented* and *over-segmented* frames. This incorrect

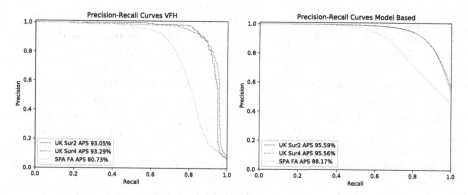

Fig. 6. Precision-Recall Curves showing the classification performance of the segmented points. The value shown is the average precision score (APS) at various discrimination threshold settings. The plots show the performance of Euclidean Clustering (EC) and VFH features from [7] on the left, and our Model-Based (MB) approach and FPFH features on the right. The plots show the performance of both methods using the same datasets.

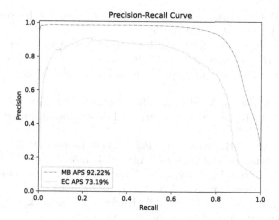

Fig. 7. Precision-Recall Curves showing the classification performance of the segmented points for *under-segmented* and *over-segmented* frames. The plot shows the performance of Euclidean Clustering (EC) from [7] and our Model-Based (MB) approach. In nearly 10% of the tested frames the EC-based method produced this incorrect segmentation.

segmentation outcome was observed in nearly 10% of all the datasets used for our experiments. Additionally, our results can also be favourably compared against the performance accuracy of 94% reported by Blok *et al.* [3].

5   Conclusion

In this paper, we discussed a method for 3D point cloud segmentation based on 3D feature descriptor matching. Comparative experimental results show that our method performed favourably against an existing 3D broccoli detection algorithm based on the Euclidean proximity of 3D points when tested on the same dataset. The results showed a promising precision score. Moreover, our results also showed that the segmentation method can be used to detect broccoli heads, as a first step in the development of a fully autonomous selective harvester.

Interesting future research directions include a more principled selection of interest points to be examined by, for instance, performing a point cloud compression that retains the original perceived distribution of 3D points. Another research direction is to adopt strategies to find or even synthesize descriptors for the reference models, so they better encode the properties of the broccoli heads we are interested to segment. Also, other state-of-the-art methods may be considered, such as CNN's and other Deep Learning related methods.

References

1. Bac, C.W., van Henten, E.J., Hemming, J., Edan, Y.: Harvesting robots for high-value crops: state-of-the-art review and challenges ahead. J. Field Robot. **31**(6), 888–911 (2014)
2. Bachche, S.: Deliberation on design strategies of automatic harvesting systems: a survey. Robotics **4**(2), 194–222 (2015)
3. Blok, P.M., Barth, R., van den Berg, W.: Machine vision for a selective broccoli harvesting robot. IFAC-PapersOnLine **49**(16), 66–71 (2016). 5th IFAC Conference on Sensing, Control and Automation Technologies for Agriculture AGRICONTROL 2016
4. Castellani, U., Cristani, M., Fantoni, S., Murino, V.: Sparse points matching by combining 3D mesh saliency with statistical descriptors. Comput. Graph. Forum **27**(2), 643–652 (2008)
5. Cousins, S., Rusu, R.B.: 3D is here: Point Cloud Library (PCL). In: IEEE International Conference on Robotics and Automation, Shanghai (China) (2011)
6. Jimenez, A.R., Ceres, R., Pons, J.L.: A survey of computer vision methods for locating fruit on trees. Trans. ASAE **43**(6), 1911 (2000)
7. Kusumam, K., Krajník, T., Pearson, S., Duckett, T., Cielniak, G.: 3D-vision based detection, localization, and sizing of broccoli heads in the field. J. Field Robot. **34**(8), 1505–1518 (2017)
8. Maggioni, L., von Bothmer, R., Poulsen, G., Branca, F.: Origin and domestication of cole crops (Brassica oleracea L.): linguistic and literary considerations. Econ. Bot. **64**(2), 109–123 (2010)
9. Orzolek, M.D., Lamont, W.J., Kime Jr., L.F., Harper, J.K.: Broccoli production. In: Agricultural Alternatives series. Agricultural Alternatives series, Penn State Cooperative Extension (2012)
10. Ramirez, R.A.: Computer vision based analysis of broccoli for application in a selective autonomous harvester. mathesis, Virginia Polytechnic Institute and State University (2006)
11. Rusu, R.B., Blodow, N., Beetz, M.: Fast point feature histograms (FPFH) for 3D registration. In: IEEE International Conference on Robotics and Automation, pp. 3212–3217 (2009)
12. Saito, T., Rehmsmeier, M.: The precision-recall plot is more informative than the ROC plot when evaluating binary classifiers on imbalanced datasets. PLoS ONE **10**(3), e0118432 (2015)

13. Tu, K., Ren, K., Pan, L., Li, H.: A study of broccoli grading system based on machine vision and neural networks. In: International Conference on Mechatronics and Automation, pp. 2332–2336. IEEE (2007)
14. Zhao, Y., Gong, L., Huang, Y., Liu, C.: A review of key techniques of vision-based control for harvesting robot. Comput. Electron. Agric. **127**, 311–323 (2016)

Mine Detonating Sphere-Bot

Rebecca Harding[(✉)], Charles Freestone, and Martin F. Stoelen

School of Computing, Electronics and Mathematics,
University of Plymouth, Plymouth, UK
{rebecca.harding, charles.freestone}
@students.plymouth.ac.uk,
martin.stoelen@plymouth.ac.uk

Abstract. The inspiration for this project came from the armadillo. This creature can curl itself into a ball, protecting its vulnerable parts with plates made of bone acting as armor. While the armadillo moves using its legs, this robot always remains in a spherical shape, and moves using wheels inside a sphere. It is theorized a robot of this design could be used in demining. The sphere rolls over a mine, detonates it, then survives the impact and can move on to detonate further mines. The robot makes use of soft materials rather than hard plates in order to survive impacts. This paper describes the design of the robot including consideration of different materials, different wheel shapes and spherical casing design. Simulations and compression testing were used to find the optimal designs. In addition, a hill climb test determines the robot's ability to traverse sloped environments. Finally, a drop test shows its ability to survive impacts.

Keywords: Demining · Spherical robot · Soft robotics · Low-cost · 3D printed

1 Introduction

The aims of this project are to design a rolling robot, optimize its ability to absorb high impacts from outside forces and to test the resulting robot. This robot can absorb impacts through the materials chosen and spread them over the design, increasing the likelihood of survival. It must be able to roam around inclined environments as this is the area of space it would have to navigate to do its job, including inclines of around 5°.

The robot consists of a carriage that houses two high torque motors, which rotate wheels that are specially designed to absorb large impacts and maintain traction within the sphere. The sphere adds an extra layer of protection that will take the initial impacts.

To reduce complexity of the design of the prototype, the robot will be remote controlled, not autonomous. This is so the focus of the project can be on the physical design. The robot will utilize mostly 3D printed parts, so that replacement parts can be reprinted from anywhere where 3D printers are available.

The robot moving inside of a sphere will allow the center of gravity of the design to be more easily shifted, this will allow for easier hill climbing in design. It will also allow the protective sphere to deform inwards more on an impact as there will be an air gap for it to deform into.

© Springer Nature Switzerland AG 2019
K. Althoefer et al. (Eds.): TAROS 2019, LNAI 11649, pp. 460–472, 2019.
https://doi.org/10.1007/978-3-030-23807-0_38

The Military suffer from a great risk when patrolling the field: mines. These devices are placed before battles to prevent troops, and at times vehicles, from travel in certain areas. This can also be the case years after wars when mines are left untriggered, leaving areas to stay remote, due to fear of loss of life. These areas need to be cleared of the devices: this removal process is called demining.

Demining is a clearance process typically carried out in military scenarios but can also take place in humanitarian situations. It is a dangerous task and needs specialized equipment to avoid endangering lives. Currently the main equipment used is large and cumbersome, using flail-like devices on the front of tanks to churn up the soil containing mines and having the tank withstand any blasts incurred from the process [1] or fling mines out of the ground without activating them. However, the equipment used is expensive and cannot navigate through woodland areas. Manual methods can also be used, whereby people with and without experience go out into the mine filled areas and remove them with crude methods such as trowels and pitchforks. This is highly dangerous and is a method used out of necessity with no other means of removing them.

Fig. 1. Completed spherical robot and the completed robot with one hemisphere removed so the internals can be viewed

A handful of demining robots exist but all existing solutions are large and expensive [2–4]. They use rigid structures to survive impacts rather than soft mechanisms. In addition, these existing robots are wheeled or legged, not spherical.

A spherical device exists for mine clearance, but it relies on wind power and has no directional control; it is purely a mechanical device, not a robot [5]. Spherical robots exist [6] but none for the application of demining.

In this project we hope to create a cheap replicable solution that could be used by anyone with access to a 3D printer, while lowering the risks associated with demining. This will be done by creating a small remote-control robot designed to drive over the mines and trigger them. The robot will then absorb or otherwise ignore the majority of the impact taken and be able to carry on with the task of mine removal (Fig. 1).

2   Design Process and Implementation

2.1   Design Tools

Autodesk Fusion 360 was used for all CAD work. Designs created needed to fit the dimension constraints of the 3D printers available, and the amount of material required was minimised where possible to reduce printing times. Designs created also account for dimensions of other hardware such as the motors, to allow a good fit.

3D printing, a type of Computer Aided Manufacture, was used to produce all designs. This meant iterations of designs could be produced relatively quickly and iterative improvements could be made. Laser cutting was also available, but this was not utilised. Only the electronics housing could have been assembled from laser cut parts, but 3D printing this as one part minimised complexity and provided a stronger solution.

2.2   Materials

A tougher material is desired if the design is to perform better. After looking at research taken into 3D printed materials it is clear to see that polylactic acid (PLA) is not a favoured material to be impact resistant compared to acrylonitrile butadiene styrene (ABS) plastic. The ABS 3D printed parts reached 304 J/m of absorbed energy in an un-notched Izod test, while the PLA part only reached 96.1 J/m [7, 8].

Creating 3D printed wheels made of ABS plastic would be desired for future iterations of the project. To achieve this a 3D printer would need to be purchased that could sustain such development.

The use of flexible NinjaFlex means that impacts can be absorbed. In addition, silicone was used to coat the inside of the sphere and the outside of the wheels. The coefficient of friction of silicone is high, meaning there is less chance of wheel slippage inside the robot. Silicone is also tacky, which means there is additional grip.

2.3   Hardware

The robot moves using two Pimoroni Micro Metal Gearmotors with a 1006:1 gear ratio. This provides a high torque allowing ease of movement and the ability to move up a slight incline. As the motors rotate the wheels, the internals move to the front of the sphere which causes the sphere to rotate due to its centre of mass being shifted. The robot is remote controlled using an HC-12 radio module inside the sphere and a radio module on a controller. The controller features four push buttons to allow the user to control the movement of the robot. The robot and the controller use an Arduino Nano.

The wheels need to be able to absorb impacts in order to protect the motors from damage. Three wheel designs were initially considered. One inspired by the complex wheel structure of the SandFlea robot [9], one inspired by a Mars Rover using spiral shapes as shock absorbers [10] and one that simply used a rigid inner part and a soft tyre on the outside made from NinjaFlex, like a car tyre. Each of these designs were tested, as shown later in this paper, and the final wheel design was altered afterwards.

2.4   Control

Code was produced using the Arduino IDE. Each of the push buttons on the controller represent a different direction. The robot does not travel while it is turning, it merely turns on the spot, by having each motor move in opposite directions. The speed of the moving motors is constant, as PWM is not used. This could be considered in the future to allow the robot to veer left or right, or to move slowly in certain situations.

2.5   Final Design

Figure 2A shows the front view of the robot without the outer sphere, Fig. 2B shows the side view and Fig. 2C shows the isometric view. Figure 2D, E and F show the same views but with one half of the outer sphere.

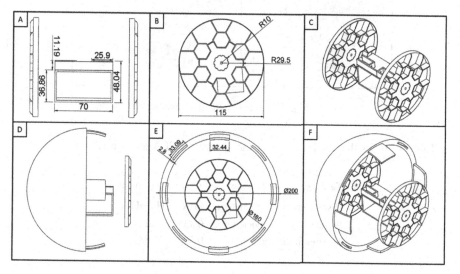

Fig. 2. Engineering drawings of the final design of the robot

3   Simulations

3.1   Finite Element Analysis: Sphere

Method. All Finite Element Analysis was completed using Autodesk Fusion 360. The 3D design was used. The sphere is made up of two interlocking hemispheres. For this test, only one hemisphere was used. The same force is applied to the sphere for both measurements, but the material of the sphere is changed to be either PLA or NinjaFlex.

Results. Figure 3A shows the result for PLA, Fig. 3B shows the result for NinjaFlex. Figure 3C and D show a different view for PLA and NinjaFlex respectively and include surface probes to show the displacement of the sphere at the location of the applied force.

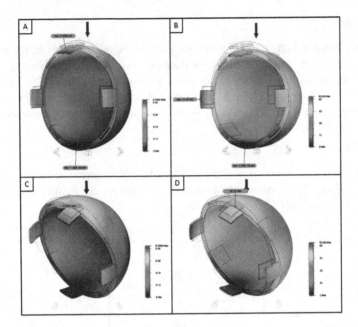

Fig. 3. Sphere simulation results

Table 1 shows the displacement of the sphere for PLA and NinjaFlex.

Table 1. Table to show measured displacement

Displacement (mm)/material	PLA	NinjaFlex
At location of applied force	0.4357	52.27
Maximum displacement	0.5086	63.88

Discussion. It can be clearly seen that the sphere deforms a lot more when made from NinjaFlex. This is a desired effect as it will protect the internals from impacts, therefore NinjaFlex was used when printing the sphere.

3.2   Finite Element Analysis: Wheels

Method. The wheel designs tested were the designs that were also 3D printed. Five wheel designs were tested. For each wheel, a range of forces were applied onto the rim with the axle as the fixed point, and the maximum displacement was observed. The forces were 50 N, 100 N, 150 N, 200 N and 250 N.

Results. Figure 4 shows the results. "SF" represents the SandFlea inspired wheels and three thicknesses of struts were tested: 1 mm, 1.2 mm and 2 mm. "Tyre" is the wheel and tyre design. "Rover/10" represents the Mars Rover inspired wheel, but the values have been scaled down by a factor of 10 as the displacement values were very large.

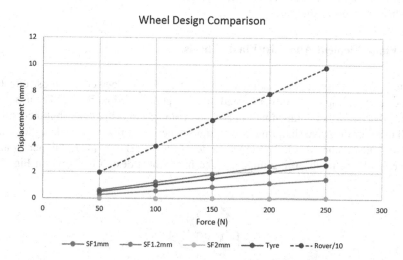

Fig. 4. Graph to show the comparison of different wheel designs

Discussion. The displacement values were smallest for the SandFlea inspired wheels with 2 mm thickness. This design is undesirable as the wheels would not provide much dampening. The displacement values for the Mars Rover inspired wheels were largest. However, part of the reason for the large values is that the values recorded were the maximum displacement. As seen in Fig. 5, the inner, spiral parts deform more than the outside of the wheel.

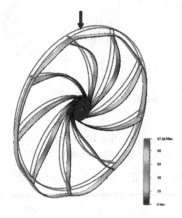

Fig. 5. Example of Rover inspired wheel results

Overall, the SandFlea inspired wheel with 1 mm thickness was deemed to be the most effective design due to the balance of dampening abilities due to deformation and the ability to hold its structure sufficiently. This decision was based on results from other tests as well as this one.

3.3   Finite Element Analysis: Final Wheels

Method. After testing, the SandFlea inspired wheel was deemed the most effective. The design was improved further by adding a NinjaFlex section. It acts like suspension for the wheels, further dampening impacts and compressions that the robot incurs. PLA is still used for the drive shaft (allowing a rigid material for the motor axle to hold onto) and the struts of the wheel. The outer circle of the wheel was made thinner to allow further flexibility in absorbing impacts. The final wheel design is shown in Fig. 6.

Fig. 6. CAD final wheel design

Results. Figure 7A shows deformation of the final wheel at 50 N. Figure 7B shows 100 N. Figure 7C shows 150 N. Figure 7D shows 200 N. Figure 7E shows 250 N.

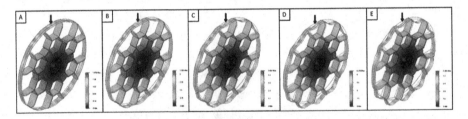

Fig. 7. FEA results for final wheel design

Figure 8 shows the comparison of the final design with the original design simulations. The results for the final design are shown by the orange line labelled "Final".

Discussion. Due to the addition of a NinjaFlex piece, this design has a greater displacement than the other SandFlea inspired wheels. This means there is a greater dampening effect in the case of impacts, so the internals will be better protected.

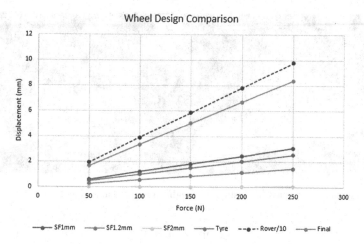

Fig. 8. Comparison including the final wheel design

4 Experiments

4.1 Preliminary Compression Testing

Method. To better understand how fractures manifest in 3D printed objects and how designs used in industry distribute force across themselves outside of simulations. The three wheel designs previously mentioned were used; Rover inspired, SandFlea inspired and Tyre. The study was carried out at the University of Plymouth's Testing Laboratory. A compression test machine was used to initially test the wheel designs until the point of breakage.

Force was applied until a deformation of 30 mm was created. The wheels were all kept the same depth (5 mm) and compressible material (struts) was also kept to a similar thickness, 0.8 mm. The depth was chosen to reduce slip in the experiment. The thickness of the material was chosen to allow adequate compressions. This meant adjusting the infill of the NinjaFlex tyre so that the outside supports became the same thickness. Figure 9A shows the compression test on the SandFlea inspired wheel and Fig. 9B shows the Rover inspired wheel.

Results. Figure 10 shows the results from the initial compression test. From these results it's clear to see that the SandFlea inspired design is the best for maintaining a uniform distribution across the test. The tyre design is best for being compliant at lower compressions (when the NinjaFlex material can be functional) but stays rigid at higher compressions. The Rover inspired design did not perform well.

Discussion. The Rover inspired design is too easily compressed and therefore is not strong enough. The tyre design outer NinjaFlex compresses very easily while the inner PLA doesn't therefore is too rigid. The SandFlea inspired design provides an optimum solution out of the three options as it is strong enough to maintain its structure while also being compliant enough to dampen the effects of impacts.

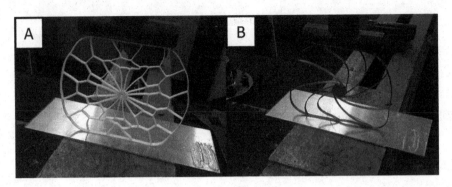

Fig. 9. Examples of compression testing for SandFlea inspired and Mars Rover inspired wheels

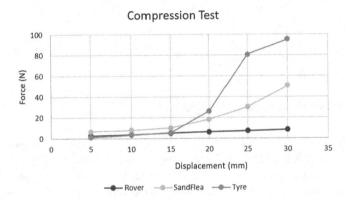

Fig. 10. Graph to show compression test of different wheel designs

4.2 Further Compression Testing

Method. After preliminary tests were taken it was noted that the SandFlea inspired wheels suited the task the best. A compression test machine was used to compare two different variations of the design: struts with a thickness of 1 mm or of 1.2 mm.

Results. In Fig. 11, Line 1 represents the SandFlea inspired wheel with thickness of 1.2 mm and Line 2 represents 1 mm. This test showed that the thicker wheels held up to greater forces than the thinner ones. As seen in the video on GitHub (see Sect. 6), the thinner wheels didn't fracture as severely as the thicker design. This was due to the wheel not fracturing down the layers like the thicker counterpart, but instead fracturing across.

Discussion. Even though the 1.2 mm wheels took a higher amount of force to break, they broke after the PLA material had already fractured between the layers. This is not feasible for the design and so the 1 mm wheels will be chosen. The fracturing can also be addressed by adding silicone over the outside of the wheels, to prevent them from peeling apart under high forces.

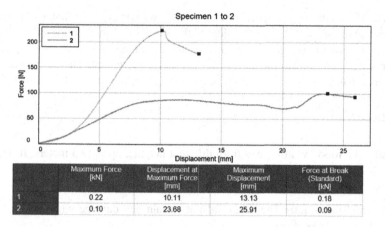

	Maximum Force [kN]	Displacement at Maximum Force [mm]	Maximum Displacement [mm]	Force at Break (Standard) [kN]
1	0.22	10.11	13.13	0.18
2	0.10	23.68	25.91	0.09

Fig. 11. Graph to show compression test of different wheel thicknesses automatically generated by the compression test machine

4.3 Hill Climb Test

Method. A test on how changing variables such as the incline, weight carried by the carriage and materials used to increase friction affect the angle the robot can climb. A plank of wood will be used as an adjustable ramp for the robot to climb. Angles of 0–10° and added weights of 0–400 g were used.

Results. Table 2 shows the results from the Hill Climb Test. From these results it's clear to see that adding silicone increased the friction enough for the sphere to increase the amount it could climb. It prevented slip from the wheels to the inside of the sphere. However, at higher weights the motors would fail to rotate. This was probably due to the amount of force that the motors had to apply being too great.

Table 2. Table to show the difference when adding silicone to inner surface of the robot for varying weights

No Silicone

Angle/Weight	0	10	20	50	60	70	80	90	100	150	200	210	220	250	300	350	400
0.0	Pass	Pass	Pass	Pass	Pass	Pass	Pass	Pass	Pass	Pass	Pass	Pass	Pass	Pass	Fail	Fail	Fail
2.5	Fail	Fail	Pass	Pass	Pass	Pass	Pass	Pass	Pass	Pass	Pass	Slip	Slip	Slip	Slip	Slip	Slip
5.0	Fail	Fail	Fail	Fail	Slip	Slip	Slip	Slip	Pass	Pass	Slip	Slip	Slip	Slip	Slip	Slip	Slip
7.5	Fail	Fail	Fail	Fail	Fail	Fail	Fail	Fail	Fail	Slip	Slip	Slip	Slip	Slip	Slip	Slip	Slip
10.0	Fail	Fail	Fail	Fail	Fail	Fail	Fail	Fail	Slip	Slip	Slip	Slip	Slip	Slip	Slip	Slip	Slip

Silicone

Angle/Weight	0	10	20	50	60	70	80	90	100	150	200	210	220	250	300	350	400
0.0	Pass	Pass	Pass	Pass	Pass	Pass	Pass	Pass	Pass	Pass	Pass	Pass	Pass	Pass	Fail	Fail	Fail
2.5	Fail	Fail	Pass	Pass	Pass	Pass	Pass	Pass	Pass	Pass	Pass	Pass	Pass	Pass	Fail	Fail	Fail
5.0	Fail	Fail	Fail	Fail	Fail	Fail	Pass	Pass	Pass	Pass	Pass	Pass	Pass	Pass	Fail	Fail	Fail
7.5	Fail	Fail	Fail	Fail	Fail	Fail	Fail	Fail	Fail	Fail	Fail	Fail	Fail	Pass	Fail	Fail	Fail
10.0	Fail	Fail	Fail	Fail	Fail	Fail	Fail	Fail	Fail	Fail	Fail	Fail	Fail	Fail	Fail	Fail	Fail

Discussion. The difference between results in the two tables shows that adding silicone to the internals of the robot (the inside of the sphere and the outside of the wheels) increases the amount of friction obtained by the design and thus increases the amount of energy transferred from the motors to the robot's movement. The tacky property of the silicone paired with the higher value for coefficient of friction allowed this change.

4.4   Drop Test

Method. The robot was dropped from different heights, up to two meters. It only had gravity acting upon it, it was not pushed. The surfaces of impact were a grass lawn and a concrete path.

Results and Discussion. The robot did not sustain any damage when dropped from any height up to two meters.

Figure 12 shows a series of images to show the drop test tests carried out on a hard surface and on a soft surface.

Fig. 12. Images of drop test on a hard surface and a soft surface

A video of the results for a hard surface at two meters can be found here:
https://youtu.be/-dnSy7yHwFQ
A video of the results for a soft surface at two meters can be found here:
https://youtu.be/0s82ZIrWDRs

The robot was not damaged after being dropped from two meters, showing a robustness to impacts.

5   Conclusion

The robot created in this project was able to climb an incline of 7.5° while being contained in a protective sphere. The design was achieved through an iterative design process, which included FEA, 3D printing, as well as compression, tensile and drop testing. The soft protective layer, in tandem with the soft wheels, allowed the robot to absorb impacts and was able to make full use of the flexible NinjaFlex material.

The robot is not yet ready for tasks in the field, but this early prototype is one step in the direction of a low-cost, 3D printable, highly mobile and potentially reusable robot for mine clearance. Future improvements are needed to develop and test the robot for real mine explosions. This would likely include a high strength outer layer similar to a flak jacket, but also to print the robot internals using ABS or Nylon plastic (to increase toughness). More experimentation is also needed to improve the quality of the NinjaFlex parts.

By scaling the robot design and incorporating a localisation method, the robot could potentially be used as part of a swarm, increasing the efficiency of mine clearing. Further sensing, such as a metal detector, could perhaps also be added to the robot to detect a mine and travel towards it.

6   Repository

This early prototype was developed as part of a group project for the ROCO504 Advanced Robot Design module at the University of Plymouth. A GitHub repository was created to support this project. This can be found at: https://github.com/ROCO504/2018-Group2

References

1. Tankmuseum.org: The Tank Museum—E1949.360 (2018). https://www.tankmuseum.org/museum-online/vehicles/object-e1949-360. Accessed 1 Dec 2018
2. Singh, S., Freese, M., Trevelyan, J.: Field characterization of humanitarian demining for future robotic assessment. In: Proceedings of the IEEE International Conference on Robotics and Automation, ICRA (2019)
3. Marques, L., et al.: Automation of humanitarian demining: the 2016 humanitarian robotics and automation technology challenge (2016). https://doi.org/10.1109/RAHA.2016.7931893
4. Mikulic, D.: Design of Demining Machines. Springer, London (2013). https://doi.org/10.1007/978-1-4471-4504-2
5. Hassani, M.: Mine Kafon Ball – Mine Kafon (2019). http://minekafon.org/index.php/mine-kafon-ball/. Accessed 27 Jan 2019
6. Guardbot.org: Guardbot (2019). http://www.guardbot.org/. Accessed 30 Oct 2018

7. Comparison of typical 3D printing materials. 2015.igem.org (2019). http://2015.igem.org/wiki/images/2/24/CamJIC-Specs-Strength.pdf. Accessed 22 Jan 2019
8. Izod Impact Strength Testing of Plastics. Matweb.com (2019). http://www.matweb.com/reference/izod-impact.aspx. Accessed 22 Jan 2019
9. SandFlea—Boston Dynamics. Bostondynamics.com (2018). https://www.bostondynamics.com/sandflea. Accessed 10 Nov 2018
10. Mars Exploration Rover Mission: Spotlight. Mars.nasa.gov (2018). https://mars.nasa.gov/mer/spotlight/wheels01.html. Accessed 10 Nov 2018

Author Index

Printed in the United States
By Bookmasters